THE AWW COOKING SCHOOL

THE AUSTRALIAN Women's Weekly

THE AWW COOKING SCHOOL

acp books

contents

Introduction 6

Recipes to know by heart 8
Showing off 48
Starters 72
Salads 92
Soups 120
Pasta 142
Rice 168
Noodles 188
Vegetables 208
Eggs 240
Sauces 262
The perfect roast 286
Stir-fries 334
Braises & stews 360
Pies 388
Curries 408
Barbecues & grills 432
Pan-fries & deep-fries 456
Pulses & grains 480
Desserts 502
Cakes 528
Teatime 554
Christmas & other celebrations 574
Preserves 602
Teaching kids to cook 614
Tricks of the trade 632

Conversion chart 640
Glossary 641
Index 664

SPECIAL FEATURES

Salad greens 106
Soup accompaniments 134
Know your pasta 146
Know your rice 172
Know your noodles 192
Know your vegetables 216, 218
Know your herbs 228
Asian vegetables 348
Stew accompaniments 386
Know your spices 416
Know your mushrooms 440
Know your seafood 446
Beans, peas & grains 496
Tropical fruit 516
Preparing cake pans 532
Drink garnishes 580
Cheeses 600

The Australian Women's Weekly has been part of our lives for more than 75 years, and I've been lucky enough to have been here for 40 of those years, in which so much has changed.

Countless recipes have been triple-tested, triple-tasted and photographed during that time by many talented and dedicated people. They came from various backgrounds – some were home-economists, others teachers or chefs, there were those with assorted catering and cooking backgrounds, and a few who just had "the passion" for food.
We pride ourselves on writing recipes clearly, we list ingredients in the order in which they're used, give specific instructions on how to handle – chop, slice, beat, whisk – those ingredients, then proceed through the cooking method in the most logical way. Weighing and measuring ingredients is vital for success, particularly for the novice cook. When it comes to baking, it's even more important to be particular about weighing and measuring accurately for guaranteed success. We even go so far as to indicate what size bowl, pan or dish to use for mixing or cooking, when to preheat the oven, and so on.
We tell the reader how many servings they can expect from a recipe or how many cookies a mixture might make. We put ourselves in the position of the shopper when we list ingredients – there's little point in saying 1 cup of chopped walnuts, if the shopper doesn't know how many walnuts to actually buy. As a bonus, all the recipes are nutritionally counted, listing the fat,

kilojoule, calorie, carbohydrate, protein and fibre content. The time taken to prepare and cook each recipe is also noted, as are tips and notes about freezing, storing and microwaving.

Creative designers are responsible for the way our cookbooks look and food stylists and photographers play an important part in the way the food looks on the page. There are no tricks, no use of fake ingredients, just good food, cooked properly and presented well.

The aim of the Weekly's Test Kitchen is to produce recipes that everyone can follow easily. The food we use in the recipes is almost always available at large supermarkets – any ingredient which might be a little different is explained and a substitute and source suggested.

In this book, we walk the cook through the recipes, giving step-by-step instructions and photos to help and guide along the way. We want to educate and inspire people to cook for themselves, their friends and families and, in so doing, promote an interest in developing their confidence and cooking skills.

Pamela Clark

Pamela Clark
Director
The Australian Women's Weekly Test Kitchen

RECIPES TO KNOW BY HEART

Recipes to know by heart

Anyone can cook, but to be a good cook – a passionate cook, and a confident cook – takes particular care and attention. Cooking is both an art and a science, requiring equal amounts of creativity and technical know-how. You should be aware that there is a reason for every instruction you read in a recipe: when the butter cake recipe warns against overbeating, for example, it's not just on a whim, it's because overbeating can make the mixture 'tough' and can effect the cooking result, and so on.

Like all of life's worthwhile endeavours, cooking requires time, dedication and persistence to do it well, but the rewards are many. The ability to confidently cook a delicious dinner for family and friends is deeply satisfying and so is turning out a perfect cake.

KEEP IT SIMPLE AND BUILD YOUR REPERTOIRE

THE BASICS

Use the freshest and best-quality ingredients: try to visit a farmers' market if you can and buy the freshest, preferably organic, produce available.

Invest in some good-quality cooking utensils: a couple of quality saucepans, a quality, heavy-based frying pan, a wok, a roasting dish and a range of different-shaped cake pans are good starting points.

Read the recipe thoroughly, a couple of times, before starting to cook and follow it carefully.

Make sure you have all the required ingredients ahead of time. Use measuring equipment, not just your own estimates, and be precise with measurements.

It's important to grasp the basics before you start getting too ambitious: a well-cooked roast chicken, for example, is much nicer than a badly cooked coq au vin.

In this chapter we have assembled a selection of recipes that, collectively, encompass a range of cooking methods you would be wise to learn.

From an easy Sunday night meal of a fluffy omelette through to a mid-week pork and vegetable stir-fry and a traditional roast chicken, these are recipes to commit to your memory's hard drive.

If you follow these recipes carefully, and learn them, then you're on your way to being a good cook.

COOKING TECHNIQUES

SOME COOKING TERMS ARE INTERCHANGEABLE ('ROAST' AND 'BAKE' ARE THE SAME, FOR EXAMPLE, WHEN TALKING ABOUT MEATS, CHICKEN AND VEGETABLES) WHILE OTHERS SEEM TO OVERLAP IN MEANING: BROWNING, SEARING AND 'LIGHT PAN-FRYING', FOR EXAMPLE, CAN CAUSE CONFUSION. HERE IS A QUICK SNAPSHOT OF SOME OF THE COOKING TECHNIQUES YOU'LL NEED IN THIS CHAPTER AND THAT YOU'LL EMPLOY IN ANY AVERAGE WEEK IN THE KITCHEN:

GRILLING Using the humble grill found in every wall oven and under some stove tops, grilling produces an even and tasty, browned surface on everything from lamb chops to an omelette and is a healthy way to cook because the fats and juices drip into the tray.

PAN-FRYING (also called shallow frying, encompasses browning and searing) refers to cooking foods in a shallow amount of cooking oil in the frying pan on the stove top. The idea is to brown the food, cooking one side first and then turning once. Heat the oil first and when it is giving off a haze, place the food in the pan. Variations in the amount of oil used and in the stove top temperature setting will produce different results: searing uses the tiniest amount of oil and a quick cooking time; pan-frying a steak or cutlet requires more oil and a medium-high heat. See the chapter on pan-frying, on page 456.

DEGLAZING This is the term used when you add liquid (water, wine or stock) to a hot frying pan or baking dish after the meat or poultry has been removed. This liquid is then stirred over moderate-hot heat to blend all the leftover cooking juices into the liquid to create a sauce that can be added to other ingredients.

STIR-FRYING This fast cooking method involves cooking meat and vegetables in oil, tossing them in a wok, over a high heat. See the chapter on stir-fries, page 334.

ROASTING The words 'roast' and 'bake' are both used to describe foods (meats, chicken and vegetables) cooked uncovered in the oven. The vessel in which we cook these roasted items can be called a roasting pan or a baking dish. Most ovens have a 'hot spot' – that is, the oven doesn't heat up completely evenly, with the heat favouring one area. Many are also hotter towards the back, so you'll need to check on your roast once or twice during cooking and turn the pan around, if necessary, to even out the cooking.

RESTING After cooking, all meat and poultry needs to 'stand' or rest in a warm place (the oven turned off). Joints of meat or whole birds should stand for 15 minutes; smaller pieces of meat and poultry require 5 minutes. This makes the meat more succulent by allowing the juices to settle into the tissues.

BULB BASTER This looks like a giant eye-dropper with a metal stem and a rubber bulb. It makes it easy to suck up pan juices and distribute them over the food as it cooks.

STEWING A perfect tonic in winter, stewing is a type of slow-cooking that involves submerging meat and vegetables in liquid (water, stock or wine or a combination of the three) and cooking slowly in a large pot on the stove top, until the meat is tender.

RECIPES TO KNOW BY HEART THE AWW COOKING SCHOOL

RECIPES TO KNOW BY HEART

herb omelette

The idea of cooking beaten eggs with butter in a pan dates back to ancient times, yet today omelettes are still one of the simplest, most nutritious meals you can whip up in the kitchen. Getting it right though requires you to follow a few basic steps.

Eggs A large number of eggs on the supermarket shelf today are labelled free range. However, many of these are actually cage or barn-laid eggs. To ensure you are buying true free-range eggs, look for a certification logo from a free-range association.

Chives The smallest member of the onion family, chives are a source of beneficial antioxidants. But their real value to the home cook is the wonderful savoury flavour and vibrant colour they can add to the most basic dish.

Parsley Fresh parsley is quite fragile so it should always be washed right before using. The flat-leaf variety has a stronger flavour than curly parsley, so it holds up better to cooking. For this reason, it is best to use flat-leaf parsley for hot dishes such as this omelette.

Sharp knife Chopping herbs to the right size can help blend in their flavours. You'll chop faster, more precisely and more safely with a very sharp chef's knife.

Water Unlike scrambled eggs, omelettes require water, not milk to give them their lightness. The water turns to steam in the pan, producing a light, airy omelette.

The right pan If you don't want your omelette to resemble a dish of scrambled eggs, equip your kitchen with a cast-iron omelette pan. This makes it easy to neatly fold the omelette in half and slide it out of the frying pan without breaking it.

Chopping board A wooden cutting surface is just as safe as plastic if cleaned properly. Scrub it after every use with hot, soapy water, rinse, dry and stand it in a dish rack to air completely. Alternatively, use a paste of bicarbonate of soda and water to clean and deodorise your board.

1. Use a clean steel or glass bowl. Crack eggs into the bowl and beat lightly with a balloon whisk or fork, taking care not to overbeat. Stir in seasoning, if using, water and any flavouring, such as herbs. We used a combination of fresh flat-leaf parsley, chervil, chives and tarragon for this omelette.

2. In a small omelette pan, over medium-high heat, add enough butter and oil to cover the base of the pan. As all stove tops vary, adjust temperature if necessary. Cook butter mixture until it starts to foam.

3. When the butter mixture foams, add a quarter of the egg mixture, gently tilting the pan to cover the base. This ensures even cooking of eggs. Continue cooking over medium heat.

herb omelette

PREP + COOK TIME 20 MINS • SERVES 4

12 eggs
2 tablespoons finely chopped fresh flat-leaf parsley
2 tablespoons finely chopped fresh chervil
2 tablespoons finely chopped fresh chives
1 tablespoon finely chopped fresh tarragon
⅓ cup (80ml) water
20g butter
1 tablespoon olive oil

TIPS

• Use room temperature eggs for an omelette.

• Overbeating eggs will make the omelette tough.

• Using a mixture of butter and oil to cook the omelette stops the butter from burning.

• Using an omelette pan makes it easier to fold and remove the omelette from the pan.

• Do not wash omelette pan with soapy water, just wipe out with a damp cloth. Washing it will make it lose its non-stick surface.

Using a palette, small spatula or fork, draw sides of eggs towards the centre of the pan, allowing the uncooked mixture to run underneath. Continue pulling the eggs from the sides until eggs are set underneath but still slightly runny on top. This also gives the omelette a plump, "crinkled" effect.

Once set, carefully flip the side of the omelette towards the centre, using a spatula, to form a neat crescent shape. Remove pan from heat.

Gently slide the cooked omelette onto a warmed serving plate. Repeat steps 1 to 6 (wiping out the pan after each omelette), until you have made four omelettes. Serve omelettes while still hot.

Use free range eggs where possible for an omelette that is richer not only in colour and flavour, but also in nutrients.

1 Lightly whisk eggs, herbs and water in large bowl until just combined.

2 Heat a quarter of the butter and 1 teaspoon of the oil in small omelette pan. When butter is just bubbling, add a quarter of the egg mixture; tilt pan to cover base with egg mixture. Cook over medium heat until omelette is just set. Use a spatula to lift and fold omelette in half; cook further 30 seconds. Carefully slide omelette onto serving plate.

3 Repeat with remaining butter, oil and egg mixture (wiping out the pan after each omelette), to make a total of four omelettes. Serve immediately.

nutritional count per serving 24.4g total fat (8.2g saturated fat); 1254kJ (300 cal); 0.6g carbohydrate; 20.1g protein; 0.2g fibre

RECIPES TO KNOW BY HEART

roast chicken with herb stuffing

Its high-protein, healthy image and sheer affordability has driven chicken to the top of the meat menu in most households, while roasting it whole gets the most votes for the tastiest method.

Serving platter Always preheat the serving dish before placing the chicken on it so it stays warm. When you have removed the stuffing from the chicken's cavity, transfer the stuffing to a separate serving dish – and let everyone help themselves.

Herb stuffing We used a fresh herb stuffing, which can be made up to one day ahead. Store in an airtight container in the refrigerator until needed. Stuff the chicken just before you are ready to cook it, otherwise there is a risk of bacteria forming.

Potatoes An essential side to roast chicken is perfect baked potatoes. In an ovenproof dish, toss unskinned new or young potatoes in 1-2 tablespoons of extra virgin olive oil and season lightly. Roast on the bottom oven rack until golden and crispy on the outside and tender inside.

Crispy skin The key to achieving a crispy, golden-brown skin on the chicken is keeping the skin and flesh intact during roasting. Exposed flesh creates steam in the oven, so avoid cutting up the chicken until roasted.

Vegetables Steam your favourite seasonal vegetables and serve with the chicken. Or, instead of cooking the chicken on a rack, tuck root vegetables around the chicken in a baking dish. This method allows the vegetables to pick up the wonderful roasting juices from the chicken.

Carving tools A well-sharpened carving knife and serving fork will take the effort out of carving chicken. Removing the legs and wings first also makes carving easier. These darker meat areas are more likely to stay moist if cut first, unlike the drier white meat parts of the chicken.

Insert the herb stuffing into the body cavity, taking care not to tear the skin. Avoid overfilling the cavity because the stuffing will expand during cooking due to the absorption of the juices from the chicken. Never stuff the cavity in advance because this will increase the risk of bacteria growth.

Pull the skin flaps back into place to enclose the cavity. Seal in the stuffing by stitching 2 to 3 wooden toothpicks through the edges of the opening, like a needle in a tapestry. This will help hold the stuffing in while the chicken is cooking.

Truss the chicken with kitchen string. Hold one end of the string in each hand, loop the centre of the string around the legs and secure a knot.

roast chicken with herb stuffing

PREP + COOK TIME 2 HOURS 15 MINS • SERVES 4

1.5kg chicken
15g butter, melted

herb stuffing
1½ cups (105g) stale breadcrumbs
1 stalk celery (150g), trimmed, chopped finely
1 small white onion (80g), chopped finely
2 teaspoons finely chopped fresh sage leaves
1 tablespoon finely chopped fresh flat-leaf parsley
1 egg, beaten lightly
30g butter, melted

TIPS

• Drying the chicken thoroughly results in a crisper skin.

• Tying the chicken's legs together helps it to keep its shape during roasting.

• Placing the chicken on a rack prevents it from sticking to the pan and causing the skin to tear.

• The water in the baking dish creates steam, keeping the chicken moist.

• Basting the chicken during baking helps the skin to brown and keeps the chicken moist.

THE AWW COOKING SCHOOL RECIPES TO KNOW BY HEART

4 Place chicken, breast-side up, on a greased oven rack in a large baking dish. Always use a heavy-based baking dish so it doesn't wobble during cooking. Half-fill the dish with water to prevent any fat from burning and creating odours.

5 Spoon the pan juices all over the chicken as it cooks in the oven. Occasional basting adds great flavour and can help the chicken brown evenly.

6 Check whether chicken is done by piercing the thigh with a wooden skewer and inspecting the juices for any signs of pinkness (blood). If there is no sign of pink juices, the chicken is done. You can also check by tugging the drumstick – if the thigh joint feels loose, the chicken is fully cooked through.

A note on hygiene: raw chicken contains harmful bacteria that can cause salmonella. In light of this, it is important to be extra careful when handling raw chicken. To avoid cross-contamination, take care to wash all utensils that have been in contact with the raw meat, especially chopping boards.

A thermometer is an easy way to check whether the chicken (and stuffing) has been cooked through. A temperature of 75°C will ensure the chicken flesh will be white and its juices run clear.

1 Preheat oven to 200°C/180°C fan-forced.
2 Make herb stuffing.
3 Remove and discard any fat from cavity of chicken. Rinse chicken inside and out with water. Pat dry cavity and skin with absorbent paper. Fill cavity of chicken with stuffing, fold over skin to enclose stuffing; secure with toothpicks. Tie legs together with kitchen string.
4 Place chicken on greased rack in large baking dish. Half-fill dish with water – it should not touch the chicken. Brush chicken with butter; roast 15 minutes.
5 Reduce oven 180°C/160°C fan-forced. Bake further 1½ hours or until chicken is cooked through, basting occasionally with pan juices. Stand 10 minutes before breaking or cutting into serving-sized pieces.
herb stuffing Combine ingredients in medium bowl.
nutritional count per serving 35.9g total fat (14.4g saturated fat); 2437kJ (583 cal); 19.4g carbohydrate; 45g protein; 1.9g fibre

RECIPES TO KNOW BY HEART

pork and vegetable stir-fry

The stir-fry has become one of our favourite mid-week meals. It's given meat and poultry more flavour, added a spark to vegetables and lured time-poor cooks into the kitchen again.

Rice The Chinese always cook more rice than is needed for the meal. Leftovers are often used for making a perfect fried rice the following day as cooked rice that has been chilled for a day works better for this classic dish than freshly cooked rice. Store in a covered container and chill.

Table etiquette If you struggle getting enough grains into your mouth with chopsticks, you'll be glad to know how the Chinese do it. The socially-acceptable method is to bring the bowl close to your mouth and quickly scoop the rice into your mouth with chopsticks.

Balanced ingredients Chinese dishes offer contrast in taste, texture and colour. But it's not only to satisfy our senses. It is believed that harmonising our taste sensations (sour, sweet, salty, bitter and piquant) is a way to keep the body balanced and maintain good health.

Vegetables The trick to shiny, crunchy vegetables is to have all the ingredients ready before you start cooking. Stir-fries happen so fast and once you have started you won't have time to peel the onions or delve in the cupboard for the soy sauce. Keep everything close at hand.

Tea Traditionally, the Chinese do not drink tea with their meal. It is served as a post-meal digestif. Three main types of tea are used. These come from the same plant but are processed to produce black tea (fermented), oolong tea (semi-fermented) or green tea (unfermented).

Essential condiments For those who like to add extra heat, salty zing or a little sweetness to their dish, place condiment servers of hot chilli oil, soy, hoisin and sweet chilli sauces on the table. All these condiments, except the chilli oil, must be refrigerated once opened.

Chopsticks Not all chopsticks are alike – those from China are different from the ones used in Japan, Korea and other Asian countries. In Chinese chopsticks, the end held in the hand is squared off, while the other end is round and blunt. They are also longer – about 25cm in length.

Pork Some cuts of pork, such as tenderloin fillet, are as low or lower in fat than chicken, and more than half of the fat is unsaturated. Tenderloin is an elongated, tender muscle from the loin. It is the most tender part of the pig. Tenderloin fillet is the ideal cut for stir-fries.

1. On a clean chopping surface, cut the pork fillet into thin slices with a sharp chef's knife. Always cut pork across the grain for stir-fries as this will keep the meat tender during cooking.

2. Remove the stem and base of the capsicum with a sharp knife. Stand upright on a chopping surface and cut down the length of the capsicum to open. Cut into wedges. Place cut-side up and cut along the inside to remove the seeds and membrane.

3. Cut the onion in half from top to root and rest one of the halves, flat-side down, on the chopping board. Holding a sharp knife parallel to the cutting surface, thinly slice the onion from head to the root. Repeat for the remaining onion half.

pork and vegetable stir-fry

PREP + COOK TIME 30 MINS • SERVES 4

2 tablespoons peanut oil
600g pork fillets, sliced
1 large brown onion (200g), sliced thinly
1 clove garlic, crushed
340g asparagus, trimmed, cut into 4cm lengths
2 medium red capsicums (400g), sliced thinly
½ cup (125ml) plum sauce
2 tablespoons light soy sauce

TIPS

• Make sure all your ingredients are prepared and immediately at hand before starting to stir-fry.

• Heat the wok to very hot before adding the oil, then tilt the wok to coat all over in oil.

• Cook food in batches so the heat of the wok does not reduce.

• Toss food constantly so it doesn't stick to the base of the wok.

• A wok chan is used to keep food moving and turning constantly. The angle and curved edge of a chan's wide, shovel-like blade are designed to fit the curve of the wok.

Swirl the oil in a very hot wok. Add the pork, in batches, to avoid overcrowding as this reduces the wok's heating capacity, stewing the meat instead of stir-frying it. Adjust the temperature up or down as needed. To allow pork to brown, wait a few seconds before tossing with a wok chan. When the pork is browned, remove from the wok and set aside.

Add vegetables according to density – the onion and garlic should be stirred in first, followed by the capsicum and asparagus. Move vegetables around immediately and continuously with the chan.

Return the pork to the wok once the vegetables are almost cooked. This prevents the meat from overcooking and allows the vegetables and meat to retain their individual flavours. Form a "well" in the centre by pushing ingredients up the sides of the wok, add sauces in the centre and stir to thicken. When stir-fry is cooked, taste and adjust seasonings.

Make sure you cut all your vegies into similar size pieces – strips or bite-sized pieces work well. This ensures that they all cook at the same rate. If you cut your vegetables on the diagonal, it not only improves the attractiveness of the dish, it maximises their exposure to the heat.

You could use chicken, beef or seafood in this recipe instead of pork.

1 Heat 1 tablespoon of the oil in wok; stir-fry pork, in batches, until browned. Remove pork from wok.
2 Heat remaining oil in wok; stir-fry onion and garlic 1 minute. Add asparagus and capsicum; stir-fry until softened.
3 Return pork to wok with combined sauces; stir-fry until pork is cooked as desired.
nutritional count per serving 13.2g total fat (2.9g saturated fat); 1647kJ (394 cal); 30g carbohydrate; 37g protein; 2.9g fibre
serving idea boiled or steamed rice.

RECIPES TO KNOW BY HEART

glazed meatloaf

A comfort food that nurtured so many of us through the fifties and sixties, meatloaf has made a return. It's a traditional dish but invites innovation, so you can try your own creative turn on the classic. As for the potential with leftovers, you'll be covered for a whole week.

Vegetable mixture By adding grated or pureed vegetables to your mixture, you are adding more moisture to the meatloaf. Not only does this make your final product juicier, it also adds lots of extra flavour and nutrients. Try grated carrot, zucchini or spinach and herbs.

Meat selections Beef mince is the standard for meatloaf as it has the right percentage of meat to fat ratio (80:20) for juicy, but not greasy, results. You can experiment with various mince combinations such as pork, veal and chicken, as well as Italian sausage.

Bread filler For a very tender, lighter-textured meatloaf, you can replace stale breadcrumbs with cubes of fresh white bread. Beat 1 egg and ⅔ cup milk together in a small bowl, pour over bread cubes and soak for 15 minutes, before mashing into small chunks with a fork.

The essential egg Should you add beaten eggs or not? Eggs help bind the loaf and also add richness. Another option is to hard-boil the egg, slice or chop it and combine it with the other ingredients, as well as parmesan cheese, for an extra tasty, high-protein meatloaf.

The glaze Coating the meatloaf with a glaze does more than just enhance its presentation. It adds wonderful flavour, which you can vary by using different ingredients. Both savoury and sweet glazes work well. Glazing also helps keep the meatloaf moist during cooking.

Matching drinks Think about the flavours in the meatloaf and glaze before pairing with drinks. Our meatloaf is lightly seasoned, so it goes well with almost any full-bodied red wine such as cabernet sauvignon. Tomato juice and mineral water make good non-alcoholic choices.

Accompaniments Meatloaf goes with most vegetables, from a winter potato mash and steamed spinach or broccoli to blanched green beans and asparagus in summer. Salads can offset the flavours of the loaf too – try rocket with tomato, tabbouleh or a robust pasta salad.

Leftovers Meatloaf is so easy to make, it's worth doubling up on the recipe and making two. A little meatloaf goes a long way. Leftovers can be sliced for wraps or sandwiches, or crumbled in a red pasta sauce, mexican chilli bean dish or even a casserole for a quick weeknight meal.

1. Lightly brush a loaf pan with oil, once you have preheated the oven to 180°C/160°C fan-forced. This is the ideal temperature for a moist meatloaf. Too hot an oven might reduce the cooking time, but it will also dry out the meat. Keep the temperature at moderate.

2. Combine the mixture until just mixed. Wet your hands with cold water beforehand to prevent mixture from sticking. A common mistake is to overmix the ingredients. Overmixing produces a compressed mixture, which will squeeze out liquid during baking, resulting in a drier meatloaf. Remember the loaf will be handled further, when it is pressed into the pan.

3. Press the mixture into the pan, after you have wet your hands again with cold water. Smooth the top of the loaf to remove any cracks, which can cause a loss of moisture during cooking.

glazed meatloaf

PREP + COOK TIME 1 HOUR • SERVES 4

750g beef mince
1 cup (70g) stale breadcrumbs
1 medium brown onion (150g), chopped finely
1 egg
2 tablespoons tomato sauce
1 tablespoon worcestershire sauce
185g can evaporated milk
2 teaspoons mustard powder
1 tablespoon brown sugar
½ teaspoon mustard powder, extra
¼ cup (60ml) tomato sauce, extra

4 Invert the loaf pan onto a foil-lined oven tray, leaving the pan in place. Bake for 15 minutes. Meanwhile, prepare the meatloaf glaze, combining the sugar, extra mustard and extra tomato sauce in a small bowl. Set the glaze aside until needed.

5 Remove the loaf from the oven after 15 minutes and carefully remove the pan. Take care not to break the meatloaf when you are lifting off the pan.

6 Brush the meatloaf generously with the glaze. Make sure you spread the glaze evenly over the top, then brush the sides lightly with the glaze. Return the meatloaf to the oven for a further 45 minutes or until well browned and cooked through. Remove the meatloaf from the oven and allow it to rest for 10 to 15 minutes before slicing and serving.

Let the meatloaf stand for 10 to 15 minutes before serving. This allows it to set and makes it much easier to slice.

Leftover meatloaf is delicious sliced cold as a sandwich filling and is a perfect addition to a picnic basket. It can also be crumbled into pasta sauces or stir-fries.

1 Preheat oven to 180°C/160°C fan-forced. Oil 14cm x 21cm loaf pan.
2 Combine beef, breadcrumbs, onion, egg, sauces, milk and mustard in medium bowl. Press mixture into pan. Turn pan upside-down onto a foil-lined oven tray; leave pan in place. Bake 15 minutes.
3 Meanwhile, combine sugar, extra mustard and extra tomato sauce in small bowl.
4 Remove loaf from oven; remove pan. Brush loaf well with glaze, return loaf to oven; bake 45 minutes or until well browned and cooked through.
5 Serve meatloaf, if desired, with rocket leaves and tomato wedges.

nutritional count per serving 19.9g total fat (10g saturated fat); 1986kJ (475 cal); 29.1g carbohydrate; 45.8g protein; 1.8g fibre

serving ideas rocket and tomato salad or steamed vegetables.

RECIPES TO KNOW BY HEART

steak with pepper sauce

Food fads come and go but beef-eaters have never lost their taste for steak with pepper sauce. A good steak is juicy and flavourful – and expensive, so you want to get it right every time. And a creamy pepper sauce is just the right accompaniment, along with some perfectly cooked chips.

Prime steak cuts For a great steakhouse-style steak at home, consider scotch fillet (rib-eye), eye-fillet (tenderloin), new-york cut (boneless sirloin), t-bone (sirloin with bone in) and rump. All can be pan-fried, grilled or barbecued. But scotch fillet is prized for its marbling effect.

The marbling advantage The key to tenderness, flavour and juiciness in a cut is marbling (when fat is distributed evenly throughout the muscle instead of being concentrated in one area). The small flecks of fat deposits dissolve and distribute throughout the meat.

Judging a rare steak If you like your steak rare, simply make a circle with your index finger and thumb, and apply pressure to the ball on the palm side of your thumb. It will feel very soft when pressed with the back of tongs. Press the centre of the steak. If it has the same texture, it is rare.

Resting the meat Never serve steak right after it is cooked. Meat is all tensed up from the heat of the cooking, so it needs to "rest" for about 10 minutes to let the juices move back into the meat. It is best if you cover it loosely and keep it at room temperature – not in the oven.

Steakhouse chips Use floury, low-moisture potatoes like idaho (russet burbank), bintje or spunta. Cut lengthways into 1cm slices; cut each slice lengthways into 1cm-wide sticks. Stand in bowl of cold water for 30 minutes. Drain; pat dry with absorbent paper. Heat peanut oil in deep frying pan; cook chips, in three batches, 4 minutes each or until just soft but not browned. Drain on absorbent paper; stand 10 minutes. Heat oil; cook chips, in three batches, until crisp and golden brown. Drain on absorbent paper. Season lightly.

Best steak pans Only by having contact with really intense heat can you cook a steak hot enough and fast enough to replicate a steakhouse-style steak. To achieve this you need a basic heavy-based frying pan or cast-iron pan, as these can hold the heat.

Pan deglazing sauce Cooking meat or vegetables in oil, then adding wine, stock, even water to the same pan is the first step to making a deglazing sauce. The idea is to loosen up the bits that have stuck to the pan and incorporate them into the liquid because they are full of flavour.

Grinding pepper Pulverising ingredients with a mortar and pestle releases flavour essence and oils. Place peppercorns inside the mortar (bowl). Sit the pestle on top of the peppercorns; apply downward pressure and grind using a circular motion. This force pulverises it.

Add half the oil to the pan over high heat. Before adding the steak, make sure the oil is hot and smoking. Mono-unsaturated oils, such as olive oil, are best for cooking steaks. Unlike butter, it won't burn and it is also low in saturated fats.

Make sure the meat is dry before adding it to the pan. Place the steaks in the pan and cook for 2 minutes or until browned. Turn over and cook until done to your liking. As the pan sears the meat's surface, it begins melting the fat, causing splattering, smoke and sometimes flames, so take care. This process caramelises the meat, making it sweet and flavourful. Remove meat, cover and allow it to rest.

Heat the remaining oil in the same pan. Add the onion and celery, and stir well to combine. Cook, stirring all the time, until the vegetables are tender.

steak with pepper sauce

PREP + COOK TIME 25 MINS • SERVES 4

1 tablespoon olive oil
4 x 200g scotch fillet steaks
1 stalk celery (150g), trimmed, chopped finely
1 medium brown onion (150g), chopped finely
½ cup (125ml) dry white wine
300ml cream
1 tablespoon mixed peppercorns, crushed
1 tablespoon coarsely chopped fresh thyme

TIPS

• Make sure the pan is hot before adding the steaks, this helps seal in the juices.

• Cook presentation side of steak first, to get the correct colour and then turn to cook the other side to desired doneness.

• Only turn steaks once during pan-frying. Continual turning will result in dry, tough steaks.

• Cook the vegetables in the same pan and then add the wine which "deglazes" the pan. This picks up all the colour and flavour from cooking the steak, resulting in a rich sauce.

Pour the liquid in all at once. We used dry white wine, but stock or water can be used. Scrape the brown bits on the bottom of the pan loose with a wooden spoon. Keep deglazing in this way, scraping and reducing. Cook until the liquid in the pan is reduced by half.

Add the cream and mixed peppercorns and bring the mixture to the boil. Reduce heat and simmer, uncovered, stirring occasionally, for about 5 minutes.

Once sauce has thickened slightly, remove the pan from the heat and stir in fresh thyme. Serve immediately with prepared steak.

1 Heat half the oil in large frying pan; cook steaks, in batches, until cooked as desired. Remove from pan; cover to keep warm.
2 Heat remaining oil in same pan; cook celery and onion, stirring, until vegetables soften. Add wine; stir until liquid is reduced by half. Add cream and peppercorns; bring to the boil. Reduce heat; simmer, uncovered, stirring occasionally, about 5 minutes or until sauce thickens slightly. Remove from heat; stir in thyme.
3 Serve steaks drizzled with sauce.
nutritional count per serving 46.7g total fat (26.3g saturated fat); 2658kJ (636 cal); 5g carbohydrate; 44.2g protein; 1.4g fibre
serving idea steakhouse chips (see page 28).

RECIPES TO KNOW BY HEART

chicken, mushroom and leek fricassee

A famous French dish, using vegetables, white meat and a creamy sauce, you will find yourself making fricassee for guests over and over again. It even makes a great base for other meals. Its virtue is not only wonderful flavour but simplicity. Once the fricassee is in the oven, you can walk away for a while and join the party.

Adding lean flavour Sometimes chicken fricassee refers to the way the chicken is cut. The French classic recipe calls for a whole chicken, which is cut into eight pieces. We've used leaner thigh fillets and given the dish an instant flavour boost with the addition of bacon.

Easy entertainer Aside from the chicken, the only items to have on hand for fricassee are some aromatic vegetables and liquids in which to braise the chicken. This can simply be the wine you didn't finish the other night, the leftover stock and that carton of cream lurking in the refrigerator.

A sauté or stew? Fricassee actually uses both these cooking methods. The chicken is cooked in oil (sautéed), then wine, stock and cream are added, and the chicken is stewed. Our recipe departs from the French classic at times but the results are still the same – a perfect fricassee.

Base to many meals A quick alternative to a slow-cooked ragout, fricassee can be served with pasta, such as tagliatelle or pappardelle. In Louisiana's Cajun country, the dish is often served with rice and kidney beans, while the Tunisians use it as a filling for a fried sandwich.

Food safety Make sure you wash all surfaces that have been used to prepare the chicken. Also wash your hands with hot, soapy water before you handle other food or utensils. When braising the chicken, don't remove it from the pan until it is cooked all the way through.

Mushrooms We used button mushrooms for this recipe but you can use swiss brown mushrooms for a richer taste. For extra flavour, try using soaked, dried wild mushrooms such as porcini, chanterelle or a mix and incorporate the soaking water into the stock mixture.

Choosing the one pot As this fricassee is finished off in the oven, you will need a flameproof baking dish. Both enamel and metal dishes work well. Heavy cast-iron dutch ovens are also a good choice because they conduct heat well on all stove tops, as well as in the oven.

Cut the chicken thigh fillets into quarters on a clean, dry surface. Make sure you have dried the chicken thoroughly beforehand by patting each fillet with absorbent paper.

Heat oil in a heavy-based flameproof dish. Cook the chicken in batches, turning every minute, for 3 to 4 minutes, until the meat has stiffened slightly and is browned all over. Remove chicken from dish.

Cook the bacon in the same dish, stirring until browned slightly. Add the butter and leek, and cook, stirring occasionally, until leek softens.

chicken, mushroom and leek fricassee

PREP + COOK TIME 50 MINS • SERVES 6

2 tablespoons olive oil
1.5kg chicken thigh fillets, quartered
3 rindless bacon rashers (195g), chopped coarsely
40g butter
3 medium leeks (1kg), trimmed, sliced thinly
3 stalks celery (450g), trimmed, sliced thinly
3 cloves garlic, crushed
¼ cup loosely packed fresh thyme sprigs
2 bay leaves
2 tablespoons plain flour
1½ cups (375ml) dry white wine
1½ cups (375ml) chicken stock
400g button mushrooms
¼ cup (60ml) cream
½ cup coarsely chopped fresh flat-leaf parsley

Stir in the celery, garlic, thyme and bay leaves. Sprinkle the flour into the vegetable and bacon mixture, and stir well to combine. By adding the flour you create a roux-like base for the dish.

Stir in the wine and stock to cover the ingredients. Bring to the boil, stirring constantly. Stir in chicken and mushrooms. Transfer dish to oven and cook for 20 minutes or until chicken is cooked through.

Return the dish to the stove top, discard bay leaves then gradually stir in the cream. Add fresh parsley and simmer, uncovered, until fricassee is heated through. Garnish with fresh thyme leaves just before serving.

This flavoursome fricassee makes a fantastic pie filling. Place the warm chicken mixture in a 24cm pie dish, top with a sheet of puff pastry and trim around the edge. Bake at 200°C/180°C fan-forced for 25 minutes or until the pastry is browned and crisp.

1 Preheat oven to 160°C/140°C fan-forced.

2 Heat oil in large heavy-based flameproof dish; cook chicken, in batches, until browned all over. Remove from pan.

3 Cook bacon in same dish, stirring, until browned lightly.

4 Add butter and leek to dish; cook, stirring occasionally, until leek softens. Stir in celery, garlic, thyme and bay leaves. Stir in flour, then wine and stock; bring to the boil, stirring. Stir in chicken and mushrooms.

5 Transfer dish to oven; cook about 20 minutes or until chicken is cooked through and sauce has thickened slightly.

6 Return dish to stove top, discard bay leaves; stir in cream and parsley. Simmer, uncovered, until fricassee is heated through. Garnish with fresh thyme leaves.

nutritional count per serving 39.2g total fat (14.6g saturated fat); 2805kJ (671 cal); 8.6g carbohydrate; 59.1g protein; 6.2g fibre

RECIPES TO KNOW BY HEART

featherlight sponge cake

Few things can impress more than a whisked up sponge cake that's light, airy – and 10cm high. The secret is a little patience, a light hand and these expert tips.

Preventing a flop Fresh ingredients are a must for a well-risen sponge. When baking, position cakes so the tops of the pans are in the oven centre; remove any upper shelves. If using two shelves, swap positions halfway through baking. Opening the oven gently won't affect the cakes at this point.

Getting it light We used wheaten cornflour, which is made from wheat rather than corn, giving this sponge a lighter texture. To achieve a fine texture, we used caster sugar, instead of granulated white sugar. Triple-sifting dry ingredients combines them and aerates them.

When is it cooked? When the sponge appears to begin to shrink from the side of the pan, you'll know the cake is ready. It should also feel slightly springy to the touch. Shake the pan gently to make sure the cake is free – turn it out immediately onto a wire rack covered with baking paper, then turn it up the right way to prevent the wire forming marks on the cake.

Better baking Shiny aluminium pans are ideal for cake-baking because they reflect heat away from the cake and produce a tender, light brown crust. If you use a pan with a dark, non-stick surface, you need to reduce the oven temperature by 10°C as these pans absorb more heat.

The adaptable sponge You can make the sponge and simply fill it with jam and cream, as we have, or cream and either lemon curd, fresh or stewed fruit.

Deep-sided cake pans give the best results as the high sides protect the delicate sponge mixture and prevent a crisp crust developing. Grease the cake pans using a pastry brush dipped in melted butter. Sprinkle the pans with flour, tap and turn the pans to coat the surface evenly. Tap the pans upside down over the sink to discard excess flour.

Triple-sift the dry ingredients. Sifting three times mixes the ingredients thoroughly and aerates them which produces a lighter, finer textured cake. Hold the sifter up high to incorporate as much air as possible into the flour.

In the bowl of an electric mixer, beat the eggs and caster sugar together until the sugar is dissolved and the mixture is thick and creamy. If the mixer has two beaters, use a small narrow-topped bowl to get the maximum volume.

featherlight sponge cake

PREP + COOK TIME 40 MINS • SERVES 10

4 eggs
¾ cup (165g) caster sugar
⅔ cup (100g) wheaten cornflour
¼ cup (30g) custard powder
1 teaspoon cream of tartar
½ teaspoon bicarbonate of soda
⅓ cup (110g) apricot jam
300ml thickened cream, whipped

TIPS

• Cake pans are best greased evenly with melted butter.

• Beating the eggs and sugar can take up to 10 minutes to get the correct volume. Using a narrow-topped bowl will allow the beaters to give volume to the egg and sugar mixture.

• Fold the flour into the cake mixture in a gentle, light circular motion for a lighter texture.

• Store unfilled sponges, wrapped well, in the freezer for up to 2 months.

Quickly transfer the mixture to a larger, wide-topped bowl – if using a small bowl – to make it easier to fold the ingredients gently together. Use a metal spoon, a knife, or a plastic or rubber spatula. Fold in triple-sifted dry ingredients.

Divide mixture between the pans, gently spreading it to the edge. The mixture will not spread once it is in the oven. The last scrapings from the bowl should be placed around the edge of the pan. If placed in the centre, a dark patch will form. To break large air bubbles, run a knife through mixture a few times.

When cooked, remove cakes from oven. Turn cakes immediately onto wire racks lined with baking paper, and then turn up the right way. This will prevent the wire racks from marking the cakes.

Sponge cakes rely heavily on eggs for their fluffiness and structure. The quality and age of the eggs used can affect the success of your sponge. Ideally, eggs are at their best for sponge-making at 2 days old.

The sugar will dissolve slightly faster if room-temperature eggs are used.

Use good quality raspberry or plum jam for a more tart filling.

1 Preheat oven to 180°C/160°C fan-forced. Grease and flour two deep 22cm-round cake pans.
2 Beat eggs and sugar in small bowl with electric mixer until thick, creamy and sugar is dissolved. Transfer mixture to large bowl; fold in triple-sifted dry ingredients. Divide mixture between pans.
3 Bake sponges about 20 minutes. Turn, top-side up, onto baking-paper-covered wire rack to cool.
4 Sandwich sponges with jam and cream.
nutritional count per serving 13.3g total fat (8g saturated fat); 1195kJ (286 cal); 37.2g carbohydrate; 3.8g protein; 0.7g fibre

VARIATIONS
ginger fluff sponge Omit custard powder, increase cornflour to ¾ cup and add 1 teaspoon cocoa powder, 2 teaspoons ground ginger and ½ teaspoon ground cinnamon. Fill sponge with whipped cream.
slab sponge Sponge can be baked in 25cm-square cake pan for 20-25 minutes.

RECIPES TO KNOW BY HEART

basic butter cake

A good butter cake should be flavourful, yet not overly sweet, tender and somewhat dense in texture, but certainly not dry. It should be able to stand on its own, or be filled and iced, or decorated to the hilt. It should become one of your "every occasion" cakes. A butter cake can be the beginning of many great desserts.

Sifting Flours are pre-sifted these days, but it's still best to sift dry ingredients especially when there is more than one – the sifting mixes the ingredients together, as well as aerates them. Use either a sifter or a fine wire or plastic strainer.

Icing the cake If you want to ice the cake, place it on a wire rack over a sheet of baking paper. Elevating the cake stops the icing from pooling around the bottom of the cake, while the baking paper catches any drips.

Essence or extract? Vanilla extract has a far superior flavour to vanilla essence. When buying, make sure it is labelled "pure". Imitation vanilla is made with synthetic vanilla and can leave a bitter aftertaste. The extract may be more expensive but you only need to use half as much.

Greasing the pan Cake pans need greasing – even non-stick surfaces – to prevent the cake from sticking. You can use either cooking oil spray or melted butter. It is best to use a pastry brush to coat the base and side(s) of the pans evenly.

Butter Using butter at room temperature makes it easier to work with and aids aeration. If you have forgotten to take the butter out of the fridge, coarsely grate it or soften it in the microwave for 10 seconds.

Cupcakes The recipe for butter cake makes the perfect mixture for cupcakes. Pour mixture into two 12-hole patty pans lined with paper cases until two-thirds full. Bake for 20 minutes. Turn cakes, top-side up, onto wire racks to cool completely. Top cakes with icing of your choice.

Ways with cake A butter cake is so versatile. Serve it plain or slightly warmed (20 seconds in a microwave oven) with fresh fruit, lightly toasted with ice-cream on the side, iced, or spread with jam or cream.

Grease and line the base and side(s) of a pan with baking paper, extending the paper a little above the edge of the pan. Always use the pan size specified in the recipe. A deep 20cm-square or 22cm-round cake pan is best for this recipe. If you use a pan that is too large, the cake will not rise properly or brown evenly. If the pan is too small, the mixture is likely to dome and crack, or worse, run over the top of the pan.

Beat the softened butter, vanilla extract and caster sugar at medium speed in an electric mixer or until fluffy and light in colour. Scrape down the sides of the bowl with a rubber spatula several times during the mixing.

Add the eggs, one at a time, with the mixer on low speed and beat for several seconds between each addition. Overbeating will soften the butter too much and will cause curdling.

basic butter cake

PREP + COOK TIME 1 HOUR 30 MINS • SERVES 12

250g butter, softened
1 teaspoon vanilla extract
1¼ cups (275g) caster sugar
3 eggs
2¼ cups (335g) self-raising flour
¾ cup (180ml) milk

TIPS

• When beating in eggs, ensure each egg is combined well in butter mixture before adding the next egg. Do this quickly to avoid curdling.

• Add any flavouring such as extracts, essences, citrus rinds etc. with the butter. The resulting flavour of the baked cake will be better than if flavourings were added with the flour and milk.

• Store butter cake at room temperature, in an airtight container for 2 days, or can be frozen for 2 months.

4 Stir in half the sifted flour and half the milk, gently stir the ingredients together using a wooden spoon; the mixture will look a little lumpy. Add the remaining flour and milk, gently stir until the ingredients combine. Still using the wooden spoon, beat the mixture quickly and firmly for a few seconds to smooth the mixture.

5 Spread the mixture evenly into the pan and bake in the preheated oven. You may need to rotate the pan to ensure even baking. Check the cake about 5 minutes before the end of baking time. If it feels firm and is browned evenly, test the cake by inserting a fine metal skewer in the centre. If the skewer is clean – free from cake mixture – the cake is cooked.

6 Remove cake from oven; stand in pan for 5 minutes. Invert the pan onto a wire rack lined with baking paper. Allow cake to cool completely before dusting with icing sugar, or topping with icing, and slicing.

1 Preheat oven to 180°C/160°C fan-forced. Grease deep 20cm-square or 22cm-round cake pan; line base and side(s) with baking paper.
2 Beat butter, extract and sugar in medium bowl with electric mixer until light and fluffy. Beat in eggs, one at a time. Stir in sifted flour and milk, in two batches.
3 Spread mixture into pan; bake about 1 hour. Stand cake 5 minutes; turn, top-side up, onto wire rack to cool.
nutritional count per serving 18.6g total fat (11.6g saturated fat); 1522kJ (364 cal); 43.5g carbohydrate; 5.1g protein; 1.1g fibre

VARIATIONS
orange cake Replace vanilla extract with 1 teaspoon finely grated orange rind and replace ¼ cup (60ml) of the milk with freshly squeezed orange juice.
chocolate cake Replace ¼ cup of the flour with ¼ cup cocoa powder.

RECIPES TO KNOW BY HEART

basic butter cookies

Baking from scratch is pure therapy and can give the home cook as much pleasure as it gives those eating the end result. Biscuits are especially rewarding. Unlike cake, which can disappear in less time than it takes to make, biscuits go a long way. Using very few ingredients, the recipe for these basic cookies is virtually failproof. But there are some secrets you need to know before you start.

Leave room to spread Place biscuits about 2cm apart on the oven tray. If they are too close together, the biscuits won't cook through properly, or they will join together.

[clockwise from top left]
chocolate and hazelnut cookies;
basic butter cookies;
dried cranberry cookies.

Keep biscuits fresh If making more than one type of biscuit, store each variety in a separate container, or they will soften quickly. To re-crisp softened biscuits, bake on a non-stick or lined oven tray in a moderate (180°C/160°C fan-forced) oven for about 5 minutes. Transfer to a wire rack to cool.

Beat the butter and sifted sugar in a bowl, using an electric mixer, until the mixture changes to a lighter colour. Take care not to overbeat the butter and sugar mixture. Overbeating can produce a very soft mixture, causing the biscuits to spread too much in the oven.

Transfer mixture to a large bowl if using a small bowl from an electric mixer with two beaters. Stir in sifted flour, in two batches, to take the effort out of mixing.

Knead dough gently on a lightly floured surface until smooth. Try not to over-handle the dough or the gluten in the flour will develop, producing a tough-textured biscuit. The dough must stay cold too. Run warm hands under cold water, then dry before kneading quickly and lightly.

basic butter cookies

PREP + COOK TIME 30 MINS (+ REFRIGERATION) • MAKES 50

250g butter, softened
1 cup (160g) icing sugar
2½ cups (375g) plain flour

TIPS

• Cookies should feel soft in the oven even though they're cooked. Check the cookies a few minutes before the end of baking time – if they feel a little soft, but firm, give one cookie a gentle push with the side of your thumb. A cooked cookie will slide easily on the tray. The cookies will become crisp on cooling.

• Store cookies in an airtight container for up to 1 week.

• Keep this dough, rolled into a log shape and tightly sealed in plastic wrap, in your fridge for up to 3 days or in your freezer for up to 3 months. Thaw in refrigerator before cutting into slices.

Divide the dough in half and roll each half into a 25cm log. If you are working in a warm kitchen, refrigerate one dough half to keep it firm. When you are ready to roll t, remove it from the refrigerator.

Cut logs into 1cm slices, using a sharp knife. Don't press down hard on the log or you will squash it and the cookies will lose their round shape.

Place cookies on greased oven trays lined with baking paper. A flat aluminium tray with little or no sides is best as it allows heat to circulate for even browning. Make sure there is enough space between biscuits so they can spread. Bake about 10 minutes or until browned lightly. Rest on trays for a few minutes before cooling on a wire rack.

1 Beat butter and sifted sugar in small bowl with electric mixer until light and fluffy. Transfer mixture to large bowl; stir in flour, in two batches.
2 Knead dough on lightly floured surface until smooth. Divide dough in half; roll each half into a 25cm log. Wrap in plastic wrap; refrigerate about 1 hour or until firm.
3 Preheat oven to 180°C/160°C fan-forced. Grease oven trays; line with baking paper.
4 Cut logs into 1cm slices; place slices on trays about 2cm apart.
5 Bake cookies about 10 minutes or until browned lightly. Transfer cookies onto wire rack to cool.
nutritional count per cookie 4g total fat (2.6g saturated fat); 314kJ (75 cal); 8.6g carbohydrate; 0.9g protein; 0.3g fibre

VARIATIONS
chocolate and hazelnut Beat 2 tablespoons sifted cocoa powder into butter and sugar mixture, then stir in ⅓ cup ground hazelnuts and ¼ cup finely chopped milk Choc Bits before adding the flour.
dried cranberry Stir in ⅔ cup finely chopped dried cranberries into butter and sugar mixture.
vanilla Beat 1 teaspoon vanilla extract into butter and sugar mixture.
lemon Beat 1 teaspoon finely grated lemon rind into butter and sugar mixture.
orange Beat 1 teaspoon finely grated orange rind into butter and sugar mixture.

SHOWING OFF

Showing off

We're going to let you in on a little secret: many of the classic dishes that you might order at a restaurant, but wouldn't dare to attempt yourself, are actually simpler than you might expect.

It's natural to feel intimidated by the thought of cooking a glazed baked ham or a beef wellington, and to assume that the time-honoured classic recipes are the preserve of master chefs and those with years of cooking experience under their belt. But often, these dishes are classics because they are so simple and dependably delicious. They still require care and attention to get them right, but they are very achievable for beginner and veteran home cooks alike.

It's good to have a repertoire of reliable recipes you can call upon for a dinner party with family or friends. The recipes in this chapter are dinner party classics: they are exquisitely presented, taste extraordinary and, best of all, are hearteningly easy to make. Dazzle your family and friends the next time you invite them around for dinner.

DINNER PARTY RULES

There are a few important, stress-reducing steps you can take to ensure your dinner party is as enjoyable for you as it is for your guests.

MAKE AHEAD OF TIME This is the key to making your dinner party as smooth-running as possible. Cook and prepare what you can ahead of time, either a few hours prior to your guests arriving, or even the day before. You don't want to be madly stirring at the stove top when people are walking through your door.

CHOOSE ONE 'STAR' COURSE that you spend time on. This should preferably be a recipe you've tried before and feel confident cooking again: you don't want to add to your stress by taking on a new, complicated dish with unknown results.

PLAN THE OTHER COURSE, OR COURSES, AROUND YOUR 'STAR' COURSE Keep them really simple and, preferably, made ahead. A lemon tart, for example, is easy to make but never fails to attract admiration from everybody. It can be made the day before and kept, perfectly poised, in the fridge until required.

REMEMBER TO THINK ABOUT THE DINNER AS A WHOLE If you're planning a rich crème brûlée for dessert, then a light, flavoursome main (such as Thai steamed fish in banana leaves) would be a wonderful prequel. Don't double up on two cream-based courses or two pastry-based courses.

DON'T FEEL PRESSURED TO MAKE EVERYTHING YOURSELF Your guests will already be impressed, so take the pressure off and include some quality store-bought items. For a fantastic antipasto platter, check your local deli for a wide selection of char-grilled vegetables. Pre-made pastry cases are ideal time-savers when teamed with a home-made filling – sweet or savoury. And for a quick dessert with maximum impact, fill chocolate dessert cups (often found near pavlova shells in supermarkets) with ready-made mousse and top with fresh berries. It'll be our little secret.

IMPRESSIVE CLASSICS

THERE ARE MANY FOODS THAT NON-COOKS (AND COOKS TOO) THINK ARE HARD BECAUSE THEY ARE EXOTIC, OR LEGENDARY, OR BOTH. THE THAI STEAMED FISH RECIPE IN THIS CHAPTER, FOR EXAMPLE, IS STRAIGHTFORWARD ENOUGH, BUT THE AROMATIC HERBS USED AND THE CREATIVE PRESENTATION OF THE DISH HELP TO LIFT THE MEAL INTO ANOTHER DIMENSION. LIKEWISE, THE TERRINE DE CAMPAGNE IS MORE THAN JUST A FANCY NAME FOR MEATLOAF: THIS FLAVOUR-PACKED DISH WITH MINCED PORK AND CHICKEN LIVERS IS EASY TO MAKE AND SUPER IMPRESSIVE. IT NEVER FAILS TO DRAW GASPS FROM EVERYONE AT THE TABLE. HERE ARE SOME OTHER SURPRISINGLY SIMPLE RECIPES:

CHICKEN LIVER PATE This silky-smooth pâté is easy and relatively inexpensive to make. The finished pâté can be made ahead and refrigerated, covered with plastic wrap, for up to 1 week.

BEEF WELLINGTON This is another dish you might naturally think you would reserve for ordering at a restaurant but it is very easy to assemble and great for dinner parties. An impressive and hearty dish of succulent beef tenderloin wrapped in golden puff pastry, it looks wonderful sitting centre stage on the dinner table and easily cuts into multiple servings. Beef wellington can be prepared and refrigerated ahead of your guests' arrival: it can cook while they have their pre-dinner drinks and nibbles.

GLAZED BAKED HAM Synonymous with Christmas entertaining and important occasions, a glazed baked ham is a grand culinary statement but surprisingly quick and easy to prepare.

SOUFFLES These elegant, special-occasion foods are famous for being lighter than air and equally famous for being temperamental. In fact, despite the mystique that surrounds them, soufflés are easy. They key is in the beating and folding of the egg whites, which takes particular care but is not really hard, and the cooking time, which can be easily monitored. Even soufflé mixtures can be made ahead of time, except for the addition of the egg whites. For a soufflé dessert, you can prepare the soufflé mixture (except the egg whites of course) ahead of time: turn on the oven as you sit down to the main course, then just before dessert, simply whip up the egg whites, fold them into the mixture and pop the soufflés into the oven.

CREME BRULEE This much-loved gourmet dessert is essentially a simple custard. The magic comes when you caramelise the sugar on the top of the cooled custard just before serving. It's the perfect dessert for entertaining because it can be made ahead of time and refrigerated overnight.

prawn and scallop tortellini

PREP + COOK TIME 40 MINS (+ STANDING) • SERVES 6

Preserved lemons are available from delis and some supermarkets. Bear in mind that only the rind is used in cooking, so discard the flesh from each piece first. Rinse the rind well before chopping finely.

500g uncooked medium king prawns, shelled, deveined
250g scallops without roe
1 tablespoon olive oil
2 tablespoons finely chopped fresh vietnamese mint
2 tablespoons finely chopped fresh chervil
2 tablespoons finely chopped preserved lemon rind
220g soft goat's cheese
2 teaspoons sea salt
1 teaspoon cracked black pepper
275g packet round gow gee wrappers

lemon dressing
¼ cup (60ml) lemon juice
½ cup (125ml) olive oil
1 tablespoon finely chopped fresh chervil
1 tablespoon finely chopped fresh flat-leaf parsley

TIPS

• Cover gow gee wrappers with a damp tea towel to stop them drying out while making the tortellini.

• The tortellini can be made a day ahead; store tortellini, in a single layer, covered in plastic wrap, in the refrigerator until ready to cook.

1 Place ingredients for lemon dressing in screw-top jar; shake well.
2 Coarsely chop prawns and scallops. Heat oil in large frying pan; cook seafood over medium heat until prawns change colour. Cool.
3 Combine seafood, herbs, lemon rind, cheese, salt and pepper in medium bowl.
4 To make tortellini, place a gow gee wrapper on bench; place 1 level tablespoon of the seafood mixture in centre, brush edge with water. Fold in half; bring two points together, to make a crescent shape, press gently to seal. Repeat with remaining wrappers and filling.
5 Cook tortellini in large saucepan of boiling water until tortellini floats to the top; drain. Transfer tortellini to large heatproof bowl; drizzle with a little dressing.
6 Serve tortellini drizzled with remaining dressing; sprinkle with extra chervil sprigs.
nutritional count per serving 28.6g total fat (7.1g saturated fat); 1346kJ (323 cal); 1.8g carbohydrate; 15.3g protein; 0.2g fibre

Using your fingers, remove the head, shell, legs and tail. Remove the intestinal vein by slitting down the back with a sharp knife and pulling it out.

Arrange gow gee wrappers on a clean suface. Place a level tablespoon of seafood mixture in the centre of each wrapper. Brush edges with a little water.

Fold the wrapper in half and pinch edge together to seal. Repeat process for remaining wrappers and filling.

Bring the ends of the straight edge together to join and form a crescent shape, pressing gently to seal. Cook tortellini in a large saucepan of water.

chicken liver pâté

PREP + COOK TIME 45 MINS (+ REFRIGERATION) • MAKES 4 CUPS

Pâté can be bought easily nowadays from delis and supermarkets. By making your own, however, you can ensure that ingredients are of a high quality and that the pâté is of the utmost freshness when served.

1kg chicken livers
200g ghee (clarified butter)
4 rindless bacon rashers (260g), chopped finely
1 small brown onion (80g), chopped finely
¼ cup (60ml) brandy
½ cup (125ml) cream
2 teaspoons finely chopped fresh thyme
pinch ground nutmeg

1 Cut any sinew from livers; pull each lobe away from connecting tissue.
2 Heat a quarter of the ghee in large frying pan; cook half the livers, stirring, until browned and barely cooked. Remove from pan. Repeat with another quarter of the ghee and remaining livers.
3 Heat 1 tablespoon of the remaining ghee in same pan; cook bacon and onion, stirring, until onion softens. Add brandy; bring to the boil.
4 Blend livers, bacon mixture, cream, thyme, nutmeg and 2 tablespoons of the remaining ghee until smooth (you may need to do this in batches).
5 Press pâté into 1-litre (4-cup) dish; melt remaining ghee, pour over pâté in dish. Refrigerate 3 hours or overnight.

nutritional count per teaspoon 1.7g total fat (1g saturated fat); 88kJ (21 cal); 0.1g carbohydrate; 1.2g protein; 0g fibre
serving ideas serve pâté with lavosh, melba toasts or water crackers.

Use a small sharp knife to cut any sinew from the chicken livers, then pull the lobes away from the connecting tissues. The chicken livers need to be as fresh as possible, so it's best to buy them on the day you intend to make the pâté.

Heat a quarter of the ghee in a frying pan and add half the livers, stirring until browned but barely cooked – the livers should be just seared. Remove from pan. Repeat with another quarter of the ghee and remaining livers. Cook bacon and onion, then add brandy and bring to the boil.

Process livers, bacon mixture, cream, thyme, nutmeg and 2 tablespoons of the remaining ghee in a blender, or with a hand blender, to a smooth paste (you may need to do this in batches).

Pour and press the pâté into a 1-litre (4-cup) dish. Melt the remaining ghee and pour over pâté in dish. Refrigerate for 3 hours or overnight to chill.

terrine de campagne

PREP + COOK TIME 2 HOURS 20 MINS (+ REFRIGERATION) • SERVES 6

"Country-style terrine" is the literal meaning of this classic dish as it is chunky and rustic.

Juniper berries, the dried fruit from the evergreen tree of the same name, can be found in specialty spice stores and good delicatessens.

350g chicken thigh fillets, chopped coarsely
400g boned pork belly, rind removed, chopped coarsely
300g calves' liver, trimmed, chopped coarsely
3 rindless bacon rashers (195g), chopped coarsely
3 cloves garlic, crushed
2 teaspoons finely chopped fresh thyme
10 juniper berries, crushed
2 tablespoons port
¼ cup (60ml) dry white wine
1 egg, beaten lightly

1 Preheat oven to 150°C/130°C fan-forced. Oil 1.5-litre (6-cup) ovenproof terrine dish.
2 Chop or process meats, separately, until coarsely minced; combine in large bowl with remaining ingredients.
3 Press meat mixture into dish; cover with foil. Place terrine dish in baking dish; pour enough boiling water into baking dish to come halfway up sides of terrine dish. Cook 1 hour. Uncover; cook a further 1 hour.
4 Remove terrine dish from baking dish; cover terrine with baking paper. Weight with another dish filled with heavy cans; cool 10 minutes then refrigerate overnight.
5 Turn terrine onto serving plate. Serve sliced terrine, at room temperature.
nutritional count per serving 28.6g total fat (9.6g saturated fat); 1839kJ (440 cal); 2.5g carbohydrate; 40.4g protein; 0.3g fibre
serving ideas serve terrine with slices of french bread and cornichons.

Chop chicken, pork belly, liver and bacon separately on a clean surface, or process in a food processor, until coarsely minced. Combine meats in a large bowl with the remaining ingredients.

Spoon the meat mixture into a heavy-based 1.5-litre terrine dish. Press into the base of the dish using your fingertips to smooth the surface.

Cover terrine dish with foil. Place in a large baking dish and pour enough boiling water into dish to come halfway up the sides of the terrine dish. Cook in a preheated oven for 1 hour. Uncover and cook for a further 1 hour.

gruyère soufflé

PREP + COOK TIME 55 MINS • SERVES 4

Always ensure the egg yolks and whites are completely separated. The smallest amount of yolk can prevent egg whites from stiffening as they should.

Gruyère is a hard, yellow, swiss cheese (named after the valley of the same name) made from cow's milk. It has a rich nutty flavour and is often used in baking due to its distinctive but not overpowering flavour.

⅓ cup (50g) plain flour
1⅔ cups (410ml) milk
20g butter, chopped
6 eggs, separated
1⅓ cups (165g) grated gruyère cheese (or strong cheddar cheese)
100g sliced smoked salmon
1½ teaspoons drained baby capers
1 tablespoon fresh chervil leaves

1 Preheat oven to 200°C/180°C fan-forced. Oil 2-litre (8-cup) ovenproof soufflé dish; place on oven tray.
2 Place flour in small saucepan; gradually whisk in milk until smooth. Cook flour mixture over medium heat, whisking constantly, until mixture boils and thickens. Remove from heat; stir in butter. Whisk in egg yolks and cheese. Transfer mixture to large mixing bowl.
3 Beat egg whites in large bowl with electric mixer until soft peaks form. Fold egg whites into cheese mixture, in two batches. Pour mixture into dish.
4 Bake soufflé about 35 to 40 minutes or until well risen and browned.
5 Arrange salmon on serving platter, top with capers and chervil; serve with soufflé.
nutritional count per serving 33.8g total fat (18.5g saturated fat); 2048kJ (490 cal); 14.5g carbohydrate; 32.3g protein; 0.5g fibre

Place flour in a saucepan and gradually whisk in the milk until smooth. Keep whisking over medium heat, until mixture boils and thickens. Remove from heat. Stir in the butter, then whisk in egg yolks and cheese. Transfer mixture to a bowl.

Beat egg whites in a separate bowl with electric mixer until soft peaks form.

Carefully fold egg whites into cheese mixture, in two batches. Pour the soufflé mixture into an ovenproof dish.

glazed baked ham

PREP + COOK TIME 1 HOUR 20 MINS • SERVES 16

Reserve the rind from the ham after it has been removed. When storing the ham (or the leftovers), re-cover the leg's cut surface with the reserved rind – this will keep it moist.

½ cup (180g) honey
½ cup (125ml) maple syrup
½ cup (110g) firmly packed brown sugar
2¼ cups (560ml) water
7kg cooked (leg) ham

1 Preheat oven to 180°C/160°C fan-forced.
2 Combine honey, syrup, sugar and ¼ cup of the water in small saucepan; bring to the boil. Stir over heat until sugar dissolves, bring to the boil; remove from heat, cool 10 minutes.
3 Cut through rind of ham 10cm from the shank end of the leg. To remove rind, run thumb around edge of rind just under skin. Start pulling rind from widest edge of ham, continue to pull rind carefully away from the fat up to the shank end. Remove rind completely. Score across the fat at about 3cm intervals, cutting through the surface of the fat (not the meat) in a diamond pattern.
4 Pour the remaining water into large baking dish; place ham on oiled wire rack over dish. Brush ham all over with honey glaze. Roast, uncovered, 1 hour or until browned, brushing frequently with glaze during cooking.

nutritional count per serving 19.4g total fat (7.1g saturated fat); 2111kJ (505 cal); 22.9g carbohydrate; 59g protein; 0g fibre

Use a small sharp knife to cut through the rind about 10cm from the shank end of the leg. Gently lift rind off in one piece by running your thumb around edge of rind just under the skin. Pull the rind from the widest edge of the ham and up to the shank end until removed.

Score the fat, about 1cm deep to cut through the surface of the fat, in a diamond pattern, taking care not to cut into the meat. The diagonal scores should be about 3cm apart.

Pour water into a large baking dish to keep the ham moist during cooking. Place ham on an oiled wire rack over the dish and brush all over with glaze. Place in a preheated oven and roast, uncovered, for 1 hour or until browned. Brush frequently with glaze during cooking.

beef wellington

PREP + COOK TIME 1 HOUR 20 MINS • SERVES 4

This classic dish was served at countless dinner parties during the 1970s. It has recently crept back onto restaurant menus due to its impressive nature and the ease of preparation.

Beef wellington should always be served with the centre slightly pink.

1 tablespoon olive oil
800g piece beef fillet
25g butter
1 small brown onion (80g), chopped finely
125g button mushrooms, chopped finely
150g chicken or duck liver pâté
2 sheets puff pastry
1 egg

1 Heat oil in large frying pan; cook beef until browned all over. Wrap in foil; cool.
2 Heat butter in same pan; cook onion and mushrooms, stirring, until tender. Cool.
3 Preheat oven to 240°C/220°C fan-forced. Line oven tray with baking paper.
4 Stir pâté in medium bowl until soft. Spread over top of beef; top with mushroom mixture, gently pushing onto pâté.
5 Roll out pastry on floured surface into a rectangle large enough to enclose beef; moisten edges with water. Place beef on one end of rectangle, fold pastry over beef; trim excess pastry and press edges to seal. Place beef on tray; brush with egg, then cut small slits in top of pastry.
6 Bake beef for 10 minutes. Reduce temperature to 200°C/180°C fan-forced; bake a further 20 minutes or until browned lightly. Slice thickly to serve.

nutritional count per serving 52.2g total fat (23g saturated fat); 3449kJ (825 cal); 31.9g carbohydrate; 56.4g protein; 2.7g fibre
serving idea serve with a leafy green salad.

Heat oil in a large frying pan and cook beef, turning occasionally, for about 8 minutes or until browned all over. Wrap in foil and allow to cool.

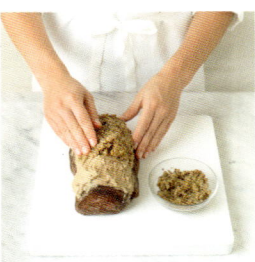

Spread the softened pâté over the beef. Top with the mushroom mixture, pressing down with your fingers until the mixture sticks to the pâté.

Roll out the puff pastry on a floured surface into a rectangle large enough to enclose the beef. Brush the edges with water to moisten. Place beef on one end of the rectangle, fold pastry over beef and trim any excess pastry. Press edges to seal.

thai steamed fish in banana leaves

PREP + COOK TIME 40 MINS (+ REFRIGERATION)
SERVES 4

You will need cotton string to wrap each fish parcel.

TIPS

• If bream is unavailable, use any of your favourite whole firm-fleshed fish for this recipe. Cooking times will vary depending on the fish you use.

• Steaming is best done in a bamboo steamer because, in a metal one, condensation on the lid can drip on to the food and spoil the appearance. If you have to use a metal steamer, cover the fish with baking paper that doesn't touch the steamer.

• Fish parcels can be cooked on a heated grill plate or barbecue for about 15 minutes or until the fish is cooked as desired.

4 medium whole bream (1.8kg)
1 large banana leaf
4 fresh small red thai chillies, sliced thinly
2 fresh kaffir lime leaves, shredded finely
2 green onions, sliced thinly
¼ cup loosely packed fresh coriander leaves
¼ cup loosely packed fresh thai basil leaves
2 x 10cm sticks fresh lemon grass (40g)

lime and sweet chilli dressing
¼ cup (60ml) sweet chilli sauce
2 tablespoons fish sauce
2 tablespoons lime juice
2 tablespoons peanut oil
1 clove garlic, crushed
1 teaspoon grated fresh ginger

1 Make lime and sweet chilli dressing.
2 Score fish both sides through thickest part of flesh; place on large tray, drizzle with half of the dressing. Cover; refrigerate 1 hour.
3 Meanwhile, trim banana leaf into four 30cm squares. Using tongs, dip one square at a time into large saucepan of boiling water; remove immediately. Rinse under cold water; pat dry with absorbent paper. Place leaves on work surface.
4 Combine chilli, lime leaves, onion, coriander and basil in medium bowl. Halve lemon grass sticks lengthways, then halve crossways; you will have eight pieces.
5 Place two pieces cut lemon grass on each leaf square; place one fish on each. Top fish with equal amounts of the herb mixture then fold opposite corners of the leaf to enclose centre part of fish; secure each parcel with cotton string.
6 Place parcels, in single layer, in large bamboo steamer; steam, covered, in two batches, over wok of simmering water about 15 minutes or until fish is cooked through. Serve fish still in parcel, drizzled with remaining dressing.

lime and sweet chilli dressing Place ingredients in screw-top jar; shake well.
nutritional count per serving 21.8g total fat (6g saturated fat); 1697kJ (406 cal); 4.1g carbohydrate; 48g protein; 1.3g fibre

Using a sharp knife, score the flesh of each bream, making several diagonal cuts on both sides. Place on tray and drizzle over the prepared dressing.

Dip banana leaf squares into a large saucepan of boiling water, one at a time, to soften. Remove, then rinse under cold water and pat dry with absorbent paper.

Lay leaves out on a clean work surface. Place lemon grass on each leaf, then fish; top with herb mixture. Fold opposite corners to enclose and tie with string.

chocolate soufflé

PREP + COOK TIME 35 MINS • SERVES 4

Egg whites are vital to a soufflé's success. They must be folded very carefully into the mixture. Use a wide-topped bowl so folding is easier for you. Use a whisk, spatula or large metal spoon for the folding – the choice is yours. Some cooks like to fold a small amount of the egg white (about a quarter) through the flavoured, more solid mixture first to "let the mixture down" a little. Fold in the remaining egg whites, in one or two batches depending on the quantity. Experiment a little to determine what works best for you and your soufflés.

⅓ cup (75g) caster sugar
50g butter
1 tablespoon plain flour
200g dark eating chocolate, melted
2 eggs, separated
2 egg whites
1 tablespoon cocoa powder

1 Preheat oven to 180°C/160°C fan-forced. Grease four ¾-cup (180ml) soufflé dishes. Sprinkle inside of dishes with a little of the sugar; shake away excess. Place dishes on oven tray.
2 Melt butter in small saucepan, add flour; cook, stirring, about 2 minutes or until mixture thickens and bubbles. Remove from heat; stir in chocolate and egg yolks. Transfer to large bowl.
3 Beat all egg whites in small bowl with electric mixer until soft peaks form. Gradually add remaining sugar, beating until sugar dissolves. Fold egg white mixture into chocolate mixture, in two batches.
4 Divide soufflé mixture among dishes; bake 15 minutes. Serve immediately, dusted with cocoa powder.

nutritional count per serving 27.1g total fat (16.1g saturated fat); 2040kJ (488 cal); 52.3g carbohydrate; 8.1g protein; 0.7g fibre

Grease four soufflé dishes, then sprinkle the insides with caster sugar, shaking away excess. Place the dishes on an oven tray.

Melt butter in a saucepan, then add flour and cook for 2 minutes. Remove the pan from the heat, add chocolate, stirring, then add egg yolks. Stir mixture well to combine.

Transfer chocolate mixture to a large mixing bowl. Fold in the egg white mixture, in two batches. Stir well to combine and divide between four soufflé dishes. Bake for 15 minutes.

SHOWING OFF THE AWW COOKING SCHOOL

crème brûlée

PREP + COOK TIME 55 MINS (+ REFRIGERATION) • SERVES 6

For many, the best part about crème brûlée is the crisp toffee on top. This is also the hardest part to get right if you don't have a blowtorch (favoured by chefs). But we've found topping the custards with pure icing sugar makes it easier to caramelise them under the grill at home.

Make sure you place the crème brûlées as close as possible to a hot grill. Surrounding the custards with ice keeps them cool as you heat the top. Of course, you can use a blowtorch if you have one. The adjustable flame melts the sugar quickly, so the filling remains cool.

Professional cooks' blowtorches are available from specialty kitchen shops.

1 vanilla bean
3 cups (750ml) thickened cream
6 egg yolks
¼ cup (55g) caster sugar
¼ cup (40g) pure icing sugar

1 Preheat oven to 180°C/160°C fan-forced. Grease six ½-cup (125ml) ovenproof dishes.
2 Split vanilla bean in half lengthways; scrape seeds into medium heatproof bowl. Place pod in small saucepan with cream; heat without boiling.
3 Add egg yolks and caster sugar to seeds in bowl; gradually whisk in hot cream mixture. Place bowl over medium saucepan of simmering water; stir over heat about 10 minutes or until custard mixture thickens slightly and coats the back of a spoon. Discard pod.
4 Place dishes in large baking dish; divide custard among dishes. Add enough boiling water to baking dish to come halfway up sides of ovenproof dishes.
5 Bake custards, uncovered, about 20 minutes or until set. Remove custards from dish; cool. Cover; refrigerate overnight.
6 Preheat grill. Place custards in shallow flameproof dish filled with ice cubes; sprinkle custards evenly with sifted icing sugar. Using finger, spread sugar over the surface of each custard, pressing in gently; place under grill until the tops caramelise.
nutritional count per serving 52.1g total fat (32.3g saturated fat); 2358kJ (564 cal); 19.8g carbohydrate; 5.8g protein; 8g fibre

Split the vanilla bean in half lengthways and scrape the seeds out with a knife. Place the seeds in a heatproof bowl. Place the pod in a small saucepan with the thickened cream and heat through, but do not boil.

Combine the egg yolk and caster sugar with the seeds in the bowl. Slowly whisk in the hot cream mixture. Place the bowl over a saucepan of simmering water. Stir the cream mixture for about 10 minutes or until it coats the back of a spoon.

Remove the chilled custards from the refrigerator and place in a shallow heatproof dish. Fill dish with ice cubes to keep custards cool when grilling the tops. Sprinkle the tops with pure icing sugar to help them caramelise under the grill.

Caramelise the sugar under a preheated hot grill, having the dishes as close as possible to the heat. If you have a blowtorch, use that to brown the sugar. The top should be hard and when cracked with a spoon, reveal a creamy custard underneath.

lemon tart

PREP + COOK TIME 1 HOUR 25 MINS (+ REFRIGERATION) • SERVES 8

Lemon tart appears on almost every restaurant menu, with varying degrees of quality. We guarantee this recipe is as good, if not better, than any lemon tart you've ever tasted. Don't overcook the filling. The custard should feel firm around the outside of the tart, but still a bit wobbly in the middle — it will set as the tart cools.

This tart is best made a day ahead and stored in the fridge.

1¼ cups (185g) plain flour
⅓ cup (55g) icing sugar
¼ cup (30g) ground almonds
125g cold butter, chopped
1 egg yolk
2 tablespoons iced water

lemon filling
3 teaspoons finely grated lemon rind
⅓ cup (80ml) lemon juice
3 eggs
½ cup (110g) caster sugar
⅔ cup (160ml) pouring cream

1 Blend or process flour, icing sugar, ground almonds and butter until crumbly. Add egg yolk and the water; process until combined. Knead dough on floured surface until smooth. Wrap in plastic wrap, refrigerate 30 minutes.
2 Roll pastry between sheets of baking paper until large enough to line shallow (2cm-deep) 24cm-round loose-based flan tin. Lift pastry into tin; press into side, trim edge. Cover; refrigerate 30 minutes.
3 Meanwhile, preheat oven to 200°C/180°C fan-forced.
4 Place flan tin on oven tray. Line pastry case with baking paper, fill with dried beans or rice. Bake, uncovered, 15 minutes. Remove paper and beans; bake about 10 minutes or until browned lightly.
5 Meanwhile, whisk ingredients for lemon filling in medium bowl; stand 5 minutes.
6 Reduce oven to 180°C/160°C fan-forced.
7 Pour lemon filling into pastry case; bake about 30 minutes or until filling has set slightly, cool. Refrigerate until cold.

nutritional count per serving 25.3g total fat (14.3g saturated fat); 1714kJ (410 cal); 38.5g carbohydrate; 6.7g protein; 1.3g fibre

serving idea whipped cream; dust tart with sifted icing sugar just before serving.

Use a rolling pin to carefully lift the pastry into a loose-based flan tin. Press the pastry into the base and side of the tin and trim the edge to fit. Cover and place in the refrigerator to chill.

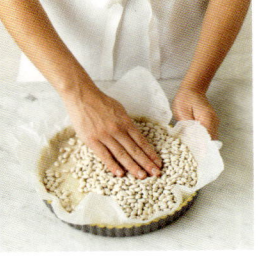

Line the pastry with baking paper and fill with dried beans. Bake for 15 minutes, remove the paper and beans, then bake for a further 10 minutes or until lightly browned. Remove from the oven and cool slightly. This process of blind baking creates a firm, dry and even crust.

Pour lemon fillng into cooled pastry case. Place in a preheated oven and bake for about 30 minutes or until the filling has just set. Allow lemon tart to cool before placing in the refrigerator to chill.

STARTERS

Starters

If you're hosting a dinner party, you'll need to plan ahead and think about the food preparations in the context of the practicalities of time and the mood of the occasion.

A traditional, three-course, sit-down meal can elevate your dining experience to a special, out-of-the-ordinary occasion, but it can place more pressure on the host's time and preparations. For a more casual and relaxed mood, have your guests mingle and help themselves to finger food before sitting down to the table for mains.

It's worth putting some thought into the starters you serve – they are the introduction, the greeting, the welcome. They need to be taste-tempting without overwhelming the rest of your meal.
The recipes in this chapter can be used as finger food, while others are more suited to a sit-down first course.

MAKING AN IMPRESSION

REMEMBER, THE FIRST COURSE IS THE INTRODUCTION TO THE MEAL, SO YOU WANT IT TO MAKE AN IMPRESSIVE ENTRANCE. PUT SOME EFFORT INTO MAKING THE FOOD LOOK TEMPTING AND VISUALLY INTERESTING. PAY ATTENTION TO THE RECIPE PHOTOGRAPHS FOR POINTERS ON PRESENTATION.

FOR PLATTERS OF MIXED APPETISERS, TRY TO ARRANGE THE FOOD IN COLOURS AND SHAPES THAT CREATE AN APPEALING VISUAL EFFECT. PLACE FOODS CLOSE TO EACH OTHER ON THE PLATE, RATHER THAN SPREADING THEM AROUND THE EDGES. USING HERBS OR FRUIT AS A GARNISH CAN ENLIVEN A PLATE.

A WINNING COMBINATION

A versatile and easy way to open a meal is to serve mixed appetisers, arranged either on individual plates or large platters for guests to help themselves. Serving a selection of appetisers is handy if you're short of time because you can mix home-made with good-quality bought items. They're suitable for sit-down or stand-up affairs and they're the perfect way to cater for a range of tastes. The idea of mixed appetisers is not new, of course, and many different cultures around the world have embraced their own versions: the traditional 'mezze' is a staple in the Middle East and Greece; the Italians have their antipasto and the French serve hors d'oeuvres.
The beauty of the mixed platter is that you can bring together any number of flavours into one taste-tempting mix. As a general rule, try to serve at least one fresh salad-derived item with one warm home-made item plus a few good-quality bought items.

THINK OF THE FLAVOURS AND TEXTURES

It's good to create a variety of flavours and textures in your meal. You don't want the first course and second course to echo each other. Think about the meal as a whole and once you have decided on one part of it – a roast dinner for main course perhaps, or a rich velvety chocolate pudding for dessert – then plan the rest of the meal around that choice. If the main course has a rich sauce, you will want to create a light, fresh first course. Or, if you're planning to serve a serious pudding for dessert, you might serve a soup first, then a lighter meal as your main course, so that your dinner guests can enjoy the finale. You also have to think of the practicalities of time and space: do you have the time to create complicated individual servings for the first course while the main course is cooking? Can you create the starters ahead of time? Will your first and second courses be competing for bench and oven space at the same time? Make sure you've thought about the cooking times and requirements of each part of the meal and feel confident that your kitchen (and you) will cope before you begin.

HOME-MADE

Perhaps you could make some bruschetta, some mini quiches, or offer some chilled or warm soup (depending on the season), served in demitasse cups containing just a few tantalising mouthfuls. Combine these home-made provisions with any of the following:

FROM THE SUPERMARKET AND DELI

A range of dips, such as hummus, baba ganoush and taramasalata.

Pâtés such as chicken liver or smoked salmon.

Salami, smoked pork or beef, ham and other cold meats.

Char-grilled vegetables such as capsicum and eggplant.

Marinated mushrooms and artichoke hearts.

Olives, plain or marinated (preferably pitted).

A range of soft cheeses: brie, camembert, blue cheese.

Marinated chicken wings or kebabs.

Savoury biscuits from a deli.

Pitta bread (cut into small triangles and grilled).

FROM THE GREENGROCER

Salad vegetables perfect for a platter, including: cucumber, radish, celery, carrot, capsicum, baby spinach leaves and watercress.

Some cooked vegetables work well as bite-sized appetisers too, such as asparagus and whole baby beans (both served warm with melted butter and lemon) and baby potatoes and carrots (served with melted butter and mint).

FROM THE FISH MARKETS OR LOCAL QUALITY SEAFOOD STORE

Prawns, oysters or scallops, served either plain or with simple light sauces.

FROM YOUR LOCAL INDIAN, THAI OR CHINESE RESTAURANT

Purchase a selection of your favourite entrees such as curry puffs, spring rolls, fish cakes, samosas or pakoras.

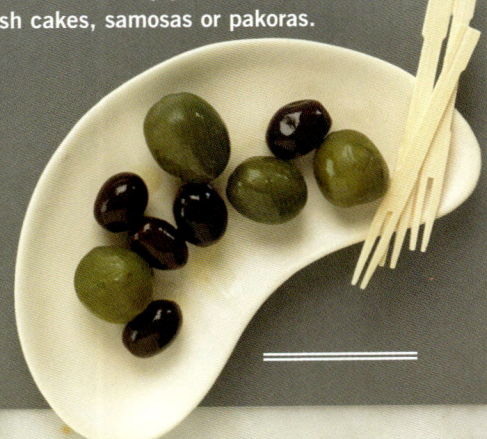

vietnamese prawn rolls

PREP + COOK TIME 20 MINS • MAKES 12

Soften rice paper in warm water, one at a time, for 15 to 20 seconds. Make sure you don't over-soak them as they will fall apart in your hands.

The rolls can be made at the table by each diner, or ahead of time and stored in the fridge for up to 3 hours. Cover rolls with a damp clean tea towel to keep the rice paper moist.

50g rice vermicelli noodles, soaked, drained
¼ small wombok (175g), shredded finely
½ cup loosely packed fresh mint leaves, torn
2 teaspoons brown sugar
2 tablespoons lime juice
500g cooked medium king prawns
12 x 21cm rice paper rounds

hoisin dipping sauce
½ cup (125ml) hoisin sauce
2 tablespoons rice vinegar

1 Combine chopped vermicelli in medium bowl with wombok, mint, sugar and juice.
2 Shell and devein prawns; chop meat finely.
3 Meanwhile, make hoisin dipping sauce.
4 Dip one rice paper round into bowl of warm water until soft; place on board covered with tea towel. Top with a little of the prawn meat and noodle filling. Fold and roll to enclose filling. Repeat with remaining rounds, prawn meat and noodle filling.
5 Serve rolls with hoisin dipping sauce.
hoisin dipping sauce Combine ingredients in bowl.
nutritional count per roll 0.9g total fat (0.1g saturated fat); 326kJ (78 cal); 10.8g carbohydrate; 5.5g protein; 1.7g fibre

Dip one rice paper round in a bowl of warm water for about 15 seconds until soft and pliable. Shake off any excess water and transfer round to a board covered with a clean tea towel.

Place a tablespoon of the prawn meat and noodle mixture at one end of the rice paper round. Make sure you leave a border at both ends to tuck in and avoid overfilling.

Fold the ends of the rice paper round over the filling, then roll up to enclose. Repeat the process for the remaining rice paper rounds and filling.

rösti stacks with prawns and mint aïoli

PREP + COOK TIME 50 MINS • SERVES 4

16 uncooked medium king prawns (720g)
800g russet burbank potatoes, grated coarsely
1 teaspoon finely chopped fresh rosemary
2 cloves garlic, crushed
2 tablespoons olive oil
30g baby rocket leaves

mint aïoli
⅓ cup coarsely chopped fresh mint
1 clove garlic, quartered
1 egg
1 tablespoon dijon mustard
½ cup (125ml) olive oil

1 Make mint aïoli.
2 Shell and devein prawns, leaving tails intact.
3 To make rösti, squeeze excess moisture from potato; combine in medium bowl with rosemary and garlic. Divide into eight portions.
4 Heat half the oil in large frying pan; cook rösti, in batches, flattening slightly, until browned both sides. Drain.
5 Heat remaining oil in pan; cook prawns until just changed in colour.
6 Serve rösti stacked alternately with prawns, mint aïoli and rocket.

mint aïoli Blend or process mint, garlic, egg and mustard until mixture is pureed. With motor operating, add oil in a thin, steady stream until aïoli thickens.

nutritional count per serving 39.8g total fat (5.8g saturated fat); 2324kJ (556 cal); 23.6g carbohydrate; 24.9g protein; 3.7g fibre

To make the rösti, use your hands to squeeze out excess liquid from the grated potato. Place in a large bowl, along with the rosemary and garlic. Divide the potato mixture into eight portions.

Heat oil in a large frying pan and add rösti, in batches. Use an egg slice to flatten each portion slightly. Cook, turning over, until both sides are browned. Transfer to a dish lined with absorbent paper to drain.

bruschetta with tomato, basil and capers

PREP + COOK TIME 15 MINS • SERVES 6

Fantastic served as an entrée, finger food, or a mid-summer snack, this simple and quick-to-prepare recipe is sure to become a family favourite.

6 medium ripe tomatoes (900g), seeded, chopped finely
¼ cup (60ml) extra virgin olive oil
¼ cup fresh baby basil leaves
2 tablespoons baby capers, rinsed, drained
500g loaf wood-fired bread, cut into 12 slices
1 clove garlic, halved

1 Combine tomatoes in medium bowl with 2 tablespoons oil, basil leaves and capers.
2 Toast bread slices both sides on heated oiled grill plate (or grill or barbecue). Rub one side of each slice with the cut side of the garlic; place toast on platter, garlic-side up.
3 Top toasts with tomato mixture; sprinkle with freshly ground black pepper and drizzle with remaining oil.

nutritional count per serving 11.4g total fat (1.6g saturated fat); 1237kJ (296 cal); 39g carbohydrate; 7.7g protein; 3.3g fibre

white bean dip

PREP TIME 5 MINS • MAKES 2 CUPS

Many varieties of cooked white beans are available canned, among them cannellini (which is what we used), butter and haricot beans – any of these are suitable for this dip.

2 x 400g cans white beans, rinsed, drained
2 cloves garlic, crushed
2 tablespoons lemon juice
⅓ cup (80ml) olive oil
1 tablespoon fresh basil leaves

1 Blend or process beans, garlic, juice and oil until almost smooth.
2 Sprinkle dip with basil.

nutritional count per tablespoon 3.1g total fat (0.4g saturated fat); 138kJ (33 cal); 0.6g carbohydrate; 0.5g protein; 0.9g fibre

serving idea wedges of toasted turkish bread.

[1] bruschetta with tomato, basil and capers
[2] white bean dip
[3] baba ghanoush [page 82]
[4] blue cheese and caramelised onion dip [page 82]

baba ghanoush

PREP + COOK TIME 45 MINS (+ STANDING) • MAKES 2 CUPS

For an extra touch of the Middle East, top baba ghanoush with chopped mint, finely chopped pistachios or pomegranate pulp.

This recipe can be refrigerated in an airtight container for up to a week.

2 large eggplants (1kg)
3 cloves garlic, crushed
2 tablespoons tahini
¼ cup (60ml) lemon juice
2 tablespoons olive oil
½ teaspoon sweet paprika

1 Preheat grill. Oil oven tray.
2 Pierce eggplants all over with fork or skewer; place on tray. Grill about 30 minutes or until skin blackens and eggplant is soft, turning occasionally. Stand 15 minutes.
3 Peel eggplants, discard skin; drain eggplants in colander 10 minutes.
4 Blend or process eggplant flesh with remaining ingredients.

nutritional count per ¼ cup 8g total fat (1g saturated fat); 431kJ (103 cal); 3.6g carbohydrate; 2.5g protein; 3.7g fibre

serving ideas crisp vegetables, pitta bread or rice crackers.

blue cheese and caramelised onion dip

PREP + COOK TIME 30 MINS • MAKES 1½ CUPS

20g butter
1 large brown onion (200g), chopped finely
2 tablespoons brown sugar
2 tablespoons white wine vinegar
100g blue cheese, crumbled
¾ cup (180g) crème fraîche
¼ cup finely chopped fresh flat-leaf parsley

1 Melt butter in medium saucepan; cook onion, stirring, until onion softens.
2 Add sugar and vinegar; cook, stirring, over low heat, about 10 minutes or until onion is caramelised.
3 Stir in cheese and crème fraîche until smooth. Cool. Cover; refrigerate until cold. Stir in parsley before serving.

nutritional count per teaspoon 1.7g total fat (1.1g saturated fat); 84kJ (20 cal); 0.7g carbohydrate; 0.4g protein; 0.1g fibre

serving idea wedges of toasted pitta bread.

chicken and olive empanadas

PREP + COOK TIME 1 HOUR 10 MINS • MAKES 24

Perfect for a party or picnic, these little pastry pockets can be individually wrapped and frozen for up to three months. And they don't require thawing before reheating – pop them straight from the freezer into the oven for a fuss-free snack.

2 cups (500ml) chicken stock
1 bay leaf
3 chicken thigh fillets (330g)
1 tablespoon olive oil
1 small brown onion (80g), chopped finely
2 cloves garlic, crushed
2 teaspoons ground cumin
½ cup (80g) sultanas
⅓ cup (40g) seeded green olives, chopped coarsely
5 sheets shortcrust pastry
1 egg, beaten lightly

1 Place stock and bay leaf in medium frying pan; bring to the boil. Add chicken, reduce heat; poach chicken, covered, about 10 minutes or until cooked through. Cool chicken in liquid 10 minutes; shred chicken finely. Reserve 1 cup of the poaching liquid; discard remainder (or keep for another use).
2 Meanwhile, heat oil in large frying pan; cook onion, stirring, until softened. Add garlic and cumin; cook, stirring, until fragrant. Add sultanas and reserved poaching liquid; bring to the boil. Reduce heat; simmer, uncovered, about 15 minutes or until liquid is almost evaporated. Stir in chicken and olives.
3 Preheat oven to 200°C/180°C fan-forced. Grease two oven trays.
4 Using 9cm cutter, cut 24 rounds from pastry sheets. Place 1 level tablespoon of the filling in centre of each round; fold round in half to enclose filling, pinching edges to seal. Using fork, press around edges of empanadas. Place on trays; brush tops with egg.
5 Bake empanadas about 25 minutes. Serve with yogurt.

nutritional count per empanada 12g total fat (5.6g saturated fat); 849kJ (203 cal); 18.3g carbohydrate; 5.5g protein; 0.9g fibre
serving idea yogurt for dipping.

prawn cocktail

PREP TIME 30 MINS • SERVES 4

32 cooked medium prawns (1.5g)
⅓ cup (100g) mayonnaise
2 tablespoons cream
1 tablespoon tomato sauce
1 teaspoon worcestershire sauce
½ teaspoon Tabasco sauce
½ teaspoon dijon mustard
2 teaspoons lemon juice
½ iceberg lettuce, shredded finely

1 Shell and devein prawns.
2 Whisk mayonnaise, cream, sauces, mustard and juice in small bowl.
3 Divide lettuce among serving glasses; top with prawns and sauce.
nutritional count per serving 14.2g total fat (4.2g saturated fat); 1254kJ (300 cal); 7.6g carbohydrate; 34.6g protein; 1.8g fibre
serving idea wedges of lemon.

crab cakes with avocado salsa

PREP + COOK TIME 30 MINS (+ REFRIGERATION) • SERVES 4

Crab meat is available from fishmongers or supermarkets. If you buy it frozen, thaw then drain well before use.

600g cooked crab meat
1 cup (70g) stale white breadcrumbs
1 egg
1 clove garlic, crushed
2 tablespoons mayonnaise
¼ cup finely chopped fresh coriander
½ teaspoon cayenne pepper
15g butter
1 tablespoon olive oil

avocado salsa
2 small avocados (400g), chopped coarsely
1 medium tomato (150g), chopped coarsely
¾ cup loosely packed fresh coriander leaves
2 teaspoons Tabasco sauce
1 tablespoon lime juice
1 tablespoon olive oil

1 Combine crab meat, breadcrumbs, egg, garlic, mayonnaise, coriander and pepper in medium bowl. Shape mixture into eight patties; place on tray. Cover; refrigerate 1 hour.
2 Meanwhile, make avocado salsa.
3 Heat butter and oil in large frying pan; cook crab cakes, in batches, until browned both sides and heated through. Serve crab cakes topped with salsa.
avocado salsa Combine ingredients in medium bowl.
nutritional count per serving 34.1g total fat (7.8g saturated fat); 2011kJ (481 cal); 17.6g carbohydrate; 25.3g protein; 2.8g fibre

[opposite] prawn cocktail

oysters with three toppings

PREP + COOK TIME 30 MINS (+ COOLING) • SERVES 6

We used pacific oysters in this recipe, because their full-bodied flavour teams well with these robust dressings.

Serving oysters on a bed of coarse rock salt (or crushed ice) prevents them from sliding around on the plate. Another way to serve them is to take them out of the shells and put them on Chinese porcelain soup spoons, then top with dressings and salsa.

36 oysters (900g), on the half shell
coarse rock salt

ponzu dressing
2 tablespoons light soy sauce
2 teaspoons peanut oil
2 teaspoons mirin
1 tablespoon brown sugar
2 tablespoons lime juice

shallot dressing
⅓ cup (80ml) white wine vinegar
3 shallots (75g), chopped finely

green mango and cucumber salsa
½ lebanese cucumber (65g), seeded, chopped finely
1 tablespoon finely shredded green mango
1 tablespoon finely chopped red onion
1 teaspoon finely grated lime rind
1 teaspoon lime juice
1 teaspoon fish sauce
1 tablespoon vegetable oil

1. Make ponzu dressing.
2. Make shallot dressing.
3. Make green mango and cucumber salsa.
4. Serve oysters on bed of rock salt with dressings.

ponzu dressing Stir sauce, oil, mirin and sugar in medium saucepan over low heat until sugar dissolves. Stir in juice; season. Cool.

shallot dressing Bring vinegar to the boil in small saucepan; remove from heat. Stir in shallots; cool.

green mango and cucumber salsa Combine ingredients in small bowl; season.

nutritional count per serving 6.2g total fat (1.2g saturated fat); 439kJ (105 cal); 4g carbohydrate; 8.1g protein; 0.3g fibre

scallops with saffron cream

PREP + COOK TIME 15 MINS (+ STANDING) • MAKES 12

12 scallops in half shell (480g)
1 teaspoon olive oil
1 small brown onion (80g), chopped finely
2 teaspoons finely grated lemon rind
pinch saffron threads
⅔ cup (160ml) cream
1 tablespoon lemon juice
2 teaspoons salmon roe

1 Remove scallops from shells; wash and dry shells. Place shells, in single layer, on serving platter.
2 Rinse scallops under cold water; discard scallop roe. Gently pat scallops dry with absorbent paper.
3 Heat oil in small saucepan; cook onion, stirring, until softened. Add rind, saffron and cream; bring to the boil. Reduce heat; simmer, uncovered, about 5 minutes or until mixture has reduced to about ½ cup. Remove from heat; stand 30 minutes. Stir in juice; stand 10 minutes. Strain cream mixture into small bowl then back into same cleaned pan; stir over low heat until heated through.
4 Meanwhile, cook scallops, in batches, on heated oiled grill plate (or grill or barbecue) until browned lightly and cooked as desired.
5 Return scallops to shells; top with cream sauce and roe.
nutritional count per scallop 6.4g total fat (4g saturated fat); 288kJ (69 cal); 0.8g carbohydrate; 2.3g protein; 0.1g fibre

black olive tapenade

PREP TIME 5 MINS • MAKES 1 CUP

Sometimes nicknamed "yuppie Vegemite", this classic Provençal preparation is used as a dip for raw vegetables, spread on bread and pizza, and served with fish and meats.

2 cups (240g) seeded black olives
1 drained anchovy fillet, rinsed
1 tablespoon drained capers, rinsed
2 teaspoons dijon mustard
2 tablespoons olive oil

1 Rinse and drain olives on absorbent paper. Blend or process olives with anchovy, capers and mustard until smooth.
2 With motor operating, add oil in a thin steady stream, processing until tapenade is smooth.
nutritional count per tablespoon 3.3g total fat (0.5g saturated fat); 213kJ (51 cal); 4.6g carbohydrate; 0.6g protein; 0.3g fibre
serving idea wedges of toasted turkish bread.

money bags

PREP + COOK TIME 50 MINS (+ COOLING) • MAKES 12 BAGS (1½ CUPS SAUCE)

Cut the upper green section of a green onion into four strips using a sharp knife. Repeat process for remaing two onions. Soften in hot water for a few seconds.

Place wrappers on a clean flat surface, topping each one with another to form a star shape.

Add teaspoonsful of filling to the centre of each wrapper and fold up sides to form a pouch. Pinch to enclose, tie with an onion strip and secure with a toothpick.

1 tablespoon peanut oil
1 small brown onion (80g), chopped finely
1 clove garlic, crushed
1 tablespoon grated fresh ginger
100g chicken mince
1 tablespoon finely grated palm sugar
1 tablespoon finely chopped roasted unsalted peanuts
2 teaspoons finely chopped fresh coriander
3 green onions
24 x 8cm-square wonton wrappers
vegetable oil, for deep-frying

peanut dipping sauce
1 tablespoon peanut oil
2 cloves garlic, crushed
1 small brown onion (80g), chopped finely
2 fresh small red chillies, chopped coarsely
10cm stick fresh lemon grass (20g), chopped finely
¾ cup (180ml) coconut milk
2 tablespoons fish sauce
¼ cup (55g) dark brown sugar
½ cup (140g) crunchy peanut butter
½ teaspoon curry powder
1 tablespoon lime juice

1 Heat oil in wok; stir-fry onion, garlic and ginger until onion softens. Add chicken; stir-fry until chicken is changed in colour. Add sugar; stir-fry about 3 minutes or until sugar dissolves. Stir nuts and coriander into filling mixture.
2 Cut upper green half of each onion into four long slices; discard remaining onion half. Submerge onion strips in hot water for a few seconds to make pliable.
3 Place 12 wrappers on board; cover each wrapper with another, placed on the diagonal to form star shape. Place rounded teaspoons of the filling mixture in centre of each star; gather corners to form pouch shape. Tie green onion slice around neck of each pouch to hold closed, secure with toothpick.
4 Make dipping sauce (freeze excess for a future use).
5 Just before serving, heat oil in wok or large saucepan; deep-fry money bags, in batches, until crisp and browned lightly. Drain on absorbent paper; serve with dipping sauce.

peanut dipping sauce Heat oil in small saucepan; cook garlic and onion until softened. Stir in remaining ingredients; bring to the boil. Reduce heat; simmer, stirring, about 2 minutes or until sauce thickens.

nutritional count per money bag 5.1g total fat (0.9g saturated fat); 435kJ (104 cal); 10.8g carbohydrate; 3.8g protein; 0.6g fibre
nutritional count per tablespoon dipping sauce 4.7g total fat (1.7g saturated fat); 251kJ (60 cal); 2.5g carbohydrate; 2.2g protein; 0.8g fibre

tuna tartare

PREP TIME 25 MINS (+ REFRIGERATION) • SERVES 6

Tuna sold as sashimi has to meet stringent guidelines regarding its handling and treatment after leaving the water, but it is still probably a good idea to buy it only from a fishmonger you trust or to seek advice from local authorities before eating any raw seafood.

200g piece sashimi tuna, trimmed
1 tablespoon drained capers, rinsed, chopped finely
2 teaspoons prepared horseradish
⅓ cup (80ml) lime juice
2 small tomatoes (180g), seeded, chopped finely
1 small avocado (200g), chopped finely
1 small red onion (100g), chopped finely
1 baby cos lettuce, trimmed, leaves separated
1 tablespoon extra virgin olive oil

1 Cut tuna into 5mm pieces; combine tuna in medium bowl with capers, horseradish and 1 tablespoon of the juice. Cover; refrigerate 30 minutes.
2 Combine tomato, avocado, onion and remaining juice in medium bowl.
3 Serve lettuce leaves topped with tomato mixture and tuna tartare; drizzle with oil.

nutritional count per serving 10.4g total fat (2.3g saturated fat); 610kJ (146 cal); 2.4g carbohydrate; 9.8g protein; 1.6g fibre

smoked salmon with capers

PREP TIME 25 MINS • SERVES 8

320g sliced smoked salmon
1 small red onion (100g), chopped finely
½ cup (90g) drained baby capers, rinsed
2 small witlof (110g), leaves separated
1 baby fennel bulb (130g), sliced thinly
2 red radishes (70g), trimmed, sliced thinly

mustard honey dressing
1 teaspoon dijon mustard
2 teaspoons honey
2 tablespoons lemon juice
1 tablespoon finely chopped fresh dill
¼ cup (60ml) olive oil

1 Make mustard honey dressing.
2 Divide salmon among serving plates; sprinkle with onion and capers. Serve with witlof, fennel and radish; drizzle with dressing.
mustard honey dressing Place ingredients in screw-top jar; shake well.
nutritional count per serving 8.8g total fat (1.3g saturated fat); 564kJ (135 cal); 3.8g carbohydrate; 9.8g protein; 1g fibre

spring rolls

PREP + COOK TIME 45 MINS (+ COOLING) • MAKES 12

Make sure the oil is quite hot before you start deep-frying the spring rolls, and don't overcrowd them in the wok or they won't cook evenly. Use a wok chan or tongs to turn them constantly in the oil for even cooking.

Keep the finished spring rolls warm by placing them on an absorbent-paper-lined oven tray in a very slow oven while you finish deep-frying the remainder.

20g rice vermicelli noodles
2 teaspoons peanut oil
100g pork mince
1 clove garlic, crushed
1 fresh small red thai chilli, chopped finely
1 green onion, chopped finely
1 small carrot (70g), grated finely
1 teaspoon fish sauce
1 teaspoon finely chopped coriander root and stem mixture
50g shelled cooked prawns, chopped finely
1 teaspoon cornflour
2 teaspoons water
12 x 12cm-square spring roll wrappers
vegetable oil, for deep-frying

1 Place noodles in medium heatproof bowl; cover with boiling water. Stand until just tender; drain. Using kitchen scissors, cut vermicelli into random lengths.
2 Heat oil in wok; stir-fry pork, garlic and chilli until pork is changed in colour. Add onion, carrot, fish sauce, coriander mixture and prawns; stir-fry until vegetables just soften. Place stir-fried mixture in small bowl with noodles; cool.
3 Blend cornflour with the water in small bowl. Place 1 level tablespoon of the filling near one corner of each wrapper. Lightly brush edges of each wrapper with cornflour mixture; roll to enclose filling, folding in ends.
4 Just before serving, heat oil in wok; deep-fry spring rolls, in batches, until golden brown. Drain on absorbent paper.

nutritional count per serving 3.4g total fat (0.6g saturated fat); 255kJ (61 cal); 4g carbohydrate; 3.3g protein; 0.4g fibre
serving idea sweet chilli dipping sauce or any favourite dipping sauce.

beef carpaccio

PREP TIME 30 MINS (+ FREEZING) • SERVES 8

400g piece beef eye fillet
2 tablespoons olive oil
2 teaspoons finely grated lemon rind
2 tablespoons lemon juice
1 clove garlic, crushed
⅓ cup finely chopped fresh flat-leaf parsley
2 tablespoons finely chopped fresh oregano
⅓ cup finely chopped baby rocket leaves
⅓ cup (25g) flaked parmesan cheese

1 Tightly wrap beef fillet in plastic wrap; freeze 1 hour or until firm.
2 Unwrap beef; slice as thinly as possible. Arrange slices on serving platter.
3 Combine oil, rind, juice, garlic, parsley, oregano and rocket leaves in small bowl. Serve beef sprinkled with herb mixture and cheese.

nutritional count per serving 7.8g total fat (2.3g saturated fat); 506kJ (121 cal); 0.3g carbohydrate; 12.3g protein; 0.3g fibre

SALADS

Salads

Sometimes, don't you just crave a salad? After a jaded week at the office or running after the kids, your body just wants to eat fresh, simple, minimally-processed, preferably raw, food.

A well-conceived salad made from fresh and ripe ingredients is a joy to taste and the best way to enjoy those all-important raw ingredients that are recommended for well being.

A salad can be anything you want it to be. It can be enjoyed on its own as a nourishing light meal or used to add a refreshing balance to another dish. It can be a first course, main course, a picnic companion, a buffet star, casual or elegant, warm or cold, vegetarian or not. Our approach to salads, like ideas on food in general, has changed over the past 20 years and the modern salad is no longer the all-purpose "mixed salad" of a generation ago, created using iceberg lettuce and a jumble of everything imaginable from the fridge. These days, a good salad consists of one or two key ingredients supported by carefully selected supporting flavours and textures.

Fresh green leaves can stand alone as the perfect green salad or they can provide the background that sets off other salad ingredients. A leafy salad should look fluffy and vibrant, not heavy and settled. To ensure this, dress the salad at the last moment and use only enough dressing to make every leaf glisten, and never enough to run off into a puddle at the bottom of the salad bowl.

BUYING, STORING AND HANDLING SALAD VEGETABLES

LETTUCE AND OTHER LEAVES Leaf vegetables should be crisp, brightly coloured and have a sheen. If you're buying iceberg or cos lettuce or cabbage, choose a size you will use within a week. If you're buying a soft-leaf lettuce or other soft leaves, buy only as much as you can use within a day or two. Witlof and radicchio should be used within 2 to 3 days. Except for watercress, leaf vegetables are best stored in a paper bag inside a plastic bag in the fridge. For watercress, cut the stems and gather into a bunch, tying loosely with a rubber band; stand in 2cm to 3cm of water in a bowl. Cover with a plastic bag and store in the fridge. Wash salad leaves up to 12 hours ahead and dry in a salad spinner – store as above until needed.

TOMATOES Ideally, you should buy tomatoes that have been fully sun-ripened on the vine but this is rarely available in supermarkets. You are more likely to find them at a farmers' market. To improve reasonably ripe tomatoes, place them in a paper bag with a banana (nature's ripening agent) at room temperature for a day or two. Never put tomatoes in the fridge as chilling them damages their cell structure. Store them at room temperature, away from sunlight and preferably, in a single layer. Fully ripened tomatoes should be used within 3 days. To peel tomatoes, cut a tiny cross at the base, place in a bowl, cover with boiling water and stand for 20 seconds. Drain and run cold water over them. Starting at the base, pull off the skin using a small knife.

CUCUMBERS, CAPSICUM, CELERY, ZUCCHINI AND MUSHROOMS should be perfectly firm with no soft or discoloured spots. Capsicums should be glossy and the other vegetables should have a sheen. Buy only as much of these vegetables as you'll use in 4 or 5 days. Store cucumbers and capsicum unwrapped in a covered crisper; store the other vegetables in a paper bag inside a plastic bag in the fridge. Vegetables should be washed and cut up as close to serving time as possible. Mushrooms should just be wiped with a damp cloth.

AVOCADOS If you want to eat an avocado the day you buy it, look for one that 'yields' all over when gently pressed. If you want an avocado suitable for the next day or so, look for one that is just starting to yield at the neck end and is firm elsewhere. Store them at room temperature and if one is slow to ripen, you can help it along by enclosing it in a paper bag with a ripe apple or banana.

VEGETABLES TO BE COOKED Beans, asparagus, artichokes and snow, sugar or ordinary peas should be firm and crisp with an almost moist-looking sheen. Corn should be brightly coloured and glossy. Ideally, these vegetables should be bought only a day or two ahead of use. Store asparagus by standing bunches upright in 2cm to 3cm of water in a jar or other container, drop a plastic bag over the top and store in the fridge. Store the other vegetables in paper bags enclosed in plastic bags in the fridge. Cook them only until they are on the firm side of tender and as close as possible to serving.

CARROTS AND BEETROOTS These and other root vegetables can be bought up to 4 or 5 days ahead and stored in a covered crisper. They are often used raw, finely sliced or grated. If cooked, they are best steamed until just tender and eaten freshly cooked and just warm.

SALAD DRESSINGS

A crisp salad tossed lightly with the perfect amount of dressing can be a match made in heaven. But a salad can be ruined if it is drowned in a strong dressing. The key ingredients in a basic dressing are olive oil and vinegar and all cooks agree that you should try to use the best quality oil and vinegar you can find. The better the quality, the better your salad will taste. Use a wine vinegar – red, white or perhaps a sherry vinegar. Good wine vinegar has been aged and this should be indicated on the label.

> THE TWO GREAT BASIC DRESSINGS ARE FRENCH DRESSING (VINAIGRETTE) AND MAYONNAISE AND TOGETHER THEY FORM THE BASIS FOR MOST SALAD DRESSINGS.

VINAIGRETTE This classic salad dressing is made by mixing together a good wine vinegar or fresh lemon juice, a good olive or nut oil (or a mixture of these two), a dollop of french mustard and a pinch of salt and pepper. This can take on many variations and additions, changing its name along the way to italian dressing (with garlic, capsicum, onion and herbs), roquefort (with crumbled roquefort whisked in) and salsa verde (garlic, herbs and anchovy). You can drizzle a vinaigrette dressing on a whole range of hot or cold salads.

MAYONNAISE Mayonnaise can be as simple as combining egg yolks, vinegar, olive oil, salt and pepper, or it can morph into various other guises with the additions of garlic (aïoli); a dollop of mustard (mustard mayonnaise); gherkins, capers and herbs (tartare sauce); or mustard, gherkins, herbs and anchovy (remoulade). Nothing beats homemade mayonnaise, although many of the expensive ones, sold under chef's names, are also good. Commercial mayonnaise whisked together with your own vinaigrette makes a nice, creamy dressing for lighter-flavoured salads.

waldorf salad

PREP TIME 20 MINS • SERVES 4

¾ cup (225g) mayonnaise (see page 118)
¼ cup (60ml) lemon juice
5 stalks celery (750g), trimmed, sliced thickly
2 medium red apples (300g), sliced thinly
1 small red onion (100g), sliced thinly
1 cup (100g) roasted walnuts
1 cup loosely packed fresh flat-leaf parsley leaves

1 Combine mayonnaise and juice in large bowl, add remaining ingredients; toss gently to combine.

nutritional count per serving 35.7g total fat (3.1g saturated fat); 1852kJ (443 cal); 22.4g carbohydrate; 5.8g protein; 6.3g fibre

chicken salad

PREP + COOK TIME 55 MINS • SERVES 4

1 litre (4 cups) boiling water
1 litre (4 cups) chicken stock
700g chicken breast fillets
1 long french bread stick (300g), sliced thinly
2 tablespoons olive oil
½ cup (150g) mayonnaise (see page 118)
½ cup (120g) sour cream
2 tablespoons lemon juice
4 stalks celery (600g), trimmed, sliced thinly
1 medium white onion (150g), chopped finely
3 large dill pickles (150g), sliced thinly
2 tablespoons finely chopped fresh flat-leaf parsley
1 tablespoon finely chopped fresh tarragon
1 large butter lettuce, leaves separated

1 Bring the water and stock to the boil in large frying pan; poach chicken, covered, about 10 minutes or until cooked through. Cool chicken in liquid 10 minutes; slice thinly. Discard liquid.
2 Meanwhile, preheat grill. Brush both sides of bread slices with oil; toast under grill until browned lightly both sides.
3 Whisk mayonnaise, cream and juice in small bowl.
4 Place chicken in large bowl with celery, onion, pickle and herbs; toss gently to combine.
5 Place lettuce leaves on serving platter; top with salad and bread, drizzle with mayonnaise mixture.

nutritional count per serving 41.1g total fat (12.5g saturated fat); 3352kJ (802 cal); 53.3g carbohydrate; 51.9g protein; 6.5g fibre

[opposite] waldorf salad

tuna salad

PREP TIME 15 MINS • SERVES 4

There are many different flavours of canned tuna available these days. In this salad we prefer to use simple, good-quality tuna in springwater and let the fresh herbs do the talking.

¼ cup (60ml) olive oil
2 tablespoons white wine vinegar
1 tablespoon lemon juice
2 teaspoons finely chopped fresh basil
2 teaspoons finely chopped fresh oregano
1 clove garlic, crushed
1 fresh long red chilli, chopped finely
1 medium iceberg lettuce, cut into wedges
425g can tuna in springwater, drained, flaked
250g cherry tomatoes, halved
1 medium avocado (250g), chopped coarsely
1 lebanese cucumber (130g), sliced thinly
1 small red onion (100g), sliced thinly

1 Place oil, vinegar, juice, herbs, garlic and chilli in screw-top jar; shake well.
2 Place lettuce wedges on serving plate; top with remaining ingredients. Drizzle with dressing.

nutritional count per serving 26.1g total fat (4.9g saturated fat); 1492kJ (357 cal); 4.6g carbohydrate; 24.4g protein; 4.9g fibre

fattoush

PREP + COOK TIME 20 MINS • SERVES 4

This traditional Lebanese salad is made interesting by satisfyingly crunchy pieces of pitta bread sprinkled throughout.

Add some freshly chopped iceberg lettuce to any leftover salad to boost its volume and crispness.

2 large pitta bread (160g)
⅓ cup (80ml) olive oil
2 tablespoons lemon juice
1 clove garlic, crushed
3 red radishes (105g), trimmed, sliced thinly
½ small daikon (200g), grated coarsely
2 medium tomatoes (300g), chopped coarsely
1 lebanese cucumber (130g), chopped coarsely
1 small red onion (100g), sliced thinly
1 small green capsicum (150g), chopped coarsely
1 cup loosely packed fresh mint leaves
1 cup loosely packed fresh flat-leaf parsley leaves

1 Preheat grill to hot.
2 Place bread on oven tray; grill until crisp. Break bread into pieces.
3 Whisk oil, juice and garlic together in large bowl. Mix in half the bread and remaining ingredients.
4 Serve fattoush sprinkled with remaining bread.

nutritional count per serving 19.7g total fat (2.7g saturated fat); 1367kJ (327 cal); 28.1g carbohydrate; 6.8g protein; 5.8g fibre

[opposite] tuna salad

coleslaw

PREP TIME 10 MINS • SERVES 6

Coleslaw is a nutritious and inexpensive alternative to regular mixed green salad. To ensure your coleslaw remains crisp and fresh for as long as possible, keep everything (including ingredients and equipment) very cold during preparation.

½ small cabbage (600g), shredded finely
1 medium carrot (120g), grated coarsely
4 green onions, sliced thinly
½ cup (150g) mayonnaise (see page 118)
1 tablespoon lemon juice

1 Combine ingredients in large bowl.

nutritional count per serving 8.1g total fat (1g saturated fat); 523kJ (125 cal); 8.8g carbohydrate; 2g protein; 4.5g fibre

tabbouleh

PREP TIME 30 MINS (+ REFRIGERATION) • SERVES 4

Traditional tabbouleh is made with a great deal of chopped parsley and varying smaller amounts of burghul, green onion and mint. Go easy on the burghul: too much and the completed dish will be overly heavy instead of fluffy and light as intended.

¼ cup (40g) burghul
3 medium tomatoes (450g)
3 cups coarsely chopped fresh flat-leaf parsley
3 green onions, chopped finely
¼ cup coarsely chopped fresh mint
¼ cup (60ml) lemon juice
¼ cup (60ml) olive oil

1 Place burghul in medium shallow bowl. Halve tomatoes, scoop pulp from tomato over burghul. Chop tomato flesh finely; spread over burghul. Cover; refrigerate 1 hour.
2 Place burghul mixture in large bowl with remaining ingredients; toss gently to combine.

nutritional count per serving 14.1g total fat (2g saturated fat); 790kJ (189 cal); 9.2g carbohydrate; 3.4g protein; 5.6g fibre

[1] coleslaw
[2] tabbouleh
[3] oak leaf and mixed herb salad [page 102]
[4] thai beef salad [page 102]

1

2

3

4

oak-leaf and mixed herb salad

PREP TIME 10 MINS • SERVES 6

1 green oak-leaf lettuce, leaves separated
¼ cup coarsely chopped fresh chives
½ cup firmly packed fresh flat-leaf parsley leaves
½ cup firmly packed fresh chervil leaves

dijon vinaigrette
2 tablespoons olive oil
2 tablespoons white wine vinegar
1 tablespoon dijon mustard
2 teaspoons white sugar

1 Place ingredients for dijon vinaigrette in screw-top jar; shake well.
2 Place salad ingredients in medium bowl with dressing; toss gently to combine.

nutritional count per serving 6.2g total fat (0.9g saturated fat); 288kJ (69 cal); 2g carbohydrate; 0.7g protein; 1.1g fibre

thai beef salad

PREP + COOK TIME 35 MINS (+ REFRIGERATION) • SERVES 4

In recent years the Western world has embraced Thai cuisine with great enthusiasm and this char-grilled salad, found on Thai menus under the name of yum nuah, deliciously explains exactly why.

¼ cup (60ml) fish sauce
¼ cup (60ml) lime juice
500g beef rump steak
3 lebanese cucumbers (390g), seeded, sliced thinly
4 fresh small red thai chillies, sliced thinly
4 green onions, sliced thinly
250g cherry tomatoes, halved
¼ cup firmly packed fresh vietnamese mint leaves
½ cup firmly packed fresh coriander leaves
½ cup firmly packed fresh thai basil leaves
1 tablespoon grated palm sugar
2 teaspoons soy sauce
1 clove garlic, crushed

1 Combine 2 tablespoons of the fish sauce and 1 tablespoon of the juice in medium bowl with beef; toss beef to coat in marinade. Cover; refrigerate 3 hours or overnight.
2 Drain beef; discard marinade. Cook beef on heated oiled grill plate (or grill or barbecue) until cooked as desired. Cover beef, stand 5 minutes; slice beef thinly.
3 Meanwhile, combine cucumber, chilli, onion, tomato and herbs in large bowl.
4 Place sugar, soy sauce, garlic, remaining fish sauce and remaining juice in screw-top jar; shake well.
5 Add beef and dressing to salad; toss gently to combine.

nutritional count per serving 8.7g total fat (3.8g saturated fat); 986kJ (236 cal); 8.2g carbohydrate; 30.6g protein; 3.4g fibre

pasta salad

PREP + COOK TIME 25 MINS • SERVES 4

Pasta salad is another one of those favourites that has as many versions as there are cooks who make it. Because it's eaten cold, it's ideal for picnics or lunchboxes, and as a side salad to grilled chops for a simple midweek meal.

250g orecchiette
2 tablespoons drained sun-dried tomatoes, chopped coarsely
1 small red onion (100g), sliced thinly
1 small green capsicum (150g), sliced thinly
½ cup coarsely chopped fresh flat-leaf parsley

sun-dried tomato dressing
1 tablespoon sun-dried tomato pesto
1 tablespoon white wine vinegar
2 tablespoons olive oil

1 Cook pasta in large saucepan of boiling water, uncovered, until just tender; drain. Rinse under cold water; drain.
2 Place ingredients for sun-dried tomato dressing in screw-top jar; shake well.
3 Place pasta in large bowl with remaining ingredients and dressing; toss gently to combine.

nutritional count per serving 12g total fat (1.9g saturated fat); 1405kJ (336 cal); 46g carbohydrate; 8.8g protein; 3.6g fibre

greek salad

PREP TIME 20 MINS • SERVES 4

This crunchy salad is found on tables all over the world, not just in Greece. The only obligatory ingredients are fetta, tomato and onion; use your imagination and add capers, hard-boiled eggs, and red or green capsicum – as long as it offers "bite", the sky's the limit.

¼ cup (60ml) olive oil
1 tablespoon lemon juice
1 tablespoon white wine vinegar
1 tablespoon finely chopped fresh oregano
1 clove garlic, crushed
3 medium tomatoes (450g), cut into wedges
2 lebanese cucumbers (260g), chopped coarsely
1 small red onion (100g), sliced thinly
1 small red capsicum (150g), sliced thinly
½ cup (75g) seeded black olives
200g fetta cheese, chopped coarsely

1 Whisk oil, juice, vinegar, oregano and garlic in large bowl.
2 Add remaining ingredients to large bowl; toss gently to combine.

nutritional count per serving 25.8g total fat (9.6g saturated fat); 1359kJ (325 cal); 10.8g carbohydrate; 11.5g protein; 3.2g fibre

classic caesar salad

PREP + COOK TIME 45 MINS • SERVES 4

Named after Caesar Cardini, the Italian-American who tossed the first caesar in Mexico during the 1920s, this salad always contains fresh croûtons, crisp cos lettuce leaves, lightly boiled eggs, lemon juice, olive oil, worcestershire and parmesan but no one ingredient should dominate.

½ loaf ciabatta (220g)
1 clove garlic, crushed
⅓ cup (80ml) olive oil
2 eggs
3 baby cos lettuces, trimmed, leaves separated
1 cup (80g) flaked parmesan cheese

caesar dressing
1 clove garlic, crushed
1 tablespoon dijon mustard
2 tablespoons lemon juice
2 teaspoons worcestershire sauce
2 tablespoons olive oil

1 Preheat oven to 180°C/160°C fan-forced.
2 Cut bread into 2cm cubes; combine garlic and oil in large bowl with bread. Toast bread on oven tray until croûtons are browned.
3 Place ingredients for caesar dressing in screw-top jar; shake well.
4 Bring water to the boil in small saucepan, add eggs; cover pan tightly, remove from heat. Remove eggs from water after 2 minutes. When cool enough to handle, break eggs into large bowl; add lettuce, mixing gently so egg coats leaves.
5 Add cheese, croûtons and dressing to bowl; toss gently to combine.

nutritional count per serving 39.1g total fat (9.1g saturated fat); 2366kJ (566 cal); 33.1g carbohydrate; 18.4g protein; 5.6g fibre

mixed cabbage coleslaw

PREP TIME 20 MINS • SERVES 4

Elongated, with pale green, crinkly leaves, wombok (also called chinese cabbage) is the most common cabbage used throughout South-East Asia. It can be shredded or chopped and eaten raw, braised, steamed or stir-fried.

You need about half a small wombok for this recipe, a quarter of a savoy cabbage and a quarter of a red cabbage.

⅓ cup (80ml) olive oil
2 tablespoons cider vinegar
2 teaspoons dijon mustard
2 cups (160g) finely shredded green cabbage
2 cups (160g) finely shredded red cabbage
2 cups (160g) finely shredded wombok
1 medium carrot (120g), grated coarsely
4 green onions, sliced thinly

1 Whisk oil, vinegar and mustard in large bowl, add remaining ingredients; toss gently to combine.

nutritional count per serving 18.4g total fat (2.6g saturated fat); 836kJ (200 cal); 4.5g carbohydrate; 2.4g protein; 4.7g fibre

[opposite] classic caesar salad

SPECIAL FEATURE

Salad greens

The meaning of salad has expanded considerably over the years, as has the variety of leaves available to us. When crisp, moist and fresh, these lettuces give us the essential ingredients to make a truly great salad that deserves the spotlight. This can be a light, simple dish or a satisfying salade composé.

MIZUNA
A mustard green from Japan where it is traditionally used in soups and other cooked main dishes. It's often found in a mesclun, but its mild, aromatic jagged green leaves can also stand alone. Refrigerate in a plastic bag, unwashed, for up to five days.

WATERCRESS
Sprigs of dark-green watercress look pretty in a bowl and give salads and sandwiches a fresh, peppery tang. Lovely dressed with walnut or hazelnut oil and lemon juice, and a sprinkling of nuts over the top. Both summer and winter varieties are available.

CORAL LETTUCE
A soft baby green with either red or green tightly crinkled leaves. Its leaves have a delicate, sweet flavour, so they're perfect with a mixture of lettuces. You'll often find coral as part of a mesclun salad. Use within two days of purchase and dress lightly.

COS LETTUCE
Also known as romaine, this spear-shaped, crispy lettuce is quite robust in flavour and goes well with rich dressings and substantial companions like egg or bacon. Its coarse outer leaves are often discarded. Baby cos, a smaller form, has less wastage.

LAMB'S LETTUCE (MACHE)
Sometimes called corn lettuce, this salad green has long, spoon-shaped dark leaves that resemble the shape of a lamb's tongue. They have a distinctive, tangy flavour and suit a light dressing. They can also be cooked. Available in the cooler months.

CURLY ENDIVE
Also known as frisée, curly endive belongs to the chicory family and has its characteristic bitterness played against grassy freshness. Particularly good with beetroot and also used in mesclun. It will keep in the refrigerator, unwashed, for five days.

Q&A

I love salads and eat them year round as a side dish or as a main meal in the warmer months. I'm constantly told, however, they're just 99 per cent water. Is this true or are salad leaves a good source of nutrients?

Most lettuces are about 95 per cent water, but some types are very high in nutrients. Watercress, for instance, contains a substance called isothiocyanates, shown to significantly improve the health of smokers' lungs and even prevent cancer. It's packed with vitamins, iron, calcium, phosphorus, potassium, and lutein, as well as mustard oil. All you need to eat is one small bowl a day to get the benefits of this peppery leaf. Rocket, radicchio, cos and endive are other nutrient-rich lettuces. Generally, dark-coloured, bitter-tasting leaves contain more beta-carotene and other antioxidants, as well as the green pigment called chlorophyll, known to purify the blood.

OAK-LEAF LETTUCE
The curly leaves vary from reddish-brown to pale green and resemble the shape of oak leaves. This popular variety of lettuce has a soft texture with a sweet, mild flavour. It is an ideal lettuce to grow because the leaves can be harvested one at a time.

MIGNONETTE LETTUCE
This is a small, soft-leafed lettuce, but crisper and glossier than coral or oak-leaf. It has a good grassy flavour with just a delicate suggestion of bitterness. Its leaves vary from red to green and are good mixed with cos, or bland-tasting lettuces such as iceberg.

WITLOF (BELGIAN ENDIVE, CHICORY)
Crisp, tightly furled witlof tastes mild and fresh with a touch of bitterness. It is grown in the dark to keep the leaves white and minimise bitterness. It comes in red- and green-tipped varieties, and is good served with vegetables such as beetroot and asparagus.

ROCKET
You'll also see this sold as rucola or arugula. It's part of the mustard family, so it's no wonder it has such a strong, peppery, mustard-like flavour. Good with char-grilled vegetables, strong cheeses and balsamic vinegar, and as a pizza topping. Use within a day.

RADICCHIO
A red-leafed Italian chicory with a refreshing bitter taste that's appreciated both raw and grilled. Its antioxidant levels rival those of blueberries. Comes in varieties named after their places of origin, such as round-headed Verona or long-headed Treviso.

MESCLUN
Sold as a pre-mixed pile or bouquet of baby greens, which may include coral, mignonette, oak-leaf or butter lettuce, rocket, spinach, curly endive, mizuna and/or radicchio. If buying loose, grab more than you need and discard the tired-looking leaves.

vietnamese chicken salad

PREP + COOK TIME 35 MINS • SERVES 4

500g chicken breast fillets
1 large carrot (180g)
½ cup (125ml) rice wine vinegar
2 teaspoons salt
2 tablespoons caster sugar
1 medium white onion (150g), sliced thinly
1½ cups (120g) bean sprouts
2 cups (160g) finely shredded savoy cabbage
¼ cup firmly packed fresh vietnamese mint leaves
½ cup firmly packed fresh coriander leaves
1 tablespoon crushed roasted peanuts
2 tablespoons fried shallots

vietnamese dressing
2 tablespoons fish sauce
¼ cup (60ml) water
2 tablespoons caster sugar
2 tablespoons lime juice
1 clove garlic, crushed

1 Place chicken in medium saucepan of boiling water; return to the boil. Reduce heat; simmer, uncovered, about 10 minutes or until cooked through. Cool chicken in poaching liquid 10 minutes; discard liquid. Shred chicken coarsely.

2 Meanwhile, cut carrot into matchstick-sized pieces. Combine carrot, vinegar, salt and sugar in large bowl, cover; stand 5 minutes. Add onion, cover; stand 5 minutes. Add sprouts, cover; stand 3 minutes. Drain pickled vegetables; discard liquid.

3 Place ingredients for vietnamese dressing in screw-top jar; shake well.

4 Place pickled vegetables in large bowl with chicken, cabbage, mint, coriander and dressing; toss gently to combine. Sprinkle with nuts and shallots.

nutritional count per serving 8.9g total fat (2.3g saturated fat); 1271kJ (304 cal); 24.3g carbohydrate; 31g protein; 5.1g fibre

Q&A

I prefer to use skinless breast fillets for recipes that call for chicken as it's quick and low in fat. But whether I'm poaching or grilling, I always end up with a tough, dry and stringy fillet. What am I doing wrong?

When it comes to chicken fillets, you need to be aware that different rules apply for moist-heat cooking (poaching or baking in parchment) and dry-heat cooking (roasting, grilling, frying). When using moist heat, as in poaching, keep the heat low and cook for a longer period of time. Grilled chicken breasts cook in 8-10 minutes, while poached breasts cook in about 20 minutes (this includes the cooling period in the pan). One way to ensure juicy, moist chicken fillets is to brine them before cooking as the salt draws moisture into the cells. To brine chicken, place breasts in a solution of salt and water for 1 hour in the refrigerator, then rinse away excess salt.

caprese salad

PREP TIME 15 MINS • SERVES 4

This simple salad is native to Campania, the largely agricultural region of Italy that's also home to "mozzarella di bufala", the fresh, stretched, buffalo milk cheese that's a key component to this classic salad. Buffalo mozzarella is available locally, but it can be hard to find and expensive, so we used fresh, good-quality bocconcini here with great results.

3 large egg tomatoes (270g), sliced thinly
300g bocconcini cheese, drained, sliced thinly
2 tablespoons olive oil
¼ cup firmly packed fresh basil leaves, torn

1 Overlap slices of tomato and cheese on serving platter.
2 Drizzle with oil; sprinkle with basil.

nutritional count per serving 20.6g total fat (8.8g saturated fat); 1028kJ (246 cal); 1.6g carbohydrate; 13.6g protein; 1.1g fibre

green papaya salad

PREP + COOK TIME 20 MINS • SERVES 4

10cm stick fresh lemon grass (20g)
1 small green papaya (650g)
2 cups (160g) bean sprouts
1 cup (100g) coarsely grated fresh coconut
¾ cup loosely packed fresh coriander leaves
¾ cup loosely packed fresh mint leaves
2 purple shallots (50g), sliced thinly
½ cup (70g) roasted unsalted peanuts, chopped coarsely

chilli citrus dressing
¼ cup (60ml) lime juice
¼ cup (60ml) lemon juice
1 tablespoon grated palm sugar
2 teaspoons fish sauce
1 fresh small red thai chilli, chopped finely

1 Soak lemon grass in medium heatproof bowl of boiling water about 4 minutes or until tender. Drain; slice lemon grass thinly.
2 Meanwhile, make chilli citrus dressing.
3 Peel papaya, quarter lengthways, discard seeds; grate papaya coarsely.
4 Place lemon grass, dressing and papaya in large bowl with sprouts, coconut, herbs and shallots; toss gently to combine. Serve salad sprinkled with nuts.

chilli citrus dressing Place ingredients in screw-top jar; shake well.

nutritional count per serving 15.5g total fat (7.3g saturated fat); 1049kJ (251 cal); 16.3g carbohydrate; 7.9g protein; 8.4g fibre

[opposite] caprese salad

salade composé

PREP + COOK TIME 35 MINS • SERVES 4

Literally meaning "composed salad", the ingredients in this dish are layered on top of each other, rather than being tossed together, and the dressing is drizzled over the top.

1 small french bread stick (150g)
2 cloves garlic, crushed
¼ cup (60ml) olive oil
6 rindless bacon rashers (480g), sliced thickly
150g mesclun
6 medium egg tomatoes (450g), sliced thinly
4 hard-boiled eggs, halved lengthways

red wine vinaigrette
¼ cup (60ml) red wine vinegar
3 teaspoons dijon mustard
⅓ cup (80ml) extra virgin olive oil

1 Preheat grill.
2 Cut bread into 1cm slices. Brush both sides with combined garlic and oil; toast under preheated grill.
3 Cook bacon in large frying pan until crisp; drain on absorbent paper.
4 Meanwhile, place ingredients for red wine vinaigrette in screw-top jar; shake well.
5 Layer bread and bacon in large bowl with mesclun and tomato, top with egg; drizzle with vinaigrette.

nutritional count per serving 51.8g total fat (11.1g saturated fat); 2859kJ (684 cal); 23.4g carbohydrate; 30.5g protein; 3.9g fibre

potato salad

PREP + COOK TIME 45 MINS (+ REFRIGERATION) • SERVES 8

Everyone has a different opinion as to what a potato salad should be – hot or cold, creamy or dressed with vinaigrette, with bacon bits or simply sprinkled with fresh herbs – but you'd be hard-pressed to find one you didn't like. Cover the saucepan while potatoes are cooking, but lift the lid and give them an occasional gentle stir to move them around. Don't overcook them or they will break apart.

2kg potatoes, peeled
2 tablespoons cider vinegar
1 cup (300g) mayonnaise (see page 118)
4 green onions, sliced thinly
¼ cup finely chopped fresh flat-leaf parsley

1 Cover potatoes with cold water in large saucepan; bring to the boil. Reduce heat; simmer, covered, until tender. Drain; cut into 3cm pieces. Spread potato on tray, sprinkle with vinegar; refrigerate until cold.
2 Place potato in large bowl with mayonnaise, onion and parsley; toss gently to combine.

nutritional count per serving 30.4g total fat (4.1g saturated fat); 1764kJ (422 cal); 29g carbohydrate; 6.2g protein; 3.7g fibre

[opposite] salade composé

witlof, pear and blue cheese salad

PREP TIME 20 MINS • SERVES 4

Witlof, also known as endive, is a perfect addition to this bitey salad. Its bitter-yet-creamy flavour goes beautifully with the sharp taste of the blue cheese, and its crisp robust nature makes it a perfect candidate for the rich dressing.

2 red witlof (250g), trimmed, leaves separated
2 yellow witlof (250g), trimmed, leaves separated
1 medium pear (230g), sliced thinly
¾ cup (90g) roasted pecans, coarsely chopped

blue cheese dressing
⅓ cup (80ml) buttermilk
100g blue cheese, crumbled
1 tablespoon lemon juice

1 Make blue cheese dressing.
2 Place salad ingredients in large bowl; toss gently to combine.
3 Serve salad drizzled with dressing.

blue cheese dressing Whisk ingredients in small jug until smooth.

nutritional count per serving 24.9g total fat (6.5g saturated fat); 1295kJ (309 cal); 9.9g carbohydrate; 9.5g protein; 5.3g fibre

salade niçoise

PREP + COOK TIME 20 MINS • SERVES 4

The original French salade niçoise was created with the finest local produce from Provence – vine-ripened tomatoes, piquant caperberries, tiny, firm black olives, hand-picked baby beans and fresh tuna caught just off the coast. Our version has adapted a modern approach more suitable to our hectic lifestyle; if you wish, however, instead of using canned tuna, char-grill four 200g tuna steaks briefly and centre one of them on each beautiful salad arrangement.

200g baby green beans, trimmed
2 tablespoons olive oil
1 tablespoon lemon juice
2 tablespoons white wine vinegar
4 medium tomatoes (600g), cut into wedges
4 hard-boiled eggs, quartered
425g can tuna in springwater, drained, flaked
½ cup (80g) drained caperberries, rinsed
½ cup (60g) seeded small black olives
¼ cup firmly packed fresh flat-leaf parsley leaves
440g can drained whole baby new potatoes, rinsed, halved

1 Boil, steam or microwave beans until tender; drain. Rinse under cold water; drain.
2 Whisk oil, juice and vinegar in large bowl; add beans and remaining ingredients, toss gently to combine.

nutritional count per serving 16.9g total fat (3.7g saturated fat); 1522kJ (364 cal); 19.5g carbohydrate; 30.9g protein; 5.2g fibre

french dressing

PREP TIME 5 MINS • MAKES 1 CUP (250ML)

Combine ⅓ cup white wine vinegar, 2 teaspoons dijon mustard and ½ teaspoon sugar in small bowl. Gradually add ⅔ cup olive oil in thin, steady stream, whisking constantly until mixture thickens.
nutritional count per tablespoon 12.2g total fat (1.7g saturated fat); 456kJ (109 cal); 0.2g carbohydrate; 0g protein; 0g fibre

italian dressing

PREP TIME 5 MINS • MAKES 1 CUP (250ML)

Place ⅔ cup olive oil, ⅓ cup lemon juice, 1 crushed garlic clove, 2 teaspoons finely chopped fresh oregano, 2 teaspoons finely chopped fresh basil and 2 teaspoons caster sugar in screw-top jar; shake well.
nutritional count per tablespoon 12.2g total fat (1.7g saturated fat); 468kJ (112 cal); 0.9g carbohydrate; 0.1g protein; 0.1g fibre

sesame soy dressing

PREP TIME 5 MINS • MAKES ½ CUP (125ML)

Combine 1 tablespoon toasted sesame seeds, 1 tablespoon sesame oil, 2 finely chopped shallots, 1 tablespoon kecap manis and ¼ cup lime juice in small bowl.
nutritional count per tablespoon 1.4g total fat (0.2g saturated fat); 63kJ (15 cal); 0.2g carbohydrate; 0.3g protein; 0.1g fibre

ranch dressing

PREP TIME 10 MINS • MAKES 1 CUP (250ML)

Whisk ½ cup mayonnaise, ¼ cup buttermilk, 1 tablespoon white wine vinegar, 1 finely chopped small brown onion, 1 crushed garlic clove, 1 tablespoon finely chopped fresh chives, 1 tablespoon finely chopped fresh flat-leaf parsley and ¼ teaspoon sweet paprika in small jug until combined.
nutritional count per tablespoon 4.2g total fat (0.5g saturated fat); 217kJ (52 cal); 3.2g carbohydrate; 0.5g protein; 0.2g fibre

balsamic and garlic dressing

PREP TIME 5 MINS • MAKES 1¼ CUPS (310ML)

Whisk 2 tablespoons balsamic vinegar, ¼ cup lemon juice, 1 crushed garlic clove and ¾ cup olive oil in small bowl until combined.
nutritional count per tablespoon 10.9g total fat (1.5g saturated fat); 406kJ (97 cal); 0.1g carbohydrate; 0g protein; 0g fibre

lemon and macadamia dressing

PREP TIME 10 MINS • MAKES 1 CUP (250ML)

Whisk ½ cup macadamia oil, ⅓ cup finely chopped roasted macadamia nuts, 2 teaspoons finely grated lemon rind, 2 tablespoons lemon juice and 1 teaspoon caster sugar in small jug until combined.
nutritional count per tablespoon 12.4g total fat (1.8g saturated fat); 477kJ (114 cal); 0.6g carbohydrate; 0.3g protein; 0.2g fibre

red berry vinaigrette

PREP TIME 5 MINS • MAKES 1 CUP (250ML)

Blend or process ¼ cup red wine vinegar, ½ cup olive oil, 150g fresh raspberries and ¼ cup whole berry cranberry sauce until smooth. Push dressing through fine sieve into small bowl.
nutritional count per tablespoon 9.5g total fat (1.3g saturated fat); 418kJ (100 cal); 3.4g carbohydrate; 0.2g protein; 0.7g fibre

thousand island dressing

PREP TIME 10 MINS • MAKES 1 CUP (250ML)

Combine ½ cup mayonnaise, 1½ tablespoons tomato sauce, ½ finely grated small white onion, 8 finely chopped pimiento-stuffed green olives and ½ finely chopped small red capsicum in small bowl.
nutritional count per tablespoon 4.3g total fat (0.5g saturated fat); 226kJ (54 cal); 3.6g carbohydrate; 0.3g protein; 0.4g fibre

green goddess dressing

PREP TIME 10 MINS • MAKES 1¼ CUP (310ML)

Combine 1 cup mayonnaise, 2 finely chopped anchovy fillets, 2 thinly sliced green onions, 2 teaspoons finely chopped fresh flat-leaf parsley, 2 teaspoons finely chopped fresh chives, 2 teaspoons finely chopped fresh tarragon and 2 teaspoons cider vinegar in small bowl.
nutritional count per tablespoon 24.2g total fat (2.9g saturated fat); 1166kJ (279 cal); 14.6g carbohydrate; 1.2g protein; 0.6g fibre

caesar dressing

PREP + COOK TIME 15 MINS • MAKES 1½ CUPS (375ML)

Bring water to the boil in small saucepan; using slotted spoon, carefully lower 1 whole egg into water. Cover pan tightly, remove from heat; after 1 minute remove egg from water using slotted spoon. When cool enough to handle, break egg into large bowl; whisk in 2 crushed garlic cloves, ½ teaspoon dijon mustard and 2 finely chopped anchovy fillets. Gradually add 1 cup olive oil in thin, steady stream; whisking until mixture thickens slightly. Stir in 2 tablespoons lemon juice.
nutritional count per tablespoon 13g total fat (1.9g saturated fat); 493kJ (118 cal); 0.1g carbohydrate; 0.5g protein; 0.1g fibre

russian dressing

PREP + COOK TIME 25 MINS • MAKES 1½ CUPS (375ML)

Boil, steam or microwave 1 large unpeeled beetroot until tender; drain, reserving ¼ cup of the cooking liquid. When cool enough to handle, peel then chop beetroot coarsely. Blend or process beetroot with 2 tablespoons coarsely chopped pickled onions, 1 tablespoon drained, rinsed capers, ½ cup sour cream and reserved liquid until smooth.
nutritional count per tablespoon 14g total fat (9.2g saturated fat); 681kJ (163 cal); 7g carbohydrate; 1.8g protein; 1.8g fibre

honey mustard dressing

PREP TIME 5 MINS • MAKES 1 CUP (250ML)

Whisk ½ cup mayonnaise, ¼ cup cider vinegar, 1 tablespoon honey and 2 teaspoons wholegrain mustard in small jug until combined.
nutritional count per tablespoon 4.1g total fat (0.5g saturated fat); 230kJ (55 cal); 4.5g carbohydrate; 0.2g protein; 0.1g fibre

citrus and poppy seed dressing

PREP TIME 10 MINS • MAKES 1 CUP (250ML)

2 teaspoons finely grated orange rind
¼ cup (60ml) orange juice
2 tablespoons apple cider vinegar
1 tablespoon poppy seeds
⅓ cup (80g) sour cream
2 teaspoons honey mustard
¼ cup (60ml) water

1 Whisk rind, juice, vinegar, seeds, sour cream and mustard in small bowl. Add water; whisk until combined.

nutritional count per tablespoon 3.1g total fat (1.8g saturated fat); 138kJ (33 cal); 0.7g carbohydrate; 0.4g protein; 0.2g fibre

serving ideas this dressing goes well with salmon and pasta salad; coleslaw; green leaf salad; and steamed asparagus.

classic mayonnaise

PREP TIME 15 MINS • MAKES 1 CUP (250ML)

Olive oil, particularly extra virgin, can be too heavy for whipping up into a good, stiff mayonnaise. It does however, offer a beautiful, rich flavour. We use two-thirds extra light olive oil, and one-third regular (or extra virgin if you like) to get the best of both worlds.

Mayonnaise can be stored in the refrigerator for up to 3 days.

2 egg yolks
½ teaspoon salt
1 teaspoon dijon mustard
⅔ cup (160ml) extra light olive oil
⅓ cup (80ml) olive oil
1 tablespoon white wine vinegar
1 tablespoon lemon juice

1 Combine egg yolks, salt and mustard in medium bowl. Gradually add oils in a thin, steady stream, whisking constantly until mixture thickens. Stir in vinegar and juice.

nutritional count per tablespoon 19.2g total fat (2.9g saturated fat); 719kJ (172 cal); 0g carbohydrate; 0.5g protein; 0g fibre

[opposite] classic mayonnaise

SOUPS

Soups

Soup is one of the world's best-loved foods and it's easy to see why: made fresh, using flavoursome ingredients and served, steaming and aromatic in generous bowls, it is both nourishing and satisfying, easy to share, easy to digest and deeply soothing, especially in winter.

There are many types of soup – from cleansing thin broths, to velvety smooth elixirs, to seriously hearty meals in a bowl. Some soups focus on a single ingredient, while others bring together a heady combination of flavours and textures. Traditionally, soup was served as the first of several courses in a meal, but these days we're just as likely to serve it as the main dish rather than a mere opener to a meal. In this chapter, you'll find recipes for some of the world's most popular soups, ranging from the robust variety to the more delicate, lighter ones suitable for serving in the traditional role as the first course.

Making a soup from scratch is not hard, but it can take a little time, which is a precious commodity for most of us, especially during the working week. So, make your soup on the weekend and reap the benefits during the week.

And don't limit your soup making to just the winter months. While it is an unbeatable heart warming food in cold weather, soup can also be a refreshing starter to a summer meal, whether it be in the form of an ice cold gazpacho, cool and elegant vichyssoise or a spicy and restorative tom yum goong.

THE STARTING POINT

A QUALITY STOCK IS AN INDISPENSABLE INGREDIENT THAT GIVES LIFE AND VIGOUR TO MANY OF OUR CULINARY STAPLES – SOUPS, CASSEROLES, GRAVIES AND SAUCES. NOT ALL SOUPS ARE MADE WITH STOCK, BUT MANY RELY ON IT AND THE ADDITION OF HOME-MADE STOCK CAN ELEVATE A SOUP FROM DELICIOUS TO SUBLIME.

STOCKS ARE FLAVOURSOME LIQUIDS THAT CAN BE MEAT-BASED OR VEGETARIAN. MEAT STOCKS ARE MADE BY SIMMERING MEAT BONES (USUALLY BEEF OR VEAL) AND THEIR TRIMMINGS, WITH AROMATIC VEGETABLES AND HERBS TO EXTRACT THEIR FLAVOUR.

CHICKEN AND FISH STOCKS ARE MADE IN THE SAME WAY. VEGETARIAN STOCKS ARE MADE FROM SIMMERING VEGETABLES AND HERBS ALONE.

MAKING YOUR OWN STOCK IS EASY AND ECONOMICAL AND ONCE MOST COOKS HAVE MADE THEIR FIRST BATCH, THEY FIND THAT HAVING A SUPPLY OF HOMEMADE STOCK ON HAND QUICKLY BECOMES A KITCHEN MUST-HAVE. THOUGH IT DOES TAKE TIME TO CREATE, IT ISN'T A COMPLICATED PROCESS AND THE RESULTS ARE WORTH IT. MAKE A GENEROUS BATCH SO YOU CAN FREEZE IT IN USER-FRIENDLY PORTIONS.

TO SERVE

While the wafts of steaming soup are usually enough to beckon your guests, the addition of a simple, well-matched garnish makes the bowl look all the more inviting. Keep it simple: a sprinkling of chopped parsley, chives or other fresh herb is all it takes to bring your soup to life. Dill is the perfect complement to borscht, fennel is good for fish soups. Cream soups can be topped with a small swirl of cream plus some chopped chives. A few thin shavings of parmesan cheese are delicious on thick vegetable soups. Potato and pumpkin soups look good with a few crisp croutons in the centre (see below). And for chilled soups, one or two slices of lemon or lime, cut paper thin, or some finely shredded lettuce or a tiny bouquet of watercress adds a sparkle.

ON THE SIDE

A generous serving of good-quality bread is an ideal partner for most soups. Warm savoury muffins or toast topped with grilled cheese are also popular companions and help to turn a bowl of soup into a satisfying meal. If you are serving an elegant soup as a first course, then melba toast is the perfect accompaniment. To make, lightly toast slices of white sandwich bread, cut off the crusts and with a thin, sharp knife, split each slice of toast through the middle. Cut into small triangles and bake in a moderately hot oven until golden, checking often so that they don't get too brown. If you're not using them immediately, you can store them in an airtight container and reheat briefly in a moderate oven.

HOW TO MAKE CROUTONS

REMOVE THE CRUSTS FROM THICKLY SLICED BREAD THEN CUT INTO SMALL CUBES.

FRY BREAD CUBES IN A MIXTURE OF OIL AND BUTTER UNTIL GOLDEN.

DRAIN CROUTONS ON ABSORBENT PAPER THEN STORE IN AN AIRTIGHT CONTAINER.

BRIEFLY REHEAT CROUTONS IN A MODERATE OVEN.

STOCK BASICS

Meat and chicken stocks require hours of simmering to extract the gelatine from the bones for a rich base flavour – brown the meat first to help enhance colours and flavours. Fish and vegetable stocks require a short amount of simmering: you won't extract any more flavour if you cook them longer and in fact, if cooked for too long, they can lose their freshness. Vegetables can also be browned before simmering for a deeper colour and flavour.

After simmering, strain out the solids and pour the liquid into a bowl. Refrigerate the liquid until chilled, then scrape the solidified fat layer from the top. Store beef, veal, chicken and vegetable stocks in the fridge for 2 to 3 days, fish stock for 2 days and all of them can be frozen for months.

A WORD ON COMMERCIAL STOCKS The packaged liquid stocks available in supermarkets are quality products and it's worth having a supply in the pantry. The same goes for the jars of concentrated stock available from delis, some butchers and gourmet food stores. Be aware that these products are inherently salty so adjust final seasonings accordingly. The advantage of home-made stocks is that they have no added salt, giving you greater control over the saltiness of your final dish.

beef stock

PREP + COOK TIME 5 HOURS 10 MINS (+ COOLING & REFRIGERATION) • MAKES 3.5 LITRES

Before simmering, brown your vegies in the oven with the bones, for a richer, more flavoursome stock.

2kg meaty beef bones
2 medium brown onions (300g), chopped coarsely
5.5 litres water (22 cups)
2 stalks celery (300g), trimmed, chopped coarsely
2 medium carrots (240g), chopped coarsely
3 bay leaves
2 teaspoons black peppercorns
3 litres water (12 cups), extra

1 Preheat oven to 200°C/180°C fan-forced.
2 Roast bones on an oven tray, uncovered, about 1 hour or until browned.
3 Place bones and onion in large saucepan or boiler with the water, celery, carrot, bay leaves and peppercorns; bring to the boil. Reduce heat; simmer, uncovered, 3 hours, skimming surface occasionally. Add extra water; simmer, uncovered, 1 hour. Strain stock through muslin-lined sieve or colander into large heatproof bowl; discard solids. Allow stock to cool, cover; refrigerate until cold. Skim and discard surface fat before using.
nutritional count per 1 cup (250ml) 2g total fat (0.9g saturated fat); 259kJ (62 cal); 2.3g carbohydrate; 8g protein; 1.1g fibre

chicken stock

PREP + COOK TIME 2 HOURS 10 MINS (+ COOLING & REFRIGERATION) • MAKES 3.5 LITRES

Apart from being the base ingredient for most soups, stock has many a useful purpose in the kitchen. For example, replace water with stock when cooking rice for a delicate infusion of favours, or add to pasta sauce for a more full-bodied result.

2kg chicken bones
2 medium onions (300g), chopped coarsely
2 stalks celery (300g), trimmed, chopped coarsely
2 medium carrots (240g), chopped coarsely
3 bay leaves
2 teaspoons black peppercorns
5 litres (20 cups) water

1 Place ingredients in large saucepan or boiler; simmer, uncovered, 2 hours, skimming surface occasionally.
2 Strain stock through muslin-lined sieve or colander into large heatproof bowl; discard solids. Allow stock to cool, cover; refrigerate until cold. Skim and discard surface fat before using.
nutritional count per 1 cup (250ml) 0.6g total fat (0.2g saturated fat); 105kJ (25 cal); 2.3g carbohydrate; 1.9g protein; 1.1g fibre

fish stock

PREP + COOK TIME 25 MINS (+ COOLING & REFRIGERATION) • MAKES 2.5 LITRES

Ask your local fishmonger or butcher to set aside bones for your stock. Alternatively, use those reserved from previous meals, such as the chicken carcass from a roast. Bones can be frozen for up to 3 months before use, however, as in most recipes, it is best to use fresh ingredients where possible.

1.5kg fish bones
3 litres (12 cups) water
1 medium onion (150g), chopped coarsely
2 stalks celery (300g), trimmed, chopped coarsely
2 bay leaves
1 teaspoon black peppercorns

1 Combine ingredients in large saucepan; simmer, uncovered, 20 minutes.
2 Strain stock through muslin-lined sieve or colander into large heatproof bowl; discard solids. Allow stock to cool, cover; refrigerate until cold. Skim and discard surface fat before using.

nutritional count per 1 cup (250ml) 0.2g total fat (0.1g saturated fat); 63kJ (15 cal); 1.1g carbohydrate; 1.9g protein; 0.6g fibre

vegetable stock

PREP + COOK TIME 1 HOUR 40 MINS (+ COOLING & REFRIGERATION) • MAKES 3.5 LITRES

It's a good idea not to go overboard when seasoning your stock – keep the flavours mild and simple at this stage. Add the appropriate amounts of zest or other flavourings to the soup once the stock is added.

2 large carrots (360g), chopped coarsely
2 large parsnips (700g), chopped coarsely
4 medium onions (600g), chopped coarsely
10 stalks celery (1.5kg), trimmed, chopped coarsely
4 bay leaves
2 teaspoons black peppercorns
6 litres (24 cups) water

1 Combine ingredients in large saucepan; simmer, uncovered, 1½ hours.
2 Strain stock through muslin-lined sieve or colander into large heatproof bowl; discard solids. Allow stock to cool, cover; refrigerate until cold. Skim and discard surface fat before using.

nutritional count per 1 cup (250ml) 0.2g total fat (0g saturated fat); 151kJ (36 cal); 5.7g carbohydrate; 1.4g protein; 2.9g fibre

minestrone

PREP + COOK TIME 4 HOURS (+ REFRIGERATION) • SERVES 6

Roast ham hock and onion in a preheated oven for about 30 minutes or until cooked. Roasted hock and onion adds a rich depth of flavour to the broth.

1 ham hock (1kg)
1 medium brown onion (150g), quartered
1 stalk celery (150g), trimmed, chopped coarsely
1 teaspoon black peppercorns
1 bay leaf
4 litres (16 cups) water
1 tablespoon olive oil
1 large carrot (180g), chopped finely
2 stalks celery (200g), trimmed, chopped finely, extra
3 cloves garlic, crushed
¼ cup (70g) tomato paste
2 large tomatoes (440g), chopped finely
1 small leek (200g), sliced thinly
1 cup (100g) small pasta shells
420g can white beans, rinsed, drained
½ cup coarsely chopped fresh flat-leaf parsley
½ cup coarsely chopped fresh basil
½ cup (40g) flaked parmesan cheese

Once the broth has been made, remove the hock and strain the broth through a muslin-lined sieve into a large heatproof bowl. Discard the remaining solids.

1. Preheat oven to 220°C/200°C fan-forced.
2. Roast ham hock and onion in baking dish, uncovered, 30 minutes.
3. Place hock and onion in large saucepan with celery, peppercorns, bay leaf and the water; bring to the boil. Reduce heat; simmer, uncovered, 2 hours.
4. Remove hock from broth. Strain broth through muslin-lined sieve or colander into large heatproof bowl; discard solids. Allow broth to cool, cover; refrigerate until cold.
5. Remove ham from hock; shred coarsely. Discard bone, fat and skin.
6. Meanwhile, heat oil in large saucepan; cook carrot and extra celery, stirring, 2 minutes. Add ham, garlic, paste and tomato; cook, stirring, 2 minutes.
7. Discard fat from surface of broth. Pour broth into a large measuring jug; add enough water to make 2 litres (8 cups). Add broth to pan; bring to the boil. Reduce heat; simmer, covered, 20 minutes.
8. Add leek, pasta and beans to pan; bring to the boil. Reduce heat; simmer, uncovered, until pasta is tender. Remove from heat; stir in herbs. Serve soup sprinkled with cheese.

nutritional count per serving 7.2g total fat (2.4g saturated fat); 865kJ (207 cal); 19.6g carbohydrate; 12.7g protein; 6.1g fibre

Remove the ham from the hock and, using two forks, shred the meat coarsely. Discard the bone, fat and skin. Add the meat to the pan to make the tomato-based broth for the minestrone.

cream of chicken soup

PREP + COOK TIME 3 HOURS • SERVES 4

2 litres (8 cups) water
1 litre (4 cups) chicken stock
1.8kg whole chicken
1 medium carrot (120g), chopped coarsely
1 stalk celery (150g), trimmed, chopped coarsely
1 medium brown onion (150g), chopped coarsely
40g butter
⅓ cup (50g) plain flour
2 tablespoons lemon juice
½ cup (125ml) cream
¼ cup finely chopped fresh flat-leaf parsley

1 Place the water and stock in large saucepan with chicken, carrot, celery and onion; bring to the boil. Reduce heat; simmer, covered, 1½ hours. Remove chicken from pan; simmer broth, covered, 30 minutes.
2 Strain broth through muslin-lined sieve or colander into large heatproof bowl; discard solids.
3 Melt butter in large saucepan, add flour; cook, stirring, until mixture thickens and bubbles. Gradually stir in broth and juice; stir over heat until mixture boils and thickens slightly. Add cream, reduce heat; simmer, uncovered, about 25 minutes, stirring occasionally.
4 Meanwhile, remove and discard skin and bones from chicken; shred meat coarsely. Add chicken to soup; stir over medium heat until hot. Serve soup sprinkled with parsley.
nutritional count per serving 59.2g total fat (26.2g saturated fat); 3327kJ (796 cal); 15.7g carbohydrate; 50.7g protein; 2.5g fibre
serving idea warm slices of crusty bread.

chicken and vegetable soup

PREP + COOK TIME 2 HOURS 40 MINS (+ REFRIGERATION) • SERVES 6

1.5kg whole chicken
1 small brown onion (80g), halved
2 litres (8 cups) water
5 black peppercorns
2 bay leaves
20g butter
2 stalks celery (300g), trimmed, sliced thinly
2 medium carrots (240g), cut into 1cm pieces
1 large potato (300g), cut into 1cm pieces
150g snow peas, trimmed, chopped coarsely
3 green onions, sliced thinly
310g can corn kernels, drained

1 Place chicken, brown onion, the water, peppercorns and bay leaves in large saucepan; bring to the boil. Reduce heat; simmer, covered, 2 hours.

2 Remove chicken from pan. Strain broth through colander into large bowl; discard solids. Allow broth to cool, cover; refrigerate overnight. When chicken is cool enough to handle, remove and discard skin and bones. Shred meat coarsely; cover, refrigerate overnight.

3 Heat butter in same cleaned pan; cook celery, carrot and potato, stirring, until onion softens. Skim and discard fat from surface of broth. Add to pan; bring to the boil. Reduce heat; simmer, covered, 10 minutes or until vegetables are just tender.

4 Add snow peas, green onion, corn and reserved chicken to soup; cook, covered, 5 minutes or until heated through.

nutritional count per serving 9.2g total fat (2.8g saturated fat); 1183kJ (283 cal); 18.8g carbohydrate; 29.1g protein; 4.2g fibre

vietnamese beef pho

PREP + COOK TIME 1 HOUR 40 MINS • SERVES 6

Large bowls of pho (noodle soup) are a breakfast favourite throughout Vietnam, but we like to eat it any time of the day.

Round steak, gravy beef (shin) and skirt steak are all suitable for this recipe.

2 litres (8 cups) water
1 litre (4 cups) beef stock
1kg chuck steak
2 star anise
8cm piece fresh ginger (40g), grated
⅓ cup (80ml) japanese soy sauce
200g bean thread noodles
1½ cups (120g) bean sprouts
¼ cup loosely packed fresh coriander leaves
⅓ cup loosely packed fresh mint leaves
4 green onions, sliced thinly
2 fresh long red chillies, sliced thinly
¼ cup (60ml) fish sauce
1 medium lemon (140g), cut into six wedges

1 Place the water and stock in large saucepan with beef, star anise, ginger and soy sauce; bring to the boil. Reduce heat; simmer, covered, 30 minutes. Uncover, simmer about 30 minutes or until beef is tender.

2 Meanwhile, place noodles in medium heatproof bowl, cover with boiling water; stand until just tender, drain. Combine sprouts, coriander, mint, onion and chilli in medium bowl.

3 Remove beef from pan. Strain broth through muslin-lined sieve or colander into large heatproof bowl; discard solids. When beef is cool enough to handle, remove and discard fat and sinew. Slice beef thinly, return to same cleaned pan with broth; bring to the boil. Stir in fish sauce.

4 Divide noodles among soup bowls; ladle hot beef broth into bowls, sprinkle with sprout mixture, serve with lemon.

nutritional count per serving 8g total fat (3.3g saturated fat); 1166kJ (279 cal); 11.8g carbohydrate; 38.3g protein; 2.4g fibre

scotch broth

PREP + COOK TIME 2 HOURS 15 MINS • SERVES 4

2.25 litres (9 cups) water
1kg lamb neck chops
¾ cup (150g) pearl barley
1 large brown onion (200g), chopped coarsely
2 medium carrots (240g), chopped coarsely
1 medium leek (350g), sliced thinly
2 cups (160g) finely shredded savoy cabbage
½ cup (60g) frozen peas
2 tablespoons finely chopped fresh flat-leaf parsley

1 Place the water, lamb and barley in large saucepan; bring to the boil. Reduce heat; simmer, covered, 1 hour, skimming fat from surface occasionally. Add onion, carrot and leek; simmer, covered, about 30 minutes or until carrot is tender.
2 Remove lamb from pan. When cool enough to handle, remove and discard bones; shred lamb meat coarsely.
3 Return lamb meat to soup with cabbage and peas; cook, uncovered, about 10 minutes or until peas are tender. Serve soup sprinkled with parsley.

nutritional count per serving 24.4g total fat (10.7g saturated fat); 2274kJ (544 cal); 32.8g carbohydrate; 43.2g protein; 10.7g fibre

vichyssoise

PREP + COOK TIME 45 MINS (+ STANDING & REFRIGERATION) • SERVES 4

Vichyssoise (pronounced vish-ee-swaz) is a French-style cold soup made with potatoes and leeks. Use only the white part of the leeks in this recipe to preserve the creamy whiteness of the soup.

30g butter
1 large brown onion (200g), chopped finely
1 large leek (500g), sliced thickly
4 medium potatoes (800g), chopped coarsely
1.5 litres (6 cups) chicken stock
300ml cream
2 tablespoons finely chopped fresh chives

1 Heat butter in large saucepan; cook onion and leek, stirring, about 10 minutes or until soft. Add potato and stock; bring to the boil. Reduce heat; simmer, covered, 15 minutes.
2 Stand soup 10 minutes then blend or process, in batches, until smooth. Stir cream into soup; cover, refrigerate 3 hours or overnight. Serve soup sprinkled with chives.

nutritional count per serving 40.6g total fat (26.3g saturated fat); 2299kJ (550 cal); 32.8g carbohydrate; 12g protein; 5.6g fibre

[1] scotch broth
[2] vichyssoise
[3] borscht [page 132]
[4] pea and ham soup [page 132]

1

2

3

4

borscht

PREP + COOK TIME 1 HOUR 40 MINS • SERVES 6

Borsht is a thick beetroot-based soup from Russia, beautifully rich in both colour and flavour. It can be refrigerated for up to three days and frozen for about three months. When reheating borscht do not bring it to the boil or it will lose its wonderful colour.

50g butter
2 medium brown onions (300g), chopped coarsely
2kg beetroot, peeled, grated coarsely
2 medium potatoes (400g), chopped coarsely
2 large tomatoes (440g), chopped coarsely
2 medium carrots (240g), chopped coarsely
2.5 litres (10 cups) water
⅓ cup (80ml) red wine vinegar
500g piece gravy beef
3 bay leaves
4 cups (320g) shredded savoy cabbage
½ cup (120g) sour cream
2 tablespoons coarsely chopped fresh flat-leaf parsley

1 Melt butter in large saucepan, add onion; cook, stirring, until soft. Add beetroot, potato, tomato, carrot, the water, vinegar, beef and bay leaves. Bring to the boil; reduce heat, simmer, covered, 1 hour.
2 Remove and discard fat from surface of soup. Remove beef from soup; shred meat using two forks. Return meat to soup with cabbage; simmer, uncovered, 20 minutes.
3 Remove and discard bay leaves. Serve soup topped with sour cream and parsley.
nutritional count per serving 19.1g total fat (11.3g saturated fat); 1952kJ (467 cal); 39.8g carbohydrate; 26.9g protein; 14.6g fibre

pea and ham soup

PREP + COOK TIME 2 HOURS 15 MINS (+ STANDING) • SERVES 6

1 medium brown onion (150g), chopped coarsely
2 stalks celery (300g), trimmed, chopped coarsely
2 bay leaves
1.5kg ham hocks
2.5 litres (10 cups) water
1 teaspoon cracked black pepper
2 cups (375g) green split peas

1 Place onion, celery, bay leaves, hocks, the water and pepper in large saucepan; bring to the boil. Reduce heat; simmer, covered, about 1½ hours. Add peas; simmer, covered, 30 minutes or until peas are tender.
2 Remove hocks from pan; when cool enough to handle, remove meat from hocks. Shred meat finely. Discard bones, fat and skin; remove and discard bay leaves.
3 Stand soup 10 minutes then blend or process half the soup mixture, in batches, until smooth. Return to pan with remaining soup mixture and ham; stir soup until heated through.
nutritional count per serving 4.9g total fat (1.4g saturated fat); 1162kJ (278 cal); 31g carbohydrate; 23.5g protein; 7.3g fibre

cream of pumpkin soup

PREP + COOK TIME 40 MINS (+ STANDING) • SERVES 6

Pumpkin soup is one of those simple, comforting classics that everyone loves. It needs nothing more than a thick slice of warm, buttered bread to dunk in and mop up the creamy pumpkin goodness.

You can use any type of pumpkin variety in this soup, but to get that sweet nutty flavour and velvety smooth texture, butternut pumpkin is the best.

40g butter
1 large brown onion (200g), chopped coarsely
3 bacon rashers (210g), chopped coarsely
1.5kg pumpkin, chopped coarsely
2 large potatoes (600g), chopped coarsely
1.25 litres (5 cups) chicken stock
½ cup (125ml) cream

1 Melt butter in large saucepan; cook onion and bacon, stirring, until onion softens. Stir in pumpkin and potato.
2 Stir in stock, bring to the boil; simmer, uncovered, about 20 minutes or until pumpkin is soft.
3 Stand soup 10 minutes then blend or process, in batches, until smooth. Return soup to same cleaned pan, add cream; stir until heated through.
nutritional count per serving 20.9g total fat (12.3g saturated fat); 1555kJ (372 cal); 28g carbohydrate; 16.2g protein; 4.2g fibre

lamb shank and vegetable soup

PREP + COOK TIME 2 HOURS • SERVES 4

Mixed dried beans, lentils or potato make a nice addition to this hearty soup.

4 lamb shanks (1kg)
2 medium white onions (300g), chopped coarsely
2 cloves garlic, crushed
2 medium potatoes (400g), chopped coarsely
2 medium carrots (240g), chopped coarsely

2 stalks celery (300g), trimmed, chopped coarsely
400g can chopped tomatoes
1.5 litres (6 cups) beef or chicken stock
½ cup (125ml) tomato paste
2 medium zucchini (240g), chopped coarsely

1 Place shanks, onion, garlic, potato, carrot, celery, undrained tomatoes, stock and paste in large saucepan; bring to the boil. Reduce heat; simmer, covered, 1 hour.
2 Add zucchini; simmer, uncovered, further 30 minutes or until shanks are tender.
3 Remove shanks from soup. When cool enough to handle, remove meat from bones, discard bones. Return meat to soup, stir until heated through.
nutritional count per serving 9.2g total fat (3.9g saturated fat); 1513kJ (362 cal); 29.2g carbohydrate; 39.7g protein; 8.5g fibre

SPECIAL FEATURE

Soup accompaniments

Soups can be a clever way to impress a crowd or soothe yourself on a cold day. For many of us though, it has become a trusty back-up in the freezer when we need some quick sustenance. What you serve with it can make or break it. Here are some ideas that will help you make a meal out of soup.

PAPRIKA BUTTER
Melt about 60g butter in a small frying pan; add 2 teaspoons ground hot paprika. Cook, stirring regularly, 2 minutes; remove from the heat. Stir in 2 finely chopped green onions and divide between serving bowls. Serve immediately.

CHILLI PARMESAN CRISPS
Combine 1 cup finely grated parmesan cheese and ½ finely chopped long red chilli; drop level tablespoons of mixture onto an oven tray lined with baking paper. Bake crisps in a hot oven about 3 minutes; stand until set before serving with soup.

GREMOLATA
Combine ⅓ cup finely chopped fresh flat-leaf parsley, 1 tablespoon finely grated lemon rind and 2 cloves finely chopped garlic in a small bowl. Keep covered with plastic wrap or in an airtight container in the fridge until ready to use.

TORTILLA CRISPS
Slice soft corn tortillas into thin strips; shallow-fry in vegetable oil, in batches, until browned lightly. Drain on absorbent paper. Serve with tomato soup, or scatter on top of pureed red kidney bean soup along with cubes of avocado or a spoonful of chilli con carne.

BACON TOASTS
Thinly slice a loaf of ciabatta; toast slices on one side under a preheated grill. Turn slices and spread with wholegrain mustard. Top with a mixture of coarsely chopped cooked crisp bacon and some finely grated parmesan cheese; grill until browned lightl.

CINNAMON CREAM
Lightly whip some thickened cream with an electric mixer until soft peaks form; sprinkle a little ground cinnamon over cream to taste. Top serving cups or soup bowls with a spoonful of cream or place in the refrigerator, covered, until needed.

Q&A

Although store-bought melba toasts are convenient, they can be quite expensive, so I would like to make them at home using a reliable recipe. What is the trick to getting them so thin, crispy and perfect?

Preheat your grill on high and use to toast 8 slices of white bread lightly on both sides. Remove the crusts from the bread and, carefully, using a sharp knife, split each slice of bread lengthways into 2 slices, so you end up with 16 slices that are only toasted on one side. Place the slices you've just made back under the grill and cook the untoasted side until crisp. The sides of the bread will curl as a result, and this is the effect you are after. You can also make Melba toast earlier in the day. Set them aside and warm in an oven preheated to 170°C/150°C fan-forced for a few minutes before serving. For best results use wire trays to allow airflow around both sides of bread.

GRUYERE TOASTS
Cut a french bread stick into thick slices; toast slices on one side under a preheated grill. Turn slices over and sprinkle tops with finely grated gruyère cheese; place under the grill until the cheese melts. Serve hot gruyère toasts alongside soup bowls.

SPICED YOGURT
Dry-fry 1 teaspoon ground coriander, 1 teaspoon ground cumin and ½ teaspoon hot paprika in a non-stick frying pan until fragrant. Combine spices in a small bowl with 1 cup yogurt and ¼ cup finely chopped fresh mint.

PISTOU
Blend or process 2 cups fresh basil leaves, 1 quartered clove garlic, ¼ cup finely grated parmesan cheese and ¼ cup extra virgin olive oil until smooth. Refrigerate, covered. If storing for a few days, omit the cheese when preparing and stir in just before serving.

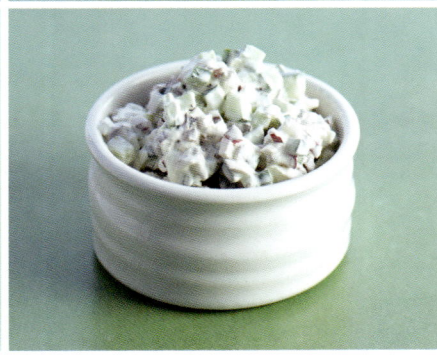

DILL CREAM
Combine ½ cup sour cream with 1 tablespoon finely chopped fresh dill in a small bowl. Place dollops of dill cream on top of soup or place in the refrigerator, covered, until needed; serve extra chopped dill sprinkled over bowl of dill cream just before serving.

ANCHOVY TOASTS
Combine 50g softened butter, 6 finely chopped anchovy fillets and 2-3 tablespoons finely chopped fresh garlic chives in a bowl. Toast bread slices on one side under a preheated grill. Spread untoasted side with anchovy butter; grill until browned lightly.

CUCUMBER AND ONION SALSA
Combine ¼ cup sour cream, 1 finely chopped, seeded lebanese cucumber, 1 finely chopped small red onion and 1 finely chopped small red thai chilli in a small bowl. Place in the refrigerator, covered, until needed or serve on the side with soup.

french onion soup with gruyère croûtons

**PREP + COOK TIME
1 HOUR 10 MINS
SERVES 4**

50g butter
4 large brown onions (800g), sliced thinly
¾ cup (180ml) dry white wine
3 cups (750ml) water
1 litre (4 cups) beef stock
1 bay leaf
1 tablespoon plain flour
1 teaspoon fresh thyme leaves

gruyère croûtons
1 small french bread (150g), cut in 1.5cm slices
½ cup (60g) coarsely grated gruyère cheese

A tablespoon of cognac, stirred into the soup at the last minute, is an excellent addition.

1 Melt butter in large saucepan, add onion; cook, stirring occasionally, about 30 minutes or until caramelised.
2 Meanwhile, bring wine to the boil in large saucepan; boil 1 minute then stir in the water, stock and bay leaf, return to the boil. Remove from heat.
3 Stir flour into onion mixture; cook, stirring, 2 minutes. Gradually add hot broth mixture to onion mixture, stirring, until mixture boils and thickens slightly. Reduce heat; simmer, uncovered, stirring occasionally, 20 minutes. Discard bay leaf; stir in thyme.
4 Meanwhile, make gruyère croûtons.
5 Serve bowls of soup topped with croûtons.
gruyère croûtons Preheat grill. Toast bread on one side then turn and sprinkle with cheese; grill croûtons until cheese browns lightly.
nutritional count per serving 16.7g total fat (10g saturated fat); 1522kJ (364 cal); 31.1g carbohydrate; 13.4g protein; 3.9g fibre
serving idea sprinkle soup with extra thyme leaves.

Q&A

When the weather turns cold, my family asks for french onion soup but chopping all those onions brings so many tears to my eyes. How do chefs stay dry-eyed? I've never seen a chef shed a tear while chopping onions.

When we chop onions, we break cells that combine with enzymes to emit gases. These gases are dissolved by the water in our eyes. Oxygen in the air converts the dissolved gas into sulfuric acid, so our eyes water to wash away the acid. Many tricks have been tried to overcome this problem, everything from keeping onions cold before cutting, and wearing goggles to chewing gum – it's believed breathing through the mouth keeps fumes away from the eyes. But chefs hold back the tears by cutting onions very fast with a sharp knife. This minimises the time for the gases to diffuse and get to their eyes. So if all the other methods fail for you, simply learn to chop like a chef.

seafood laksa

PREP + COOK TIME 1 HOUR 15 MINS • SERVES 6

To make the laksa paste, soak the dried chillies in a small heatproof bowl of boiling water for about 10 minutes or until softened. Always wear rubber gloves whenever handling chilli.

On a clean chopping board, coarsely chop the root and stems of fresh coriander using a sharp knife. You need to chop enough to make 1 tablespoon of root and stem mixture.

Place rice stick noodles in a large heatproof bowl and cover with boiling water. Soak noodles until tender, stirring with a fork to separate.

12 uncooked medium king prawns (540g)
1 litre (4 cups) chicken stock
3¼ cups (810ml) coconut milk
4 fresh kaffir lime leaves, shredded finely
150g rice stick noodles
300g scallops, roe removed
150g marinated tofu, cut into 2cm pieces
2 tablespoons lime juice
2 cups (160g) bean sprouts
4 green onions, sliced thinly
1 fresh long red chilli, sliced thinly
½ cup loosely packed fresh coriander leaves

laksa paste
3 dried medium chillies
⅓ cup (80ml) boiling water
2 teaspoons peanut oil
1 small brown onion (80g), chopped coarsely
2 cloves garlic, quartered
2cm piece fresh ginger (10g), grated
10cm stick fresh lemon grass (20g), chopped finely
1 tablespoon halved unroasted, unsalted macadamias
1 tablespoon coarsely chopped fresh coriander root and stem mixture
½ teaspoon ground turmeric
½ teaspoon ground coriander
¼ cup loosely packed fresh mint leaves

1 Shell and devein prawns, leaving tails intact.
2 Make laksa paste.
3 Cook paste in large saucepan, stirring, about 5 minutes or until fragrant. Stir in stock, coconut milk and lime leaves; bring to the boil. Reduce heat; simmer, covered, 20 minutes.
4 Meanwhile, place noodles in large heatproof bowl, cover with boiling water; stand until tender, drain.
5 Add prawns to laksa mixture; simmer, uncovered, about 5 minutes or until prawns change colour. Add scallops and tofu; simmer, uncovered, about 3 minutes or until scallops change colour. Remove from heat; stir in juice.
6 Divide noodles among serving bowls; ladle laksa into bowls, top with sprouts, onion, chilli and coriander.
laksa paste Cover chillies with the water in small heatproof bowl, stand 10 minutes; drain. Blend or process chillies with remaining ingredients until smooth.
nutritional count per serving 35.4g total fat (25.9g saturated fat); 2207kJ (528 cal); 25.1g carbohydrate; 25.7g protein; 5g fibre

gazpacho

PREP TIME 25 MINS (+ REFRIGERATION) • SERVES 4

Gazpacho is a chilled soup originating in the southern province of Andalusia in Spain where long, sunny summers produce an explosion of vegetables. It has a wonderfully refreshing flavour that only gets better when made a day ahead. Refrigerate, covered, overnight to taste it at its best.

3 cups (750ml) tomato juice
8 medium egg tomatoes (600g), chopped coarsely
1 medium red onion (170g), chopped coarsely
1 clove garlic
1 lebanese cucumber (130g), chopped coarsely
1 small green capsicum (150g), chopped coarsely
2 slices white bread, crusts removed, chopped coarsely
2 teaspoons Tabasco sauce
1 small white onion (80g), chopped finely
½ lebanese cucumber (65g), seeded, chopped finely, extra
½ small yellow capsicum (75g), chopped finely
2 teaspoons olive oil
1 tablespoon vodka
2 tablespoons finely chopped fresh coriander

1 Blend or process juice, tomato, red onion, garlic, coarsely chopped cucumber, green capsicum, bread and sauce, in batches, until pureed. Strain through sieve into large bowl, cover; refrigerate 3 hours.
2 Combine white onion, finely chopped cucumber, yellow capsicum, oil, vodka and coriander in small bowl.
3 Serve soup topped with vegetable mixture.
nutritional count per serving 2.6g total fat (0.3g saturated fat); 548kJ (131 cal); 16.9g carbohydrate; 4.8g protein; 4.9g fibre
serving idea slices of crusty bread.

tom yum goong

PREP + COOK TIME 1 HOUR • SERVES 4

Tom yums are the most popular soups in Thailand. Translated loosely as broth or stock (tom) and combined spicy sour (yum), this soup is far more than the name would indicate. Sour and tangy, without the sweetness of coconut, tom yum goong's unique taste comes from the combination of spicy ingredients, like chilli and curry paste, with sour ones, like lime juice and tamarind.

900g uncooked large king prawns
1 tablespoon peanut oil
1.5 litres (6 cups) water
2 tablespoons red curry paste
1 tablespoon tamarind concentrate
10cm stick fresh lemon grass (20g), chopped finely
1 teaspoon ground turmeric
2 fresh small red thai chillies, chopped coarsely
1cm piece fresh ginger (5g), grated
6 fresh kaffir lime leaves, shredded finely
1 teaspoon grated palm sugar
100g fresh shiitake mushrooms, halved
2 tablespoons fish sauce
2 tablespoons lime juice
¼ cup loosely packed vietnamese mint leaves
¼ cup loosely packed fresh coriander leaves

1 Shell and devein prawns, leaving tails intact; reserve heads and shells.
2 Heat oil in large saucepan; cook prawn shells and heads, stirring, about 5 minutes or until a deep orange in colour.
3 Add 1 cup of the water and curry paste to pan; bring to the boil, stirring. Add remaining water; return to the boil. Reduce heat; simmer, uncovered, 20 minutes. Strain broth through muslin-lined sieve or colander into large heatproof bowl; discard solids.
4 Return broth to same cleaned pan. Add tamarind, lemon grass, turmeric, chilli, ginger, lime leaves and sugar; bring to the boil. Boil, stirring, 2 minutes. Add mushrooms, reduce heat; cook, stirring, 3 minutes. Add prawns; simmer, uncovered, about 5 minutes or until prawns are cooked as desired. Remove from heat; stir in sauce and juice.
5 Serve bowls of soup sprinkled with mint and coriander.
nutritional count per serving 9g total fat (1.3g saturated fat); 849kJ (203 cal); 3.9g carbohydrate; 25.2g protein; 2.3g fibre

fish chowder

PREP + COOK TIME 45 MINS • SERVES 4

Chowder is thought to have originated on the Atlantic seacoast of North America where fishermen at sea would cook a portion of each day's catch in a flour-thickened stew and eat it with any available bread on board, no matter how stale. Thankfully, the tradition has evolved, and today the standard accompaniment is a salty cracker or a water biscuit, crumbled by the handful into each serving bowl.

40g butter
1 large brown onion (200g), chopped coarsely
1 clove garlic, crushed
2 rindless bacon rashers (130g), chopped coarsely
2 tablespoons plain flour
3 cups (750ml) milk
2 cups (500ml) vegetable stock
2 medium potatoes (400g), chopped coarsely
400g firm white fish fillets, chopped coarsely
2 tablespoons finely chopped fresh chives

1 Melt butter in large saucepan; cook onion, garlic and bacon, stirring, until onion softens.
2 Add flour to pan; cook, stirring, 1 minute. Add milk, stock and potato; bring to the boil. Reduce heat; simmer, covered, about 10 minutes or until potato is tender.
3 Add fish; simmer, uncovered, about 4 minutes or until fish is barely cooked. Sprinkle soup with chives.
nutritional count per serving 19.5g total fat (11.6g saturated fat); 1810kJ (433 cal); 28.4g carbohydrate; 34.8g protein; 2.4g fibre
serving idea slices of crusty bread.

PASTA

Pasta

Thankfully, the Italians took their pasta with them when they began migrating around the globe. Now, their gift to the world is an international staple and most households couldn't imagine living without it. It's quick and easy to cook, can be matched with endless varieties of sauce, and appeals to children and adults alike.

ITALIANS LOVE THEIR PASTA AND EAT IT WITH MUCH LESS SAUCE THAN WE DO: THEY REGARD THE PASTA ITSELF AS THE MAIN ATTRACTION AND THE SAUCE AS A DRESSING. GIVE IT A TRY AND MAKE SURE YOU INVEST IN GOOD QUALITY PASTA TO REALLY ENJOY ITS AUTHENTIC FLAVOUR.

 ## COOKING PASTA

ALL PASTA NEEDS TO BE BOILED, EVEN IF YOU ARE THEN BAKING IT. THE ONLY EXCEPTION TO THIS IS INSTANT LASAGNE SHEETS, WHICH CAN BE USED STRAIGHT FROM THE PACKET. FRESH PASTA WILL TAKE LESS TIME TO COOK THAN DRIED PASTA.

THE STARTING POINT FOR PERFECT PASTA IS TO USE A LARGE SAUCEPAN AND PLENTY OF WATER. BRING THE WATER TO A ROLLING BOIL, THEN ADD SALT (THE ITALIANS USE PLENTY OF SALT AT THIS POINT). ADD THE PASTA GRADUALLY SO THE WATER DOES NOT GO OFF THE BOIL. FOR LONG PASTA, HOLD THE STRANDS AND FEED THEM IN GRADUALLY INTO THE SAUCEPAN AS THEY SOFTEN IN THE WATER. KEEP THE WATER BOILING FAST TO KEEP THE PASTA MOVING. TEST THE PASTA BY SCOOPING OUT A PIECE AND BITING IT. FOR PERFECTLY COOKED PASTA, IT NEEDS TO BE AL DENTE – LITERALLY TRANSLATED AS "TO THE TOOTH" – COOKED THROUGH BUT FIRM TO BITE. FRESH PASTA SHOULD ONLY TAKE 2 TO 3 MINUTES; DRIED PASTA WILL TAKE BETWEEN 5 AND 12 MINUTES, DEPENDING ON FRESHNESS AND THICKNESS. DRAIN THE COOKED PASTA INTO A COLANDER IN THE SINK, SAVING A LITTLE OF THE STARCHY COOKING WATER TO ADD TO THE SAUCE YOU ARE MAKING. DON'T RINSE THE PASTA: YOU WILL DIMINISH ITS FLAVOUR IF YOU WASH AWAY THE STARCH AND SALT.

KINDS OF PASTA

THERE ARE HUNDREDS OF DIFFERENT VARIETIES OF PASTA, BUT THEY ARE ALL GENERALLY MADE OF A SIMPLE DOUGH OF FLOUR AND WATER. AVAILABLE FRESH OR DRY, THEY CAN BE MADE FROM A VARIETY OF DIFFERENT FLOURS, SOME ENRICHED WITH EGG, AND OTHERS ARE COLOURED WITH INGREDIENTS SUCH AS SPINACH AND TOMATO.

STORING PASTA

DRIED PASTA WILL KEEP INDEFINITELY, IN A COOL, DRY PLACE, IN ITS UNOPENED PACKAGING OR IN AN AIRTIGHT CONTAINER AFTER OPENING. FRESH PASTA WILL KEEP FOR 3 TO 4 DAYS IN THE REFRIGERATOR; IT WILL STICK TOGETHER IF KEPT ANY LONGER. PASTA CAN BE FROZEN BUT MAY GLUE TOGETHER AS IT THAWS.

DRIED PASTA This is the most widely recognisable type of pasta, available in mass-produced packets and boxes in your local supermarket. Good quality dried pasta is made with semolina flour made from durum wheat (in fact, this is enshrined in law in Italy). When you're selecting your pasta, look for "100% durum wheat". You'll find both Italian and Australian-made products of this quality. Mass-produced does not necessarily mean lesser quality: some of the biggest pasta manufacturers make top-quality pasta.

FRESH PASTA Soft and pliable, fresh pasta is found in the refrigerated section of most supermarkets, delicatessens or gourmet grocery stores. You can also make it at home using a small hand-operated or electric machine with rollers and cutters. Fresh pasta is usually made with plain flour and eggs. It is not superior to dried pasta: both have the same taste and consistency when cooked properly.

EGG PASTA Made with egg and soft wheat flour, egg pasta is available dried or fresh.

WHOLEMEAL PASTA Part wholemeal and part white flour, this variety is light-brown in appearance and has a slightly different texture and nuttier flavour. It contains more fibre than refined-wheat pasta.

FLAVOURED PASTA These are the coloured dried pasta available alongside other pasta. They are lightly flavoured with spinach, tomato or basil.

SHAPES OF PASTA

Dried pasta is available in an abundance of shapes, from small tubes, to spirals to more elaborate shapes. Some tube pastas have ridges and these, together with the more complex shapes, are designed for grabbing and holding onto the sauce.

LONG STRANDS spaghetti, spaghettoni (thicker), spaghettini (thinner), capellini (very thin) and angel hair (fine, delicate, usually shaped into a nest).

TUBULAR macaroni (short and thick), elbow macaroni (with a bend in the middle), rigatoni (short and wide, with ridged surface) and bucatini (long and thin).

FLAT RIBBONS fettuccine (plain or coloured), tagliatelle (wider), tagliolini (narrower) and linguine (narrower still).

LARGE SHEETS lasagne, flat or with ripple edges, plain or verde (green, spinach flavoured).

STUFFED PASTA ravioli (square or round), agnolotti (turnovers), tortellini (turnovers twisted into a ring).

PASTA FOR SOUP tiny shapes such as stelline (stars) and orzo or risoni (rice-grain shapes).

PASTA SHAPES DESIGNED TO 'GRAB AND HOLD' CHUNKY SAUCES penne, conchiglie (shells – available in several sizes), fusilli (corkscrews), orecchiette (little ears) and farfalle (butterflies or bow-ties).

SPECIAL FEATURE

Know your pasta

Nobody can argue when it comes to pasta, the home cook is spoilt for choice. Along with the huge variety of shapes available, in both dried and fresh form, there's a profusion of sauces that go with them. However, before we can do a good job matching these, we need to know our fusilli from our fettuccine.

PENNE
Italian for "pen", this dried pasta resembles a quill, and has angled ends and ridges to hold chunky sauces. Penne are also available in a smooth variety to complement finer sauces.

CONCHIGLIE
"Shellfish" or "shells", have concave, ridged shapes that hold sauces well. A dried type, great in hearty soups like minestrone, or added to a vegetable salad. Available in different sizes: conchigliette (small), conchiglioni (larger).

FARFALLE
"Butterflies" are rectangular pieces of dried pasta that are pinched in the centre to resemble bow ties. This pretty shape is thick enough for a host of sauces. Also good in soups and salads.

LASAGNE
From the Latin word *lasanum* ("pot"), these sheets are designed to be baked between layers of sauce in the oven. Also comes with rippled edges. Available fresh or dried – fresh is best if you want to assemble and bake the lasagne without par-boiling the sheets.

FETTUCCINE
"Little slices" are ribbon-shaped strands of pasta, traditionally made with egg. It is northern Italy's most famous fresh pasta, though it now comes in a dried version, with or without egg. Suits creamy sauces – as in the rich, buttery alfredo sauce.

TORTELLINI
"Little tarts" are ring-shaped pasta, typically filled with meat, cheese or minced vegetables. Tortellini is commonly served in a broth or a cream-based sauce. Fresh tortellini has more filling inside, so it is plumper and cooks faster than dried tortellini.

Q&A

When I order pasta at restaurants, I end up with an oversauced dish, so I can't actually taste or feel the pasta. I'm having some Italian friends over for dinner and want to know the correct way to sauce pasta.

In Italy, just enough sauce is added to lightly cling to the pasta – no extra sauce is seen at the bottom of the bowl. To avoid this problem, don't ladle the sauce over the serving bowls or in a big mixing bowl as the pasta and sauce will not combine well. The best method is to drain the pasta, return it to the drained pan, add only enough sauce to coat the pasta and briefly combine over moderate heat for about 30 seconds. Never run cold water over the drained pasta to keep it from cooking further as this removes much of the flavour. Pasta should be cooked for just enough time so it remains al dente (firm in the centre) by the time it arrives on the table.

GNOCCHI
Derived from *nocchio*, "knot in wood", gnocchi are small dumplings made from flour, semolina or potato. They should be fresh and can be boiled, grilled or used as in *gnocchi alla romana*, where they are oven-baked with butter and parmesan.

RAVIOLI
"Little turnips", squares of pasta stuffed with cheese, vegetables or meat. Usually made from fresh pasta either by hand or in moulds. Ravioli are a match for tomato-based sauces, including bolognese, or they can be served with butter, olive oil or cream.

RIGATONI
Italian for "large, ridged", this dried ribbed, tubular pasta is perfect with any sauce, from cream or cheese (especially ricotta) to the chunkiest meat sauces – a tomato and sausage one matches beautifully. Rigatoni is also good for pasta bakes.

FUSILLI
"Little spindles", also known as corkscrews, are a ridged spiral pasta. Fusilli can be topped with any sauce, makes a great addition to casseroles or can be turned into a wonderful salad. Also comes in a larger, coil-like shape, called *fusilli col buco*.

PAPPARDELLE
From the Italian verb *pappare*, meaning "to gobble up", pappardelle are broad, flat or frilly ribbons of pasta. Goes well with red meat sauces (rabbit is a Tuscan favourite), chunky tomato and mushroom sauces as in *pappardelle boscaiola*, or with cream.

ORECCHIETTE
"Little ears" are named after their shape, resembling tiny human ears. It's a chewy pasta that's traditional in southern Italy's Puglia region, where it is made from semolina. There it is served with oil, sausage and leafy greens. Good with ragu and in salads too.

fresh pasta

PREP TIME 40 MINS • MAKES 500G

Making fresh pasta is a lot simpler than many people think. The few ingredients needed are readily available and inexpensive, and the process can be really satisfying. Once you have mastered the basics, have some fun experimenting with colours and flavours by adding pureed vegetables to the mix.

2 cups (300g) plain flour
2 teaspoons salt
3 eggs

1 Sift flour and salt onto work bench or into large bowl; make a well in the centre.
2 Break eggs into well; using fingers, gradually mix flour into eggs. Press mixture into a ball. Knead dough on floured surface 10 minutes or until smooth and elastic.
3 Cut dough in half; roll each half through pasta machine set on thickest setting. Fold dough in half; roll through machine again. Repeat folding and rolling, adjusting setting on machine to become less thick with each roll, dusting dough with a little extra flour when necessary. Roll until 1mm thick or until desired thickness is reached. Cut pasta sheets into desired pasta shape.

nutritional count per 100g 4.1g total fat (1.2g saturated fat); 1145kJ (274 cal); 46.2g carbohydrate; 11.2g protein; 2.4g fibre

Press the dough into a ball, then roll and stretch it on a floured surface. Using the heel of your hand, push the dough gently along the surface. After about 10 minutes, the dough should be smooth and springy.

Adjust the hand roller to the thickest setting. Cut the dough in half and feed each half through the roller. Fold dough in half and feed the pieces through the roller again. Begin rolling the dough thinner, by turning the dial to the next thinnest setting. Guide the dough through the roller again, dusting it with flour if necessary.

The pasta should be 1mm thick. You might find it easier to work with a helper, so one person can turn the crank and the other can guide the dough into the roller with one hand and catch it with the other hand. Be careful not to stretch or tear the sheet.

Attach the cutting attachment to the hand roller according to your manual's instructions. Drape the sheet of pasta over one hand as you feed it through the roller.

Q&A

I'd like to start making my own pasta at home because store-bought fresh pasta can be expensive and not always great quality. Should I invest in a motorised machine or stick to a traditional hand-operated model?

If you want to make pasta at home, avoid electric machines and stick to the manual types. The electric ones might make light, fast work of rolling and cutting the dough but they have their drawbacks too. On a machine, the rolling is done by squeezing the dough to thinness (compression), whereas hand rollers combine compression and stretching. This makes the pasta's texture more resilient. Hand rollers create a more mottled surface, which picks up sauces more efficiently, so the pasta tastes even better. You'll also get more satisfaction cutting the pasta yourself and deciding its length. Hand-rolled pasta is easier to manage too, compared with machine-cut pasta.

spaghetti bolognese

PREP + COOK TIME 2 HOURS 35 MINS • SERVES 6

Pasta-lovers the world over have made this dish, originally from Bologna in northern Italy, their own. The biggest secret of a good bolognese is long, slow cooking to concentrate the complex flavour.

2 teaspoons olive oil
6 slices pancetta (90g), chopped finely
1 large white onion (200g), chopped finely
1 medium carrot (120g), chopped finely
2 stalks celery (300g) trimmed, chopped finely
600g beef mince
150g chicken livers, trimmed, chopped finely
1 cup (250ml) milk
50g butter
1½ cups (375ml) beef stock
1 cup (250ml) dry red wine
410g can tomato puree
2 tablespoons tomato paste
¼ cup finely chopped fresh flat-leaf parsley
750g fresh spaghetti
½ cup (40g) shaved parmesan cheese

1 Heat oil in large heavy-based frying pan; cook pancetta, stirring, until crisp. Add onion, carrot and celery; cook, stirring, until vegetables soften.
2 Add beef and liver to pan; cook, stirring, until beef changes colour. Stir in milk and butter; cook, stirring occasionally, until liquid reduces to about half.
3 Add stock, wine, puree and paste to pan; simmer, covered, 1 hour. Uncover; simmer 1 hour. Remove from heat; stir in parsley.
4 Meanwhile, cook pasta in large saucepan of boiling water until tender; drain.
5 Serve pasta topped with bolognese sauce and cheese.

nutritional count per serving 26.6g total fat (13g saturated fat); 2504kJ (599 cal); 41g carbohydrate; 39.2g protein; 5.5g fibre

fettuccine alfredo

PREP + COOK TIME 30 MINS • SERVES 4

This sauce is named after the Roman restaurateur Alfredo di Lello who created the dish in the 1920s. Do not reduce the cream mixture too rapidly or by too much as this sauce can burn. Check and stir once or twice and take the pan off the heat when it is reduced correctly.

500g fresh fettuccine pasta
80g butter
300ml cream
½ cup (40g) finely grated parmesan cheese

1 Cook pasta in large saucepan of boiling water until tender; drain. Return to pan.
2 Meanwhile, melt butter in medium frying pan, add cream; bring to the boil. Reduce heat; simmer, uncovered, about 5 minutes or until sauce reduces by half. Stir in cheese, over low heat, about 2 minutes or until cheese melts.
3 Add sauce to pasta; toss gently to coat.

nutritional count per serving 53.4g total fat (34.5g saturated fat); 3821kJ (914 cal); 87.5g carbohydrate; 19.4g protein; 4.1g fibre

[opposite] spaghetti bolognese

fettuccine carbonara

PREP + COOK TIME 20 MINS • SERVES 4

Italian recipes vary from region to region, reflecting the ingredients available there. While "charcoal burners' fettuccine" is made without cream in the south, it includes cream, as our recipe does, in the north of the country.

500g fresh fettuccine pasta
60g butter
6 rindless bacon rashers (390g), sliced thinly
1 clove garlic, crushed
½ teaspoon cracked black pepper
300ml cream
2 eggs, beaten lightly
½ cup (40g) finely grated parmesan cheese
½ cup (40g) finely grated romano cheese
2 teaspoons coarsely chopped fresh chives

1 Cook pasta in large saucepan of boiling water until tender; drain.
2 Meanwhile, melt butter in medium frying pan; cook bacon, stirring, 5 minutes.
3 Add garlic, pepper and cream to pan; simmer, uncovered, until sauce reduces by half. Remove from heat. Stir in egg and cheeses.
4 Add pasta to sauce; stir to coat. Serve pasta sprinkled with chives.

nutritional count per serving 66.7g total fat (39g saturated fat); 3662kJ (876 cal); 33.6g carbohydrate; 53.7g protein; 2.4g fibre

spaghetti with pesto

PREP + COOK TIME 25 MINS • SERVES 4

Pesto can be made in advance and stored in the refrigerator for up to one week. If doing this, omit the parmesan cheese when blending and stir it through just before serving.

2 cloves garlic, chopped coarsely
⅓ cup (50g) roasted pine nuts
½ cup (40g) finely grated parmesan cheese
2 cups firmly packed fresh basil leaves
½ cup (125ml) olive oil
500g spaghetti
½ cup (40g) flaked parmesan cheese

1 Blend or process garlic, nuts, grated cheese and basil until almost smooth. Gradually add oil in a thin, steady stream, processing until thick.
2 Cook pasta in large saucepan of boiling water, until just tender; drain, reserving ¼ cup of the cooking liquid.
3 Combine pasta, pesto and reserved cooking liquid in large bowl. Serve with flaked cheese.

nutritional count per serving 45.2g total fat (8.9g saturated fat); 3578kJ (859 cal); 86.2g carbohydrate; 23.6g protein; 5.6g fibre

serving ideas pesto also goes well with both creamy and grilled polenta, barbecued fish, pan-fried lamb and beef.

[1] fettuccine carbonara
[2] spaghetti with pesto
[3] macaroni cheese [page 154]
[4] spinach and ricotta cannelloni [page 154]

1

2

3

4

macaroni cheese

PREP + COOK TIME 1 HOUR • SERVES 4

This recipe freezes well; you could double the recipe and freeze one batch for a rainy day.

300g macaroni pasta
4 rindless bacon rashers (260g), chopped finely
50g butter
⅓ cup (50g) plain flour
1 litre (4 cups) milk
1 cup (120g) coarsely grated cheddar cheese
½ cup (40g) finely grated pecorino cheese
2 tablespoons wholegrain mustard
½ cup (35g) stale breadcrumbs
20g butter, extra

1 Preheat oven to 180°C/160°C fan-forced. Oil deep 2-litre (8-cup) ovenproof dish.
2 Cook pasta in large saucepan of boiling water until tender; drain.
3 Meanwhile, cook bacon in medium saucepan, stirring, until crisp; drain on absorbent paper.
4 Melt butter in same pan, add flour; cook, stirring, 1 minute. Gradually stir in milk; cook, stirring, until sauce boils and thickens. Cool 2 minutes; stir in cheeses and mustard.
5 Combine pasta, sauce and bacon in large bowl; pour mixture into dish. Top with breadcrumbs, dot with extra butter. Bake about 30 minutes or until browned.

nutritional count per serving 47.5g total fat (27.8g saturated fat); 3854kJ (922 cal); 78.8g carbohydrate; 43.1g protein; 3.5g fibre
serving idea serve with a baby spinach, grape tomato and celery salad.

spinach and ricotta cannelloni

PREP + COOK TIME 1 HOUR • SERVES 6

The cannelloni can be prepared completely up to a day ahead, ready to go into the oven. Keep it covered in the refrigerator overnight.

1kg spinach, trimmed, chopped coarsely
500g ricotta cheese
2 eggs
1½ cups (120g) coarsely grated parmesan cheese
¼ cup finely chopped fresh mint
3 teaspoons finely chopped fresh thyme
2 teaspoons finely chopped fresh rosemary
250g cannelloni tubes

creamy tomato sauce
1 tablespoon olive oil
1 medium brown onion (150g), chopped finely
4 cloves garlic, crushed
4 x 400g cans diced tomatoes
½ cup (125ml) cream
1 teaspoon white sugar

1 Make creamy tomato sauce.
2 Meanwhile, preheat oven to 180°C/160°C fan-forced.
3 Cook washed, drained (not dried) spinach in heated large saucepan, stirring, until wilted. Drain; when cool enough to handle, squeeze out excess moisture.
4 Combine spinach in large bowl with ricotta, eggs, ½ cup of the parmesan cheese and the herbs. Using a large piping bag, fill pasta with spinach mixture.
5 Spread a third of the tomato sauce into shallow 25cm x 35cm ovenproof dish; top with pasta, in single layer, then top with remaining sauce. Bake, covered, 20 minutes. Uncover, sprinkle pasta with remaining parmesan; cook further 15 minutes or until pasta is tender and cheese is browned lightly.

creamy tomato sauce Heat oil in large saucepan; cook onion, stirring, until softened. Add garlic; cook, stirring, until fragrant. Add undrained tomatoes; bring to the boil. Reduce heat; simmer, uncovered, stirring occasionally, about 20 minutes or until sauce thickens slightly. Cool 10 minutes; blend or process sauce with cream and sugar until smooth.

nutritional count per serving 31g total fat (17.1g saturated fat); 2412kJ (577 cal); 41.8g carbohydrate; 28.7g protein; 8.3g fibre

spaghetti and meatballs

PREP + COOK TIME 50 MINS • SERVES 4

Anchovies are always a feature in this popular Italo-American pasta dish, however, if you're cooking for someone who doesn't like them, you can omit them. A teaspoon of baby capers can be added to the tomato mixture for an extra-salty sensation.

500g pork and veal mince
½ cup (35g) stale breadcrumbs
1 egg
¼ cup (20g) finely grated
   parmesan cheese
1 tablespoon olive oil
1 medium brown onion (150g),
   chopped coarsely
2 cloves garlic, quartered
1 fresh small red thai chilli

6 anchovy fillets
1 cup (150g) drained
   sun-dried tomatoes
¼ cup (70g) tomato paste
1 cup (250ml) chicken stock
12 pimiento-stuffed olives,
   sliced thinly
375g spaghetti
⅓ cup coarsely chopped fresh
   flat-leaf parsley

1 Combine mince, breadcrumbs, egg and cheese in medium bowl; roll level tablespoons of mixture into balls.
2 Heat oil in medium frying pan; cook meatballs, uncovered, until browned.
3 Blend or process onion, garlic, chilli, anchovy, tomatoes and paste until smooth. Combine tomato mixture with stock in medium saucepan; bring to the boil. Add meatballs and olives; simmer, uncovered, 15 minutes.
4 Meanwhile, cook spaghetti in large saucepan of boiling water until tender; drain.
5 Serve spaghetti topped with meatballs and sauce; sprinkle with parsley.

nutritional count per serving 20.6g total fat (6.3g saturated fat); 2964kJ (709 cal); 78.8g carbohydrate; 47.5g protein; 7.9g fibre

vegetarian lasagne

PREP + COOK TIME 2 HOURS 10 MINS • SERVES 4

This is traditional lasagne redesigned for vegetarians, but the flavours are so rich that meat-eaters will love it too.

3 medium red capsicums (600g)
1 medium eggplant (300g), sliced thinly
1 tablespoon coarse cooking salt
3 medium zucchini (360g), sliced thinly
1 medium kumara (400g), sliced thinly
cooking-oil spray
2 cups (500g) bottled tomato pasta sauce
250g instant lasagne sheets
2½ cups (250g) coarsely grated mozzarella cheese
⅓ cup (25g) coarsely grated parmesan cheese

white sauce
40g butter
2 tablespoons plain flour
1¼ cups (310ml) milk
¼ cup (20g) coarsely grated parmesan cheese

1 Quarter capsicums; discard seeds and membranes. Roast under grill or in very hot oven, skin-side up, until skin blisters and blackens. Cover capsicum pieces in plastic or paper for 5 minutes; peel away skin.

2 Reduce oven to 200°C/180°C fan-forced. Place eggplant in colander, sprinkle all over with salt; stand 20 minutes. Rinse eggplant under cold water; drain on absorbent paper.

3 Meanwhile, make white sauce.

4 Place eggplant, zucchini and kumara, in single layer, on oven trays; spray with oil. Roast about 20 minutes or until browned and tender.

5 Oil deep rectangular 2-litre (8-cup) ovenproof dish. Spread ⅔ cup of the pasta sauce into dish; top with a quarter of the lasagne sheets, ⅓ cup of the pasta sauce, eggplant and a third of the mozzarella. Layer cheese with another quarter of the lasagne sheets, ⅓ cup of the pasta sauce, capsicum, and another third of the mozzarella. Layer mozzarella with another quarter of the lasagne sheets, ⅓ cup of the pasta sauce, zucchini, kumara, remaining mozzarella, remaining lasagne sheets and remaining pasta sauce. Top with white sauce, sprinkle with parmesan.

6 Bake lasagne, uncovered, about 30 minutes or until browned lightly. Stand 10 minutes before serving.

white sauce Heat butter in small saucepan, add flour; cook, stirring, until mixture thickens and bubbles. Gradually stir in milk; stir until mixture boils and thickens. Remove from heat; stir in cheese.

nutritional count per serving 32.5g total fat (19g saturated fat); 3189kJ (763 cal); 82g carbohydrate; 37.5g protein; 9.9g fibre

penne puttanesca

PREP + COOK TIME 30 MINS • SERVES 4

According to one folk legend, this dish is prepared in the style of prostitutes in Rome; deliberately robust in scent and hearty in flavour so as to attract clients. Another spin on the same legend says that this sauce was a favourite among the ladies because, as it was so quick to prepare, they could cook it from ingredients kept in their cupboards without wasting time between clients.

500g penne pasta
⅓ cup (80ml) extra virgin olive oil
3 cloves garlic, crushed
1 teaspoon chilli flakes
5 medium tomatoes (950g), chopped coarsely
200g seeded kalamata olives
8 drained anchovy fillets, chopped coarsely
⅓ cup (65g) drained capers, rinsed
⅓ cup coarsely chopped fresh flat-leaf parsley
2 tablespoons finely shredded fresh basil

1 Cook pasta in large saucepan of boiling water, uncovered, until just tender; drain.
2 Meanwhile, heat oil in large frying pan; cook garlic, stirring, until fragrant. Add chilli and tomato; cook, stirring, 5 minutes. Add remaining ingredients; cook, stirring occasionally, about 5 minutes or until sauce thickens slightly.
3 Add pasta to sauce; toss gently to coat.

nutritional count per serving 21.1g total fat (3.1g saturated fat); 2884kJ (690 cal); 10.2g carbohydrate; 18.6g protein; 7.9g fibre

fettuccine boscaiola

PREP + COOK TIME 30 MINS • SERVES 4

500g fresh fettuccine pasta
2 teaspoons olive oil
200g button mushrooms, sliced thickly
2 cloves garlic, crushed
200g shaved ham, chopped coarsely
¼ cup (60ml) dry white wine
1¼ cups (310ml) cream
2 tablespoons coarsely chopped fresh chives

1 Cook pasta in large saucepan of boiling water until tender; drain.
2 Meanwhile, heat oil in large saucepan; cook mushrooms, garlic and ham, stirring, until ingredients are browned lightly. Add wine; boil, uncovered, until wine reduces by half.
3 Add cream to mushroom mixture; reduce heat. Simmer, uncovered, until sauce thickens slightly.
4 Add chives and pasta to sauce; toss to combine.

nutritional count per serving 38.1g total fat (22.7g saturated fat); 3436kJ (822 cal); 87.8g carbohydrate; 26.8g protein; 5.7g fibre

chilli prawn linguine

PREP + COOK TIME 30 MINS • SERVES 4

500g linguine pasta
⅓ cup (80ml) olive oil
400g uncooked medium king prawns, peeled
3 fresh small red thai chillies, chopped finely
2 cloves garlic, crushed
½ cup finely chopped fresh flat-leaf parsley
2 teaspoons finely grated lemon rind

1 Cook pasta in large saucepan of boiling water until tender; drain.
2 Meanwhile, heat oil in large frying pan; cook prawns, chilli and garlic, stirring, until prawns are just cooked through. Remove from heat; stir in parsley and rind.
3 Combine pasta with prawn mixture in large bowl; toss gently.

nutritional count per serving 20.8g total fat (3g saturated fat); 2851kJ (682 cal); 85.5g carbohydrate; 34.7g protein; 4.8g fibre

chicken and mushroom pasta bake

PREP + COOK TIME 50 MINS • SERVES 4

Rigatoni, a ridged, tube-shaped pasta, is ideal for 'pasta al forno' (baked dishes) because it is wide and the hearty fillings cling to the indentations around the edges.

375g rigatoni pasta
60g butter
600g chicken breast fillets, cut into 1cm pieces
100g button mushrooms, sliced thinly
2 tablespoons plain flour
2 cups (500ml) milk
½ cup (40g) coarsely grated romano cheese
1¼ cups (150g) coarsely grated cheddar cheese
170g asparagus, trimmed, chopped coarsely
¼ cup chopped fresh flat-leaf parsley

1 Preheat oven to 200°C/180°C fan-forced.
2 Cook pasta in large saucepan of boiling water, uncovered, until just tender; drain.
3 Meanwhile, heat 20g of the butter in large frying pan; cook chicken, in batches, until browned and cooked through. Remove from pan.
4 Heat remaining butter in same pan; cook mushrooms, stirring, until tender. Add flour; cook, stirring, 1 minute. Gradually stir in milk. Stir over medium heat until mixture boils and thickens. Stir in chicken, ¼ cup of the romano cheese, ¾ cup of the cheddar cheese and the asparagus.
5 Combine chicken mixture and drained pasta in 2.5 litre (10-cup) ovenproof dish; sprinkle with remaining cheeses. Bake about 15 minutes or until top browns lightly. Serve pasta bake sprinkled with parsley.

nutritional count per serving 37.3g total fat (22.3g saturated fat); 3775kJ (903 cal); 75.2g carbohydrate; 64g protein; 4.8g fibre

beef lasagne

PREP + COOK TIME 2 HOURS 50 MINS • SERVES 6

Instant lasagne sheets are thinner than the dried uncooked version and do not require any pre-boiling. Just layer them in an ovenproof dish (large in area and shallow, rather than high-sided, is best) with a favourite meat, chicken or vegetable sauce, various cheeses and a béchamel sauce or similar. Make sure the filling is saucy enough to provide the pasta with enough moisture to rehydrate it to tooth-tenderness.

1 tablespoon olive oil
1 medium brown onion (150g), chopped finely
1 medium carrot (120g), chopped finely
1 stalk celery (150g), trimmed, chopped finely
2 cloves garlic, crushed
500g beef mince
⅓ cup (80ml) dry red wine
850g can crushed tomatoes
2 tablespoons tomato paste
½ cup (125ml) water
4 slices prosciutto (60g), chopped finely
1 tablespoon coarsely chopped fresh oregano
2 tablespoons coarsely chopped fresh flat-leaf parsley
18 instant lasagne sheets
½ cup (40g) grated parmesan cheese

cheese sauce
60g butter
⅓ cup (50g) plain flour
1 litre (4 cups) milk
¾ cup (60g) grated parmesan cheese
pinch ground nutmeg

1 Heat oil in large frying pan; cook onion, carrot, celery and garlic, stirring, until onion is soft. Add beef; cook, stirring, until browned. Add wine; bring to the boil. Stir in undrained tomatoes, paste and the water; reduce heat. Simmer, uncovered, about 1 hour or until mixture is thick. Stir in prosciutto and herbs; cool slightly.
2 Meanwhile, make cheese sauce.
3 Preheat oven to 180°C/160°C fan-forced. Oil shallow 3-litre (12-cup) ovenproof dish.
4 Place six lasagne sheets into dish. Spread with half the meat sauce; drizzle with 1 cup of the cheese sauce. Repeat layering; top with remaining pasta sheets then spread with remaining cheese sauce and sprinkle with cheese.
5 Bake lasagne about 45 minutes or until pasta is tender and cheese is browned lightly.

cheese sauce Melt butter in heated large saucepan, add flour; cook, stirring, until mixture bubbles and thickens. Remove from heat; gradually stir in milk. Cook, stirring, until mixture boils and thickens. Remove from heat; stir in cheese and nutmeg. Cool 10 minutes.

nutritional count per serving 32.5g total fat (17.2g saturated fat); 2993kJ (716 cal); 62g carbohydrate; 38.7g protein; 5.6g fibre

pastitsio

PREP + COOK TIME 2 HOURS 15 MINS (+ STANDING) • SERVES 6

Pastitsio is to the Greek kitchen as lasagne is to an Italian cucina – a rich and comforting layered meat, tomato and pasta bake traditionally smothered with a creamy béchamel sauce. Some recipes do not call for cinnamon in the meat sauce, but it's a classic signature flavour that has made it one of the most well-known of all Greek baked dishes. If you can find bucatini, a long, hollow pasta slightly thicker than spaghetti, use it instead of a shorter macaroni.

250g macaroni pasta
2 eggs, beaten lightly
¾ cup (60g) coarsely grated parmesan cheese
2 tablespoons stale breadcrumbs

meat sauce
1 tablespoon olive oil
2 medium brown onions (300g), chopped finely
750g beef mince
400g can chopped tomatoes
⅓ cup (95g) tomato paste
½ cup (125ml) beef stock
¼ cup (60ml) dry white wine
½ teaspoon ground cinnamon
1 egg, beaten lightly

cheese topping
90g butter
½ cup (75g) plain flour
3½ cups (875ml) milk
1 cup (80g) coarsely grated parmesan cheese
2 egg yolks

1 Preheat oven to 180°C/160°C fan-forced. Oil shallow 2.5-litre (10-cup) ovenproof dish.
2 Make meat sauce. Make cheese topping.
3 Cook pasta in large saucepan of boiling water until tender; drain.
4 Combine warm pasta, egg and cheese in large bowl. Press pasta over base of dish; top with meat sauce, pour over cheese topping, smooth surface then sprinkle with breadcrumbs.
5 Bake pastitsio about 1 hour or until browned lightly. Stand 10 minutes before serving.

meat sauce Heat oil in large saucepan; cook onion, stirring, until soft. Add beef; cook, stirring, until well browned. Stir in undrained tomatoes, paste, stock, wine and cinnamon; simmer, uncovered, until thick. Cool 10 minutes; stir in egg.

cheese topping Melt butter in medium saucepan, add flour; cook, stirring, until mixture thickens and bubbles. Gradually stir in milk; cook, stirring, until sauce boils and thickens. Remove from heat; stir in cheese. Cool 5 minutes; stir in egg yolks.

nutritional count per serving 41.6g total fat (21.8g saturated fat); 3436kJ (822 cal); 54.4g carbohydrate; 54g protein; 3.8g fibre

vegetable gnocchi with cheese sauce

PREP + COOK TIME
2 HOURS 40 MINS
(+ REFRIGERATION)
SERVES 6

1.2kg russet burbank potatoes
1 medium kumara (400g)
300g spinach, trimmed, chopped
3 eggs
½ cup (40g) coarsely grated parmesan cheese
2 cups (300g) plain flour, approximately
2 tablespoons olive oil
100g blue cheese, crumbled
⅓ cup (25g) finely grated pecorino cheese

cheese sauce
30g butter
2 tablespoons plain flour
2½ cups (625ml) milk
⅔ cup (160ml) cream
½ cup (50g) finely grated gruyère cheese
⅔ cup (50g) finely grated pecorino cheese

On a lightly floured surface, roll the kneaded parmesan mixture, and kumara and spinach mixture into three sausage shapes. Cut each sausage into 2cm balls.

Roll the front of a fork over each ball, pressing lightly, to create grooves. The grooves on gnocchi are not only for presentation – they help pick up the sauce.

1 Boil or steam unpeeled potatoes until tender; drain. When cool enough to handle, peel potatoes; chop coarsely.
2 Meanwhile, microwave unpeeled kumara on HIGH (100%) about 8 minutes or until tender; drain. Peel when cool enough to handle. Boil, steam or microwave spinach until wilted; drain.
3 Using wooden spoon, push potato through fine sieve or mouli into large bowl. Divide potato mash among three medium bowls; stir one egg into each bowl until mixture is combined. Using wooden spoon, stir parmesan cheese into one of the bowls. Push kumara through fine sieve into the second bowl; stir to combine. Stir spinach into the third bowl. Stir about ⅓ cup of flour into parmesan-flavoured mixture to make a firm dough. Stir about ½ cup of flour into both the kumara and spinach mixtures to make a firm dough.
4 Roll each portion of dough on floured surface into 2cm-thick sausage shape. Cut each sausage shape into 2cm pieces; roll pieces into balls. Roll each ball along the inside tines of a fork, pressing lightly on top of ball with index finger to form classic gnocchi shape – grooves on one side and a dimple on the other. Place gnocchi, in single layer, on floured trays; cover, refrigerate 1 hour.
5 Cook gnocchi, in batches, in large saucepan of boiling water about 2 minutes or until gnocchi float to surface. Remove from pan with slotted spoon; drain. Gently toss gnocchi in large bowl with oil.
6 Make cheese sauce. Pour sauce over gnocchi; toss gently to coat.
7 Divide gnocchi among six oiled 1½-cup (375ml) ovenproof dishes; sprinkle with blue cheese then pecorino cheese. Place under hot grill about 3 minutes or until cheese browns lightly.

cheese sauce Melt butter in medium saucepan, add flour; cook, stirring, until mixture thickens and bubbles. Gradually add milk and cream; stir until mixture boils and thickens. Remove from heat; stir in cheeses.

nutritional count per serving 40.4g total fat (22.4g saturated fat); 3285kJ (786 cal); 74.6g carbohydrate; 27.5g protein; 7.1g fibre

cheese and spinach tortellini with gorgonzola sauce

PREP + COOK TIME 20 MINS
SERVES 4

30g butter
2 tablespoons plain flour
1 cup (250ml) milk
¾ cup (180ml) cream
100g gorgonzola cheese, chopped coarsely
750g packaged cheese and spinach tortellini
¼ cup loosely packed fresh flat-leaf parsley

This sauce is also delicious served with pumpkin gnocchi or steaks. Or to make a quick starter, place a canned pear half in a ramekin, top with the sauce and some breadcrumbs and grill until golden.

1 Melt butter in medium saucepan, add flour; cook, stirring, about 2 minutes or until mixture bubbles and thickens. Gradually stir in milk and cream; bring to the boil. Reduce heat; simmer, uncovered, until sauce boils and thickens. Remove from heat; stir in cheese.
2 Meanwhile, cook pasta in large saucepan of boiling water until pasta floats to the top; drain.
3 Combine pasta with sauce; sprinkle with parsley.
nutritional count per serving 58.5g total fat (37.4g saturated fat); 3741kJ (895 cal); 56.2g carbohydrate; 34g protein; 5.8g fibre

angel hair with rocket and chilli

PREP + COOK TIME 20 MINS • SERVES 4

Also known as capelli d'angelo, angel hair is sold as small, circular nests of very fine, delicate pasta strands; its cooking time is minimal because it's extremely thin.

2 tablespoons olive oil
1 teaspoon dried chilli flakes
2 cloves garlic, crushed
½ teaspoon cracked black pepper
¼ cup (60ml) lemon juice
375g angel hair pasta
80g rocket leaves
2 medium tomatoes (300g), seeded, chopped coarsely
⅔ cup firmly packed fresh basil leaves

1 Heat oil in large frying pan; cook chilli and garlic, stirring, until fragrant. Add pepper and juice; stir until hot.
2 Meanwhile, cook pasta in large saucepan of boiling water until tender; drain.
3 Combine chilli mixture and pasta in large bowl with rocket, tomato and basil.
nutritional count per serving 10.4g total fat (1.5g saturated fat); 1756kJ (420 cal); 66.4g carbohydrate; 12.1g protein; 4.8g fibre

spaghetti alla vongole

PREP + COOK TIME 1 HOUR 10 MINS (+ STANDING) • SERVES 6

This delicate and decorative pasta dish is a specialty of Venice.

1.5kg clams
1 tablespoon coarse cooking salt
¼ cup (60ml) olive oil
1 medium brown onion (150g), chopped finely
2 cloves garlic, crushed
2 drained anchovy fillets, chopped finely
1 fresh red thai chilli, chopped finely
2 teaspoons chopped fresh thyme
20 medium egg tomatoes (1.5kg), peeled, seeded, chopped finely
2 tablespoons chopped fresh flat-leaf parsley
500g spaghetti

1 Rinse clams under cold water and place in large bowl. Sprinkle with salt, cover with cold water and soak for 2 hours (this purges them of any grit). Discard water, then rinse clams thoroughly; drain.
2 Heat 2 tablespoons of the oil in large saucepan, add clams; cover with tight-fitting lid. Cook over high heat about 8 minutes or until all clams have opened.
3 Strain clam cooking liquid through muslin or clean tea-towel. Return liquid to same cleaned pan; cook, uncovered, until liquid is reduced to 1 cup (250ml). Reserve clam stock.
4 Heat remaining oil in another saucepan; cook onion, garlic, anchovy, chilli and thyme, stirring, until onion is soft. Add tomato and reserved clam stock; cook, uncovered, about 10 minutes or until sauce is thickened. Add clams, stir until heated through. Stir in parsley.
5 Meanwhile, cook pasta in large saucepan of boiling water, uncovered, until just tender; drain.
6 Toss clam sauce through spaghetti.

nutritional count per serving 10.5g total fat (1.5g saturated fat); 1789kJ (428 cal); 60.8g carbohydrate; 19.8g protein; 4.5g fibre

The last time I cleaned clams with cold water and salt, it didn't work so well and my guests were left to eat a slightly gritty pasta dish. What did I do wrong and can you recommend another cleaning method?

The cold water method should work as clams filter water as they breathe, pushing salt and sand out of their shells. You need to leave the clams in the water for at least 20 minutes, then pull them up and out of the bowl – do not pour them into a strainer because you will be pouring the expelled sand at the bottom of the bowl back over the clams. If you want to try another method however, add a handful of polenta to the bowl of water. The clams feed on the polenta and this causes them to burp. As they burp, they emit any debris inside the shell. Always make sure the water is cold – warm water will cause the shells to open and spoil the meat.

RICE

Rice

It's hard to think of a more versatile ingredient than rice: used by cultures around the globe, it adpats itself to both savoury and sweet dishes, appearing in the most exotic of Eastern and Asian dishes through to an old-fashioned rice pudding.

Look at our supermarket shelves and the story of our love affair with rice is evident in the different varieties now available. Many of the specialist rices – arborio, basmati, jasmine, sushi rice – were once only available as imports, but are now grown in Australia.

When it is first harvested, rice has a rough outside layer, or hull: under the hull is a bran layer and under the bran is the grain of rice. Most of the rice eaten around the world is white (polished) rice, which has been hulled and had its bran layer removed. It is tender and easily digested. Rice that has been hulled but still has the bran layer intact is brown rice. It has a nutty taste and a chewy texture and takes longer to cook than white. Brown rice is more filling and more nutritious because the bran layer is rich in B vitamins and dietary fibre.

HOW TO COOK RICE

Ideally, you want to cook rice so that the grains are tender but separate rather than stuck together or lumpy. There are two methods for cooking rice:

BOILED RICE This method makes it very easy to keep the grains separate, but you do throw away some of the rice flavour with the cooking water. Bring a large saucepan of lightly salted water to a rolling boil. Slowly sprinkle in the rice, stir once then cook, uncovered, keeping the water at a brisk boil. Start testing the rice after 10 minutes. The rice should be tender but firm in the centre, not mushy. Drain and run hot water through to separate the grains.

ABSORPTION METHODS This method retains all the flavour of the rice and is therefore often preferred. There are two ways to cook rice by absorption. Many cooks recommend rinsing the rice first in a sieve, rubbing it with your fingers, to help dislodge surface starch.

i) In a large saucepan, place double the amount of lightly salted water, by volume, as the amount of rice. Cover and bring to the boil over high heat. Uncover and slowly sprinkle in the rice, keeping the heat high so the water does not go off the boil. Stir once, then cover again with a tight-fitting lid; turn the heat to very low. Cook for 10 minutes without removing the lid. Remove from the heat, stand with the lid on for at least another 10 minutes, then fluff up with a fork.

ii) Place the rice in a large saucepan, add a pinch of salt and cold water to cover. Shake the pan from side to side to level the surface. Place the tip of your index finger on the surface of the rice and add more cold water until it comes up to your first finger joint. This applies regardless of the quantity you are cooking. Bring to the boil and cook until the water evaporates, leaving steam holes in the rice; cover with a tight-fitting lid and turn the heat to very low. Cook for about 10 minutes or until the rice is tender but firm in the centre. Don't lift the lid until the last minute or two of cooking, then quickly remove a few grains of rice to test and replace the lid immediately. When cooked, remove the pan from the heat, stand with the lid on for 10 minutes, then fluff up with a fork.

TYPES OF RICE

LONG-GRAIN RICE When cooked, this rice looks light and fluffy and the grains remain separate. Available in both white and brown rice varieties, long grain rice is suitable for most savoury dishes and is perfect for pilafs, salads and stuffings and for Indian, Middle Eastern, Italian and Spanish dishes. Long-grain rices include:

• BASMATI A fragrant, long-grain white rice with a nutty aroma, favoured for Indian dishes. When cooked, the grains are firm, separate and dry.

• JASMINE A fragrant, long-grain white rice with a delicate floral aroma that is used throughout South-East Asia. It is softer than basmati and when cooked, its grains are slightly sticky.

• JASMATI A hybrid, aromatic rice that is a cross between basmati and jasmine rice. It is soft textured with a mild flavour.

MEDIUM-GRAIN RICE The grains of this rice are rounded and a little longer than they are fat. When cooked, it is slightly clingy, making it ideal for rice croquettes and moulds and also for eating with chopsticks. It's favoured in Chinese cooking. Varieties of medium-grain rice include:

• ARBORIO, CARNAROLI AND VIALONE NANO These are rices used specifically for risotto. They have a soft texture and their special quality is that they can absorb liquid and stand up to long cooking and stirring without becoming soft and mushy. At the same time, they release just enough starch to give creaminess. Arborio is the best known and least expensive of these risotto rices. Carnaroli is the aristocrat of risotto rices because of its fine flavour and texture. Vialone nano has a stubbier grain. Risotto rices are also good for paella.

• CALROSE is the brand-name of an Australian medium-grain white rice that has been developed as an all-purpose rice. It gives different results according to how it is cooked – separate and fluffy after short cooking and rinsing, moist and easily compacted after longer cooking without rinsing. Calrose brown rice is also available.

SHORT-GRAIN RICE The round, fat grains of this rice cook to a soft, moist texture and cling together, making it perfect for puddings and a good food for babies before they get teeth. Short-grain rice is favoured in Spain for paella and in Japan for sushi. The moist, sticky grains are ideal for eating with chopsticks. In south-east Asia, sticky short-grain rice (both white and black) is used to make desserts such as black sticky rice pudding. Short-grain rice includes:

• GLUTINOUS Also known as sticky rice, its short, fat grains become sticky and cling together when cooked, allowing it to be easily formed into small balls. It is used mainly for desserts and rice cakes.

• KOSHIHIKARI AND NISHIKI Also called sushi rices, these rices are moist and tender when cooked, but still firm and clingy enough to be picked up with chopsticks.

• BLACK RICE A variety of glutinous rice, black-brown when raw and deep purple when cooked.

• CALASPARRA A short-grain Spanish rice suited to making paella as it can absorb 2½ to 3 times its own volume of liquid.

NOTE Some medium/short-grain varieties are interchangeable. If short-grain is called for, you can use medium. If medium if called for, use long for dishes like croquettes, and short for puddings.

STORING RICE

WHITE RICE WILL KEEP IN AN AIRTIGHT CONTAINER IN A COOL, DRY PLACE FOR UP TO 2 YEARS. THE OIL IN THE BRAN COATING OF BROWN RICE SHORTENS ITS STORAGE LIFE: IT WILL KEEP IN THE SAME CONDITIONS AS WHITE RICE FOR 6 MONTHS. ONCE COOKED, KEEP RICE IN A COVERED CONTAINER IN THE REFRIGERATOR AND USE WITHIN A WEEK. LEFTOVER LONG-GRAIN RICE IS PERFECT FOR FRIED RICE.

SPECIAL FEATURE

Know your rice

The whole world loves rice. It all started with Asian fried rice. Then the Italians showed us risotto, the Spaniards gave us paella, sushi made its way from Japan and the Near East introduced us to pulao. But despite our love for the grain, not all rice is created equal. Each has its virtues and uses.

LONG-GRAIN
Long and slender, the grains stay dry, separate and fluffy after cooking, so it is the right choice for most savoury uses. Perfect as a plain accompaniment or a bed for sauces. Great in rice salads, Indian and Middle Eastern pulaos, and Mediterranean soups.

BASMATI
A fragrant long-grain rice, originally from Pakistan. It should be cooked by the absorption method to retain its warm aroma and taste. The grain is prized for its low-GI rating, which means it helps control blood glucose levels and keeps you satisfied for longer.

JASMINE
A long-grain Thai rice that is also aromatic but is softer and a little more clingy than basmati once cooked. Jasmine is the perfect accompaniment for South-East Asian food. It should be cooked by the absorption method to preserve its aroma and taste.

BROWN
Brown rice retains the high-fibre, nutritious bran coating that's removed from white rice when hulled. It takes longer to cook than white rice and has a chewier texture. Once cooked, the long grains stay separate, while the short grains are soft and stickier.

WILD RICE
Not a member of the rice family at all but the seed of an aquatic grass native to the cold regions of North America. Wild rice has a strong nutty taste and can be expensive, so it is best used combined with brown and white rices in pulaos, stuffings and salads.

WILD RICE BLEND
A packaged blend of white long-grain rice and wild rice. With its dark brown, almost black grains, crunchy, resilient texture and smoky flavour, wild rice contrasts nicely with mild-tasting white rice. Perfect with lentils, fish, in pulaos or added to soups.

Q&A

My family eats lots of rice but we can't agree on variety. I prefer brown long-grain because it is so nutritious, has great flavour and is non-sticky. The drawback is the longer cooking time. My husband and children, however, don't like its strong taste and prefer softer, milder white rices. Can you suggest a compromise?

A good compromise between nutrient-rich brown rice and tender, fast-cooking white rice is parboiled (converted) rice. Although it might sound like a modern product, parboiling was discovered in ancient India, where the process was used to preserve rice and retain the nutrients that are lost during milling. Parboiled rice stores better than brown rice because it has no bran or germ oil, so it won't go rancid. It cooks to a firm, separate grain and doesn't become gluggy if overcooked. The rice can be used in most dishes (except desserts) and reheats well.

ROSE
edium grain developed in California in the 1950s then by Australian growers. The variety is no er grown, but many brands use "calrose" as a eric name for their medium-grain rice. It's easier ork with than sushi rice as it's not as clingy.

ARBORIO
The best-known of the Italian risotto rices, which partly dissolve when cooked to achieve a clinging, creamy texture but, at the same time, remain firm to the bite (al dente), so the rice won't become mushy. Other risotto rices include carnaroli and vialone nano.

GLUTINOUS
Also known as sticky rice, this variety is a stickier version of short-grain rice. Its plump, distinctively flavoured grains cling together when cooked, so they can be easily formed into small balls for dipping into savoury dishes and soaking up the sauce.

ACK
so known as purple rice, black rice is unmilled, ving the dark husk in place which colours the ain when cooked. It has a nutty taste and crunchy ture. There are hundreds of varieties across Asia, m Chinese black rice to Thai black sticky rice.

NISHIKI
A Japanese variety that's often sold as medium-grain rice, but is actually a slightly longer short-grain rice. Like Koshihikari (right), Nishiki cooks to the tender and lightly clinging texture that is right for sushi. This light, fresh-tasting grain is also grown in California.

KOSHIHIKARI
A premium Japanese short-grain rice, distinguished by its aroma, sweet flavour and sticky texture. Its small, round grains cook to a softness with just enough cling to be eaten with chopsticks. Perfect for sushi and rice desserts. Also sold as "sushi rice".

mushroom risotto

PREP + COOK TIME 40 MINS • SERVES 4

Unlike some other rice dishes, risotto does not require you to rinse the rice before you begin to cook. In fact, the starch is essential to the dish. The initial toasting of the rice loosens the starch in each grain. As liquid is added to the rice and stirred in, gently and almost constantly, more starch is released. This process will eventually leave you with a soft, creamy and evenly cooked risotto.

10g dried chanterelle mushrooms
10g dried porcini mushrooms
1 litre (4 cups) chicken or vegetable stock
2 cups (500ml) water
50g butter
100g chestnut mushrooms, trimmed
100g button mushrooms, sliced thickly
2 flat mushrooms (160g), halved, sliced thickly
4 shallots (100g), chopped finely
2 cloves garlic, crushed
2 cups (400g) arborio rice
½ cup (125ml) dry white wine
½ cup (40g) finely grated parmesan cheese
2 tablespoons finely chopped fresh chives

1 Combine chanterelle and porcini mushrooms, stock and the water in medium saucepan; bring to the boil. Reduce heat; simmer, covered.
2 Meanwhile, melt 30g of the butter in large saucepan; add remaining mushrooms to pan. Cook, stirring, until mushrooms are tender and liquid evaporates; remove from pan.
3 Melt remaining butter in same pan; cook shallots and garlic, stirring, until shallots soften. Add rice; stir to coat rice in butter mixture. Return mushrooms cooked in butter to pan with wine; bring to the boil. Reduce heat; simmer, uncovered, until liquid has almost evaporated. Add 1 cup simmering stock mixture; cook, stirring, over low heat, until stock is absorbed. Continue adding stock mixture, in 1 cup batches, stirring, until absorbed between additions. Total cooking time should be about 25 minutes or until rice is tender. Stir in cheese and chives.

nutritional count per serving 15.4g total fat (9.4g saturated fat); 2391kJ (572 cal); 82.2g carbohydrate; 17.9g protein; 4.4g fibre

Using a sharp knife, cut both the flat and button mushrooms into thick slices, and trim the edges of the chestnut mushrooms.

Once the vegetables are cooked and softened, stir in the rice. Cook, stirring constantly, to coat the rice with butter.

Add 1 cup of simmering stock mixture and cook, stirring constantly, over a low heat, until stock is absorbed. Continue adding stock, 1 cup at a time, stirring constantly and allowing each addition to be absorbed before adding the next cup.

prawn and asparagus risotto

PREP + COOK TIME 1 HOUR 10 MINS • SERVES 4

500g uncooked medium king prawns
3 cups (750ml) chicken stock
3 cups (750ml) water
10g butter
1 tablespoon olive oil
1 small brown onion (80g), chopped finely
2 cups (400g) arborio rice
½ cup (125ml) dry sherry
10g butter, extra
2 teaspoons olive oil, extra
2 cloves garlic, crushed
500g asparagus, chopped coarsely
⅓ cup (25g) coarsely grated parmesan cheese
⅓ cup coarsely chopped fresh basil

1 Shell and devein prawns; chop prawn meat coarsely.
2 Place stock and the water in large saucepan; bring to the boil. Reduce heat; simmer, covered.
3 Meanwhile, heat butter and oil in large saucepan; cook onion, stirring, until soft. Add rice; stir rice to coat in onion mixture. Add sherry; cook, stirring, until liquid is almost evaporated. Stir in 1 cup simmering stock mixture; cook, stirring, over low heat until liquid is absorbed. Continue adding stock mixture, in 1-cup batches, stirring, until absorbed after each addition. Total cooking time should be about 35 minutes or until rice is tender.
4 Heat extra butter and extra oil in medium frying pan; cook prawn meat and garlic, stirring, until prawn just changes colour.
5 Boil, steam or microwave asparagus until just tender; drain. Add asparagus, prawn mixture and cheese to risotto; cook, stirring, until cheese melts. Stir in basil.

nutritional count per serving 14.7g total fat (5.5g saturated fat); 2516kJ (602 cal); 82.8g carbohydrate; 26.3g protein; 2.6g fibre

baked pumpkin and spinach risotto

PREP + COOK TIME 50 MINS • SERVES 4

500g butternut pumpkin, chopped coarsely
2 tablespoons olive oil
1½ cups (375ml) chicken stock
1.25 litres (5 cups) water
1 large brown onion (200g), chopped coarsely
2 cloves garlic, crushed
2 cups (400g) arborio rice
½ cup (125ml) dry white wine
500g spinach, trimmed, chopped coarsely
½ cup (80g) pine nuts, roasted
½ cup (40g) coarsely grated parmesan cheese
½ cup (125ml) cream

1 Preheat oven to 220°C/200°C fan-forced.

2 Combine pumpkin with half of the oil in baking dish. Bake, uncovered, about 20 minutes or until tender.

3 Meanwhile, combine stock and the water in large saucepan; bring to the boil. Reduce heat; simmer.

4 Heat remaining oil in large saucepan; cook onion and garlic, stirring, until onion is soft. Add rice; stir to coat in mixture. Add wine; stir until almost evaporated. Stir in 1 cup simmering stock mixture; cook, stirring, over low heat until liquid is absorbed. Continue adding stock mixture, in 1-cup batches, stirring, until liquid is absorbed after each addition. Total cooking time should be about 30 minutes or until rice is just tender.

5 Add spinach, pine nuts, cheese and cream; cook, stirring, until spinach wilts. Gently stir in baked pumpkin.

nutritional count per serving 41.6g total fat (13.8g saturated fat); 3490kJ (835 cal); 91.5g carbohydrate; 19.3g protein; 5.7g fibre

jambalaya

PREP + COOK TIME 1 HOUR 30 MINS • SERVES 4

This dish is a real one-pot-wonder. Very similar to the Spanish paella, jambalaya is the US-version and, like paella, often contains seafood.

Jalapeño chillies are fairly hot green chillies, sold finely chopped or whole, bottled in vinegar, as well as fresh from specialty greengrocers; we used the chopped, medium-hot, sweetish bottled version here.

1 tablespoon olive oil
4 smoked chorizo sausages (680g)
400g chicken breast fillets
1 medium red onion (170g), chopped finely
1 medium red capsicum (200g), chopped finely
2 cloves garlic, crushed
2 tablespoons finely chopped bottled jalapeño chillies

1 teaspoon dried oregano
¼ teaspoon cayenne pepper
1 bay leaf
2 tablespoons tomato paste
1½ cups (300g) white long-grain rice
400g can crushed tomatoes
2 cups (500ml) chicken stock

1 Heat oil in large saucepan; cook sausages, turning occasionally, until browned. Remove from pan; slice thickly. Add chicken to pan; cook, turning occasionally, until browned. Remove from pan; slice thickly.

2 Cook onion, capsicum and garlic in same pan, stirring, until capsicum softens. Add chilli; cook, stirring, 1 minute. Add spices, bay leaf and paste; cook, stirring, 2 minutes. Add rice; stir to coat in mixture.

3 Add undrained tomatoes and stock, bring to a simmer. Return sausage and chicken to pan; cook, covered, about 45 minutes or until rice is tender and liquid is absorbed.

nutritional count per serving 62.3g total fat (21.2g saturated fat); 4648kJ (1112 cal); 73g carbohydrate; 63.3g protein; 4.5g fibre

khitcherie

PREP + COOK TIME 35 MINS (+ STANDING TIME) • SERVES 6

Khitcherie, a classic Indian rice and lentil dish, was anglicised by the Raj to make that English breakfast staple, kedgeree.

1 cup (200g) yellow split peas
2 tablespoons ghee
1 medium brown onion (150g), chopped finely
2 cloves garlic, crushed
2 long green chillies, sliced thinly
3cm piece fresh ginger (15g), grated
½ teaspoon ground turmeric
1 teaspoon cumin seeds
½ teaspoon garam masala
1 teaspoon ground coriander
1 cinnamon stick
4 fresh curry leaves
1½ cups (300g) basmati rice, rinsed, drained
1 cup (150g) raisins
1 litre (4 cups) hot water
1 tablespoon lime juice
½ cup (75g) roasted unsalted cashews

1 Place split peas in small bowl; cover with cold water, stand 1 hour, drain.
2 Heat ghee in large deep frying pan; cook onion, garlic, chilli, ginger, spices and curry leaves, stirring, until onion softens.
3 Add peas, rice, raisins and the hot water to pan; bring to the boil. Reduce heat; simmer, covered, about 15 minutes or until rice is tender.
4 Remove pan from heat, discard cinnamon stick, stir in juice; stand, covered, 5 minutes. Sprinkle khitcherie with nuts before serving.

nutritional count per serving 13.2g total fat (5.1g saturated fat); 2073kJ (496 cal); 76.3g carbohydrate; 14.3g protein; 6.5g fibre

classic pulao

PREP + COOK TIME 30 MINS (+ STANDING) • SERVES 4

Pulau, pilaf, pilav or pellao, all are the same cooked grain (usually rice) dish with different spellings in their respective countries of origin. The secret of a perfect pulao is to rinse the grain thoroughly, to remove excess starch, then soak it briefly. Soaking before cooking softens the grains and results in a fluffier pulao.

1⅓ cups (265g) basmati rice, rinsed, drained
2½ cups (625ml) chicken stock
pinch saffron threads
50g butter
1 medium brown onion (150g), chopped finely
2 cloves garlic, crushed
1 cinnamon stick
6 cardamom pods
1 bay leaf
⅓ cup (55g) sultanas
½ cup (75g) roasted unsalted cashews

1 Place rice in medium bowl, cover with cold water; stand 20 minutes, drain.
2 Heat stock and saffron in small saucepan.
3 Meanwhile, melt butter in large saucepan; cook onion and garlic, stirring, until onion softens. Stir in cinnamon, cardamom and bay leaf; cook, stirring, 2 minutes.
4 Add rice; cook, stirring, 2 minutes. Add stock mixture and sultanas; simmer, covered, about 10 minutes or until rice is tender and liquid is absorbed.
5 Sprinkle pulao with nuts just before serving.

nutritional count per serving 20.6g total fat (8.8g saturated fat); 2128kJ (509 cal); 68.7g carbohydrate; 10.5g protein; 3g fibre

[1] khitcherie
[2] classic pulao

steamed jasmine rice

PREP + COOK TIME 15 MINS (+ STANDING) • SERVES 4

Jasmine rice is a fragrant long-grain white rice with a delicate floral aroma; it is softer than basmati and, when cooked, its grains are slightly sticky. Store leftover cooked rice in a covered container in the refrigerator and use within a week.

2 cups (400g) jasmine rice
1 litre (4 cups) cold water

1 Place rice and the water in large saucepan with a tight-fitting lid; bring to the boil, stirring occasionally.
2 Reduce heat as low as possible; cook rice, covered tightly, about 12 minutes or until all water is absorbed and rice is cooked as desired. Do not remove lid or stir rice during cooking time. Remove from heat; stand, covered, 10 minutes before serving.

nutritional count per serving 0.5g total fat (0.1g staurated fat); 1480kJ (354 cal); 79g carbohydrate; 6.6g protein; 0.8g fibre

coconut rice with coriander

PREP + COOK TIME 35 MINS • SERVES 4

Calrose is the brand-name of an Australian medium-grain white rice that has been developed to serve as an all-purpose rice, as it gives different results according to how it is cooked – separate and fluffy after short cooking and rinsing, moist and easily compacted after longer cooking without rinsing. Calrose brown rice is also available.

½ cup (40g) shredded coconut
2 tablespoons vegetable oil
2 teaspoons chilli oil
1 medium brown onion (150g), chopped coarsely
1 medium red capsicum (200g), chopped coarsely
3 cloves garlic, crushed
3cm piece fresh ginger (15g), grated
1½ cups (300g) calrose rice
1½ cups (375ml) chicken stock
1 cup (250ml) water
140ml can coconut milk
3 green onions, chopped coarsely
¼ cup coarsely chopped fresh coriander
¼ cup (60ml) lemon juice
¼ cup fresh coriander leaves

1 Heat wok; add coconut, stir constantly until browned lightly. Remove from wok.
2 Heat oils in wok; stir-fry brown onion, capsicum, garlic and ginger until onion softens. Add rice; stir-fry 2 minutes. Add stock, the water and coconut milk; simmer, covered, about 20 minutes or until liquid is absorbed and rice is tender.
3 Remove wok from heat; stir in green onion, chopped coriander, juice and half the toasted coconut. Sprinkle with remaining toasted coconut and coriander leaves.

nutritional count per serving 26.2g total fat (13.9g saturated fat); 2282kJ (546 cal); 66.4g carbohydrate; 9g protein; 4.5g fibre

yellow coconut rice

PREP + COOK TIME 20 MINS (+ STANDING) • SERVES 4

1¾ cups (350g) long-grain white rice
1¼ cups (310ml) water
400ml can coconut cream
½ teaspoon salt
1 teaspoon sugar
½ teaspoon ground turmeric
pinch saffron threads

TIP

• This recipe is easy to cook in a microwave oven. Place ingrecients in a large microwave-safe bowl; cover with absorbent paper and cook on HIGH (100%) for 10 minutes. Pause, stir; cook, covered with absorbent paper, a further 2 minutes on HIGH (100%). Pause and mix with a fork; cook uncovered on MEDIUM (50%) for 2 minutes.

1 Soak rice in large bowl of cold water for 30 minutes. Pour rice into strainer; rinse under cold water until water runs clear. Drain.

2 Place rice and remaining ingredients in large heavy-based saucepan; cover, bring to the boil, stirring occasionally. Reduce heat; simmer, covered, about 15 minutes or until rice is tender. Remove from heat; stand, covered, 5 minutes.

nutritional count per serving 21.1g total fat (18.2g staurated fat); 2186kJ (523 cal); 73.9g carbohydrate; 7.7g protein; 2.4g fibre

salmon kedgeree

PREP + COOK TIME 25 MINS • SERVES 6

1½ cups (300g) white long-grain rice
415g can red salmon
80g butter
⅓ cup coarsely chopped fresh flat-leaf parsley
2 teaspoons lemon juice
3 hard-boiled eggs, chopped coarsely

1 Cook rice in large saucepan of boiling water until tender; drain.
2 Drain salmon; discard skin and bones. Flake flesh.
3 Melt butter in large frying pan, add rice, parsley and juice; cook, stirring, until heated through. Add salmon and eggs; cook, stirring gently, until heated through.

nutritional count per serving 20.5g total fat (9.9g saturated fat); 1760kJ (421 cal); 39.7g carbohydrate; 19.1g protein; 0.6g fibre

serving idea lemon wedges.

paella

PREP + COOK TIME 2 HOURS (+ STANDING) • SERVES 6

Calasparra rice is a short-grain rice available from gourmet food stores, and Spanish delicatessens. If you can't find calasparra, any short-grain rice can be substituted.

500g clams
1 tablespoon coarse cooking salt
500g uncooked medium prawns
500g small black mussels
2 tablespoons olive oil
3 cups (750ml) chicken stock
pinch saffron threads
220g chicken thigh fillets, chopped coarsely
1 chorizo sausage (170g), sliced thickly
1 large red onion (300g), chopped finely
1 medium red capsicum (200g), chopped finely
2 cloves garlic, crushed
2 teaspoons smoked paprika
2 medium tomatoes (300g), peeled, seeded, chopped finely
1½ cups (300g) calasparra rice
1 cup (120g) frozen peas
2 tablespoons finely chopped fresh flat-leaf parsley

1 Rinse clams under cold water, place in large bowl with salt; cover with cold water, stand 2 hours. Drain then rinse.
2 Shell and devein prawns, leaving tails intact. Reserve shells. Scrub mussels and remove beards.
3 Heat 2 teaspoons of the oil in large saucepan, add prawn shells; cook, stirring, until red. Add stock; bring to the boil. Reduce heat; simmer, uncovered, 20 minutes. Strain through fine sieve into jug or bowl; add saffron to the liquid. Discard prawn shells.
4 Heat another 2 teaspoons of the oil in 45cm paella pan or large frying pan, add chicken; cook until browned all over, remove from pan. Add chorizo to same pan; cook until browned all over. Remove chorizo from pan; drain on absorbent paper.
5 Heat remaining oil in pan, add onion, capsicum, garlic, paprika and tomato; cook, stirring, until soft. Add rice; stir to coat in mixture.
6 Add chicken, chorizo and stock to pan; stir until combined. Bring mixture to the boil; reduce heat, simmer, uncovered, about 15 minutes or until rice is almost tender.
7 Sprinkle peas over rice; place clams, prawns and mussels evenly over surface of paella. Cover pan with a lid or large sheets of foil; simmer about 5 minutes or until prawns are cooked and mussels and clams have opened (discard any that do not). Sprinkle with parsley; serve immediately.

nutritional count per serving 18.9g total fat (5.2g saturated fat); 2128kJ (509 cal); 49.1g carbohydrate; 33.6g protein; 3.7g fibre

brown rice sushi

PREP + COOK TIME 1 HOUR 20 MINS (+ COOLING) • SERVES 4

Spread rice in a non-metallic dish, slicing it with a spatula to break up lumps and separate grains. At the same time, pour in the sushi vinegar gradually.

Place a nori sheet, shiny-side down, across mat 2cm from the edge closest to you. Dip fingers into bowl of vinegared water, pick up a third of the rice, place across centre of nori sheet.

Pick up mat with thumb and index fingers, holding filling in place with remaining fingers, and roll mat away from you. Press gently, wrapping the nori around the rice and filling.

1 cup (200g) brown short-grain rice
2 cups (500ml) water
1 tablespoon rice vinegar
3 sheets toasted nori (yaki-nori)
1 lebanese cucumber (130g), seeded, cut into matchsticks
20g snow pea sprouts, trimmed
2 tablespoons japanese soy sauce

sushi vinegar
2 tablespoons rice vinegar
2 teaspoons white sugar
¼ teaspoon fine salt

chicken teriyaki
120g chicken breast fillet, sliced thinly
2 tablespoons teriyaki sauce
1 clove garlic, crushed
cooking-oil spray

1 Wash rice several times in large bowl with cold water until water is almost clear. Drain rice in strainer for at least 30 minutes.
2 Meanwhile, make sushi vinegar and chicken teriyaki.
3 Place rice and the water in medium saucepan, cover tightly; bring to the boil. Reduce heat; simmer, covered, about 30 minutes or until water is absorbed. Remove from heat; stand, covered, 10 minutes.
4 Spread rice in a large, non-metallic, flat-bottomed bowl. Using plastic spatula, repeatedly slice through rice at a sharp angle to break up lumps and separate grains, gradually pouring in sushi vinegar at the same time.
5 Continue to slice and turn the rice mixture with one hand; fan the rice with the other hand about 5 minutes or until it is almost cool. Cover rice with damp cloth to stop it drying out while making sushi.
6 Add rice vinegar to medium bowl of cold water. Place one nori sheet, shiny-side down, lengthways across bamboo mat about 2cm from edge of mat closest to you. Dip fingers of one hand into bowl of vinegared water, shake off excess; pick up a third of the rice, place across centre of nori sheet.
7 Wet fingers again, then, working from left to right, gently rake rice evenly over nori, leaving 2cm strip on far side of nori uncovered. Build up rice in front of uncovered strip to form a mound to keep filling in place.
8 Place one-third of the cucumber, sprouts and chicken in a row across centre of rice, making sure the filling extends to both ends of the rice.
9 Starting with edge closest to you, pick up mat using thumb and index fingers of both hands; use remaining fingers to hold filling in place as you roll mat away from you. Roll forward, pressing gently but tightly, wrapping nori around rice and filling. Working quickly, repeat process to make a total of three rolls. Cut each roll into four pieces. Serve with sauce, and wasabi, if you like.

sushi vinegar Combine ingredients in small jug.

chicken teriyaki Combine chicken, sauce and garlic in small bowl. Spray heated small frying pan with cooking-spray oil for 1 second. Cook chicken, stirring, until cooked through. Cool.

nutritional count per serving 2.3g total fat (0.5g saturated fat); 1058kJ (253 cal); 43.1g carbohydrate; 12.8g protein; 3.4g fibre

combination fried rice

PREP + COOK TIME 20 MINS • SERVES 4

You will need to cook 1⅓ cups (260g) white long-grain rice the day before making this recipe. Spread it in a thin layer on a tray and refrigerate it overnight.

Dried chinese sausages, also called lap cheong, are usually made from pork and sold, several strung together, in all Asian food stores.

2 teaspoons peanut oil
3 eggs, beaten lightly
1 tablespoon peanut oil, extra
2 cloves garlic, crushed
2 teaspoons grated fresh ginger
6 green onions, sliced thinly
4 cups cooked white long-grain rice
200g cooked shelled small prawns
200g chinese barbecued pork, sliced thinly
3 dried chinese sausages (100g), sliced thinly
¾ cup (90g) frozen peas, thawed
1 cup (80g) bean sprouts
2½ tablespoons light soy sauce

1 Heat half of the oil in wok, add half of the egg; swirl wok so egg forms an omelette over base. Cook omelette until set; remove, cool. Repeat with remaining oil and remaining egg. Roll omelettes, slice thinly.
2 Heat extra oil in wok; stir-fry garlic, ginger and onion until fragrant. Add rice, prawns, pork, sausage, peas, sprouts, sauce and omelette strips; stir-fry until heated through.

nutritional count per serving 24.8g total fat (7.9g staturated fat); 2571kJ (615 cal); 58.7g carbohydrate; 36.1g protein; 5.8g fibre

nasi goreng

PREP + COOK TIME 40 MINS • SERVES 4

Nasi goreng, which translates simply as "fried rice" in Indonesia and Malaysia, was first created to use up yesterday's leftovers. You will need to cook 2 cups (400g) white long-grain rice the day before making this recipe. Spread it in a thin layer on a tray and refrigerate it overnight.

720g cooked medium king prawns
1 tablespoon peanut oil
175g dried chinese sausages, sliced
1 medium brown onion (150g), sliced thinly
1 medium red capsicum (200g), sliced thinly
2 fresh long red chillies, sliced thinly
2 cloves garlic, crushed
2cm piece fresh ginger (10g), grated
1 teaspoon shrimp paste
4 cups cold cooked white long-grain rice
2 tablespoons kecap manis
1 tablespoon light soy sauce
4 green onions, sliced thinly
1 tablespoon peanut oil, extra
4 eggs

1 Shell and devein prawns.
2 Heat half the oil in wok; stir-fry sausage, in batches, until brown. Remove from wok.
3 Heat remaining oil in wok; stir-fry onion, capsicum, chilli, garlic, ginger and paste, until vegetables soften. Add prawns and rice; stir-fry 2 minutes. Return sausage to wok with sauces and half the green onion; stir-fry until combined.
4 Heat extra oil in large frying pan; fry eggs, one side only, until just set. Divide nasi goreng among serving plates, top each with an egg; sprinkle with remaining green onion.

nutritional count per serving 25.7g total fat (7.4g saturated fat); 2730kJ (653 cal); 48.5g carbohydrate; 54.7g protein; 3.3g fibre

lamb biryani

PREP + COOK TIME 2 HOURS 35 MINS (+ REFRIGERATION) • SERVES 4

An elaborate layered dish inspired by moghul royalty, the regal biryani is still a spectacular Indian curry fit for a king. Perfect for entertaining, our version takes time but is worth every bit of effort.

Masala simply means blended flavours, so it can be whole spices, a paste or a powder, and can include herbs as well as spices and other seasonings. Traditional dishes are usually based on and named after particular masalas. Garam masala, used here, is a North Indian blend of spices containing varying proportions of cloves, cinnamon, cardamom, coriander, fennel and cumin, roasted and ground together. Black pepper and chilli can also be added for a hotter version.

1kg lamb shoulder, cut into 3cm pieces
3cm piece fresh ginger (15g), grated
2 cloves garlic, crushed
2 fresh small red thai chillies, chopped finely
2 teaspoons garam masala
1 tablespoon finely chopped fresh coriander
¼ teaspoon ground turmeric
½ cup (140g) yogurt
2 tablespoons ghee
½ cup (40g) flaked almonds
¼ cup (40g) sultanas
2 medium brown onions (300g), sliced thickly
½ cup (125ml) water
pinch saffron threads
1 tablespoon hot milk
1½ cups (300g) basmati rice
¼ cup firmly packed fresh coriander leaves

1 Combine lamb, ginger, garlic, chilli, garam masala, chopped coriander, turmeric and yogurt in medium bowl. Cover; refrigerate overnight.
2 Heat half the ghee in large saucepan; cook nuts and sultanas, stirring, until nuts brown lightly. Remove from pan.
3 Heat remaining ghee in same pan; cook onion, covered, 5 minutes. Uncover; cook, stirring occasionally, about 5 minutes or until browned lightly. Reserve half of the onion.
4 Add lamb mixture to pan; cook, stirring, until browned. Add the water; bring to the boil. Reduce heat; simmer, covered, 1 hour. Uncover; simmer about 30 minutes or until lamb is tender and sauce is thickened.
5 Meanwhile, combine saffron and milk in small bowl; stand 15 minutes.
6 Cook rice in medium saucepan of boiling water, uncovered, 5 minutes; drain.
7 Preheat oven to 180°C/160°C fan-forced.
8 Spread half the lamb mixture into oiled deep 2-litre (8-cup) ovenproof dish. Layer with half the rice; top with remaining lamb mixture then remaining rice. Drizzle milk mixture over rice; cover tightly with greased foil and lid.
9 Bake biryani about 30 minutes or until rice is tender. Serve biryani topped with reserved onion, nut and sultana mixture and coriander leaves.

nutritional count per serving 38.6g total fat (17.4g saturated fat); 3703kJ (886 cal); 73.8g carbohydrate; 58.7g protein; 3.4g fibre

NOODLES

Noodles

Noodles are a perfect food for modern times: they're quick and easy to prepare and when teamed with vegetables and meat, they make a nutritious, balanced and delicious meal. The Chinese have known this for 2000 years and are as passionate about their noodles as the Italians are about their pasta. Like pasta, noodles are made from a simple dough, but they differ from their European counterparts because they're not solely wheat-based: they are also made from rice, buckwheat and vegetable starches such as mung bean. Noodles are incredibly versatile: they can be eaten hot or cold, boiled, deep-fried, stir-fried, or added to a fragrant soup. They play a prominent role in all Asian cooking but the Chinese and Japanese cuisines are particularly devoted to them and have developed a glorious array of varieties. Check out the growing display of noodles at the supermarket – or visit an Asian grocery store – and you'll discover a whole new world of possibilities.

STORING NOODLES

LIKE PASTA, DRIED NOODLES CAN BE STORED INDEFINITELY IN THEIR UNOPENED PACKAGES OR IN AIRTIGHT CONTAINERS. FRESH NOODLES LIKE HOKKIEN SHOULD BE STORED IN THE REFRIGERATOR, WHERE THEY WILL KEEP FOR WEEKS UNOPENED. ONCE OPENED, WRAP THEM IN PLASTIC WRAP, ENCLOSE IN A PLASTIC BAG AND THEY'LL KEEP UNTIL THE USE-BY DATE.

TYPES OF NOODLES

WHEAT NOODLES

EGG NOODLES Also called yellow noodles or ba mee, these all-purpose noodles are made from wheat flour and eggs. They are available fresh or dried, and range from very fine strands to spaghetti-like lengths. Dried noodles are often sold in nest-like swirls. To prepare, soak in hot water for 10 minutes. Drain, loosening the strands, then cook in a large saucepan of boiling water with a little peanut oil.

FRIED NOODLES Also called crispy noodles, these deep-fried egg noodles are sold often in 100g packs. Add straight to dishes, no cooking required.

HOKKIEN NOODLES These long, fat Chinese noodles are also called stir-fry noodles. They're thick and soft, having been parboiled before packing. The beauty of these noodles is that they don't need cooking, just reheating: cover them in boiling water, gently separating the strands with a fork.

RAMEN This was traditionally the name of a Japanese soup with noodles, but now refers to the instant, wavy-shaped noodles sold with a sachet of soup base. These are very popular in Japan.

SOMEN These fine, delicate, white Japanese noodles are cooked in the same way as pasta, only they need to be rinsed after draining.

UDON NOODLES These thick white wheat noodles are sold fresh or dried. To cook, add them to a large saucepan of boiling water, stir, add cold water, boil, then reduce heat and cook until tender (3 minutes for fresh udon; 8-10 minutes for dried). Drain and run under cold water.

RICE NOODLES

FRESH RICE NOODLES These white, flat Chinese noodles are prized for their chewy, satiny texture and mild flavour, which lets stronger flavours shine. They come in various widths or in sheets to be cut as desired. They do not need preliminary boiling, only a short soak in hot water to soften them and remove excess starch.

RICE PAPER SHEETS Used to create the wrappings for summer rolls (a popular Vietnamese snack) these sheets are round and translucent. To use them, soften them briefly in hot water then wrap them around fresh ingredients such as vegetables, shredded chicken, seafood and herbs and serve with a dipping sauce.

RICE STICKS These are available in various widths – thin for soups and wide for stir-fries. Dried white rice noodles need to be soaked and softened in hot water before they are added to dishes to prevent them from sticking together.

RICE VERMICELLI These fine, dried noodles are often used instead of wheat noodles in the popular stir-fry dish, singapore noodles – a combination of noodles, vegetables, chicken and prawns. They can be prepared in two ways. Vermicelli can be soaked in hot water until softened, boiled briefly, then rinsed with hot water. They can also be cut into shorter lengths and deep-fried until puffed up and crunchy, and then used in chinese chicken salad, or as a garnish or bed for sauces.

BUCKWHEAT NOODLES

SOBA NOODLES These fresh or dried Japanese noodles are made from pure buckwheat or a combination of buckwheat and wheat flour. Some also contain green tea powder or dried mugwort leaves. Soba are not as simple to cook as other noodles (see Q&A, page 193).

MUNG BEAN NOODLES

BEAN THREAD NOODLES Also called cellophane or glass noodles (they become transparent when cooked), these fine, dried noodles are made from ground mung beans. Sold in bundles, they must be soaked in hot water before use. They can also be deep-fried like rice vermicelli.

SPECIAL FEATURE

Know your noodles

Along with the pasta craze came the noodle boom. Asian noodles were soon everywhere. Long, skinny ones, short fat ones, white rice ones and yellow wheat ones. These nutritious ribbons can keep our meals light or can extend a meal. And when done right, they can also give us that delicious hawker experience.

HOKKIEN
These plump, yellow, fresh wheat noodles are the most popular stir-fry noodles as they soak up sauce so easily. They are good in meat-based soups, too. Hokkien also come in a thin version, which can be used interchangeably with fresh singapore noodles.

FRIED
Also known as crispy noodles, these wheat flour and egg noodles have been deep-fried until crisp, then dried and packaged. They are often used in the popular Chinese dish sang choy bow and the Thai stir-fry, mee krob. Or, add them straight to salads.

BEAN THREAD
Also called fen si, sai fun or cellophane noodles because their long, thin strands resemble clear plastic. They are made from mung bean flour, and have a gelatinous, springy texture that is perfect for soaking up dressings. Also used in Thai desserts.

SOBA
These thin, grey-brown buckwheat noodles can be eaten chilled with a Japanese-style dipping sauce and as a salad with various sea vegetables, blanched vegetables and tofu. Also served cold with a topping of seafood, fish or meat, or add them to hot broths.

SHANGHAI
Fresh thick, round wheat noodles, similar to hokkien but paler in colour, and usually sold unoiled. Also available as dried thin white noodles, which need to be boiled for up to 15 minutes, or until soft. Shanghai noodles are often used in stir-fries.

RAMEN
Popular Japanese wheat noodles, sold in dried, fresh, steamed and instant forms. Common toppings are negi (leek), shinachiku (seasoned bamboo shoots), nori (dried seaweed), yakibuta (grilled pork), narutomaki (fish cake) and soft-boiled egg.

Q&A

My diet already includes plenty of wheat and rice, so I'd like to start eating other grains. I know soba noodles are high in protein and fibre, and I've enjoyed them at Japanese restaurants. Are they fiddly to prepare?

Soba or buckwheat noodles can be made with 100 per cent buckwheat (gluten-free) or a blend of buckwheat and wheat. Those that contain wheat are less "floury" in texture and easier to prepare. Whole soba noodles need a little more attention. Bring a large pan of water to the boil – the pan should be large enough to allow water to circulate around the noodles. Add noodles gradually so the water doesn't stop boiling, then cook until just tender. Drain. Rinse noodles under cold water then drain again.

SH RICE
e white, shiny noodles are chewy and slippery in re. When cut very thin, they are known as mei - as in the stir-fry dish with shrimp. The thicker les are named hor fun or chow fun, after the ese stir-fry containing meat, fish or vegetables.

RICE STICK
These have a little less chew than the fresh versions. The thin noodles are used in soups, while the wide flat ones are added to stir-fries, including the famous South-East Asian dish, pad thai. They can also be fried until crisp and puffed, and used as a garnish.

RICE VERMICELLI
Made of rice flour and water, vermicelli are often compressed into tablets and dried, and are slightly longer than bean threads. They are used in spring rolls and cold salads, and when deep-fried until crispy can be used in chicken salad or as a garnish.

MEN
emely thin noodles made from hard wheat – if 'ess, they are labelled somen, and tamago if made egg. These Japanese noodles are traditionally n in cold dishes but can be served in warm h. Avoid overcooking, as they become gluggy.

UDON
Broad, creamy-white Japanese wheat noodles with a mild taste and slippery texture. Particularly popular in southern Japan, udon are known as soup noodles, but are also good in stir-fries and hotpots. Available fresh and dried, in round, square or ribbon shapes.

FRESH EGG
Made from wheat flour and eggs, these golden noodles are available fresh or dried. They range in width from fine vermicelli to wide flat ribbons, and are mainly used in Chinese stir-fries and soups. Can also be crispy-fried and used to garnish stir-fries.

singapore noodles

PREP + COOK TIME 15 MINS • SERVES 4

You need to purchase a large barbecued chicken weighing about 900g to get the amount of shredded meat needed for this recipe.

Fresh singapore noodles are pre-cooked wheat noodles best described as a thinner version of hokkien. Sold packaged in the refrigerated section of the supermarket.

450g fresh singapore noodles
1 teaspoon peanut oil
1 small brown onion (80g), sliced finely
2 rindless bacon rashers (130g), chopped finely
3cm piece fresh ginger (15g), grated
1 tablespoon mild curry powder
3 cups (480g) shredded barbecued chicken
200g chinese barbecued pork, sliced thinly
6 green onions, sliced thinly
½ cup (125ml) sweet sherry
¼ cup (60ml) light soy sauce

1 Place noodles in large heatproof bowl, cover with boiling water; separate with fork, drain.

2 Heat oil in wok; stir-fry brown onion, bacon and ginger, about 2 minutes or until onion softens and bacon is crisp. Add curry powder; stir-fry until fragrant.

3 Add noodles and remaining ingredients; stir-fry until hot.

nutritional count per serving 18.6g total fat (5.6g saturated fat); 2341kJ (560 cal); 37.0g carbohydrate; 50.9g protein; 3.3g fibre

Place the barbecued pork on a clean chopping board. Using a very sharp knife, cut the pork into thin slices.

To prepare singapore noodles, place them in a heatproof bowl, pour over boiling water and separate strands with a fork.

pad thai

PREP + COOK TIME 40 MINS (+ STANDING) • SERVES 4

Place soaked tamarind pulp in a fine strainer over a bowl and push as much pulp as possible through the strainer by pressing down with the back of a spoon.

Place preserved turnip, flat-side down, on a clean chopping board and, using a sharp knife, cut into slices. Chop slices into very small pieces.

Place turnip, garlic, dried shrimp and chilli in a mortar (bowl), grinding each ingredient with a pestle before adding the next one, to make a paste. Or process the ingredients using a hand blender or food processor.

40g tamarind pulp
½ cup (125ml) boiling water
2 tablespoons grated palm sugar
⅓ cup (80ml) sweet chilli sauce
⅓ cup (80ml) fish sauce
375g rice stick noodles
12 uncooked medium prawns (500g)
2 cloves garlic, crushed
2 tablespoons finely chopped preserved turnip
2 tablespoons dried shrimp
1 tablespoon grated fresh ginger
2 fresh small red thai chillies, seeded, chopped coarsely
1 tablespoon peanut oil
250g pork mince
3 eggs, beaten lightly
2 cups (160g) bean sprouts
4 green onions, sliced thinly
⅓ cup coarsely chopped fresh coriander
¼ cup (35g) coarsely chopped roasted unsalted peanuts
1 lime, quartered

1 Soak tamarind pulp in the boiling water 30 minutes. Pour tamarind into fine strainer over small bowl; push as much tamarind pulp through strainer as possible, scraping underside of strainer occasionally. Discard any tamarind solids left in strainer; reserve pulp liquid in bowl. Mix sugar and sauces into bowl with pulp liquid.
2 Meanwhile, place noodles in large heatproof bowl; cover with boiling water. Stand until just tender; drain.
3 Shell and devein prawns, leaving tails intact.
4 Blend or process garlic, turnip, shrimp, ginger and chilli until mixture forms a paste.
5 Heat oil in wok; stir-fry garlic paste until fragrant. Add pork; stir-fry until just cooked through. Add prawns; stir-fry 1 minute. Add egg; stir-fry until egg just sets. Add noodles, tamarind mixture, sprouts and half of the onion; stir-fry, tossing gently until combined. Remove from heat; add remaining green onion, coriander and nuts, toss gently until combined. Serve with lime wedges.

nutritional count per serving 19.7g total fat (4.5g saturated fat); 2608kJ (624 cal); 65.6g carbohydrate; 42.6g protein; 5.4g fibre

tip Preserved turnip is also called hua chai po or cu cai muoi, or dried radish because of its similarity to daikon. Sold packaged whole or sliced, it is very salty and must be rinsed and dried before use.

vegetarian pad thai

PREP + COOK TIME 30 MINS • SERVES 4

Soaking the rice stick noodles (sen lek) in hot water before stir-frying makes them tender and helps prevent them from sticking together. Sen lek are the traditional noodles used in pad thai, and before soaking measure about 5mm in width; other thin rice noodles can be substituted.

200g rice stick noodles
2 cloves garlic, quartered
2 tablespoons finely chopped preserved turnip
2 fresh small red thai chillies, chopped coarsely
¼ cup (60ml) peanut oil
2 eggs, beaten lightly
1 cup (90g) fried shallots
125g fried tofu, cut into small pieces
¼ cup (35g) coarsely chopped roasted unsalted peanuts
3 cups (240g) bean sprouts
6 green onions, sliced thinly
2 tablespoons soy sauce
1 tablespoon lime juice
2 tablespoons coarsely chopped fresh coriander

1 Place noodles in large heatproof bowl; cover with boiling water, stand until noodles just soften, drain.
2 Meanwhile, using mortar and pestle, crush garlic, turnip and chilli until mixture forms a paste.
3 Heat 2 teaspoons of the oil in wok. Pour egg into wok; cook over medium heat, tilting wok, until almost set. Remove omelette from wok; roll tightly, slice thinly.
4 Heat remaining oil in wok; stir-fry garlic paste and fried onion until fragrant. Add tofu; stir-fry 1 minute. Add half of the nuts, half of the sprouts and half of the green onion; stir-fry until sprouts are just wilted. Add noodles, sauce and juice; stir-fry, tossing gently until combined. Remove from heat; toss omelette strips, coriander and remaining nuts, sprouts and green onion through pad thai.

nutritional count per serving 24.3g total fat (4.4g saturated fat); 1417kJ (339 cal); 15.2g carbohydrate; 13.4g protein; 4.3g fibre

mee krob

PREP + COOK TIME 50 MINS • SERVES 4

Thais serve mee krob by dividing the vermicelli among bowls, then presenting the sauce in a separate bowl. Onion, omelette and coriander are also served in separate small bowls, with each diner taking as much as desired of the three to sprinkle over the top of his or her dish.

150g fresh firm silken tofu
vegetable oil, for deep-frying
125g rice vermicelli noodles
2 tablespoons peanut oil
2 eggs, beaten lightly
1 tablespoon water
2 cloves garlic, crushed
2 fresh small red thai chillies, chopped finely
1 small green thai chilli, chopped finely
2 tablespoons grated palm sugar
2 tablespoons fish sauce
2 tablespoons tomato sauce
1 tablespoon rice wine vinegar
200g pork mince
200g cooked small prawns, shelled, chopped coarsely
6 green onions, sliced thinly
¼ cup firmly packed fresh coriander leaves

Be careful when deep-frying the vermicelli: slide rather than drop them into the oil to help prevent splattering. Add them in small batches so the oil temperature doesn't reduce. Vermicelli puff immediately and must be removed from the oil quickly with a metal slotted spoon or tongs.

1 Pat tofu all over with absorbent paper; cut into slices, then cut each slice into 1cm-wide matchsticks. Spread tofu, in single layer, on absorbent-paper-lined tray; cover with more absorbent paper, stand at least 20 minutes.
2 Meanwhile, heat vegetable oil in wok; deep-fry noodles quickly, in batches, until puffed. Drain on absorbent paper.
3 Using same heated oil, deep-fry drained tofu, in batches, until browned lightly. Drain on absorbent paper. Discard oil from wok.
4 Heat 2 teaspoons of the peanut oil in cleaned wok. Pour half of the combined egg and water into wok; cook over medium heat, tilting wok, until almost set. Remove omelette from wok; roll tightly, slice thinly. Heat 2 more teaspoons of the peanut oil in wok; repeat with remaining egg mixture.
5 Combine garlic, chillies, sugar, sauces and vinegar in small bowl; pour half of the chilli mixture into small jug, reserve.
6 Combine pork in bowl with remaining half of the chilli mixture. Heat remaining peanut oil in wok; stir-fry pork mixture about 5 minutes or until pork is cooked through. Add prawns; stir-fry 1 minute. Add tofu; stir-fry, tossing gently to combine.
7 Remove wok from heat; add reserved chilli mixture and half of the onion, toss to combine. Add noodles; toss gently to combine. Sprinkle with remaining onion, omelette strips and coriander.
nutritional count per serving 20.7g total fat (4.5g saturated fat); 1509kJ (361 cal); 17.6g carbohydrate; 25.6g protein; 1.9g fibre

beef chow mein

PREP + COOK TIME 25 MINS • SERVES 4

1 tablespoon vegetable oil
500g beef mince
1 medium brown onion (150g), chopped finely
2 cloves garlic, crushed
1 tablespoon curry powder
1 large carrot (180g), chopped finely
2 stalks celery (300g), trimmed, sliced thinly
150g mushrooms, sliced thinly
1 cup (250ml) chicken stock
⅓ cup (80ml) oyster sauce
2 tablespoons dark soy sauce
440g thin fresh egg noodles
½ cup (60g) frozen peas
½ small wombok (350g), shredded coarsely

1 Heat oil in wok; stir-fry beef, onion and garlic until beef is browned. Add curry powder; stir-fry about 1 minute or until fragrant. Add carrot, celery and mushrooms; stir-fry until vegetables soften.
2 Add stock, sauces and noodles; stir-fry 2 minutes. Add peas and wombok; stir-fry until wombok just wilts.
nutritional count per serving 15.7g total fat (4.6g saturated fat); 2571kJ (615 cal); 70.6g carbohydrate; 42.3g protein; 8.4g fibre

vietnamese noodle and chicken salad

PREP + COOK TIME 40 MINS • SERVES 6

You can poach, shred and refrigerate the chicken a day ahead. The dressing and salad vegetables can also be prepared a day ahead; store separately, in the refrigerator. Simply combine the prepared ingredients with the noodles when you're ready. Or, poach and shred the chicken, and use it warm with the salad ingredients and noodles.

2 litres (8 cups) water
800g chicken breast fillets
200g vermicelli noodles
150g snow peas, trimmed
8 green onions
2 medium carrots (240g)
½ medium wombok (500g), shredded finely
2 cups (160g) bean sprouts
1 cup firmly packed fresh mint leaves
1 cup firmly packed fresh coriander leaves
½ cup (70g) roasted unsalted peanuts, chopped coarsely

sweet chilli dressing
½ cup (125ml) lime juice
2 tablespoons fish sauce
3 teaspoons sambal oelek
2 teaspoons sesame oil
1 tablespoon brown sugar
1 clove garlic, crushed

1 Bring the water to the boil in large saucepan; add chicken. Simmer, uncovered, about 10 minutes or until chicken is cooked. Cool chicken in poaching liquid 10 minutes; drain. Using two forks, shred chicken coarsely.
2 Place noodles in large heatproof bowl, cover with boiling water; stand until tender, drain. Rinse under cold water, drain.
3 Meanwhile, make sweet chilli dressing.
4 Slice snow peas and onions diagonally into thin strips. Halve carrots crossways; cut into matchsticks. Combine peas, onion, carrot, wombok, sprouts, herbs and chicken in large bowl with noodles; drizzle with dressing. Serve sprinkled with nuts.
sweet chilli dressing Place ingredients in screw-top jar; shake well.
nutritional count per serving 15.1g total fat (3.1g saturated fat); 1772kJ (424 cal); 30.9g carbohydrate; 37.7g protein; 6.4g fibre

Q&A

I've always used plain rice vermicelli for vietnamese noodle salad but can I use bean thread noodles instead? I have a packet in the pantry but the cooking instructions are not in English. How do I prepare them?

Bean thread or cellophane noodles are even thinner than vermicelli. These crystal-clear dried noodles are made from the flour of the green mung bean. Like vermicelli, you can fry them straight from the packet, for a garnish or soften them until white and slippery. There are two ways to do this – place them in a pan of boiling water for about 30 seconds, remove them from the heat and leave them for 1 to 2 minutes; or simply soak them in warm water until tender. The latter method will preserve their texture better. Whereas vermicelli are good in both hot and cold dishes, bean threads are better suited to cold dishes as their web-like strands are harder to separate.

mee goreng

PREP + COOK TIME 50 MINS • SERVES 4

500g fresh wheat noodles
vegetable oil, for deep-frying
1 small white onion (80g), sliced thinly
2 tablespoons raw peanuts
2 tablespoons peanut oil
500g pork fillets, sliced thinly
5 cloves garlic, crushed
2 tablespoons grated fresh ginger
3 fresh red thai chillies, chopped finely
10 fresh water chestnuts, sliced thinly
18 snake beans (180g), sliced thickly
2 stalks celery (300g), trimmed, chopped finely
2 baby buk choy, chopped coarsely
2 green onions, chopped coarsely
⅓ cup (80ml) kecap manis
2 tablespoons sweet chilli sauce
1 tablespoon thick tamarind concentrate
⅓ cup (80ml) vegetable stock
1 teaspoon sesame oil

1 Cook noodles in large saucepan of boiling water, uncovered, until just tender; drain.
2 Heat vegetable oil in small saucepan. Deep-fry white onion until browned; drain on absorbent paper. Deep-fry peanuts until browned lightly; drain on absorbent paper. Blend or process onion and peanuts until chopped finely.
3 Heat half of the peanut oil in heated large wok; stir-fry pork until browned and cooked as desired. Remove pork; cover to keep warm.
4 Heat remaining peanut oil in wok; stir-fry garlic, ginger and chilli until fragrant. Add water chestnuts and vegetables; stir-fry 2 minutes.
5 Return pork to pan with noodles, kecap manis, sauce, tamarind, stock and sesame oil; stir-fry until heated through. Serve sprinkled with onion and peanut mixture.

nutritional count per serving 43.3g total fat (14.9g saturated fat); 3867kJ (925 cal); 81.7g carbohydrate; 44.3g protein; 16.2g fibre

fried noodles with chinese sausage

PREP + COOK TIME 35 MINS • SERVES 4

450g wide fresh rice noodles
2 teaspoons peanut oil
300g dried chinese sausages, sliced thickly
1 medium brown onion (150g), chopped coarsely
2 cloves garlic, crushed
100g shiitake mushrooms, chopped coarsely
1 small wombok (700g), chopped coarsely
¼ cup (60ml) chicken stock
¼ cup (95g) char siu sauce
2 tablespoons lime juice
½ cup loosely packed fresh coriander leaves
¼ cup loosely packed fresh mint leaves
⅓ cup (50g) coarsely chopped roasted unsalted cashews
1 fresh long red chilli, sliced thinly

1 Place noodles in large heatproof bowl, cover with boiling water; separate with fork, drain.
2 Heat oil in wok; stir-fry sausage, onion, garlic and mushrooms until sausage is browned and vegetables tender.
3 Add wombok; stir-fry until wombok wilts. Add stock, sauce, juice and noodles; stir-fry until hot. Remove from heat; sprinkle with coriander and mint. Serve with nuts and chilli.

nutritional count per serving 28.4g total fat (7.8g saturated fat); 2161kJ (517 cal); 43.6g carbohydrate; 17.6g protein; 9.8g fibre

hokkien mee

PREP + COOK TIME 30 MINS • SERVES 4

Hokkien mee is a flavourful fried noodle, vegetable and beef dish that has become synonymous with fried noodles and is eaten all over the world wherever noodle shops are found.

450g hokkien noodles
1 tablespoon peanut oil
600g piece eye fillet, sliced thinly
1 medium brown onion (150g), sliced thinly
2 cloves garlic, crushed
1 medium red capsicum (200g), sliced thinly
115g baby corn, halved lengthways
150g snow peas, trimmed, halved diagonally
2 baby buk choy (300g), chopped coarsely
¼ cup (60ml) char siu sauce
1 tablespoon dark soy sauce
¼ cup (60ml) chicken stock

1 Place noodles in medium heatproof bowl, cover with boiling water; separate with fork, drain.
2 Heat half the oil in wok; stir-fry beef, in batches, until browned. Remove from wok.
3 Heat remaining oil in wok; stir-fry onion, garlic and capsicum until tender.
4 Return beef to wok with noodles, corn, snow peas, buk choy, sauces and stock; stir-fry until vegetables are tender and beef is cooked as desired.

nutritional count per serving 32.3g total fat (13.8g saturated fat); 3382kJ (809 cal); 75.5g carbohydrate; 47.1g protein; 13.3g fibre

char kway teow

PREP + COOK TIME 35 MINS • SERVES 4

Dried chinese sausages, also called lap cheong, are usually made from pork but can also be made with duck liver or beef. Red-brown in colour and sweet-spicy in flavour, the 12cm dried links are sold, several strung together, in all Asian food stores.

450g wide fresh rice noodles
250g uncooked small prawns
250g squid hoods
⅓ cup (80ml) peanut oil
250g firm white fish fillets, skinned, cut into 3cm pieces
2 cloves garlic, crushed
2 fresh small red thai chillies, chopped finely
4cm piece fresh ginger (20g), grated
2 eggs, beaten lightly
5 green onions, sliced thinly
2 cups (160g) bean sprouts
120g dried chinese sausage, sliced thinly
2 tablespoons dark soy sauce
1 tablespoon kecap manis
1 tablespoon light soy sauce

1 Place noodles in large heatproof bowl; cover with boiling water, separate with fork, drain.
2 Shell and devein prawns, leaving tails intact. Cut squid down centre to open out; score inside in diagonal pattern, then cut into 2cm-wide strips.
3 Heat 1 tablespoon of the oil in wok; stir-fry fish and squid, in batches, until browned lightly. Place in large bowl; cover to keep warm.
4 Heat another tablespoon of the oil in wok; stir-fry prawns, garlic, chilli and ginger until prawns just change colour. Add to bowl with fish and squid; cover to keep warm.
5 Heat remaining oil in wok; stir-fry egg, onion and sprouts until egg is just set. Slide egg mixture onto plate; cover to keep warm.
6 Stir-fry sausage in wok until crisp; drain. Return sausage to wok with seafood, egg mixture, sauces and noodles; stir-fry until hot.

nutritional count per serving 29.9g total fat (6.9g saturated fat); 2291kJ (548 cal); 27g carbohydrate; 41.1g protein; 3.3g fibre

Q&A

I recently became vegetarian and tried making char kway teow, using tofu instead of sausage and seafood. The result was very bland. What other meat substitutes can I use to create more complex flavours? I still eat eggs.

It is possible to make a good hawker-style dish without meat. In fact, you can find hawker stalls in the streets of Singapore that sell vegetarian versions of char kway teow. Plain tofu is great for soaking up flavour but won't add any flavour to the dish. Try using smoked tofu or the nutty-like tofu-tempeh – tofu speckled with chunky tempeh (semi-fermented soy beans). You can also use frozen baked taro balls. All these products are sold at health food shops. The chicken eggs can be replaced with richer-tasting duck eggs, and peanuts will add both crunch and flavour. Vegetarians often use mushrooms (shiitake) and root vegetables (sweet potato) as flavour enhancers, too.

crab and soba salad

PREP + COOK TIME 30 MINS • SERVES 4

Soba are fresh or dried Japanese noodles made from buckwheat and wheat flour, sometimes with egg yolks; called matcha soba when Japanese green tea is added.

Serve cold with a dipping sauce and side dishes of tempura, or in a hot broth, plain or with clams, chicken, mushroom or other meats or vegetables, and various garnishes. They are a popular fast food.

270g soba noodles
1 lebanese cucumber (130g), seeded, sliced thinly
1 small red onion (100g), chopped finely
1 medium carrot (120g), cut into matchsticks
50g baby spinach leaves, sliced thinly
400g fresh crab meat
1 tablespoon drained pickled ginger, sliced thinly

ginger miso dressing
6cm piece fresh ginger (30g), chopped coarsely
2 tablespoons drained pickled ginger
2 cloves garlic
⅓ cup (100g) yellow miso paste
½ teaspoon wasabi paste
½ cup (125ml) rice vinegar
½ cup (125ml) vegetable oil
2 tablespoons water

1. Make ginger miso dressing.
2. Cook noodles in large saucepan of boiling water, uncovered, until just tender; drain. Rinse under cold water; drain.
3. Combine noodles in large bowl with cucumber, onion, carrot, spinach, half the crab and half the dressing. Divide salad among serving plates; top with remaining crab, ginger and remaining dressing.

ginger miso dressing Blend or process ingredients until smooth.

nutritional count per serving 32.4g total fat (4g saturated fat); 2805kJ (671 cal); 55.9g carbohydrate; 35.9g protein; 5.9g fibre

sweet soy fried noodles

PREP + COOK TIME 35 MINS • SERVES 4

Known as "pad sieu" this traditional Thai dish is similar to the famous "pad thai", but uses kecap manis (a thick, sweet soy sauce) to give it its special flavour. Fresh rice noodles can be purchased in various widths or large sheets weighing about 500g, which are cut into the noodle width desired.

450g fresh wide rice noodles
1 tablespoon peanut oil
3 cloves garlic, sliced thinly
2 eggs, beaten lightly
280g gai lan, chopped coarsely
200g snake beans, cut into 5cm lengths

⅓ cup (80ml) kecap manis
2 tablespoons light soy sauce
½ teaspoon dried chilli flakes
350g packet fried tofu, cut into 2cm cubes
4 green onions, sliced thinly
¾ cup loosely packed thai basil leaves

1. Place noodles in large heatproof bowl, cover with boiling water; separate with fork, drain.
2. Heat oil in wok; stir-fry garlic until fragrant. Add egg; stir-fry until set. Add vegetables, sauces and chilli; stir-fry until vegetables are tender. Add noodles, tofu, onion and basil; stir-fry until hot.

nutritional count per serving 18.2g total fat (4g saturated fat); 2036kJ (487 cal); 55.4g carbohydrate; 20.1g protein; 9.8g fibre

udon noodle and prawn broth

PREP + COOK TIME 30 MINS • SERVES 4

Udon noodles are broad, white Japanese wheat noodles. Particularly popular in southern Japan, udon are best known as soup noodles, but are also good in stir-fries and hotpots. Available fresh and dried, in round, square or ribbon shapes.

3 cups (750ml) fish stock
3 cups (750ml) water
10cm stick fresh lemon grass (20g), chopped coarsely
4 fresh kaffir lime leaves, shredded
8cm piece fresh ginger (40g), sliced thinly
2 fresh small red thai chillies, chopped coarsely
1 tablespoon fish sauce
1kg uncooked medium king prawns
200g fresh udon noodles
230g can sliced bamboo shoots, rinsed, drained
100g fresh shiitake mushrooms, sliced thickly
60g baby spinach leaves

1 Combine stock, the water, lemon grass, lime leaves, ginger, chilli and sauce in large saucepan; bring to the boil. Reduce heat, simmer broth, uncovered, 10 minutes.
2 Meanwhile, shell and devein prawns.
3 Strain broth through sieve into large bowl; discard solids. Return broth to pan with prawns, noodles, bamboo shoots and mushrooms. Simmer, uncovered, about 5 minutes or until prawns are changed in colour and noodles are cooked as desired. Remove from heat; stir in spinach.

nutritional count per serving 1.5g total fat (0.3g saturated fat); 861kJ (206 cal); 16.2g carbohydrate; 30.3g protein; 2.3g fibre

chilled soba

PREP + COOK TIME 20 MINS (+ CHILLING) • SERVES 4

The Japanese celebrate New Year's Eve by eating soba noodles as the clock strikes midnight. This is known as "Toshi-koshi soba", which literally means "Across the Years Noodles". The noodles symbolise longevity.

250g dried soba noodles
¾ cup (180ml) dashi
2 tablespoons japanese soy sauce
2 tablespoons mirin
½ teaspoon sugar
2 green onions, chopped finely
1 teaspoon wasabi
½ toasted seaweed sheet (yaki-nori), sliced thinly

1 Cook noodles in large saucepan of boiling water, uncovered, until just tender; drain. Rinse under cold water; drain.
2 Heat dashi, sauce, mirin and sugar in small saucepan, stirring, until sugar dissolves; cool dipping sauce.
3 Divide dipping sauce, onion and wasabi among individual side dishes.
4 Just before serving, place noodles in a strainer and immerse in iced water to chill. Drain and divide among serving baskets or dishes; top with seaweed strips.
5 Add onion and wasabi to dipping sauce according to taste then dip noodles in sauce before eating.

nutritional count per serving 0.8g total fat (0.2g saturated fat); 953kJ (228 cal); 44.1g carbohydrate; 7.7g protein; 2.3g fibre

VEGETABLES

Vegetables

There'll always be times in your life when you've eaten an excess of fast or rich food, and all you want is a plate of steamed vegetables for a dose of sheer, unadulterated goodness. And for the rest of the time, you can enjoy vegetables in all their multiple guises: trusty accompaniments to the main dish; the star attraction in a fragrant curry; crunchy just-cooked ingredients in a tasty Asian stir-fry; or sliced and char-grilled on the barbecue. The possibilities are endless.

BUYING VEGETABLES

When they are fresh, vegetables should appear healthy-looking and upstanding, and most have a sheen. Greens should be taut and bright, the cabbage family firm and tightly packed, tomatoes should be gleaming and richly coloured, eggplant and capsicum should be smooth and glossy, root vegetables such as carrots, potatoes and beetroot should be well shaped and unmarked (potatoes are actually better tasting if they still have some dirt on them as the high pressure hoses used to clean them can damage their skins).

When you're selecting potatoes, think about the way in which you want to cook them because different varieties are better for different uses. For example, high starch, floury varieties that boil well will not bake satisfactorily. Desiree, pontiac, or bintje varieties are best for boiling and mashing while spunta, russet burbank, kipfler and king edward are good for baking. Greens and vegetable flowers and fruits – such as globe artichokes, broccoli, cauliflower, eggplant, capsicum and zucchini – are best used within a few days of buying them. Root vegetables should be used within a week or so. Peas and sweetcorn should be eaten the day you buy them because they gradually lose sweetness and tenderness.

STORING AND HANDLING VEGETABLES

Store leaf vegetables, peas, beans, corn, globe artichokes, broccoli, cauliflower, cut pumpkin and beetroot in paper bags or loosely wrapped in greaseproof paper, enclosed in plastic bags.

Store carrots, eggplant and capsicum unwrapped in a covered crisper.

Store onions and potatoes in a cool, dark place on racks or in baskets off the floor.

Canned Asian vegetables can be kept in a container of water in the fridge, changing the water daily, for 2 or 3 days. Fresh water chestnuts can be stored unpeeled and uncut in the fridge crisper for up to 3 days. Fresh bamboo shoots and lotus root should be enclosed in a paper bag, then a plastic one, and refrigerated for up to 3 days.

ASIAN VEGETABLES

THERE IS A WHOLE EXTENDED FAMILY OF VEGETABLES TO DISCOVER AT YOUR ASIAN GROCERY STORE AND FOR AUTHENTICITY IN YOUR ASIAN COOKING IT'S REWARDING TO EXPLORE THEM. ASIAN VEGETABLES CAN SOMETIMES REQUIRE CONSIDERABLE PREPARATION AHEAD, BUT ONCE PREPARED THEY ARE COOKED QUICKLY TO PRESERVE THEIR TEXTURES WHICH ARE AS IMPORTANT AS FLAVOURS IN ASIAN COOKING.

THREE POPULAR ASIAN VEGETABLES

BAMBOO SHOOTS available canned and sometimes fresh in Asian food shops, they are tender mild-flavoured shoots (from the base of bamboo plants) used in soups and stir-fries.

LOTUS ROOT is the crisp, delicately flavoured root of a waterlily, used in salads and stir-fries. It can be bought canned or frozen and sometimes fresh. Fresh lotus root is usually cut crossways into slices which are decoratively patterned with holes and are often used for their visual appeal.

WATER CHESTNUTS are the corms (solid bulbs) of an aquatic plant native to South-East Asia. Available fresh and canned, they are the size of a walnut and are prepared by peeling off the dark skin to reveal a crunchy white flesh. They are used in a variety of ways: chopped to go in minced meat dishes and wontons, sliced for stir-fries and boiled whole as a street snack.

COOKING VEGETABLES

BOILING There's an old-fashioned rule of thumb when boiling vegetables: those that grow 'in the cold and the dark' (root vegetables) should be boiled 'in the cold and the dark' – that is, placed in cold salted water and heated to boiling with the lid on. Vegetables that grow above-ground 'in the heat and the light' should be boiled 'in the heat and the light' – that is, placed in boiling water from the start and cooked without a lid. Once cooked, drain the vegetables, return to the saucepan and shake briefly over low heat to dry.

STEAMING While it takes almost as long as boiling, steaming your vegetables is preferred by most cooks because the vegetables retain all their flavour without leaching out the goodness into the cooking water. Place the vegetables in a steamer (the water should not touch the steamer or the vegetables) and cover with a tight-fitting lid.

ROASTING/BAKING For vegetables to accompany a roast, par-boil for 5 minutes, dry as for boiled root vegetables and score the surface with a fork. Place around roast meat for half an hour before the roast is done, spooning with pan juices and turning once. For a crunchier roast potato, roast on an oiled oven tray by themselves.

CHAR-GRILLING OR BARBECUING These cooking methods give vegetables a smoky flavour. Slice vegetables such as eggplant and zucchini, and brush with olive oil. Place on a hot ridged grill or barbecue, press down with tongs, turning, until barely tender and marked with char stripes.

STIR-FRYING Vegetables are usually diced or cut into strips for stir-frying and added to a steaming hot wok in the order of the time they take to par-cook – that is, the longest-cooking vegetables go first, the quickest-cooking last. Stir-fried vegetables should still be crunchy at the end of the cooking.

PAN-FRYING Heat a little oil or butter, or a little of both, over medium heat until the oil gives off a haze or the butter stops sizzling. Fry the vegetables until browned and tender, turning once; remove and drain on absorbent paper.

VEGETABLES THE AWW COOKING SCHOOL

hasselback potatoes

PREP + COOK TIME 1 HOUR 30 MINS • SERVES 4

This Swedish version of roasted potatoes produces a wonderfully crisp crust and makes an excellent accompaniment to roast beef or lamb.

You could also use ruby lou potatoes for this recipe.

4 medium desiree potatoes (800g), halved horizontally
20g butter, melted
1 tablespoon olive oil
¼ cup (25g) packaged breadcrumbs
½ cup (60g) finely grated cheddar cheese

1 Preheat oven to 180°C/160°C fan-forced.
2 Place one potato half, cut-side down, on chopping board; place a chopstick on board along each side of potato. Slice potato thinly, cutting through to chopsticks to prevent cutting all the way through. Repeat with remaining potato halves.
3 Coat potatoes in combined butter and oil in medium baking dish; place, rounded-side up, in single layer. Roast 1 hour, brushing frequently with oil mixture.
4 Sprinkle combined breadcrumbs and cheese over potatoes; roast about 10 minutes or until browned.

nutritional count per serving 14.1g total fat (6.6g saturated fat); 1225kJ (293 cal); 30.4g carbohydrate; 9.5g protein; 3.5g fibre

Place a potato half, cut-side facing down, on a chopping surface. Position a chopstick on either side of potato half.

Using a very sharp knife, slice the potato half thinly – the chopsticks will prevent you from cutting right through to the bottom. Repeat for remaining potato halves.

Roast potatoes, cut-side down, in a preheated oven for 1 hour, brushing regularly with oil and butter mixture. Turn potatoes over and sprinkle breadcrumb and cheese mixture on top. Roast for a further 10 minutes or until browned.

asparagus hollandaise

PREP + COOK TIME 35 MINS • SERVES 4

1kg asparagus, trimmed
hollandaise sauce
2 tablespoons water
2 tablespoons white wine vinegar
¼ teaspoon cracked black pepper
2 egg yolks
200g unsalted butter, melted

1 Make hollandaise sauce.
2 Boil, steam or microwave asparagus until tender. Serve asparagus on a large platter drizzled with hollandaise sauce.
hollandaise sauce Bring the water, vinegar and pepper to the boil in small saucepan. Reduce heat; simmer, uncovered, until liquid is reduced to 1 tablespoon. Strain mixture through fine sieve into medium heatproof bowl; cool 10 minutes. Whisk egg yolks into vinegar mixture. Set bowl over medium saucepan of simmering water; do not allow water to touch base of bowl. Whisk mixture over heat until thickened. Remove bowl from heat; gradually whisk in melted butter in a thin, steady stream, whisking constantly until sauce is thick and creamy.
nutritional count per serving 44g total fat (26.9g saturated fat); 1797kJ (430 cal); 2.8g carbohydrate; 6.1g protein; 2.6g fibre
serving ideas add a poached egg and some fresh dill for a gourmet breakfast. Spoon hollandaise sauce over globe artichokes, and steamed or poached fish.

roasted capsicums

PREP + COOK TIME 30 MINS • SERVES 8

4 large red capsicums (1.4kg)
1 sprig rosemary
2 cloves garlic, sliced thinly
1 cup (250ml) olive oil, approximately

TIP

• When using roasted capsicum, remove from oil and drain on absorbent paper to remove as much oil as possible.

1 Preheat oven to 250°C/230°C fan-forced.
2 Quarter capsicums; discard seeds and membranes. Place in large baking dish. Roast, skin-side up, until skin blisters and blackens.
3 Cover capsicum pieces with plastic or paper for 5 minutes; peel away skin. Place capsicum quarters in large sterilised jar; add rosemary and garlic. Pour in enough oil to cover capsicums. Store in refrigerator for up to 2 months.
nutritional count per serving 28.7g total fat (4g saturated fat); 1216kJ (291 cal); 6g carbohydrate; 2.4g protein; 1.8g fibre

[opposite] asparagus hollandaise

SPECIAL FEATURE

Know your vegetables

Today's vegetables bear little resemblance to the limp, grey-green culinary selections before us only two decades ago. They have now become a source of pleasure appreciated for their bright colours, crisp or tender textures and distinctive flavours. Some greens are still seasonal delicacies.

GLOBE ARTICHOKE
Part of the thistle family and not to be confused with jerusalem artichokes (the tubers). Globes have round or conical-shaped heads made up of leathery-like petals. You can eat the tender heart and juicy base of the petals. Best from late winter to spring.

GREEN BEANS
There are a few varieties of green or french beans. Most have been bred to be stringless – to check, nip off an end with a thumbnail and and test if you can pull down a string. Tender baby greens are simply green beans picked young. Available year-round.

SNAKE BEANS
Sometimes known as yard-long beans, this variety is stronger flavoured than the common green bean, but can be used interchangeably in recipes. You'll find them in Asian shops, if not in ordinary greengrocers. They peak in the summer and autumn months.

BROAD BEANS
Broad or fava beans have bright green, slightly furry pods. When young, the beans inside can be eaten raw with their skin intact. The skin on the large, mature beans becomes tough and bitter, and must be removed. Mostly available from winter to spring.

BORLOTTI BEANS
Distinguished by their reddish-brown streaked pods and seeds. Only the seeds are cooked, and these lose their streaks once cooked. Their mealy texture makes them perfect for minestrone or stews. Fresh borlotti are available in autumn. Also sold dried.

BEETROOT
The rich maroon flesh of this root vegetable is sweet and nutritious. It can be baked or boiled and added to salads, or served with other roasted vegetables. It has an earthier flavour when eaten raw, grated in salads. Peaks mid-winter to early summer.

Q&A

Each time celeriac comes into season – from autumn to early spring – I'm tempted to buy it. Friends have served it up as a zesty salad bed for squid and a prawn remoulade, and it has the most amazing taste. Its hairy, gnarly roots and tough knotted skin have always put me off, though. How difficult is it to remove?

It's not too hard, once you know how, and it's well worth the effort. Wash the roots to remove as much dirt as possible. Then use a sharp knife to trim away the roots and skin. Slice the celeriac and immediately toss it into a bowl of water acidulated with lemon juice or the flesh will turn brown. Because the roots and dirt-filled crevices have to be trimmed away, you'll lose about a quarter of the celeriac during peeling. A 500g celeriac will yield about two cups once peeled and sliced. Pat dry and use a processor or hand grater to shred the celeriac.

BROCCOLI
of the cabbage family, along with cauliflower, coli is high in beneficial antioxidants, and ins C and A. Cook, uncovered, to preserve its nt green colour, and until it is tender but still Best from midwinter to spring.

BROCCOLINI
A Japanese cross-breed of gai lan and broccoli, but sweeter and more tender than the latter. Can be substituted for broccoli, although the whole vegetable is used – trim by cutting off the very ends of the stalks and washing well, just before cooking.

CAULIFLOWER
The most delicately flavoured member of the cabbage family, cauliflower is good boiled or steamed and served with white or cheese sauces, broken into florets and stir-fried, or made into fritters or a creamy soup. Available year-round but peak in winter.

VER BEET
ely related to and often mistaken for spinach, r beet, sometimes called swiss chard, has an ier, slightly bitter taste. Its ribbed leaves can be d and added to salads, soups, meat stews, rice, a, stir-fries or cheese pies. Available year-round.

CELERIAC
Also called celery root, celeriac is the bulb of a type of celery. Under the brown knobby skin is an ivory-coloured flesh with a faint celery flavour. Peel, grate and use in a remoulade, a citrus-dressed salad, or add to soup or mash. Its season is autumn to spring.

CHOKO
Chayote or christophine are the other names for this South American tuber. Some describe its taste as bland, others say it is subtle. It can be used like a potato in recipes, but the skin has a tacky sap, so wear gloves when peeling it. Available early winter.

SPECIAL FEATURE

Know your vegetables

Vegetables are a welcome addition to any meal, often becoming the central focus, especially as their nutritional value is now better understood. From elaborate salads to soufflés and casseroles to pasta dishes, using plant-based sauces, vegetables have become a daily source of discovery.

FENNEL
A vegetable and herb in one with a licorice-like taste. The bulb can be eaten raw or cooked, the fronds can be used to flavour salmon or salads, while the seeds can be added to sauces, vegetables and breads. Winter is its season; baby fennel is picked in spring.

JERUSALEM ARTICHOKE
This knobbly tuber is actually native to the Americas and belongs to the sunflower family. Its flavour is delicately earthy, nutty and sweet, and it is tender when cooked. Great in soups, or baked like a potato, or pureed for a side dish. Available autumn to spring.

KALE
This strong-flavoured member of the cabbage family is very high in antioxidants. In the southern USA it's known as collard greens, while the Italians call it cavolo nero. Used like cabbage, kale is best during winter. The summer variety is paler and thinner.

KOHLRABI
This round purple or green globe is a member of the cabbage family and develops a bulbous stem above ground. The bulb has a delicate cauliflower/turnip flavour and can be added to soups and casseroles, or used like potatoes. It comes into season in winter.

OKRA
These green pods feature in the cuisine of India, East Asia, the Middle East and the Mississippi area of the USA. It tastes like eggplant but is part of the mallow family, which explains its gummy texture. Add to rice, stews and curries. In season summer and autumn.

PARSNIP
Their nutty sweetness is especially good when steamed and dressed with a garlic and cream sauce or in a curried parsnip soup, or simply baked. Can be substituted for potatoes. Available all year but the cold develops their sweet/savoury flavour in winter.

Q&A

When I shop at the greengrocers, I usually have a rough idea of what I'll be cooking for the week and select my fruit and vegetables accordingly. Is this a bad way to shop? Should I be thinking more about seasonality?

Determining your grocery list from a weekly menu is a smart way to shop – but only if you are buying in season. When vegetables come into season, supply is high, so the prices drop. Over a year, you can make significant savings. Vegetables that have been grown and harvested during peak condition will also be fresher, taste better as a result and last longer. Most greengrocers have in-store flyers on what's in season, so pick one up next time you are there. You can refer to it when you think about your weekly menu and compile your shopping list. And don't forget that buying locally grown seasonal produce will reduce your carbon imprint, too.

EN PEAS
ods of this variety of pea are not eaten. Select ully and use promptly as peas deteriorate soon being picked. Serve boiled with any meat or or pureed with potato. Good in soups, pastas risottos, too. Best in spring and summer.

SNOW PEAS
Flat edible pods, enclosing tiny peas that do not mature. Eaten whole or sliced, snow peas can be blanched and served with meat or fish, or used raw in salads, stir-fries or noodle dishes. Can also be added to soups at the end. Available year-round.

SUGAR SNAP PEAS
Not to be mistaken for green peas, snap or sugar snap peas have an edible crisp, sweet pod. They can be briefly boiled, used raw in salads, or added raw to stir-fries and noodle dishes. Small ones can be used in risottos and pasta sauces. Available all year.

KON
ry large Asian radish, daikon can be served raw alads, pickled, grated as a garnish, simmered in os or added to stir-fries. The Japanese cook it e water in which rice has been washed to keep hite and reduce any bitterness. Best in winter.

ZUCCHINI
Also known as courgette, zucchini has a subtle, sweet flavour when steamed, grilled, fried and baked – they should never be boiled for too long. Best in winter to spring, available in green and yellow, and as the yellow round variety called patty pan squash.

ZUCCHINI FLOWERS
The flowers of zucchini are harvested before they are fully grown and still young enough to have tender edible seeds. A summer treat to dip into batter and deep-fry or stuff with a savoury cheese mixture, coat with egg and breadcrumbs, and pan-fry.

artichoke hearts vinaigrette

PREP + COOK TIME 1 HOUR 30 MINS (+ COOLING) • SERVES 4

The classic artichoke season runs from the end of winter to early summer, peaking in early to mid-spring, though some varieties introduced in recent years may appear as early as autumn. Size does not indicate quality. The important thing is that the leaves be tightly closed around the head, the stem firm and rigid and the artichoke plump and heavy for its size. Tiny artichokes may have looser leaves, but they should be firm and springy and when pulled back, make a definite snap.

1 medium lemon (140g), chopped coarsely
20 small globe artichokes (2kg)
2 cups (500ml) dry white wine
¼ cup loosely packed fresh thyme leaves
5 cloves garlic, unpeeled
½ cup (125ml) lemon juice
2 teaspoons sea salt flakes
1 cup (250ml) white wine vinegar
2 cups (500ml) water
1 tablespoon extra virgin olive oil

1 Place lemon in large bowl half-filled with water. Discard outer leaves from artichokes; cut tips from remaining leaves. Trim, then peel stalks; place artichokes in lemon water.
2 Cut a piece of baking paper into a round to fit inside a large saucepan.
3 Place wine, thyme, garlic, juice, salt, vinegar, the water and drained artichokes in large saucepan; cover with baking-paper round. Bring to the boil then simmer, covered, about 25 minutes or until artichokes are tender. Cool in poaching liquid about 30 minutes.
4 Whisk ½ cup of the poaching liquid in small bowl with oil (discard remaining liquid).
5 Halve artichokes lengthways; using small knife, remove chokes. Divide artichokes among serving bowls; drizzle with poaching mixture. If you like, sprinkle with extra thyme leaves and serve with crusty bread.

nutritional count per serving 5.5g total fat (0.7g saturated fat); 865kJ (207 cal); 6.7g carbohydrate; 10.4g protein; 4.4g fibre

To prepare an artichoke, remove any tough outer leaves by pulling them off with your fingers.

Using a sharp knife, trim the stalk and the top. Trim tips of remaining leaves. Place peeled artichokes in a bowl of water with some chopped lemons to stop artichoke from discolouring.

Place artichokes in a large pan, along with poaching ingredients. Cover pan with a round of baking paper to fit pan. Cook artichokes until tender, then cool in pan.

Using a small, sharp knife, cut artichokes in half, lengthways. Carefully remove the choke in the centre and divide artichokes among serving bowls.

caramelised red onion

PREP + COOK TIME 50 MINS • MAKES 1½ CUPS

This recipe makes enough to go with six servings of grilled steak, but it is worth making double the quantity or more because it is so useful to have on hand.

You can also use brown onions in this recipe.

Caramelised onion will keep for weeks in a lidded container in the refrigerator.

50g butter
4 medium red onions (680g), sliced thinly
1 tablespoon brown sugar
⅓ cup (80ml) dry red wine
¼ cup (60ml) beef stock
1 tablespoon balsamic vinegar

1 Melt butter in large frying pan; cook onion over low heat, stirring occasionally, about 30 minutes.
2 Add sugar; cook, stirring, about 5 minutes or until onion has caramelised. Add wine, stock and vinegar; bring to the boil then remove from heat.

nutritional count per tablespoon 2.3g total fat (1.5g saturated fat); 159kJ (38 cal); 2.8g carbohydrate; 0.6g protein; 0.5g fibre

serving ideas this goes well wtih chicken, burgers, for a pizza topping, a quiche, omelette or sandwich filling, or a garnish for barbecued swordfish.

caramelised fennel tarts

PREP + COOK TIME 45 MINS • SERVES 4

These tarts are easy but impressive. They can be served alone or as part of a vegetarian table, or with delicate fillets of whiting or trout. The caramelised fennel can be prepared ahead but place it on the pastry bases only when they are to go in the oven.

50g butter
4 baby fennel bulbs (520g), trimmed, halved lengthways
1 teaspoon finely grated orange rind
½ cup (125ml) orange juice
1 sheet puff pastry
2 teaspoons finely chopped fresh thyme

1 Preheat oven to 220°C/200°C fan-forced. Oil and line two oven trays.
2 Melt butter in large frying pan; cook fennel until browned lightly. Add rind and juice; bring to the boil. Reduce heat; simmer, uncovered, about 5 minutes or until fennel is caramelised and tender.
3 Cut pastry sheet into four squares; place on oven trays. Remove fennel from pan, leaving behind the pan juices; divide among pastry squares. Bake about 20 minutes or until pastry is browned.
4 Meanwhile, return pan juices to the boil. Reduce heat; simmer, uncovered, until sauce thickens slightly.
5 Serve tarts drizzled with sauce and sprinkled with thyme.

nutritional count per serving 19.8g total fat (11.9g saturated fat); 1145kJ (274 cal); 19.9g carbohydrate; 3.3g protein; 2.7g fibre

caramelised onion and beetroot tart

PREP + COOK TIME 1 HOUR 10 MINS (+ FREEZING)
SERVES 6

50g butter
4 medium red onions (680g), halved, sliced thinly
1 tablespoon red wine vinegar
1 teaspoon fresh thyme leaves
3 medium beetroot (500g), trimmed
1 sheet butter puff pastry
cooking-oil spray
120g baby rocket leaves

chive oil
½ cup coarsely chopped fresh chives
¾ cup (180ml) olive oil
1 ice cube

horseradish cream
¾ cup (180ml) cream
1 tablespoon horseradish cream

1 Melt butter in medium frying pan; cook onion, stirring occasionally, over medium heat about 30 minutes or until caramelised. Stir in vinegar and thyme.
2 Meanwhile, boil, steam or microwave unpeeled beetroot until just tender; drain. When cool enough to handle, peel then slice beetroot thinly.
3 Preheat oven to 250°C/230°C fan-forced.
4 Place pastry sheet on flat surface; cut a 24cm circle out of pastry. Place on oiled oven tray, prick all over with fork; freeze 10 minutes. Bake pastry about 5 minutes or until browned lightly.
5 Make chive oil. Make horseradish cream.
6 Spread onion mixture over pastry; top with slightly overlapping beetroot slices. Spray tart lightly with oil; bake 10 minutes.
7 Meanwhile, combine rocket in medium bowl with half of the chive oil; divide among serving plates.
8 Cut tart into six wedges. Place each wedge on rocket, drizzle with remaining chive oil; serve with horseradish cream.
chive oil Blend or process ingredients until smooth.
horseradish cream Beat cream in small bowl with electric mixer until soft peaks form; fold in horseradish cream.
nutritional count per serving 54.5g total fat (20.6g saturated fat); 2558kJ (612 cal); 24.2g carbohydrate; 5.8g protein; 4.6g fibre

For years, I've been making do with canned or bottled beetroot. Until I tasted tarts and salads at cafés using fresh beets, I didn't realise what I was missing out on. Now I can't go back to packaged sweetened beets and want to start cooking the fresh variety – any tips on how to do this, mess-free?

You need to boil, bake or steam beetroot without peeling it first to retain its nutrients and keep the colour from running or "bleeding". Trim the root before cooking, but make sure you don't cut it too close to the beet itself or it will "bleed". Once cooked, the skin will easily rub off, either under cold running water or simply by peeling with your hands after it has cooled slightly. Always wear rubber gloves so you don't stain your skin. An easy way to bake them is to wrap each beet in foil, roast on a tray, then unwrap and peel.

broad beans and thyme

PREP + COOK TIME 40 MINS • SERVES 4

The flavour of these beans is musky and fresh, and they combine beautifully with mint and fetta in a salad, or slip easily into a spring vegetable soup. Early in the season they are sweet; later in the season, when they become mealy, they should be pureed.

600g frozen broad beans, thawed
10g butter
2 shallots (50g), chopped finely
150g speck, chopped finely
1 tablespoon fresh thyme leaves
1 tablespoon lemon juice

1 Drop beans into medium saucepan of boiling water, return to the boil; drain. When beans are cool enough to handle, peel away grey-coloured outer shells.
2 Heat butter in large frying pan; cook shallot and speck, stirring, until speck is browned lightly. Add beans and thyme; cook, stirring, until beans are heated through. Stir in juice.

nutritional count per serving 7.7g total fat (3.5g saturated fat); 589kJ (141 cal); 2g carbohydrate; 13.9g protein; 4.8g fibre

roasted caramelised parsnips

PREP + COOK TIME 1 HOUR 10 MINS • SERVES 4

Caramelising deepens a parsnip's natural sweetness but doesn't make it oversweet because the more sugar is cooked, the more its sweetness is transformed into deep, roasted flavours.

1kg parsnips, halved lengthways
2 tablespoons olive oil
¼ cup (55g) brown sugar
1 teaspoon ground nutmeg
1 tablespoon finely chopped fresh flat-leaf parsley

1 Preheat oven to 220°C/200°C fan-forced.
2 Combine parsnip, oil, sugar and nutmeg in large baking dish; roast about 1 hour or until parsnip is browned and tender.
3 Serve parsnip sprinkled with parsley.

nutritional count per serving 9.6g total fat (1.3g saturated fat); 1074kJ (257 cal); 35.8g carbohydrate; 4.1g protein; 5.7g fibre

[1] broad beans and thyme
[2] roasted caramelised parsnips
[3] glazed carrots with hazelnuts [page 226]
[4] braised baby leeks [page 226]

1

2

3

4

glazed carrots with hazelnuts

PREP + COOK TIME 25 MINS • SERVES 4

A most elegant side dish to grace roast duck, pork or game birds such as quail or guinea fowl.

30g butter
800g baby carrots, trimmed, peeled
2 teaspoons finely grated orange rind
¼ cup (60ml) orange juice
2 tablespoons dry white wine
2 tablespoons maple syrup
½ cup (70g) coarsely chopped roasted hazelnuts

1 Melt butter in large frying pan; cook carrots, turning occasionally, until almost tender.
2 Add rind, juice, wine and syrup; bring to the boil. Reduce heat; simmer, uncovered, until liquid has almost evaporated and carrots are tender and caramelised.
3 Serve carrots sprinkled with nuts.

nutritional count per serving 17.2g total fat (4.5g saturated fat); 1145kJ (274 cal); 20.8g carbohydrate; 4.1g protein; 7.7g fibre

braised baby leeks

PREP + COOK TIME 40 MINS • SERVES 4

You could serve these leeks on their own as a first course, or as an impressive side to veal or fish. Be sure to supply diners with sharp knives, as even baby leeks can be hard to cut with blunt ones.

16 baby pencil leeks (1.3kg)
30g butter
⅔ cup (160ml) chicken stock
2 tablespoons dry white wine
1 teaspoon finely grated lemon rind
2 tablespoons lemon juice
¼ cup (20g) flaked parmesan cheese
¼ cup coarsely chopped fresh flat-leaf parsley

1 Carefully trim root end from leeks, leaving each leek in one piece. Trim leeks into 15cm lengths; halve lengthways. Rinse under cold water; drain.
2 Melt butter in large frying pan; cook leeks, 1 minute. Add stock, wine, rind and juice; bring to the boil. Reduce heat; simmer, covered, 15 minutes or until leeks are tender. Uncover; simmer about 5 minutes or until liquid has reduced by half.
3 Serve leeks drizzled with cooking liquid then sprinkled with cheese and parsley.

nutritional count per serving 8.7g total fat (5.2g saturated fat); 644kJ (154 cal); 8.3g carbohydrate; 6.5g protein; 6g fibre

creamed spinach

PREP + COOK TIME 15 MINS • SERVES 4

20g butter
600g spinach, trimmed
½ cup (125ml) cream

1 Melt butter in large frying pan; cook spinach, stirring, until wilted.
2 Add cream; bring to the boil. Reduce heat; simmer, uncovered, until liquid reduces by half.

nutritional count per serving 38.7g total fat (25.4g saturated fat); 1555kJ (372 cal); 2.8g carbohydrate; 3.5g protein; 2.1g fibre

brussels sprouts with cream and almonds

PREP + COOK TIME 10 MINS • SERVES 4

Brussels sprouts look just like mini cabbages. Possibly the least-liked vegetable, they are in fact little mouthfuls of nutritional goodness. Avoid overcooking and you will be surprised at how delicious they can be. Usually served as a side dish, their sweet cabbage flavour goes well with nuts, bacon, butter and herbs.

50g butter
⅓ cup (25g) flaked almonds
1kg brussels sprouts, trimmed, halved
2 cloves garlic, crushed
300ml cream

1 Melt 10g of the butter in large frying pan; cook nuts, stirring, until browned lightly; remove from pan.
2 Melt remaining butter in same pan; cook sprouts and garlic, stirring, until sprouts are browned lightly. Add cream; bring to the boil. Reduce heat; simmer, uncovered, until sprouts are tender and sauce thickens slightly. Serve sprinkled with nuts.

nutritional count per serving 46.7g total fat (28.4g saturated fat); 2061kJ (493 cal); 6.6g carbohydrate; 9.5g protein; 7.3g fibre

chilli and herb swede crush

PREP + COOK TIME 30 MINS • SERVES 4

The swede is thought to be a hybrid (cross) of the cabbage and the turnip. It is a relatively "modern" vegetable, having been known only since the 17th century, unlike its parents which have both been cultivated for thousands of years.

1kg swedes, chopped coarsely
40g butter
¼ cup (60ml) cream
1 fresh long red chilli, chopped finely
1 tablespoon finely chopped fresh flat-leaf parsley
2 teaspoons finely grated lemon rind

1 Boil, steam or microwave swede until tender; drain.
2 Crush swede with butter and cream in medium bowl; stir in remaining ingredients.

nutritional count per serving 14.7g total fat (9.7g saturated fat); 773kJ (185 cal); 8.6g carbohydrate; 2.3g protein; 5.8g fibre

SPECIAL FEATURE

Know your herbs

Dried herbs certainly have their place in the kitchen, especially when the home cook is caught off guard. However, once you start using fresh herbs, you'll never want go back to using just the dried varieties again. One of nature's little surprise packages, fresh herbs pack a big flavour punch.

CHERVIL
A herb belonging to the parsley family, chervil has a faint fennel flavour. It is elegant enough to use in salads, or added to fish, poultry and vegetable dishes. Chervil is one of the classic French fines herbes (along with parsley, chives and tarragon).

DILL
The dark-green feathery, anise-flavoured fronds of the dill plant look decorative and are often used as a garnish. Tastes wonderful with fresh, smoked and cured fish, shellfish, cucumber, beetroot, potatoes and rice, and in a vinaigrette or mayonnaise.

VIETNAMESE MINT
Not really a mint, but a smooth-leafed herb with a flavour that resembles peppery coriander. It is used widely throughout South-East Asia in laksas, salads stir-fries and curries. The pretty leaf is also shredded and used as a garnish for many dishes.

CORIANDER
Coriander is essential to South-East Asian, South American and Middle Eastern cooking. Every part of the plant has its distinctive lemon/anise/sage flavour, and all parts are used – leaves, stems and roots.

OREGANO
The big savoury taste and scent of oregano speak of Mediterranean cooking, from Greek moussaka and zucchini or eggplant dishes to Italian pizza and pasta sauces. Unlike most other herbs, it has the best taste and greatest pungency when dried.

GARLIC CHIVES
Their flat, dark-green leaves are a great Asian ingredient, used in soups, stir-fries, egg dishes and noodle dishes. Also good for snipping over salads and into mayonnaise and cream cheese.

Q&A

I always prefer to use fresh herbs over dried ones, but there are times when I simply can't make it to the greengrocer's in time, or the potted herbs on my balcony aren't doing so well. I then reach for the spice pantry but never quite know how much dried herb to use as a substitute. Are there any rules here?

Generally, a ratio of one part dried herbs to three parts fresh herbs works because most dried herbs have a more intense, concentrated flavour than the fresh ones. For example, when a recipe calls for 1 tablespoon of fresh herbs, 1 teaspoon of dried herbs can be substituted. Of course if your jar of dried herbs has been sitting on the shelf for three years and it has lost its potency, it may take a little more than this. It's also a good idea to add the dried herbs near the beginning of food preparation, unlike fresh herbs, which are added near the end.

BASIL
different from common or sweet basil, its green es are smaller with a serrated edge and the stem rplish. Thai basil leaves have a strong aniseed ur, and are an essential ingredient in many Thai es, soups and stir-fries. Also used as garnish.

TARRAGON
French tarragon, with its subtle aniseed flavour, complements chicken, eggs and veal, and is essential in a béarnaise sauce. It is also one of the herbs that make up the French fines herbs. Russian and mexican tarragons are slightly coarser in taste.

BASIL
One of the most valuable culinary herbs, basil features in Mediterranean dishes. Its clove-and-anise perfume works magically with tomatoes and in pesto sauce. Although it is a summer annual, basil can be processed with olive oil and stored in the freezer.

SAGE
pungent, balsamic taste and scent of sage are sic in stuffings for duck and pork, or with veal prosciutto for the Italian saltimbocca dish. p-fried sage leaves are a delicious garnish for and liver and pumpkin ravioli in a butter sauce.

PARSLEY
The trusty workhorse of herbs, parsley works just as well as a garnish as it does in scrambled eggs, a potato salad or in a sauce for corned beef. Flat-leaf (also called continental) parsley has a stronger taste than the curly variety.

MARJORAM
Closely related to and similar in flavour to oregano, but milder and sweeter. Delicious in herb mixtures for omelettes, stuffings, herb scones and herb and cream cheese sandwiches. As with oregano, many chefs prefer dried marjoram to fresh.

scalloped potatoes

PREP + COOK TIME 1 HOUR 30 MINS (+ STANDING) • SERVES 6

This scrumptious layered dish of potato, ham, cream and cheese is certain to become a family favourite.

You could use coliban or sebago potatoes for this recipe.

1.2kg desiree potatoes, peeled
150g leg ham, chopped finely
300ml cream
¾ cup (180ml) milk
¾ cup (90g) coarsely grated cheddar cheese

1 Preheat oven to 180°C/160°C fan-forced; oil 1.5-litre (6-cup) baking dish.
2 Using sharp knife, mandoline or V-slicer, cut potatoes into very thin slices; pat dry with absorbent paper. Layer a quarter of the potato in prepared dish; top with a third of the ham. Continue layering remaining potato and ham, finishing with potato.
3 Heat cream and milk in small saucepan until almost boiling; pour over potato mixture. Cover with foil; bake 30 minutes. Remove foil; bake 20 minutes. Top with cheese; bake, uncovered, about 20 minutes or until potato is tender. Stand 10 minutes before serving.

nutritional count per serving 28.9g total fat (18.6g saturated fat); 1764kJ (422 cal); 25.2g carbohydrate; 14.6g protein; 2.7g fibre

the perfect rösti

PREP + COOK TIME 25 MINS • MAKES 8

TIPS

• The perfect rösti have a thick crunchy crust and are moist and buttery inside.

• Rösti are best served immediately but can be kept, loosely covered with foil, in a slow oven for up to an hour.

• Do not grate the potato until ready to cook the rösti to avoid discolouring.

• Use the largest holes of a four-sided grater to grate the potatoes coarsely.

1kg russet burbank potatoes, peeled
1 teaspoon salt
80g unsalted butter
2 tablespoons vegetable oil

1 Grate potatoes coarsely into large bowl; stir in salt, squeeze excess moisture from potatoes. Divide potato mixture into eight portions.
2 Heat 10g of the butter and 1 teaspoon of the oil in medium non-stick frying pan; spread one portion of the potato mixture over base of pan, flatten with spatula to form a firm pancake. Cook, uncovered, over medium heat, until golden brown on underside; shake pan to loosen rösti, then invert onto large plate. Gently slide rösti back into pan; cook, uncovered, until other side is golden brown and potato centre is tender. Drain on absorbent paper; cover to keep warm. Repeat with the same amounts of remaining butter, oil and potato mixture.

nutritional count per rösti 12.9g total fat (6g saturated fat); 823kJ (197 cal); 16.4g carbohydrate; 3.1g protein; 2g fibre

[1] scalloped potatoes
[2] the perfect rösti
[3] potato wedges [page 232]
[4] the perfect potato chip [page 232]

1

2

3

4

potato wedges

PREP + COOK TIME 50 MINS • SERVES 4

You could also use coliban or sebago potatoes for this recipe.

1kg kipfler potatoes, unpeeled
2 tablespoons olive oil

1 Preheat oven to 220°C/200°C fan-forced. Lightly oil two oven trays.
2 Cut each potato into wedges; toss wedges and oil in large bowl. Place wedges, in single layer, on trays; roast, uncovered, turning occasionally, about 40 minutes or until crisp and cooked through.

nutritional count per serving 9.4g total fat (1.3g saturated fat); 1041kJ (249 cal); 32.8g carbohydrate; 6g protein; 5g fibre

VARIATIONS These spice combinations can be tossed with the oil and potato wedges before roasting:
lemon pepper Combine 1 tablespoon finely grated lemon rind, 1 tablespoon lemon juice and ½ teaspoon freshly ground black pepper in small bowl.
cajun Combine ½ teaspoon ground oregano, 2 teaspoons ground cumin, 1 teaspoon hot paprika, ½ teaspoon ground black pepper, 1 teaspoon ground turmeric, 1 teaspoon ground coriander and ¼ teaspoon chilli powder in small bowl.

the perfect potato chip

PREP + COOK TIME 30 MINS (+ STANDING) • SERVES 4

TIP

• After the first cooking, the chips can stand for several hours before the final deep-frying.

• Corn oil or vegetable oil can also be used.

1kg russet burbank potatoes, peeled
peanut oil, for deep-frying

1 Cut potatoes lengthways into 1cm slices; cut each slice lengthways into 1cm-wide pieces. Stand potato pieces in large bowl of cold water for 30 minutes to avoid discolouration. Drain; pat dry with absorbent paper.
2 Heat oil in deep-fryer, wok or large saucepan; cook chips, in three batches, about 4 minutes each batch or until just tender but not browned. Drain on absorbent paper; stand 10 minutes.
3 Reheat oil; cook chips again, in three batches, separating any that stick together by shaking deep-fryer basket or with a slotted spoon, until crisp and golden brown. Drain on absorbent paper.

nutritional count per serving 12.8g total fat (2.3g saturated fat); 1162kJ (278 cal); 32.8g carbohydrate; 6g protein; 4g fibre

perfect mashed potato

PREP + COOK TIME 30 MINS • SERVES 4

This recipe makes the most lusciously smooth, fluffy, irresistible mash. Use potatoes high in starch and take care not to overcook them. Push the potato through a sieve, as suggested here, or through a potato ricer or food mill (mouli). You can also use pink-eye or sebago potatoes for this recipe.

1kg spunta potatoes, chopped coarsely
40g butter
¾ cup (180ml) hot milk

1 Boil, steam or microwave potatoes until tender; drain.
2 Using the back of a wooden spoon; push potato through fine sieve into large bowl. Stir in butter and milk.

nutritional count per serving 10.2g total fat (6.6g saturated fat); 1028kJ (246 cal); 30.1g carbohydrate; 6.7g protein; 3.4g fibre

celeriac puree

PREP + COOK TIME 35 MINS • SERVES 4

For celeriac mash to serve with meats, make this recipe with 500g of celeriac and use a wooden spoon to beat it into 500g of boiled, mashed potato – don't use a food processor as it will turn the potato to glue.

2 cups (500ml) chicken stock
1kg celeriac, trimmed, peeled, chopped coarsely
½ cup (125ml) pouring cream
1 tablespoon finely chopped fresh chives

1 Bring stock to the boil in medium saucepan; add celeriac, return to the boil. Reduce heat; simmer, covered, about 30 minutes or until celeriac is tender. Drain.
2 Blend or process celeriac in batches with cream until smooth.
3 Serve sprinkled with chives.

nutritional count per serving 14.4g total fat (9.2g saturated fat); 815kJ (195 cal); 7.4g carbohydrate; 5.2g protein; 8.8g fibre

serving ideas seafood, poultry or game birds such as quail or squab pigeon.

peas with mint butter

PREP + COOK TIME 10 MINS • SERVES 4

You need approximately 1kg fresh pea pods to get the required amount of shelled peas for this recipe.

2¼ cups (350g) fresh shelled peas
40g butter, softened
1 tablespoon finely chopped fresh mint
1 teaspoon finely grated lemon rind

1 Boil, steam or microwave peas until tender; drain.
2 Meanwhile, combine remaining ingredients in small bowl.
3 Serve peas topped with butter mixture.

nutritional count per serving 8.6g total fat (5.4g saturated fat); 589kJ (141 cal); 8.6g carbohydrate; 5.2g protein; 5g fibre

eggplant parmigiana

PREP + COOK TIME 1 HOUR • SERVES 6

This is Italian cooking at its rich and gorgeous best. And it's worth every kilojoule.

2 large eggplants (1kg)
olive oil, for shallow-frying
½ cup (75g) plain flour
4 eggs, beaten lightly
2 cups (200g) packaged breadcrumbs
750ml bottled tomato pasta sauce
1 cup (100g) coarsely grated mozzarella cheese
¼ cup (20g) finely grated parmesan cheese
⅓ cup loosely packed fresh oregano leaves

1 Using vegetable peeler, peel random strips of skin from eggplants; discard skins. Slice eggplants thinly.
2 Heat oil in large frying pan.
3 Coat eggplant in flour; shake off excess. Dip in egg, then in breadcrumbs. Shallow-fry eggplant, in batches, until browned lightly. Drain on absorbent paper.
4 Preheat oven to 200°C/180°C fan-forced.
5 Spread about one-third of the pasta sauce over base of greased 2.5-litre (10-cup) ovenproof dish. Top with about one-third of the eggplant, one-third of the cheeses and one-third of the oregano. Repeat layering.
6 Bake eggplant, covered, 20 minutes. Uncover; bake about 10 minutes or until browned lightly.

nutritional count per serving 27.5g total fat (6.8g saturated fat); 2257kJ (540 cal); 49.4g carbohydrate; 19.9g protein; 8.3g fibre

Using a vegetable peeler, peel off random strips of skin from the eggplant. Slice eggplant thinly with a sharp knife. Repeat steps for the remaining eggplant.

Dip eggplant slices in flour to coat all over and shake off excess. Dip into beaten egg, then coat with breadcrumbs.

Arrange one-third of the fried eggplant slices over pasta sauce in an ovenproof dish. Top with one-third of the cheese mixture and one-third of the oregano. Repeat layering until ingredients have been used up.

corn fritters

PREP + COOK TIME 40 MINS • MAKES 18

These corn fritters are perfect for a light meal or afternoon snack that kids will love. Add bacon, sweet chilli sauce or an assortment of fresh herbs for variation.

1 cup (150g) self-raising flour
½ teaspoon bicarbonate of soda
1 teaspoon ground cumin
¾ cup (180ml) milk
2 eggs, separated
2 cups (330g) fresh corn kernels
2 green onions, sliced finely
2 tablespoons finely chopped fresh coriander

1 Sift flour, soda and cumin into medium bowl. Gradually whisk in milk and egg yolks until batter is smooth.
2 Beat egg whites in small bowl with electric mixer until soft peaks form.
3 Stir corn, onion and coriander into batter; fold in egg whites.
4 Pour 2 tablespoons of the batter for each fritter into heated oiled large frying pan; spread batter into round shape. Cook fritters about 2 minutes each side. Remove from pan; cover to keep warm.
5 Repeat step 4 to make a total of 18 fritters. Fritters can be served with tomato chutney and fresh coriander leaves.

nutritional count per fritter 1.3g total fat (0.5g saturated fat); 263kJ (63 cal); 9.9g carbohydrate; 2.7g protein; 1.2g fibre

TIP
• You can use 425g can corn kernels, rinsed and drained, instead of the fresh corn kernels, if you like.

roasted balsamic onions

PREP + COOK TIME 1 HOUR • SERVES 4

These onions can be made ahead and served hot with steak, pan-fried veal, liver and bacon or roast beef, or cold with any cold meat or poultry.

2 medium red onions (340g), quartered
2 medium brown onions (300g), quartered
2 bulbs garlic, halved horizontally
2 tablespoons olive oil
1 tablespoon balsamic vinegar
1 tablespoon brown sugar

1 Preheat oven to 220°C/200°C fan-forced.
2 Combine ingredients in medium baking dish.
3 Roast, brushing occasionally with pan juices, about 40 minutes or until onions and garlic are tender and caramelised.

nutritional count per serving 9.8g total fat (1.4g saturated fat); 702kJ (168 cal); 13.9g carbohydrate; 3.5g protein; 5.6g fibre

[opposite] corn fritters

sautéed mushrooms

PREP + COOK TIME 30 MINS • SERVES 4

Peeling mushrooms is time-consuming and unnecessary; many nutrients and much of the flavour is found in the skin. The best way to prepare mushrooms is to wipe them over using damp absorbent paper. This removes any grit and prevents them becoming soggy. They become waterlogged if washed, making them difficult to sauté (they tend to steam in the pan and lose their beautiful flavour).

50g butter, chopped
1 small brown onion (80g), chopped finely
500g button mushrooms, halved
1 tablespoon malt vinegar
⅓ cup coarsely chopped fresh chives

1 Melt butter in large frying pan; cook onion, stirring, until soft.
2 Add mushrooms; cook, stirring occasionally, 10 minutes or until mushrooms are tender. Add vinegar; bring to the boil. Remove from heat; stir in chives.
3 Serve mushrooms on thick toast, if desired.

nutritional count per serving 10.7g total fat (6.8g saturated fat); 531kJ (127 cal); 1.7g carbohydrate; 4.9g protein; 3.5g fibre

steamed asian greens with char siu sauce

PREP + COOK TIME 15 MINS • SERVES 4

Almost every vegetable can be steamed, and this is an excellent way to cook them because they retain their shape, flavour, colour and goodness. Trim and prepare the vegetables as you would normally then layer them evenly in the steamer basket. Food can still be overcooked in a steamer, especially green vegetables which will lose their bright colour and look dull and dry, so keep an eye on them.

1 fresh long red chilli, sliced thinly
350g broccolini, trimmed
150g snow peas, trimmed
2 baby buk choy (300g), halved
2 tablespoons char siu sauce
2 teaspoons sesame oil
1 tablespoon peanut oil
1 tablespoon toasted sesame seeds

1 Layer chilli, broccolini, snow peas and buk choy in baking-paper-lined bamboo steamer. Steam, covered, over wok of simmering water about 5 minutes or until vegetables are just tender.
2 Combine vegetables, sauce and sesame oil in large bowl.
3 Heat peanut oil in small saucepan until hot; pour oil over vegetable mixture then toss to combine. Serve sprinkled with seeds.

nutritional count per serving 9.5g total fat (1.4g saturated fat); 635kJ (152 cal); 7g carbohydrate; 6.6g protein; 6.6g fibre

lemon and ricotta-filled zucchini flowers

PREP + COOK TIME 45 MINS • SERVES 4

250g ricotta cheese
2 tablespoons finely grated parmesan cheese
1 teaspoon finely grated lemon rind
1 tablespoon lemon juice
1 tablespoon finely chopped fresh mint
2 tablespoons roasted pine nuts
12 zucchini flowers with stem attached (240g)

1 Combine cheeses, rind, juice, mint and nuts in small bowl.
2 Discard stamens from inside zucchini flowers; fill flowers with cheese mixture, twist petal tops to enclose filling.
3 Place zucchini flowers, in single layer, in large bamboo steamer, over large saucepan of boiling water. Steam, covered, about 20 minutes or until zucchini are tender.
nutritional count per serving 13.4g total fat (5.5g saturated fat); 711kJ (170 cal); 2.2g carbohydrate; 9.6g protein; 1.4g fibre

cauliflower gratin

PREP + COOK TIME 30 MINS • SERVES 6

This is a delicious way to enjoy nutritious cauliflower and fantastic for introducing the unusual tasting vegie to the kids. Serve as a side-dish to a roast or on its own as a healthy alternative to macaroni cheese.

Of course you can use 750g of regular-sized cauliflower, cut into florets, in place of the babies.

6 baby cauliflowers (750g), trimmed
50g butter
¼ cup (35g) plain flour
1½ cups (375ml) hot milk
½ cup (60g) coarsely grated cheddar cheese
¼ cup (20g) finely grated parmesan cheese
1 tablespoon packaged breadcrumbs

1 Preheat oven to 220°C/200°C fan-forced.
2 Boil, steam or microwave cauliflowers until tender; drain. Place in medium shallow ovenproof dish.
3 Meanwhile, melt butter in medium saucepan, add flour; cook, stirring, until mixture bubbles and thickens. Gradually stir in milk until smooth; cook, stirring, until mixture boils and thickens. Remove from heat, stir in cheeses.
4 Pour cheese sauce over cauliflower in dish; sprinkle with breadcrumbs. Bake about 15 minutes or until browned lightly.
nutritional count per serving 14.1g total fat (9g saturated fat); 865kJ (207 cal); 10.2g carbohydrate; 9.1g protein; 2.2g fibre

EGGS

Eggs

Late Saturday breakfasts just wouldn't be the same without the scrumptious promise of scrambled eggs on toast. And isn't it always comforting to have the fall-back of a hard-boiled egg for an easy Sunday night snack or a toddler's dinner? Eggs provide us with so many simple pleasures. And delicious ones, too: where would we be without soothing custards, melt-in-the-mouth quiches, sublime hollandaise, dreamy soufflés and meringues, perfectly rich cakes and creamy sauces made silky by the inclusion of our beloved egg?

EGG VARIETIES AND SIZES

HEN EGGS These are the eggs most commonly used in cooking and they are available in small (about 50g), medium (about 55g) and large (about 60g) sizes. Most recipes call for the larger size to be used. For cakes, use the large size unless the recipe specifies otherwise.

DUCK EGGS These are larger than hen eggs, with an average size of 90g, and are richer-tasting. They're harder to find than hen eggs, and you'll need to do your research to find a local supplier. They can be used in the same way as hen eggs but are used mainly for baking and making custards: duck egg whites do not whisk up well.

QUAIL EGGS Regarded more as a gourmet ingredient, quail eggs are available from specialist suppliers. These little eggs taste like hen eggs and are prized for their miniature charm.

BUYING AND STORING

You can taste and see the difference in eggs gathered fresh from the chook shed. Free-range eggs come from happier hens and do taste much better. But the 'free-range' label you see in big supermarkets is not always all you'd imagine. If you're buying free-range eggs because you're concerned about animal welfare, look for eggs that are certified by the RSPCA or you could buy certified organic eggs (check the labels) or go to a farmers' market to find eggs with independent free-range certification.

Eggs are perishable and need to be stored in the fridge in their carton to protect them from odours which might penetrate their porous shells. Always check eggs for cracks and leaks before placing the carton in your shopping trolley. If you find cracks or leaks once you're back home, throw the egg away.

Fresh eggs, stored in their carton, should keep for 3 to 4 weeks. Hard-boiled eggs will keep for a week and leftover egg dishes need to be consumed within 3 to 4 days. To check the freshness of a raw egg, place it in a bowl of water: fresh eggs will sink to the bottom while stale eggs will float with the big end upward.

HOW DO YOU LIKE YOUR EGGS?

POACHED The chefs' method of gently lowering eggs, one at a time, into a deep, large saucepan of simmering water works well, but it takes practice to perfect. Here's how you can do it at home: half-fill a lidded frying pan with water, add a dash of white vinegar and bring to the boil. Break each egg into a cup. When the water boils, add the eggs; allow the water to return to the boil then immediately move the pan off the heat, put the lid on and stand for 4 minutes or until a light film of egg white has set over the yolks. Use a slotted spoon to lift out each egg, place it for a moment (still on the spoon) on absorbent paper and serve immediately. Poach no more than three or four eggs at a time.

FRIED Over medium heat, melt enough butter, bacon fat or oil in a frying pan to cover the bottom. Break each egg into a cup. When the butter begins to give off a haze, slide the eggs into the pan – the butter should sizzle gently; if not, adjust the heat. Spoon butter over the yolks to set the "veil" of white. When the whites are set but the yolks still wobble, use a spatula to remove eggs. Serve at once.

BOILED There are two methods for boiled eggs:
1. Place eggs in salted boiling water, boil gently for 3 minutes for soft yolks and firm whites, or 7 minutes for hard-boiled eggs. Drain and place immediately into cold water. Tap eggs all over to crack the shell then stand in water a few minutes before peeling.
2. Place eggs snugly in a saucepan, barely cover with cold water, cover with a lid and bring to the boil. As soon as the water boils, remove lid and boil gently 2½ minutes for soft or 7 minutes for hard-boiled.

SCRAMBLED For this Saturday breakfast favourite, whisk two to three eggs per person with salt, pepper and a tablespoon of milk or cream per egg. Have ready any additional ingredients such as herbs or smoked fish. Over low heat, melt enough butter in a frying pan to cover the bottom generously. When the butter foams slightly, add the eggs and stir with a wooden spoon, reaching right to the edges. When the eggs are a little softer than you want them, add the herbs etc, stir once more, remove from heat and serve immediately.

SEPARATING EGGS

Have ready two non-plastic bowls and a cup – dry and grease-free. Crack an egg open and, holding your hand over the cup, tip the contents of the egg onto your hand, allowing the white to run through your fingers into the cup, and gently cradling the yolk. Carefully drop the yolk into a bowl. Check the white is free of shell and yolk, then tip it into the other bowl. Scoop tiny bits of shell in the white out with a larger piece of shell. If any yolk spills into the white it will prevent it from beating up properly, so must be discarded.

BEATING EGG WHITES

Place the egg whites in clean, dry bowl. A copper bowl is ideal (copper reacts with whites to form a very stable foam), though glass, stainless steel or china bowls are also fine. A stand-alone electric mixer is recommended for beating egg whites, though a whisk or hand-held electric beater also work well. All utensils must be dry and grease-free. Whisk plain whites until they form foamy, drooping peaks. For meringue, start adding sugar gradually at the soft-foam stage and continue whisking until the mixture forms soft upright peaks.

poached egg

PREP + COOK TIME 5 MINS • MAKES 4

Fresh eggs are essential for perfect poaching. Most store-bought eggs will have a best-before date, however if in doubt place the egg in question in a bowl of water. A fresh egg will lie on the bottom, while a stale egg will float, big end up.

2 teaspoons white vinegar
4 eggs

1 Half-fill a large shallow frying pan with water; add vinegar. Bring to the boil.
2 Break 1 egg into a small bowl or cup. Swirl the boiling water with a spoon, then slide egg into pan. Repeat with three more eggs. When all eggs are in pan, allow water to return to the boil.
3 Cover pan, turn off heat; stand about 4 minutes or until a light film of egg white sets over yolks.
4 Remove the egg with a slotted spoon and drain on absorbent paper.
nutritional count per egg 5.3g total fat (1.6g saturated fat); 309kJ (74 cal); 0.2g carbohydrate; 6.7g protein; 0g fibre

Make a whirlpool in the pan of boiling water using a wooden spoon. Putting the eggs into the whirlpool will help keep the whites in a neat shape.

Break one egg into a small bowl or cup and gently slide it into the whirlpool. Continue with remaining eggs. Return the water to the boil.

Use a slotted spoon to remove the eggs and drain them on absorbent paper. At this stage you can trim the whites if they look ragged.

Q&A

My poached eggs always look untidy, never like the eggs I get in cafés.

Most poached eggs come out of the pan with ragged edges. Once you've drained them, place them on a cutting board and quickly trim the edges of the whites with a small sharp knife – it's what chefs do.

poached eggs and smoked salmon on blini

PREP + COOK TIME 30 MINS • SERVES 4

This luxurious café style breakfast is just as good for a casual lunch or Sunday supper.

8 eggs
200g sliced smoked salmon
2 tablespoons sour cream
1 tablespoon coarsely chopped fresh chives

blini
⅓ cup (50g) buckwheat flour
2 tablespoons plain flour
1 teaspoon baking powder
1 egg
½ cup (125ml) buttermilk
30g butter, melted

1 Make blini.
2 To poach eggs, half-fill a large shallow frying pan with water; bring to the boil. Break 1 egg into a small bowl or cup then slide into pan. Working quickly, repeat process with three more eggs. When all 4 eggs are in pan, return water to the boil. Cover pan, turn off heat; stand about 4 minutes or until a light film of white sets over each yolk. Remove each egg with a slotted spoon and drain on absorbent paper; cover to keep warm. Repeat with remaining eggs.
3 Serve blini topped with eggs, salmon, sour cream and chives.
blini Sift flours and baking powder into medium bowl; gradually whisk in combined egg and buttermilk until mixture is smooth. Stir in butter. Cook blini, in batches, by dropping 1 tablespoon of the batter into heated oiled large frying pan. Cook blini until browned both sides; you will have 12 blini. Cover to keep warm.
nutritional count per serving 25.9g total fat (11.3g saturated fat); 1731kJ (414 cal); 14.1g carbohydrate; 31.5g protein; 1.6g fibre

boiled eggs

PREP + COOK TIME 10 MINS • MAKES 4

To peel boiled eggs, crack the shells gently and leave immersed in cold water at least 5 minutes or until cold. Remove shells, starting from broad end. Wash the eggs, then pat dry using absorbent paper.

4 eggs

1 Place eggs in medium saucepan; add enough cold water to cover eggs. Stir constantly using wooden spoon over high heat until water boils; this will centralise each yolk.
2 Boil, uncovered, until yolks are as soft or as firm as you like. As a guide, 3 minutes will give you set egg white and soft yolk. After 5 minutes, the yolk will be set.
3 Place saucepan of eggs under cold running water about 1 minute or until eggs are cool. This will stop a dark ring forming around the yolk.
nutritional count per egg 5.3g total fat (1.6g saturated fat); 309kJ (74 cal); 0.2g carbohydrate; 6.7g protein; 0g fibre

[opposite] poached eggs and smoked salmon on blini

eggs benedict

PREP + COOK TIME 50 MINS • SERVES 4

8 eggs
4 english muffins
200g shaved leg ham
¼ cup finely chopped fresh chives
hollandaise sauce
1½ tablespoons white wine vinegar
1 tablespoon lemon juice
½ teaspoon black peppercorns
2 egg yolks
125g unsalted butter, melted

1 Make hollandaise sauce.
2 To poach eggs, half-fill a large shallow frying pan with water; bring to the boil. Break 1 egg into a cup then slide into pan. Working quickly, repeat process with three more eggs. When all 4 eggs are in pan, return water to the boil. Cover pan, turn off heat; stand about 4 minutes or until a light film of white sets over each yolk. Remove each egg with a slotted spoon and drain on absorbent paper; cover to keep warm. Repeat with remaining eggs.
3 Meanwhile, split muffins in half and toast. Serve muffins topped with ham, poached eggs, sauce and chives.
hollandaise sauce Bring vinegar, juice and peppercorns to the boil in small saucepan. Reduce heat; simmer, uncovered, until liquid is reduced by half. Strain through a fine sieve into small heatproof bowl; cool 10 minutes. Whisk egg yolks into vinegar mixture. Set bowl over small saucepan of simmering water; do not allow water to touch base of bowl. Whisk mixture over heat until thickened. Remove bowl from heat; gradually whisk in melted butter in a thin steady stream, whisking constantly until sauce is thick and creamy.
nutritional count per serving 40.6g total fat (21.2g saturated fat); 2450kJ (586 cal); 24.2g carbohydrate; 30.8g protein; 2g fibre

Can hollandaise sauce be made in advance and warmed up just before serving? I'd love to make eggs benedict when I'm having friends around for breakfast, but I'm not confident that I can make the hollandaise when I'm short of time.

Hollandaise can be kept warm for about an hour (place the bowl of hollandaise in a larger bowl of warm water) but it really is a sauce that has to be eaten fresh. We suggest you make eggs benedict for a late (rather than early) breakfast to allow yourself time to make the sauce.

creamy scrambled eggs

PREP + COOK TIME 20 MINS • SERVES 4

For light, fluffy scrambled eggs cook them over medium heat and stir gently-yet-consistently. Add chives (parsley is great too) when the eggs are a bit softer than you would like. Once cooked, be sure to remove the mixture from the pan immediately so it does not continue to cook and become dry.

8 eggs
½ cup (125ml) pouring cream
2 tablespoons finely chopped fresh chives
30g butter

1 Place eggs, cream and chives in medium bowl; beat lightly with fork.
2 Heat butter in large frying pan over low heat. Add egg mixture, wait a few seconds, then use a wide spatula to gently scrape the set egg mixture along the base of the pan; cook until creamy and barely set.
3 Serve eggs immediately, with toast, if you like.

nutritional count per serving 30.2g total fat (16.2g saturated fat); 1375kJ (329 cal); 1.3g carbohydrate; 14g protein; 0g fibre

Whisk the eggs, cream and chives together lightly with a fork.

Melt the butter and add the egg mixture. The heat should not be too high otherwise the eggs will become dry instead of creamy.

Fold the egg mixture from the edge of the pan to the centre. Remove from heat when eggs are still creamy and barely set.

Q&A

My scrambled eggs break into big pieces and are always a bit dry. I make them with low-fat milk and butter. Is there any way I can make them soft and creamy without using cream?

The softest, creamiest and most luxurious scrambled eggs are made with cream, but that does make them high in fat. You'll never get really creamy scrambled eggs using low-fat milk, but they'll still be good if you cook them slowly. Don't think of scrambled eggs as a quick dish. Instead, cook them over a low heat, stirring all the time, until they are set – this will take about 10 minutes.

asian crab and rice omelette

PREP + COOK TIME 40 MINS • SERVES 4

Water is added to the eggs because, when heated, the water turns to steam giving the omelette a light texture.

If you prefer the filling to be more evenly distributed throughout the omelette, add the rice mixture to the whisked eggs, before adding them to the pan.

¼ cup (60ml) peanut oil
4 green onions, chopped finely
2 fresh small red thai chillies, chopped finely
1 tablespoon red curry paste
2 cups cold cooked jasmine rice
250g fresh crab meat, shredded
2 tablespoons lime juice
2 tablespoons fish sauce
8 eggs
2 tablespoons water

1 Heat 1 tablespoon of the oil in wok; stir-fry onion and chilli until onion softens. Add curry paste; stir-fry until fragrant.
2 Add rice; stir-fry until heated through. Place fried rice in large bowl; add crab, juice and sauce, toss to combine.
3 Whisk eggs with the water in medium bowl. Heat about a quarter of remaining oil in same cleaned wok. Pour a quarter of the egg mixture into wok; cook over medium heat, tilting pan, until almost set.
4 Spoon a quarter of the rice mixture into centre of omelette; using spatula, fold four sides of omelette over to enclose filling. Press omelette firmly with spatula; turn carefully to brown other side. Remove omelette from wok; cover to keep warm. Repeat with remaining oil, egg and crab fried rice a further three times.
nutritional count per serving 26.6g total fat (5.9g saturated fat); 1927kJ (461 cal); 29.4g carbohydrate; 24.9g protein; 2g fibre
serving idea serve with a mixed green salad.

Add the cold cooked rice in batches to the onion mixture in the wok and stir in before adding the next batch. This prevents the rice from clumping together as it fries.

When the omelette is almost set, place a quarter of the rice mixture in the centre.

Use a spatula (or your hands, carefully) to fold the four sides of the omelette over the filling to form a parcel. Remove from pan and cover to keep warm.

spinach scrambled eggs

PREP + COOK TIME 20 MINS • SERVES 4

20g butter
75g spinach leaves
8 slices pancetta
8 eggs
½ cup (125ml) light pouring cream
4 slices crusty bread

1 Heat half of the butter in large frying pan, add spinach; cook until spinach just wilts. Drain on absorbent paper; cover to keep warm.
2 Preheat grill. Place pancetta under grill until crisp; cover to keep warm.
3 Whisk eggs and cream in medium bowl until combined.
4 Heat remaining butter in same cleaned pan over medium heat. Add egg mixture; wait a few seconds, then using a wide spatula, gently scrape the set egg mixture along the base of the pan; cook until creamy and just set.
5 Meanwhile, toast bread. Top toast with pancetta, scrambled eggs and spinach.
nutritional count per serving 25.7g total fat (11.7g saturated fat); 1559kJ (373 cal); 14.4g carbohydrate; 21.7g protein; 1.1g fibre

fried eggs and bacon

PREP + COOK TIME 25 MINS • SERVES 2

For a good fried egg, place a non-stick frying pan over medium heat, melt enough butter, bacon fat or oil to cover the bottom. Break each egg into a small bowl or cup. When the butter begins to give off a haze, slide the eggs into the pan – the butter should sizzle gently; if not, adjust the heat. Spoon butter over the yolks to set the "veil" of white. When the whites are set but the yolks still wobble, use a spatula to lift the eggs out and serve at once.

4 rindless bacon rashers (260g)
1 tablespoon vegetable oil
4 eggs
1 medium tomato (190g), halved

1 Cook bacon in oiled medium frying pan until browned and cooked as desired. Remove from pan; cover to keep warm.
2 Add oil to same pan; break eggs into pan or into greased egg rings in pan. Cook, uncovered, until egg white has set and yolk is cooked as desired.
3 Meanwhile, preheat grill. Place tomato, cut-side up, onto baking tray; season to taste. Place tomato under grill until browned lightly and just tender.
4 Divide eggs, bacon and tomato among serving plates.
nutritional count per serving 26.3g total fat (6.8g saturated fat); 1522kJ (364 cal); 2.4g carbohydrate; 29.4g protein; 1.1g fibre
serving ideas slices of toast.

[opposite] spinach scrambled eggs

denver omelette

PREP + COOK TIME 25 MINS • SERVES 4

This omelette is called a "western" in most states east of the Mississippi River and a "denver" in the western half of the United States. Its origins are based more on folklore than fact, but it's believed to have been an Americanisation of the classic egg foo yung served by Chinese cooks to the work gangs building the east-to-west-coast railway link in the 1840s. Today in the USA, the denver is often cooked, cooled, doused in tomato sauce then eaten between slices of white bread.

10 eggs
⅓ cup (80g) sour cream
2 fresh small red thai chillies, chopped finely
2 teaspoons vegetable oil
3 green onions, sliced thinly
1 medium green capsicum (200g), chopped finely
100g leg ham, chopped finely
2 small tomatoes (260g), seeded, chopped finely
½ cup (60g) coarsely grated cheddar cheese

1 Break eggs in large bowl, whisk lightly; whisk in sour cream and chilli.
2 Heat oil in large non-stick frying pan; cook onion and capsicum, stirring, until onion softens. Place onion mixture in medium bowl with ham, tomato and cheese; toss to combine.
3 Pour ½ cup of the egg mixture into same lightly oiled frying pan; cook, tilting pan, over low heat until almost set. Sprinkle about ⅓ cup of the filling over half of the omelette; using spatula, fold omelette over to completely cover the filling.
4 Pour ¼ cup of the egg mixture into empty half of pan; cook over low heat until almost set. Sprinkle about ⅓ cup of the filling over folded omelette, fold omelette over top of first omelette to cover filling. Repeat twice more, using ¼ cup of the egg mixture each time, to form one large layered omelette. Carefully slide omelette onto plate; cover to keep warm.
5 Repeat steps 3 and 4 to make second omelette, using remaining egg and filling. Cut each denver omelette in half.

nutritional count per serving 30.2g total fat (13.4g saturated fat); 1639kJ (392 cal); 3.5g carbohydrate; 26.7g protein; 1.3g fibre

zucchini and mushroom omelette

PREP + COOK TIME 20 MINS • SERVES 1

10g butter
1 clove garlic, crushed
25g button mushrooms, sliced thinly
¼ cup (50g) coarsely grated zucchini
1 green onion, chopped finely
2 eggs
1 tablespoon water
¼ cup (30g) coarsely grated cheddar cheese

Drain the zucchini well before stirring into the pan by either squeezing it in your hands or in absorbent paper. This is a single serving omelette but you can increase the ingredients proportionately with no problem. If doubling it, the omelette can be cooked all at once but if you want the finished product to serve four, make two omelettes.

1 Heat half of the butter in small frying pan; cook garlic and mushroom, stirring, over medium heat about 2 minutes or until mushroom is lightly browned. Add zucchini and onion; cook, stirring, about 1 minute or until zucchini begins to soften. Remove vegetable mixture from pan; cover to keep warm.
2 Beat eggs and the water in small bowl. Add cheese; whisk until combined.
3 Heat remaining butter in same pan; swirl pan so butter covers base. Pour egg mixture into pan; cook, tilting pan, over medium heat until almost set.
4 Place vegetable mixture evenly over half of the omelette; using spatula, flip other half over vegetable mixture. Using spatula, slide omelette gently onto serving plate.

nutritional count per serving 11.7g total fat (6.1g saturated fat); 606kJ (145 cal); 0.8g carbohydrate; 8.9g protein; 0.9g fibre

egg-white omelette

PREP + COOK TIME 45 MINS • SERVES 4

It's criminal to waste the 12 egg yolks here, especially when you can freeze them for another day. Drop a single yolk into each section of an ice cube tray then cover the tray and freeze, popping out the yolks as your needs dictate.

Some recipes that call for lots of egg yolks are hollandaise, aïoli, custard, lemon curd, crème brûlée, pots de crème, crème anglaise and zabaglione.

12 egg whites
4 green onions, chopped finely
¼ cup finely chopped fresh chives
¼ cup finely chopped fresh chervil
½ cup finely chopped fresh flat-leaf parsley
½ cup (60g) coarsely grated cheddar cheese
½ cup (50g) coarsely grated mozzarella cheese

1 Preheat grill.
2 Beat a quarter of the egg white in small bowl with electric mixer until soft peaks form; fold in a quarter of the combined onion and herbs.
3 Pour mixture into heated oiled 20cm non-stick frying pan; cook over low heat until omelette is just browned lightly on the bottom.
4 Sprinkle a quarter of the combined cheeses on half of the omelette. Place pan under grill until cheese begins to melt and omelette sets; fold omelette over to completely cover cheese. Carefully slide onto serving plate; cover to keep warm.
5 Repeat process three times with remaining egg white, onion and herb mixture, and cheeses.

nutritional count per serving 7.9g total fat (5g saturated fat); 620kJ (148 cal); 1.1g carbohydrate; 18.2g protein; 0.7g fibre

baked eggs

PREP + COOK TIME 25 MINS • SERVES 4

This is the perfect brunch dish for entertaining, as you don't have to stand over it while it cooks. Sprinkle chopped fresh parsley over the top of the baked eggs to add gorgeous colour and flavour.

1 tablespoon olive oil
100g prosciutto, chopped finely
100g button mushrooms, chopped finely
4 green onions, chopped finely
100g slightly underripe brie cheese, chopped coarsely
8 eggs

1 Preheat oven to 200°C/ 180°C fan-forced. Grease four ¾-cup (180ml) shallow ovenproof dishes.
2 Heat oil in medium frying pan; cook prosciutto and mushrooms, stirring, until onion softens. Remove pan from heat; stir in half of the cheese. Divide prosciutto mixture among dishes; break two eggs into each dish.
3 Bake, uncovered, 5 minutes. Increase oven to 220°C/200°C fan-forced.
4 Sprinkle remaining cheese over eggs; bake, uncovered, about 5 minutes or until eggs set and cheese melts.

nutritional count per serving 25.3g total fat (9.5g saturated fat); 1388kJ (332 cal); 1.3g carbohydrate; 25.6g protein; 0.9g fibre

mini pea and pancetta frittatas

PREP + COOK TIME 30 MINS • MAKES 36

Use fresh peas when you can on this recipe for a burst of flavour.

1 teaspoon olive oil
4 slices pancetta (60g), chopped finely
1 clove garlic, crushed
6 eggs
⅔ cup (160ml) pouring cream
½ cup (60g) frozen peas
⅓ cup (25g) finely grated parmesan cheese
1 tablespoon finely chopped fresh mint
1 teaspoon finely grated lemon rind
2 tablespoons crème fraîche
36 small fresh mint leaves

1 Preheat oven to 200°C/180°C fan-forced. Grease three 12-hole (1-tablespoon/20ml) mini muffin pans.
2 Heat oil in small frying pan; cook pancetta and garlic, stirring, until pancetta is crisp. Cool.
3 Whisk eggs and cream in large jug; stir in pancetta mixture, peas, cheese, mint and rind. Pour egg mixture into pan holes.
4 Bake frittatas about 12 minutes or until set. Stand in pan 5 minutes before serving topped with crème fraîche and mint leaves.

nutritional count per frittata 3.8g total fat (2.1g saturated fat); 178kJ (43 cal); 0.4g carbohydrate; 1.9g protein; 0.1g fibre

[1] baked eggs
[2] mini pea and pancetta frittatas
[3] goat's cheese soufflé [page 260]
[4] spanish tortilla [page 260]

1

2

3

4

goat's cheese soufflé

PREP + COOK TIME 40 MINS (+ COOLING) • SERVES 6

Many cooks believe the key to perfectly risen soufflés is "bottom heat". Preheat an oven tray, place the filled ramekins onto this, and return to the oven immediately.

cooking-oil spray
¼ cup (25g) packaged breadcrumbs
30g butter
2 tablespoons plain flour
1 cup (250ml) milk
4 eggs, separated
¼ teaspoon cayenne pepper
150g firm goat's cheese, crumbled

creamed spinach sauce
180g baby spinach leaves
⅔ cup (160ml) pouring cream, warmed

1 Preheat oven to 200°C/ 180°C fan-forced. Spray six 1-cup (250ml) soufflé dishes with cooking-oil spray, sprinkle with breadcrumbs; place on oven tray.
2 Melt butter in small saucepan, add flour; cook, stirring, until mixture bubbles and thickens. Gradually add milk; stir until mixture boils and thickens. Transfer to large bowl; stir in egg yolks, pepper and cheese. Cool 5 minutes.
3 Beat egg whites in small bowl with electric mixer until soft peaks form; gently fold whites, in two batches, into cheese mixture. Divide mixture among dishes.
4 Bake soufflés about 15 minutes or until puffed and browned lightly.
5 Meanwhile, make creamed spinach sauce.
6 Serve soufflés with sauce.
creamed spinach sauce Boil, steam or microwave spinach until just wilted; drain. Using hand, squeeze out excess liquid. Blend or process spinach until almost smooth. With motor operating, gradually add cream; process until smooth.
nutritional count per serving 26g total fat (15.2g saturated fat); 1315kJ (314 cal); 8.8g carbohydrate; 11.4g protein; 1.1g fibre

spanish tortilla

PREP + COOK TIME 45 MINS • SERVES 4

800g russet burbank potatoes, peeled, sliced thinly
1 tablespoon olive oil
1 large brown onion (200g), sliced thinly
200g chorizo sausage, sliced thinly
6 eggs, beaten lightly
300ml pouring cream
4 green onions, sliced thickly
¼ cup (25g) coarsely grated mozzarella cheese
¼ cup (30g) coarsely grated cheddar cheese

A Spanish tortilla is an omelette made predominantly with potato. It tastes great served warm or at room temperature, and makes an excellent breakfast, lunch, dinner or appetiser with drinks.

1 Boil, steam or microwave potato until just tender; drain.
2 Meanwhile, heat oil in medium frying pan; cook brown onion, stirring, until softened. Add chorizo; cook, stirring, until crisp. Remove from pan; drain on absorbent paper.
3 Whisk eggs in large bowl with cream, green onion and cheeses; stir in potato and chorizo mixture.
4 Pour mixture into heated oiled medium non-stick frying pan; cook, covered, over low heat about 10 minutes or until tortilla is just set. Carefully invert tortilla onto plate, then slide back into pan; cook, uncovered, about 5 minutes or until cooked through.

nutritional count per serving 64.1g total fat (32.5g saturated fat); 3390kJ (811 cal); 29.1g carbohydrate; 30g protein; 3.8g fibre

potato frittata with smoked salmon

PREP + COOK TIME 45 MINS • SERVES 4

You will need a medium ovenproof frying pan with a 17cm base for this recipe.

20g butter
1 tablespoon olive oil
2 medium potatoes (400g), cut into 1cm pieces
1 green onion, chopped finely
8 eggs

¼ cup (60ml) pouring cream
⅓ cup (25g) finely grated parmesan cheese
1 tablespoon finely chopped fresh dill
200g smoked salmon
2 tablespoons sour cream

1 Preheat oven to 220°C/200°C fan-forced.
2 Heat butter and oil in medium frying pan; cook potato, stirring occasionally, until browned and tender. Add onion; cook, stirring gently, 1 minute.
3 Meanwhile, whisk eggs, cream, cheese and dill in medium jug. Pour into pan; stir gently. Cook frittata over medium heat, about 2 minutes or until bottom sets. Place pan in oven; cook, uncovered, about 10 minutes or until frittata sets.
4 Slide frittata onto serving plate; serve topped with salmon, sour cream and some extra dill, if you like.

nutritional count per serving 34.1g total fat (15.2g saturated fat); 2031kJ (486 cal); 14.3g carbohydrate; 30.2g protein; 2.1g fibre

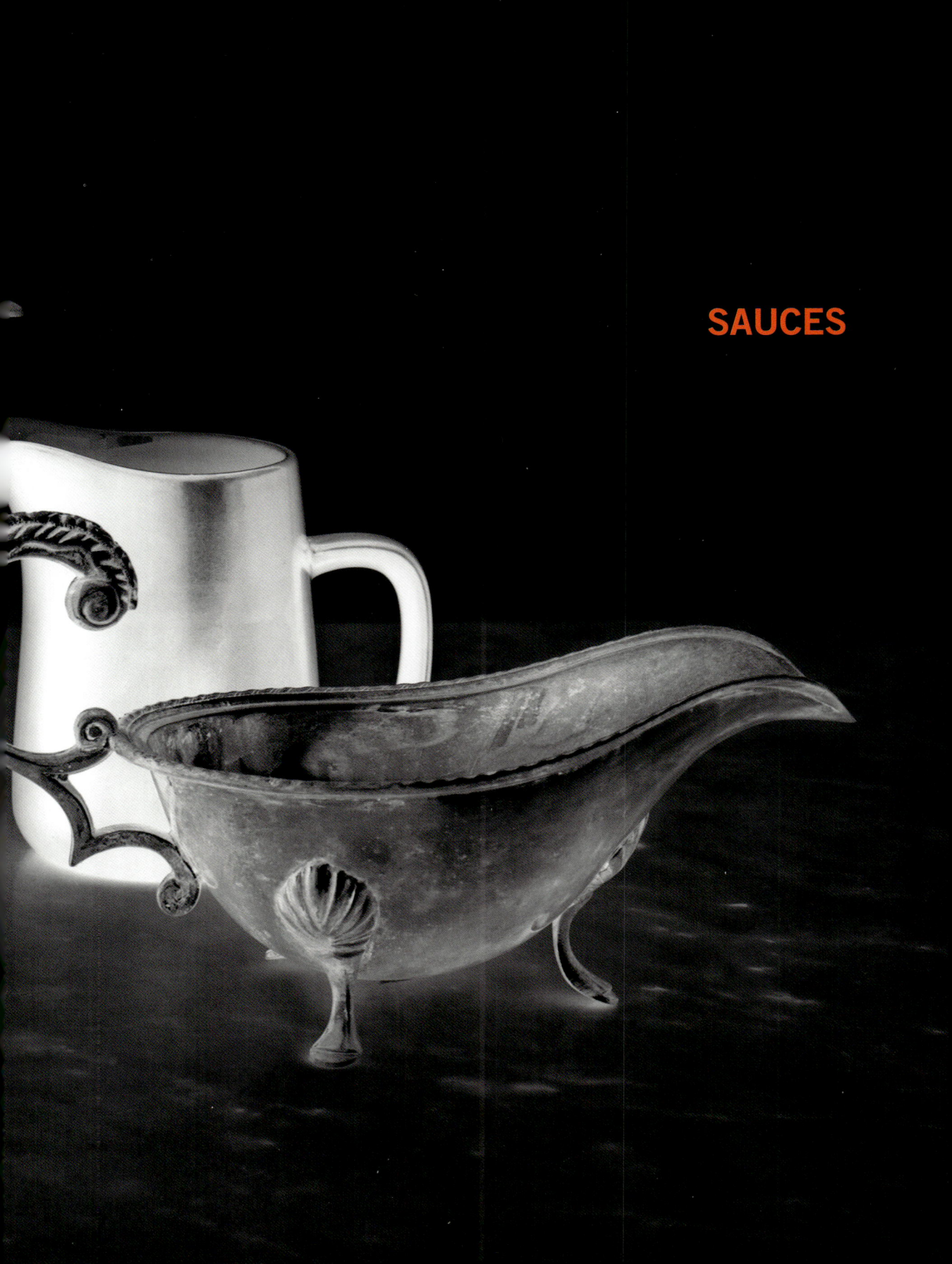

SAUCES

Sauces

A great sauce can add the perfect finishing touch to a dish, lifting it from merely more-ish to memorable. Having a few classic sauce recipes up your sleeve is a valuable asset: it can help you to whip up a tasty snack, liven up a meal or create something exciting out of leftovers in the fridge.

SOME OF THE SAUCES IN THIS CHAPTER HAVE BEEN FAMILIAR TREASURES FOR GENERATIONS; OTHERS ARE FAIRLY NEW TO WESTERN COOKERY ALTHOUGH THEY HAVE A LONG HISTORY IN OTHER PARTS OF THE WORLD. ALL OF THEM CONTAIN THE PROMISE TO TRANSFORM YOUR BASIC DISHES INTO FOOD THAT SINGS. LEARNING TO MAKE YOUR OWN SAUCES IS NOT HARD AND ONCE YOU HAVE A REPERTOIRE OF CLASSICS YOU WILL NEVER GO BACK TO THE COMMERCIAL PRODUCTS.

EGG AND BUTTER SAUCES

Hollandaise sauce is famous for its rich, velvety texture which is derived from a combination of egg yolks and butter. Most commonly seen drizzled over eggs benedict in cafès, it is also the perfect partner for asparagus spears and artichoke hearts.

Hollandaise sauce is also the basis of béarnaise sauce, which contains the addition of tarragon – it is the classic accompaniment to a fillet of beef.

Both of these sauces [see pages 266 and 269] can be made by hand or in a blender or food processor. When making by hand, it's important to whisk the egg yolk mixture until it thickens enough to cling to the whisk when it is raised, and that you incorporate the butter completely before adding more. It is crucial to keep the heat low and steady.

Many cooks prefer to make these sauces in a ceramic bowl over a saucepan rather than in a double boiler, as it provides a gentler heat for the delicate ingredients. If the sauces are too thick, or separate, whisk in a tablespoon or two of hot water until the mixture becomes smooth and creamy.

SALSAS

It is no coincidence that these sauces share the name of a South American dance because they are similarly lively and spirited – and can make you break out in a sweat.

While we have only recently embraced the concept of salsas as spicy accompaniments to traditional main courses, they have been relished by generations of Latin Americans and equally enthusiastically incorporated into cuisines around the world – such as the Mediterranean's pesto, salsa verde and skordalia and South Asia's raita, sambal and satay sauce. While these accompaniments are all very different from each other and made from culturally-specific ingredients, they all share the same reason for being: they are all condiments designed to bring excitement to the food they're served with, to enliven the flavours and give them a kick.

Salsas are a wonderful complement to barbecued meats and fish.

THE CLASSICS

THERE ARE WHITE SAUCES, BROWN SAUCES AND BUTTER SAUCES,
AND EACH OF THESE CAN HAVE ANY NUMBER OF VARIATIONS.

White and brown sauces are based on a 'roux' – a paste made from equal parts of melted butter and flour – to which a hot liquid is added. White sauce is based on a blond roux (in which the flour is not browned) and brown sauce is based on a brown roux (where the flour is deliberately browned to a nutty colour) and the sauces they create are determined by the type of hot liquid added to the roux. It's important to stir the sauces continually while you're making them so they don't get too thick. All sauces intended for spooning over food should run freely off the spoon.

GOOD, CLASSIC SAUCES FOR YOUR REPERTOIRE INCLUDE

BÉCHAMEL The addition of hot milk to a blond roux produces a basic béchamel or the kind of white sauce we're accustomed to seeing drizzled over cauliflower or used in lasagne. Grated cheese is a popular addition to this sauce. Other variations include onion sauce for corned beef, and mushroom sauce for chicken and steak. The key thing to watch with these white sauces is that they do not get too thick.

VELOUTÉ This is a pale golden sauce produced when hot stock is added to a blond roux. It's a lovely sauce on chicken, fish or veal.

ESPAGNOLE This lovely rich and silky brown sauce is created when veal stock is added to a brown roux. Good restaurants create espagnole made with meat stock and pan drippings.

GRAVY While it mightn't sound as aristocratic as espagnole, gravy is still a distant cousin of the classic brown sauces. Deglazing is the term used when you add liquid (water, wine or stock) to a hot frying pan or baking dish after the meat (or whatever you have been roasting) has been removed. This liquid is stirred over medium-high heat to blend the cooking juices into the liquid, creating a sauce.

DEGLAZING

THE PROCESS OF DEGLAZING IS AT THE HEART OF MAKING A FLAVOURSOME GRAVY. YOU CAN MAKE A THIN GRAVY (THE FRENCH TERM IS JUS) BY POURING OFF ALL THE FAT FROM THE BAKING DISH AND DEGLAZING THE PAN WITH STOCK PLUS A LITTLE WINE IF YOU WISH. SCRAPE AND STIR THE COAGULATED PAN JUICES INTO THE LIQUID AS IT HEATS. START WITH TWICE AS MUCH LIQUID AS YOU WANT TO END UP WITH; WHEN IT HAS REDUCED BY HALF, STRAIN THE LIQUID INTO A SAUCEPAN, SEASON LIGHTLY WITH SALT AND PEPPER, AND BRING BACK TO SIMMERING POINT AND ADD BITS OF BUTTER, SWIRLING OR WHISKING THEM IN TO GIVE THE GRAVY A BIT OF BODY.

hollandaise sauce

PREP + COOK TIME 20 MINS • MAKES 1 CUP (250ML)

This recipe makes enough for six servings of eggs benedict (see recipe page 248), a breakfast or brunch specialty consisting of toasted english muffin halves topped with ham, poached egg and hollandaise sauce.

2 tablespoons water
2 tablespoons white vinegar
¼ teaspoon cracked black pepper
2 egg yolks
200g unsalted butter, melted

1 Bring the water, vinegar and pepper to the boil in small saucepan. Reduce heat; simmer, uncovered, until liquid reduces to 1 tablespoon. Strain through fine sieve into medium heatproof bowl; cool 10 minutes.

2 Whisk egg yolks into vinegar mixture until combined. Set bowl over medium saucepan of simmering water; do not allow water to touch base of bowl. Whisk mixture over heat until thickened.

3 Remove bowl from heat; gradually add melted butter in thin, steady stream, whisking constantly until sauce has thickened.

nutritional count per tablespoon 14.5g total fat (9.2g saturated fat); 548kJ (131 cal); 0.1g carbohydrate; 0.5g protein; 0g fibre

serving ideas goes well with steamed asparagus and grilled fish.

TIP

• If the sauce is too thick, or separates, whisk in up to 2 tablespoons of hot water until mixture is smooth and creamy.

Whisk the mixture over a pan of simmering water. This is when the sauce could curdle so make sure the water doesn't touch the bottom of the bowl.

Gradually add melted butter in a steady stream, whisking all the time until the sauce is smooth and thick.

Q&A

What's the difference between hollandaise and béarnaise sauce and how do you use each of them?

Béarnaise is started with a reduction of vinegar, shallots, tarragon and pepper – this gives it a stronger flavour than hollandaise, which begins with a reduction of vinegar and pepper. After this initial reduction the two sauces are made in the same way. Béarnaise goes best with beef – it's the perfect complement. Hollandaise, being milder in flavour, goes well with asparagus, eggs and fish.

béarnaise sauce

PREP + COOK TIME 25 MINS • MAKES 1 CUP (250ML)

2 tablespoons white vinegar
2 tablespoons water
1 shallot (25g), chopped finely
2 teaspoons coarsely chopped fresh tarragon
½ teaspoon black peppercorns
3 egg yolks
200g unsalted butter, melted
1 tablespoon finely chopped fresh tarragon

TIP
- If sauce separates, whisk in about 1 tablespoon boiling water until mixture is smooth.

1 Bring vinegar, the water, shallot, coarsely chopped tarragon and peppercorns to the boil in small saucepan. Reduce heat; simmer, uncovered, about 2 minutes or until liquid reduces by half. Strain over medium heatproof bowl; discard solids. Cool 10 minutes.
2 Whisk egg yolks into vinegar mixture until combined. Set bowl over medium saucepan of simmering water; do not allow water to touch base of bowl. Whisk mixture over heat until thickened. Remove bowl from heat; gradually whisk in melted butter in thin, steady stream until béarnaise thickens slightly. Stir finely chopped tarragon into sauce.

nutritional count per tablespoon 15.1g total fat (9.5g saturated fat); 577kJ (138 cal); 0.2g carbohydrate; 0.8g protein; 0g fibre
serving ideas goes well with grilled beef steaks, pan-fried chicken breast fillets, white fish fillets and steamed or boiled vegetebls.

mint sauce

PREP + COOK TIME 10 MINS (+ STANDING) • MAKES 1 CUP (250ML)

This sauce makes enough for a 2kg roast leg of lamb.

2 cups firmly packed fresh mint leaves
¼ cup (60ml) water
¾ cup (180ml) white wine vinegar
2 tablespoons caster sugar

1 Chop half of the mint coarsely; place in small heatproof bowl.
2 Combine the water, vinegar and sugar in small saucepan; stir over heat, without boiling, until sugar dissolves. Pour liquid over chopped mint in bowl, cover; stand 3 hours.
3 Strain liquid into bowl; discard mint. Chop remaining mint coarsely; stir into liquid. Blend or process until chopped finely.

nutritional count per tablespoon 0.3g total fat (0.1g saturated fat); 234kJ (56 cal); 10.1g carbohydrate; 0.9g protein; 1.9g fibre
serving ideas goes well with felafel, mixed bean salad or rice salad.

[opposite] béarnaise sauce

roast beef with espagnole sauce

**PREP + COOK TIME
1 HOUR 25 MINS
SERVES 4
(MAKES 1 CUP SAUCE)**

2 teaspoons olive oil
900g beef sirloin
2 medium carrots (240g), chopped coarsely
4 shallots (100g), quartered
2 stalks celery (300g), trimmed, chopped coarsely
2 teaspoons plain flour
1 tablespoon tomato paste
2 cups (500ml) beef stock
1 cup (250ml) water

1 Preheat oven to 200°C/180°C fan-forced.
2 Heat oil in large flameproof dish; cook beef, uncovered, over high heat until browned. Place dish in oven; roast, uncovered, about 45 minutes or until beef is cooked as desired.
3 Remove beef from dish; cover to keep warm. Place dish with pan juices over high heat, add carrot, shallot and celery; cook, uncovered, stirring occasionally, about 10 minutes or until vegetables are well-browned. Add flour; cook, stirring, about 4 minutes or until mixture is dark brown. Add paste, stock and the water; bring to the boil. Boil, uncovered, about 10 minutes or until sauce thickens.
4 Strain sauce, discard vegetables. Slice beef; serve with espagnole.
nutritional count per serving 23.2g total fat (9.7g saturated fat); 1831kJ (438 cal); 6.4g carbohydrate; 49.7g protein; 2.9g fibre
serving ideas serve this recipe with roasted kipfler potatoes and shallots.
This sauce also goes well with roast venison and roast kangaroo.

Cook the piece of sirloin over high heat in a heavy pan until it is brown all over. Roast the beef in the same pan until cooked to your liking.

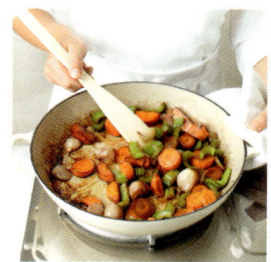

Keep the beef warm while you make the sauce. Heat the juices in the pan and add carrots, shallots and celery.

Add flour and cook until the mixture browns – this gives the espagnole its depth of flavour. Pour in the stock.

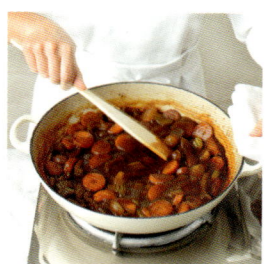

Stir for about 10 minutes over high heat while the sauce reduces and thickens. Strain the sauce and serve it with the beef.

This recipe makes enough for six 180g servings of pan-fried ocean perch fillets.

1 Melt butter in medium frying pan; cook shallot and mustard powder, stirring, about 3 minutes or until shallot softens. Add wine; cook, uncovered, until wine reduces by two-thirds. Add stock; bring to the boil. Boil, uncovered, about 7 minutes or until reduced by half.
2 Add cream to pan; bring to the boil, then reduce heat. Simmer, uncovered, about 15 minutes or until sauce thickens slightly.
nutritional count per tablespoon 12.4g total fat (8.1g saturated fat); 531kJ (127 cal); 1g carbohydrate; 0.9g protein, 0g fibre
serving ideas goes well with grilled or barbecued prawns and grilled lobster.

seafood sauce

PREP + COOK TIME 25 MINS • MAKES 2 CUPS (500ML)

This recipe makes enough for eight 220g servings of pan-fried salmon fillets.

1 cup (250ml) dry white wine
1 cup (250ml) béchamel sauce (see page 273)
¾ cup (180ml) cream
250g marinara mix, drained
2 tablespoons finely chopped fresh dill
1 tablespoon lemon juice

1 Bring wine to the boil in medium frying pan then reduce heat. Simmer, uncovered, until reduced by half.
2 Add béchamel, cream and marinara mix to pan; bring to the boil then reduce heat. Simmer, uncovered, about 5 minutes or until seafood is cooked through. Stir in dill and juice.
nutritional count per tablespoon 5g total fat (3.2g saturated fat); 293kJ (70 cal); 2.1g carbohydrate; 2.7g protein; 0.1g fibre
serving ideas goes well with grilled fish fillets, pasta and grilled beef fillets.

mornay

PREP + COOK TIME 10 MINS • MAKES 2 CUPS (500ML)

A mornay is identified by the addition of cream and cheese (traditionally emmentaler) to the béchamel, and is the basis of a good gratin.

This recipe makes enough for four servings of steamed cauliflower.

1 cup (250ml) béchamel sauce (see page 273)
¼ cup (60ml) cream
1 egg yolk
1 cup (120g) coarsely grated emmentaler cheese

1 Bring béchamel to the boil in medium saucepan; add cream and egg yolk, whisk 1 minute.
2 Remove sauce from heat; add cheese, stir until cheese melts.
nutritional count per tablespoon 4.4g total fat (2.8g saturated fat); 222kJ (53 cal); 1.4g carbohydrate; 2.2g protein; 0g fibre
serving ideas goes well with oysters, lobster and grilled fish fillets.

chicken and mushroom velouté

PREP + COOK TIME 35 MINS • MAKES 2½ CUPS (625ML)

Velouté, which translates from the French as "the texture of velvet", is similar to a béchamel except for the fact that a light stock is added to the roux instead of milk. If you're serving this sauce with fish, replace the chicken stock with fish stock; for a vegetarian version, use vegetable stock. Velouté should be served as soon as it is made.

2¼ cups (560ml) chicken stock
60g butter
2 tablespoons plain flour
1 small brown onion (80g), chopped finely
150g button mushrooms, sliced thinly
¼ cup (60ml) dry white wine
¼ cup (60ml) pouring cream

1 Place stock in small saucepan; bring to the boil then remove from heat.
2 Melt 40g of the butter in medium saucepan, add flour; cook, stirring, about 2 minutes or until mixture bubbles and thickens. Stir in hot stock gradually; bring to the boil. Cook, stirring, until sauce boils and thickens.
3 Reduce heat; simmer, uncovered, about 20 minutes or until reduced by half. Strain sauce into small bowl.
4 Melt remaining butter in medium saucepan; cook onion, stirring, until softened. Add mushrooms; cook, stirring, about 5 minutes or until softened.
5 Add wine to pan; cook, stirring, until almost all liquid evaporates. Add velouté; bring to the boil. Add cream; reduce heat, stir until sauce is heated through.

nutritional count per tablespoon 2.6g total fat (1.7g saturated fat); 130kJ (31 cal); 0.9g carbohydrate; 0.6g protein; 0.2g fibre
serving ideas goes well with pasta and as a chicken and bacon pie filling.

tomato sauce

PREP + COOK TIME 50 MINS (+ COOLING) • MAKES 3½ CUPS (875ML)

Also called ketchup, this thick, spicy sauce is a traditional American accompaniment to french fries, scrambled eggs, hamburgers and hot dogs.

If tomatoes are in season, coarsely chop 1.8kg and substitute for the canned variety.

This sauce can be kept, covered, in the refrigerator for up to one month; it's also suitable to freeze.

[opposite] chicken and mushroom velouté

1 tablespoon olive oil
1 large brown onion (200g), chopped coarsely
2 tablespoons brown sugar
3 x 400g cans diced tomatoes
¼ teaspoon ground allspice
½ teaspoon celery salt
2 tablespoons tomato paste
⅓ cup (80ml) white vinegar

1 Heat oil in large saucepan; cook onion, stirring, until soft. Add sugar, undrained tomatoes, allspice and celery salt; bring to the boil then reduce heat. Simmer, uncovered, stirring occasionally, about 30 minutes or until mixture thickens. Stir in paste and vinegar; cook, uncovered, 5 minutes.
2 Blend or process sauce until smooth; push through fine sieve into medium bowl. Discard solids. Serve sauce cold.

nutritional count per tablespoon 0.5g total fat (0.1g saturated fat); 63kJ (15 cal); 1.9g carbohydrate; 0.3g protein; 0.5g fibre
serving ideas goes well with grilled white fish fillets, sirloin steak, pork sausages, meat pies and sausage rolls.

napoletana sauce

PREP + COOK TIME 1 HOUR 15 MINS • MAKES 1 LITRE (4 CUPS)

Makes enough sauce for 500g pasta, to serve four people.

An equal quantity of canned diced tomatoes can be used instead of fresh tomatoes.

This sauce will keep, covered, in the fridge for up to three days. Freeze in sealed containers for up to three months.

⅓ cup (80ml) olive oil
1 medium brown onion (150g), chopped finely
3 cloves garlic, crushed
¼ cup loosely packed fresh basil leaves
1 teaspoon sea salt
2 tablespoons tomato paste
1.5kg ripe tomatoes, chopped coarsely

1 Heat half of the oil in large saucepan; cook onion, garlic, basil and salt, stirring, until onion softens. Add paste; cook, stirring, 1 minute.

2 Add tomato; bring to the boil then reduce heat. Simmer, uncovered, stirring occasionally, about 45 minutes or until sauce thickens. Stir in remaining oil; simmer, uncovered, 5 minutes.

nutritional count per tablespoon 1.6g total fat (0.2g saturated fat); 84kJ (20 cal); 0.9g carbohydrate; 0.4g protein; 0.5g fibre

arrabbiata sauce

PREP + COOK TIME 25 MINS • MAKES 1.25 LITRES (5 CUPS)

Makes enough sauce for 500g pasta, to serve four people.

Arrabbiata sauce is traditionally served with penne – combining to make the well-known Italian dish Penne all'Arrabbiata, literally meaning 'angry pasta'. Its name is derived from the fuming spicy flavour that the chillies provide. If you can't take the heat, remove some of the chilli seeds for a milder dish.

¼ cup (60ml) olive oil
2 fresh small red thai chillies, chopped finely
1 litre (4 cups) napoletana sauce (see recipe above)
½ cup coarsely chopped fresh flat-leaf parsley

1 Heat half of the oil in large saucepan; cook chilli, stirring, 2 minutes.

2 Add sauce; bring to the boil. Stir in remaining oil and parsley.

nutritional count per tablespoon 2.2g total fat (0.3g saturated fat); 100kJ (24 cal); 0.7g carbohydrate; 0.3g protein; 0.4g fibre

[opposite] napoletana sauce

aïoli

PREP TIME 20 MINS • MAKES 1 CUP (300G)

This garlic-flavoured mayonnaise originated in the Provence region of southern France, where for centuries, it has been a traditional accompaniment to bouillabaisse. These days, it is often enjoyed with chips and seafood as an alternative to traditional mayonnaise or tartare sauce.

4 cloves garlic, quartered
1 teaspoon sea salt
2 teaspoons lemon juice
1 cup (250ml) mayonnaise (see page 118)

1 Using mortar and pestle, crush garlic and salt to a smooth paste.
2 Combine garlic mixture and remaining ingredients in small bowl.
nutritional count per tablespoon 19.1g total fat (2.8g saturated fat); 719kJ (172 cal); 0.2g carbohydrate; 0.6g protein; 0.2g fibre
serving ideas goes well with grilled fish fillets, crudités, and fried or boiled potatoes.

tartare sauce

PREP TIME 20 MINS • MAKES 1 CUP (300G)

1 cup (250ml) mayonnaise (see page 118)
2 tablespoons finely chopped cornichons
1 tablespoon drained, rinsed baby capers, chopped finely
1 tablespoon finely chopped fresh flat-leaf parsley
2 teaspoons finely chopped fresh dill
2 teaspoons lemon juice

1 Combine ingredients in small bowl.
nutritional count per tablespoon 9.5g total fat (1.4g saturated fat); 364kJ (87 cal); 0.3g carbohydrate; 0.3g protein; 0g fibre
serving ideas goes well with grilled chicken breast fillets, and smoked or fried fish.

skordalia

PREP + COOK TIME 20 MINS (+ STANDING) • MAKES 1 CUP (300G)

This recipe makes enough for four servings of lamb kebabs.

If skordalia becomes too thick, add small amounts of hot water until the desired consistency is reached.

[1] aïoli
[2] tartare sauce
[3] skordalia
[4] tangy barbecue sauce [page 282]

1 medium potato (200g), quartered
3 cloves garlic, quartered
2 tablespoons cold water
1 tablespoon lemon juice
1 tablespoon white wine vinegar
⅓ cup (80ml) olive oil

1 Boil, steam or microwave potato until tender; drain. Cool 10 minutes.
2 Blend or process potato, garlic, the water, juice and vinegar until mixture is pureed. With motor operating, gradually add oil in thin, steady stream, processing until mixture thickens.
nutritional count per tablespoon 6.1g total fat (0.9g saturated fat); 280kJ (67 cal); 2.3g carbohydrate; 0.5g protein; 0.4g fibre
serving ideas goes well with lamb kebabs, fried zucchini or eggplant, and battered fish.

tangy barbecue sauce

PREP + COOK TIME 30 MINS • MAKES 2 CUPS (500ML)

This sauce is best made a day ahead. Keep, refrigerated, for up to three days in a screw-top jar.

This recipe makes enough for six beef burgers or 2kg of braised short ribs.

1 cup (250ml) tomato sauce
½ cup (125ml) apple cider vinegar
¼ cup (60ml) worcestershire sauce
⅔ cup (150g) firmly packed brown sugar
2 tablespoons american-style mustard
1 fresh small red thai chilli, chopped finely
1 clove garlic, crushed
1 tablespoon lemon juice

1 Combine ingredients in medium saucepan; bring to the boil then reduce heat. Simmer, uncovered, stirring occasionally, 20 minutes.

nutritional count per tablespoon 0.1g total fat (0g saturated fat); 163kJ (39 cal); 9.3g carbohydrate; 0.3g protein; 0.3g fibre

serving ideas goes well with roasted potato wedges or as a sauce for home-made baked beans.

pork cutlets with charcuterie sauce

PREP + COOK TIME 35 MINS
SERVES 4
(MAKES 1 CUP SAUCE)

1 tablespoon olive oil
4 pork cutlets (950g)
1 small brown onion (80g), chopped finely
2 rindless bacon rashers (130g), sliced thinly
⅔ cup (160ml) dry white wine
⅔ cup (160ml) chicken stock
⅓ cup (60g) cornichons, sliced thinly lengthways
⅓ cup (40g) seeded green olives, sliced thinly
2 teaspoons dijon mustard
2 tablespoons finely chopped fresh flat-leaf parsley

1 Heat oil in large frying pan; cook pork, in batches, until browned both sides and cooked as desired. Cover to keep warm.
2 Add onion and bacon to pan; cook, stirring, until onion softens.
3 Deglaze pan with wine, stirring until mixture reduces by half.
4 Stir in remaining ingredients; bring to the boil. Boil, uncovered, about 1 minute or until sauce thickens slightly.

nutritional count per serving 24.1g total fat (7.4g saturated fat); 1697kJ (406 cal); 7.7g carbohydrate; 33g protein; 0.9g fibre

serving ideas charcuterie sauce also goes well with grilled pork sausages, barbecued veal steaks and pan-fried chicken breast fillets.

strawberry coulis

PREP + COOK TIME 10 MINS • MAKES 1 CUP (250ML)

For a delicious dessert, fold ½ cup coulis, the pulp of 2 passionfruit, ½ cup lightly crushed biscotti, 250g yogurt and 250g vanilla custard together until just combined. Serve in four glass tumblers.

300g frozen strawberries, thawed
1 tablespoon icing sugar

1 Push berries through fine sieve into small bowl; discard seeds.
2 Stir sifted icing sugar into sauce.

nutritional count per tablespoon 0.3g total fat (0g saturated fat); 42kJ (10 cal); 1.6g carbohydrate; 0.4g protein; 0.6g fibre
serving ideas goes well with puddings, slices and poached fruits.

crème anglaise

PREP + COOK TIME 30 MINS (+ REFRIGERATION) • MAKES 1½ CUPS (375ML)

Low heat and constant whisking are the key elements to a successful crème anglaise.

Try flavouring the custard with liqueurs, finely grated citrus rind, chocolate, spices or coffee.

1 vanilla bean
1½ cups (375ml) milk
⅓ cup (75g) caster sugar
4 egg yolks

1 Split vanilla bean in half lengthways; scrape seeds into medium saucepan, add pod, milk and one tablespoon of the sugar. Bring to the boil then strain into large jug. Discard pod.
2 Meanwhile, combine egg yolks and remaining sugar in medium heatproof bowl set over medium saucepan of simmering water; do not allow water to touch base of bowl. Whisk until thick and creamy; gradually whisk in hot milk mixture.
3 Return custard mixture to pan; stir, over low heat, until mixture is just thick enough to coat the back of a spoon.
4 Return custard to bowl; refrigerate about 1 hour or until cold.

nutritional count per tablespoon 2.1g total fat (0.9g saturated fat); 184kJ (44 cal); 5.2g carbohydrate; 1.4g protein; 0g fibre
serving ideas goes well with fresh figs, chocolate cake and apple pie.

chocolate fudge sauce

PREP + COOK TIME 15 MINS • MAKES 1 CUP (250ML)

This sauce will keep under refrigeration, covered, for up to three days. To serve, reheat sauce briefly in microwave oven on HIGH (100%) or over low heat in small saucepan until it reaches the desired consistency.

200g dark eating chocolate
20g butter
¼ teaspoon vanilla extract
½ cup (125ml) cream

1 Place chocolate and butter in small heatproof bowl set over small saucepan of simmering water; do not allow water to touch base of bowl. Stir until chocolate is melted. Add extract and cream; stir until combined. Serve sauce warm.

nutritional count per tablespoon 10.6g total fat (6.7g saturated fat); 585kJ (140 cal); 10.7g carbohydrate; 1.1g protein; 0.2g fibre
serving ideas goes well with ice-cream, puddings, mousses and poached fruit.

sabayon

PREP + COOK TIME 10 MINS • MAKES 2 CUPS (500ML)

Sabayon is a light, frothy custard sauce. Ensure you whisk the mixture vigorously to incorporate as much air as possible or your sabayon will be flat. Cooking the mixture too quickly though will make it too thick – prevent this by keeping the water in the saucepan at a low simmer.

3 egg yolks
¼ cup (55g) caster sugar
¼ cup (60ml) dry white wine

1 Place ingredients in medium bowl set over medium saucepan of simmering water; do not allow water to touch base of bowl. Whisk vigorously and continually about 5 minutes or until sauce is thick and creamy.
nutritional count per tablespoon 0.6g total fat (0.2g saturated fat); 71kJ (17 cal); 2.3g carbohydrate; 0.3g protein; 0g fibre
serving ideas goes well with poached pears, grilled peaches or nectarines, and fresh mango slices.

orange butterscotch sauce

PREP + COOK TIME 15 MINS • MAKES 1 CUP (250ML)

For a lavish touch, add ¼ cup raisins and 1 tablespoon rum or brandy. Serve over ice-cream or baked apples.

½ cup (125ml) thickened cream
½ cup (110g) firmly packed brown sugar
60g cold butter, chopped
1 teaspoon finely grated orange rind

1 Stir ingredients in small saucepan over low heat, without boiling, until sugar dissolves. Bring to the boil then reduce heat; simmer, uncovered, 3 minutes.
nutritional count per tablespoon 8g total fat (5.2g saturated fat); 456kJ (109 cal); 9.3g carbohydrate; 0.3g protein; 0g fibre
serving ideas goes well with pancakes, waffles, sweet crêpes and poached oranges.

Q&A

I've heard of people melting Mars bars in cream to make a sauce for ice-cream. Is that really possible and if so, how do I do it?

It is indeed possible and it makes a super-quick and easy sauce for ice-cream. All you do is gently heat a chopped up Mars bar in ½ cup of pouring cream. Stir all the time until the chocolate melts and don't allow it to boil. You could also use coarsely chopped After-dinner Mints.

[opposite] sabayon

THE PERFECT ROAST

The perfect roast

Many of us have fond memories of weekly roast dinners as we were growing up. They were often a favourite ritual on Sundays at our parents' or grandparents' homes and they were all about bringing family together as much as nourishing our bodies.

And for many of us, that's where they have stayed – a cherished memory from our past, only occasionally reprised for special occasions. Many of us have got out of the habit of making what our mothers called a "baked dinner" because we think it takes too long (and yes, it does take time, but you don't have to hang around the kitchen while the roast is in the oven – you can continue tapping away at the computer or read a book) or because it's too formal or traditional. But ask your family and friends what their idea of a perfect meal is and many of them will vouch for the nostalgic baked dinner.

The only upside about not having roasts as often as we used to is that, when they do appear it is memorable. Serve up a roast chicken or a leg of lamb with gravy and melt-in-the-mouth baked vegetables for friends and family and watch their delight. And if you don't want to cook a traditional-size roast, there are mini roasts available in all the major supermarkets.

So now, there's no excuse: a roast dinner needn't be reserved only for ceremonial occasions. It's a sumptuous meal you can revisit at any time – and you get the added benefit of having delicious leftovers to enjoy.

COOKING TIPS

CHICKEN Roast chicken requires a preheated hot oven for the first 15 to 20 minutes then reduced heat for another 60 minutes or so. You need to baste occasionally to ensure the meat remains moist. Roast chicken should be cooked through, but not overdone (see When Is Your Roast Done?, opposite).

BEEF Allow 125g to 150g of meat per person of boneless beef and 150g to 200g for a bone-in roast. The exact cooking times, and frequency of basting, will depend on the cut. To judge when beef is cooked to your taste, insert a fine skewer into the centre and check the juices (see When Is Your Roast Done?, opposite).

LAMB Today, most people enjoy roast lamb best when it is browned outside but still pink and juicy inside. When it is medium-done, it will be fairly firm and blush-pink, with clear or slightly pinkish juice; when medium-rare, the interior will be soft and reddish pink and the juices "bloody".

ROAST LAMB requires a preheated hot oven. Roast for 20 minutes, then reduce to moderate for the remaining cooking time. Baste with pan juices every 20 minutes. Trimmed roasts, being lean, need to be brushed with oil before cooking and basted every 10 minutes. Allow 10 to 15 minutes per 500g, depending on whether you want rare or firm but pink lamb; 20 minutes per 500g will give well-done lamb that is just pink in the middle. Start checking for doneness towards the end of cooking time.

CHOOSING YOUR ROAST

CHICKEN Try to find a fresh, free-range, organic chicken. Second-best is fresh, but not free-range, chicken. If cooking a frozen chicken, give it time to thaw out in the fridge first. It will lose some of its juices as it thaws, but will lose less this way. Thaw, uncovered, on several thicknesses of absorbent paper on a plate in the fridge. Never cook a partially frozen bird: it may appear to be cooked through, but unless the internal temperature reached 75°C or higher during cooking, dangerous micro-organisms such as salmonella may have survived. The same considerations apply for other poultry – duck, quail and turkey.

BEEF The best cuts for roasting are fillet, scotch fillet, rump, sirloin and rib, either on the bone (a "standing" roast) or boned and rolled. Fillet is the most tender cut of all and is fatless, so it is perfect for serving with a rich sauce, but rump, sirloin or rib will give more flavour in their own right. You may see cheaper cuts marked "roasting" but these are often tough.

LAMB The best roasting cuts are the leg, which may be bone-in or partly boned (called easy-carve); trimmed roasts, which are usually individual leg muscles seamed out for small, fatless roasts; loin on the bone or boned and rolled; saddle, which is two loins still joined; chump, a choice, small, compact roast with some bone; a rack (ribs), which consists of 8 cutlets still joined or can be ordered by the number of cutlets required (usually 3 or 4 per person, depending on size); the rump; the shoulder, either on the bone, which is tricky to carve, or boned and rolled; the forequarter, which consists of forequarter chops still joined but is usually sold boned and rolled; and for slow-roasting only, a rolled breast, which is a fatty cut.

PORK Roasting cuts are the loin, bone-in or boned and sometimes rolled, which serves 8–10 and is often cut into two smaller roasts; the leg, also very large and often divided into the fillet end and the shank end, which is often boned and rolled; rump; fillet; individual leg muscles seamed out for small, boneless roasts; shoulder, either on the bone or boned and rolled; and rack or rib on the bone, consisting of 6–8 cutlets in one piece. You may see cheaper cuts than these marked "roasting", but they are often tough.

Suckling pig is the supreme roast pork for a special celebration. A 6–7kg one will serve 12 to 15 people. It must be ordered well ahead – ensure you measure your oven before ordering, to make sure the pig will fit.

WHEN IS YOUR ROAST DONE?

CHICKEN, DUCK AND TURKEY should be cooked through but not overdone. Check by inserting a fine skewer into the thickest part of the thigh near the body; juices should run clear with no tinge of pink. Pink juice means it is underdone.

MEAT To judge when your roasted meat is done to your taste, use a meat thermometer or run a fine skewer into the thickest part of the meat and check the juice that comes out. Red juice means it is rare, pink juice is medium and clear juice is well done.

PORK Don't overcook pork. A hint of pink is fine. Allow 30 minutes per 500g if it is over 3kg and 40 minutes per 1kg if under 3kg. Use a meat thermometer or check by inserting a fine skewer into the centre towards the end of cooking time. It is done if the skewer goes in easily and juices run clear.

ALL ROASTS SHOULD BE RESTED in a warm place, loosely covered with foil, 15 minutes before serving, to allow the juices to settle and the meat to become more succulent.

THE PERFECT ROAST

roast beef with yorkshire puddings

Roast beef with yorkshire puddings is the most traditional British roast and in fact probably the most famous of all British food. While the beef is resting, make the gravy and yorkshire puddings and serve the roast with crispy baked potatoes, boiled baby carrots and steamed green vegetables.

Checking for doneness To judge when a roast is done to your taste, use a meat thermometer or run a fine skewer into the centre and check the juice that comes out. Red juice means rare, pink means medium and clear means well done.

Timing Many people think a roast is one of the simplest meals to put together. And it is – as long as you've got the timing right. Cold plates, cold vegetables, gravy that has sat for too long – all of these things will spoil what is one of the crowning glories of British cooking.

The beef We've used a corner piece of beef topside, but you can use rump, sirloin or scotch fillet if you prefer. Fillet of beef is not usually used in roast beef with yorkshire pudding because while tender, it doesn't have as much flavour as the other cuts.

Crispy roast potatoes Boil or microwave the potatoes until just cooked. Run the tines of a fork over the surface to rough it up, then place the potatoes in a roasting pan covered with a thin layer of very hot olive oil. Roast in a hot oven for approximately 40 minutes or until crisp.

Hot vegetables Boil, steam or microwave your other vegetables last. Boiled vegetables get cold very quickly, so they should be brought to the table and passed around at the last minute.

1. Marinate the beef in the wine and herb mixture for 3 hours or overnight, covered, in the refrigerator.

2. Drain the beef and discard the herb mixture. Reserve 1 cup of the marinade to use in the gravy. Place the beef on a bed of vegetables and roast for about 1½ hours.

3. Pour the pan juices into a jug – the oil will rise to the surface. Remove 1½ tablespoons of this oil for cooking the yorkshire puddings. Discard the remaining oil.

roast beef with yorkshire puddings

**PREP + COOK TIME
2 HOURS 35 MINS
(+ REFRIGERATION &
STANDING) • SERVES 8**

2kg corner piece beef topside roast
2 cups (500ml) dry red wine
2 bay leaves
6 black peppercorns
¼ cup (70g) wholegrain mustard
4 cloves garlic, sliced
4 sprigs fresh thyme
1 medium brown onion (150g), chopped coarsely
2 medium carrots (240g), chopped coarsely
1 large leek (500g), chopped coarsely
2 stalks celery (300g), trimmed, chopped coarsely
2 tablespoons olive oil

yorkshire puddings
1 cup (150g) plain flour
2 eggs
½ cup (125ml) milk
½ cup (125ml) water

gravy
2 tablespoons plain flour
1½ cups (375ml) beef stock

4 ...e the roast s cooking, mix the batter for yorkshire puddings and leave to stand for minutes.

5 Heat the reserved oil in muffin pan until quite hot, then pour in the yorkshire pudding batter. Return the pan to the hot oven quickly so the puddings will start to cook right away.

6 To make the gravy, add flour to the reserved pan juices and gradually add combined stock and reserved marinade, stirring constantly until mixture is thick and smooth.

Try adding 1 tablespoon horseradish cream or 1 teaspoon english dry mustard or dried thyme to the yorkshire pudding mixture. You can also add ale or beef stock instead of the water.

For light fluffy yorkshire puddings it is essential that the batter is well rested and cold, and that the oven and reserved oil are both very hot.

1 Combine beef, wine, bay leaves, peppercorns, mustard, garlic, thyme and onion in large shallow dish. Cover; refrigerate 3 hours or overnight.
2 Preheat oven to 180°C/160°C fan-forced.
3 Drain beef over medium bowl; reserve 1 cup (250ml) of marinade. Combine carrot, leek and celery in large baking dish, top with beef; brush beef with oil.
4 Roast beef, uncovered, about 1½ hours. Remove beef from dish, wrap in foil; stand 20 minutes before serving. Increase oven to 220°C/200°C fan-forced.
5 Remove vegetables with slotted spoon; discard vegetables. Pour pan juices into jug; stand 2 minutes. Reserve 1½ tablespoons oil from the surface for yorkshire puddings, discard remaining oil; reserve 2 tablespoons of the pan juices for gravy.
6 Make yorkshire puddings and gravy. Serve beef with puddings and gravy.
yorkshire puddings Sift flour into medium bowl; whisk in combined eggs, milk and water all at once until smooth. Stand batter 30 minutes. Spoon reserved oil into eight holes of 12-hole (⅓-cup/80ml) muffin pan; heat in oven 2 minutes. Divide batter into pan holes. Bake about 20 minutes or until puffed and golden.
gravy Heat reserved pan juices in same baking dish, add flour; cook, stirring, until browned. Gradually add stock and reserved marinade; cook, stirring, until mixture boils and thickens. Strain gravy into heatproof jug.
nutritional count per serving 15.4g total fat (4.8g saturated fat); 2169kJ (519 cal); 21.1g carbohydrate; 61.2g protein; 4g fibre

THE PERFECT ROAST

standing rib roast with roast vegetables

Cooking a rib roast is at once simple and confusing. The meat itself is so flavourful, it doesn't need much seasoning – just a little salt and pepper, and its own natural juices. This much is simple. The hard part is getting the oven temperature and timing right.

Adjusting to size If using a very large roast (more than five ribs), check the temperature when the cooking time is a little way from up. Take the roast out of the oven just short of the goal, as larger roasts, and the bone in them, continue to cook and rise in temperature as they rest.

Slicing it You'll be surprised at the difference between the chew of a thickly cut piece of rib roast and a thin slice. For a truly good chew, cut the slices 3-4cm thick. Also, as you cut the roast away from the bones, leave some meat on them, so you can gnaw on the juicy bones.

Standing rib roast It gets its name from the fact that the bones are included in the roast, so the roast can stand by itself. The bones give the meat great flavour. A rib roast comprises seven ribs, from the shoulder down the back to the loin. We used a 1.2kg (three-rib) roast.

Probing for doneness The best way to judge a standing rib roast's degree of doneness is with a meat thermometer. The internal temperature should be: 55-60°C for rare; 60-65°C for medium-rare; 65-70°C for medium; 70-75°C for medium-well; and 75°C for well-done.

The tong test If you don't have a meat thermometer handy, you can use tongs to test the roast's doneness. Gently prod or squeeze the roast – rare is very soft; medium-rare is soft; medium is springy but soft; medium-well is firm; and well-done is very firm.

Adding flavour When the roast is done, remove it from the oven, set aside, and let it rest so it can redistribute its juices for at least 20 minutes. This is the time to make the sauce.

1. Using a simple knot, tie kitchen string between each rib bone to ensure the outer layers of meat do not pull away from the rib-eye during roasting.

2. Brush oil all over the roast and season with pepper. Heat oil in a large flameproof baking dish and add the roast, fat-side down, and brown. Turn the roast and cook until browned all over.

Heat oil in a separate flameproof baking dish, add potatoes and cook, stirring, until browned. Add the pumpkin and kumera. Place the dish in oven, with the beef, and roast uncovered until cooked.

standing rib roast with roast vegetables PREP + COOK TIME 1 HOUR 50 MINS • SERVES 4

1.2kg beef standing rib roast
¼ cup (60ml) olive oil
2 teaspoons cracked black pepper
500g potatoes, chopped coarsely
500g pumpkin, chopped coarsely
500g kumara, chopped coarsely
½ cup (125ml) brandy
1½ cups (375ml) beef stock
1 tablespoon cornflour
¼ cup (60ml) water
1 tablespoon finely chopped fresh chives

sfer the beef juices left in the baking dish to a l saucepan. Add brandy and bring to the boil.

Once you have added the stock, pour in the blended cornflour and water, and continue cooking until the mixture comes to the boil and starts to thicken.

Hold an end rib with one hand to keep the roast steady. Using a very sharp knife, with the other hand, cut between the rib bones to release the slice.

A standing rib roast is also known as a bone-in rib roast.

1 Preheat oven to 200°C/180°C fan-forced.
2 Brush beef with 1 tablespoon of the oil; sprinkle with pepper. Heat 1 tablespoon of the oil in large shallow flameproof baking dish; cook beef, uncovered, over high heat until browned all over. Roast, uncovered, in oven about 45 minutes or until cooked as desired.
3 Meanwhile, heat remaining oil in another large flameproof baking dish; cook potatoes, stirring, over high heat until browned lightly. Add pumpkin and kumara, place dish in oven with beef; roast, uncovered, about 35 minutes or until vegetables are browned.
4 Place beef on vegetables, cover; return to oven to keep warm. Drain juices from beef baking dish into medium saucepan, add brandy; bring to the boil. Add stock and blended cornflour and water; cook, stirring, until sauce boils and thickens slightly. Stir in chives; pour into medium heatproof jug.
5 Serve beef and vegetables with sauce.
nutritional count per serving 29.2g total fat (8.5g saturated fat); 3114kJ (745 cal); 41.1g carbohydrate; 60.4g protein; 5.4g fibre

THE PERFECT ROAST

lemon and thyme baked chicken

If you only ever learn to cook one great dish in life, make sure it's a roast chicken. Easy, impressive and utterly delicious, this recipe will see you through many dinner parties and family meals.

Thawing poultry Always thaw frozen chicken in the fridge overnight – never on the kitchen bench or in the sink. Place the chicken in a large dish to catch any juices. Once thawed, use within 24 hours.

Keeping meat moist Avoid overcooking the chicken or it will dry out. As a guide, a 1.5kg whole stuffed chicken takes about 30 minutes per 500g to cook in a 180°C/160°C fan-forced oven.

Chicken When buying poultry, keep in mind that birds free to roam outside and fed a natural diet without additives, usually taste better. Their proportion of meat to fat is higher compared with intensely farmed chickens. Check the label for free-range or organic certification logos.

Leftovers This chicken is great cold the next day. If using the breast, shred it with clean hands or, using a sharp knife, cut it into slices. Add it to a baguette or sandwich bread, and top it with lettuce and mayonnaise, or put it in a wrap. Also delicious scattered in an avocado salad.

Matching wine A fresh, lemony semillon pairs beautifully with this roast chicken, as does a dry sparkling white or even a fresh riesling. Although light reds such as pinot noir usually go with chicken, the roast's citrus flavourings may interfere with the pinot's delicate notes.

Hold the gravy This recipe is better without any gravy as it will only detract from the thyme and lemon flavoured juices coming from the chicken. Roasted or steamed vegetables and crusty bread is all else that's needed.

Once you have rinsed the chicken, pat it dry with absorbent paper. This will help the skin to brown more evenly during the roasting process.

Rub oil all over the chicken with clean hands before rubbing with the salt, pepper and thyme mixture.

Push the garlic, fresh thyme sprigs and lemon quarters into the cavity of the chicken.

lemon and thyme baked chicken PREP + COOK TIME 1 HOUR 45 MINS (+ STANDING) • SERVES 4

1.5kg chicken
1 tablespoon olive oil
1 tablespoon fine salt
2 teaspoons finely cracked black pepper
2 tablespoons fresh thyme leaves
1 bulb garlic, halved crossways
1 medium lemon (140g), cut into wedges
½ bunch fresh thyme sprigs
50g butter, softened

rate the skin from the chicken breast with your
rs, taking care not to tear the skin. Spread the
r and thyme mixture over the entire breast,
r the skin.

Once you have secured the skin over the cavity with fine skewers or toothpicks, place the chicken on an oiled wire rack in a roasting pan. Roast, uncovered, for 1 hour 20 minutes or until cooked.

To test chicken for doneness, insert a skewer into the thickest part of the leg, then pull it out and wait for the juices to bubble up to the surface. If the juices are clear, the chicken is done.

Take care to dry the chicken completely after rinsing – if there is moisture present when you put it in the oven, it will turn to steam which can prevent the skin from turning a lovely golden brown.

1 Preheat oven to 200°C/180°C fan-forced.
2 Wash chicken under cold water; pat dry inside and out with absorbent paper. Rub chicken with oil. Combine salt, pepper and half the thyme in small bowl; rub onto skin and inside cavity. Place garlic, lemon and thyme sprigs inside cavity.
3 Combine butter and remaining thyme in small bowl. Carefully separate skin from chicken breast with your fingers; spread butter under skin covering breast. Secure skin over cavity with fine skewers or toothpicks.
4 Place chicken on oiled wire rack in shallow roasting pan; roast, uncovered, 1 hour 20 minutes or until chicken is cooked through. Remove chicken from oven, cover loosely with foil; stand 10 minutes.

nutritional count per serving 39.2g total fat (15.1g saturated fat); 2144kJ (513 cal); 1g carbohydrate; 39.4g protein; 1.4g fibre

THE PERFECT ROAST

slow-roasted duck marylands

Most cooks put roasted duck into the "leave it to the chefs" basket, but it's really not that different from roasting a chicken. Once you give it a go, crispy, tender roast duck will become a new favourite.

Buying duck fresh It wasn't long ago when the only duck you could find was frozen whole duck. Today you can buy whole duck or pieces from butchers and good poultry shops. If using for a dinner party, it's a good idea to place an order with the butcher, so you don't miss out.

Reheating duck Duck reheats really well. Simply place in an ovenproof dish in a hot oven or even under a hot grill and heat through. If you want the skin to be crispier, dab the skin with absorbent paper before placing in the oven or under the grill.

A red or white meat? Many people think duck, like chicken, must be well done. However, this rule doesn't apply to duck breast, which should be treated more like a steak. Cook it past medium-rare, and you'll lose flavour and compromise texture.

Testing for doneness The duck is done to medium-rare if the juices from the fattest part of the thigh or drumstick run faintly rosy when the duck is pricked with a skewer. For well done, cook until the juices run clear.

The good fat Duck has always been considered the richest of all poultry meats. However, duck meat comprises only about 2 per cent fat – most of the fat is found in the skin. Duck fat is also more like olive oil than butter or beef fat. Whereas chicken and turkey both contain high levels of polyunsaturated fats, duck has more monosaturated fat, which is high in linoleic acid – one of the healthy fats found in heart-friendly olive oil.

1. Place bottled morello cherries in a metal sieve, over a large bowl, to strain.

2. Pour chicken stock into combined cherry juice, port, cinnamon, cloves and garlic in a large baking dish.

3. Arrange the duck marylands on a metal rack placed in the baking dish with the cherry juice mixture.

slow-roasted duck marylands

PREP + COOK TIME 2 HOURS 20 MINS • SERVES 4

680g jar morello cherries
½ cup (125ml) port
1 cinnamon stick
3 whole cloves
1 clove garlic, sliced thinly
½ cup (125ml) chicken stock
4 duck marylands (1.2kg), excess fat removed

the pan liquid into a medium bowl through a sieve to strain.

Using a large metal spoon, skim the fat from the top of the pan juices.

Transfer the skimmed pan juices to a frying pan, add the cherries and bring the mixture to the boil. Reduce heat and allow the mixture to simmer, uncovered, for 5 minutes or until the sauce thickens slightly.

1 Preheat oven to 160°C/140°C fan-forced.
2 Strain cherries over small bowl. Combine cherry juice with port, cinnamon, cloves, garlic and stock in large baking dish. Place duck on metal rack in baking dish; cover tightly with oiled foil. Roast, covered, in oven about 2 hours or until duck meat is tender.
3 Strain pan liquid into medium bowl; skim away fat. Transfer mixture to medium frying pan. Add cherries; bring to the boil. Reduce heat; simmer, uncovered, 5 minutes or until sauce thickens slightly.
4 Serve duck with cherry sauce.
nutritional count per serving 47.3g total fat (12.4g saturated fat); 3156kJ (755 cal); 39.5g carbohydrate; 47.3g protein; 2g fibre
serving idea serve with an apple, roasted walnut and parsley salad.

THE PERFECT ROAST

chicken pot roast with mustard cream sauce

This is warming comfort food at its best. Don't let the long cooking time put you off. You'll spend very little time at the stove before the pan goes in the oven.

Browning the meat The initial cooking on the stove top, until the chicken is lightly browned, is an important step in pot roasts. Some recipes skip the step altogether. This browning process intensifies the flavours as the dish cooks, and provides it with wonderful colour, too.

Use whole chicken There are a few reasons why it is better to buy a whole chicken, and not pieces, for this recipe. Chickens cost less per kilogram when bought whole. Pre-cut meat is sometimes poorly trimmed, too, and you end up getting less meat per kilogram.

Cast-iron cookware A heavy ovenproof casserole dish is a must for today's cooks. These stove-to-oven pans come in raw cast-iron (Dutch ovens) and enamelled cast-iron (French ovens). Enamelled surfaces don't need to be seasoned and provide a non-stick surface.

Time is the essence Pot roasts are a convenience food in that everything happens in one pan, – but they're not a quick-fix. Pot roasts only work with long, slow cooking, so you can't take a short cut and turn up the oven heat, hoping it will work its magic in just 45 minutes.

1. Using a sharp knife, peel the shallots. Then, on a clean chopping board, cut each shallot in half.

2. Place a flameproof casserole dish over a high heat, add the oil and, when hot, add the chicken and cook, turning occasionally, until brown all over. Remove chicken and set aside.

3. Add the shallots, carrots and parsnips to the same dish and stir to combine. Cook for about 5 minutes, stirring, until the vegetables are browned lightly.

chicken pot roast with mustard cream sauce

PREP + COOK TIME 2 HOURS 15 MINS • SERVES 4

1.6kg chicken
1 tablespoon olive oil
12 shallots (300g), halved
20 baby carrots (400g), trimmed
3 small parsnips (360g), chopped coarsely
1 cup (250ml) dry white wine
2 cups (500ml) chicken stock
2 dried bay leaves
200g swiss brown mushrooms
2 tablespoons pouring cream
2 tablespoons wholegrain mustard

4 ...rn chicken to the casserole dish with wine, ...k and bay leaves. Bring to the boil, then cover ...place in the oven for the first 30 minutes.

5 To serve, place chicken on a board, breast side up. Pull one leg away from the body so joint is exposed. Carve through socket with a sharp knife to separate leg and thigh from the body. Repeat for the other leg. To remove the wings, tug them from the carcass.

6 To carve the breast, feel for the breastbone on the top of the chicken. Carve along the breastbone on one side with your knife. Repeat on the other side of the breastbone.

Swiss brown mushrooms, also known as roman or cremini, are light-to-dark brown in colour with a full bodied flavour. Store on a tray in a single layer, covered with damp, absorbent paper and keep where cool air can circulate around them.

1 Preheat oven to 200°C/180°C fan-forced.

2 Wash chicken under cold water; pat dry inside and out with absorbent paper.

3 Heat oil in large flameproof casserole dish; cook chicken until browned all over. Remove chicken. Cook shallots, carrots and parsnips in same dish, stirring, about 5 minutes or until vegetables are browned lightly.

4 Return chicken to dish with wine, stock and bay leaves; bring to the boil. Cook, covered, in oven 30 minutes. Uncover; cook about 30 minutes or until chicken is cooked through. Add mushrooms; cook, uncovered, about 10 minutes or until mushrooms are tender.

5 Remove chicken and vegetables from dish; cover to keep warm. Add cream and mustard to dish; bring to the boil. Boil, uncovered, about 5 minutes or until sauce thickens slightly.

6 Serve chicken, cut into pieces, with vegetables and mustard cream sauce.

nutritional count per serving 42.2g total fat (13.8g saturated fat); 2859kJ (684 cal); 16.9g carbohydrate; 46.7g protein; 6.6g fibre

THE PERFECT ROAST

roast turkey with forcemeat stuffing

Roasting a whole turkey with the stuffing is an annual tradition for most households. But, every year, when it comes to the table dry and stringy we complain. For too long we've blamed the bird but the problem is in the cooking. White meat, when prepared properly, can be juicy, tender and delicious.

Food safety tips Thaw frozen turkeys in the fridge – never on the kitchen bench. A large turkey can take more than three days to thaw. Once thawed, leave it in the fridge until it is ready to cook. Stuff the turkey just before cooking.

Stuffing the turkey Stuffing a turkey helps it to cook evenly and provides the bonus of a tasty side dish. Of course, it means you need to allow more time for the turkey to cook (see Cooking guide below) but the wait is well worth it. If, however, you get to the point where the stuffing is not near done but the turkey is, scoop out the stuffing and finish in a dish in the oven.

Cooking guide A **2.5kg (size 25)** serves 4-6, takes 2-2½ days to thaw, and 1½-2 hours to cook. A **4.5kg (size 45)** serves 8-10, takes 3 days to thaw and 3-3½ hours to cook. A **6.75kg (size 67)** serves 10-12, takes 3-3½ days to thaw and 4½-5 hours to cook. A **9kg (size 90)** serves 15-20, takes 3½ days to thaw and 6-6½ hours to cook.

Storing leftovers Remove the meat from the carcass and store in an airtight container in the refrigerator for up to one week. You can also use the carcass to make stock. To freeze leftover meat, wrap in plastic wrap and place in an airtight container. Freeze for up to a month. Thaw in the fridge overnight.

Creating oven space The sheer size of a turkey means it can take up the whole oven, leaving no room for the vegetables. Cook the vegetables first, cover with foil and set aside while the turkey cooks. When the turkey is resting, return vegetables to the oven and reheat, uncovered.

To make the forcemeat stuffing, combine the cooked and cooled onion and bacon mixture in a bowl with the breadcrumbs, parsley and mince.

Pull open the neck cavity with your fingers and, using a large metal spoon, fill it loosely with the forcemeat stuffing.

Fill the large cavity until it is loosely stuffed. Make sure you do not over-stuff the cavity as the stuffing needs room to expand during cooking.

roast turkey with forcemeat stuffing

**PREP + COOK TIME
3 HOURS 45 MINS
(+ COOLING & STANDING)
SERVES 8**

4.5kg turkey
1 cup (250ml) water
80g butter, melted
¼ cup (35g) plain flour
3 cups (750ml) chicken stock
½ cup (125ml) dry white wine

forcemeat stuffing

40g butter
3 medium brown onions (450g), chopped finely
2 rindless bacon rashers (130g), chopped coarsely
1 cup (70g) stale breadcrumbs
½ cup coarsely chopped fresh flat-leaf parsley
250g pork mince
250g chicken mince

the skin over the stuffing and secure with ~~vers~~. Tie the legs together with kitchen string.

After the turkey has been cooking for 2 hours, remove it from the oven, uncover and baste with the remaining melted butter. Return to the oven, uncovered and cook until done.

Hold the turkey below the breast with a carving fork. Using a sharp knife, slice straight down one side of the breastbone with an even stroke. The slices will fall away as they are cut. Continue carving the breast until enough meat has been carved for first servings.

To test if the turkey is cooked, insert a skewer sideways into the thickest part of the thigh, then remove and press flesh to release the juices. If the juice runs clear, the turkey is cooked. Alternatively, insert a meat thermometer into the thickest part of the thigh, without touching the bone; the turkey is cooked when the thermometer reaches 90°C.

1 Preheat oven to 180°C/160°C fan-forced. Make forcemeat stuffing.

2 Discard neck from turkey. Rinse turkey under cold water; pat dry inside and out with absorbent paper. Fill neck cavity loosely with stuffing; secure skin over opening with small skewers. Fill large cavity loosely with stuffing; tie legs together with kitchen string.

3 Place turkey on oiled wire rack in large shallow baking dish; pour the water into dish. Brush turkey all over with half the butter; cover turkey tightly with two layers of greased foil. Roast 2 hours. Uncover turkey; brush with remaining butter. Roast, uncovered, about 1 hour or until cooked through. Remove turkey from dish, cover loosely with foil; stand 20 minutes.

4 Pour juice from dish into large jug; skim 1 tablespoon of fat from juice, return fat to same dish. Skim and discard fat from remaining juice; reserve juice. Add flour to dish; cook, stirring, until mixture bubbles and is well-browned. Gradually stir in stock, wine and reserved juice; cook, stirring, until gravy boils and thickens. Strain gravy into jug; serve with turkey.

forcemeat stuffing Melt butter in medium frying pan; cook onion and bacon, stirring, over low heat until onion is soft. Cool. Combine onion mixture and remaining ingredients in large bowl; season to taste.

nutritional count per serving 54.7g total fat (21g saturated fat); 3641kJ (871 cal); 12.8g carbohydrate; 79.6g protein; 1.4g fibre

THE PERFECT ROAST

herbed rack of lamb with potato smash

A fresh herb crust for lamb takes an already-succulent meat to the next level. This coating leaves out the breadcrumbs, so when you tuck in, the coating won't crumble off, and you can savour every mouthful. All it needs is a simple side of smashed potatoes.

Flavouring potatoes Smashed roasted potatoes are delicious on their own, so if you want to dress them up, go easy. After smashing the potatoes, you can toss them lightly with olive oil and lemon rind, and season with sea salt and black pepper.

Serving sizes We've used a rack with three ribs for each diner. Vary the size depending on the appetite of your guests.

Leaner cuts This recipe uses a french-trimmed lamb cutlet rack. This means the meat and fat from the ends of the bones have been trimmed. The result is a leaner cut of meat and a more elegant presentation.

Salt to serve For those who like extra salt on their food, place a small serving dish of "gourmet" salt on the table. Sea salt flakes deliver the best crunch – don't use fine salt or table salt for this purpose, as small, solid crystals taste sharp and acrid when sprinkled over cooked food.

Herb variations Anchovies have a very distinct briny flavour, so they won't complement all herbs and spices. If you want to vary the flavours in the crust of this recipe, a good blend is fresh rosemary, marjoram, garlic and peppercorns. Process with oil to make a paste and coat lamb.

THE PERFECT ROAST   THE AWW COOKING SCHOOL

To make the herb crust, place the herbs, anchovy, garlic and oil in the bowl of a small food processor and process until a paste forms.

Using your hands, press herb mixture evenly over the flesh side of each lamb rack to cover.

Use a potato masher to lightly crush the cooked potatoes, just enough to break the skin and flatten them slightly.

herbed rack of lamb with potato smash

PREP + COOK TIME 1 HOUR • SERVES 6

½ cup firmly packed fresh flat-leaf parsley leaves
½ cup firmly packed fresh mint leaves
¼ cup loosely packed fresh oregano leaves
6 drained anchovy fillets, chopped coarsely
4 cloves garlic, chopped coarsely
⅓ cup (80ml) olive oil
6 x 3 french-trimmed lamb cutlet racks (900g)
1kg baby new potatoes

...fer the smashed potatoes to an oiled oven tray drizzle the remaining olive oil over the top.

To test if the lamb is done, press the flesh with clean fingers or a pair of tongs. Rare is soft; medium feels springy; and well done is very firm.

Once the lamb has been allowed to rest for about 10 minutes, loosely covered with foil, carve into single cutlets. Using a sharp knife, cut through the meat between each rib.

The herb mixture can be made up to 8 hours ahead; cover the surface with plastic wrap and refrigerate until needed. Prepare the rest of the meal on the day of serving.

1 Preheat oven to 200°C/180°C fan-forced.
2 Blend or process herbs, anchovy, garlic and half the oil until smooth. Place lamb in large, shallow baking dish; press herb mixture onto each rack.
3 Meanwhile, boil, steam or microwave potatoes until just tender; drain. Using potato masher, smash potato roughly; spread potatoes on an oiled oven tray, drizzle with remaining oil.
4 Roast lamb and potatoes, uncovered, about 20 minutes or until lamb is cooked as desired. Remove lamb from oven, cover; stand 10 minutes.
5 Increase oven to 220°C/200°C fan-forced; roast potatoes, uncovered, further 10 minutes or until browned lightly.
6 Serve lamb with potatoes.
nutritional count per serving 25.4g total fat (7.7g saturated fat); 1697kJ (406 cal); 22.2g carbohydrate; 20.5g protein; 4.2g fibre

THE PERFECT ROAST

roast lamb

The baked dinner is as popular today as it has been for generations, though there are a few things we do differently from our grandmothers. For starters, we cook lamb a little less, so it remains juicy and pink.

Best roasting cut Leg of lamb is the favourite when it comes to roasting. A whole leg serves large numbers, and yields plenty of lean, tender meat. It can be divided into two joints – and the fillet end has the best flavour.

Buying guide Recognising quality in lamb is as important as deciding on the right cut. Choose the leanest lamb with firm, creamy-white fat. Avoid meat with excessive fat or with fat that looks crumbly, brittle and yellowish, which indicates it is not a fresh piece of meat.

Setting the temperature Some cuts of lamb suit a high oven temperature, while others are better if they are roasted at low temperatures. Leg of lamb is best roasted at low to moderate temperatures. This results in less shrinkage, better serving yields and juicier meat.

Meat thermometer Checking the degree of doneness in a leg of lamb can be trickier than other cuts. Using a thermometer is by far the safest and most accurate way to check. Avoid piercing the meat more than twice or too much juice will be lost, drying out the meat.

When to salt lamb Although lamb can be seasoned with herbs and spices up to a day before it is baked, never salt it until just before cooking. Adding salt at this stage will draw moisture out of the meat, resulting in a tough, dry roast.

Removing the fat You should avoid removing all the fat from a roasting joint, as it helps to flavour and baste the meat as it cooks. If you roast it properly, most of the fat will disappear in the cooking, leaving a nice crispy outside on the roast.

Roast your vegetables Steamed greens have their place on the table but roast lamb needs roasted vegetables to support it. We used potato, pumpkin and onion for winter, but you can use just about any seasonal combination: try jerusalem artichokes and carrots in spring, capsicum and eggplant in summer, celeriac and zucchini in autumn, and so on.

1. Using a sharp knife, make incisions in the surface of the meat at about 2cm intervals.

2. Liberally sprinkle the combined rosemary and ground sweet parprika all over the lamb. You can rub some of the mixture into the slits, if you like.

To check whether the lamb is done to your liking, insert a meat thermometer into the centre of the thickest part of the meat, away from bone and fat.

roast lamb

PREP + COOK TIME 1 HOUR 30 MINS • SERVES 6

2kg leg of lamb
3 sprigs fresh rosemary, chopped coarsely
½ teaspoon sweet paprika
1kg potatoes, chopped coarsely
500g piece pumpkin, chopped coarsely
3 small brown onions (240g), halved
2 tablespoons olive oil
2 tablespoons plain flour
1 cup (250ml) chicken stock
¼ cup (60ml) dry red wine

some of the strained lamb pan juices back into ame baking dish and, with a wooden spoon or la, stir in flour over heat.

Stir the juice and flour mixture for about 5 mintutes or until the mixture begins to bubble and brown.

Slowly add the stock and wine, and stir over a high heat until the gravy starts to boil and becomes thick in consistency. Strain the gravy into a heatproof jug.

A roast joint should be rested before serving to allow the meat to relax. The heat of the oven causes the meat fibres to tighten, so as meat rests the fibres will relax, allowing the meat juices to redistribute themselves throughout the joint. Try to carve the joint across the grain so that each slice has short fibres which feel tender to eat.

1 Preheat oven to 200°C/180°C fan-forced.
2 Place lamb in oiled large baking dish; using sharp knife, score skin at 2cm intervals, sprinkle with rosemary and paprika. Roast lamb 15 minutes.
3 Reduce oven to 180°C/160°C fan-forced; roast lamb about 45 minutes or until cooked as desired.
4 Meanwhile, place potatoes, pumpkin and onions, in single layer, in large shallow baking dish; drizzle with oil. Roast for last 45 minutes of lamb cooking time.
5 Remove lamb and vegetables from oven; strain pan juices from lamb into medium jug. Cover lamb and vegetables to keep warm. Return ¼ cup of the pan juices to baking dish, stir in flour; stir over heat about 5 minutes or until mixture bubbles and browns. Gradually add stock and wine; stir over high heat until gravy boils and thickens. Strain gravy into medium heatproof jug.
6 Slice lamb; serve with roasted vegetables and gravy.
nutritional count per serving 17.9g total fat (6.6g saturated fat); 2086kJ (499 cal); 32.3g carbohydrate; 47.7g protein; 5g fibre

THE PERFECT ROAST

greek roast lamb with skordalia and potatoes

There's more than one tradition when it comes to roast lamb. The Greeks cook theirs slowly until it is well done and mouth-wateringly tender. And the accompaniment? Forget subtlety, only a robust garlic spread and lemony potatoes will do.

When is lamb, lamb? Every country uses a different system to classify lamb. Generally, the term indicates sheep under 12 months old. The best way to know what you're really buying is to look at the meat itself. True lamb is light pink in colour with white fat and marbling. It also feels "springy" to the touch.

Hogget and mutton If the meat is a darker shade of pink going on red, it may still be good to eat, but check the price. You may well find you are buying hogget (generally, 13-15 months old) or even mutton (at least 2 years old) instead of lamb, and paying a premium for it.

Adjusting the garlic Skordalia is a matter of taste. Some prefer a mild garlic taste, while others love a little extra garlic. If the taste is too strong, adjust the quantities of potatoes or bread. If the taste is not strong enough, increase the amount of garlic.

Add some nuts In some regions of Greece, walnuts or almonds are added to the skordalia. If you like, add a cup of chopped walnuts or almonds to the food processor at the beginning, with the potatoes, and add the lemon juice to the liquids. The texture will be thick and granular.

Make ahead Skordalia can be prepared up to 1 day ahead. Store in an airtight container and refrigerate. Remove from the refrigerator 3 hours ahead. Just before serving, transfer to a serving bowl and sprinkle with extra lemon thyme, if you like.

Cube the potatoes Lamb roast done the Greek way calls for crunchy potato cubes. The key to this side dish is the lemony cooking liquid, which actually dries out during roasting. Add a little more liquid towards the end of cooking, if needed, to prevent the potatoes from sticking.

THE PERFECT ROAST   THE AWW COOKING SCHOOL

Place a leg of lamb in a large shallow dish and combine with garlic, lemon juice, olive oil, thyme and oregano. Refrigerate for 3 hours or overnight to allow the marinade to flavour the meat.

Transfer lamb to a large baking dish and place in a preheated oven. Cook, uncovered, for 4 hours.

Remove lamb from oven, cover loosely with foil to keep warm and set aside to rest.

greek roast lamb with skordalia and potatoes

**PREP + COOK TIME
4 HOURS 50 MINS
(+ REFRIGERATION)
SERVES 4**

2kg leg of lamb
2 cloves garlic, crushed
½ cup (125ml) lemon juice
2 tablespoons olive oil
1 tablespoon fresh oregano leaves
1 teaspoon fresh lemon thyme leaves
5 large potatoes (1.5kg),
   cut into 3cm cubes
1 tablespoon finely grated lemon rind
2 tablespoons lemon juice, extra
2 tablespoons olive oil, extra
1 teaspoon fresh lemon thyme leaves, extra

skordalia

1 medium potato (200g), quartered
3 cloves garlic, crushed
1 tablespoon lemon juice
1 tablespoon white wine vinegar
2 tablespoons water
⅓ cup (80ml) olive oil

ake the skordalia, push the cooked potatoes ugh a food mill or fine sieve over a medium bowl. side and allow potato to cool for 10 minutes.

Combine garlic, lemon juice, vinegar and the water in a separate bowl with a balloon whisk. Pour the lemon juice mixture into mashed potato, whisking until ingredients are incorporated.

Gradually pour the olive oil, in a slow and steady stream, into the potato mixture, continually whisking until the mixture thickens. If skordalia becomes too thick, add a tablespoon of warm water to thin it out.

Skordalia is a pungent Greek sauce or dip made with bread (or, like we have here, with potato), garlic, lemon juice and olive oil. It can be served with almost any kind of dish, from grilled meats and poultry to fish and raw vegetables.

1 Combine lamb with garlic, juice, oil, oregano and thyme in large shallow dish. Cover; refrigerate 3 hours or overnight.
2 Preheat oven to 160°C/140°C fan-forced.
3 Place lamb in large baking dish; roast, uncovered, 4 hours.
4 Meanwhile, make skordalia.
5 Combine potatoes in large bowl with rind and extra juice, oil and thyme. Place potatoes, in single layer, on oven tray. Roast potatoes for last 30 minutes of lamb cooking time.
6 Remove lamb from oven; cover to keep warm.
7 Increase oven to 220°C/200°C fan-forced; roast potatoes a further 20 minutes or until browned lightly and cooked through. Serve potatoes and lamb with skordalia.
skordalia Boil, steam or microwave potato until tender; drain. Push potato through food mill or fine sieve into medium bowl; cool 10 minutes. Whisk combined garlic, juice, vinegar and the water into potato. Gradually whisk in oil in a thin, steady stream; continue whisking until skordalia thickens. Stir in about a tablespoon of warm water if skordalia is too thick. Serve sprinkled with extra lemon thyme leaves, if you like.
nutritional count per serving 57g total fat (14g saturated fat); 4556kJ (1090 cal); 51.5g carbohydrate; 91.2g protein; 6.7g fibre

THE PERFECT ROAST

roast leg of pork with apple sauce

Roast pork with crackling tastes too good to be eaten only on special occasions. With a little know-how, you can cook succulent, tender meat and crispy rind at any time of year. And forget those too-sweet store-bought apple sauces – making one yourself is too easy.

Make-ahead sauce Apple sauce can be made one day ahead. Simply store in an airtight container or glass jar and place in the refrigerator until needed. Reheat sauce before serving.

Sauce variations You can add a handful of cranberries to the apples and increase the sugar to reduce any tartness. For a brandied apple sauce, add raisins, chopped roasted hazelnuts and a little brandy.

Storing pork As soon as you get home, store pork in the coldest part of the fridge. If you're not cooking it within two days, you can freeze pork for up to six months. Place the pork in an airtight container or sealable plastic bag. To thaw, place the frozen pork in the fridge for 24 to 48 hours, depending on the size, or until thawed.

The right cut A pork roast with crackling requires a different cut of meat from one without crackling. Look for a pork cut with good coverage of fat and rind. This recipe uses pork leg, but other suitable cuts include rack, rolled loin and rolled shoulder.

Make it medium To enjoy roast pork at its juicy best, cook it to medium so there is still a hint of pink in the centre. Contrary to popular belief, pork doesn't have to be cooked all the way through. Overcooking pork makes the meat tough and dry.

Perfect crackling The three magic ingredients for crispy savoury crackling are oil, salt and heat. Make sure the rind is dry and rubbed well with oil and salt. The pork must be placed in a very hot oven for the skin to start bubbling and browning up.

Tying the pork leg Roasts are tied for two reasons – to keep the roast in an attractive round shape and to hold any stuffing or seasoning inside of the roast. It's important to tie the knots properly – if they are too loose, the muscle in the meat will relax and gravity will cause the roast to form into an oval shape. If the knot is too tight, too much juice will seep out of the meat.

1. Place pork on a clean chopping board and score the rind at regular intervals, using a sharp knife. This allows moisture and fat to run out of the rind, which makes it crisp.

2. Tie the pork at 5cm intervals with kitchen string to secure. Avoid slipping the string into the slits.

3. Place pork in a shallow baking dish and, using your fingers, rub the oil all over the skin. Rub the salt over the skin, working it into the slits. This helps to draw any moisture out of the rind and makes it crackle.

roast leg of pork with apple sauce

**PREP + COOK TIME
2 HOURS 40 MINS
(+ STANDING)
SERVES 8**

2.5kg boneless pork leg roast, rind on
2 tablespoons olive oil
1 tablespoon sea salt flakes
6 medium potatoes (1.2kg), quartered
2 tablespoons olive oil, extra
2 tablespoons fresh sage leaves
2 tablespoons fresh rosemary leaves

apple sauce
3 large green apples (600g)
½ cup (125ml) water
1 teaspoon white sugar
pinch ground cinnamon

4 and core the apples. On a clean surface, the apples into quarters, then into thick slices.

5 Place the apples in a medium saucepan on the stove top and add ½ cup of water.

6 Bring the water to a simmer and cook the apples, uncovered, for about 10 minutes, or until the apple is soft enough to crush with a spoon.

The ancient pairing of pork and apple dates way back to the classical cookery book *Apicius*, a surviving text of the Roman Empire, in which a recipe for diced pork with apple was offered. The combination remains a favourite today, as the sweet crisp flavour of the apple counteracts the creamy fatty texture of the pork beautifully.

1 Preheat oven to 220°C/200°C fan-forced.

2 Score pork rind with sharp knife; tie pork at 5cm intervals with kitchen string. Place pork in large shallow baking dish; rub with oil, then salt. Roast, uncovered, 20 minutes.

3 Reduce oven to 180°C/160°C fan-forced; roast pork, uncovered, further 2 hours.

4 Meanwhile, combine potato with extra oil and herbs in large bowl. Place in single layer on oven tray. Roast, uncovered, about 35 minutes.

5 Make apple sauce.

6 Stand pork, covered loosely with foil, 10 minutes before slicing. Serve pork and potatoes with apple sauce.

apple sauce Peel and core apples; slice thickly. Place apples and the water in medium saucepan; simmer, uncovered, about 10 minutes or until apple is soft. Remove pan from heat; stir in sugar and cinnamon.

nutritional count per serving 34g total fat (9.7g saturated fat); 2976kJ (712 cal); 27.4g carbohydrate; 71.9g protein; 4.1g fibre

THE PERFECT ROAST

roast loin of pork

Give the modern generation of leaner, milder-tasting pork an old-fashioned roasting to put the rich, juicy chew back into the meat. In keeping with the traditional theme, this dish begs for a sweet, tangy apple sauce you can make in no time.

Quick apple sauce You can take a shortcut using the microwave oven. Place apple, water, sugar and cinnamon in a heatproof, microwave-safe bowl. Cover with a lid and cook on HIGH/800watts/100% for 3 minutes. Remove cover and cook on HIGH/800watts/100%, stirring every 4 minutes, for 8 minutes or until apples are soft.

Vegetables on the side This pork recipe avoids overpowering flavours, so you can accompany it with just about any vegetable. Try yellow and green squash, baked alongside the pork, to offset the sweetness of the apple sauce. Baked carrots, potatoes and mushrooms work well too.

Salad to serve For a light side dish, toss together a raw vegetable salad. Try shredded spinach, red cabbage and carrot, sprinkled with flaked almonds and raisins, and dressed with apple cider vinegar and oil. Just add a sliced french baguette for a complete meal.

Herb flavourings The simple Mediterranean essence of rosemary and olive oil does extraordinary things to a juicy pork loin roast. Fresh rosemary is always better than dried, but if you're caught out, substitute a teaspoon dried rosemary for a tablespoon fresh. Other good fresh substitutes for rosemary are sage and thyme.

Preparing the rind Make sure the pork is well chilled, as cold rind and fat is firm and easier to cut. Pork loin has just one rectangular piece of skin to score, which makes the job much easier. You need a very sharp knife to do the job with precision, cutting right through into the fat but not the meat.

Pork rolls Leftover roast pork makes a great filling for Vietnamese pork rolls. Spread combined pâté and mayonnaise inside a warm bread roll, then fill with pork slices and top with grated carrot, green onion and chilli. Top with sweet chilli sauce, soy sauce, and coriander.

Storing leftovers Allow any leftover pork to cool to room temperature, then store in an airtight container and place in the refrigerator. The pork should be consumed within 2 days.

1. Place pork loin on a cutting board and score the rind at 1cm intervals, using a sharp knife.

2. Tie the pork at 2cm intervals with kitchen string to secure. Avoid slipping the string into the slits.

3. Slide a few sprigs of fresh rosemary under the string that holds the pork so that they are well secured.

roast loin of pork with apple sauce

PREP + COOK TIME 2 HOURS • SERVES 8

2.5kg boneless loin of pork, rind on
2 sprigs rosemary
1 tablespoon olive oil
1 tablespoon coarse cooking salt
apple sauce
3 large apples (600g)
½ cup (125ml) water
1 teaspoon white sugar
pinch ground cinnamon

TIP

- Ask your butcher to roll and tie the pork at 2cm intervals for you, and to score the rind, if it isn't already done.

pork in a shallow baking dish and, using your s, rub the oil all over the skin. Rub the salt over in, working it into the slits.

When pork is cooked, remove from the oven and cover loosely with foil. Allow the pork to rest for about 15 minutes before cutting into slices.

Transfer the pork to a clean chopping board and, using a sharp knife, cut into slices to serve.

As always when buying meat, your best bet is a supplier you can trust. In general, pork should have fine-grained, pale pink flesh, white fat and thin, smooth skin. Avoid any that has waxy fat or is wet, meaning it has been badly handled and may be from an animal in poor condition.

1 Preheat oven to 250°C/230°C fan-forced.
2 Score pork rind with sharp knife. Tie pork at 2cm intervals with kitchen string; tuck rosemary under string. Place pork in large baking dish; rub with oil, then salt. Roast about 40 minutes or until rind blisters. Drain excess fat from dish.
3 Reduce oven to 180°C/160°C fan-forced. Roast pork about 1 hour. Transfer pork to plate; cover loosely with foil, stand 15 minutes before carving.
4 Meanwhile, make apple sauce.
5 Serve pork with apple sauce.

apple sauce Peel and core apples; slice thickly. Place apples and the water in medium saucepan; simmer, uncovered, about 10 minutes or until apple is soft. Remove pan from heat; stir in sugar and cinnamon. Blend or process mixture until almost smooth.

nutritional count per serving 72g total fat (24.1g saturated fat); 3762kJ (900 cal); 7.7g carbohydrate; 56.7g protein; 1.1g fibre

STIR-FRIES

Stir-fries

The art of stir-frying is one of Asia's many gifts to the world, and the perfect answer to modern living's weeknightly call for quick, healthy meals.

Using a wok over a high heat, the technique of stir-frying evolved in China where traditionally firewood was a precious commodity – and cooking over a fire had to be quick and efficient. Stir-frying emerged, along with the wok itself, as the best way to cook over a very high heat in a very short time.

Stir-frying is fast and fun and you can have a fragrant bowl of perfectly seared meat, crisp vegetables and noodles ready within minutes. But the key is in the preparation: make sure you have all your ingredients chopped, and spices and sauces on hand, before you turn the wok on. Then, you simply turn up the heat, splash your wok with oil, and begin cooking. Stir-fries make great main courses or you can toss your favourite vegetables together for a side dish.

It's a dynamic way to cook: it's possible to feel the hassles of your day lift from your shoulders as you toss and stir your sizzling, aromatic ingredients into a casual masterpiece.

THE WOK

The uniquely-shaped, round-bottomed wok is the tool of trade for stir-fries. The best ones are those found in Chinese food stores (you'll find loads of these in any Chinatown district, in any major city). Designer woks are usually too heavy and often too shallow, and electric woks just don't get hot enough. Some woks have flat bottoms, which do make the wok stand straight on an electric or ceramic burner without support, but this defeats the purpose of the classic design, which is to concentrate intense heat at the centre.

Stir-frying works better on gas burners than an electric stove top because the gas flames surround the wok with the intense heat needed. For cooking on gas, choose a wok made from carbon steel. For an electric stove top, use a cast-iron wok because it holds the heat better than carbon steel.

To clean a wok, wash with hot water only, removing any stuck-on food with a non-metal brush. Dry with a cloth, then place over low heat to dry thoroughly. With repeated use, the wok will acquire a dark, slightly slick surface or patina making it increasingly non-stick.

THE TECHNIQUE

The key to a successful stir-fry is in the preparation: have all the required ingredients chopped, diced, measured and immediately at hand. Remember to cut all the food into small, bite-sized pieces.

Heat the wok until it is very hot before adding the oil, then heat the oil until it just starts to smoke before adding any food. Before adding the food, use the chan or spatula to swirl the oil around the sides of the wok as well as the base.

KEEP THE HEAT HIGH THROUGHOUT THE COOKING.

Meat should go in first, ahead of vegetables. Stir constantly, and once all pieces of the meat are seared (this should only take a minute), add the vegetables. You might add some liquid at this point and cover the wok with a lid for the briefest moment, to help steam the vegetables. Green vegetables (buk choy, snow peas etc) only require the merest toss in the wok at the end of the cooking. Remember, you want the vegetables to come out of the wok just-cooked and still crisp and glistening.

Get physical in the kitchen. Stir-frying requires active participation and focus. Keep tossing and stirring constantly so that different pieces of the food are being seared on the bottom of the wok at any one time. Keep one hand on the wok handle while the other hand briskly moves the chan or spatula. Feel free to tilt and move the wok as you need to, to help toss the ingredients.

THE ACCESSORIES

MANY GAS STOVE TOPS THESE DAYS ARE FITTED WITH WOK BURNERS (OR EVEN TWO – SUCH IS IMPORTANCE OF WOK COOKING IN OUR KITCHENS TODAY) THAT ARE SPECIALLY DESIGNED TO HOLD A WOK AND EMIT AN ESPECIALLY ROBUST FLAME. BUT IF YOU DON'T HAVE A SPECIALISED BURNER, THEN YOU'LL NEED A WOK STAND TO STOP THE WOK FROM TIPPING OVER.

FOR ELECTRIC OR CERAMIC STOVE TOPS, GET A STAND THAT IS A SOLID METAL RING PUNCHED WITH ABOUT SIX VENTILATION HOLES. FOR A GAS STOVE TOP, GET ONE THAT IS A CIRCULAR WIRE FRAME, AS THE GAS FLAME MIGHT NOT GET ENOUGH AIR TO FUNCTION INSIDE THE MORE SOLID STAND.

FROM THE MOMENT YOUR INGREDIENTS ENTER THE WOK, YOU'LL NEED TO BE TOSSING THEM. THE AUTHENTIC TOOL FOR DOING THIS IS CALLED A 'CHAN', AVAILABLE FROM ASIAN FOOD STORES. YOU CAN USE A WOODEN SPATULA OR LARGE SPOON, BUT A CHAN IS INEXPENSIVE AND WORKS BETTER BECAUSE ITS BLADE IS THE RIGHT SIZE AND ITS CURVE IS DESIGNED TO FIT THE CURVE OF THE WOK.

singapore chilli crab

PREP + COOK TIME 30 MINS • SERVES 4

Notoriously difficult to eat, but irresistibly delicious. Have finger bowls filled with warm water and lemon slices – and plenty of large napkins – with this dish. And don't wear a white shirt or eat this on a first date.

4 x 325g uncooked blue swimmer crabs
2 tablespoons peanut oil
3 cloves garlic, chopped finely
4cm piece fresh ginger (20g), grated
1 fresh small red thai chilli, sliced thinly
⅓ cup (85ml) bottled tomato pasta sauce
2 tablespoons chilli sauce
2 tablespoons japanese soy sauce
⅓ cup (80ml) water
2 teaspoons white sugar
½ cup firmly packed fresh coriander leaves

1 Lift flap under body of each crab; turn crab over, hold body with one hand while pulling off top part of shell with the other. Discard shell and gills on either side of body. Rinse crab under cold water; chop body into quarters.
2 Heat oil in wok; stir-fry garlic, ginger and chilli; stir-fry until fragrant. Add sauces, the water and sugar; stir-fry 2 minutes.
3 Add crab; cook, covered, over medium heat, about 10 minutes or until crab has changed colour. Serve sprinkled with coriander.
nutritional count per serving 10.1g total fat (1.8g saturated fat); 723kJ (173 cal); 8.2g carbohydrate; 11.6g protein; 1.6g fibre

Lift the tail flap then, with a peeling motion, pull off the top shell.

Remove and discard the whitish gills (these are known as dead men's fingers), plus the liver and brain matter.

Rinse the crab well then chop into quarters.

crispy shredded beef

PREP + COOK TIME 2 HOURS (+ STANDING) • SERVES 4

Corned silverside is beef that is first pickled in brine then cooked submerged in water with spices, herbs, etc. Here we poach the silverside in milk to draw out as much salt as possible.

750g piece corned silverside
1 litre (4 cups) milk, approximately
1 fresh long red chilli, chopped coarsely
2 kaffir lime leaves, torn
3cm piece fresh ginger (15g), chopped coarsely
2 cloves garlic, quartered
450g wide fresh rice noodles
¼ cup (60ml) peanut oil
1 fresh small red thai chilli, sliced thinly
3 cloves garlic, crushed
3cm piece fresh ginger (15g), grated
1 medium red capsicum (200g), sliced thinly
150g sugar snap peas, trimmed
1 tablespoon fish sauce
2 tablespoons kecap manis
½ cup loosely packed fresh coriander leaves

1 Place beef with as much milk as needed to cover in large saucepan; bring to the boil. Reduce heat; simmer, uncovered, 10 minutes. Drain beef; discard milk.
2 Place beef, chopped chilli, lime leaves, chopped ginger and quartered garlic in same cleaned pan. Cover with cold water; simmer, covered, 1½ hours. Remove beef from pan; discard pan ingredients. Drain beef on wire rack over tray 15 minutes.
3 Meanwhile, place noodles in large heatproof bowl, cover with boiling water; separate with fork, drain.
4 Trim excess fat from beef. Using two forks, shred beef finely. Heat oil in wok; stir-fry beef, in batches, until browned and crisp. Drain.
5 Stir-fry sliced chilli, crushed garlic, grated ginger, capsicum and peas in wok until vegetables soften. Add sauces; stir-fry 1 minute.
6 Return beef to wok with noodles; stir-fry until hot. Remove from heat; sprinkle with coriander.

nutritional count per serving 29.4g total fat (11.2g saturated fat); 2571kJ (615 cal); 41g carbohydrate; 45.8g protein; 2.8g fibre

Place the beef in a pan with chilli, lime, ginger and garlic, cover with water and simmer until tender.

Drain the beef on a wire rack for about 15 minutes to allow it to dry completely.

Slice the beef and using two forks, shred it finely.

Stir-fry beef in batches in hot oil until it is brown and crisp.

char siu lamb and noodle stir-fry

PREP + COOK TIME 35 MINS • SERVES 4

Char siu sauce, salty and flavoured with chinese five-spice, has a dominant anise flavour. It turns the surface of meat red.

2 cloves garlic, crushed
2cm piece fresh ginger (10g), grated
1 tablespoon finely grated orange rind
1 teaspoon sesame oil
750g lamb strips
450g hokkien noodles
2 tablespoons peanut oil
200g sugar snap peas
115g baby corn, halved lengthways
2 fresh long red chillies, sliced thinly
⅓ cup (120g) char siu sauce
2 tablespoons water
1 tablespoon rice wine vinegar

1 Combine garlic, ginger, rind, sesame oil and lamb in medium bowl.
2 Place noodles in large heatproof bowl, cover with boiling water; separate with fork, drain.
3 Heat half the peanut oil in wok; stir-fry peas and corn until just tender. Remove from wok.
4 Heat remaining peanut oil in wok; stir-fry lamb, in batches, until browned all over and cooked as desired. Remove from wok. Return peas, corn and lamb to wok with noodles, chilli and combined sauce, water and vinegar; stir-fry until heated through.
nutritional count per serving 29.2g total fat (9.6g saturated fat); 2725kJ (652 cal); 46.6g carbohydrate; 47.1g protein; 8g fibre

beef in satay sauce

PREP + COOK TIME 30 MINS • SERVES 4

1 tablespoon peanut oil
750g beef strips
1 fresh long red chilli, sliced thinly
1 medium brown onion (150g), sliced thinly
1 medium red capsicum (200g), sliced thinly
½ cup (140g) peanut butter
½ cup (125ml) coconut cream
¼ cup (60ml) sweet chilli sauce
1 tablespoon japanese soy sauce

1 Heat half the oil in wok; stir-fry beef, in batches, until cooked. Remove beef from wok.
2 Heat remaining oil in wok; stir-fry chilli, onion and capsicum until soft; remove from wok.
3 Combine peanut butter, coconut cream and sauces in wok; bring to the boil. Return beef and onion mixture to wok; stir-fry until hot.
nutritional count per serving 42.2g total fat (15g saturated fat); 2629kJ (629 cal); 10.6g carbohydrate; 49.8g protein; 6.1g fibre

[1] char siu lamb and noodle stir-fry
[2] beef in satay sauce
[3] chiang mai pork and eggplant [page 344]
[4] cantonese lamb [page 344]

1

2

3

4

chiang mai pork and eggplant

PREP + COOK TIME 45 MINS • SERVES 4

You can also use a mortar and pestle to make the garlic paste. The theory when using a mortar and pestle is that, by adding and processing the ingredients one at a time, each builds on the next to form a well-integrated mixture. The grinding motion releases the essential oils and flavour of each of the ingredients.

3 fresh small red thai chillies, halved
6 cloves garlic, quartered
1 medium brown onion (150g), chopped coarsely
500g baby eggplants
¼ cup (60ml) peanut oil
700g pork leg steaks, sliced thinly
1 tablespoon fish sauce
1 tablespoon dark soy sauce
1 tablespoon grated palm sugar
4 purple thai shallots (100g), sliced thinly
150g snake beans, cut into 5cm lengths
1 cup loosely packed thai basil leaves

1 Blend or process chilli, garlic and onion until mixture forms a paste.
2 Quarter eggplants lengthways; slice each piece into 5cm lengths. Cook eggplant in large saucepan of boiling water until just tender; drain, pat dry.
3 Heat half the oil in wok; stir-fry eggplant, in batches, until browned lightly. Drain.
4 Heat remaining oil in wok; stir-fry pork, in batches, until cooked. Remove from wok.
5 Stir-fry garlic paste in wok about 3 minutes or until fragrant and browned lightly. Add sauces and sugar; stir-fry until sugar dissolves.
6 Add shallot and beans; stir-fry until beans are tender. Return eggplant and pork to wok; stir-fry until hot. Remove from heat; sprinkle with basil.

nutritional count per serving 19.3g total fat (4.1g saturated fat); 1672kJ (400 cal); 10.1g carbohydrate; 43.6g protein; 5.8g fibre

cantonese lamb

PREP + COOK TIME 35 MINS • SERVES 4

Char siu sauce can also be labelled chinese barbecue sauce. You can use lamb backstrap for this recipe, if you prefer, slicing it thinly before use.

1 tablespoon peanut oil
800g lamb strips
1 medium brown onion (150g), sliced thinly
1 clove garlic, crushed
150g snow peas, trimmed
150g sugar snap peas, trimmed
⅔ cup (80g) frozen peas
115g baby corn, halved lengthways
1 tablespoon dark soy sauce
1 tablespoon char siu sauce
¼ cup (60ml) chicken stock
1 tablespoon cornflour
2 tablespoons lime juice

1 Heat half the oil in wok; stir-fry lamb, in batches, until browned.
2 Heat remaining oil in wok; stir-fry onion and garlic until onion softens. Add peas and corn; stir-fry until corn is almost tender.
3 Return lamb to wok with sauces and stock; stir-fry 2 minutes or until lamb is cooked. Stir in blended cornflour and juice; stir-fry until sauce boils and thickens.

nutritional count per serving 23.2g total fat (8.9g saturated fat); 1977kJ (473 cal); 16g carbohydrate; 47.6g protein; 5.4g fibre

teriyaki beef

PREP + COOK TIME 25 MINS • SERVES 4

Mirin is a Japanese sweet rice wine used only for cooking. Sake is also a rice wine but is made for drinking, used as an ingredient only in certain dishes. If mirin is unavailable, dry sherry, vermouth or brandy can be used as a substitute.

⅓ cup (80ml) teriyaki sauce
½ cup (125ml) hoisin sauce
2 tablespoons mirin
1 tablespoon peanut oil
750g beef strips
250g broccoli, cut into florets
250g sugar snap peas, trimmed
115g fresh baby corn, halved lengthways
4cm piece fresh ginger (20g), grated
1½ cups (120g) bean sprouts

1 Combine sauces and mirin in small jug.
2 Heat half the oil in wok; stir-fry beef, in batches, until browned.
3 Heat remaining oil in wok; stir-fry broccoli until almost tender.
4 Return beef to wok with sauce mixture, peas, corn and ginger. Stir-fry until vegetables and beef are cooked. Remove from heat; sprinkle with sprouts.

nutritional count per serving 20.7g total fat (7.2g saturated fat); 2073kJ (496 cal); 23.2g carbohydrate; 48g protein; 10.5g fibre

sang choy bow

PREP + COOK TIME 30 MINS • SERVES 4

Sang choy bow is eaten with your fingers – the lettuce wrapped around the savoury mince filling. You can use chicken mince or a pork and veal mix instead; you can also serve the pork mixture in small witlof or betel leaves as cocktail food.

2 teaspoons sesame oil
1 small brown onion (80g), chopped finely
2 cloves garlic, crushed
2cm piece fresh ginger (10g), grated
500g lean pork mince
2 tablespoons water
100g shiitake mushrooms, chopped finely
2 tablespoons light soy sauce
2 tablespoons oyster sauce
1 tablespoon lime juice
2 cups bean sprouts
4 green onions, sliced thinly
¼ cup coarsely chopped fresh coriander
12 large butter lettuce leaves

1 Heat oil in wok; stir-fry brown onion, garlic and ginger until onion softens. Add pork; stir-fry until changed in colour.
2 Add the water, mushrooms, sauces and juice; stir-fry until mushrooms are tender. Remove from heat. Add sprouts, green onion and coriander; toss to combine.
3 Spoon sang choy bow into lettuce leaves to serve.

nutritional count per serving 11.5g total fat (3.6g saturated fat); 1112kJ (266 cal); 8.9g carbohydrate; 29.3g protein; 4.1g fibre

beef sukiyaki

PREP + COOK TIME 30 MINS • SERVES 4

In Japan, sukiyaki is traditionally shared at the table from the pan in which it was cooked, making it a great dish for a fun dinner party. Diners use their chopsticks to dip the piping hot ingredients into their individual bowls of egg.

400g fresh udon noodles
300g fresh firm silken tofu
4 eggs
¼ cup (60ml) vegetable oil
600g beef rump steak, trimmed, sliced thinly
8 oyster mushrooms
4 green onions, sliced thinly
300g spinach, trimmed, chopped coarsely
2 cups (160g) bean sprouts

broth
1 cup (250ml) japanese soy sauce
½ cup (125ml) sake
½ cup (125ml) mirin
½ cup (125ml) water
½ cup (110g) white sugar
2 cloves garlic, crushed

1 Combine ingredients for broth in medium saucepan; cook over medium heat, stirring, until sugar dissolves. Remove from heat; cover to keep warm.
2 Place noodles in heatproof bowl, cover with boiling water; separate with fork, drain. Cut into random lengths.
3 Cut tofu into 2cm cubes; spread, in single layer, on absorbent-paper-lined-tray. Cover tofu with more absorbent paper, stand 10 minutes.
4 Break eggs into individual serving bowls; beat lightly.
5 Heat half the oil in wok; stir-fry beef, in batches, until browned.
6 Heat half the remaining oil in wok; stir-fry tofu, in batches, until browned.
7 Add remaining oil to wok; stir-fry mushrooms, onion, spinach and sprouts until vegetables are just tender.
8 Return beef and tofu to wok with noodles and broth; stir-fry until hot.
Serve sukiyaki from wok, with each diner using chopsticks to pick up sukiyaki ingredients and dip in their individual bowl of egg and eat.

nutritional count per serving 52g total fat (17.2g saturated fat); 4811kJ (1151 cal); 87.4g carbohydrate; 65.7g protein; 13.6g fibre

Do you have to dip the sukiyaki in raw egg? I worry about the health risks of eating raw egg.

It's true that there are some people in the community who should avoid eating raw eggs: pregnant women, the elderly and those with immune deficiencies. However, if you don't like the idea of eating raw egg, then simply eat the sukiyaki just as it is.

SPECIAL FEATURE

Asian vegetables

Asian greens, herbs, mushrooms and other vegetables are becoming more and more common in our supermarkets and greegrocers. And it's a good thing too because nothing can satisfactorily replace them in Asian recipes.

TAT SOI
A mild-flavoured cabbage also known as rosette, flat or spoon cabbage because of its spoon-shaped leaves and the way it grows. Eaten raw in salads.

BUK CHOY
Usually sold in bundles of three or four plants, buk choy has crisp white stems and tender, mildly cabbage-flavoured leaves with an acid tang. Often used in stir-fries or cooked alone and dressed with Chinese sauces.

CHOY SUM
Also called flowering buk choy or buk choy sum, this has small yellow flowers which are eaten with the leaves and stems. It has a mild mustard sort of flavour; can be steamed or stir-fried.

LEMON GRASS
A very fibrous plant, so only the inner stem is used. Cut the stalks short and peel away the tough outer layers until you come to the more tender white part at the base.

OYSTER MUSHROOMS
These mushrooms are delicate in flavour and texture, so should not be used with strong-flavoured ingredients likely to overwhelm them. Use them raw or cook briefly – they become unpleasantly slippery if cooked for too long.

GREEN PAPAYA
This is simply underripe papaya. It varies in length and shape, and is mostly used, raw or cooked, in Thai recipes. Grated green papaya features in many Thai salads.

Q&A

Is there a general rule for cooking Asian greens? I'd really like to cook them in the way they do in yum cha restaurants.

The trick is brief cooking – whether steaming or stir-frying. Gai Lan is the vegetable you most often find at yum cha – it's steamed just until wilted, the stalks remain crisp and then it's drizzled with oyster sauce.

BOK
crunchy cabbage is delicious raw, stir-fried, ned or braised for Asian dishes, but you might want to try serving it instead of european age as part of a Western-style meal.

KAFFIR LIME LEAVES
Quite different in scent and flavour from ordinary lime leaves, these give a heady citrus freshness to soups, curries, fish and poultry dishes. They are rather tough, so shred finely or, if used whole, remove them before serving.

SHIITAKE MUSHROOMS
The earthy fragrance and flavour of shiitake are quite different from those of any other mushroom. Available fresh or dried; soak dried caps in warm water and discard the tough stems.

LAN
known as chinese broccoli, this vegetable is d for its crunchy texture and flavour, resembling of european broccoli. The white flowers, stems eaves are eaten. Often cooked with oyster e; can be steamed, boiled or stir-fried.

KANG KONG
Also known as water spinach, this delicate green vegetable has long, hollow stems and thin leaves. Use the leaves and top half of the stems, cut into 5cm lengths. Stir-fry, dip in batter and deep-fry, or serve steamed with kecap manis or a savoury paste.

BETEL LEAVES
Sold in bunches, often under their Vietnamese name, lá lôp; these leaves are used as a wrapping for rice, minced meat etc. The betel used for chewing is related but a different plant.

thai basil chicken and snake bean stir-fry

PREP + COOK TIME 40 MINS (+ REFRIGERATION)
SERVES 4

800g chicken thigh fillets, sliced thinly
¼ cup (60ml) fish sauce
1 tablespoon grated palm sugar
¼ teaspoon ground white pepper
1 tablespoon peanut oil
3 cloves garlic, sliced thinly
2cm piece fresh ginger (10g), sliced thinly
½ teaspoon dried chilli flakes
250g snake beans, cut into 5cm lengths
2 medium yellow capsicums (400g), sliced thinly
⅓ cup (80ml) chinese cooking wine
⅓ cup (80ml) lemon juice
1 tablespoon dark soy sauce
½ cup loosely packed thai basil leaves

There are more than two dozen varieties of basil, and the one used here is thai basil, also known as horapa. It has very small leaves and purplish stems, with a slight licorice or aniseed taste. It's one of the basic flavours of Thai cuisine.

1 Combine chicken, fish sauce, sugar and pepper in large bowl. Cover; refrigerate 1 hour.
2 Heat oil in wok; stir-fry chicken mixture 10 minutes or until almost cooked. Add garlic, ginger, chilli, beans and capsicum; stir-fry until beans are tender.
3 Add wine, juice and soy sauce; bring to the boil. Reduce heat; simmer, uncovered, 2 minutes. Remove from heat; stir in basil.

nutritional count per serving 19.4g total fat (5.2g saturated fat); 1622kJ (388 cal); 8.6g carbohydrate; 42.4g protein; 3.3g fibre

Use a clean board and a sharp knife to thinly slice the chicken thigh fillets.

Use a fine grater to grate the palm sugar (you can use brown sugar if you can't find palm sugar, but palm sugar gives the authentic Thai taste).

Peel the ginger and slice it thinly using a small, very sharp knife.

Pour in the chinese cooking wine, lemon juice and soy sauce and bring to the boil.

peking duck

PREP + COOK TIME 20 MINS • SERVES 4

This famous Chinese dish is prized for the crunchy duck skin. Chinese restaurants serve two dishes using peking duck: pancakes, which are served with skin and little meat, while the remaining duck meat is often served in a noodle or stir-fry dish.

You can buy pancakes in several sizes at Asian grocery stores. The small pancakes make great canapé bases.

1kg chinese barbecued duck
24 peking duck pancakes (240g)
4 green onions, cut into thin strips
⅔ cup (160ml) hoisin sauce
2 cups (160g) bean sprouts
2 lebanese cucumbers (260g), halved lengthways, seeded, cut into thin strips

1 Remove meat and skin from duck; discard bones. Chop meat and skin coarsely.
2 Heat pancakes by folding each into quarters, place in steamer set over large pan of simmering water; steam until warm and pliable.
3 Heat wok; stir-fry duck and onion until onion just softens. Add half the sauce; stir-fry until hot. Remove from heat; stir in sprouts.
4 Serve duck mixture with pancakes, cucumber and remaining sauce.

nutritional count per serving 40.6g total fat (11.6g saturated fat); 2713kJ (649 cal); 35.1g carbohydrate; 33.5g protein; 7.3g fibre

mongolian garlic lamb

PREP + COOK TIME 25 MINS • SERVES 4

This popular Chinese restaurant dish has its origins in the campfire-braised meats, packed with masses of garlic, eaten by Mongol herders in the vast expanses of the Euro-Asian steppes.

3 cloves garlic, crushed
1 tablespoon cornflour
¼ cup (60ml) dark soy sauce
⅓ cup (80ml) sweet sherry
800g lamb backstraps, sliced thinly
2 tablespoons peanut oil
1 tablespoon brown sugar
1 teaspoon sesame oil
8 green onions, sliced thinly

1 Combine garlic, cornflour, half the sauce and half the sherry in large bowl; add lamb, mix well.
2 Heat peanut oil in wok; stir-fry lamb mixture, in batches, until browned.
3 Return lamb to wok with sugar, sesame oil and remaining sauce and sherry; stir-fry until sauce thickens slightly. Remove from heat; serve stir-fry sprinkled with onion.

nutritional count per serving 28g total fat (9.8g saturated fat); 2057kJ (492 cal); 12.4g carbohydrate; 43.1g protein; 0.8g fibre

sweet chilli plum chicken with noodles

**PREP + COOK TIME 25 MINS
(+ REFRIGERATION)
SERVES 4**

Water chestnuts are the corms (solid bulbs) of an aquatic plant native to South-East Asia. They are about the size of a walnut and have been eaten in China for centuries, especially in the south where they are sometimes grown in paddies between rice plants. Peel off the dark outer skin to reveal crunchy white flesh. Sometimes available fresh, they are more commonly sold canned.

¼ cup (60ml) sweet chilli sauce
2 tablespoons plum sauce
750g chicken thigh fillets, sliced thinly
450g hokkien noodles
227g can water chestnuts, rinsed, halved
8 green onions, sliced thickly
1 fresh long red chilli, sliced thinly
2 cloves garlic, crushed
300g buk choy, trimmed, chopped coarsely

1 Combine sauces with chicken in large bowl. Cover; refrigerate 1 hour.
2 Heat oiled wok; stir-fry chicken mixture, in batches, until browned. Remove from wok.
3 Meanwhile, place noodles in medium heatproof bowl; cover with boiling water, separate with fork, drain.
4 Stir-fry chestnuts, onion, chilli and garlic in wok 2 minutes. Return chicken to wok with buk choy; stir-fry until chicken is cooked. Serve with noodles.

nutritional count per serving 14.9g total fat (4.2g saturated fat); 2011kJ (481 cal); 43.1g carbohydrate; 41g protein; 5.4g fibre

pork larb with broccolini

PREP + COOK TIME 25 MINS • SERVES 4

Larb is the national dish of Laos and is also a staple of Thai cuisine.

Palm sugar is an unrefined sugar used in Asian and Indian cooking. If you can't find it, you can use brown sugar instead.

1 tablespoon peanut oil
2 cloves garlic, crushed
600g pork mince
⅓ cup (90g) grated palm sugar
2 tablespoons fish sauce
4 kaffir lime leaves, sliced finely
½ cup (40g) fried shallots
⅓ cup (45g) roasted unsalted peanuts
350g broccolini, trimmed, halved lengthways
1 tablespoon lime juice
1 cup loosely packed fresh coriander leaves
1 fresh long red chilli, sliced thinly
2 tablespoons coarsely chopped roasted unsalted peanuts

1 Heat oil in wok; stir-fry garlic and pork until pork is browned through. Remove from wok with slotted spoon.
2 Add sugar, sauce, lime leaves, shallots and nuts to wok; bring to the boil. Reduce heat; simmer, uncovered, 1 minute. Return pork to wok; cook, uncovered, about 2 minutes or until larb mixture is slightly dry and sticky.
3 Meanwhile, boil, steam or microwave broccolini; drain.
4 Stir juice and three-quarters of the coriander into larb off the heat; serve tossed with broccolini and sprinkled with remaining coriander, chilli and coarsely chopped nuts.

nutritional count per serving 23.9g total fat (6g saturated fat); 2006kJ (480 cal); 25g carbohydrate; 39.5g protein; 5.5g fibre

salt and pepper tofu

PREP + COOK TIME 35 MINS (+ STANDING) • SERVES 4

It is important that the tofu is as well drained as possible before it is deep-fried. If you have the time, a few hours before you want to make the dish, pat the whole piece of tofu with absorbent paper, then place it in a strainer or colander lined with absorbent paper set over a large bowl. Weight the tofu piece with a saucer topped with a heavy can; allow to drain for up to 3 hours. Chop the tofu just before deep-frying.

2 x 300g packets fresh firm tofu
1 small red capsicum (150g), sliced thinly
1 small yellow capsicum (150g), sliced thinly
100g snow peas, sliced thinly
1 small carrot (70g), sliced thinly
1 cup (80g) bean sprouts
½ cup loosely packed fresh coriander leaves
1 teaspoon coarsely ground black pepper
1 tablespoon sea salt
¼ teaspoon five-spice powder
⅓ cup (50g) plain flour
peanut oil, for deep-frying

chilli lime dressing
2 tablespoons peanut oil
¼ cup (60ml) lime juice
2 tablespoons sweet chilli sauce

1 Dry tofu with absorbent paper. Cut each piece in half horizontally; cut each half into quarters (you will have 16 pieces). Place tofu pieces, in single layer, on absorbent paper. Cover with more absorbent paper; stand 15 minutes.
2 Meanwhile, combine capsicums, snow peas, carrot, sprouts and coriander in large bowl.
3 Make chilli lime dressing by whisking ingredients together in small bowl.
4 Combine pepper, salt, five-spice and flour in medium bowl; coat tofu in mixture, shake away excess. Heat oil in wok; deep-fry tofu, in batches, until browned lightly. Drain on absorbent paper.
5 Serve salad topped with tofu; drizzle with dressing.

nutritional count per serving 28.2g total fat (4.7g saturated fat); 1772kJ (424 cal); 17.8g carbohydrate; 22g protein; 6.1g fibre

Can you tell me the difference between different tofus? I know there's silken tofu and firm tofu but don't know when to use which.

This recipe for salt and pepper tofu uses firm tofu because it's dry and when floured will fry to a crispy finish. Silken tofu on the other hand, is soft and moist and is usually used instead of cream or soft cheese by people who want to avoid dairy products.

sweet and sour pork

PREP + COOK TIME 40 MINS • SERVES 4

Sweet and sour sauce is often described as the "yin yang" of Chinese cooking. The Chinese consider the two flavours essential to a well-balanced meal.

800g pork fillet, sliced thinly
1 tablespoon sweet sherry
½ cup (125ml) light soy sauce
¾ cup (110g) plain flour
vegetable oil, for deep-frying
1 tablespoon vegetable oil, extra
1 medium red onion (170g), chopped coarsely
2 cloves garlic, crushed
1 medium red capsicum (200g), chopped coarsely
1 medium green capsicum (200g), chopped coarsely
1 medium carrot (120g), sliced thinly
500g fresh pineapple, chopped coarsely
150g sugar snap peas, trimmed
⅓ cup (80ml) chicken stock
¼ cup (70g) tomato sauce
¼ cup (60ml) white vinegar
¼ cup (55g) white sugar
½ cup loosely packed fresh coriander leaves

1 Combine pork with sherry and 2 tablespoons of the soy sauce in medium bowl; coat pork in flour, shake off excess.
2 Heat oil in wok; deep-fry pork, in batches, until browned and crisp. Drain on absorbent paper. (Strain oil, save for another use.)
3 Heat extra oil in wok; stir-fry onion and garlic until onion softens. Add capsicums and carrot; stir-fry until vegetables are tender. Return pork to wok with pineapple, peas, remaining soy sauce, stock, tomato sauce, vinegar and sugar; stir-fry until hot. Remove from heat; stir in coriander.

nutritional count per serving 20.2g total fat (3.6g saturated fat); 2717kJ (650 cal); 57.7g carbohydrate; 53.7g protein; 7.5g fibre

Q&A

What's the difference between dark soy sauce, light soy sauce and tamari? And when should you use each of them?

Dark soy sauce is used as a table condiment (in much the same way as Westerners use salt) and in dipping sauces. Light soy sauce has a lighter colour and flavour but is saltier – it's good in stir-fries. Tamari is a thick japanese soy sauce used as a dipping sauce and for basting.

burmese clam and mussel stir-fry

PREP + COOK TIME 35 MINS (+ STANDING) • SERVES 4

It is important to check that fresh mussels are alive when you buy them; it is equally important to be sure that they were still alive when cooked, this time by discarding any that have not opened, as live ones open when heated.

500g large black mussels
500g clams
2 teaspoons shrimp paste
1 small red onion (100g), quartered
2 x 10cm sticks fresh lemon grass (40g), chopped finely
4 fresh kaffir lime leaves
2cm piece fresh galangal (10g), sliced thinly
2 tablespoons sambal oelek
1 tablespoon grated palm sugar
2 tablespoons peanut oil
¼ cup (60ml) lime juice
1 tablespoon cornflour
¼ cup (60ml) water
2 green onions, sliced thickly
1 fresh long red chilli, sliced thinly

1 Scrub mussels; remove beards.
2 Rinse clams under cold water; place in large bowl, sprinkle with salt, cover with water. Soak 1½ hours; rinse, drain.
3 Meanwhile, wrap shrimp paste securely in small piece of foil. Heat wok; stir-fry shrimp paste parcel until fragrant. Discard foil; blend or process shrimp paste with red onion, lemon grass, lime leaves, galangal, sambal and sugar until mixture forms a smooth paste.
4 Heat oil in wok; stir-fry paste 5 minutes. Add mussels, clams and juice; stir-fry 2 minutes. Cover wok; cook about 5 minutes or until mussels and clams open (discard any that do not).
5 Uncover wok, stir in blended cornflour and the water; stir-fry until sauce boils and thickens. Sprinkle with green onion and chilli.

nutritional count per serving 10.5g total fat (1.8g saturated); 723kJ (173 cal); 12.2g carbohydrate; 6.9g protein; 0.9g fibre

garlic and chilli seafood stir-fry

PREP + COOK TIME 45 MINS • SERVES 4

720g uncooked medium king prawns
2 cleaned squid hoods (300g)
540g octopus, quartered
¼ cup (60ml) peanut oil
6 cloves garlic, sliced thinly
2cm piece fresh ginger (10g), sliced thinly
2 fresh long red chillies, sliced thinly
2 tablespoons chinese cooking wine
1 teaspoon caster sugar
4 green onions, cut in 4cm pieces

chilli fried shallots
1 tablespoon fried shallots
1 teaspoon sea salt flakes
½ teaspoon dried chilli flakes

1 Shell and devein prawns, leaving tails intact. Cut squid down centre to open out; score inside in diagonal pattern then cut into thick strips. Quarter octopus lengthways.
2 Combine ingredients for chilli fried shallots in small bowl.
3 Heat 1 tablespoon of the oil in wok; stir-fry prawns until changed in colour, remove from wok. Heat another tablespoon of the oil in wok; stir-fry squid until cooked through, remove from wok. Heat remaining oil in wok; stir-fry octopus until tender.
4 Stir-fry garlic, ginger and chilli in wok until fragrant. Return seafood to wok with remaining ingredients; stir-fry until hot.
5 Serve stir-fry sprinkled with chilli shallots.

nutritional count per serving 4.7g total fat (0.8g saturated fat); 460kJ (110 cal); 0.8g carbohydrate; 15.5g protein; 0.3g fibre

thai vegetable stir-fry

PREP + COOK TIME 30 MINS (+ STANDING) • SERVES 4

Pour juice and sauce down the side of the wok rather than directly into the centre of the food, so that it is already sizzling by the time it touches the food and therefore won't lower the temperature.

1 large eggplant (400g)
300g fresh firm silken tofu
1 medium brown onion (150g)
2 tablespoons peanut oil
1 clove garlic, crushed
2 fresh small red thai chillies, sliced thinly
1 tablespoon grated palm sugar
850g gai lan, chopped coarsely
2 tablespoons lime juice
⅓ cup (80ml) soy sauce
⅓ cup coarsely chopped fresh thai basil

1 Cut unpeeled eggplant in half lengthways; cut each half into thin slices. Place eggplant in colander, sprinkle with salt; stand 30 minutes.
2 Meanwhile, pat tofu all over with absorbent paper; cut into 2cm squares. Spread tofu, in single layer, on absorbent-paper-lined tray; cover tofu with more absorbent paper, stand at least 10 minutes.
3 Cut onion in half, then cut each half into thin even-size wedges. Rinse eggplant under cold water; pat dry with absorbent paper.
4 Heat oil in wok; stir-fry onion, garlic and chilli until onion softens. Add sugar; stir-fry until dissolved. Add eggplant; stir-fry, 1 minute. Add gai lan; stir-fry until just wilted. Add tofu, juice and sauce; stir-fry, tossing gently until combined. Remove from heat; toss basil through stir-fry.

nutritional count per serving 14.8g total fat (2.4g saturated fat); 1150kJ (275 cal); 13g carbohydrate; 17g protein; 12.3g fibre

BRAISES & STEWS

Braises & stews

Some of the best things in life take time. Casseroles and other slow-cooked meals are among them, providing us with replenishing, heavenly meals infused with flavour and melt-in-your-mouth tenderness. Many of the world's best-loved dishes are slow-cooked meals: the classic French offerings of beef bourguignon and coq au vin, Hungarian goulash, Irish stew, chilli con carne, and even humble curried sausages, which taste extraordinary when cooked with extra time.

WHETHER IT'S A CASSEROLE, BRAISE, POT ROAST OR STEW, SLOW-COOKED FOODS ARE LUXURIOUS, FLAVOURFUL AND HEART-WARMING – AND RELISHED EQUALLY AT DINNER PARTIES OR AS FAMILY FAVOURITES. CASSEROLES ALSO FREEZE BEAUTIFULLY, GIVING YOU A WONDERFUL COMFORTING MEAL AT THE READY WHEN YOU CRAVE IT.

SLOW-COOKED STYLES

The guiding principle of slow cooking is that the ingredients are cooked slowly with liquid so they become tender and their flavours blend. We tend to call all these dishes casseroles but there are, in fact, a few subtle variations on the theme, with slight differences in technique and liquid/meat ratios:

CASSEROLE Casseroling is the generic term for all food cooked slowly with liquid in a covered vessel in the oven.

BRAISE A type of casserole, this particular method begins with browning the meat on the stove top first before adding the liquid and then transferring it to the oven. The liquid usually consists of water, stock or wine (or a combination of these) and it is added until the food is half-submerged (a braise uses a small amount of liquid in relation to the quantity of meat). As the dish begins to cook, steam releases from the liquid and works to flavour and tenderise the food. Additional liquid is sometimes added during cooking to ensure adequate moisture. Braises generally use smaller pieces of meat or small cuts with bone-in such as lamb shanks.

POT-ROASTING This is another kind of braise, and uses the same technique as described above, the difference being that the meat is in one large piece, such as a whole chicken or a joint of beef, lamb or pork. Braising can be carried out entirely on the stove top, but most cooks find they get a better result by transferring the ingredients to the oven once liquid is added.

STEW Generally, a stew uses more liquid and takes less time to cook as the meat is completely submerged. The key difference is that it is cooked on the stove top and served directly in its cooking liquid.

CHOOSING A CASEROLE DISH

When you're choosing a casserole dish, you should consider getting a flameproof one: this means a dish that is not only ovenproof but has the versatility of going directly onto the stove top in the same way as a saucepan or frying pan. Many casserole dishes call for browning recipes on the stove top first before adding the liquid and cooking in the oven (braising). A flameproof casserole dish allows you to do all this in one utensil. But it needs to have a thick, cast base, like a good frying pan, so that it will distribute the heat, and brown the meat, evenly.

If you buy an ovenproof, but not a flameproof, casserole dish, then you will need to do the browning in a frying pan and then transfer the food to the dish before continuing with the recipe.

Buy a casserole dish big enough to take a whole chicken comfortably: if that is sometimes too large for your recipe, make more and freeze the rest (see Freezing, opposite).

BRAISING TECHNIQUES

Many beef and chicken dishes we know and love are braises. For browning on the stove top, use a flameproof casserole dish and heat half of the butter or oil; brown the meat in small batches and give the meat plenty of room. Add the rest of the butter as needed. Steam will not escape as readily as it would from a frying pan as a casserole dish is deeper, so keep the heat high and allow more space for the steam to escape or the meat will stew and not brown. If the butter becomes very dark, remove and use a fresh lot for the vegetables if they also require browning.

Some recipes coat the meat in flour before browning – the flour thickens the pan juices slightly, creating a lovely gravy.

REDUCED-FAT BRAISING

If you find your braises are too fatty, don't reduce the butter or oil in the recipe as this helps produce flavour; instead, make the casserole at least a few hours ahead. When cooked, pour off the liquid into a bowl; refrigerate the liquid until the fat solidifies on the surface. Remove the fat, return the juices to the casserole then reheat.

FREEZING

Casseroles and stews – and all of these slow-cooked meals – freeze beautifully. The only ingredient that tends not to freeze so well is potato, which goes mushy when thawing, so if you know ahead of time that you're freezing, leave out the potato and add freshly-cooked pieces when you come to eat it.

SLOW COOKERS

These are electrical appliances that are specially designed to slowly simmer food. They are equipped with low cooking settings which allow the food to gently simmer for a long time – all day if you choose – or you can reduce the cooking time by about half if using the high setting. These appliances are available in various shapes and sizes, and with a host of different features. The 4.5-litre size cookers are the most popular size. If you're in the market for a slow cooker, research the subject fully: check out the cookers and their features carefully to make sure the appliance suits your needs.

Most soup, stew, casserole, tagine and curry recipes are perfect to use in the slow cooker. The trick is to make sure there is enough liquid in the cooker for the long, slow, cooking time. Once you get to know the cooker, you'll be able to adapt a lot of your favourite recipes. Some roasts work well in the slow cooker, too. Use recipes that would normally slow cook, well-covered in an oven set at a low temperature.

Getting the best from your slow cooker

There's something wonderful about the aroma, flavour and texture of a slow-cooked meal. Slow cookers are perfect for this way of cooking. First, read the manufacturer's instruction manual carefully, it will advise you to NOT leave the appliance on unattended at any time; this, of course, is a safety measure.

These appliances are available in various shapes and sizes, and with a host of different features. For example, some have timers that cut off after the cooking time has expired, some don't; some have timers that reduce the temperature and keep the food warm until you decide to eat. If you're in the market for a slow cooker, research the subject fully: check out the cookers and their features carefully to make sure the appliance suits your needs. They are all "safe" in terms of making sure the food reaches the correct temperatures to destroy any harmful bacteria during the long slow cooking times.

We used a 4.5-litre (18-cup) slow cooker for the slow-cooker recipes in this chapter as it's the most popular size. If you have a smaller or larger slow cooker than the one we used, you will have to decrease or increase the quantity of food, and almost certainly the liquid content, in the recipes.

HANDY HINTS

MOST RECIPES USING RED MEAT RECOMMEND that the meat is browned first, as if you were making a casserole. Do this in a heated oiled large frying pan, adding the meat in batches, and turning the meat so it browns all over. Over-crowding the pan will result in stewed, not browned, meat. If you're pushed for time, the meat and/or vegetables can be browned the night before. Once everything is browned, put it into a sealable container, along with any juices, and refrigerate until the next day.

SOME RECIPES SUGGEST TOSSING THE MEAT IN FLOUR before browning, some don't. Usually when the meat is floured, the finished sauce will be thick enough to make a light coating of gravy. If the meat is not floured, it might be necessary to thicken the sauce. Usually plain flour or cornflour are used for thickening; cornflour results in a less-cloudy sauce than if flour is used. The flour, or cornflour, needs to be blended with butter or a cold liquid such as water or some of the cooled sauce from the slow cooker. Stir the flour mixture into the sauce at the end of the cooking time, while the slow cooker is on the highest setting, then put the lid back on and leave the sauce to thicken – this will take 10 to 20 minutes.

AS A GENERAL RULE for casserole, stew, curry and tagine recipes, place the vegetables into the cooker, put the meat on top of the vegetables, then add the liquid. Soups are easy, just make sure the cooker is at least half-full. Roasts, using whole pieces of meat or poultry and pot roasts are sometimes cooked with hardly any liquid – especially if the meat is cooking on a bed of vegetables – sometimes a little liquid is added simply to make a sauce or gravy. Corned meats are usually cooked in enough liquid to barely cover them.

SOME MEATS PRODUCE A LOT OF FAT IF COOKED OVER A LONG PERIOD OF TIME There are a couple of gadgets available in kitchen/cookware shops for removing fat: one is a type of "brush" that sweeps away the fat; the other is a type of jug that separates the fat from the liquid. However, one of the easiest ways to remove fat is to soak it up using sheets of absorbent kitchen paper on the surface. The best way of all is to refrigerate the food, the fat will set on top of the liquid, then it can simply be lifted off and discarded.

WHAT SETTING DO I USE?

Use the low setting for long, all-day, cooking, or reduce the cooking time by about half if using the high setting. The food will reach simmering point on either setting. If your slow cooker has a warm setting, this is not used for cooking; it's used to keep the cooked food warm until you're ready to serve. If you need to add ingredients or thicken the sauce after cooking time, turn the covered slow cooker to high. Remove the lid and add the ingredients or thickening, replace the lid and leave the cooker to heat the added ingredients or to thicken the sauce, between 10 and 20 minutes.

WHAT CUTS OF MEAT SHOULD I USE?

Use secondary, cheaper, tougher cuts of red meat. The long, slow, cooking time will tenderise the cuts, and the flavours will be excellent; it's simply a waste to use expensive primary cuts. Other types of meat (secondary/stewing cuts) such as venison, goat, rabbit, hare, kangaroo etc, are suitable to use in the slow cooker.
All kinds of poultry cook well in a slow cooker; but be careful not to overcook it, as it will become stringy. If you can access mature birds, such as boiling fowls or wild duck etc, the long, slow, cooking times will tenderise the flesh making it very flavoursome.
Seafood is generally not suitable to use in a slow cooker as it toughens quickly. However, there are many sauces that go well with seafood, and can be cooked in the slow cooker; add the seafood just before you're ready to serve. Large octopus will cook and become tender in a slow cooker.

CAN I USE MY FAVOURITE RECIPES?

Most soup, stew, casserole, tagine and curry recipes are perfect to use in the slow cooker. The trick is to make sure there is enough liquid in the cooker for the long, slow, cooking time. Once you get to know the cooker, you'll be able to adapt a lot of your favourite recipes. Some roasts work well in the slow cooker, too. Use recipes that you would normally slow cook, well-covered in an oven set at a low temperature. Also, some conventionally slow-cooked desserts, and steamed pudding recipes, can be used.

A NOTE ON DRIED BEANS

We use canned beans, but should you want to use dried beans instead, there are few things you must do to prevent food poisoning.
All kidney-shaped beans of all colours and sizes, are related to each other and must be washed, drained, then boiled in fresh water until tender – there's no need for overnight soaking; the time depends on the type of bean. Then, like canned beans, add them to the food in the slow cooker. Soya beans and chickpeas are fine to use raw in the slow cooker, just rinse them well first; there's no need for overnight soaking.

FREEZING LEFTOVERS

The slow cooker's capacity allows you to cook quite a lot of food at once, so if there's any left over, it's smart to freeze some for another time. There is always a lot of liquid to contend with in the slow cooker, so remove the meat and vegetables to appropriate-sized freezer-friendly containers, pour in enough of the liquid to barely cover the meat etc, seal the container, and freeze – while it's hot is fine – for up to three months. Any leftover liquid can be frozen separately and used as a base for another recipe, such as soup or a sauce.

IMPORTANT SAFETY TIPS

- Read the instruction manual carefully.
- Make sure the cooker is sitting flat on the bench away from water, any heat source (gas flames, stove tops, ovens), curtains, walls, children and pets.
- Make sure the electrical cord is away from any water or heat source, and not dangling on the floor.
- Do not touch any metal part of the cooker while it's in use, as they get very hot.

GENERAL CLEANING

Most slow cooker inserts can be washed in hot soapy water. To remove cooked-on food, soak in warm water, then scrub lightly with a plastic or nylon brush. Never put a hot insert under cold water, as this can cause the insert to break. The outer metal container should never be placed in water; wipe the outside with a damp cloth and dry.

boeuf bourguignon

PREP + COOK TIME 2 HOURS 45 MINS • SERVES 6

A French classic, this was a favourite dinner-party dish 20 or 30 years ago. Thanks to the resurgence in popularity of rich and rustic comfort food, it has now reappeared on restaurant menus and in the repertoire of many home cooks.

300g baby brown onions
2 tablespoons olive oil
2kg gravy beef, trimmed, chopped coarsely
30g butter
4 rindless bacon rashers (260g), chopped coarsely
400g button mushrooms, halved
2 cloves garlic, crushed
¼ cup (35g) plain flour
1¼ cups (310ml) beef stock
2½ cups (625ml) dry red wine
2 bay leaves
2 sprigs fresh thyme
½ cup coarsely chopped fresh flat-leaf parsley

1 Peel onions, leaving root end intact so onion remains whole during cooking.
2 Heat oil in large flameproof dish; cook beef, in batches, until browned.
3 Add butter to dish; cook onions, bacon, mushrooms and garlic, stirring, until onions are browned lightly.
4 Sprinkle flour over onion mixture; cook, stirring, until flour mixture thickens and bubbles. Gradually add stock and wine; stir over heat until mixture boils and thickens. Return beef and any juices to dish, add bay leaves and thyme; bring to the boil. Reduce heat; simmer, covered, about 2 hours or until beef is tender, stirring every 30 minutes.
5 Remove from heat; discard bay leaves. Stir in parsley.
nutritional count per serving 31.4g total fat (12.1g saturated fat); 2658kJ (636 cal); 6.6g carbohydrate; 80.3g protein; 2.8g fibre

Peel the baby brown onions, but leave the root intact. It's important to this dish that the onions remain whole during the long cooking.

Cook the beef chunks in batches in a flameproof dish until they're browned. If you cook too many pieces at a time they'll stew rather than brown.

Sprinkle the flour over the softened onion-bacon mixture and stir until the flour mixture bubbles and thickens.

Gradually add stock and wine, stirring all the time, until the mixture comes to the boil and starts to thicken.

beef stroganoff

PREP + COOK TIME 35 MINS • SERVES 4

A classic Russian recipe known for at least two centuries, "Stroganov" was first brought to Europe by those fleeing the country after the fall of Imperial Russia. It became a popular dinner party dish, cooked at the table in a chafing dish. It remains a favourite in many families' weeknight repertoires because it's so quick to make.

2 tablespoons vegetable oil
600g beef rump steak, sliced thinly
1 medium brown onion (150g), sliced thinly
2 cloves garlic, crushed
1 teaspoon sweet paprika
400g button mushrooms, sliced thickly
2 tablespoons dry red wine
1 tablespoon lemon juice
2 tablespoons tomato paste
1¼ cups (300g) sour cream
1 tablespoon coarsely chopped fresh dill

1 Heat half the oil in large frying pan; cook beef, in batches, until browned lightly.
2 Heat remaining oil in same pan; cook onion and garlic, stirring, until onion softens. Add paprika and mushrooms; cook, stirring, until mushrooms are tender.
3 Return beef to pan with wine and juice; bring to the boil. Reduce heat; simmer, covered, about 5 minutes or until beef is tender. Add paste, sour cream and dill; cook, stirring, until heated through.

nutritional count per serving 43.3g total fat (22.4g saturated fat); 2462kJ (589 cal); 5.9g carbohydrate; 41.4g protein; 3.7g fibre
serving ideas steamed rice, mashed potato or fettuccine.

hungarian veal goulash

PREP + COOK TIME 8 HOURS 30 MINS • SERVES 6

TIP
• To cook goulash on the stove top, follow the method using a large saucepan. Simmer the goulash, covered, over low heat, excluding potato and carrot, for 40 minutes. Add potato and carrot; simmer for 30 minutes or until veal and vegetables are tender.

1kg boned veal shoulder, chopped coarsely
¼ cup (35g) plain flour
1 tablespoon sweet paprika
2 teaspoons caraway seeds
½ teaspoon cayenne pepper
2 tablespoons olive oil
15g butter
1 large brown onion (200g), chopped coarsely
2 cloves garlic, crushed
2 tablespoons tomato paste
1½ cups (375ml) beef stock
400g can crushed tomatoes
3 small potatoes (360g), quartered
2 medium carrots (240g), chopped coarsely
½ cup coarsely chopped fresh flat-leaf parsley

1 Toss veal in combined flour and spices to coat; shake away excess flour. Heat half the oil and half the butter in large frying pan; cook veal, in batches, until browned all over. Transfer to 4.5-litre (18-cup) slow cooker.
2 Heat remaining oil and butter in same pan; cook onion and garlic, stirring, until onion is soft. Stir in paste and stock; bring to the boil. Stir into cooker with undrained tomatoes, potato and carrot; cook, covered, on low, 8 hours.
3 Season to taste. Serve goulash sprinkled with parsley.

nutritional count per serving 12.6g total fat (3.5g saturated fat); 1505kJ (360 cal); 19g carbohydrate; 40.2g protein; 4.1g fibre

[1] beef stroganoff
[2] hungarian veal goulash
[3] chilli con carne [page 370]
[4] lamb with kumara and raisins [page 370]

1

2

3

4

chilli con carne

PREP + COOK TIME 3 HOURS 45 MINS (+ STANDING) • SERVES 8

Use leftover chilli con carne (a Mexican dish meaning meat stew with chilli bean sauce) as a topping for nachos, a filling for tacos or even served solo on a piece of toasted turkish bread topped with coleslaw for an easy dinner.

1 cup (200g) dried kidney beans
1.5kg beef chuck steak
2 litres (8 cups) water
1 tablespoon olive oil
2 medium brown onions (300g), chopped coarsely
2 cloves garlic, crushed
2 teaspoons ground cumin
2 teaspoons ground coriander
½ teaspoon cayenne pepper
2 teaspoons sweet paprika
2 x 400g cans crushed tomatoes
1 tablespoon tomato paste
4 green onions, chopped coarsely
2 tablespoons coarsely chopped fresh coriander
⅓ cup (65g) finely chopped bottled jalapeño chillies

1 Place beans in medium bowl, cover with water; stand overnight, drain.
2 Combine beef with the water in large saucepan; bring to the boil. Reduce heat, simmer, covered, 1½ hours.
3 Drain beef in large muslin-lined strainer over bowl; reserve 3½ cups (875ml) of the cooking liquid. Using two forks, shred beef.
4 Heat oil in same pan; cook brown onion and garlic, stirring, until onion is soft. Add spices; cook, stirring, until fragrant. Add beans, undrained tomatoes, paste and 2 cups of the reserved liquid; bring to the boil. Reduce heat, simmer, covered, 1 hour.
5 Add beef and remaining reserved liquid to pan; simmer, covered, 30 minutes or until beans are tender. Remove from heat; stir in green onions, coriander and chilli.
nutritional count per serving 11.4g total fat (3.9g saturated fat); 1496kJ (358 cal); 14.7g carbohydrate; 45.1g protein; 7.6g fibre
serving idea steamed rice.

lamb with kumara and raisins

PREP + COOK TIME 4 HOURS 25 MINS • SERVES 6

Ras el hanout is a blend of Moroccan spices, it's available in delis and specialist food stores. If you can't find it, use a moroccan seasoning available in supermarkets.

2 tablespoons olive oil
1.2kg boned lamb shoulder, chopped coarsely
1 large brown onion (200g), sliced thickly
4 cloves garlic, crushed
2 tablespoons ras el hanout
2 cups (500ml) chicken stock
½ cup (125ml) water
1 tablespoon honey
2 medium kumara (800g), chopped coarsely
400g can chickpeas, rinsed, drained
1 cinnamon stick
3 cardamom pods, bruised
⅓ cup (50g) raisins, halved
⅓ cup (55g) coarsely chopped blanched almonds, roasted
½ cup loosely packed fresh coriander leaves

TIP

• To cook casserole on stove top, follow method using a large saucepan. Simmer casserole, covered, over low heat, excluding kumara and chickpeas, for 50 minutes. Add kumara and chickpeas; simmer 30 minutes or until lamb and kumara are tender.

1 Heat half the oil in large frying pan; cook lamb, in batches, until browned all over. Remove lamb from pan.
2 Heat remaining oil in same pan; cook onion and garlic, stirring, until onion is soft. Add ras el hanout; cook, stirring, until fragrant. Remove from heat; stir in stock, the water and honey.
3 Place kumara in 4.5-litre (18-cup) slow cooker; mix in chickpeas, cinnamon, cardamom, lamb and onion mixture. Cook, covered, on low, 4 hours. Season.
4 Stir in raisins; serve sprinkled with nuts and coriander.
nutritional count per serving 24.1g total fat (6.9g saturated fat); 2358kJ (564 cal); 35g carbohydrate; 48.6g protein; 6.2g fibre

lamb shank stew

PREP + COOK TIME 3 HOURS 10 MINS • SERVES 8

The term "to french" in cooking means "cut in the French manner". Shanks, racks, crown roasts and cutlets are sold "frenched". French-trimmed shanks have had the upper ends of the bones trimmed slightly short and scraped (the point being to expose the cleaned bone), while the shank meat itself has been trimmed of excess fat, membrane and sinew. Shanks require long cooking to bring out their best taste and texture, and frenching them makes the end result more tender, less fatty and totally delicious.

8 french-trimmed lamb shanks (1.6kg)
8 cloves garlic, halved
2 medium lemons (280g)
2 tablespoons olive oil
3 large brown onions (600g), chopped coarsely
2 cups (500ml) dry red wine
3 medium carrots (360g), quartered lengthways
3 stalks celery (450g), trimmed, chopped coarsely
4 bay leaves
8 sprigs fresh thyme
1.75 litres (7 cups) chicken stock
½ cup finely chopped fresh flat-leaf parsley
¼ cup finely chopped fresh mint leaves

1 Pierce meatiest part of each shank in two places with sharp knife; press garlic into cuts.
2 Grate rind of both lemons finely; reserve. Halve lemons; rub cut sides all over shanks.
3 Preheat oven to 180°C/160°C fan-forced.
4 Heat oil in large flameproof dish; cook shanks, in batches, over heat until browned. Cook onion, stirring, in same dish until softened. Add wine; bring to the boil, then remove dish from heat.
5 Place carrot, celery and shanks, in alternate layers, on onion mixture in dish. Top with bay leaves and thyme; carefully pour stock over the top. Cover dish tightly with lid or foil; cook in oven about 3 hours or until meat is tender.
6 Combine reserved grated rind and herbs in bowl.
7 Transfer shanks to platter; cover to keep warm. Strain pan juices through muslin-lined sieve into medium saucepan; discard solids. Boil pan juices, uncovered, stirring occasionally, until reduced by half.
8 Serve shanks sprinkled with rind-herb mixture, drizzle with pan juices.
nutritional count per serving 15.5g total fat (5.6g saturated fat); 1375kJ (329 cal); 8.8g carbohydrate; 26.8g protein; 3.8g fibre

corned beef with parsley sauce

**PREP + COOK TIME
2 HOURS (+ STANDING &
COOLING) • SERVES 4**

1.5kg whole piece beef corned silverside
2 bay leaves
6 black peppercorns
1 large brown onion (200g), quartered
1 large carrot (180g), chopped coarsely
1 tablespoon brown malt vinegar
¼ cup (50g) firmly packed brown sugar

parsley sauce
30g butter
¼ cup (35g) plain flour
2½ cups (625ml) milk
⅓ cup (40g) grated cheddar cheese
⅓ cup finely chopped fresh flat-leaf parsley
1 tablespoon mild mustard

The 'corn' in corned beef actually refers to the large grains (or, in old-English, 'corns') of salt that were originally used to preserve the beef without refrigeration. We still corn beef today because of the delicious flavour and texture that comes from the extended brining of the meat.

1 Place beef, bay leaves, peppercorns, onion, carrot, vinegar and half of the sugar in large saucepan. Add enough water to just cover beef; simmer, covered, about 1½ hours or until beef is tender. Cool beef 1 hour in liquid in pan.
2 Remove beef from pan; discard liquid. Sprinkle sheet of foil with remaining sugar, wrap beef in foil; stand 20 minutes before serving.
3 Make parsley sauce.
4 Serve sliced corned beef with parsley sauce.
parsley sauce Melt butter in small saucepan, add flour; cook, stirring, until bubbling. Gradually stir in milk; cook, stirring, until sauce boils and thickens. Remove from heat; stir in cheese, parsley and mustard.
nutritional count per serving 35.8g total fat (19.3g saturated fat); 3520kJ (842 cal); 31g carbohydrate; 97g protein; 2.5g fibre

I've heard of corned beef hash – a friend had it for breakfast in America, but I've never tasted it. How do you make it?

Many people cook corned beef just so they can make corned beef hash. Bought corned beef just doesn't make the grade. Corned beef hash is a mixture of cold boiled potato, chopped finely, cooked corned beef, chopped finely or shredded and a few finely chopped green onions. Mix it all together and make one big flat patty or several smaller patties, cook in hot olive oil until brown and crisp on both sides and serve with a poached egg on top, drizzled with some sweet chilli sauce.

braised sweet ginger duck

PREP + COOK TIME 2 HOURS 10 MINS • SERVES 4

Star anise is the dried, star-shaped seed pod of a small evergreen tree grown from Southwest China through South-East Asia to Japan. Each fruit's pod has, as a rule, eight points having a total span of about 2cm, and each point contains a seed. The star-shaped pod can be used whole as a flavouring or the seeds alone as a spice; both can be used ground.

2kg duck
3 cups (750ml) water
½ cup (125ml) chinese cooking wine
⅓ cup (80ml) soy sauce
¼ cup (55g) firmly packed brown sugar
1 whole star anise
3 green onions, halved
3 cloves garlic, quartered
10cm piece fresh ginger (50g), unpeeled, chopped coarsely
2 teaspoons sea salt
1 teaspoon five-spice powder
800g baby buk choy, halved

1 Preheat oven to 180°C/160°C fan-forced.
2 Discard neck from duck, wash duck; pat dry with absorbent paper. Score duck in thickest parts of skin; cut duck in half through breastbone and along both sides of backbone, discard backbone. Tuck wings under duck.
3 Place duck, skin-side down, in medium shallow baking dish; add combined water, wine, soy, sugar, star anise, onion, garlic and ginger. Cover; roast about 1 hour or until duck is cooked as desired.
4 Increase oven temperature to 220°C/200°C fan-forced. Remove duck from braising liquid; strain liquid through muslin-lined sieve into large saucepan. Place duck, skin-side up, on wire rack in same dish. Rub combined salt and five-spice all over duck; roast duck, uncovered, about 30 minutes or until skin is crisp.
5 Skim fat from surface of braising liquid; bring to the boil. Reduce heat; simmer, uncovered, 10 minutes. Add buk choy; simmer, covered, about 5 minutes or until buk choy is just tender.
6 Cut duck halves into two pieces; divide bok choy, braising liquid and duck among plates.

nutritional count per serving 105.7g total fat (31.7g saturated fat); 4974kJ (1190 cal); 17.9g carbohydrate; 40.8g protein; 3.5g fibre
serving idea steamed jasmine rice.

Score the duck through the skin and fat. There are two reasons for this: it helps the flavours to be absorbed more easily into the flesh and it aids in crisping up the skin.

Cut along both sides of the backbone using poultry shears. Discard the backbone. You now have two duck halves.

Once the duck has been braised and is cooked through, place the halves, skin-side up on a wire rack and rub in the five-spice and salt mixture.

cassoulet

PREP + COOK TIME 2 HOURS 50 MINS (+ STANDING) • SERVES 6

Our version of this classic takes its lead from the traditional versions of Languedoc and Castelnaudary, but we've given it an update to make it a simpler, quicker and healthier dish. Haricot, great northern, cannellini or navy beans can be used in this recipe.

1½ cups (300g) dried white beans
300g boned pork belly, rind removed, sliced thinly
150g piece streaky bacon, rind removed, diced into 1cm pieces
800g piece boned lamb shoulder, diced into 3cm pieces
1 large brown onion (200g), chopped finely
1 small leek (200g), sliced thinly
2 cloves garlic, crushed
3 sprigs fresh thyme
400g can crushed tomatoes
2 bay leaves
1 cup (250ml) water
1 cup (250ml) chicken stock
2 cups (140g) stale breadcrumbs
⅓ cup coarsely chopped fresh flat-leaf parsley

1 Place beans in medium bowl, cover with water; soak overnight, drain. Rinse under cold water; drain. Place beans in medium saucepan of boiling water; bring to the boil. Reduce heat; simmer, covered, about 15 minutes or until beans are just tender. Drain.
2 Preheat oven to 160°C/140°C fan-forced.
3 Cook pork in large flameproof casserole dish over heat, pressing down with back of spoon on pork until browned all over; remove from dish. Cook bacon in same pan, stirring, until crisp; remove from dish. Cook lamb, in batches, in same pan, until browned all over.
4 Cook onion, leek and garlic in same dish, stirring, until onion softens. Add thyme, undrained tomatoes, bay leaves, the water, stock, beans and meat; bring to the boil. Cover; cook in oven 45 minutes. Remove from oven; sprinkle with combined breadcrumbs and parsley. Return to oven; cook, uncovered, about 45 minutes or until liquid is nearly absorbed and beans are tender.

nutritional count per serving 28g total fat (10.7g saturated fat); 2734kJ (654 cal); 39.5g carbohydrate; 54.9g protein; 12.1g fibre

braised pork with pears and cider

PREP + COOK TIME 2 HOURS 25 MINS • SERVES 4

2 tablespoons olive oil
1kg piece pork neck
3cm piece fresh ginger (15g), sliced thinly
2 cloves garlic, sliced thinly
½ teaspoon ground fennel
3 cups (750ml) sweet cider
2 cups (500ml) chicken stock
2 large pears (660g), peeled, cut into thick wedges
½ cup coarsely chopped fresh flat-leaf parsley

1 Preheat oven to 160°C/140°C fan-forced.
2 Heat oil in large flameproof dish; cook pork until browned all over. Remove from dish.
3 Cook ginger and garlic in same dish, stirring, until fragrant. Add fennel; cook, stirring, 1 minute. Add cider and stock; bring to the boil. Return pork to dish, cover; cook in oven 1 hour. Uncover; cook in oven 30 minutes. Add pear; cook, uncovered, about 30 minutes or until pear is tender. Remove pork, cover, stand 5 minutes before slicing thickly. Stir parsley into braising liquid.
4 Serve pork with drizzled braising liquid.

nutritional count per serving 29.8g total fat (8.3g saturated fat); 2805kJ (671 cal); 34.7g carbohydrate; 55.1g protein; 3.5g fibre

beef stew with parsley dumplings

PREP + COOK TIME 2 HOURS 50 MINS • SERVES 4

This recipe can be made, up to step 4, in a slow cooker or a pressure cooker if you have one; make sure you follow the instructions stated in your cooker's manual.

1kg beef chuck steak, diced into 5cm pieces
2 tablespoons plain flour
2 tablespoons olive oil
20g butter
2 medium brown onions (300g), chopped coarsely
2 cloves garlic, crushed
2 medium carrots (240g), chopped
1 cup (250ml) dry red wine
2 tablespoons tomato paste
2 cups (500ml) beef stock
4 sprigs fresh thyme

parsley dumplings
1 cup (150g) self-raising flour
50g butter
1 egg, beaten lightly
¼ cup (20g) coarsely grated parmesan cheese
¼ cup finely chopped fresh flat-leaf parsley
⅓ cup (50g) drained sun-dried tomatoes, chopped finely
¼ cup (60ml) milk

1 Preheat oven to 180°C/160°C fan-forced.
2 Coat beef in flour; shake off excess. Heat oil in large flameproof casserole dish; cook beef, in batches, until browned all over.
3 Melt butter in same dish; cook onion, garlic and carrot, stirring, until vegetables soften. Add wine; cook, stirring, until liquid reduces to ¼ cup. Return beef to dish with paste, stock and thyme; bring to the boil. Cover; cook in oven 1¾ hours.
4 Meanwhile, make parsley dumpling mixture.
5 Remove dish from oven; uncover. Drop level tablespoons of the dumpling mixture, about 2cm apart, onto top of stew. Cook, uncovered, in oven further 20 minutes or until dumplings are browned lightly and cooked through.
parsley dumplings Place flour in medium bowl; rub in butter. Stir in egg, cheese, parsley, tomato and enough milk to make a soft, sticky dough.

nutritional count per serving 39.7g total fat (17.4g saturated fat); 3457kJ (827 cal); 43g carbohydrate; 63.9g protein; 6.7g fibre

irish stew

PREP + COOK TIME 3 HOURS • SERVES 4

This is a classic peasant dish from Ireland that traditionally uses mutton and the cheapest local ingredients available, which are root vegetables and barley.

750g lamb neck chops
2 large brown onions (400g), chopped coarsely
1 large carrot (180g), chopped coarsely
1 large parsnip (350g), chopped coarsely
1kg potatoes, chopped coarsely
3½ cups (625ml) beef stock
2 tablespoons tomato paste
1 tablespoon worcestershire sauce
2 sprigs thyme
¼ cup coarsely chopped fresh flat-leaf parsley

1 Preheat oven to 160°C/140°C fan-forced.
2 Layer chops and vegetables in large ovenproof dish; pour over combined stock, paste and sauce. Add thyme. Cook, covered, 2 hours. Uncover; cook 30 minutes or until lamb and vegetables are tender.
3 Serve stew sprinkled with parsley.

nutritional count per serving 19.3g total fat (8.6g saturated fat); 2249kJ (538 cal); 46.8g carbohydrate; 39.7g protein; 8.5g fibre

chicken cacciatore

PREP + COOK TIME 1 HOURS 30 MINS • SERVES 4

Anchovies are a "secret" ingredient in many savoury dishes, merging into the flavours of the other ingredients to add depth and richness. Soaking them first in milk removes their fishy taste and some of their saltiness.

2 tablespoons olive oil
1.5kg chicken thigh cutlets, skin on
1 medium brown onion (150g), chopped finely
1 clove garlic, crushed
½ cup (125ml) dry white wine
2 tablespoons white wine vinegar
½ cup (125ml) chicken stock
410g can crushed tomatoes
¼ cup (70g) tomato paste
2 drained anchovy fillets, chopped finely
½ cup (60g) seeded black olives, chopped coarsely
½ cup coarsely chopped fresh flat-leaf parsley

1 Heat half the oil in large saucepan; cook chicken, in batches, until browned all over. Remove chicken from pan.
2 Heat remaining oil in same pan; cook onion and garlic, stirring, until onion softens. Stir in wine, vinegar, stock, undrained tomatoes, paste and anchovies.
3 Return chicken to pan, fitting pieces tightly together in a single layer; bring to the boil. Reduce heat; simmer, covered, 20 minutes. Uncover; simmer about 30 minutes or until chicken is tender and sauce is reduced. Skim fat from surface; stir in olives and parsley.

nutritional count per serving 39.9g total fat (10.8g saturated fat); 2454kJ (587 cal); 10.8g carbohydrate; 40.5g protein; 3.1g fibre

[1] irish stew
[2] chicken cacciatore
[3] coq au vin [page 380]
[4] osso buco [page 380]

1

2

3

4

coq au vin

PREP + COOK TIME 1 HOUR 30 MINS • SERVES 4

800g spring onions
¼ cup (60ml) olive oil
6 rindless bacon rashers (390g), chopped coarsely
300g button mushrooms
2 cloves garlic, crushed
8 chicken thigh fillets (880g)
¼ cup (35g) plain flour
2 cups (500ml) dry red wine
1½ cups (375ml) chicken stock
2 tablespoons tomato paste
3 bay leaves
4 sprigs fresh thyme
2 sprigs fresh rosemary

1 Trim green ends from onions, leaving about 4cm of stem attached; trim roots. Heat 1 tablespoon of the oil in large frying pan; cook onions, stirring, until browned all over. Remove onions from pan.
2 Add bacon, mushrooms and garlic to pan; cook, stirring, until bacon is crisp, remove from pan.
3 Coat chicken in flour; shake off excess. Heat remaining oil in same pan. Cook chicken, in batches, until browned all over; drain on absorbent paper.
4 Return chicken to pan with wine, stock, paste, bay leaves, herbs, onions and bacon mixture. Bring to the boil; reduce heat, simmer, uncovered, about 35 minutes or until chicken is tender and sauce has thickened slightly.
nutritional count per serving 43.6g total fat (11.8g saturated fat); 3428kJ (820 cal); 16.3g carbohydrate; 67.8g protein; 6.4g fibre

osso buco

PREP + COOK TIME 2 HOURS 45 MINS • SERVES 6

As it has become more fashionable, gremolata has morphed into many guises well removed from its original form. Originally, as we've shown here, it was the garnish strewn over steaming osso buco so the scent of its combined ingredients would excite the palate once they hit the heat. Now, it's made from any number of aromatic ingredients and sprinkled over many different dishes, from soups to steamed vegetables.

12 pieces veal osso buco (3.5kg)
¼ cup (35g) plain flour
¼ cup (60ml) olive oil
40g butter
1 medium brown onion (150g), chopped coarsely
2 cloves garlic, crushed
3 stalks celery (450g), trimmed, chopped coarsely
2 large carrots (360g), chopped coarsely
4 medium tomatoes (600g), chopped coarsely
2 tablespoons tomato paste
1 cup (250ml) dry white wine
1 cup (250ml) beef stock
400g can crushed tomatoes
3 sprigs fresh thyme
¼ cup coarsely chopped fresh flat-leaf parsley

gremolata
1 tablespoon finely grated lemon rind
⅓ cup finely chopped fresh flat-leaf parsley
2 cloves garlic, chopped finely

1 Coat veal in flour, shake off excess.
2 Heat oil in large flameproof dish; cook veal, in batches, until browned all over.
3 Melt butter in same flameproof dish; cook onion, garlic, celery and carrot, stirring, until vegetables soften. Stir in remaining ingredients.
4 Return veal to dish, fitting pieces upright and tightly together in a single layer; bring to the boil. Cover, reduce heat; simmer 1¾ hours. Uncover; cook 30 minutes.
5 Meanwhile, make gremolata.
6 Remove veal from dish; cover to keep warm. Bring sauce to the boil; boil, uncovered, about 10 minutes or until sauce thickens slightly.
7 Divide veal among serving plates; top with sauce, sprinkle with gremolata. Osso buco can be served with mashed potato or soft polenta, if you like.
gremolata Combine ingredients in small bowl.
nutritional count per serving 16.3g total fat (5.2g saturated fat); 2056kJ (492 cal); 14g carbohydrate; 63.2g protein; 6g fibre

octopus braised in red wine

PREP + COOK TIME 2 HOURS • SERVES 8

Octopus belongs to the same family as cuttlefish and squid, and can be cooked in the same ways. Baby octopus are tender but larger ones are tough and must be tenderised by pounding – this will usually have been done by the fishmonger.

1 tablespoon olive oil
1 medium brown onion (150g), chopped finely
2 cloves garlic, crushed
2 baby fennel bulbs (260g), trimmed, chopped coarsely
5 medium vine-ripened tomatoes (560g), chopped coarsely

3 bay leaves
1 teaspoon dried chilli flakes
680g whole octopus
⅔ cup (160ml) dry red wine
2 tablespoons finely chopped fresh flat-leaf parsley

1 Preheat oven to 200°C/180°C fan-forced.
2 Heat oil in large frying pan; cook onion and garlic, stirring, until onion softens. Add fennel; cook, stirring, 5 minutes. Add tomato, bay leaves and chilli; cook, stirring occasionally, about 10 minutes or until mixture thickens and fennel softens.
3 Combine fennel mixture, octopus and wine in medium baking dish; bake, covered, about 45 minutes. Uncover; bake about 40 minutes or until octopus is tender and browned lightly.
4 Cut octopus into bite-sized pieces. Stir in parsley. Serve with crusty bread.
nutritional count per serving 3g total fat (0.3g saturated fat); 493kJ (118 cal); 3.1g carbohydrate; 15.2g protein; 1.8g fibre

pork cabbage rolls

PREP + COOK TIME 2 HOURS 40 MINS • SERVES 4

18 large cabbage leaves
½ cup (100g) uncooked white long-grain rice
250g pork mince
1 medium brown onion (150g), chopped finely
¼ cup finely chopped fresh dill
1 clove garlic, crushed
1 tablespoon tomato paste
2 teaspoons ground cumin
1 teaspoon ground coriander
1 teaspoon ground allspice
4 cloves garlic, quartered
2 medium tomatoes (300g), chopped coarsely
2 x 400g cans crushed tomatoes
¼ cup (60ml) lemon juice

1 Discard thick stems from 12 cabbage leaves; reserve remaining leaves. Boil, steam or microwave trimmed leaves until just pliable; drain. Rinse under cold water; drain. Pat dry with absorbent paper.
2 Combine rice, pork, onion, dill, crushed garlic, paste and spices in medium bowl.
3 Place one trimmed leaf, vein-side up, on board; cut leaf in half lengthways. Place a level tablespoon of the pork mixture at stem end of each half; roll each half firmly to enclose filling. Repeat with remaining trimmed leaves.
4 Place reserved leaves in base of large saucepan. Place only enough rolls, seam-side down, in single layer, to completely cover leaves in base of saucepan. Top with quartered garlic, chopped fresh tomato then remaining rolls.
5 Pour undrained tomatoes and juice over cabbage rolls; bring to the boil. Reduce heat; simmer, covered, 1 hour. Uncover; simmer about 30 minutes or until cabbage rolls are cooked through.
6 Divide cabbage rolls and sauce among serving plates.

nutritional count per serving 3.6g total fat (1.1g saturated fat); 803kJ (192 cal); 24.7g carbohydrate; 14.3g protein; 9.7g fibre

serving idea serve rolls with thick greek-style yogurt flavoured with a little finely chopped preserved lemon rind.

Cut off and discard the thick stems from 12 cabbage leaves. The filling will be rolled in these leaves so make sure there are no tears in them.

Place level tablespoons of the filling mixture at one end of the softened leaves and roll up neatly, folding in the sides, to enclose the filling.

Place cabbage rolls, seam-side down in one layer in pan. Add garlic and tomato and then put remaining rolls on top. Pour over the tomato mixture.

seafood stew with chermoulla

PREP + COOK TIME 1 HOUR • SERVES 4

Chermoulla is a Moroccan blend of fresh herbs, spices and condiments traditionally used for preserving or seasoning meat and fish. We used our chermoulla blend here as a quick flavouring for the stew, but you can also use it as a sauce or marinade. You can keep freshly made chermoulla in the refrigerator, covered with a thin layer of olive oil to preserve it, for up to a month.

500g black mussels
800g uncooked medium king prawns
300g kingfish fillet, skinned
1 squid hood (150g)
1 tablespoon olive oil
1 large brown onion (200g), chopped finely
3 cloves garlic, crushed
1 medium red capsicum (200g), chopped finely
½ cup (125ml) dry white wine
1 cup (250ml) fish stock
400g can diced tomatoes

chermoulla
½ cup finely chopped fresh coriander
½ cup finely chopped fresh flat-leaf parsley
1 clove garlic, crushed
2 tablespoons white wine vinegar
2 tablespoons lemon juice
½ teaspoon ground cumin
2 tablespoons olive oil

1 Scrub mussels; remove beards. Shell and devein prawns, leaving tails intact. Dice fish into 3cm pieces. Cut squid down centre to open out; score inside in diagonal pattern then cut into thick strips.
2 Heat oil in large saucepan; cook onion, garlic and capsicum, stirring, until onion softens. Stir in wine; cook, uncovered, until wine is almost evaporated. Add stock and undrained tomatoes; bring to the boil. Add seafood, reduce heat; simmer, covered, about 5 minutes or until squid is tender and mussels open (discard any that do not).
3 Meanwhile, combine ingredients for chermoulla in small bowl.
4 Stir half of the chermoulla into stew. Divide stew among bowls; divide remaining chermoulla over the top of each bowl. Serve with a warmed baguette, if desired.
nutritional count per serving 17.5g total fat (3g saturated fat); 1714kJ (410 cal); 8.7g carbohydrate; 48.6g protein; 3.5g fibre

curried sausages

PREP + COOK TIME 55 MINS • SERVES 4

800g thick beef sausages
20g butter
1 medium brown onion (150g), chopped coarsely
1 tablespoon curry powder
2 teaspoons plain flour
2 large carrots (360g), chopped coarsely
2 stalks celery (300g), trimmed, chopped coarsely
500g baby new potatoes, halved
2 cups (500ml) beef stock
1 cup loosely packed fresh flat-leaf parsley leaves

1 Cook sausages, in batches, in heated deep large frying pan until cooked through. Cut each sausage into thirds.
2 Melt butter in same cleaned pan; cook onion, stirring, until soft. Add curry powder and flour; cook, stirring, 2 minutes.
3 Add vegetables and stock; bring to the boil. Reduce heat; simmer, covered, about 15 minutes or until vegetables are tender. Add sausages; simmer, uncovered, until sauce thickens slightly. Stir in parsley.
nutritional count per serving 55.8g total fat (27.3g saturated fat); 3177kJ (760 cal); 29.8g carbohydrate; 30.1g protein; 12.8g fibre

chicken, olive and preserved lemon tagine

PREP + COOK TIME
2 HOURS 15 MINS
(+ STANDING)
SERVES 8

1 cup (200g) dried chickpeas
2 tablespoons plain flour
2 teaspoons hot paprika
8 chicken drumsticks (1.2kg)
8 chicken thigh cutlets (1.3kg)
40g butter
2 medium red onions (340g), sliced thickly
3 cloves garlic, crushed
1 teaspoon cumin seeds
½ teaspoon ground turmeric
½ teaspoon ground coriander
¼ teaspoon saffron threads
1 teaspoon dried chilli flakes
1 teaspoon ground ginger
3 cups (750ml) chicken stock
2 tablespoons finely sliced preserved lemon rind
⅓ cup (40g) seeded green olives
2 tablespoons finely chopped fresh coriander

For a traditional accompaniment bring 1½ cups chicken stock to the boil in a small saupcean; remove from the heat. Stir in 1½ cups couscous; rest about 5 minutes, fluffing with a fork. Stir in 2 tablespoons lemon juice and ½ cup chopped fresh coriander.

1 Place chickpeas in medium bowl, cover with water; stand overnight, drain. Rinse under cold water; drain. Place chickpeas in medium saucepan of boiling water; return to the boil. Reduce heat; simmer, uncovered, about 40 minutes or until chickpeas are tender.
2 Preheat oven to 160°C/140°C fan-forced.
3 Place flour and paprika in paper or plastic bag, add chicken pieces, in batches; shake gently to coat chicken in flour mixture.
4 Melt butter in large flameproof casserole dish; cook chicken pieces, in batches, until browned. Cook onion in same dish, stirring, until softened. Add garlic, cumin, turmeric, ground coriander, saffron, chilli and ginger; cook, stirring, until fragrant. Return chicken with stock to dish; bring to the boil, then cook, covered, in oven 30 minutes. Add drained chickpeas; cook tagine, covered, 1 hour.
5 Remove tagine from oven. Stir in lemon rind, olives and fresh coriander just before serving.
nutritional count per serving 32g total fat (11.5g saturated fat); 2057kJ (492 cal); 16.4g carbohydrate; 39.8g protein; 2.6g fibre

SPECIAL FEATURE

Stew accompaniments

Stews are only half-finished without an accompaniment.

SOFT POLENTA
Combine 3 cups water and 2 cups vegetable stock in large saucepan; bring to the boil. Gradually stir in 2 cups polenta. Reduce heat; simmer, stirring, about 10 minutes or until polenta thickens. Add 1 cup milk, 30g butter and ¼ cup finely grated parmesan cheese; stir until cheese melts.

PARSNIP MASH
Boil, steam or microwave 1kg coarsely chopped parsnip until tender; drain. Ma parsnip in medium bowl with ¾ cup hot milk until smooth; stir in 2 crushed ga cloves and 40g soft butter. The same amount of celeriac, kumara or pumpkin c be used instead of parsnip.

ROAST POTATOES
Preheat oven to 200°C/180°C fan-forced. Lightly oil oven tray. Boil, steam or microwave 6 halved medium potatoes 5 minutes; drain. Pat dry with absorbent paper; cool 10 minutes. Gently rake rounded sides of potatoes with tines of fork; place potato in single layer, cut-side down, on oven tray. Brush with 2 tablespoons olive oil; roast, uncovered, in oven about 50 minutes or until potatoes are browned lightly and crisp.

COUSCOUS
Combine 1½ cups couscous with 1½ cups boiling water in large heatproof bowl cover; stand about 5 minutes or until water is absorbed, fluffing with fork occasionally. Stir in 60g finely shredded baby spinach leaves or some coarsely chopped fresh herbs of your choice, or 2 finely chopped green onions.

CREAMY MASHED POTATOES

Boil, steam or microwave 750g coarsely chopped potatoes until tender; drain. Mash potato with 60g soft butter and ½ cup hot pouring cream in medium bowl until smooth.

STEAMED GAI LAN IN OYSTER SAUCE

Boil, steam or microwave 1kg halved gai lan until tender; drain. Heat 1 tablespoon peanut oil in wok; stir-fry gai lan, 2 tablespoons oyster sauce and 1 tablespoon light soy sauce about 2 minutes or until gai lan is tender.

PILAF

Melt 30g butter in medium saucepan; cook 1 crushed garlic clove, stirring, until fragrant. Add 1 cup basmati rice; cook, stirring, 1 minute. Add 1 cup chicken stock and 1 cup water; bring to the boil. Reduce heat; simmer, covered, about 15 minutes or until rice is tender. Remove from heat; fluff rice with fork. Stir in ¼ cup coarsely chopped fresh flat-leaf parsley and ¼ cup roasted flaked almonds.

TOMATO AND HERB SALAD

Place 5 coarsely chopped medium tomatoes, 2 tablespoons chopped fresh mint, ¼ cup chopped fresh flat-leaf parsley and 2 tablespoons chopped fresh dill in medium bowl. Place 2 cloves crushed garlic, 2 tablespoons lemon juice, 1 tablespoon olive oil and 2 teaspoons white vinegar in screw-top jar; shake well. Drizzle dressing over salad; toss to combine.

PIES

Pies

Nothing says good, honest food like a pie. The sight of one, with its golden pastry lid bulging with goodness, is a sure way to make everyone smile on a cold day. Pie fillings can be made from a huge range of vegetables and meats and they are a great way of giving new life to leftovers. Pies can also be made in smaller, single-serving sizes, which are perfect for picnics and casual meals on cosy nights.

WHEN IS A PIE A PIE?

THE USUAL DEFINITION OF A PIE, AS OPPOSED TO A TART, IS THAT A PIE HAS A TOP CRUST, ALTHOUGH THERE ARE EXCEPTIONS – THE PRIME EXAMPLE BEING THE QUICHE WHICH CONSISTS OF A SAVOURY CUSTARD IN AN OPEN PASTRY CASE.

A PIE MAY ALSO HAVE A BOTTOM CRUST AS WELL. PIES WITH A TOP CRUST, OR LID, BUT NO BASE, ARE CALLED ONE-CRUST PIES. PIES WITH A LID AND A BOTTOM CRUST ARE CALLED TWO-CRUST OR DOUBLE-CRUST PIES. THE CLASSIC AUSTRALIAN MEAT PIE IS A TWO-CRUST PIE.

THE PIE DISH

YOU CAN MAKE A PIE IN JUST ABOUT ANY OVENPROOF CASSEROLE OR BAKING DISH, THOUGH THE TRADITIONAL PIE DISH IS ROUND AND HAS SLIGHTLY SLOPING SIDES WITH A RIM TO ANCHOR THE PASTRY BASE TO THE LID – WITH THE PASTRY FLUTED OR DECORATIVELY MARKED IN SOME WAY TO MAKE THE PIE LOOK HANDSOME AND IMPRESSIVE. BUT YOU DON'T NEED A SPECIAL PIE DISH: RAMEKINS, A PUDDING BASIN, A CAKE PAN OR EVEN A BAKING DISH CAN BE USED TO COOK A PIE.

METAL PIE DISHES ARE CONSIDERED BETTER FOR BROWNING BOTTOM CRUST PIES. CERAMIC PERFORMS WELL FOR ONE-CRUST PIES BECAUSE IT TAKES UP HEAT SLOWLY, WHICH HEATS THE FILLING GENTLY AND EVENLY. CERAMIC DISHES ALSO WORK WELL FOR TWO-CRUST PIES WITH A LONG COOKING PERIOD.

PASTRY

RESTING IT ONCE YOU'VE MADE THE PASTRY, WRAP IT IN PLASTIC WRAP AND REFRIGERATE IT FOR 30 MINUTES (OR AS DIRECTED) SO ITS MOISTURE CONTENT WILL EVEN OUT AND THE GLUTEN WILL HAVE TIME TO RELAX. THIS MINIMISES THE PASTRY SHRINKING DURING BAKING.

ROLLING IT AFTER RESTING, PASTRY IS BEST ROLLED ON A COOL SURFACE (MARBLE IS IDEAL). ROLL ON A FLOURED SURFACE OR BETWEEN TWO SHEETS OF BAKING PAPER, GREASEPROOF PAPER OR PLASTIC WRAP. IF ROLLING DIRECTLY ON THE WORK SURFACE, KEEP TURNING THE PASTRY TO ENSURE THAT IT IS NOT STICKING. USE SHORT, LIGHT STROKES, STARTING FROM THE CENTRE EACH TIME, TO ROLL THE PASTRY TOWARDS YOU OR AWAY FROM YOU. ROLL TO THE EDGE OF THE PASTRY, NOT OVER THE EDGE.

REST AGAIN REST THE PASTRY AGAIN ONCE IT IS ROLLED OUT AND ASSEMBLED IN THE PIE DISH, BEFORE BAKING. THIS WILL ALLOW THE GLUTEN TO RELAX AND MINIMISE PASTRY SHRINKAGE.

STORING PASTRY

COOL COOKED PASTRIES COMPLETELY BEFORE STORING. THEY KEEP WELL IN AIRTIGHT CONTAINERS, BUT AFTER A WEEK OR SO THEY SLOWLY BECOME "TIRED" – IT IS BEST TO FREEZE THEM IF YOU WANT TO KEEP THEM LONGER.

PIE CRUSTS

For pies with only a bottom crust (called pies because they're too deep to be a tart) the bottom crust may be shortcrust, puff or even fillo pastry. A top crust may be shortcrust or puff pastry.

TWO-CRUST PIES Roll out two-thirds of the pastry, allowing a 2cm overhang on the dish. Drape the pastry over the rolling pin and gently transfer it to the dish, without stretching (if the pastry breaks, patch it up with a pastry off-cut). Press the pastry evenly over base and side of the dish, pushing out any air pockets. Fill with prepared cooled filling. Roll out the remaining pastry about 2cm larger than the pie dish, moisten the outer edge of the base pastry, then drape the lid over the filling. Press the edges together firmly to seal. Trim off the overhanging pastry, angling the knife slightly under the rim as you turn the dish. Mark the pastry along the rim with a fork. Brush the top with an egg wash to glaze and help brown the pastry.

ONE-CRUST PIES If the filling of a lidded pie is not firm enough to mound in the centre to support the top crust, place a greased pie funnel or an upside down egg cup in the centre of the pie. Roll out the pastry to about 4cm larger than the top of the dish; cut a 1cm strip from around the edge of the rolled-out pastry, as wide as the rim of the pie dish, to make a collar for the rim. Moisten the rim of the dish with water and press the pastry collar onto it. Moisten the pastry collar and, using the rolling pin, lay the pastry lid over the pie filling, pressing together the pastry strip and lid, without stretching the pastry (over-stretching the pastry will make it shrink during baking). Trim away any excess using the method described for two-crust pies. A pie funnel – also called a pastry bird – will serve the added role of venting the pie. Alternatively, cut a few slashes in the pastry to allow the steam to escape.

quiche lorraine

PREP + COOK TIME 1 HOUR 30 MINS (+ REFRIGERATION) • SERVES 6

Named after the region straddling the French-German border, the classic quiche lorraine is thought to be the original quiche. The pastry used for the first quiches is thought to have been a bread dough, which morphed over the centuries to the crisp shortcrust identified with the open tart today. With its creamy custardy filling and buttery shell, it's still practically everyone's favourite.

1 medium brown onion (150g), chopped finely
3 rindless bacon rashers (195g), chopped finely
3 eggs
300ml cream
½ cup (125ml) milk
¾ cup (120g) coarsely grated gruyère cheese

pastry
1¾ cups (260g) plain flour
150g cold butter, chopped coarsely
1 egg yolk
2 teaspoons lemon juice
⅓ cup (80ml) iced water, approximately

1 Make pastry.
2 Preheat oven to 200°C/180°C fan-forced.
3 Roll pastry between sheets of baking paper large enough to line a deep 23cm loose-based flan tin. Lift pastry into tin; gently press pastry around side. Trim edge, place tin on oven tray. Cover pastry with baking paper; fill with dried beans or rice. Bake 10 minutes; remove paper and beans. Bake pastry a further 10 minutes or until golden brown; cool.
4 Reduce oven to 180°C/160°C fan-forced.
5 Cook onion and bacon in heated oiled small frying pan until onion is soft; drain on absorbent paper, cool. Sprinkle bacon mixture over pastry case.
6 Whisk eggs in medium bowl; whisk in cream, milk and cheese.
7 Pour egg mixture into pastry case. Bake about 35 minutes or until filling is set. Stand 5 minutes before removing from tin.

pastry Sift flour into bowl; rub in butter. Add egg yolk, juice and enough water to make ingredients cling together. Knead gently on lightly floured surface until smooth; cover, refrigerate 30 minutes.

nutritional count per serving 51.8g total fat (35.4g saturated fat); 3139kJ (751 cal); 35.4g carbohydrate; 22.1g protein; 2g fibre

Use the rolling pin to gently lift the pastry dough into the flan tin. Press the pastry into the sides of the tin and trim the edges.

Place a sheet of baking paper in the tin and sprinkle in some dried beans to weigh it down and keep the pastry from rising.

Once the pastry case is cooked and cooled, sprinkle cooled bacon mixture over it and pour over the custard mix.

curried chicken pies

PREP + COOK TIME 2 HOURS 30 MINS (+ STANDING) • SERVES 6

The filling for this recipe has only a mild curry-flavour. If you want to make it hotter, either use a hot curry powder or increase the amount of chilli powder.

1.6kg chicken
90g butter
1 small leek (200g), chopped finely
1 medium white onion (150g), chopped finely
1 medium red capsicum (200g), chopped finely
2 stalks celery (300g), trimmed, chopped finely
3 teaspoons curry powder
¼ teaspoon chilli powder
¼ cup (35g) plain flour
⅓ cup (80g) sour cream
½ cup finely chopped fresh flat-leaf parsley
2 sheets puff pastry
1 egg, beaten lightly

1 Place chicken in large saucepan, add enough water to just cover chicken; bring to the boil. Reduce heat; simmer, uncovered, 1 hour. Remove pan from heat; when cool enough to handle, remove chicken from stock. Reserve 1¾ cups (430ml) of the stock for this recipe.
2 Preheat oven to 200°C/180°C fan-forced.
3 Remove skin and bones from chicken; chop chicken flesh roughly.
4 Heat butter in large frying pan, add leek, onion, capsicum and celery; cook, stirring, until vegetables are soft.
5 Add curry powder and chilli powder; cook, stirring, until fragrant. Stir in flour. Add reserved stock, stir over heat until mixture boils and thickens; reduce heat, simmer 1 minute, remove from heat. Stir in sour cream, chicken and parsley. Spoon mixture into six 1¼-cup (310ml) ovenproof dishes.
6 Cut pastry into six rounds large enough to cover top of each dish. Lightly brush pastry with egg. Place pies on oven tray.
7 Bake pies 10 minutes. Reduce oven to 180°C/160°C fan-forced; bake further 15 minutes or until pastry is golden brown.

nutritional count per serving 52.8g total fat (25.4g saturated fat); 3001kJ (718 cal); 28.5g carbohydrate; 33.3g protein; 3g fibre

chicken and leek pie

PREP + COOK TIME 1 HOUR 35 MINS • SERVES 6

2 cups (500ml) chicken stock
600g chicken breast fillets
1 tablespoon olive oil
40g butter
1 large leek (500g), sliced thinly
2 stalks celery (300g), trimmed, chopped finely
2 tablespoons plain flour
2 teaspoons fresh thyme leaves
½ cup (125ml) milk
1 cup (250ml) cream
2 teaspoons wholegrain mustard
2 sheets shortcrust pastry
1 sheet puff pastry
1 egg yolk

The part of the leek that is eaten is the thick white stem and the first, pale part of the green top. Because leeks are planted deep to keep them white, they harbour soil between the leaves and have to be washed thoroughly to remove it.

1 Bring stock to the boil in medium saucepan. Add chicken; return to the boil. Reduce heat; simmer, covered, about 10 minutes or until chicken is cooked. Remove from heat; stand chicken in poaching liquid 10 minutes. Remove chicken; chop coarsely. Reserve ⅓ cup of the poaching liquid; keep remainder for another use, or discard.

2 Heat oil and butter in medium saucepan; cook leek and celery, stirring, until leek softens. Add flour and thyme; cook, stirring, 1 minute. Gradually stir in reserved poaching liquid, milk and cream; cook, stirring, until mixture boils and thickens. Stir in chicken and mustard. Cool 10 minutes.

3 Preheat oven to 200°C/180°C fan-forced. Oil 1.5-litre (6-cup) ovenproof dish.

4 Line base and side of dish with shortcrust pastry, trim to fit; prick well all over with fork. Bake 10 minutes; cool 5 minutes.

5 Spoon chicken mixture into pastry case; place puff pastry over filling, trim to fit dish. Brush pastry with egg yolk; cut two small slits in top of pastry. Bake about 20 minutes or until browned lightly.

nutritional count per serving 56g total fat (30.1g saturated fat); 3344kJ (800 cal); 42.5g carbohydrate; 31.1g protein; 3.6g fibre

farmhouse chicken pie

PREP + COOK TIME 1 HOUR 15 MINS • SERVES 6

60g butter
1 medium leek (350g), sliced thickly
⅓ cup (50g) plain flour
¾ cup (180ml) milk
1 cup (250ml) chicken stock
3 cups (480g) coarsely chopped cooked chicken
1 cup (85g) chopped broccoli
1 small red capsicum (150g), chopped finely
310g can corn kernels, drained
¼ cup coarsely chopped fresh flat-leaf parsley
2 sheets puff pastry
1 egg

1 Melt butter in medium saucepan; cook leek, stirring, about 1 minute or until leek is soft. Add flour; cook, stirring, until mixture bubbles. Remove from heat, gradually stir in milk and stock; cook, stirring, over heat until mixture boils and thickens. Remove from heat; stir in chicken, broccoli, capsicum, corn and parsley.

2 Preheat oven to 200°C/180°C fan-forced.

3 Spoon filling into 23cm pie dish. Cut 3cm wide strips from one sheet of pastry and place them around the lip of dish. Brush strips lightly with egg. Place second sheet of pastry over filling and lip to cover dish. Trim edge, scallop edge firmly to seal, decorate with pastry scraps, if desired. Brush top of pastry with egg.

4 Bake pie about 10 minutes; reduce oven to 180°C/160°C fan-forced, bake further 20 minutes or until pastry is brown.

nutritional count per serving 29.4g total fat (9.1g saturated fat); 2291kJ (548 cal); 37.3g carbohydrate; 29.3g protein; 4.2g fibre

chunky beef and vegetable pie

PREP + COOK TIME 2 HOURS 40 MINS • SERVES 8

You may choose not to buy a special pie dish or dishes, but to use ramekins, an ovenproof dish, a pudding basin, a soufflé dish, a cake pan or even a baking dish for your pies. The purpose of the wide rim on a classic pie dish is to hold an extended double crust, fluted or decoratively marked in some way to make the pie look handsome and impressive.

1 tablespoon olive oil
1.5kg gravy beef, cut into 2cm pieces
60g butter
1 medium brown onion (150g), chopped finely
1 clove garlic, crushed
¼ cup (35g) plain flour
1 cup (250ml) dry white wine
3 cups (750ml) hot beef stock
2 tablespoons tomato paste
2 stalks celery (300g), trimmed, cut into 2cm pieces
2 medium potatoes (400g), cut into 2cm pieces
1 large carrot (180g), cut into 2cm pieces
1 large zucchini (150g), cut into 2cm pieces
150g mushrooms, quartered
1 cup (120g) frozen peas
½ cup finely chopped fresh flat-leaf parsley
2 sheets puff pastry
1 egg, beaten lightly

1 Heat oil in large saucepan; cook beef, in batches, until browned all over. Remove from pan.
2 Melt butter in same pan; cook onion and garlic, stirring, until onion softens. Add flour; cook, stirring, until mixture thickens and bubbles. Gradually stir in wine and stock; stir until mixture boils and thickens slightly.
3 Return beef to pan with paste, celery, potato and carrot; bring to the boil. Reduce heat; simmer, covered, 1 hour.
4 Add zucchini and mushrooms; simmer, uncovered, about 30 minutes or until beef is tender. Add peas; stir until heated through. Remove from heat; stir in parsley.
5 Preheat oven to 220°C/200°C fan-forced.
6 Divide warm beef mixture between two deep 25cm pie dishes; brush outside edge of dishes with a little egg. Top each pie with a pastry sheet, pressing edges to seal. Trim pastry; brush pastry with egg.
7 Bake pies about 20 minutes or until browned.

nutritional count per serving 27.6g total fat (13.3g saturated fat); 2412kJ (577 cal); 28.6g carbohydrate; 46.4g protein; 4.9g fibre

Sometimes when I make a pie, especially a large one, it sags in the middle. How can I prevent this?

The best way is by mounding the filling in the centre of the pie dish – if the filling is not firm enough to mound (or too chunky), use a funnel, pie bird or upturned eggcup in the centre of the dish and ease the pastry over that. A china pie bird looks the best, with its little head and open beak poking through a slit in the pastry, but they're not used often anymore and are hard to come by – look for them in antique and junk shops.

crab, fennel and herb quiche

PREP + COOK TIME 50 MINS • MAKES 12

When you trim the fennel for slicing, put the leaves aside to be chopped later. We used lump crab meat from the fish market, but well-drained canned crab meat will work quite well.

3 sheets shortcrust pastry
1 tablespoon olive oil
1 medium fennel bulb (300g), sliced
250g crab meat
2 tablespoons finely chopped fennel fronds
2 tablespoons finely chopped fresh flat-leaf parsley
½ cup (60g) coarsely grated cheddar cheese

quiche filling
300ml cream
¼ cup (60ml) milk
3 eggs

1 Preheat oven to 200°C/180°C fan-forced. Oil 12-hole (⅓-cup/80ml) muffin pan.
2 Cut twelve 9cm rounds from pastry; press into pan holes.
3 Heat oil in large frying pan; cook fennel, stirring, about 5 minutes or until fennel softens and browns slightly. Divide fennel among pastry cases; top with combined crab, fronds, parsley and cheese.
4 Make quiche filling; pour into pastry cases.
5 Bake quiches about 25 minutes. Stand in pan 5 minutes before serving.
quiche filling Whisk ingredients in large jug.

nutritional count per quiche 27.1g total fat (15g saturated fat); 1509kJ (361 cal); 20.3g carbohydrate; 9g protein; 1.3g fibre

steak and kidney pie

PREP + COOK TIME 2 HOURS 30 MINS • SERVES 6

The French name for puff pastry is mille-feuille, meaning a thousand leaves. It consists of hundreds of tissue-paper-thin layers of crisp pastry, which, when baked, separate and puff up to make a crisp, fragile pastry.

300g beef ox kidneys
1.5g beef chuck steak, chopped coarsely
2 medium brown onions (300g), sliced thinly
1 cup (250ml) beef stock
1 tablespoon soy sauce
¼ cup (35g) plain flour
½ cup (125ml) water
2 sheets puff pastry
1 egg, beaten lightly

1 Remove fat from kidneys; chop kidneys finely. Place kidneys, steak, onion, stock and sauce in large saucepan; simmer, covered, about 1 hour or until steak is tender.
2 Preheat oven to 200°C/180°C fan-forced.
3 Stir blended flour and water into beef mixture; stir until mixture boils and thickens. Transfer to 1.5-litre (6-cup) ovenproof dish.
4 Cut pastry into 6cm rounds. Overlap rounds on beef mixture; brush with egg. Bake pie about 30 minutes or until browned.

nutritional count per serving 25.8g total fat (12.2g saturated fat); 2546kJ (609 cal); 27.2g carbohydrate; 65.9g protein; 1.6g fibre

[1] crab, fennel and herb quiche
[2] steak and kidney pie
[3] shepherd's pie [page 400]
[4] roasted vegetable tart [page 400]

1

2

3

4

shepherd's pie

PREP + COOK TIME 1 HOUR • SERVES 4

Shepherd's pie is traditionally made from cooked lamb (and any of the vegies, too, leftover with the Sunday roast). A similar potato-topped pie but usually made with minced beef is called cottage pie.

30g butter
1 medium brown onion (150g), chopped finely
1 medium carrot (120g), chopped finely
½ teaspoon dried mixed herbs
4 cups (750g) finely chopped cooked lamb
¼ cup (70g) tomato paste
¼ cup (60ml) tomato sauce
2 tablespoons worcestershire sauce
2 cups (500ml) beef stock
2 tablespoons plain flour
⅓ cup (80ml) water

potato topping
5 medium potatoes (1kg), chopped coarsely
60g butter
¼ cup (60ml) milk

1 Preheat oven to 200°C/180°C fan-forced. Oil shallow 2.5-litre (10-cup) ovenproof dish.
2 Make potato topping.
3 Meanwhile, heat butter in large saucepan; cook onion and carrot, stirring, until tender. Add mixed herbs and lamb; cook, stirring, 2 minutes. Stir in paste, sauces and stock, then blended flour and water; stir over heat until mixture boils and thickens. Pour mixture into dish.
4 Drop heaped tablespoons of potato topping onto lamb mixture. Bake in oven about 20 minutes or until browned and heated through.
potato topping Boil, steam or microwave potato until tender; drain. Mash with butter and milk until smooth.
nutritional count per serving 36.2g total fat (20.2g saturated fat); 2976kJ (712 cal); 44.7g carbohydrate; 48.8g protein; 6g fibre

roasted vegetable tart

PREP + COOK TIME 1 HOUR 40 MINS (+ REFRIGERATION) • SERVES 16

Garlic is easy to roast and has a more mellow taste than it does raw or fried. Make it and freeze it by the tablespoon wrapped tightly in plastic wrap. Roasted garlic beaten with softened butter adds a whole new dimension of flavour to mashed potato or steamed corn cobs.

90g cold butter, chopped
1¼ cups (185g) plain flour
½ cup (40g) grated parmesan cheese
1 egg yolk
1 tablespoon chopped fresh chives
3 teaspoons iced water
½ large butternut pumpkin (600g), chopped coarsely
10 baby beetroot (300g), trimmed
10 french shallots (250g), peeled
8 cloves garlic
2 tablespoons olive oil

roast garlic cream
1 tablespoon finely chopped fresh dill
¾ cup (180g) sour cream
2 tablespoons milk

1 Process butter, flour and cheese until butter is combined. Add egg yolk, chives and water, process until mixture just clings together. Wrap in plastic; refrigerate for 30 minutes.
2 Preheat oven to 200°C/180°C fan-forced. Combine pumpkin, beetroot, shallots and garlic with oil in large baking dish; bake about 45 minutes or until tender.
3 Meanwhile, roll dough between two sheets of baking paper until large enough to fit the base and sides of 10cm x 34cm rectangular, loose-based flan tin. Lift pastry into tin, press into sides; trim edges. Place tin on oven tray; refrigerate 30 minutes.
4 Peel beetroot, wearing disposable gloves. Squeeze flesh from garlic skins; reserve garlic for roast garlic cream. Cover vegetables to keep warm.
5 Reduce oven to 180°C/160°C fan-forced. Line pastry with baking paper; fill with dried beans or rice. Bake 15 minutes. Remove paper and beans; bake further 10 minutes or until browned and crisp.
6 Combine reserved garlic with all ingredients for roast garlic cream in small bowl.
7 Fill tart shell with roasted vegetables; serve warm with roast garlic cream.
nutritional count per serving 12.9g total fat (7.1g saturated fat); 777kJ (186 cal); 12.9g carbohydrate; 4g protein; 1.7g fibre

fish mornay pies

PREP + COOK TIME 55 MINS • SERVES 4

Make these pies in advance for a dinner party, but do not grill. When your guests arrive, place the pies in a moderate oven for 20 to 25 minutes until heated through and lightly browned.

2½ cups (625ml) milk
½ small brown onion (40g)
1 bay leaf
6 black peppercorns
4 x 170g trevally fillets, skinned
3 large potatoes (900g), chopped coarsely
600g celeriac, chopped coarsely
1 egg yolk
½ cup (40g) finely grated parmesan cheese
¾ cup (180ml) pouring cream
60g butter
¼ cup (35g) plain flour
2 tablespoons coarsely chopped fresh flat-leaf parsley

1 Place milk, onion, bay leaf and peppercorns in large saucepan; bring to the boil. Add fish, reduce heat; simmer, covered, about 5 minutes or until cooked through. Remove fish from pan; divide fish among four 1½-cup (375ml) ovenproof dishes. Strain milk through sieve into medium jug. Discard solids; reserve milk.
2 Boil, steam or microwave potato and celeriac, separately, until tender; drain. Push potato and celeriac through sieve into large bowl; stir in yolk, cheese, ¼ cup of the cream and half of the butter until smooth. Cover to keep warm.
3 Meanwhile, melt remaining butter in medium saucepan; add flour, cook, stirring, about 3 minutes or until mixture bubbles and thickens slightly. Gradually stir in reserved milk and remaining cream; cook, stirring, until mixture boils and thickens. Stir in parsley.
4 Divide mornay mixture among dishes; cover each with potato mixture. Place pies on oven tray; place under hot grill until browned lightly.
nutritional count per serving 47.8g total fat (28.9g saturated fat); 3748kJ (832 cal); 42.8g carbohydrate; 53.9g protein; 8.7g fibre

meat pies

PREP + COOK TIME 1 HOUR 35 MINS (+ REFRIGERATION) • MAKES 6

The Australian meat pie is a national icon; there is even an official "Great Aussie Pie Competition" held annually, with thousands of entries. Australians consume the greatest number of pies per head of population anywhere in the world.

1½ cups (225g) plain flour
100g cold butter, chopped coarsely
1 egg
1 tablespoon iced water, approximately
2 sheets puff pastry
1 egg, extra

beef filling
1 tablespoon vegetable oil
1 small brown onion (80g), chopped finely
600g beef mince
415g can crushed tomatoes
2 tablespoons tomato paste
2 tablespoons worcestershire sauce
¾ cup (180ml) beef stock

1 Process flour and butter until crumbly. Add egg and enough of the water to make ingredients cling together. Knead pastry on floured surface until smooth. Cover; refrigerate 30 minutes.
2 Meanwhile, make beef filling.
3 Oil six ⅔-cup (160ml) pie tins. Divide pastry into six portions; roll each between sheets of baking paper until large enough to line tins. Lift pastry into tins, gently press over base and sides; trim edges. Refrigerate 30 minutes.
4 Cut six 11cm rounds from puff pastry; refrigerate until required.
5 Preheat oven to 200°C/180°C fan-forced.
6 Place pastry cases on oven tray; line pastry with baking paper then fill with dried beans or rice. Bake 10 minutes. Remove paper and beans; bake a further 5 minutes. Cool.
7 Fill pastry cases with beef filling; brush edges of pastry with extra egg. Top with puff pastry rounds; press edges to seal. Brush tops with egg. Cut steam holes in top of pies. Bake about 20 minutes or until pastry is golden. Serve pies with tomato sauce, if you like.
beef filling Heat oil in large saucepan; cook onion and beef, stirring, until beef is well browned. Stir in undrained tomatoes, paste, sauce and stock; bring to the boil. Reduce heat; simmer, uncovered, about 20 minutes or until thick. Cool.
nutritional count per pie 38.7g total fat (13.8g saturated fat); 2876kJ (688 cal); 52.4g carbohydrate; 31.2g protein; 3.5g fibre

What's the best way to reheat a pie?

Pies are best reheated in a slow oven. If you reheat them on too high a temperature the pastry will burn before the filling heats. It's always best to thaw a frozen pie before reheating. The microwave oven does not reheat pies successfully – it makes the pastry become soggy. However, you can defrost a frozen pie in the microwave and then gently reheat it in the oven.

gruyère, leek and bacon tart

PREP + COOK TIME 55 MINS • SERVES 4

A firm, pale yellow, cow-milk cheese from the Fribourg canton in Switzerland, gruyère is also produced in many regions of France. It has a sweet, nutty taste and is delicious eaten as is or used in cooking – try making macaroni cheese with gruyère for a flavour sensation.

50g butter
2 medium leeks (700g), sliced thinly
2 rindless bacon rashers (130g), chopped finely
2 sheets puff pastry

2 eggs
½ cup (125ml) cream
1 teaspoon fresh thyme leaves
½ cup (60g) finely grated gruyère cheese

1 Preheat oven to 220°C/200°C fan-forced. Oil 24cm-round loose-based flan tin; place tin on oven tray.
2 Melt butter in medium frying pan; cook leek, stirring occasionally, 15 minutes or until soft. Remove from pan. Cook bacon in same pan, stirring, until crisp; drain on absorbent paper.
3 Meanwhile, place one pastry sheet in flan tin; overlap with second sheet to form cross shape, trim away overlapping pastry. Prick pastry base with fork, line with baking paper; fill with dried beans or rice. Bake 20 minutes. Remove paper and beans; cool pastry case. Reduce oven to 200°C/180°C fan-forced.
4 Whisk eggs, cream and thyme in small bowl.
5 Spread leek into pastry case; top with bacon. Pour in egg mixture; sprinkle with cheese. Bake tart about 20 minutes or until filling sets. Cool 10 minutes before serving.

nutritional count per serving 34.8g total fat (20.2g saturated fat); 1948kJ (466 cal); 24.5g carbohydrate; 14.4g protein; 2.8g fibre

spanakopita

PREP + COOK TIME 1 HOUR 10 MINS • MAKES 16

Fillo pastry consists of paper-thin sheets of raw pastry which are used by brushing with oil or melted butter and stacking one on another, then cutting or folding as the recipe directs. It makes a distinctly layered, crackling-crisp, airy crust or wrapping for small pastries such as spanakopita.

1.5kg silver beet, trimmed
1 tablespoon olive oil
1 medium brown onion (150g), chopped finely
2 cloves garlic, crushed
1 teaspoon ground nutmeg
200g fetta cheese, crumbled
1 tablespoon finely grated lemon rind
¼ cup chopped fresh mint leaves

¼ cup chopped fresh flat-leaf parsley
¼ cup chopped fresh dill
4 green onions, chopped finely
16 sheets fillo pastry
125g butter, melted
2 teaspoons sesame seeds

1 Boil, steam or microwave silver beet until just wilted; drain. Squeeze out excess moisture; drain on absorbent paper. Chop coarsely; spread out on absorbent paper.
2 Heat oil in small frying pan; cook brown onion and garlic, stirring, until onion is soft. Add nutmeg; cook, stirring, until fragrant. Combine onion mixture and silver beet in large bowl with fetta, rind, herbs and green onion.
3 Preheat oven to 180°C/160°C fan-forced.
4 Brush one sheet of fillo with butter; fold lengthways into thirds, brushing with butter between each fold. Place rounded tablespoon of silver beet mixture at the bottom of one narrow edge of folded fillo sheet, leaving a border. Fold opposite corner of fillo diagonally across the filling to form large triangle; continue folding to end of fillo sheet, retaining triangular shape. Place on oiled oven tray, seam-side down; repeat with remaining ingredients.
5 Brush spanakopita with remaining butter; sprinkle with sesame seeds. Bake about 15 minutes or until browned lightly.

nutritional count per spanakopita 11.1g total fat (6.4g saturated fat); 690kJ (165 cal); 11g carbohydrate; 4.7g protein; 1.5g fibre

beef pasties

PREP + COOK TIME 1 HOUR 15 MINS • MAKES 16

Coliban potatoes are a round, smooth variety, with white skin and white flesh. They are great for baking and mashing.

500g coliban potatoes, peeled, chopped coarsely
1 tablespoon olive oil
1 small brown onion (80g), chopped finely
2 cloves garlic, crushed
1 medium carrot (120g), chopped finely
1 stalk celery (150g), trimmed, chopped finely

350g beef mince
⅓ cup (80ml) dry red wine
1 cup (250ml) beef stock
¼ cup (70g) tomato paste
½ cup (60g) frozen peas
8 sheets puff pastry, thawed
1 egg, beaten lightly

1 Boil, steam or microwave potato until tender; drain. Mash in medium bowl.
2 Meanwhile, heat oil in medium saucepan; cook onion and garlic, stirring, until onion softens. Add carrot and celery; cook, stirring, until vegetables are tender. Add beef; cook, stirring, until changed in colour.
3 Stir in wine, stock, paste and peas; cook, uncovered, about 5 minutes or until mixture thickens slightly. Stir potato into beef mixture; cool 10 minutes.
4 Preheat oven to 180°C/160°C fan-forced. Oil two oven trays.
5 Cut two 14cm-rounds from each pastry sheet. Spoon filling evenly in centre of each round. Brush edge of pastry with egg; fold over to enclose filling, pressing around edge with fork to seal. Place pasties on oven trays.
6 Bake pasties about 30 minutes or until browned lightly.

nutritional count per pasty 22g total fat (11.1g saturated fat); 1626kJ (389 cal); 34.9g carbohydrate; 10.9g protein; 2.3g fibre

lamb and rosemary pies

PREP + COOK TIME 45 MINS • SERVES 4

Diced lamb can be bought from supermarkets and butchers. If you prefer to dice the lamb yourself, shoulder meat is very good. Ask the butcher to bone the shoulder for you, and discard as much fat as possible.

2 tablespoons olive oil
400g diced lamb
4 baby onions (100g), quartered
1 tablespoon plain flour
¼ cup (60ml) dry red wine
¾ cup (180ml) beef stock
1 tablespoon tomato paste
1 tablespoon fresh rosemary leaves

2 sheets puff pastry
1 egg, beaten lightly
4 fresh rosemary sprigs
20g butter
2½ cups (300g) frozen peas
1 tablespoon lemon juice
½ cup (125ml) water

1 Heat half of the oil in large saucepan; cook lamb, in batches, uncovered, until browned all over. Heat remaining oil in same pan; cook onion, stirring, until soft. Add flour; cook, stirring, until mixture bubbles and thickens. Gradually add wine, stock, paste and rosemary leaves; stir until mixture boils and thickens. Stir in lamb; cool 10 minutes.

2 Preheat oven to 200°C/180°C fan-forced. Oil four holes of 6-hole (¾-cup/180ml) texas muffin pan.

3 Cut two 13cm rounds from opposite corners of each pastry sheet; cut two 9cm rounds from remaining corners of each sheet. Place larger rounds in prepared holes to cover bases and sides; trim any excess pastry, prick bases with fork.

4 Spoon lamb mixture into pastry cases; brush around edges with a little egg. Top pies with smaller rounds; gently press around edges to seal. Brush pies with remaining egg; press one rosemary sprig into top of each pie.

5 Bake pies about 15 minutes or until browned lightly. Stand 5 minutes in pan before serving.

6 Meanwhile, heat butter in medium saucepan; cook peas, juice and the water, uncovered, stirring occasionally, about 5 minutes or until peas are just tender.

nutritional count per serving 42.7g total fat (18.6g saturated fat); 2868kJ (686 cal); 40.4g carbohydrate; 33.1g protein; 6.1g fibre

Which pies do you suggest I take on a picnic?

The obvious picnic pies are quiches – keep them in the dish they were cooked in and wrap them loosely in foil. That way they'll travel well and stay warm. Individual meat, fish or vegetable pies are also great for picnics and apple turnovers, cooked the day before, heated in the oven in the morning and wrapped in foil make the perfect road trip breakfast with a thermos of coffee.

CURRIES

Curries

Yes, curry recipes usually involve a long list of exotic ingredients. But that doesn't mean they're hard to make – they're just more of an adventure. And once you have your pantry stocked with all those fragrant, earthy-toned spices, you'll want to use them again and again.

The word curry is derived from a Tamil (southern Indian) word literally meaning 'gravy', and is used to describe a whole range of savoury, stew-like dishes flavoured with herbs and/or spices. While Indian and Thai curries are the most familiar to us, curries also feature strongly in the cuisines of Pakistan, Sri Lanka, Africa, South-East Asia (Vietnam, Malaysia, Indonesia, Cambodia, Burma) and the Pacific Islands.

While all curries are based on curry pastes – aromatic mixtures of fresh or dried herbs and spices – the content of those pastes is very different on the Indian subcontinent from those made in South-East Asia. Indian curry pastes are generally quite powdery, made from ground dried spices and few, if any, herbs.

Thai curry pastes on the other hand – and those of Indonesia, Malaysia, Cambodia and Vietnam – are moister blends of mainly fresh herbs and spices. The dry, aromatic spices that feature so prominently in Indian curries are used much more sparingly in Thai cooking.

Indian curries are generally cooked for longer than their Thai counterparts and tend to be thicker and more stew-like while Thai curries are more soup-like. Indian curries generally have deeper, smokier, flavours while Thai curries are often sweeter. All of them are delicious and there are literally hundreds of different curry recipes to choose from, featuring meat, poultry, seafood and vegetables. Explore them all.

GRINDING SPICES

Many Asian chefs and home cooks insist that, for the very best results, you need to grind your own spices from whole seeds just before using them. And certainly, if you have the time, grinding your spices in a mortar and pestle is one of those rewarding, back-to-basics activities that brings you closer to the food you're making – and it's stimulating for the olfactory nerves, too, as the aromas of all the spices and herbs are released.

But this is not always possible, so if you need to purchase your curry powders and spices then try to source them from an Asian grocery store (preferably one where the stock is continually renewed) or failing that, from the spice section at your supermarket. Your ground spices and curry powders must be kept fresh in airtight containers. Older stale spices lose their taste, will add nothing to your dish and leave you feeling disappointed with the result.

THAI CURRIES	INDIAN CURRIES
IN THAILAND, CURRY IS CALLED 'GAENG PHET' (LITERALLY MEANING 'HOT LIQUID') AND REFERS TO SOUPS AND CURRIES. THAI CURRIES USUALLY CONSIST OF CURRY PASTE, COCONUT MILK OR WATER, AND MEAT AND VEGETABLES. THERE ARE DOZENS OF VARIATIONS DEPENDING ON THE TYPE OF CURRY PASTE, LIQUID AND COMBINATION OF MEATS, HERBS, VEGETABLES AND FRUITS USED.	SPICES ARE THE HEART AND SOUL OF ALL INDIAN CURRY RECIPES. A BASIC CURRY BEGINS WITH MAKING A FRAGRANT MIXTURE OF ONIONS, GARLIC AND SPICES IN A BIG POT, TO WHICH YOU ADD WATER, STOCK OR COCONUT MILK (OR A COMBINATION OF THESE) AND THEN THE CHICKEN, MEAT AND/OR VEGETABLES.

The key ingredients in most Thai curry pastes are 'wet' (ie. produced from fresh herbs) and fragrant: fresh chillies, lemon grass, galangal, garlic, shallot, kaffir lime, coriander and shrimp paste.

There is a huge range of spices that can be used but a few crucial star performers: cumin seeds, coriander seeds, fenugreek, turmeric, and cardamom. These usually form the basic ingredients for an Indian curry.

Thai curries use more fresh herbs and garlic and fewer dry spices than Indian curries. In fact, there are only two curry dishes in Thailand that are based mainly on dried herbs and spices, rather then fresh ones: the popular Massaman and Panang curries. When spices are used, they are most likely to be hot chilli peppers, cumin seeds, coriander seeds and/or turmeric.

Other aromatic ingredients such as asafoetida, allspice, garam masala (a mixed blend), clove, cinnamon, nutmeg, green or red chilli, aniseed and black pepper are also prominent in Indian recipes and might be included for specific types of curry powder. Onion, ginger and garlic are essential ingredients in any curry, but Indian dishes typically make very little use of herbs. The most frequent is coriander leaf, and this is always used fresh, never dried. In fact, coriander leaves are usually added towards the end of cooking and most often only as a garnish.

Thai curries are most commonly categorised by their colour – red, green and yellow – which is determined by the curry paste.

GREEN CURRY Usually considered the hottest (spiciest) of Thai curries, green curry is based on a curry paste made from fresh green chillies, shallots, lemon grass, white pepper, coriander root, garlic, kaffir lime rind and shrimp paste with sweet basil leaves, round green eggplant and kaffir lime leaves adding to the attractive green colour of the final curry dish.

To thicken a curry sauce, Indian cooking often includes pureed vegetables, yogurt, cream, coconut milk or ground nuts such as almonds and pistachios to give it body.

There is a huge range of Indian curries: every region of India has its own dishes with their own distinct flavours and spice combinations.

RED CURRY While it looks more fiery than green curry, red curry is usually milder and made with dried long red chillies, garlic, fresh lemon grass, fresh turmeric and shrimp paste and any of the following: coriander, cumin, shallots, kaffir lime rind and galangal.

Indian curries don't have to be hot: they range from the very mild to only-for-the brave (the famous Vindaloo, for example). If you are a beginner curry eater, start with the mild options and work your way up from there.

YELLOW CURRY Yellow curry paste is a more mellow sweet-spicy blend based on turmeric and curry powder with coriander, cumin, lemon grass, galangal, shrimp paste and dry red chillies to create a curry that is a lovely rich golden colour.

green curry paste

PREP + COOK TIME 20 MINS • MAKES 1 CUP

These four curry paste recipes make 1 cup. Use the amount of paste required in each curry recipe then freeze the rest, in one tablespoon batches, for up to 3 months.

- 2 teaspoons ground coriander
- 2 teaspoons ground cumin
- 10 long green chillies, chopped coarsely
- 10 small green chillies, chopped coarsely
- 1 teaspoon shrimp paste
- 1 clove garlic, quartered
- 4 green onions, chopped coarsely
- 10cm stick fresh lemon grass (20g), chopped finely
- 1cm piece fresh galangal (5g), chopped finely
- ¼ cup coarsely chopped fresh coriander root and stem mixture
- 1 tablespoon peanut oil

1 Dry-fry ground coriander and cumin in small frying pan over medium heat, stirring until fragrant.
2 Blend or process spices with chillies, paste, garlic, onion, lemon grass, galangal and coriander mixture until mixture forms a paste.
3 Add oil to paste; continue to blend until smooth.

nutritional count per tablespoon 1.6g total fat (0.3g saturated fat); 67kJ (16 cal); 0.3g carbohydrate; 0.2g protein; 0.2g fibre

red curry paste

PREP + COOK TIME 30 MINS (+ STANDING) • MAKES 1 CUP

Commercial curry pastes can't compare to the amazing blend of flavours created by homemade ones; however, they do save time. Jars of Thai and Indian curry pastes are available in most supermarkets, but you may have to adjust the amounts used to those called for in our recipes.

- 20 dried long red chillies
- 1 teaspoon ground coriander
- 2 teaspoons ground cumin
- 1 teaspoon hot paprika
- 2 teaspoons finely chopped fresh ginger
- 3 large cloves garlic, quartered
- 1 medium red onion (170g), chopped coarsely
- 2 x 10cm sticks fresh lemon grass (40g), sliced thinly
- 1 fresh kaffir lime leaf, sliced thinly
- 2 tablespoons coarsely chopped fresh coriander root and stem mixture
- 2 teaspoons shrimp paste
- 1 tablespoon peanut oil

1 Place whole chillies in small heatproof jug, cover with boiling water; stand 15 minutes, drain.
2 Meanwhile, dry-fry ground coriander, cumin and paprika in small frying pan over medium heat until fragrant.
3 Blend or process chillies and spices with ginger, garlic, onion, lemon grass, lime leaf, coriander mixture and paste until mixture forms a paste.
4 Add oil to paste; continue to blend until smooth.

nutritional count per tablespoon 1.6g total fat (0.3g saturated fat); 92kJ (22 cal); 1.2g carbohydrate; 0.5g protein; 0.5g fibre

panang curry paste

PREP + COOK TIME 20 MINS (+ STANDING) • MAKES 1 CUP

25 dried long red chillies
1 teaspoon ground coriander
2 teaspoons ground cumin
2 cloves garlic, quartered
8 green onions, chopped coarsely
2 x 10cm sticks fresh lemon grass (40g), sliced thinly
2cm piece fresh galangal (10g), chopped finely
2 teaspoons shrimp paste
½ cup (75g) roasted unsalted peanuts
2 tablespoons peanut oil

1 Place chillies in small heatproof jug, cover with boiling water; stand 15 minutes, drain.
2 Meanwhile, dry-fry ground coriander and cumin in small frying pan over medium heat, stirring until fragrant.
3 Blend or process chillies and spices with remaining ingredients until mixture forms a paste.

nutritional count per tablespoon 6.1g total fat (0.9g saturated fat); 288kJ (69 cal); 1.3g carbohydrate; 1.9g protein; 0.9g fibre

massaman curry paste

PREP + COOK TIME 30 MINS • MAKES 1 CUP

20 dried red chillies
1 teaspoon ground coriander
2 teaspoons ground cumin
2 teaspoons ground cinnamon
½ teaspoon ground cardamom
½ teaspoon ground clove
5 cloves garlic, quartered
1 large brown onion (200g), chopped coarsely
2 x 10cm sticks fresh lemon grass (40g), sliced thinly
3 fresh kaffir lime leaves, sliced thinly
4cm piece fresh ginger (20g), chopped coarsely
2 teaspoons shrimp paste
1 tablespoon peanut oil

1 Place chillies in small heatproof jug, cover with boiling water; stand 15 minutes. Drain; reserve chillies.
2 Meanwhile, dry-fry ground coriander, cumin, cinnamon, cardamom and clove in small frying pan, stirring, until fragrant.
3 Preheat oven to 160°C/140°C fan-forced.
4 Place chillies and roasted spices in small shallow baking dish with remaining ingredients. Roast, uncovered, in oven 15 minutes.
5 Blend or process roasted mixture until smooth.

nutritional count per tablespoon 6.7g total fat (1.2g saturated fat); 376kJ (90 cal); 4.5g carbohydrate; 2.1g protein; 2.4g fibre

butter chicken

PREP + COOK TIME 1 HOUR 40 MINS (+ REFRIGERATION) • SERVES 4

For a great pie filling add 2 large cooked potatoes, chopped, and 100g baby spinach leaves to the butter chicken. Spoon the filling into a deep pie dish and top with a sheet of puff pastry. Brush with beaten egg, snip two air holes in the top and bake in a hot oven for 25 minutes or until the pastry is golden.

1 cup (150g) unsalted raw cashews
2 teaspoons garam masala
2 teaspoons ground coriander
½ teaspoon chilli powder
3 cloves garlic, chopped coarsely
4cm piece fresh ginger (20g), grated
2 tablespoons white vinegar
⅓ cup (95g) tomato paste
½ cup (140g) yogurt
1kg chicken thigh fillets, halved

80g butter
1 large brown onion (200g), chopped finely
1 cinnamon stick
4 cardamom pods, bruised
1 teaspoon hot paprika
400g can tomato puree
¾ cup (180ml) chicken stock
¾ cup (180ml) cream

1 Dry-fry nuts in small frying pan, stirring, until nearly brown. Add garam masala, coriander and chilli, continue stirring, until nuts are browned lightly.

2 Blend or process nut mixture with garlic, ginger, vinegar, paste and half the yogurt until mixture forms a paste. Transfer to large bowl, stir in remaining yogurt and chicken. Cover; refrigerate 3 hours or overnight.

3 Melt butter in large saucepan; cook onion, cinnamon and cardamom, stirring, until onion is browned lightly. Add chicken mixture; cook, stirring, 10 minutes.

4 Stir in paprika, puree and stock; simmer, uncovered, 45 minutes, stirring occasionally.

5 Discard cinnamon and cardamom. Add cream; simmer, uncovered, 5 minutes.

nutritional count per serving 74g total fat (33.3g saturated fat); 4138kJ (990 cal); 20.8g carbohydrate; 59.3g protein; 6.5g fibre

Cardamom pods must be bruised (crushing with the side of a knife is the easiest way) to release their fragrance and warm subtle taste.

Fry the cashews in a small dry frying pan, shaking the pan and stirring until almost brown. Watch constantly – a moment's inattention now and the nuts will burn.

Blend or process the spiced nuts with ginger, garlic, vinegar, tomato paste and yogurt until smooth. Transfer the paste to a large bowl.

SPECIAL FEATURE

Know your spices

The trick with spices is to buy them fresh and never keep them for more than year. Spices go stale and lose their sparkle, so buy them in small quantities and store them in airtight containers. Spices such as cinnamon, nutmeg and vanilla beans have the strongest and most intense flavour if bought whole.

RAS EL HANOUT
The name means "top of the shop" and the mixture varies from one merchant to another, but is always subtly savoury with a touch of heat. Excellent with lamb or chicken.

FENUGREEK
The seeds of a herb of the pea family. Used in curry powder, good with seafood and in chutneys. The aroma of fenugreek is known for its characteristic of masking unpleasant odours.

SAFFRON
Expensive because it consists of the hand-gathered stigmas from a crocus flower. Buy it only from a reputable source. It colours food golden and has a bittersweet almondy taste.

STAR ANISE
The dried, star-shaped fruit of a small Asian tree with a pungent liquorice/clove/cinnamon flavour. Used whole or ground, it is the main spice in chinese five-spice. Use sparingly with pork or duck or in a fruit compote.

ASAFOETIDA
The dried and ground resin of a giant fennel, notorious for its penetrating "rotten" smell but this is toned down in cooking. Its pungent flavour suggests fermented garlic. Use this spice sparingly with lentils and in fish and vegetable curries.

BAHARAT
A spice blend used throughout the Middle East. It typically includes ground paprika, black pepper, cumin, coriander, cassia, cloves, cardamom and nutmeg. Rub on fish, beef or lamb before cooking.

Q&A

Many curry recipes ask for the spice paste to be fried for several minutes 'or until fragrant'. What does this mean exactly and why do you have to do it?

You fry a spice paste to rid it of its 'raw' taste. It needs about 5 minutes frying over gentle heat to develop a deeper, richer flavour and a noticeable 'fragrance'. If you use a curry paste, either home-made or purchased without giving it this preliminary frying, you'll really notice the difference in taste.

...AC
...ple-red sp ce ground from the berries of a small ...terranean t ee. Adds a tart, lemony flavour to ...and dressings and goes well with meat, chicken ...sh, tomato and avocado.

GARAM MASALA
The name simply means "spice blend" and the mixture varies, but is always savoury with a touch of pepper bite. Used as a seasoning in Indian cooking and is sometimes sprinkled over the finished dish.

HARISSA
A fiery Tunisian paste made by pounding chilli with spices, garlic and mint. Used to season meats such as kebabs and traditionally placed on the table as an all-purpose condiment.

...ONJI
...called nigella, these are the seeds of a plant ...d to buttercups. The flavour is sharp/metallic ...uced by cooking), nutty, peppery. Used in or ...urkish and India n breads, and in the Indian ...e mix, panch phora.

SICHUAN PEPPERCORNS
No relation to other peppercorns, sichuan (also spelt szechuan) peppercorns are the dried berries of a small tree native to the Sichuan province of south-west China, where highly spiced foods are much appreciated. They smell and taste peppery/lemony.

ZA'ATAR
A blend of roasted dried oregano, marjoram, thyme, sumac and sesame seeds found in the Lebanese and Syrian kitchen. Traditionally sprinkled on toast spread with ricotta, it's great tossed with roasted potato wedges too.

pork and vegetable vindaloo

PREP + COOK TIME 1 HOUR 30 MINS • SERVES 6

This is often the hottest dish on a restaurant menu. To counteract the heat or "chilli burn", drink milk or a lassi (yogurt drink).

- 2 teaspoons cumin seeds
- 2 teaspoons garam masala
- 1 teaspoon ground cinnamon
- 2 cloves garlic, quartered
- 4 fresh small red thai chillies, chopped coarsely
- 2cm piece fresh ginger (10g), sliced thinly
- 1 large brown onion (200g) chopped coarsely
- 2 tablespoons white vinegar
- 2 tablespoons vegetable oil
- 1kg boneless pork shoulder, cut into 2cm pieces
- 2 cups (500ml) beef stock
- 2 medium potatoes (400g), cut into 2cm pieces
- 2 medium carrots (240g), cut into 2cm pieces
- 150g green beans, trimmed, chopped coarsely

1 Dry-fry spices in small frying pan, stirring, until fragrant; cool.
2 Blend or process spices, garlic, chilli, ginger, onion and vinegar until mixture forms a smooth paste.
3 Heat half the oil in large saucepan; cook pork, in batches, until browned.
4 Heat remaining oil in same pan; cook paste, stirring, 5 minutes. Return pork to pan with stock; bring to the boil. Reduce heat; simmer, covered, 30 minutes. Add potato, carrot and beans; simmer, uncovered, about 30 minutes or until pork is tender and sauce thickens slightly.

nutritional count per serving 19.9g total fat (5.4g saturated fat); 1664kJ (398 cal); 13.6g carbohydrate; 39.3g protein; 3.8g fibre

tandoori chicken

PREP + COOK TIME 50 MINS (+ REFRIGERATION) • SERVES 4

The tandoori curry paste is spicy but not hot. Here it is mixed with yogurt and used as a marinade. Classically, it would then be baked on the wall of a tandoor, a round clay oven – it can be baked in an ordinary hot oven or, better still, baked and then finished on a barbecue.

- 200g yogurt
- 1 medium brown onion (150g), chopped coarsely
- 2 tablespoons lemon juice
- 1 tablespoon vegetable oil
- 2cm piece fresh ginger (10g), grated
- 3 cloves garlic, crushed
- 2 teaspoons chilli powder
- 1 teaspoon garam masala
- 1 teaspoon ground cumin
- ½ teaspoon red food colouring
- 1.5kg chicken pieces
- 1 cup loosely packed fresh coriander leaves

1 Blend or process yogurt, onion, juice, oil, ginger, garlic, spices and colouring until smooth. Combine paste with chicken in large bowl. Cover; refrigerate overnight.
2 Remove chicken from marinade; cook, covered, on heated oiled grill plate (or grill or barbecue) until cooked through. Serve chicken sprinkled with coriander leaves and with lemon wedges.

nutritional count per serving 26.5g total fat (7.7g saturated fat); 2512kJ (601 cal); 5.9g carbohydrate; 84g protein; 1.3g fibre

[opposite] pork and vegetable vindaloo

easy lamb curry

PREP + COOK TIME 1 HOUR 30 MINS • SERVES 4

- 2 cloves garlic, crushed
- 2 long green chillies, chopped
- 5cm piece fresh ginger (25g), peeled, chopped
- 2 tablespoons vegetable oil or ghee
- 2 medium brown onions (300g), chopped coarsely
- 1½ teaspoons turmeric
- 1 teaspoon ground cumin
- 3 teaspoons ground coriander
- 1 teaspoon ground chilli powder
- 1kg diced lamb shoulder
- 1 teaspoon salt
- 400g can peeled tomatoes
- ¼ cup (60ml) coconut cream

1 Using a mortar and pestle (or small processor), pound garlic, chilli and ginger to form a paste.
2 Heat oil or ghee in large saucepan; cook onion, stirring, about 10 minutes or until browned lightly. Add garlic paste; cook, stirring, over low heat, 3 minutes or until fragrant but not browned.
3 Blend spices with a little water to make a smooth paste, add to pan; cook, stirring, 5 minutes.
4 Add lamb to pan, in batches, cooking until browned. Return all lamb to pan with salt. Add undrained tomatoes; mix well.
5 Cook lamb curry, covered, stirring occasionally, about 50 minutes or until lamb is tender. Stir in coconut cream in the last 20 minutes of cooking time.

nutritional count per serving 26.9g total fat (10.6g saturated fat); 2052kJ (491 cal); 8.4g carbohydrate; 52.4g protein; 3g fibre

fish curry with lime and coconut

PREP + COOK TIME 50 MINS • SERVES 4

Coriander, also known as cilantro or chinese parsley, is a bright-green-leafed herb with a pungent flavour. Often stirred into or sprinkled over a dish just before serving for maximum impact. The stems and roots of coriander are also used in Thai cooking; wash well before chopping.

- 6 fresh small red thai chillies, chopped coarsely
- 2 cloves garlic, quartered
- 10 shallots (250g), chopped coarsely
- 10cm stick fresh lemon grass (20g), chopped coarsely
- 5cm piece fresh galangal (25g), quartered
- ¼ cup coarsely chopped fresh coriander root and stem mixture
- ¼ teaspoon ground turmeric
- 1 tablespoon peanut oil
- 2 x 400ml cans coconut milk
- 2 tablespoons fish sauce
- 4 fresh kaffir lime leaves, shredded
- 1 tablespoon lime juice
- 4 x 200g kingfish fillets
- ½ cup loosely packed fresh coriander leaves

1 Blend or process chilli, garlic, shallot, lemon grass, galangal, coriander root and stem mixture, turmeric and oil until mixture forms a smooth paste.
2 Cook paste in large frying pan, stirring, over medium heat, about 3 minutes or until fragrant. Add coconut milk, sauce and lime leaves; bring to the boil. Reduce heat; simmer, uncovered, about 15 minutes or until thickened slightly. Stir in juice.
3 Add fish to pan; simmer, uncovered, about 10 minutes or until cooked. Serve curry sprinkled with coriander leaves.
nutritional count per serving 50.6g total fat (38.5g saturated fat); 2867kJ (686 cal); 10.6g carbohydrate; 45.9g protein; 4.9g fibre

pork jungle curry

PREP + COOK TIME 40 MINS • SERVES 4

This fiery curry got its name from the originating cooks who, travelling through the jungle in Thailand's central plains, had to make do with what was available there. It has remained popular because it's easy to prepare and has such strong links to Thai history.

2 tablespoons peanut oil
¼ cup (75g) red curry paste (see page 412)
750g pork fillet, sliced thinly
⅓ cup firmly packed fresh thai basil leaves
40g pickled ka chai, sliced thinly
150g thai eggplants, chopped coarsely
1 medium carrot (150g), sliced thinly
100g snake beans, chopped coarsely
227g can bamboo shoots, rinsed, drained
2 x 5cm stems pickled green peppercorns (10g)
2 fresh kaffir lime leaves, torn
1 litre (4 cups) vegetable stock
4 fresh small red thai chillies, chopped coarsely

1 Place oil and curry paste in large saucepan; stir over heat until fragrant.
2 Add pork; cook, stirring, about 5 minutes or until browned all over.
3 Reserve about four large whole basil leaves for garnish. Add remaining basil leaves, ka chai, eggplant, carrot, beans, bamboo shoots, peppercorns, lime leaves and stock to pan; bring to the boil. Reduce heat; simmer, uncovered, about 10 minutes or until vegetables are tender. Stir in chilli.
4 Place curry in serving bowl; sprinkle with reserved thai basil leaves.
nutritional count per serving 31.2g total fat (7.8g saturated fat); 2073kJ (496 cal); 6.5g carbohydrate; 45.3g protein; 5g fibre

beef massaman curry

PREP + COOK TIME 2 HOURS 30 MINS • SERVES 4

Massaman curry is a staple in the Muslim communities in the south of Thailand close to the Malaysian border. It is a fragrant, hot curry with an acid note, showing the influence of traders who came from further west to that coast.

1kg skirt steak, cut into 3cm pieces
2 cups (500ml) beef stock
5 cardamom pods, bruised
¼ teaspoon ground clove
2 star anise
1 tablespoon grated palm sugar
2 tablespoons fish sauce
2 tablespoons tamarind concentrate
2 x 400ml cans coconut milk
2 tablespoons massaman curry paste (see page 413)
8 baby brown onions (200g), halved
1 medium kumara (400g), chopped coarsely
¼ cup (35g) coarsely chopped roasted unsalted peanuts
2 green onions, sliced thinly

1 Place beef, 1½ cups of the stock, cardamom, clove, star anise, sugar, sauce, 1 tablespoon of the tamarind and half of the coconut milk in large saucepan; simmer, uncovered, about 1½ hours or until beef is almost tender.
2 Strain beef over large bowl; reserve braising liquid, discard solids. Cover beef to keep warm.
3 Cook curry paste in same pan, stirring, until fragrant. Add remaining coconut milk, tamarind and stock; bring to the boil. Cook, stirring, about 1 minute or until mixture is smooth. Return beef to pan with brown onion, kumara and 1 cup of the reserved braising liquid; simmer, uncovered, about 30 minutes or until beef and vegetables are tender.
4 Stir nuts and green onion into curry off the heat.

nutritional count per serving 52.7g total fat (39.5g saturated fat); 3645kJ (872 cal); 29.2g carbohydrate; 67.4g protein; 7.2g fibre

Place the beef in a large saucepan with the coconut milk and spices and cook over low heat for about 1½ hours.

Strain the cooked beef over a bowl. Discard spices but reserve the cooking liquid.

Fry the massaman curry paste, stirring, for about 5 minutes until it becomes deliciously fragrant.

rogan josh

PREP + COOK TIME 2 HOURS 20 MINS • SERVES 4

Rogan josh, traditionally made with lamb, is an Indian tomato-based curry, and literally means "meat in spicy red sauce". It is slightly milder than many curries due in equal part to the fairly large amount of tomato used and the very little chilli found in the paste.

2 teaspoons ground cardamom
2 teaspoons ground cumin
2 teaspoons ground coriander
1kg boned leg of lamb, trimmed, diced into 3cm pieces
20g butter
2 tablespoons vegetable oil
2 medium brown onions (300g), sliced thinly
4cm piece fresh ginger (20g), grated
4 cloves garlic, crushed
2 teaspoons sweet paprika
½ teaspoon cayenne pepper
½ cup (125ml) beef stock
425g can crushed tomatoes
2 bay leaves
2 cinnamon sticks
200g yogurt
¾ cup (110g) roasted slivered almonds
1 fresh long red chilli, sliced thinly

cucumber raita
1 cup (280g) thick "country-style" yogurt
1 lebanese cucumber (130g), seeded, chopped finely
1 tablespoon finely chopped fresh mint
pinch ground cumin

1 Combine cardamom, cumin and coriander in medium bowl, add lamb; toss lamb to coat in spice mixture.
2 Heat butter and half of the oil in large deep saucepan; cook lamb, in batches, until browned all over. Remove from pan.
3 Heat remaining oil in same pan; cook onion, ginger, garlic, paprika and cayenne over low heat, stirring, until onion softens.
4 Return lamb to pan with stock, undrained tomatoes, bay leaves and cinnamon. Add yogurt, 1 tablespoon at a time, stirring well between each addition; bring to the boil. Reduce heat; simmer, covered, about 1½ hours or until lamb is tender.
5 Meanwhile, make cucumber raita.
6 Sprinkle lamb with nuts and chilli off the heat; serve with raita and, if desired, warmed naan bread.

cucumber raita Combine ingredients in small bowl with salt and pepper to taste.
nutritional count per serving (incl. raita) 48.1g total fat (15.3g saturated fat); 3219kJ (770 cal); 15.7g carbohydrate; 68.9g protein; 5.5g fibre

panang fish curry

PREP + COOK TIME 45 MINS • SERVES 4

Panang is the English adaptation of the Thai word "phanoeng" or "panaeng" meaning curry. The paste is a complex, sweet and milder variation of an authentic Thai red curry paste, which is especially good with seafood. Kaffir lime leaves, aromatic leaves of a citrus tree, are used similarly to bay leaves or curry leaves. They are available from Asian food stores.

2 x 400ml cans coconut milk
¼ cup (60g) panang curry paste (see page 413)
¼ cup (60ml) fish sauce
2 tablespoons grated palm sugar
4 fresh kaffir lime leaves, torn
2 tablespoons peanut oil
500g ling fillets, cut into 3cm pieces
500g uncooked medium king prawns
250g scallops
200g snake beans, chopped coarsely
½ cup loosely packed fresh thai basil leaves
½ cup (70g) coarsely chopped roasted unsalted peanuts
2 fresh long red chillies, sliced thinly

1 Place coconut milk, paste, sauce, sugar and lime leaves in wok; simmer, stirring, about 15 minutes or until mixture reduces by a third.
2 Meanwhile, heat oil in large frying pan; cook seafood, in batches, until just changed in colour. Drain on absorbent paper.
3 Add beans and seafood to curry mixture; cook, uncovered, stirring occasionally, about 5 minutes or until beans are just tender and seafood is cooked as desired.
4 Serve curry sprinkled with basil, nuts and chilli.

nutritional count per serving 64.3g total fat (39.8g saturated fat); 3716kJ (889 cal); 18.3g carbohydrate; 57.1g protein; 7.2g fibre

green chicken curry

PREP + COOK TIME 50 MINS • SERVES 4

Green curry paste is one of the hottest of the Thai traditional pastes, but this doesn't stop it being one of the favourite curries among non-Thai cooks and diners. Coconut milk tempers the fire, but doesn't dilute the beautiful flavour of this curry. You can use ready-made green curry paste available in most supermarkets instead of making your own.

1 tablespoon peanut oil
¼ cup (75g) green curry paste (see page 412)
3 long green chillies, chopped finely
1kg chicken thigh fillets, cut into 3cm pieces
2 x 400ml cans coconut milk
2 tablespoons fish sauce
2 tablespoons lime juice
1 tablespoon grated palm sugar
150g pea eggplants
1 large zucchini (150g), sliced thinly
⅓ cup loosely packed fresh thai basil leaves
¼ cup loosely packed fresh coriander leaves
2 green onions, chopped coarsely

1 Heat oil in large saucepan; cook paste and about two-thirds of the chilli, stirring, about 2 minutes or until fragrant. Add chicken; cook, stirring, until browned.
2 Add coconut milk, sauce, juice, sugar and eggplants; simmer, uncovered, about 10 minutes or until eggplants are just tender.
3 Add zucchini, basil and coriander; simmer, uncovered, until zucchini is just tender.
4 Serve curry sprinkled with remaining chilli and green onion.

nutritional count per serving 67.3g total fat (43.2g saturated fat); 3716kJ (889 cal); 17g carbohydrate; 52.9g protein; 6g fibre

[1] panang fish curry
[2] green chicken curry
[3] beef rendang [page 428]
[4] dhal and paneer vegetable curry [page 428]

1

2

3

4

beef rendang

PREP + COOK TIME 2 HOURS 15 MINS • SERVES 6

Serve this curry with steamed jasmine rice, accompanied by combined finely chopped cucumber and finely sliced fresh red chilli in rice vinegar.

You can make the curry a day or two before you need it.

1.5kg beef chuck steak, trimmed, cut into 3cm cubes
400ml can coconut milk
½ cup (125ml) water
10cm stick fresh lemon grass (20g), bruised
3 fresh kaffir lime leaves, torn

spice paste
2 medium red onions (340g), chopped coarsely
4 cloves garlic, chopped coarsely
5cm piece fresh ginger (25g), chopped coarsely
2 fresh long red chillies, chopped coarsely
3 teaspoons grated fresh galangal
3 teaspoons ground coriander
1½ teaspoons ground cumin
1 teaspoon ground turmeric
1 teaspoon salt

1 Blend or process spice paste ingredients until combined.
2 Combine paste in wok with beef, coconut milk, the water, lemon grass and lime leaves; bring to the boil. Reduce heat; simmer, covered, stirring occasionally, about 2 hours or until mixture thickens and beef is tender.

nutritional count per serving 25.2g total fat (16.9g saturated fat); 1952kJ (467 cal); 6.1g carbohydrate; 52.9g protein; 2.5g fibre

dhal and paneer vegetable curry

PREP + COOK TIME 1 HOUR 40 MINS • SERVES 4

The word dhal is the Hindi word for legumes and pulses; regarded as meat substitutes, they feature widely in Indian cooking because they are a good source of protein for this largely vegetarian nation.

2 tablespoons ghee
1 medium brown onion (150g), chopped finely
2 cloves garlic, crushed
2cm piece fresh ginger (10g), grated
2 teaspoons ground cumin
1 tablespoon ground coriander
1 teaspoon ground turmeric
2 teaspoons garam masala
2 cardamom pods, bruised
2 tablespoons mild curry paste
1 cup (200g) yellow split peas
810g can crushed tomatoes
2 cups (500ml) vegetable stock
2 cups (500ml) water
250g cabbage, chopped coarsely
2 medium carrots (240g), cut into 2cm pieces
½ cup (60g) frozen peas
2 x 100g packets paneer cheese, cut into 2cm pieces
⅓ cup loosely packed fresh coriander leaves

1 Heat ghee in large saucepan; cook onion, garlic and ginger, stirring, until onion softens. Add spices; cook, stirring, until fragrant. Add curry paste; cook, stirring, until fragrant.
2 Add split peas, undrained tomatoes, stock and the water; bring to the boil. Reduce heat; simmer, covered, 30 minutes, stirring occasionally. Uncover, add cabbage and carrot; cook, stirring occasionally, about 30 minutes or until split peas soften.
3 Add frozen peas and cheese; cook, uncovered, about 5 minutes or until cheese is heated through. Serve curry sprinkled with coriander.
nutritional count per serving 20.1g total fat (10g saturated fat); 1923kJ (460 cal); 39.6g carbohydrate; 23.4g protein; 14.2g fibre

chicken korma

PREP + COOK TIME 1 HOUR 10 MINS (+ REFRIGERATION) • SERVES 4

Also known as nigella, kalonji are angular purple-black seeds which are a creamy colour inside and possess a sharp, nutty taste. They are the seeds sprinkled over the top of freshly made pide, Turkish bread, that give it a special sharp, peppery flavour. Kalonji are found in spice shops and Middle-Eastern and Asian food stores.

¼ cup (35g) unsalted cashews
1 teaspoon sesame seeds
500g yogurt
3 cloves garlic, crushed
2cm piece fresh ginger (10g), grated
1 teaspoon dried chilli flakes
½ teaspoon ground turmeric
1kg chicken thigh fillets, diced into 3cm pieces
2 tablespoons vegetable oil
2 medium brown onions (300g), sliced thinly
2 cardamom pods
2 whole cloves
½ teaspoon black cumin seeds
½ cinnamon stick
2 tablespoons lemon juice
⅓ cup (15g) flaked coconut
⅓ cup (50g) unsalted cashews, extra
2 teaspoons kalonji seeds
¼ cup loosely packed fresh coriander leaves

1 Process nuts and sesame seeds until ground finely. Combine nut mixture with yogurt, garlic, ginger, chilli and turmeric in large bowl; add chicken, toss to coat in marinade. Cover; refrigerate 3 hours or overnight.
2 Heat oil in large saucepan; cook onion, stirring, until soft. Add chicken mixture. Reduce heat; simmer, uncovered, 40 minutes, stirring occasionally.
3 Using mortar and pestle, crush cardamom, cloves and cumin seeds.
4 Add spice mixture, cinnamon and juice to chicken mixture; cook, uncovered, about 10 minutes or until chicken is cooked through.
5 Meanwhile, dry-fry coconut and extra nuts in small frying pan, stirring, until browned lightly. Remove from heat; stir in kalonji seeds.
6 Discard cinnamon from curry; serve curry, sprinkled with coconut mixture and coriander, accompanied by steamed basmati rice, if desired.
nutritional count per serving 45.7g total fat (13.6g saturated fat); 2918kJ (698 cal); 13.2g carbohydrate; 58.1g protein; 3.7g fibre

pumpkin and eggplant curry

PREP + COOK TIME 1 HOUR • SERVES 6

2 tablespoons olive oil
1 medium brown onion (150g), sliced thickly
1 clove garlic, crushed
2cm piece fresh ginger (10g), grated
2 fresh small red thai chillies, chopped finely
1 teaspoon ground cumin
½ teaspoon ground turmeric
¼ teaspoon ground cardamom
¼ teaspoon ground fennel
8 baby eggplants (480g), sliced thickly
1kg butternut pumpkin, cut into 2cm pieces
400g can diced tomatoes
400ml can coconut cream
1 cup (250ml) vegetable stock
1 tablespoon tomato paste
400g can chickpeas, rinsed, drained
½ cup coarsely chopped fresh mint

1 Heat oil in large saucepan; cook onion, garlic, ginger and chilli, stirring, until onion softens. Add spices and eggplant; cook, stirring, 2 minutes.
2 Add pumpkin, undrained tomatoes, coconut cream, stock and paste; bring to the boil. Reduce heat; simmer, uncovered, 20 minutes. Add chickpeas; simmer, uncovered, about 10 minutes or until vegetables are tender.
3 Serve bowls of curry sprinkled with mint.
nutritional count per serving 22.3g total fat (13.6g saturated fat); 1467kJ (351 cal); 24.5g carbohydrate; 9.5g protein; 8.6g fibre

chicken tikka

PREP + COOK TIME 25 MINS • SERVES 4

Tikka paste is a mild paste which, in Indian cookery, is made to its maker's choice of spices and oils and sometimes tomatoes or coconut cream; it is frequently coloured red. It is usually used for marinating or for basting the food as it cooks, rather than as an ingredient. It is most often used with chicken.

2 cups (400g) jasmine rice
2 tablespoons tikka masala paste
2 tablespoons mango chutney
1kg chicken thigh fillets, sliced thinly
⅓ cup (80ml) vegetable stock
½ cup (140g) yogurt
½ cup loosely packed, coarsely chopped fresh coriander
2 teaspoons lime juice
1 red thai chilli, sliced thinly

1 Cook rice in large saucepan of boiling water, uncovered, until just tender; drain.
2 Meanwhile, combine paste, chutney and chicken in large bowl. Heat wok or large frying pan; stir-fry chicken mixture, in batches, until chicken is browned all over.
3 Add remaining ingredients to wok; bring to the boil. Reduce heat; simmer, uncovered, about 5 minutes or until chicken is cooked through. Serve with rice.
nutritional count per serving 23.4g total fat (6.8g saturated fat); 3290kJ (787 cal); 86.3g carbohydrate; 55.8g protein; 2.4g fibre

[opposite] pumpkin and eggplant curry

BARBECUES & GRILLS

Barbecues & grills

Barbecues are synonymous with summer, salads and languid meals spent around the outdoor table with family and friends. Few things say relaxed summer entertaining better than platters of steaming, char-grilled meat and fish, delivered straight from the barbecue to the outdoor table, alongside the salads.

People love the distinctive flavours and charming appearance of char-grilled foods. That's why we love barbecues and that's why we have embraced the arrival of grill pans, which allow you to cook food in a way similar to barbecuing, but indoors on your kitchen stove top, all year-round. And then, of course, there's the traditional griller that is part of every kitchen: when it's Sunday night at home, and you don't want any fuss, nothing beats the humble griller for a trusty grilled snack.

ON THE BARBECUE

Brush or spray food for barbecuing with oil or melted butter just before cooking. Also oil the grill, unless the manufacturer's instructions direct otherwise. Baste the food frequently with more oil (or with a marinade or sauce according to the recipe) while it is cooking.

STEAKS, CHOPS AND CHICKEN PIECES Cook the first side until browned to your liking, turn only once and cook the other side to your liking. Rest meat and chicken in the warmth next to the barbecue for 5 minutes before serving.

SAUSAGES Cook at a moderate heat, moving to the side of grill or plate if over-browning before they are cooked through. Or poach sausages beforehand, then brown them quickly on the barbecue.

ROASTS Follow the manufacturer's directions for roasting on your barbecue.

FISH Pay close attention to fish and remove it as soon as the flesh turns white (or pink for salmon or trout). Whole fish is cooked when a skewer slides easily into the thickest part. For whole fish, slash sides two or three times before cooking and use a greased fish-shaped hinged wire grill to help turn it without breaking. If you don't have one, lift it carefully with two spatulas, one at each end.

UNDER THE GRILL

Grilling produces an even and deliciously browned surface on everything from lamb chops to an omelette. Ubiquitously housed in every wall oven or stovetop, the grill consists of a pierced tray or rack fitted over a shallow pan. Grilling is healthy because the fats and juices drip into the pan.

The key is to pre-heat the grill on high so that when the food goes under, it starts to brown immediately. Even if a recipe calls for medium heat, have the griller hot then turn it down when you start to grill.

If you're grilling small pieces of tender foods, grill on high heat, making sure you coat them with oil first. Larger items, like half a chicken, are usually cooked on medium-hot heat and may still be uncooked although they look golden-brown on the outside. If a recipe says to reduce the heat and continue cooking, it is best to lower the food away from the grill rather than reduce the temperature. If this is too hard to do mid-grilling, then finish cooking in a moderate oven.

GRILL CARE

High heat 'cooks on' any food residue on a grill tray. Soaking to loosen these bits is better for the tray than scouring it. Or, to minimise cleaning, cover the tray with heavy foil before use.

IN THE GRILL PAN

People love grill pans (which sit on the hotplate of your stove top) because they cook the food in a similar way to a barbecue – complete with those distinctive dark-barred markings, which are created by the ridges in the pan. The food chars where it makes contact with the very hot ridges, while the heat rising from the base of the pan cooks the parts in between. Char-grilling is a fast cooking method, best suited to small, tender items of food. It is a healthy way to cook because excess fat seeps off into the gutters between the ridges while the food is held above it. And it looks stylish and tastes marvellous.

GRILL PANS are available in round, square and rectangular shapes, in various sizes. They are made from a number of different materials including enamelled cast iron, titanium, bare iron and toughened aluminium.

FOODS Char-grilling in a grill pan is suitable for a whole range of foods: seafood (thick, meaty fish fillets); meat (steaks, fillets, chops or cutlets); chicken thighs and breasts; vegetables, fruits and thickly-sliced breads.

GRILL PAN MUST-DOS

Grill pans can create smoky fumes so you need a strong exhaust fan, preferably ducted to the outside, to avoid a smoke-filled kitchen.

Brush both food and grill pan with melted butter or oil. Place food, slightly apart, across the ridges of the grill, pressing each piece down lightly with tongs to ensure it has full contact with the ridges. Allow the food to grill for a few minutes without moving it so that char marks will be clearly defined. Lift an edge to check when food is done to your liking and turn over. Turn food only once.

Seafood, thin steaks or cutlets, may be nearly cooked by the time they are well marked on the first side. If so, cook them only briefly on the second side, then take them off the heat. Serve with the well-marked side up.

Thick foods, such as steak, may not be cooked through even when they look well-charred on the outside. Rather than continuing in the grill pan (which could scorch or dry it out), finish cooking in a moderate oven, turning it once, if necessary.

Coat fish in melted butter or oil before cooking to protect it and help it colour quickly. All seafood should be removed from the grill pan while it is still a little underdone: its own heat will finish cooking it by the time it is served. Tuna and salmon are often served barely seared.

GRILL PAN CARE

After cooking, immediately plunge the grill pan into a sink of very hot water to loosen any food residue, then brush with a stiff brush (not metal). Dry with a cloth and place over very low heat for a few minutes to dry thoroughly.

BARBECUE CARE

CLEAN BARBECUE ACCORDING TO MANUFACTURER'S DIRECTIONS, OR CLEAN WHILE HOT – BUT TURNED OFF – WITH HOT WATER AND A WIRE BRUSH; DRY WITH A CLOTH AND LEAVE FOR AN HOUR OR TWO IN THE OPEN AIR TO DRY THOROUGHLY. SPRAY METAL PARTS WITH OIL AND WIPE OFF SURPLUS BEFORE COVERING.

garlic and rosemary smoked lamb

PREP + COOK TIME 1 HOUR (+ REFRIGERATION & SOAKING) • SERVES 6

1kg boned loin of lamb
4 cloves garlic, halved
8 fresh rosemary sprigs
1 teaspoon dried chilli flakes
1 tablespoon olive oil
250g smoking chips

When using indirect heat with a gas burner, place the food in a preheated, covered barbecue, then turn the burners directly under the food off, while keeping the side burners on. With a charcoal barbecue, metal bars hold two layers of coals against the sides of the barbecue, leaving the centre of the barbecue rack empty. A disposable aluminium baking dish can be placed here to catch fat drips.

Ask your butcher to bone the lamb loin for you.

1 Pierce lamb in eight places with sharp knife; push garlic and rosemary into cuts. Sprinkle lamb with chilli; rub with oil. Roll and tie at intervals with kitchen string. Cover; refrigerate 3 hours or overnight.
2 Soak smoking chips in large bowl of water 2 hours.
3 Cook lamb, uncovered, on heated oiled barbecue until browned all over. Place drained smoking chips in smoke box on barbecue next to lamb. Cook lamb in covered barbecue, using indirect heat and following manufacturer's instructions, about 40 minutes or until cooked as desired.

nutritional count per serving 17.8g total fat (7.1g saturated fat); 1250kJ (299 cal); 0.2g carbohydrate; 35g protein; 0.3g fibre

TIP

• Smoking chips and smoke box are available from barbecue specialty shops.

Make eight slits in the lamb with a small sharp knife and insert the garlic and rosemary into the slits.

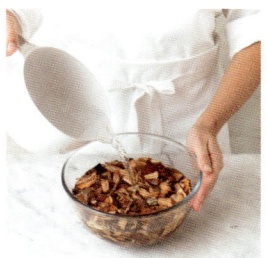

Smoking chips must be soaked in water for 2 hours before being used on the barbecue. This helps them to smoulder slowly and prevents them from burning.

Drain the smoking chips and place them in the smoke box. Put the smoke box on the barbecue next to the lamb.

cajun chickens

PREP + COOK TIME 1 HOUR 20 MINS • SERVES 6

A small chicken like this is also known as spatchcock (or poussin); they are no more than 6 weeks old and weigh a maximum of 500g. Spatchcock is also the cooking term to describe cutting a small chicken along the backbone and flattening it for grilling.

6 x 500g small chickens
2 tablespoons olive oil
1 small white onion (80g), grated coarsely
2 cloves garlic, crushed
2 tablespoons sweet paprika
2 teaspoons ground cinnamon
2 teaspoons ground fennel
2 teaspoons dried oregano

spicy tomato salsa
6 large egg tomatoes (540g), halved
1 tablespoon olive oil
1 medium brown onion (150g), chopped finely
2 cloves garlic, crushed
1 tablespoon sweet paprika
1 teaspoon smoked paprika
1 tablespoon red wine vinegar
1 fresh long red chilli, chopped finely

1 Discard necks from chickens. Using scissors, cut along each side of each chicken's backbone; discard backbones. Turn chickens skin-side up; press down on breastbone to flatten.
2 Rub chickens all over with combined remaining ingredients. Cook chickens on heated oiled grill plate, turning midway through cooking time, about 1 hour or until cooked.
3 Meanwhile, make spicy tomato salsa.
4 Serve chickens with spicy tomato salsa.
spicy tomato salsa Cook tomato on heated oiled grill plate, turning, until softened; chop tomato coarsely. Heat oil in medium saucepan; cook onion and garlic, stirring, until onion softens. Add spices; cook, stirring, until fragrant. Stir in tomato, vinegar and chilli; cook, uncovered, stirring occasionally, 20 minutes or until thickened.
nutritional count per serving 48.8g total fat (13.6g saturated fat); 2746kJ (657 cal); 4g carbohydrate; 50.6g protein; 2.1g fibre

salmon with dill and caper dressing

PREP + COOK TIME 20 MINS • SERVES 4

¼ cup (60g) sour cream
1 tablespoon drained tiny capers
2 teaspoons finely chopped fresh dill
2 teaspoons horseradish cream
1 teaspoon lime juice
4 small salmon fillets (600g)

1 Combine sour cream, capers, dill, horseradish and juice in medium bowl.
2 Cook salmon on heated oiled grill plate (or grill or barbecue) until browned both sides and cooked as desired.
3 Serve salmon with dill and caper dressing.
nutritional count per serving 13.8g total fat (4.5g saturated fat); 1041kJ (249 cal); 1.4g carbohydrate; 29.9g protein; 0.1g fibre

[opposite] cajun chickens

SPECIAL FEATURE

Know your mushrooms

There are a lot of mushroom varieties to choose from these days at farmers' markets, and many are even available from supermarkets. If your only experience with mushrooms has been button and field mushrooms, you're in for a culinary treat.

STRAW
These small and globe-shaped mushrooms have an internal stem and are so named for the straw on which they are grown. They are so fragile and deteriorate so quickly after harvesting that they are not a commercial proposition fresh so are usually canned.

ENOKI
These cultivated mushrooms also called enokitake, are tiny long-stemmed, pale mushrooms that grow and are sold in clusters, and can be used that way or separated by slicing off the base. They have a mild fruity flavour and are slightly crisp in texture.

FLAT
Large, white mushrooms that are fully open, dark and more robust in flavour than the smaller white varieties (buttons, caps). Their size makes them ideal for filling, and their rich, earthy flavour makes them a great addition to hearty soups and casseroles.

PINK OYSTER
Also called abalone mushrooms when large. These fan-like shaped mushrooms are prized for their smooth texture and subtle, oyster-like flavour, making them ideal to combine with veal, seafood and poultry. They become unpleasantly slippery if cooked too long so should be added near the end of cooking.

PINE
Also called the australian cep, these mushrooms are wild-picked in forests of introduced pine species. They are related to but not the same as the true european cep but their fruity scent and deep, earthy flavour explain the common name. They are best served simply: fried quickly or added in the last few minutes of cooking to a soup.

DRIED PORCINI
The richest-flavoured mushrooms, also known as ceps. They are expensive but, because they are so strongly flavoured, you only need to use a small amount for any particular dish. Rehydrate before use by soaking in hot water for 20-60 minutes, depending on the thickness of the caps. Strain the soaking water and use for soup or as stock for a risotto.

Q&A

I've always been a bit afraid of trying 'new' types of mushrooms, worrying that they might be slimy or have a very strong taste. What's the best way of experimenting with different mushroom types?

If you like mushrooms cooked in butter and cream, buy small quantities of enoki and swiss brown, as well as field and button mushrooms. Cook them all up together in butter with a little crushed garlic and some chopped parsley. It's a delicious combination. After that, experiment with other combinations until you find the ones you like the most.

NTERELLE

called girolles or pfifferling, this trumpet-shaped mushroom, ranges in colour from yellow to ge. Their delicate flavour and chewy texture es them a good all-round mushroom. Rehydrate e use by soaking in water for 15-20 minutes.

SHIMEJI

Also called beech mushrooms, these cultivated small oyster mushrooms grow and are sold in clumps. They have a delicate, sweet flesh with a nutty flavour and are suitable for stir-frying and pan-frying. When cooked, they are slightly crunchy in texture.

SWISS BROWN

Also known as roman or cremini, swiss browns are light to dark brown in colour with a full-bodied flavour. Their firm flesh means they hold their shape well when cooked so are an excellent choice for use in risottos, casseroles or being stuffed and baked.

TON

se are the youngest type of cultivated white hrooms, and are tightly enclosed around the . The name refers to the shape and stage of rowth, not the size (cap and flat are the larger es). They have a delicate flavour and fine texture h lends them to take on other flavours. When ipe in this book calls for an unspecified type ushroom, these are the ones to use.

CHESTNUT

Are cultivated mushrooms with a brown outer skin, a firm texture and a strong, nutty flavour. They are available infrequently.

PORTOBELLO

Portobellos are fully mature swiss browns, being larger and bigger in flavour. With an open, flat cap that can easily measure up to 15cm in diameter, they are often served whole and grilled. Their stems are woody and should be removed.

grilled t-bone with three butters

PREP + COOK TIME 20 MINS (+ REFRIGERATION) • SERVES 8

8 large t-bone steaks (2kg)

peppercorn butter
100g butter, softened
1 tablespoon canned drained green peppercorns
½ teaspoon mustard powder

mustard butter
100g butter, softened
3 green onions, chopped finely
1 tablespoon seeded mustard
2 teaspoons lemon juice

satay butter
100g butter, softened
1 small red capsicum (150g), chopped finely
⅓ cup (50g) salted peanuts, chopped finely
2 teaspoons light soy sauce

1 Make butters.
2 Cook steaks on heated oiled grill plate until cooked as desired.
3 Serve steaks with butters in small serving dishes.
butters Prepare each butter by combining ingredients in small bowl; mix well. Spoon each mixture onto a piece of foil; press each into triangle shape using two rulers or roll into sausage shape. Wrap foil firmly around butters to enclose; refrigerate 30 minutes or until firm.
nutritional count per serving 45.4g total fat (25.7g saturated fat); 2312kJ (553 cal); 2.3g carbohydrate; 34.7g protein; 0.7g fibre

piri piri chicken thigh fillets

PREP + COOK TIME 45 MINS • SERVES 4

The Afro-Portuguese chilli paste called piri piri seems made to enliven grilled poultry. The name originally came from the tiny, hot piri piri chilli which the Portuguese introduced to their former colonies of Angola and Mozambique.

4 fresh long red chillies, chopped coarsely
1 teaspoon dried chilli flakes
2 cloves garlic, quartered
1 teaspoon sea salt
2 tablespoons olive oil
1 tablespoon apple cider vinegar
2 teaspoons brown sugar
8 x 125g chicken thigh fillets

1 Using mortar and pestle, grind fresh chilli, chilli flakes, garlic and salt to make piri piri paste.
2 Combine paste with oil, vinegar, sugar and chicken in medium bowl. Cook chicken on heated oiled grill plate (or grill or barbecue) until cooked through.
3 Serve chicken with lime wedges, if desired.
nutritional count per serving 27.2g total fat (6.8g saturated fat); 1822kJ (436 cal); 1.8g carbohydrate; 46.6g protein; 0.3g fibre

chilli and honey barbecued steak

PREP + COOK TIME 25 MINS • SERVES 4

All grilled meat should be rested in a warm place, loosely covered with foil, for 5 minutes to allow the juices to settle and the meat to become more succulent.

2 tablespoons barbecue sauce
1 tablespoon worcestershire sauce
1 tablespoon honey
1 fresh long red chilli, chopped finely
1 clove garlic, crushed
4 x 200g new-york cut steaks

1 Combine sauces, honey, chilli and garlic in large bowl, add steaks; turn to coat steaks in honey mixture.
2 Cook steaks on heated oiled grill plate (or grill or barbecue) until browned both sides and cooked as desired.
3 Serve steaks with coleslaw or warm potato salad.

nutritional count per serving 12.1g total fat (5g saturated fat); 1354kJ (324 cal); 11.7g carbohydrate; 42.4g protein; 0.3g fibre

cheeseburgers with caramelised onion

PREP + COOK TIME 55 MINS • SERVES 4

The first step in many recipes is to fry chopped onion slowly to a soft, golden mass, which takes about 20 minutes and needs frequent checking and stirring. A quicker way is to warm the butter or oil, stir in the onion until well coated, then barely cover with warm water; cook over high heat until the water has evaporated. Stir the now softened onion on medium to low heat for a few minutes until it is golden, adding a little more butter or oil if needed.

500g beef mince
4 thin slices (40g) cheddar cheese
4 hamburger buns, split
1 small tomato (90g), sliced thinly
8 large butter lettuce leaves
4 large dill pickles (240g), sliced thinly
1 tablespoon american-style mustard
⅓ cup (95g) tomato sauce

caramelised onion
2 tablespoons olive oil
2 medium white onions (300g), sliced thinly
1 tablespoon brown sugar
2 tablespoons balsamic vinegar
2 tablespoons water

1 Make caramelised onion.
2 Shape mince into four patties; cook on heated oiled grill plate (or grill or barbecue) until cooked through. Top each patty with cheese slices during last minute of cooking time.
3 Meanwhile, toast buns, cut-sides down, on grill plate.
4 Place cheeseburgers, onion, tomato, lettuce and pickle between buns; serve with mustard and tomato sauce.

caramelised onion Heat oil in large frying pan; cook onion, stirring, until soft. Add sugar, vinegar and the water; cook, stirring, until onion is caramelised.

nutritional count per serving 23.6g total fat (7.4g saturated fat); 2378kJ (569 cal); 51.6g carbohydrate; 34.9g protein; 5g fibre

lemon-chilli butterflied chicken

PREP + COOK TIME 1 HOUR 15 MINS • SERVES 4

This shortcut to a perfect grilled chicken takes very little time but guarantees even cooking through the whole bird. To butterfly means, after you cut out and remove the backbone, you can open the chicken like a book (this shape rather resembles a butterfly) and press it flat. This easy technique will result in a grilled chicken that cooks faster and uniformly.

80g butter, softened
½ teaspoon dried chilli flakes
½ teaspoon cracked black pepper
1 tablespoon finely grated lemon rind
1 tablespoon finely chopped fresh rosemary
1.6kg whole chicken
½ cup (35g) stale breadcrumbs
2 teaspoons finely grated lemon rind, extra
¼ cup (20g) coarsely grated parmesan cheese

1 Move oven shelf to second-bottom position. Preheat grill.
2 Combine butter, chilli, pepper, rind and rosemary in small bowl.
3 Cut along each side of chicken's backbone; discard backbone. Turn chicken skin-side up; press down to flatten. Loosen and lift chicken skin; push butter mixture between skin and flesh.
4 Place chicken, skin-side down, on oiled wire rack in shallow flameproof baking dish. Grill chicken 40 minutes. Turn chicken; cook about 10 minutes or until chicken is cooked.
5 Meanwhile, combine remaining ingredients in small bowl.
6 Remove chicken from dish; strain juices from dish into small heatproof jug. Return chicken to dish; sprinkle with crumb mixture, drizzle ¼ cup (60ml) of the juices over crumb mixture.
7 Grill chicken about 5 minutes or until topping is browned lightly. Quarter chicken; serve with mixed green salad.

nutritional count per serving 50.5g total fat (21.9g saturated fat); 2705kJ (647 cal); 6g carbohydrate; 43.1g protein; 0.5g fibre

To butterfly the chicken, cut along each side of the backbone with poultry shears. Remove and discard the backbone.

Press down on the butterflied chicken with the heel of your hand to flatten it.

Gently loosen and lift the chicken skin and push the butter mixture between the flesh and the skin.

SPECIAL FEATURE

Know your seafood

Seafood that is freshly caught and simply cooked is one of life's great pleasures. But you need to know your seafood. Here are some of the more unusual varieties with information on how to prepare and cook them to bring out their best.

SCALLOPS
Available on the half-shell or shelled, their beautiful shell is usually used as part of the presentation. Often eaten raw or barely seared, they should never be cooked more than 30 seconds as they will lose their juicy tenderness and become tough.

ABALONE
This harvested single-shelled deep-water shellfish has a reputation for toughness, so is usually sliced and pounded before cooking. If bought live and used the same day by shelling, slicing and dropping into hot oil for seconds only, it tastes like lobster and is not tough.

BABY OCTOPUS
Usually tenderised before you buy them; both octopus and squid require either long slow cooking (usually for the large molluscs) or quick cooking over high heat (usually for the small molluscs) – anything in between will make the octopus tough and rubbery.

YABBIES
Yabbies are the most common type of Australian freshwater crayfish, specifically found throughout south eastern Australia. They are found in creeks and dams, but those available commercially are now mostly farmed. Its fresh-tasting, moist meat is in the tail and claws.

MARRON
One of the three types of Australian freshwater crayfish, marron is native to south western Australia and is the largest of these varieties. It is important to undercook, rather than overcook crayfish as they will continue cooking in residual heat. They are ideal to steam, poach, deep-fry, pan-fry, stir-fry, bake, grill or barbecue.

PIPIS
A variety of clam, pipis are the more commonly-used term in Australia for these small edible bivalves. Available from fish markets and large seafood outlets. They can be eaten raw from the shell with a squeeze of lemon juice, shelled and added to soup, or opened but left in the shell, to top a bowl of pasta. They can be substituted with vongole and cockles.

Q&A

Can you tell me about mussels? I've never cooked them but I believe they can make you sick if they're not prepared properly.

Mussels must be alive when cooked. The way you can tell is that their shells should be tightly closed when you buy them. Throw out any that have open shells – they're dead. Scrub them with a small scrubbing brush under running water and pull off their beard (the piece of string that protrudes from the shell), you'll need to give it a strong yank. Cook them in a large pan with a little liquid (wine or water) – not much because the mussels will lose some of their liquid as they cook. As soon as the mussels open, remove from the pan. Discard any that do not open – they are also dead.

MUSSELS
Mussels are found clustered on rocks or under jetties, the main Australasian varieties being the greenlip and black mussels. It is important to make sure fresh mussels are alive when you buy them, and equally important that they are still alive when you cook them.

BALMAIN BUGS
These crustaceans are a type of crayfish, also called slipper or shovelnose lobster, or southern bay lobster. Their flesh, which is mostly in the tail, resembles lobster in taste and texture. Can be substituted with moreton bay bugs, king prawns or scampi.

BLUE SWIMMER CRAB
Also known as sand crab, blue manna crab, bluey, sand crab or sandy, this crab turns orange-red when cooked. Its fine-textured, sweet meat is found in the legs and claws. Can be substituted with lobster, balmain or moreton bay bugs.

OYSTERS
Sydney rock oysters are among the finest in the world, while other varieties include pacific, bay/clip and New Zealand rock oysters. Ideally, oysters should be bought alive in their closed shells and opened just before they are eaten, but most people jib at opening them themselves – your fishmonger can do this for you. Fresh oysters can also be bought shelled and bottled and these are useful for soups or stews.

SQUID
Also known as calamari, squid are shellfish without an external shell but with a long, bony "quill" inside. To prepare squid, gently pull the head and entrails away from the squid body, then remove and discard the quill. Cut the tentacles from the head just below the eyes, then remove the beak. Gently pull away the outer membrane from the hood and flaps, then wash the hood, tentacles and flaps well. You can also buy squid hoods to make preparation and cooking faster.

KING PRAWNS
These large prawns are also known as ocean king, blueleg, sand, western, and western king prawn. They have a sweet true-prawn flavour, moist firm flesh and are available uncooked (green) or cooked, with or without shells. When buying prawns, look for good colour and lustre and make sure shells are free of discolouration. They can be substituted with scampi or farmed tiger prawns.

balmain bugs with garlic herbed butter

PREP + COOK TIME 50 MINS • SERVES 4

These small sand lobsters can be bought cooked or alive. Their flesh, which is mostly in the tail, resembles lobster in taste and texture. Allow one large or two small bugs per serving.

8 uncooked balmain bugs (1.6kg)
4 large flat mushrooms (360g)
100g curly endive, chopped coarsely

garlic herbed butter
125g butter, softened
2 teaspoons finely grated lemon rind
2 tablespoons lemon juice
2 tablespoons finely chopped fresh chives
2 tablespoons coarsely chopped fresh flat-leaf parsley
2 tablespoons coarsely chopped fresh tarragon
1 clove garlic, crushed

1 Place bugs upside down on board; cut tail from body, discard body. Using scissors, cut soft shell from underneath tails to expose meat; cut tails in half lengthways. Discard back vein.
2 Make herbed butter.
3 Melt half the herb butter in small saucepan. Brush mushrooms with half the melted butter; cook on heated oiled grill plate until tender.
4 Brush bugs with remaining melted butter mixture; cook on grill plate.
5 Serve endive and mushrooms with bug halves; top with remaining herb butter.
garlic herbed butter Beat butter, rind and juice in small bowl with electric mixer until light and fluffy. Stir in herbs and garlic.

nutritional count per serving 27.1g total fat (17.1g saturated fat); 1584kJ (379 cal); 2.1g carbohydrate; 30.4g protein; 3.2g fibre

The tail is the only part of the bug that is eaten. Place bugs upside down on a board and cut the tail away from the body. Discard the body.

Cut the shell from underneath the tail to expose the flesh. It's best to do this with scissors or poultry shears. Cut the tails in half lengthways.

There's a black vein down the centre of the tails which should be removed before cooking the bugs.

veal cutlets with green olive salsa

PREP + COOK TIME 35 MINS • SERVES 4

Kipfler poatoes, being small, are quick and easy to cook on a barbecue. Prick the scrubbed potatoes, rub with butter or olive oil then double-wrap individually in foil (with a sprig of herb or an unpeeled clove of garlic, if you wish) and place directly on the coals. After about 30 minutes, stick a bamboo skewer through the foil to see if it's cooked through.

2 tablespoons olive oil
2 cloves garlic, crushed
1 tablespoon finely chopped fresh oregano
2 teaspoons finely grated lemon rind
1 tablespoon lemon juice
4 x 125g veal cutlets

green olive salsa
1 tablespoon lemon juice
¼ cup coarsely chopped fresh flat-leaf parsley
½ cup (80g) finely chopped large green olives
1 small green capsicum (150g), chopped finely
1 tablespoon olive oil
1 clove garlic, crushed
1 tablespoon finely chopped fresh oregano

1 Make green olive salsa.
2 Combine oil, garlic, oregano, rind and juice in small bowl; brush mixture over veal. Cook veal on heated oiled grill plate (or grill or barbecue) until browned both sides and cooked as desired.
3 Serve veal with salsa and barbecued kipflers or mashed potato.
green olive salsa Combine ingredients in small bowl.
nutritional count per serving 16.3g total fat (2.7g saturated fat); 1112kJ (266 cal); 5.8g carbohydrate; 23.4g protein; 1.2g fibre
serving idea barbecued kipfler potatoes.

barbecued baby octopus

PREP + COOK TIME 25 MINS (+ REFRIGERATION) • SERVES 6

Rigani is a type of wild oregano. It has a stronger flavour than regular oregano and is used in many Greek dishes. You can find rigani at specialty supermarkets and delicatessens. If it is hard to find, use dried oregano.

Octopus is best cooked just before serving.

1kg baby octopus
⅓ cup (80ml) lemon juice
⅓ cup (80ml) olive oil
2 cloves garlic, crushed
2 teaspoons dried rigani
1 medium lemon, cut into wedges

1 Clean octopus, remove eyes and beaks. Combine octopus with juice, oil, garlic and rigani in medium bowl. Cover, refrigerate 3 hours or overnight.
2 Drain octopus; discard marinade. Cook octopus on heated oiled barbecue (or grill or grill plate) until tender. Serve with lemon wedges.
nutritional count per serving 13.4g total fat (1.7g saturated fat); 982kJ (235 cal); 1g carbohydrate; 27.6g protein; 0.2g fibre

texan-style spareribs

PREP + COOK TIME 1 HOUR 50 MINS (+ REFRIGERATION) • SERVES 8

3kg american-style pork spareribs
2 tablespoons sweet paprika
1 tablespoon ground cumin
1 teaspoon cayenne pepper
2 x 800ml bottles beer
1 cup (250ml) barbecue sauce
¼ cup (60ml) water
¼ cup (60ml) maple syrup
¼ cup (60ml) cider vinegar

1 Place ribs on large tray. Combine spices in small bowl, rub spice mixture all over ribs. Cover; refrigerate 3 hours or overnight.
2 Bring beer to the boil in medium saucepan. Reduce heat; simmer, uncovered, 20 minutes. Divide beer and ribs between two large shallow disposable baking dishes. Cook, covered, on barbecue, using indirect heat for 1¼ hours. Drain ribs; discard beer.
3 Meanwhile, combine sauce, the water, syrup and vinegar in small saucepan; bring to a boil. Reduce heat; simmer, uncovered, 5 minutes.
4 Cook ribs, in batches, directly on heated barbecue, turning and brushing with sauce occasionally, about 20 minutes until browned all over.
nutritional count per serving 17.5g total fat (6.1g saturated fat); 2123kJ (508 cal); 25.4g carbohydrate; 49.8g protein; 0.4g fibre

pork cutlet with fennel and apple salsa

PREP + COOK TIME 35 MINS • SERVES 4

To make crushed potatoes: boil, steam or microwave 1kg unpeeled new potatoes; drain. Mash half the potatoes with ½ cup sour cream and 40g butter in a large bowl until smooth and stir in ¼ cup coarsely chopped flat-leaf parsley and 2 tablespoons chopped fresh dill. Roughly crush the remaining potatoes with the back of a fork until the skins burst and the flesh is just crushed; stir into herbed mash.

2 tablespoons cider vinegar
¼ cup (60ml) olive oil
1 tablespoon dijon mustard
2 teaspoons caster sugar
4 x 235g pork cutlets
1 large unpeeled green apple (200g), chopped finely
1 small red onion (100g), chopped finely
1 medium fennel (300g), trimmed, chopped finely

1 Whisk vinegar, oil, mustard and sugar in medium bowl; transfer 2 tablespoons of dressing to large bowl. Add pork to large bowl; turn to coat cutlets in dressing.
2 To make salsa, combine apple, onion and fennel in bowl with remaining dressing.
3 Meanwhile, cook drained pork on heated oiled grill plate (or grill or barbecue) until browned both sides and cooked as desired, brushing occasionally with dressing.
4 Serve pork with salsa, and with mashed potato or roasted potato chips.
nutritional count per serving 31.2g total fat (7.9g saturated fat); 1877kJ (449 cal); 9.6g carbohydrate; 32g protein; 2.3g fibre
serving idea crushed potatoes.

grilled pork chops with apples

PREP + COOK TIME 30 MINS • SERVES 4

As always when buying meat, your best bet is a supplier you can trust. In general, pork should have fine-grained, pale pink flesh, white fat and thin, smooth skin. Avoid any that has waxy fat or is wet, meaning it has been badly handled and may be from an animal in poor condition.

2 medium apples (300g)
1 tablespoon olive oil
1 medium red onion (170g), cut into thin wedges
4 x 280g pork loin chops
½ cup (125ml) plum sauce
¼ cup (60ml) lemon juice
⅓ cup (80ml) chicken stock

1 Cut each unpeeled, uncored apple horizontally into four slices. Heat oil in grill pan; cook apple and onion, turning, until softened.
2 Meanwhile, cook pork on heated oiled grill plate until cooked.
3 Stir sauce, juice and stock into apple mixture; simmer 1 minute.
4 Serve pork with sauce.

nutritional count per serving 29.7g total fat (9.1g saturated fat); 2404kJ (575 cal); 32g carbohydrate; 45g protein; 1.8g fibre

barbecued scotch fillet

PREP + COOK TIME 1 HOUR 40 MINS (+ REFRIGERATION & STANDING) • SERVES 6

American mustard is very mild. If you have trouble finding it, use 1 tablespoon of french mustard instead.

¼ cup (60ml) barbecue sauce
2 tablespoons american mustard
4 cloves garlic, crushed
½ cup (125ml) beer
1.4kg piece beef scotch fillet

1 Combine sauce, mustard, garlic and beer in large bowl, add beef; turn beef to coat in mixture. Cover; refrigerate 3 hours or overnight.
2 Place beef and marinade in oiled disposable aluminium baking dish. Cook, covered, on barbecue, using indirect heat, about 1½ hours or until cooked as desired. Cover; stand 15 minutes, slice thinly.

nutritional count per serving 14.2g total fat (5.9g saturated fat); 1488kJ (356 cal); 5.9g carbohydrate; 49.7g protein; 0.6g fibre

[1] grilled pork chops with apples
[2] barbecued scotch fillet
[3] lemon and garlic kebabs [page 454]
[4] barbecued whole snapper [page 454]

lemon and garlic lamb kebabs

PREP + COOK TIME 30 MINS • SERVES 4

It's a good idea to pierce lamb with metal or bamboo skewers first to make threading the rosemary stalks easier.

8 x 15cm stalks fresh rosemary
800g lamb fillets, diced into 3cm pieces
3 cloves garlic, crushed
2 tablespoons olive oil
2 teaspoons finely grated lemon rind
1 tablespoon lemon juice

1 Remove leaves from bottom two-thirds of each rosemary stalk; sharpen trimmed ends to a point.
2 Thread lamb onto rosemary skewers. Brush kebabs with combined garlic, oil, rind and juice. Cover; refrigerate until required.
3 Cook kebabs on heated oiled grill plate, brushing frequently with remaining garlic mixture, until cooked.
nutritional count per serving 16.4g total fat (4.5g saturated fat); 1313kJ (314 cal); 0.4g carbohydrate; 41.2g protein; 0.4g fibre

barbecued whole snapper

PREP + COOK TIME 1 HOUR • SERVES 8

We used snapper in this recipe, but a fish like salmon would work well, too – it may need slightly less cooking time, depending on how you like your salmon cooked.

1 whole snapper (2kg)
1 clove garlic, sliced thinly
3 sprigs fresh rosemary, cut into 3cm lengths
1 medium lemon (140g), sliced thinly
40g butter
2 large zucchini (300g)
2 trimmed corn cobs (500g), sliced thickly
2 medium red capsicums (400g), sliced thickly
1 large red onion (300g), cut into wedges

lemon herb butter
160g butter, softened
1 clove garlic, crushed
2 teaspoons finely grated lemon rind
2 teaspoons finely chopped fresh rosemary

1 Make lemon herb butter.
2 Meanwhile, place fish on board; score fish both sides through thickest part of flesh. Push garlic and rosemary into cuts; fill cavity with a third of the lemon slices.
3 Place a long piece of baking paper on bench; place half of the remaining lemon slices on paper. Place fish on lemon; top with remaining lemon then butter. Fold paper over fish to completely enclose, then wrap tightly in foil.
4 Cook fish on heated oiled grill plate (or grill or barbecue) 20 minutes; turn, cook about 20 minutes.
5 Meanwhile, cut zucchini in half crossways; cut each half lengthways into six. Combine zucchini with remaining ingredients in large bowl. Place eight 30cm foil squares on bench; divide vegetable mixture among foil squares. Gather corners of squares together; fold to enclose vegetables securely.
6 Cook parcels on heated oiled flat plate until vegetables are tender.
7 Open vegetable parcels; top with slices of lemon herb butter. Serve with fish.
lemon herb butter Combine ingredients in small bowl. Place on piece of plastic wrap; shape into 6cm log, wrap tightly. Freeze until firm; cut into eight slices.
nutritional count per serving 24.2g total fat (14.5g saturated fat); 1664kJ (398 cal); 12.4g carbohydrate; 30.9g protein; 4.2g fibre

grilled vegetables with garlic herb dressing

PREP + COOK TIME 1 HOUR • SERVES 4

1 medium red capsicum (200g)
1 medium yellow capsicum (200g)
¼ cup (60ml) olive oil
1 clove garlic, crushed
1 teaspoon finely grated lemon rind
2 teaspoons finely chopped fresh rosemary
1 medium red onion (170g), cut into wedges
2 small leeks (400g), trimmed, cut into 2cm pieces
1 medium eggplant (300g), sliced thickly
2 medium zucchini (240g), sliced thickly
4 flat mushrooms (320g), quartered
3 cloves garlic, unpeeled
⅓ cup (100g) mayonnaise
1 tablespoon lemon juice

1 Quarter capsicums, discard seeds and membranes. Roast under grill or in very hot oven, skin-side up, until skin blisters and blackens. Cover capsicum pieces in plastic or paper for 5 minutes; peel away skin, slice thickly.
2 Combine oil, crushed garlic, rind and half the rosemary in small bowl.
3 Brush onion, leek, eggplant, zucchini, mushrooms and unpeeled garlic with oil mixture; cook vegetables, in batches, on heated oiled grill plate until tender.
4 Squeeze cooked garlic into small jug; discard skins. Whisk in remaining rosemary, mayonnaise and juice. Serve vegetables with dressing.
nutritional count per serving 22.8g total fat (2.9g saturated fat); 1325kJ (317 cal); 16.9g carbohydrate; 7.9g protein; 8.4g fibre

PAN-FRIES & DEEP-FRIES

Pan-fries & deep-fries

Pan-frying and deep-frying are like very different siblings: they share a common name and trait (they're both 'dry cooking' methods that rely on hot oil to cook the food) but they operate differently, and produce different results.

PAN-FRYING

PAN-FRYING (ALSO CALLED SHALLOW FRYING) IS A COOKING METHOD IN WHICH FOOD IS FRIED IN A SHALLOW LAYER OF OIL IN A FRYING PAN. WITH PAN-FRYING, THE IDEA IS TO BROWN ONE SIDE FIRST, THEN TURN THE FOOD. THIS METHOD IS USED FOR DISHES SUCH AS CHICKEN SCHNITZEL AND CRUMBED LAMB CUTLETS.

Pan-frying produces a tasty, golden-brown crust around the food while also retaining the moisture inside. To ensure the food is moist inside, rather than greasy, the oil needs to be at a consistently medium-hot temperature. The amount of oil used in pan-frying can vary anywhere from a light coating on the base of the frying pan to half the height of the food.

TO PAN-FRY VEGETABLES Heat a little oil or butter, or a mixture of both, over medium heat until the oil gives off a haze or the butter stops sizzling. Fry the vegetables until browned and tender, turning once; remove with a slotted spoon or tongs and drain on absorbent paper.

PAN-FRIED FOODS Food suitable for pan-frying include tender cuts of meat, chicken, fish and vegetables. Meats are usually coated in breadcrumbs before cooking; vegetables are not. All the foods must be cut thinly because they won't cook through if too thick (the surface will cook but the centre will remain uncooked).

Place the food in the heated pan and cook until the first side is brown; turn and brown the other side. If cooking in batches, scoop out any errant food bits and add fresh oil in between batches.

Drain all pan-fried foods on absorbent paper.

THE FRYING PAN

A good frying pan is indispensible. A medium-sized one (20 to 22cm across the base) is the most useful. If you think you require greater capacity, then a second medium-sized pan is more versatile than one huge one.

The key is to make sure your pan is solid and feels heavy. It should be thick so that it can take up and hold the heat, and made of a material that is a good conductor of heat – that is, it transmits heat rapidly and evenly to the whole cooking surface, and responds quickly when the heat is turned up.

WHAT TO LOOK FOR If money is no object, then you could invest in a titanium pan (which provides fast and even heat distribution and retention) but copper, aluminium, stainless steel or cast iron are more realistic options. Each of these has its advantages and disadvantages and your decision should come down to performance, not looks. Make sure the handle is riveted or welded on, not just attached with screws, and a handle that can go into the oven makes it more versatile. A lid is also useful because browning is often only the first step in a recipe, followed by covered cooking.

DEEP-FRYING

THE GOAL OF DEEP-FRYING – PLUNGING FOOD INTO DEEP, HOT OIL – IS THAT THE FOOD GETS QUICKLY CRISPED ON THE OUTSIDE WHILE STEAMING ON THE INSIDE. FOR THIS TO HAPPEN, IT IS VITAL THAT THE OIL STAYS AT THE CORRECT TEMPERATURE (BETWEEN 175°C AND 190°C) THROUGHOUT COOKING. IF THE OIL IS NOT HOT ENOUGH, THE FOOD WILL BE SOGGY AND GREASY.

Deep-frying is a cooking method avoided by the health conscious although, in its defence, it doesn't (or shouldn't) make the food itself greasy or heavy if it is done properly. That said, no one can deny you're eating some oil when you're enjoying hot fish and chips: moderation is the order of the day as far as these foods go.

If the oil is too hot, the food will be burned on the outside by the time the interior is cooked. As long as the oil is hot enough and the food isn't immersed in it for too long, no oil will enter the interior and the food will remain light and digestible, encased in a crispy exterior. Be careful not to overcrowd the deep fryer (or saucepan or wok) because this can lower the temperature of the oil, leading to greasy food. Fry in batches rather than in huge quantities.

DEEP-FRIED FOODS are usually coated with batter or egg and breadcrumbs. After breadcrumbing, rest the pieces for about 20 minutes before frying to allow the egg to set. This ensures the coating adheres better during cooking. Pat off excess breadcrumbs before placing the food in the oil.

OILS suitable for deep frying include peanut, safflower, sunflower and most blended oils.

Change the oil after every few batches or if it darkens.

Cut food pieces to a uniform size so they will cook at the same time

Fry in batches small enough for the pieces to float free without touching each other.

Drain the food after frying on absorbent paper.

WHAT YOU NEED

A DEEP PAN you need a container deep enough to cover your food with oil as it fries. You don't have to have an electric deep fryer: a saucepan or wok serves perfectly well for this purpose.

A THERMOMETER for stove top deep-frying, use a special deep-frying thermometer with a clamp on it so you can attach it to the side of the pan. (Electric deep fryers have in-built thermostatic controls to keep the oil at a steady temperature.)

A SLOTTED SPOON OR LONG-HANDLED METAL TONGS to handle and remove items.

FRYING BASKET if you're deep-frying on the stove top on a regular basis, it's worth having one of these, to add and remove the food from the pan as a batch. Use a wire basket with a long handle.

OVEN GLOVES for handling the metal frying basket.

SAFETY

Deep frying involves very hot oil, so make sure children and pets are out of the way.

Avoid splashing hot oil: place food items gently into the oil either in batches (using a basket) or individually using long tongs.

Never fill the pan or fryer more than half-full of oil because it bubbles up when the food is added.

Never lift or move the fryer until it and the oil are completely cooled.

chicken schnitzel

PREP + COOK TIME 30 MINS • SERVES 4

The breadcrumb mixture lends itself to the addition of extra flavours, such as grated parmesan, finely grated lemon rind, chopped thyme or rosemary, chilli or mustard powder.

4 chicken breast fillets (800g)
¼ cup (35g) plain flour
2 eggs
1 tablespoon milk
2½ cups (175g) stale white breadcrumbs
2 teaspoons finely grated lemon rind
2 tablespoons finely chopped fresh flat-leaf parsley
2 tablespoons finely chopped fresh basil
⅓ cup (25g) finely grated parmesan cheese
vegetable oil, for shallow-frying

1 Using meat mallet, gently pound chicken, one piece at a time, between sheets of plastic wrap until 5mm thick; cut each piece in half.
2 Whisk flour, eggs and milk in shallow bowl; combine breadcrumbs, rind, herbs and cheese in another shallow bowl. Coat chicken pieces, one at a time, in egg mixture then breadcrumb mixture.
3 Heat oil in large frying pan; shallow-fry chicken, in batches, until cooked. Drain on absorbent paper.
4 Serve chicken schnitzel with lemon wedges, if you like.
nutritional count per serving 41.5g total fat (9g saturated fat); 3097kJ (741 cal); 35.4g carbohydrate; 55.7g protein; 2.3g fibre

Dip the pounded out chicken fillets in a batter made from flour, eggs and milk.

Put the breadcrumb mixture in a shallow dish and coat the chicken fillets on both sides.

Heat enough oil to coat the bottom of the pan and shallow-fry the chicken schnitzels, turning once until golden brown and cooked through.

steak diane

PREP + COOK TIME 20 MINS • SERVES 4

No one really knows the origin of steak diane; chefs in Australia, Brazil and the US have all claimed to be its creators. The dish was extremely popular in restaurants in the 1950s and 1960s, often being cooked at the table. Steak diane now features on pub and bistro menus.

1 tablespoon olive oil
4 x 125g beef fillet steaks
⅓ cup (80ml) brandy
2 cloves garlic, crushed
¼ cup (60ml) worcestershire sauce
1 cup (250ml) cream
1 tablespoon finely chopped fresh flat-leaf parsley

1 Heat oil in large frying pan; cook steaks until cooked as desired. Remove from pan; cover to keep warm.
2 Add brandy to pan; bring to the boil. Add garlic, sauce and cream; cook, stirring, about 3 minutes or until sauce thickens slightly. Remove pan from heat; stir in parsley.
3 Serve steaks with sauce, and accompany with chips and a green salad, if you like.
nutritional count per serving 39.1g total fat (21.6g saturated fat); 2182kJ (522 cal); 5.2g carbohydrate; 27.9g protein; 0.4g fibre

veal saltimbocca

PREP + COOK TIME 35 MINS • SERVES 4

Saltimbocca is a classic Italian veal dish that literally means "jump in the mouth" – just the sensation the wonderful flavours will produce with your first bite.

8 veal schnitzels (800g)
8 slices prosciutto (120g)
16 fresh sage leaves
40g butter
1 cup (250ml) dry white wine
1 tablespoon lemon juice
2 tablespoons coarsely chopped fresh sage

1 Top each piece of veal with prosciutto and sage leaves. Fold in half to secure filling; secure with toothpicks or small skewers.
2 Melt half the butter in large frying pan; cook veal, in batches, until cooked as desired. Cover to keep warm.
3 Add wine to pan; bring to the boil. Boil, uncovered, until reduced by half. Stir in remaining butter, juice and sage.
4 Serve saltimbocca with sauce, and accompany with steamed green beans and baby new potatoes, if you like.
nutritional count per serving 13g total fat (6.8g saturated fat); 1509kJ (361 cal); 0.5g carbohydrate; 50.3g protein; 0g fibre

[1] steak diane
[2] veal saltimbocca
[3] veal parmigiana [page 464]
[4] pork chops with apple and calvados [page 465]

veal parmigiana

PREP + COOK TIME 1 HOUR 45 MINS • SERVES 4

Veal comes from calves and may be milk-fed, meaning that the animal never ate grass, or grass-fed, meaning that the animal spent some time on pasture before slaughter. Milk-fed veal is very pale and delicate in flavour and grass-fed is pink and fuller-flavoured.

4 veal steaks (320g)
¼ cup (35g) plain flour
1 egg
1 tablespoon water
⅓ cup (25g) stale breadcrumbs
30g butter
⅓ cup (80ml) olive oil
1½ cups (150g) coarsely grated mozzarella cheese
⅓ cup (25g) finely grated parmesan cheese

tomato sauce
1 tablespoon olive oil
1 medium brown onion (150g), chopped finely
1 stalk celery (150g), trimmed, chopped finely
1 medium red capsicum (200g), chopped finely
1 clove garlic, crushed
400g can crushed tomatoes
2 teaspoons white sugar
1 tablespoon tomato paste
1½ cups (375ml) chicken stock
1 tablespoon finely chopped fresh flat-leaf parsley
1 tablespoon finely chopped fresh basil

1 Make tomato sauce.
2 Pound veal out thinly between layers of plastic wrap. Coat veal in flour; shake off excess. Dip veal in combined beaten egg and the water; press breadcrumbs firmly onto veal. Refrigerate 10 minutes.
3 Preheat oven to 180°C/160°C fan-forced.
4 Heat butter and half the oil in large frying pan; cook veal, in batches, until browned both sides. Place veal in large shallow ovenproof dish; top veal with mozzarella, drizzle with tomato sauce then sprinkle evenly with parmesan. Drizzle over remaining oil.
5 Bake parmigiana, in oven, about 20 minutes or until browned lightly. Serve with a green salad, if you like.
tomato sauce Heat oil in medium frying pan; cook onion, celery, capsicum and garlic, stirring, until onion is soft. Remove pan from heat. Push undrained tomatoes through a sieve into the pan; discard solids. Add sugar, paste and stock. Cover; bring to the boil. Reduce heat; simmer, covered, 30 minutes. Uncover; simmer until sauce is thick. Stir in herbs.
nutritional count per serving 42g total fat (14.8g saturated fat); 2592kJ (620 cal); 21g carbohydrate; 37g protein; 3.7g fibre

pork chops with apples and calvados

PREP + COOK TIME 30 MINS • SERVES 4

Calvados is an expensive apple brandy – use brandy instead of calvados if you like.

4 x 280g pork loin chops
50g butter
2 medium apples (300g), peeled, cut into thin wedges
4 shallots (100g), sliced thinly
1 tablespoon plain flour
½ cup (125ml) calvados
1 cup (250ml) cider vinegar
1 cup (250ml) chicken stock
⅔ cup (160ml) cream

1 Cook pork in heated oiled large frying pan until cooked as desired. Remove from pan; cover to keep warm. Drain and discard excess fat from pan.
2 Heat half the butter in pan; cook apples, stirring, until browned lightly. Remove from pan.
3 Heat remaining butter in pan; cook shallots, stirring, until soft. Add flour; cook, stirring, 1 minute. Add calvados; bring to the boil. Stir in cider, stock and cream; simmer, uncovered, until sauce thickens slightly. Return apples to pan; cook until heated through.
4 Serve pork topped with apples and sauce.

nutritional count per serving 47.5g total fat (25g saturated fat); 2947kJ (705 cal); 18.1g carbohydrate; 35.7g protein; 1.4g fibre

salt and pepper squid

PREP + COOK TIME 45 MINS • SERVES 4

For a quick way to coat squid, place the flour, salt and pepper in a strong plastic bag with the squid; grip the bag tightly closed, then gently shake. Remove the squid from the bag; shake off any excess flour.

Tenderising squid in coconut milk with 1 tablespoon fish sauce will impart a wonderful flavour. Drain well and pat dry with absorbent paper before tossing it in the flour.

600g squid hoods, cleaned
¼ cup (35g) plain flour
1½ teaspoons sea salt flakes
1½ teaspoons cracked black pepper
1 teaspoon dried chilli flakes
vegetable oil, for deep-frying
40g baby rocket leaves
1 large tomato (220g), seeded, chopped finely

lemon aïoli
2 egg yolks
1 teaspoon dijon mustard
⅔ cup (160ml) extra light olive oil
⅓ cup (80ml) olive oil
2 tablespoons lemon juice
2 cloves garlic, crushed

1 Make lemon aïoli.
2 Cut squid down centre to open out; score the inside in a diagonal pattern. Halve squid lengthways; slice halves crossways into thick strips.
3 Combine flour, salt, pepper and chilli in medium bowl, add squid; toss squid to coat in flour mixture. Shake off excess.
4 Heat oil in wok; deep-fry squid, in batches, until tender, drain.
5 Serve squid with rocket, tomato and aïoli.

lemon aïoli Whisk egg yolks and mustard in medium bowl. Gradually whisk in combined oils, in a thin, steady stream until thickened. Stir in juice and garlic.

nutritional count per serving 67.1g total fat (10.1g saturated fat); 3118kJ (746 cal); 8.2g carbohydrate; 28.6g protein; 1.6g fibre

steak sandwich

PREP + COOK TIME 30 MINS • MAKES 4

2 cloves garlic, crushed
2 tablespoons olive oil
4 thin beef scotch fillet steaks (500g)
2 medium brown onions (200g), sliced thinly
1 tablespoon brown sugar
1 tablespoon balsamic vinegar
8 thick slices white bread (560g)
1 baby cos lettuce (180g), leaves separated
2 dill pickles (40g), sliced thinly
¼ cup (80g) tomato chutney

1 Combine garlic and half the oil in medium bowl, add steaks; rub both sides of steak with mixture.
2 Heat remaining oil in medium frying pan; cook onion over low heat, stirring occasionally, about 10 minutes or until soft. Add sugar and vinegar; cook, stirring, about 5 minutes or until caramelised. Remove from pan.
3 Meanwhile, cook steaks in heated oiled large frying pan.
4 Toast bread both sides. Sandwich lettuce, steaks, onion, pickle and chutney between toast slices.

nutritional count per sandwich 20.5g total fat (5g saturated fat); 2809kJ (672 cal); 78.1g carbohydrate; 39.7g protein; 6.4g fibre

seared calves' liver with persillade

PREP + COOK TIME 30 MINS • SERVES 4

Persillade is a mixture of chopped garlic and parsley traditionally used either as a garnish or to flavour a sauce, as we have done here.

400g piece calves' liver, sliced thinly
50g butter
1 clove garlic, chopped finely
1 shallot (25g), chopped finely
½ cup (125ml) chicken stock
1 tablespoon lemon juice
⅓ cup finely chopped fresh flat-leaf parsley

1 Pat liver dry with absorbent paper. Melt about 1 tablespoon of the butter in large frying pan; cook liver quickly, in batches, over high heat until browned both sides and cooked as desired (do not overcook). Remove from pan; cover to keep warm.
2 To make persillade, heat remaining butter in same pan; cook garlic and shallot, stirring, until shallot softens. Add stock and juice; bring to the boil, stirring. Remove from heat; stir in parsley. Serve sliced liver with persillade.

nutritional count per serving 18g total fat (9.1g saturated fat); 1087kJ (260 cal); 3g carbohydrate; 21.6g protein; 0.3g fibre

[opposite] steak sandwich

garlic prawns

PREP + COOK TIME 30 MINS • SERVES 4

Prawns are deveined because the vein, which is the gut, may contain grit as prawns are bottom-feeders.

1kg uncooked medium king prawns
4 cloves garlic, crushed
2 fresh small red thai chillies, chopped finely
2 tablespoons olive oil
1 medium red capsicum (200g), sliced thinly
1 medium green capsicum (200g), sliced thinly
½ cup (125ml) chicken stock
300ml cream
1 tablespoon lemon juice
1 tablespoon finely chopped fresh flat-leaf parsley

1 Shell and devein prawns, leaving tails intact. Combine prawns, garlic and chilli in medium bowl.
2 Heat half the oil in large frying pan; cook prawns, stirring, until changed in colour. Remove from pan.
3 Heat remaining oil in same pan; cook capsicums, stirring, until tender. Return prawns to pan with stock, cream and juice; bring to the boil. Reduce heat; simmer, uncovered, about 5 minutes or until sauce thickens slightly. Remove from heat; stir in parsley.
nutritional count per serving 42.6g total fat (22.9g saturated fat); 2169kJ (519 cal); 5.4g carbohydrate; 28.9g protein; 1.4g fibre
serving ideas good-quality bread, steamed rice, pasta.

crumbed lamb cutlets

PREP + COOK TIME 40 MINS (+ REFRIGERATION) • SERVES 4

12 lamb cutlets (900g)
¼ cup (60ml) soy sauce
2 cloves garlic, crushed
½ cup (70g) plain flour
2 eggs, beaten lightly
¼ cup (60ml) milk
1 cup (70g) stale breadcrumbs
1 cup (100g) packaged breadcrumbs
vegetable oil, for shallow-frying

1 Trim excess fat from cutlets. Using meat mallet, pound each cutlet between sheets of plastic wrap until cutlets are flattened slightly.
2 Combine soy sauce and garlic in large dish, add cutlets. Cover; refrigerate, turning cutlets several times, 30 minutes.
3 Place flour in plastic bag; add cutlets; toss until cutlets are well coated. Dip cutlets in combined egg and milk, then coat with combined breadcrumbs.
4 Heat oil in large frying pan; shallow-fry cutlets until cooked as desired. Drain on absorbent paper.
nutritional count per serving 63.7g total fat (22.4g saturated fat); 3988kJ (954 cal); 59.4g carbohydrate; 35g protein; 3.7g fibre

sausages with pea and bacon mash

PREP + COOK TIME 25 MINS • SERVES 4

It's not necessary to oil a frying pan when cooking bacon as the fat renders in the hot pan, creating its own frying medium.

3 rindless bacon rashers (195g), chopped
1 tablespoon olive oil
2 medium onions (300g), sliced thinly
8 thick beef sausages (640g)
1kg potatoes, peeled, quartered
1 cup (250ml) milk, warmed
40g butter
½ cup (60g) frozen peas

1 Add the bacon to a heated frying pan, cook until browned and crisp; remove.
2 Heat oil in same pan, add onions and sausages; cook until onions are soft and the sausages are cooked through.
3 Meanwhile, boil or steam the potatoes until soft; drain. Mash potatoes with milk, butter and salt and pepper to taste.
4 Boil, steam or microwave peas until just tender; drain. Add peas and bacon to mash.
5 Serve mash topped with sausages and onion.

nutritional count per serving 60.5g total fat (28.8g saturated fat); 3624kJ (867 cal); 39.7g carbohydrate; 37.7g protein; 9.4g fibre

caramelised crispy-skin duck

PREP + COOK TIME 30 MINS • SERVES 4

4 duck breast fillets (600g)
¼ cup (55g) brown sugar
1 teaspoon finely grated orange rind
2 tablespoons orange juice
1 fresh long red chilli, chopped finely
2cm piece fresh ginger (10g), grated
1 tablespoon balsamic vinegar

1 Cook duck, skin-side down, in heated large frying pan about 5 minutes or until skin is browned and crisp. Turn duck; cook about 5 minutes or until cooked as desired. Remove from pan; cover to keep warm.
2 Drain all but 2 tablespoons of duck fat from pan; reheat. Add sugar, rind, juice, chilli, ginger and vinegar; bring to the boil. Reduce heat; simmer sauce, uncovered, 2 minutes.
3 Serve with duck topped with sauce.

nutritional count per serving 29.1g total fat (8.7g saturated fat); 1868kJ (447 cal); 14.3g carbohydrate; 32.4g protein; 0.1g fibre

classic fish and chips

PREP + COOK TIME 50 MINS • SERVES 4

This dish is traditionally served with tartare sauce. To make your own, combine ⅔ cup whole-egg mayonnaise, ½ finely chopped small brown onion, 2 tablespoons finely chopped cornichons, 1 tablespoon finely chopped drained and rinsed capers, 1 tablespoon finely chopped fresh flat-leaf parsley and 1 tablespoon lemon juice in a medium bowl.

1 cup (150g) self-raising flour
1 cup (250ml) dry ale
1 tablespoon sea salt
1kg potatoes, peeled
peanut oil, for deep-frying
4 x 150g blue-eye fillets, halved lengthways

1 Sift flour into medium bowl; whisk in beer and salt until smooth.
2 Cut potatoes lengthways into 1cm slices; cut each slice lengthways into 1cm-chips; dry with absorbent paper.
3 Heat oil in large saucepan. Cook chips, in three batches, about 2 minutes or until tender but not brown. Drain on absorbent paper.
4 Dip fish in batter; drain away excess. Deep-fry fish, in batches, until cooked. Drain on absorbent paper.
5 Deep-fry chips, in three batches, until crisp and golden brown; drain on absorbent paper. Serve fish and chips with tartare sauce and lemon wedges.
nutritional count per serving 14.6g total fat (3.1g saturated fat); 2261kJ (541 cal); 55.1g carbohydrate; 39.6g protein; 4.8g fibre

Add beer to the flour and salt and whisk together until it becomes a smooth batter.

Dip the fish fillets into the batter and shake off the excess.

Deep-fry the fish in batches until golden and cooked through. Drain the fillets well on absorbent paper.

vegetable tempura

PREP + COOK TIME 50 MINS • SERVES 4

Adjust the size or thickness of slower-cooking vegetables (such as sweet potato and pumpkin) to ensure they cook at the same rate as faster-cooking vegetables (such as mushrooms). Always use fresh, clean oil and keep at a constant temperature during cooking. Optimum oil temperature for vegetables is fairly hot, about 170°C and for seafood slightly higher; seafood is usually cooked after vegetables.

Lotus root has a crisp texture and delicate flavour. It has small holes throughout its length, which, when sliced into rounds, looks like a flower. Fresh lotus root must be peeled and cooked before eating. Also available prepared and ready for cooking in cans, vacuum packs and frozen.

1 medium brown onion (150g)
1 small fresh or frozen lotus root (200g)
8 fresh shiitake mushrooms
2 sheets toasted seaweed (yaki-nori)
20g cellophane noodles (harusame), cut in half
vegetable oil, for deep-frying
½ cup (75g) plain flour
120g pumpkin, sliced thinly
50g green beans, halved
1 small kumara (250g), sliced thinly
1 baby eggplant (60g), sliced thinly
1 small red capsicum (150g), cut into 3cm pieces
1 medium carrot (120g), sliced thinly, diagonally
250g firm tofu, pressed, cut into 2cm cubes

batter
1 egg, beaten lightly
2 cups (500ml) iced soda water
1 cup (150g) plain flour
1 cup (150g) cornflour

dipping sauce
1 cup (250ml) primary dashi
⅓ cup (80ml) mirin
⅓ cup (80ml) light soy sauce
½ cup (120g) finely grated daikon
5cm piece fresh ginger (10g), grated finely

1 Make batter and dipping sauce.
2 Halve onion from root end. Insert toothpicks at regular intervals to hold onion rings together and slice in between.
3 Peel lotus root and slice. Place slices in water with a dash of vinegar to prevent browning. If using canned lotus, drain and slice. Remove and discard mushroom stems; cut a cross in the top of caps.
4 Cut one sheet seaweed into 5cm squares, halve the other sheet and cut into 2cm-wide strips. Brush seaweed strips with water and wrap tightly around about 10 noodles, either at one end or in the middle; reserve noodle bunches.
5 Heat oil in wok or large saucepan. Toss vegetables in flour to coat; shake off excess flour. Dip seaweed squares and vegetables in batter, in batches; drain excess batter. Deep-fry ingredients, in batches, until browned lightly and crisp. Drain on absorbent paper. Deep-fry reserved noodle bundles.
6 Serve tempura with individual bowls of warm dipping sauce.
batter Combine egg in a bowl with iced water. Add sifted flours all at once, mixing lightly until just combined, but still very lumpy.
dipping sauce Place dashi, mirin and sauce in medium saucepan and heat gently; divide among four individual serving bowls. Shape daikon into four pyramid shapes. Place a pyramid in each serving bowl; top with even amounts of ginger.
nutritional count per serving 62g total fat (8.2g saturated fat); 4289kJ (1026 cal); 93.4g carbohydrate; 20.7g protein; 8.6g fibre

zucchini fritters

PREP + COOK TIME 1 HOUR (+ STANDING) • SERVES 6

The smaller, the better is a good rule for buying zucchini and small squash, unless a certain size is required for stuffing. Whatever the size, they should be brightly coloured with a sheen on the skin, and firm with no soft spots.

4 medium zucchini (480g)
2 teaspoons coarse cooking salt
peanut oil, for deep-frying

skordalia
4 slices stale white sandwich bread (180g), crusts removed
4 cloves garlic, crushed
½ cup (125ml) olive oil
1 tablespoon lemon juice
1 tablespoon water, approximately

batter
1 cup (150g) self-raising flour
¾ cup (180ml) warm water
1 tablespoon olive oil
1 egg yolk

1 Make skordalia.
2 Cut zucchini into 1cm diagonal slices. Place zucchini in colander, sprinkle with salt; stand 30 minutes. Rinse zucchini under cold water; drain on absorbent paper.
3 Make batter.
4 Heat oil in large saucepan. Dip zucchini into batter, carefully lower into hot oil; cook zucchini until browned and crisp. Drain on absorbent paper.
5 Serve zucchini fritters with skordalia.

skordalia Briefly dip bread into a bowl of cold water, then gently squeeze out the water. Blend or process bread and garlic until combined. With motor operating, gradually add oil, juice and enough of the water, in a thin steady stream, until mixture is smooth and thick. Transfer to serving bowl.

batter Sift flour into medium bowl; whisk in combined remaining ingredients until smooth. Stand batter 10 minutes. If batter thickens too much, whisk in a little extra water to give it a coating consistency.

nutritional count per serving 28g total fat (4.2g saturated fat); 1601kJ (383 cal); 26.5g carbohydrate; 5.4g protein; 3g fibre

pan-seared scallops with anchovy butter

PREP + COOK TIME 15 MINS • SERVES 4

Scallops are often eaten raw or barely seared, and should never be cooked for more than about 30 seconds as they will lose their juicy tenderness and become tough. Cooked scallops are often served on the natural half-shells (which can be washed and used again) or on porcelain shell-shaped dishes.

2 teaspoons olive oil
12 scallops (300g), roe removed
30g butter
3 drained anchovy fillets
2 cloves garlic, crushed
2 teaspoons lemon juice
1 tablespoon finely chopped fresh chives

1 Heat oil in large frying pan; cook scallops, both sides, until browned lightly. Remove from pan; cover to keep warm.
2 Add butter, anchovies and garlic to pan; cook, stirring, until garlic is browned lightly. Return scallops to pan with juice; cook until scallops are heated through. Serve scallops drizzled with anchovy butter and sprinkled with chives.
nutritional count per serving 9.1g total fat (4.8g saturated fat); 514kJ (123 cal); 0.8g carbohydrate; 9.6g protein; 0.3g fibre

pancakes with lemon and sugar

PREP + COOK TIME 25 MINS • SERVES 4

This simple yet delicious combination makes a perfect Sunday breakfast or after-dinner treat. Use brown sugar in place of white for a more caramel flavour.

2 cups (300g) plain flour
4 eggs, beaten lightly
2 cups (500ml) milk, approximately
40g butter
¼ cup (60ml) lemon juice, approximately
2 tablespoons sugar, approximately

1 Place flour in medium bowl. Make well in centre; gradually whisk or stir in egg and enough of the milk to make a thin, smooth batter.
2 Heat large frying pan over high heat a few minutes. Place ½ teaspoon butter in pan; swirl around pan until greased all over. Pour ¼ cup of the batter from jug into centre of pan; quickly tilt pan so that batter runs from centre around edge.
3 When pancake is browned lightly underneath, turn and brown other side. This can be done using spatula or egg slide, or pancake can be tossed and flipped over back into the pan; this takes a little practice.
4 Serve pancakes, as they are made, on warm plates; spread one side with a little of the butter. Drizzle with juice; sprinkle with sugar.
nutritional count per pancake 19.3g total fat (10.4g saturated fat); 2245kJ (537 cal); 69.7g carbohydrate; 19.2g protein; 2.9g fibre

[opposite] pan-seared scallops with anchovy butter

french toast

PREP + COOK TIME 20 MINS • SERVES 4

For a delicious alternative to icing sugar, sprinkle french toast with vanilla or cinnamon sugar. Simply combine ¼ cup caster sugar with the seeds of half a vanilla pod or a good pinch of ground cinnamon.

4 eggs
½ cup (125ml) cream
¼ cup (60ml) milk
1 teaspoon ground cinnamon
¼ cup (55g) caster sugar
100g butter, melted
8 thick slices white bread (360g)
2 tablespoons icing sugar
⅓ cup (80ml) maple syrup

1 Whisk eggs in medium bowl, then whisk in cream, milk, cinnamon and sugar.
2 Heat a quarter of the butter in medium frying pan. Dip two bread slices into egg mixture, one at a time; cook bread until browned both sides. Remove french toast from pan; keep warm.
3 Repeat step 2 to make a total of 8 french toasts.
4 Serve toasts dusted with sifted icing sugar and drizzled with maple syrup. Top with sliced strawberries, if you like.

nutritional count per serving 42.2g total fat (24.8g saturated fat); 3194kJ (764 cal); 79.4g carbohydrate; 15.5g protein; 2.6g fibre

banana fritters

PREP + COOK TIME 30 MINS • SERVES 4

The word fritter comes from the Latin word "frictura", meaning fried. You can serve these fritters drizzled with pure maple syrup, sprinkled with chopped roasted pecans and topped with a scoop (or two) of vanilla ice-cream. They are also delicious drizzled with coconut liqueur and sprinkled with roasted shredded coconut.

¼ cup (40g) icing sugar
2 teaspoons ground cinnamon
1 egg, beaten lightly
¾ cup (50g) japanese breadcrumbs
vegetable oil, for deep-frying
4 large bananas (920g), halved lengthways

1 Combine sugar and cinnamon in shallow medium bowl. Beat egg in shallow medium bowl; place breadcrumbs in another bowl.
2 Heat oil in medium saucepan.
3 Meanwhile, dip bananas in sugar mixture; shake off excess. Dip banana in egg, then in crumbs to coat.
4 Deep-fry bananas, in batches, until browned. Drain on absorbent paper.

nutritional count per serving 9.7g total fat (1.5g saturated fat); 1329kJ (318 cal); 49.2g carbohydrate; 6g protein; 3.9g fibre

[opposite] french toast

crêpes suzette

PREP + COOK TIME 1 HOUR 40 MINS (+ STANDING) • SERVES 4

¾ cup (110g) plain flour
3 eggs
2 tablespoons vegetable oil
¾ cup (180ml) milk

orange sauce
125g unsalted butter
½ cup (110g) caster sugar
1½ cups (375ml) orange juice
2 tablespoons lemon juice
⅓ cup (80ml) orange-flavoured liqueur

TIPS

• Be very careful when igniting the sauce – use extra long matches, available from most supermarkets or camping stores. Igniting the sauce burns off the alcohol, leaving a more intense flavour. If you prefer, the sauce can be served as is, without first igniting it.

• Make sure overhead exhaust fans are turned off before igniting the orange sauce.

1 Sift flour into medium bowl, make well in centre; add eggs and oil then gradually whisk in milk until smooth. Pour batter into large jug, cover; stand 1 hour.

2 Heat greased heavy-based crêpe pan or small frying pan; pour ¼ cup of batter into pan, tilting pan to coat base. Cook, over low heat, until browned lightly, loosening edge of crêpe with spatula. Turn crêpe; brown other side. Remove crêpe from pan; cover to keep warm. Repeat with remaining batter to make a total of 8 crêpes, greasing pan each time.

3 Make orange sauce.

4 Fold crêpes in half then in half again, place in sauce; warm over low heat. Remove crêpes to serving plates; pour hot sauce over crêpes. Serve with orange segments, if you like.

orange sauce Melt butter in large frying pan, add sugar; cook, stirring, until mixture begins to brown. Add strained juices; bring to the boil. Reduce heat; simmer, uncovered, about 3 minutes or until a golden colour. Remove from heat; add liqueur, ignite.

nutritional count per serving 41g total fat (20.5g saturated fat); 3039kJ (727 cal); 66.9g carbohydrate; 10.3g protein; 1.3g fibre

Q&A

How do you cut orange segments so that they have no skin? They always look wonderful in photographs and I've had them in cafés too, but have never learned the trick myself.

It's harder (and probably takes longer) to describe than it would be to demonstrate this. Peel the orange, leaving no white pith at all. Then, with a small very sharp knife, cut down through a segment to the centre of the orange, and with a flicking movement, cut up the other side of the segment. The segment will fall out, minus its skin. (Do it over a bowl to catch all the juices.) Continue all the way around the orange.

PULSES & GRAINS

Pulses & grains

They used to be called "poor man's meats" because they were cheap and filling, but pulses (dried beans, peas and lentils) together with grains (such as couscous, polenta, rye and oats) are now prized around the world for their nutritional value and enjoyable eating. Collectively, they deliver rich supplies of protein, dietary fibre, vitamins and minerals and have little or no fat.

PULSES

OVER GENERATIONS, THESE HUMBLE INGREDIENTS HAVE BEEN TRANSFORMED INTO SOME OF THE WORLD'S MOST POPULAR DISHES SUCH AS ITALY'S FAMOUS MINESTRONE, FILLED WITH BEANS AND VEGETABLES; INDIA'S SOOTHING DHALS MADE FROM LENTILS; THE MIDDLE EAST'S CHICKPEA DIP, HUMMUS; AND MEXICO'S REFRIED BEANS, TO NAME A FEW.

BEANS Adzuki beans; black beans (turtle beans); black-eyed beans (black-eyed peas); borlotti beans; broad beans (fava beans); butter (lima) beans; chickpeas; flageolet beans; haricot beans (encompassing cannellini and navy beans, different varieties of mild-flavoured white beans that are interchangeable with each other in recipes); kidney beans; mung beans (the bean usually used for sprouts); pinto beans; and soybeans.

PEAS Blue boilers (whole peas, grey-green colour, used for mushy peas, pea and ham soup); split peas (skinless, yellow or green, sweet, with a definite pea flavour).

LENTILS Are usually described by colour:
- Brown lentils (also called 'green' and 'continental' lentils): pale brown to greenish in colour, and come in various sizes, with their skin on. They have a warm, slightly spicy flavour.
- Red lentils: these tiny, orange-red lentils come skinned and split. They have a spicy flavour, and cook to a puree.
- Puy lentils (also called french green lentils): small, dark blue-green, and exceptionally fine in flavour and texture; originally from the Le Puy district in France.

SOAKING

Dried beans and peas are best soaked before cooking, but lentils don't need soaking.
LONG SOAKING Soak pulses in cold water, covered, for at least 6-8 hours. Chickpeas need up to 12 hours and broad beans need 24 hours. Refrigerate when soaking so they don't ferment.
QUICK SOAKING To quicken the soaking process, cover the pulses generously with cold water in a large saucepan, bring to the boil, then cover and cook for 2 minutes. Remove the pan from the heat and stand for an hour.

COOKING

Cover pulses with cold water and bring to the boil. Do not add salt, sugar or other flavouring as this will toughen them; add towards the end of cooking. Once boiling, cover, reduce heat to low and simmer until tender. Lentils may take 20 minutes or less to cook; beans and peas 1-2 hours or longer. When tender, drain and use. Store cooked pulses, covered, in the fridge for 2-3 days.

GRAINS

LIKE PULSES, GRAINS ARE INTEGRAL TO SOME OF THE WORLD'S GREAT DISHES AND THANKFULLY, THEY'RE NOW INGRAINED IN OUR OWN FOOD: WHERE WOULD WE BE WITHOUT OATS (EITHER IN MUESLI OR PORRIDGE) AT BREAKFAST? OR THE CHEWY GOODNESS OF PEARL BARLEY IN OUR WINTER SOUPS? OR TABBOULEH SALAD IN SUMMER?

BARLEY Pearl barley is the type usually used for cooking. Delicious in soups, pearl barley has a robust, nutty flavour.

BUCKWHEAT Not a true grain, but the fruit of a plant related to rhubarb and sorrel. It is, however, used as a grain, being cooked into a porridge or ground into a flour which is used for pancakes and noodles.

BURGHUL The star of tabbouleh, burghul is made from cracked wheat which is hulled, par-boiled or steamed, then dehydrated. Before use, it should be soaked in cold water to soften and swell the grains. Drain and squeeze as dry as possible and spread on a tea-towel or absorbent paper to dry further.

COUSCOUS The staple cereal of north Africa, couscous is made from fine semolina (the first, grainy millings of the floury part of wheat grains), combined with flour, salt and water to make tiny pellets. Traditionally, couscous is first moistened to allow the grains to swell, then steamed over the pot in which the meat and vegetables for the meal are simmering. Pre-cooked "instant" couscous is also available.

OATS A very nutritious grain, oats are milled into oatmeal (of varying degrees of fineness) for various uses, including rolled oats which are used in porridge, muesli and baking.

POLENTA The Italian name for cornmeal, polenta is made from dried corn ground to various degrees of fineness. It is prepared by boiling with water to make a porridge. It can be eaten like this (soft or wet polenta) or spread in a shallow pan, chilled to firm it, then brushed with oil and grilled, pan-fried or barbecued. Pre-cooked "instant" polenta is also available.

QUINOA Pronounced 'keen-wa', this is a very nutritious south American cereal-like grain: the quality of its protein is equal to that of milk. It can be served instead of rice or couscous.

RYE A favourite grain in breads, including pumpernickel and rye crispbreads. Cracked whole rye, soaked overnight, can be made into porridge. Rye flakes can be used in the same way as rolled oats (for porridge, muesli and cooking).

STORING

IN STORAGE, PULSES HARDEN AND TAKE LONGER TO COOK, SO BUY FROM SHOP WITH A HIGH TURNOVER. STORE IN AIRTIGHT CONTAINERS IN A COOL, DRY PLACE FOR NO MORE THAN A YEAR. MANY OF THE DRIED BEANS ARE AVAILABLE READY-COOKED IN CANS. THEY NEED TO BE DRAINED AND RINSED BEFORE USE. STORE GRAINS AWAY FROM HEAT OR LIGHT, IN LIDDED CONTAINERS TO PREVENT MOUSE OR INSECT DAMAGE.

grain and seed loaf

PREP + COOK TIME 1 HOUR 10 MINS (+ STANDING) • MAKES 18 SLICES

1 cup (160g) burghul
3 teaspoons (10g) dry yeast
1 teaspoon sugar
¾ cup (180ml) warm milk
¼ cup (60ml) warm water
2¼ cups (335g) white plain flour
½ cup (80g) wholemeal plain flour
1 teaspoon salt
2 tablespoons linseeds
2 teaspoons olive oil
1 tablespoon milk, extra
1 tablespoon sesame seeds

1 Place burghul in medium heatproof bowl, cover with boiling water. Cover; stand 30 minutes. Rinse well; drain well.
2 Combine yeast, sugar, milk and the water in small bowl, whisk until yeast dissolves. Cover; stand in warm place about 10 minutes or until mixture is frothy.
3 Sift flours and salt into large bowl, add burghul and linseeds. Stir in oil and yeast mixture; mix to a soft dough. Knead dough on floured surface about 10 minutes or until dough is smooth and elastic. Place dough in large oiled bowl; cover, stand in warm place about 1 hour or until dough has doubled in size.
4 Preheat oven to 220°C/200°C fan-forced. Oil 14cm x 21cm loaf pan.
5 Using fist, punch dough to expel air. Turn dough onto floured surface, knead until smooth. Divide dough into three pieces. Shape each piece into a 30cm sausage. Plait sausages together, place into pan. Cover; stand in warm place about 30 minutes or until risen.
6 Brush dough with extra milk, sprinkle evenly with sesame seeds. Bake bread about 45 minutes; turn onto wire rack to cool.

nutritional count per slice 1.9g total fat (0.5g saturated fat); 539kJ (129 cal); 22.3g carbohydrate; 4.1g protein; 2.8g fibre

Stand the yeast mixture in a warm place to allow it to become frothy. It's important that the spot you choose is warm, not hot. If it's too hot you'll kill the yeast.

Once the dough has doubled in size, punch it and knead it until it's smooth and elastic – you should be able to stretch the dough without it breaking.

Plait the three lengths of dough together loosely and place the dough in the oiled loaf pan.

Once the dough has risen above the top of the pan, brush it with milk and sprinkle with sesame seeds before baking.

hummus

PREP + COOK TIME 25 MINS • MAKES 2 CUPS

Hummus can be served as a sauce with kebabs or meatballs or as a dip with pitta bread. It is classically served in a shallow dish, drizzled with extra oil and sometimes sprinkled with paprika.

2 cups (500ml) water
2 x 300g cans chickpeas, rinsed, drained
¼ cup (60ml) lemon juice
¼ cup (60ml) olive oil
⅓ cup (80ml) tahini
3 cloves garlic, crushed
1 tablespoon olive oil, extra

1 Place the water and chickpeas in medium saucepan; bring to the boil. Boil, uncovered, about 10 minutes or until tender. Strain chickpeas over medium bowl; reserve 1 cup cooking liquid.
2 Blend or process chickpeas and reserved cooking liquid with juice, oil, tahini and garlic until just smooth.
3 Serve hummus drizzled with extra oil.
nutritional count per ¼ cup 13.9g total fat (1.9g saturated fat); 752kJ (180 cal); 7.2g carbohydrate; 5.2g protein; 3.8g fibre

felafel

PREP + COOK TIME 1 HOUR (+ STANDING) • MAKES 50

These savoury chickpea balls are a popular snack and street food in many parts of the Middle East, whether dipped in spices and yogurt, as in this recipe, or wrapped in pitta bread with hummus and salad.

Dukkah is an Egyptian blend of nuts, spices and seeds, often mixed with oil or mayonnaise for a dip. You can make your own or buy it ready-made from speciality spice shops and delicatessens.

2 cups (400g) dried chickpeas
1 medium brown onion (150g), chopped coarsely
2 cloves garlic, quartered
½ cup fresh flat-leaf parsley, chopped coarsely
2 teaspoons ground coriander
1 teaspoon ground cumin
1 teaspoon bicarbonate of soda
2 tablespoons plain flour
1 teaspoon salt
vegetable oil, for deep frying

1 Place chickpeas in large bowl, cover with cold water; stand overnight, drain.
2 Combine chickpeas, onion, garlic, parsley and spices in large bowl. Blend or process, in two batches, until almost smooth; return mixture to large bowl.
3 Add soda, flour and salt to chickpea mixture; knead on lightly floured surface for 2 minutes. Stand 30 minutes.
4 Roll level tablespoons of mixture into balls; stand 10 minutes.
5 Deep-fry balls in hot oil, in batches, until golden brown.
nutritional count per felafel 0.9g total fat (0.1g saturated fat); 79kJ (19 cal); 1.8g carbohydrate; 0.7g protein; 0.6g fibre
serving ideas serve with separate bowls of dukkah and yogurt for dipping.

grilled parmesan polenta triangles

**PREP + COOK TIME 25 MINS
(+ REFRIGERATION)
SERVES 4**

1 litre (4 cups) water
1 cup (170g) polenta
20g cold butter, chopped
1 cup (80g) finely grated parmesan cheese

Grilled polenta is made by spreading soft polenta into an even layer, then chilling, cutting into shapes, oiling and grilling until crisp.

1 Oil deep 19cm-square cake pan.
2 Bring the water to the boil in large saucepan. Gradually stir in polenta; simmer, stirring, about 10 minutes or until polenta thickens. Stir in butter and cheese.
3 Spread polenta into cake pan; cool 10 minutes. Cover; refrigerate 3 hours or until firm.
4 Turn polenta onto board. Cut polenta into four squares; cut squares into triangles. Cook polenta, both sides, in heated oiled grill pan (or grill or barbecue) until browned and heated through.
nutritional count per serving 11.4g total fat (6.9g saturated fat); 1120kJ (268 cal); 29.3g carbohydrate; 11.1g protein; 1.2g fibre

soft polenta

PREP + COOK TIME 40 MINS • SERVES 4

This goes beautifully with meat casseroles, especially those that include red wine.

1 litre (4 cups) milk
1 large brown onion (200g), quartered
4 bay leaves
4 cloves garlic, quartered
8 black peppercorns
1 cup (170g) instant polenta
40g butter, chopped
1 cup (80g) finely grated parmesan cheese

1 Bring milk, onion, bay leaves, garlic and peppercorns to the boil in large saucepan. Strain milk mixture; discard solids. Return milk to same pan.
2 Gradually whisk in polenta; cook, stirring, over medium heat about 20 minutes.
3 Whisk in butter and cheese; season to taste with salt and freshly ground black pepper. Serve immediately.
nutritional count per serving 25.4g total fat (16.1g saturated fat); 2065kJ (494 cal); 44.5g carbohydrate; 20.5g protein; 2.4g fibre

mixed dhal

PREP + COOK TIME 1 HOUR 25 MINS • SERVES 4

If you are unable to buy ghee, also known as "clarified butter", make your own. Heat some butter in a small pan until a white foamy layer appears on the surface; skim and discard. Pour off the butter leaving the sediment (milk solids) at the bottom of the pan; discard. Ghee will keep for several months in the fridge.

2 tablespoons ghee
1 medium brown onion (150g), chopped finely
2 cloves garlic, crushed
4cm piece fresh ginger (20g), grated
1½ tablespoons black mustard seeds
1 long green chilli, chopped finely
1 tablespoon ground cumin
1 tablespoon ground coriander
2 teaspoons ground turmeric
½ cup (100g) brown lentils
⅓ cup (65g) red lentils
⅓ cup (85g) yellow split peas
⅓ cup (85g) green split peas
400g can crushed tomatoes
2 cups (500ml) vegetable stock
1½ cups (375ml) water
140ml can coconut cream

1 Heat ghee in large saucepan; cook onion, garlic and ginger, stirring, until onion softens. Add seeds, chilli and spices; cook, stirring, until fragrant.
2 Add lentils and peas to pan. Stir in undrained tomatoes, stock and the water; simmer, covered, stirring occasionally, about 1 hour or until lentils are tender.
3 Just before serving, add coconut cream; stir over low heat until heated through.
nutritional count per serving 18.4g total fat (12.5g saturated fat); 1898kJ (454 cal); 42.6g carbohydrate; 23.3g protein; 12.7g fibre

split pea and vegetable tagine

PREP + COOK TIME 1 HOUR • SERVES 6

Like the word casserole, the word tagine means both the food and the pot in which it is cooked, an attractive pottery vessel with a shallow circular base and a tall, conical lid which collects and condenses the steam so that it drips or slides back into the food in a continuous cycle.

2 tablespoons olive oil
1 large red onion (300g), sliced thinly
¾ cup (150g) yellow split peas
2 cloves garlic, crushed
5cm piece fresh ginger (25g), grated
3 teaspoons ground coriander
2 teaspoons ground cumin
2 teaspoons sweet paprika
1 teaspoon caraway seeds
1 litre (4 cups) vegetable stock
400g can diced tomatoes
750g butternut pumpkin, cut into 2cm pieces
350g yellow patty pan squash, quartered
200g green beans, trimmed, halved widthways
½ cup (125ml) water
½ cup coarsely chopped fresh coriander

1 Heat oil in large saucepan; cook onion, stirring, until softened. Add peas, garlic, ginger, spices and seeds; cook, stirring, until fragrant.
2 Add stock and undrained tomatoes; bring to the boil. Reduce heat; simmer, uncovered, stirring occasionally, 15 minutes. Add pumpkin; simmer 15 minutes or until peas are tender. Stir in squash, beans and the water, cover; cook 5 minutes or until vegetables are tender.
3 Serve tagine sprinkled with chopped coriander.
nutritional count per serving 8.3g total fat (1.6g saturated fat); 1070kJ (256 cal); 27.8g carbohydrate; 13.5g protein; 7.9g fibre

[1] mixed dhal
[2] split pea and vegetable tagine
[3] baked lima beans [page 490]
[4] black bean, corn and chipotle stew [page 490]

1

2

3

4

baked lima beans

PREP + COOK TIME 1 HOUR 50 MINS (+ STANDING & REFRIGERATION) • SERVES 4

Also known as butter beans, lima beans are small and pale green if picked young or large, flat and white if picked when fully grown.

The baked beans are even better if made a day in advance, as this allows the flavours to develop.

1½ cups (285g) dried lima beans
2 cups (500ml) vegetable stock
½ cup (85g) polenta
1 tablespoon dijon mustard
½ cup (40g) finely grated parmesan cheese
2 tablespoons finely chopped fresh flat-leaf parsley

2 teaspoons olive oil
1 large brown onion (200g), chopped finely
2 cloves garlic, crushed
400g can crushed tomatoes
1 tablespoon tomato paste
2 tablespoons brown sugar
1½ cups (375ml) vegetable stock, extra

1 Place beans in medium bowl, cover with water; soak overnight, drain. Rinse under cold water; drain. Place beans in medium saucepan of boiling water; return to the boil. Reduce heat; simmer, covered, 15 minutes or until beans are just tender. Drain.
2 Preheat oven to 200°C/180°C fan-forced. Oil 19cm-square loaf pan; line base with baking paper.
3 Bring stock to the boil in medium saucepan. Gradually add polenta, stirring constantly. Reduce heat; simmer, stirring, 10 minutes or until polenta thickens. Stir in mustard, cheese and parsley. Spread polenta into pan; cover, refrigerate about 3 hours or until firm.
4 Heat oil in large flameproof dish; cook onion and garlic, stirring, until onion softens. Add beans, undrained tomatoes, paste, sugar and extra stock; bring to the boil. Cook, uncovered, in oven about 40 minutes or until sauce thickens.
5 Preheat grill.
6 Turn polenta onto board; trim edges. Cut into four squares, cut each square into two triangles. Grill polenta until browned both sides. Serve polenta with bean mixture.
nutritional count per serving 8.4g total fat (3g saturated fat); 1689kJ (404 cal); 55.3g carbohydrate; 25.2g protein; 15.8g fibre

---

black bean, corn and chipotle stew

PREP + COOK TIME 2 HOURS 15 MINS (+ STANDING) SERVES 4

1½ cups (300g) dried black beans
2 chipotle chillies
½ cup (125ml) boiling water
1 tablespoon cumin seeds
2 trimmed corn cobs (500g)
2 teaspoons olive oil
1 large brown onion (200g), chopped finely
810g can crushed tomatoes
8 small white corn tortillas

salsa
1 small red onion (100g), chopped coarsely
1 small tomato (90g), chopped coarsely
½ cup coarsely chopped fresh coriander
1 lebanese cucumber (130g), chopped coarsely
1 tablespoon olive oil
2 tablespoons lemon juice

1 Place beans in medium bowl, cover with water; stand overnight, drain. Rinse under cold water; drain. Place beans in medium saucepan of boiling water; return to the boil. Reduce heat; simmer, uncovered, about 15 minutes or until beans are just tender.
2 Preheat oven to 200°C/180°C fan-forced.
3 Place chillies and the boiling water in small bowl; stand 15 minutes. Discard stalks; blend or process chilli and its soaking liquid until smooth.
4 Meanwhile, dry-fry cumin seeds in small frying pan, stirring, until fragrant.
5 Cook corn on heated oiled grill plate (or grill or barbecue) until browned lightly and just tender. When cool enough to handle, cut kernels from cobs with sharp knife.
6 Heat oil in large flameproof dish; cook onion, stirring, until soft. Add drained beans, chilli mixture, cumin, undrained tomatoes and half of the corn; bring to the boil. Cook, uncovered, in oven about 20 minutes or until sauce thickens.
7 Meanwhile, heat tortillas according to manufacturer's instructions.
8 Combine remaining corn with salsa ingredients in medium bowl.
9 Serve stew with tortillas and salsa.

nutritional count per serving 10.4g total fat (1.3g saturated fat); 1839kJ (440 cal); 61.3g carbohydrate; 26.2g protein; 19.5g fibre

pumpernickel bread

PREP + COOK TIME 1 HOUR 15 MINS (+ STANDING) • MAKES 24 SLICES

This pumpernickel is milder in flavour than the classic version, which uses rye flour only, but still has the characteristic sweet-sour tang of this popular German bread.

2 teaspoons dried yeast
1 teaspoon caster sugar
1 cup (250ml) warm water
50g butter, melted
1 tablespoon molasses
1 tablespoon caraway seeds
½ cup (85g) polenta
1½ cups (185g) rye flour
1 cup (150g) plain flour
2 tablespoons cocoa powder
1 teaspoon salt

1 Whisk yeast, sugar and the water in large bowl until yeast dissolves, cover; stand in warm place about 10 minutes or until mixture is frothy.
2 Stir in butter and molasses, then seeds, polenta and sifted flours, cocoa and salt. Turn dough onto floured surface; knead about 10 minutes or until smooth. Place dough into large greased bowl, cover; stand in warm place about 2 hours or until dough has doubled in size.
3 Grease 8cm x 26cm bar cake pan; line sides of pan with baking paper, extending 5cm above edge. Turn dough onto floured surface; knead until smooth. Press dough into pan, cover loosely; stand in warm place about 45 minutes or until dough has risen to top of pan.
4 Preheat oven to 180°C/160°C fan-forced. Cover pan with foil.
5 Bake 15 minutes. Uncover; bake about 30 minutes. Turn onto wire rack to cool.

nutritional count per slice 2.1g total fat (1.2g saturated); 334kJ (80 cal); 12.3g carbohydrate; 2.2g protein; 1.4g fibre

lentil and bean burger

PREP + COOK TIME 45 MINS (+ REFRIGERATION & COOLING) • SERVES 4

The relish is best made a day or two ahead and stored, covered, in the refrigerator to allow the flavours to blend. You can add a finely chopped, fresh red chilli to the mixture if you want it hotter.

1 cup (200g) red lentils
420g can four-bean mix, rinsed
1 egg
4 green onions, chopped coarsely
2 tablespoons coarsely chopped fresh coriander
½ cup (35g) stale wholemeal breadcrumbs
4 hamburger buns
8 butter lettuce leaves
40g bean sprouts
40g snow pea sprouts, trimmed
1 lebanese cucumber (130g), sliced

chilli tomato relish
2 medium tomatoes (300g), chopped coarsely
1 small brown onion (80g), chopped finely
1 clove garlic, crushed
⅓ cup (80ml) sweet chilli sauce
2 tablespoons malt vinegar

Process the cooked lentils, canned beans and egg until the mixture is smooth.

Divide the mixture into four portions and, using floured hands, shape them into flattened patties.

1 Make chilli tomato relish.
2 Meanwhile, cook lentils in medium saucepan of boiling water until tender; drain. Cool 10 minutes.
3 Blend or process lentils, beans and egg until smooth. Combine in medium bowl with onion, coriander and breadcrumbs; season to taste. Cover; refrigerate 1 hour.
4 Using floured hands, shape lentil mixture into four patties; cook patties in large heated lightly oiled non-stick frying pan until browned both sides and heated through. Remove from pan; cover to keep warm.
5 Split buns in half; toast cut-sides of buns. Spread buns with relish; sandwich lettuce, sprouts, cucumber, patties and remaining relish between buns.

chilli tomato relish Cook tomato, onion and garlic in small saucepan, stirring, about 10 minutes or until tomato has softened. Add sauce and vinegar; bring to the boil. Reduce heat; simmer, uncovered, stirring occasionally, about 10 minutes or until relish thickens. Cool 15 minutes.

nutritional count per serving 6.5g total fat (1.2g saturated fat); 2282kJ (546 cal); 82g carbohydrate; 29.4g protein; 19.1g fibre

dhansak with caramelised onion rice

PREP + COOK TIME
2 HOURS 55 MINS
(+ STANDING)
SERVES 8

1 cup (200g) yellow split peas
½ cup (100g) dried chickpeas
½ cup (100g) red lentils
⅓ cup (80ml) vegetable oil
1kg diced lamb
1 large eggplant (500g), chopped
800g pumpkin, chopped coarsely
5 medium tomatoes (750g), peeled, chopped coarsely
1kg medium brown onions, sliced

garam masala
1 tablespoon ground coriander
2 teaspoons ground cumin
2 teaspoons ground turmeric
½ teaspoon ground cinnamon
½ teaspoon ground cardamom
½ teaspoon black mustard seeds
¼ teaspoon ground clove

masala paste
6 dried small red chillies
6 long green chillies, seeded
4cm piece fresh ginger (20g), chopped coarsely
6 cloves garlic, quartered
½ cup firmly packed fresh mint leaves
½ cup firmly packed fresh coriander leaves
¼ cup (60ml) hot water

caramelised onion rice
2½ cups (500g) basmati rice
1.25 litres (5 cups) water
2 tablespoons vegetable oil
20g butter
4 medium brown onions (600g), sliced thinly

Dhansak, a lentil and meat stew, is a tantalisingly complex mixture of traditional Persian and Indian food. It is always served with "brown" rice – white rice cooked with caramelised onion until it changes colour.

1 Place split peas and chickpeas in large bowl, cover with water; stand overnight, drain. Rinse under cold water; drain. Rinse lentils under cold water; drain. Combine lentils, split peas and chickpeas in large saucepan of boiling water; return to the boil. Reduce heat; simmer, uncovered, 40 minutes or until chickpeas are tender.
2 Meanwhile, make garam masala and masala paste.
3 Heat half of the oil in large frying pan; cook lamb, in batches, until just browned. Remove from pan; cover to keep warm.
4 Drain pea mixture through sieve over large bowl. Return 1 litre cooking liquid to same pan, discard remainder. Reserve pea mixture in same bowl.
5 Place eggplant, pumpkin, tomato and about a third of the sliced onion in pan with reserved cooking liquid, cover; bring to the boil. Reduce heat; simmer dhansak, covered, 10 minutes, stirring occasionally. Drain vegetable mixture through sieve over another large bowl; reserve 2 cups of the cooking liquid, discard remainder.
6 Combine half of the split pea mixture and half of the vegetable mixture in large bowl; mash until smooth.
7 Heat same cleaned pan; dry-fry garam masala and masala paste, stirring, until fragrant. Add mashed and whole split pea and vegetable mixtures, lamb and reserved cooking liquid to pan; bring to the boil. Reduce heat; simmer, uncovered, 45 minutes, stirring occasionally.
8 Meanwhile, make caramelised onion rice.
9 Heat remaining oil in large frying pan; cook remaining sliced onion, stirring, about 15 minutes or until softened and caramelised lightly. Sprinkle onion over dhansak; serve with rice, and lemon wedges.

garam masala Combine all ingredients in small bowl.
masala paste Blend or process ingredients until mixture forms a smooth paste.
caramelised onion rice Wash rice in strainer under cold water until water runs clear; drain. Heat oil and butter in medium saucepan; cook onion, stirring, about 15 minutes or until softened and lightly caramelised. Carefully add the water to pan; bring to the boil. Stir in rice; return to the boil. Reduce heat; simmer rice, partially covered, about 10 minutes or until steam holes appear on the surface. Cover rice tightly, reduce heat to as low as possible; steam 10 minutes (do not remove lid). Remove from heat; stand 10 minutes without removing lid. Fluff with fork before serving.

nutritional count per serving 18g total fat (3.5g saturated fat); 2604kJ (623 cal); 87.9g carbohydrate; 20.4g protein; 12.3g fibre

chickpea and vegetable gratin

PREP + COOK TIME 1 HOUR • SERVES 6

- 2 tablespoons olive oil
- 1 large brown onion (200g), chopped finely
- 4 cloves garlic, crushed
- ½ teaspoon ground allspice
- ½ teaspoon chilli flakes
- 2 x 400g cans diced tomatoes
- 2 large red capsicums (700g)
- 2 medium eggplants (600g), cut into 5mm slices
- 3 medium zucchini (360g), cut into 5mm slices
- 2 x 400g cans chickpeas, rinsed, drained
- ½ cup coarsely chopped fresh flat-leaf parsley
- ⅓ cup coarsely chopped fresh basil
- 1 teaspoon fresh thyme leaves
- 1 teaspoon white sugar
- 1 cup (80g) finely grated parmesan cheese

1 Heat half the oil in medium saucepan; cook onion, stirring, until softened. Add garlic, allspice and chilli; cook, stirring, until fragrant. Add undrained tomatoes; simmer, uncovered, about 15 minutes or until sauce thickens slightly.
2 Meanwhile, quarter capsicums; discard seeds and membranes. Roast under preheated grill or in very hot oven, skin-side up, until skin blisters and blackens. Cover capsicum pieces with plastic or paper 5 minutes; peel away skin then cut capsicum into 3cm pieces.
3 Combine eggplant, zucchini and remaining oil in large bowl; place vegetables on two oven trays, grill both sides until tender.
4 Preheat oven to 200°C/180°C fan-forced.
5 Stir chickpeas, herbs and sugar into tomato sauce. Place half the combined capsicum, eggplant and zucchini in shallow 10-cup (2.5-litre) ovenproof dish; pour half the chickpea sauce over vegetables. Repeat layering; sprinkle with cheese. Cook, uncovered, about 20 minutes or until browned lightly.

nutritional count per serving 13.3g total fat (3.9g saturated fat); 1296kJ (310 cal); 26.4g carbohydrate; 15.8g protein; 11.2g fibre

SPECIAL FEATURE

Beans, peas & grains

Beans, peas and grains, collectively called pulses, are some of the most nutritious foods we can eat. Unfortunately they have a reputation for being bland and boring. This is simply not the case – some of the world's great dishes are made from pulses.

ADZUKI BEANS
Small russet beans with a cream stripe. Thin-skinned and sweetish, they are used in Japan in a paste for desserts and cakes, and are also good in stews and for sprouting.

BLACK BEANS
Also called turtle beans. Their big, savoury flavour makes them the stars of Caribbean and Latin-American cooking, famously for black-bean soup. Not the same as chinese black beans, which are salted, fermented soybeans.

BLACK-EYED BEANS
Also called black-eyed peas or cow peas. Mild-flavoured and thin-skinned, so they cook faster than most other beans. Often served in the American south with pork and cornbread.

HARICOT BEANS
The haricot bean family includes navy beans for boston baked beans and soissons for French cassoulet as well as cannellini. All are mild-flavoured white beans which can be interchanged with each other.

BURGHUL
Best-known in the refreshing Middle Eastern salad, tabbouleh, burghul is hulled, steamed or par-boiled and dried cracked wheat ground to various degrees of fineness. Before use, it is soaked briefly in water to soften and swell the grains, then squeezed dry.

PUY LENTILS
From the Le Puy district in southern France, these tiny dark grey-green lentils are delicious and very expensive. Local versions are available, sold under the name of french green or bondi lentils.

Q&A

I'm a vegetarian and I've read that we should eat pulses and grains to make up the nutrients we are missing by not eating meat. Is this right?

Vegetarians should make a particular point of eating pulses and grains – when eaten together they form a complete protein. Interestingly many cultures have always known this: tacos and beans; dhal and rice, even baked beans on toast are all combinations of grains and pulses.

AD BEANS
called fava beans. Large and mealy-textured, fresh and dried. Used with chickpeas for l. Ful medames (egyptian brown beans) are all, nutty-flavoured variety.

SPLIT PEAS
Yellow or green varieties, both with a sweet, strong pea flavour. Best known for pea and ham soup and for traditional pease pudding (mashed with butter, mint, parsley and eggs, then steamed) to serve with corned beef.

CHICKPEAS
Also called garbanzos, channa or hummus, prized for their full, nutty flavour and crisp texture. Essential for the Italian soup pasta e ceci, and for the Middle Eastern hummus bi tahini.

  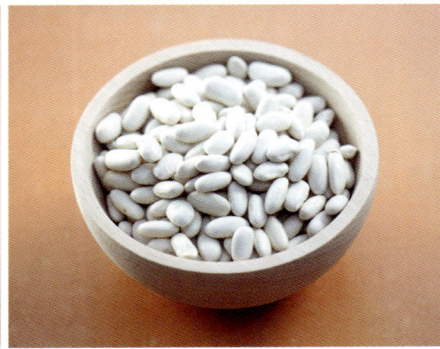

ENTA
known as cornmeal, made from dried corn nd to various degrees of fineness. It is boiled water to a porridge (soft polenta), which may be chilled, cut into shapes, oiled and grilled.

COUSCOUS
The staple cereal of North Africa, made from fine semolina. It is steamed over the pot in which the meat and vegetables are cooking, or, for sweet couscous, over water, then mixed with sugar, nuts and fruits.

CANNELLINI BEANS
Small, white Italian members of the haricot bean family. Used in minestrone and other soups and in Tuscan dishes such as beans baked with pancetta and garlic or chilled beans with tuna.

bircher muesli

PREP TIME 20 MINS (+ REFRIGERATION) • SERVES 6

Try to find plain full-cream yogurt, sometimes called country-style or greek-style yogurt, for this recipe. Other types, especially the low-fat kind, are not suitable. Additional milk can be added if the muesli is too thick.

Use a tart, crisp green apple, such as a granny smith, for this recipe.

2 cups (180g) rolled oats
1¼ cups (310ml) apple juice
1 cup (280g) yogurt
2 medium apples (300g)
¼ cup (35g) roasted slivered almonds
¼ cup (40g) currants
¼ cup (20g) toasted shredded coconut
1 teaspoon ground cinnamon
½ cup (140g) yogurt, extra

1 Combine oats, juice and yogurt in medium bowl. Cover; refrigerate overnight.
2 Peel, core and coarsely grate one apple; stir into oat mixture with nuts, currants, coconut and cinnamon.
3 Core and thinly slice remaining apple. Serve muesli topped with extra yogurt and apple slices.

nutritional count per serving 10.4g total fat (4.1g saturated fat); 1187kJ (284 cal); 37g carbohydrate; 8.2g protein; 4.3g fibre

roasted muesli with dried fruit and honey

PREP + COOK TIME 30 MINS • SERVES 6

Oats have a tendency to go rancid more quickly than other grains, as they contain more oils. Therefore only make enough muesli to last a couple of weeks. Keep muesli in a sealed container in a cool place; it will keep longest if stored in the fridge.

2 cups (180g) rolled oats
1 cup (110g) rolled rice
¼ cup (15g) unprocessed wheat bran
¼ cup (50g) pepitas
1 teaspoon ground cinnamon
⅓ cup (115g) honey
1 tablespoon vegetable oil
¾ cup (35g) flaked coconut
⅓ cup (50g) coarsely chopped dried apricots
⅓ cup (20g) coarsely chopped dried apples
⅓ cup (55g) sultanas
¼ cup (35g) dried cranberries, chopped coarsely

1 Preheat oven to 180°C/160°C fan-forced.
2 Combine oats and rice in large bowl, then spread evenly between two oven trays. Roast, uncovered, in oven 5 minutes.
3 Stir bran, pepitas and cinnamon into oat mixtures, then drizzle evenly with combined honey and oil; stir to combine. Roast, uncovered, 5 minutes. Stir in coconut. Roast, uncovered, 5 minutes.
4 Remove trays from oven; place muesli mixture in same large bowl, stir in remaining ingredients. Serve with milk or yogurt.

nutritional count per serving 16.1g total fat (4.8g saturated); 1768kJ (423 cal); 52.8g carbohydrate; 7.3g protein; 11.1g fibre

[opposite] bircher muesli

white bean puree

PREP + COOK TIME 20 MINS • SERVES 4

This recipe calls for white beans, a generic term we use for canned or dried cannellini, haricot, navy or great northern beans which are all of the same family, *phaseolus vulgaris*, and are all interchangeable.

20g butter
1 small brown onion (80g), chopped finely
1 clove garlic, crushed
¼ cup (60ml) dry white wine
¾ cup (180ml) chicken stock
2 x 400g cans white beans, rinsed, drained
2 tablespoons cream

1 Melt butter in medium frying pan; cook onion and garlic, stirring, until onion softens. Add wine; cook, stirring, until liquid is reduced by half.
2 Add stock and beans; bring to the boil. Reduce heat; simmer, uncovered, about 10 minutes or until liquid is almost evaporated.
3 Blend or process bean mixture and cream until smooth.

nutritional count per serving 8.9g total fat (5.8g saturated fat); 548kJ (131 cal); 4.9g carbohydrate; 4.2g protein; 3.1g fibre

semolina slice

PREP + COOK TIME 2 HOURS 5 MINS (+ REFRIGERATION) • MAKES 28

Known in Middle Eastern and North African countries as basboosa, namoura or harisi, these sweets are appreciated for their lovely orange perfume. Cover the slice loosely with foil if it starts to overbrown while cooking.

1kg coarsely ground semolina
2½ cups (550g) sugar
1 cup (250ml) milk
125g butter
¼ cup (40g) blanched almonds

sugar syrup
3 cups (750ml) water
2 teaspoons lemon juice
1½ cups (330g) caster sugar
2 teaspoons orange flower water

1 Make sugar syrup.
2 Preheat oven to 160°C/140°C fan-forced. Grease 20cm x 30cm lamington pan.
3 Combine semolina and sugar in large bowl. Place milk and butter in small saucepan; stir over low heat until butter melts. Pour into semolina mixture; stir to combine.
4 Spread semolina mixture into pan; smooth the top with a wet hand. Score slice into 4cm diamond shapes; centre one almond on each diamond. Bake about 1 hour 20 minutes or until slice is golden brown and slightly firm to the touch.
5 Cut through diamond shapes to bottom of slice; gradually pour cooled syrup over hot slice. Cool in pan.
sugar syrup Bring the water, juice and sugar to the boil in medium saucepan. Reduce heat; simmer, uncovered, about 20 minutes or until syrup reduces to about 2½ cups. Cool to room temperature. Add orange flower water, cover; refrigerate 3 hours or overnight.

nutritional count per piece 5.2g total fat (2.8g saturated fat); 1225kJ (293 cal); 55.6g carbohydrate; 4.4g protein; 1.3g fibre

[opposite] semolina slice

DESSERTS

Desserts

When you're eating dessert, it's impossible to have anything but pleasant thoughts. For most of us, eating dessert is not an everyday occurrence but rather a little luxury we reserve for dinner parties and special family meals, and we relish every blissful mouthful.

THE RECIPES IN THIS CHAPTER ARE BELOVED CLASSICS AND ALL-TIME FAVOURITES. SOME ARE SIMPLE AND QUICK TO CREATE. OTHERS ARE MORE COMPLICATED AND TIME-CONSUMING, BUT WORTH IT. SOME ARE IMPRESSIVE STATEMENTS THAT COMMAND CENTRE STAGE AT A DINNER PARTY, OTHERS FIT MORE COMFORTABLY WITH A QUIET FAMILY DINNER. TRY THEM ALL, FROM THE SUMPTUOUS SUMMER PUDDING, TO THE ELEGANT CHOCOLATE TART, TO THE UNMATCHED PAVLOVA AND THE HOMELY BREAD AND BUTTER PUDDING LIKE YOUR GRANDMOTHER USED TO MAKE.

BAKING TIPS

It's important to get to know your oven. Every nuance and quirk will have an impact on your baking. Every oven bakes differently but as a general rule it's good to position the dish so the top of the dessert is at the centre of the oven.

Check the accuracy of your oven's temperature gauge with an oven thermometer. Most domestic ovens have hotspots, so don't be nervous about opening the oven door to reposition the dish. But any dessert or cake full of air, like a soufflé or sponge, should be treated carefully – they might deflate if moved at the wrong time.

A WATER BATH is used to insulate baked desserts, making the baking process gentler. The water also adds humidity, which can prevent the top of the dessert from cracking. If the recipe calls for a water bath, place the dessert dish in a larger baking dish and pour boiling water into the larger dish until the water comes halfway up the side(s) of the dessert dish. Do this while they are on a shelf in the oven – it's safer than trying to get both dishes in the oven. While baking, keep an eye on the water level – if it looks low, top it up.

MERINGUE DESSERTS

Everyone needs to make a pavlova at least once in their lives – that wonderful symphony of melt-in-your-mouth meringue, cream and strawberries. Lemon meringue is another family favourite with its memorable combination of tangy lemon custard crowned by meringue.

The main point to watch when making meringue is that all utensils are dry and free of grease and that egg whites are completely free of yolk, as even a hint of grease or a speck of yolk will prevent the whites from beating up properly.

TO MAKE THE MERINGUE Beat egg whites only until soft peaks form before you start adding the sugar: if you beat the whites until they are stiff and dry, the sugar will take longer to dissolve. If the sugar doesn't dissolve properly the meringue can "weep" droplets of moisture during and after baking.

The meringue case for pavlova can be made up to 4 days ahead and stored in an airtight container at room temperature. Fill with cream and fruit about an hour before serving.

CHEESECAKES

No wonder cheesecakes are so wonderful: they had their genesis in ancient Greek times, so we've had time to perfect them. Back then, a combination of cheese and honey was served on an oaten base. Today's cheesecakes can be baked or fridge-set and many countries claim to have the supreme recipe. Our baked new york cheesecake combining a creamy, not-too-sweet filling with a crunchy biscuit is hard to surpass.

You'll need a springform tin for cheesecakes: these are special round tins that come in two parts – the base and the ring – that attach and detach using a special catch on the side of the ring. Springform tins eliminate all the uncertainties of turning out the cheesecake: you simply release the ring and it slips off the dessert.

For a smooth-textured filling, have the cream cheese and all the other ingredients at room temperature before you start to mix.

You need fine, evenly-sized crumbs to make a good crust. This can be achieved by using a blender, or a food processor or by crushing them in a plastic bag with a rolling pin. When the biscuit mixture is made, you'll need about one third of it for the base and the rest for the side.

DON'T OVER-BEAT MIXTURES THAT CONTAIN CREAM AND MASCARPONE CHEESE AS THE MIXTURE CAN CURDLE

For an extra smooth side to an unbaked 'biscuit-base only' cheesecake, you can line the tin with plastic wrap: remove the base of the tin then drape a piece of plastic wrap over the lightly greased side of the tin. Position and secure the base back into the tin, stretching the wrap neatly and leaving a little of the wrap hanging over the edge.

Follow cooking times carefully and don't overcook.

Leave the cheesecake to cool in the oven: this will allow it to cool slowly and avoid shrinking, sinking in the middle or cracking as it cools.

Use a hot, dry knife to cut the cheesecake.

FROZEN DESSERTS

HOME-MADE ICE-CREAM, LIKE THE VANILLA BEAN ICE-CREAM IN THIS CHAPTER, SHOULD BE STORED IN THE FREEZER TO ALLOW IT TO DEVELOP (LET THE FLAVOURS BECOME STRONGER) FOR AT LEAST AN HOUR AFTER IT IS MADE. IT IS BEST EATEN WITHIN 48 HOURS OF BEING MADE. HOME-MADE ICE-CREAM IS HARDER THAN COMMERCIAL ICE-CREAM AND SHOULD BE TRANSFERRED FROM THE FREEZER TO THE FRIDGE ABOUT HALF AN HOUR BEFORE SERVING, TO SOFTEN.

crème caramel

PREP + COOK TIME 1 HOUR (+ REFRIGERATION) • SERVES 8

¾ cup (165g) caster sugar
½ cup (125ml) water
6 eggs
1 teaspoon vanilla extract
⅓ cup (75g) caster sugar, extra
300ml cream
1¾ cups (430ml) milk

There is a great sense of achievement once you've mastered crème caramel. Home cooks are usually concerned about the toffee, but it's not as tricky as you think. Use a heavy pan and stir the sugar and water over medium heat. Once the sugar has been dissolved and the mixture starts to boil, watch it carefully. As soon as it starts to brown, tilt the pan until the brown areas merge. Keep tilting and turning the pan until the toffee is a rich golden colour. Remove the pan from the heat, let the bubbles subside, then pour toffee over the base of the cake pan. There is no need to coat the side of the pan, or even grease it. An aluminium cake pan gives the best results for even baking of the custard. Refrigerating the crème caramel overnight breaks down and liquefies the toffee which will make it easier to turn the crème caramel out of the pan. When you're ready to serve, use your fingers to ease the custard away from the side of the pan, gently wriggle the pan and you'll "feel" the custard floating on the caramel. Put the serving plate on top of the cake pan and quickly invert.

1 Preheat oven to 160°C/140°C fan-forced.
2 Combine sugar and the water in medium heavy-based frying pan; stir over heat, without boiling, until sugar dissolves. Bring to the boil; boil, uncovered, without stirring, until mixture is a deep caramel colour. Remove from heat; allow bubbles to subside. Pour toffee into deep 20cm-round cake pan.
3 Whisk eggs, extract and extra sugar in large bowl.
4 Combine cream and milk in medium saucepan; bring to the boil. Whisking constantly, pour hot milk mixture into egg mixture. Strain mixture into cake pan.
5 Place pan in baking dish; add enough boiling water to come halfway up side of pan. Bake, in oven, about 40 minutes or until set. Remove custard from baking dish, cover; refrigerate overnight.
6 Gently ease crème caramel from side of pan; invert onto deep-sided serving plate.

nutritional count per serving 22.3g total fat (13.3g saturated fat); 1526kJ (365 cal); 33.8g carbohydrate; 7.5g protein; 0g fibre

All the sugar needs to be dissolved when you're making caramel. Some sugar will stick to the sides of the pan – brush these off using a dampened pastry brush.

When the caramel is a deep, rich brown, pour it into the base of a deep 20cm cake pan.

Put the custard into a baking dish and pour enough boiling water around the cake pan to come halfway up its side.

apple pie

PREP + COOK TIME 1 HOUR 45 MINS (+ REFRIGERATION) • SERVES 8

Make sure your apples are drained well and are cooled to room temperature. Brushing the inside of the pastry case with egg white will also help stop the apples from making the pastry soggy.

10 medium apples (1.5kg)
½ cup (125ml) water
¼ cup (55g) caster sugar
1 teaspoon finely grated lemon rind
¼ teaspoon ground cinnamon
1 egg white
1 tablespoon caster sugar, extra

pastry
1 cup (150g) plain flour
½ cup (75g) self-raising flour
¼ cup (35g) cornflour
¼ cup (30g) custard powder
1 tablespoon caster sugar
100g cold butter, chopped coarsely
1 egg yolk
¼ cup (60ml) iced water

1 Make pastry.
2 Peel, core and slice apple thickly. Place apple and the water in large saucepan; bring to the boil. Reduce heat; simmer, covered, about 10 minutes or until apples soften. Drain; stir in sugar, rind and cinnamon. Cool.
3 Preheat oven to 220°C/200°C fan-forced. Grease deep 25cm pie dish.
4 Divide pastry in half. Roll one half between sheets of baking paper until large enough to line dish. Lift pastry into dish; press into base and side. Spoon apple mixture into pastry case; brush edge with egg white.
5 Roll remaining pastry large enough to cover filling; lift onto filling. Press edges together; trim away excess pastry. Brush pastry with egg white; sprinkle with extra sugar.
6 Bake pie 20 minutes. Reduce oven to 180°C/160°C fan-forced; bake further 25 minutes or until golden brown. Serve with vanilla custard, or scoops of vanilla ice-cream, if you like.
pastry Process dry ingredients with butter until crumbly. Add egg yolk and the water; process until combined. Knead on floured surface until smooth. Cover; refrigerate 30 minutes.
nutritional count per serving 11.4g total fat (7g saturated fat); 1438kJ (344 cal); 53.9g carbohydrate; 4.3g protein; 3.7g fibre

What are the best apples to use for an apple pie?

Granny smiths are the traditional apple pie apple because they have just enough tartness to complement the sweet pastry, and they soften beautifully. For tarte tartin and other open-faced apple tarts, golden delicious are a better choice, because they keep their shape even when they're fully cooked.

baked custard

PREP + COOK TIME 50 MINS • SERVES 6

We heat the milk to decrease the baking time. The milk should be hot, not boiling, but certainly much more than warm. Be careful to avoid overcooking. The custard is done when it still looks and feels a bit wobbly in the middle. The heat within the custard will continue to cook, heat and thicken the rest of the custard as it cools down.

6 eggs
1 teaspoon vanilla extract
⅓ cup (75g) caster sugar
1 litre (4 cups) hot milk
¼ teaspoon ground nutmeg

1 Preheat oven to 160°C/140°C fan-forced. Grease shallow 1.5-litre (6-cup) ovenproof dish.
2 Whisk eggs, extract and sugar in large bowl; gradually whisk in hot milk. Pour custard mixture into dish; sprinkle with nutmeg.
3 Place dish in larger baking dish; add enough boiling water to come halfway up sides of dish. Bake, uncovered, about 45 minutes. Remove custard from large dish; stand 5 minutes before serving.

nutritional count per serving 11.8g total fat (5.9g saturated fat); 995kJ (238 cal); 20.7g carbohydrate; 12.3g protein; 0g fibre

golden syrup steamed pudding

PREP + COOK TIME 1 HOUR 15 MINS • SERVES 6

Honey, treacle or molasses can be substituted for the golden syrup here. Don't use pouring honey or pouring golden syrup because they're not stable or thick enough for this recipe.

Make sure the baking paper and foil (pleated to allow room for the pudding to expand) are tied tightly around the bowl.

60g butter
¼ cup (90g) golden syrup
½ teaspoon bicarbonate of soda
1 cup (150g) self-raising flour
2 teaspoons ground ginger
½ cup (125ml) milk
1 egg

syrup
⅓ cup (115g) golden syrup
2 tablespoons water
30g butter

1 Grease 1.25-litre (5-cup) pudding steamer.
2 Stir butter and syrup in small saucepan over low heat until smooth. Remove from heat, stir in soda; transfer mixture to medium bowl. Stir in sifted dry ingredients then combined milk and egg, in two batches.
3 Spread mixture into steamer. Cover with pleated baking paper and foil; secure with lid. Place pudding steamer in large saucepan with enough boiling water to come halfway up side of steamer; cover pan with tight-fitting lid. Boil 1 hour, replenishing water as necessary to maintain level. Stand pudding 5 minutes before turning onto serving plate.
4 Meanwhile, make syrup.
5 Serve pudding topped with syrup and, if desired, cream.

syrup Stir ingredients in small saucepan over heat until smooth; bring to the boil. Reduce heat; simmer, uncovered, 2 minutes.

nutritional count per serving 14.3g total fat (9g saturated fat); 1367kJ (327 cal); 44.5g carbohydrate; 4.5g protein; 1g fibre

[1] baked custard
[2] golden syrup steamed pudding
[3] vanilla bean ice-cream [page 512]
[4] chocolate self-saucing pudding [page 512]

1

2

3

4

vanilla bean ice-cream

PREP + COOK TIME 25 MINS (+ REFRIGERATION, CHURNING & FREEZING)
SERVES 8

2 vanilla beans
1⅔ cups (410ml) milk
600ml thickened cream
8 egg yolks
¾ cup (165g) caster sugar

When you want to finish freezing ice-cream in a hurry, remove it from your ice-cream churn when it's only partially frozen, spread it into a thin layer in a lamington pan, cover it well with foil and put it in your freezer. It will become solidly frozen in about an hour.

1 Split vanilla beans lengthways; scrape out seeds into medium saucepan. Add pods, milk and cream; bring to the boil.
2 Meanwhile, whisk egg yolks and sugar in medium bowl until creamy; gradually whisk into hot milk mixture. Stir over low heat, without boiling, until mixture thickens slightly.
3 Strain mixture into medium heatproof bowl; discard pods. Cover surface of custard with plastic wrap; refrigerate about 1 hour or until cold.
4 Pour custard into ice-cream maker, churn according to manufacturer's instructions (or place custard in shallow container, such as an aluminium slab cake pan, cover with foil; freeze until almost firm). Place ice-cream in large bowl, chop coarsely then beat with electric mixer until smooth. Pour into deep container, cover; freeze until firm. Repeat process two more times.
nutritional count per serving 35.5g total fat (21.4g saturated fat); 1856kJ (444 cal); 25.5g carbohydrate; 6.5g protein; 0g fibre

chocolate self-saucing pudding

PREP + COOK TIME 55 MINS • SERVES 6

60g butter
½ cup (125ml) milk
½ teaspoon vanilla extract
¾ cup (165g) caster sugar
1 cup (150g) self-raising flour

1 tablespoon cocoa powder
¾ cup (165g) firmly packed brown sugar
1 tablespoon cocoa powder, extra
2 cups (500ml) boiling water

1 Preheat oven to 180°C/160°C fan-forced. Grease 1.5-litre (6-cup) ovenproof dish.
2 Melt butter with milk in medium saucepan. Remove from heat; stir in extract and caster sugar then sifted flour and cocoa.
3 Spread pudding mixture into dish. Sift brown sugar and extra cocoa over mixture; gently pour boiling water over mixture.
4 Bake pudding about 40 minutes or until centre is firm. Stand 5 minutes before serving.
nutritional count per serving 9.7g total fat (6.2g saturated fat); 1676kJ (401 cal); 73.4g carbohydrate; 3.8g protein; 1.1g fibre

chocolate tart

PREP + COOK TIME 1 HOUR 10 MINS (+ REFRIGERATION) • SERVES 12

Use unsalted butter and good-quality eating chocolate for this tart. Dust lightly with good-quality cocoa powder just before serving. A small dollop of cream on each serving, despite its added richness, somehow cuts through the rich chocolate filling.

2 eggs
2 egg yolks
¼ cup (55g) caster sugar
250g dark eating chocolate, melted
200g butter, melted

pastry
1½ cups (225g) plain flour
½ cup (110g) caster sugar
140g cold butter, chopped
1 egg, beaten lightly

1 Make pastry.
2 Grease 24cm-round loose-based flan tin. Roll dough between sheets of baking paper until large enough to line tin. Lift pastry into tin, ease into base and side; trim edge, prick base all over with fork. Refrigerate 30 minutes.
3 Preheat oven to 200°C/180°C fan-forced.
4 Place tin on oven tray. Line pastry case with baking paper; fill with dried beans or rice. Bake 10 minutes. Remove paper and beans; bake 5 minutes. Cool.
5 Reduce oven to 180°C/160°C fan-forced.
6 Whisk eggs, egg yolks and sugar in medium heatproof bowl over medium saucepan of simmering water about 15 minutes or until light and fluffy. Gently whisk chocolate and butter into egg mixture; pour into pastry shell.
7 Bake tart 10 minutes or until filling is set; cool 10 minutes. Refrigerate 1 hour.
pastry Process flour, sugar and butter until crumbly. Add egg; process until ingredients come together. Knead pastry on floured surface until smooth. Wrap in plastic wrap; refrigerate 30 minutes.
nutritional count per serving 32g total fat (21.8g saturated fat); 1952kJ (467 cal); 39.4g carbohydrate; 5.2g protein; 1.7g fibre

chocolate mousse

PREP + COOK TIME 35 MINS (+ REFRIGERATION) • SERVES 6

TIP
• The eggs must be at room temperature for success with this recipe.

200g dark eating chocolate, chopped coarsely
30g unsalted butter
3 eggs, separated
300ml thickened cream, whipped

1 Melt chocolate and butter in large glass heatproof bowl over large saucepan of simmering water (do not allow water to touch base of bowl). Remove from heat. Stir in egg yolks; cool.
2 Beat egg whites in small bowl with electric mixer until soft peaks form.
3 Meanwhile, fold cream into chocolate mixture; fold in egg whites in two batches.
4 Spoon mousse mixture into serving dishes; refrigerate 3 hours or overnight.
nutritional count per serving 34.8g total fat (21.4g saturated fat); 1777kJ (425 cal); 22.5g carbohydrate; 6.1g protein; 0.4g fibre
serving ideas top mousse with whipped cream and chocolate curls.

lemon meringue pie

PREP + COOK TIME 1 HOUR 10 MINS (+ REFRIGERATION) • SERVES 10

Use a rolling pin to gently ease the pastry into the flan tin, being careful not to stretch it.

Spread the lemon filling evenly into the cooked and cooled pie shell. A spatula is the best implement to use for this.

Roughen the surface of the lemon filling before you spread the meringue on top. This will help prevent the meringue from shrinking away from the filling as it cooks.

½ cup (75g) cornflour
1 cup (220g) caster sugar
½ cup (125ml) lemon juice
1¼ cups (310ml) water
2 teaspoons finely grated lemon rind
60g unsalted butter, chopped
3 eggs, separated
½ cup (110g) caster sugar, extra

pastry
1½ cups (225g) plain flour
1 tablespoon icing sugar
140g cold butter, chopped
1 egg yolk
2 tablespoons cold water

1 Make pastry.
2 Grease 24cm-round loose-based fluted flan tin. Roll pastry between sheets of baking paper until large enough to line tin. Ease pastry into tin, press into base and side; trim edge. Cover; refrigerate 30 minutes.
3 Preheat oven to 240°C/220°C fan-forced.
4 Place tin on oven tray. Line pastry case with baking paper; fill with dried beans or rice. Bake 15 minutes; remove paper and beans carefully from pie shell. Bake about 10 minutes; cool pie shell, turn oven off.
5 Meanwhile, combine cornflour and sugar in medium saucepan; gradually stir in juice and the water until smooth. Cook, stirring, over high heat, until mixture boils and thickens. Reduce heat; simmer, stirring, 1 minute. Remove from heat; stir in rind, butter and egg yolks. Cool 10 minutes.
6 Spread filling into pie shell. Cover; refrigerate 2 hours.
7 Preheat oven to 240°C/220°C fan-forced.
8 Beat egg whites in small bowl with electric mixer until soft peaks form; gradually add extra sugar, beating until sugar dissolves.
9 Roughen surface of filling with fork before spreading with meringue mixture. Bake about 2 minutes or until browned lightly.

pastry Process flour, icing sugar and butter until crumbly. Add egg yolk and the water; process until ingredients come together. Knead dough on floured surface until smooth. Cover; refrigerate 30 minutes.

nutritional count per serving 18.9g total fat (11.6g saturated fat); 1772kJ (424 cal); 57.7g carbohydrate; 5g protein; 0.9g fibre

SPECIAL FEATURE

Tropical fruit

Tropical fruit are considered by many to be the closest thing to heaven that food can provide. All tropical fruits are at their best served ripe and just as they are – it seems a sacrilege to mess about with perfection.

RAMBUTAN
A relative of the lychee, with similar luscious, perfumed, grape-like flesh. To remove the leathery, tendril-covered shell, break open with a fingernail and peel like an egg.

GOLDEN BANANA
These are small, golden-skinned bananas from Asia. The flesh is sweet and creamy. These bananas are usually sold in bunches in Asian food shops. Do not store in the fridge as the skin will turn black.

STAR FRUIT
Also called carombola and belimbing (a smaller variety). Some ripen to yellow or pinky yellow, most to a yellow-green. Very crisp and juicy, with a mild sweet flavour.

LYCHEE
Its juicy, translucent flesh tastes like a more luscious, perfumed grape. Will keep, unshelled, for weeks in the fridge. Ambrosial alone, in fruit salads or as a touch of delicate sweetness in a duck salad.

JACKFRUIT
A huge fruit containing numerous seeds surrounded by golden, richly flavoured, sharp-sweet flesh. Used in fruit salads, ice-cream, milk drinks and soups. The seeds are edible boiled, then roasted in a pan with a little oil.

DRAGON FRUIT
The fruit of a pitaya cactus. The flesh, eaten raw, is tasty and mildly sweet, a little like the flavour of kiwifruit. Scoop the flesh and seeds out of the chilled fruit with a teaspoon.

Q&A

Many recipes call for green papaya and green mango. Are they a different fruit from the ones we normally see in the greengrocer?

No, the green fruit are simply unripe. They are both used, usually grated, in Thai and Vietnamese salads. Served with a spicy, lime juice-laden dressing, they are refreshing and really delicious. And it's reassuring to know that green papapa and green mango won't give you a stomach ache.

GREEN MANGO
This is the unripe fruit of the mango tree. The flesh is deliciously tart. Used raw in many Asian salads or as a vegetable; it can also be bought pickled or dried.

MANGO
Paradise flavour, texture and fragrance – wonderful alone, in desserts and also with curries. Buy fully coloured but not oversoft, or with a touch of green, then ripen at room temperature.

PAPAYA
The papaya family includes both the yellow-fleshed fruit called pawpaw and the pink-fleshed fruit called papaya. Their mild, sweet flavour is best with a squeeze of lime.

BANANA PASSIONFRUIT
A member of the berry family, this fruit is filled with sweet pulp with small black seeds. It is not as tart as the more common purple variety of passionfruit.

MANGOSTEEN
The shiny, purple-brown skin peels to reveal segments of white flesh whose refreshing, sweet-sour flavour is reminiscent of pineapple. Delicious eaten out of hand, like an orange, or chilled and mixed with other tropical fruits.

DURIAN
Famous as the fruit which "smells like hell and tastes like heaven". One recommendation for enjoying the taste without the smell is to cut the flesh into pieces and soak for a day in coconut milk.

tarte tatin

PREP + COOK TIME 1 HOUR 30 MINS (+ REFRIGERATION) • SERVES 8

Be prepared for a bit of work if you're going to make this sensational dessert. Golden delicious apples are the best apples to use, granny smith the second best.

100g unsalted butter, chopped
6 large apples (1.2kg), peeled, cored, quartered
1 cup (220g) firmly packed brown sugar
2 tablespoons lemon juice

pastry
1 cup (150g) plain flour
2 tablespoons caster sugar
80g cold unsalted butter, chopped
2 tablespoons sour cream

1 Melt butter in large heavy-based frying pan; add apples, sprinkle evenly with sugar and juice. Cook, uncovered, over low heat, about 40 minutes, turning apples as they caramelise.
2 Meanwhile, make pastry.
3 Preheat oven to 200°C/180°C fan-forced.
4 Place apples, rounded-sides down, in 23cm pie dish, packing tightly to ensure there are no gaps; drizzle with 1 tablespoon of the caramel in pan. Reserve remaining caramel.
5 Roll pastry between sheets of baking paper until large enough to cover apples. Peel away one sheet of baking paper; cut pastry to fit dish. Remove remaining paper. Place pastry carefully over hot apples; tuck pastry around apples.
6 Bake tarte tatin about 30 minutes or until pastry is browned. Carefully turn onto serving plate, apple-side up; drizzle apple with reheated reserved caramel.
pastry Process flour, sugar, butter and sour cream until ingredients just come together. Knead on floured surface until smooth. Cover; refrigerate 30 minutes.
nutritional count per serving 21.1g total fat (13.7g saturated fat); 1860kJ (445 cal); 59.5g carbohydrate; 2.7g protein; 2.9g fibre

Place the caramelised apples, rounded-side down, in the pie dish. Remember, this is an upside-down pie, so be careful to arrange the apples in a decorative pattern.

Cut the pastry round to fit snugly into the pie dish and place it over the hot apples.

Tuck the pastry carefully and evenly down the sides of the dish – this will form the pastry base when the pie is inverted.

Turn the pie out onto the serving plate, apple-side up and drizzle the tart with the reheated reserved caramel.

classic trifle

PREP + COOK TIME 40 MINS (+ REFRIGERATION) • SERVES 8

85g packet raspberry jelly crystals
250g sponge cake, cut into 3cm pieces
¼ cup (60ml) sweet sherry
¼ cup (30g) custard powder
¼ cup (55g) caster sugar
½ teaspoon vanilla extract
1½ cups (375ml) milk
825g can sliced peaches, drained
300ml thickened cream
2 tablespoons flaked almonds, roasted

1 Make jelly according to directions on packet; pour into shallow container. Refrigerate 20 minutes or until jelly is almost set.
2 Arrange cake in 3-litre (12-cup) bowl; sprinkle with sherry.
3 Blend custard powder, sugar and extract with a little of the milk in small saucepan; stir in remaining milk. Stir over heat until mixture boils and thickens. Cover surface with plastic wrap; cool.
4 Pour jelly over cake; refrigerate 15 minutes. Top with peaches. Stir a third of the cream into custard; pour over peaches.
5 Whip remaining cream; spread over custard, sprinkle with nuts. Refrigerate 3 hours or overnight.

nutritional count per serving 19.7g total fat (10.9g saturated fat); 1689kJ (404 cal); 47g carbohydrate; 7.1g protein; 1.6g fibre

plum clafoutis

PREP + COOK TIME 1 HOUR 10 MINS (+ COOLING) • SERVES 6

This is a rustic dessert from the Limousin region of central France; in the local dialect it translates as "brimming over". It is usually made in the cherry season, when a baking dish is filled with the ripe fruit and a sweet batter is poured over and baked. Other stone fruits or plumped prunes can be used instead of cherries. We have used plums in this recipe but you could use apricots, peeled peaches or caramelised apple instead.

10 small plums (750g), halved, seeded
1 cinnamon stick, halved
¼ cup (60ml) water
¼ cup (55g) brown sugar
⅔ cup (160ml) milk
⅔ cup (160ml) cream
1 teaspoon vanilla extract
4 eggs
½ cup (110g) caster sugar
¼ cup (35g) plain flour

1 Preheat oven to 200°C/180°C fan-forced. Grease shallow 2.5-litre (10-cup) ovenproof dish.
2 Place plums in medium baking dish with cinnamon and the water; sprinkle with brown sugar. Cook about 15 minutes or until plums soften.
3 Remove cinnamon from dish and add to medium saucepan with milk, cream and extract; bring to the boil. Cool; remove cinnamon stick.
4 Whisk eggs and caster sugar in medium bowl until light and frothy; whisk in flour then whisk mixture into cream mixture.
5 Place drained plums in shallow ovenproof dish; pour cream mixture over plums. Bake about 30 minutes or until browned lightly. Serve dusted with icing sugar.

nutritional count per serving 16.1g total fat (9.3g saturated fat); 1417kJ (339 cal); 46.2g carbohydrate; 7.1g protein; 2.4g fibre

new york cheesecake

PREP + COOK TIME 1 HOUR 50 MINS (+ REFRIGERATION) • SERVES 12

We've added some orange rind as well as the lemon rind to this famous cheesecake. If you prefer the lemon flavour you can increase the amount of finely grated lemon rind up to 1 tablespoon and leave the orange rind out completely – or add 1 teaspoon vanilla extract instead of the orange rind, for that lovely lemon/vanilla combination.

250g plain sweet biscuits
125g butter, melted
750g cream cheese, softened
2 teaspoons finely grated orange rind
1 teaspoon finely grated lemon rind
1 cup (220g) caster sugar
3 eggs
¾ cup (180g) sour cream
¼ cup (60ml) lemon juice

sour cream topping
1 cup (240g) sour cream
2 tablespoons caster sugar
2 teaspoons lemon juice

1 Process biscuits until fine. Add butter, process until combined. Press mixture over base and side of 24cm springform tin; place on oven tray. Refrigerate 30 minutes.
2 Preheat oven to 180°C/160°C fan-forced.
3 Beat cheese, rinds and sugar in medium bowl with electric mixer until smooth. Beat in eggs, one at a time, then cream and juice. Pour filling into tin.
4 Bake cheesecake 1¼ hours. Remove from oven; cool 15 minutes.
5 Make sour cream topping by combining ingredients in small bowl; spread topping over cheesecake.
6 Bake cheesecake 20 minutes; cool in oven with door ajar. Refrigerate 3 hours or overnight.
nutritional count per serving 39.3g total fat (24.4g saturated fat); 2270kJ (543 cal); 38.9g carbohydrate; 9.2g protein; 0.4g fibre

apple crumble

PREP + COOK TIME 50 MINS • SERVES 4

5 large apples (1kg)
¼ cup (55g) caster sugar
¼ cup (60ml) water

crumble
½ cup (75g) self-raising flour
¼ cup (35g) plain flour
½ cup (110g) firmly packed brown sugar
100g cold butter, chopped
1 teaspoon ground cinnamon

1 Preheat oven to 180°C/160°C fan-forced. Grease deep 1.5-litre (6-cup) baking dish.
2 Peel, core and quarter apples. Cook apples, sugar and the water in large saucepan over low heat, covered, about 10 minutes. Drain; discard liquid.
3 Meanwhile, make crumble.
4 Place apples in dish; sprinkle with crumble. Bake about 25 minutes.
crumble Blend or process ingredients until combined.
nutritional count per serving 21g total fat (13.6g saturated fat); 2245kJ (537 cal); 80.7g carbohydrate; 3.6g protein; 4.5g fibre

summer pudding

PREP + COOK TIME 35 MINS (+ REFRIGERATION) • SERVES 6

Mix and match the berries and the jam to suit your tastes. You can use fresh berries instead of frozen, if you like. A combination of fresh and frozen is good too.

⅓ cup (75g) caster sugar
½ cup (125ml) water
2 cups (300g) frozen blackberries
3⅓ cups (500g) frozen mixed berries
10 thick slices stale white bread (760g)
¼ cup (80g) blackberry jam

1 Bring sugar and the water in medium saucepan to the boil. Stir in berries; return to the boil. Reduce heat; simmer, uncovered, until berries soften. Strain over medium bowl; reserve syrup and berries separately.

2 Line 1.25-litre (5-cup) pudding bowl with plastic wrap, extending wrap 10cm over side of bowl. Remove crusts from bread. Place two slices of bread on top of each other, then cut into a rounded wedge shape (see step pic 2, below); repeat with another two slices of bread. Cut a round from another slice of bread to fit the base of the bowl. Cut remaining bread into 10cm long strips.

3 Place small bread round in base of bowl; use bread strips to line side of bowl.

4 Pour ⅔ cup of the reserved syrup into small jug; reserve. Fill pudding bowl with berries; cover with remaining syrup, top with rounded wedge shapes. Cover pudding with overhanging plastic wrap, weight pudding with saucer; refrigerate 3 hours or overnight.

5 Stir jam and 2 tablespoons of the reserved syrup in small saucepan until heated through. Turn pudding onto serving plate; brush with remaining reserved syrup then jam mixture. Serve with extra fresh berries and whipped cream.

nutritional count per serving 3.5g total fat (0.5g saturated fat); 1856kJ (444 cal); 84.6g carbohydrate; 12.8g protein; 8.9g fibre

Line the pudding basin with plastic wrap to make it easier to remove the pudding from the basin and to help keep its shape.

Line the bottom and sides of the basin with bread slices, overlapping slightly and making sure there are no gaps for the filling to ooze out.

Fill the bread-lined basin with fruit and pour the syrup over it. Top with bread slices until completely covered.

Cover the pudding with a saucer that will fit inside the pudding basin and place weights (tins of food are good) on top. This compresses the pudding.

bread and butter pudding

PREP + COOK TIME 1 HOUR 15 MINS • SERVES 6

Change the bread in this classic dish for something different – good-quality fruit loaf, croissants or panettone. You can also add chunks of chocolate to the mixture, any dried fruit you like, or even jam. Try using brown instead of white sugar, or replacing some of the sugar with maple syrup, honey or golden syrup. For a richer pudding you might also substitute cream or coconut cream for some of the milk – the variations are endless.

6 slices white bread (270g)
40g butter, softened
½ cup (80g) sultanas
¼ teaspoon ground nutmeg

custard
1½ cups (375ml) milk
2 cups (500ml) cream
⅓ cup (75g) caster sugar
1 teaspoon vanilla extract
4 eggs

1 Preheat oven to 160°C/140°C fan-forced. Grease shallow 2-litre (8-cup) ovenproof dish.
2 Make custard.
3 Trim crusts from bread. Spread each slice with butter; cut into four triangles. Layer bread, overlapping, in dish; sprinkle with sultanas. Pour custard over bread; sprinkle with nutmeg.
4 Place ovenproof dish in large baking dish; add enough boiling water to come halfway up side of ovenproof dish.
5 Bake pudding about 45 minutes or until set. Remove pudding from baking dish; stand 5 minutes before serving. Serve dusted with sifted icing sugar, if you like.
custard Combine milk, cream, sugar and extract in medium saucepan; bring to the boil. Whisk eggs in large bowl; whisking constantly, gradually add hot milk mixture to egg mixture.

nutritional count per serving 48.6g total fat (30.4g saturated fat); 2859kJ (684 cal); 49.3g carbohydrate; 12.4g protein; 1.8g fibre

lemon delicious puddings

PREP + COOK TIME 1 HOUR • SERVES 6

This is the all-time best lemon delicious pudding. It needs to be served straight from the oven or the pudding will sink and absorb all the sauce.

125g butter, melted
2 teaspoons finely grated lemon rind
1½ cups (330g) caster sugar
3 eggs, separated
½ cup (75g) self-raising flour
⅓ cup (80ml) lemon juice
1⅓ cups (330ml) milk

1 Preheat oven to 180°C/160°C fan-forced. Grease six 1-cup (250ml) ovenproof dishes; place in large baking dish.
2 Combine butter, rind, sugar and yolks in large bowl. Whisk in sifted flour then juice. Gradually whisk in milk; mixture should be smooth and runny.
3 Beat egg whites in small bowl with electric mixer until soft peaks form; fold into lemon mixture in two batches.
4 Divide lemon mixture among dishes. Add enough boiling water to baking dish to come halfway up side of ovenproof dishes. Bake about 30 minutes or until puddings have risen and are a light golden colour.

nutritional count per serving 22g total fat (13.5g saturated fat); 2069kJ (495 cal); 67.1g carbohydrate; 6.7g protein; 0.5g fibre

[1] bread and butter pudding
[2] lemon delicious pudding
[3] marshmallow pavlova [page 526]
[4] tiramisu [page 526]

1

2

3

4

marshmallow pavlova

PREP + COOK TIME 1 HOUR 50 MINS (+ COOLING) • SERVES 8

4 egg whites
1 cup (220g) caster sugar
½ teaspoon vanilla extract
¾ teaspoon white vinegar

300ml thickened cream, whipped
250g strawberries, halved
¼ cup (60ml) passionfruit pulp

1 Preheat oven to 120°C/100°C fan-forced. Line oven tray with foil; grease foil, dust with cornflour, shake away excess. Mark 18cm-circle on foil.
2 Beat egg whites in small bowl with electric mixer until soft peaks form; gradually add sugar, beating until sugar dissolves. Beat in extract and vinegar until combined.
3 Spread meringue into circle on foil, building up at the side to 8cm in height. Smooth side and top of pavlova gently. Using spatula blade, mark decorative grooves around side of pavlova; smooth top again.
4 Bake pavlova about 1½ hours. Turn oven off; cool pavlova in oven with door ajar.
5 Cut around top edge of pavlova (the crisp meringue top will fall on top of the marshmallow centre). Top with whipped cream, strawberries and passionfruit.

nutritional count per serving 14g total fat (9.2g saturated fat); 1095kJ (262 cal); 30g carbohydrate; 3.3g protein; 1.7g fibre

tiramisu

PREP TIME 30 MINS (+ REFRIGERATION) • SERVES 8

People are often confused about whether to regard mascarpone as a cheese or a thick cream. It is, in fact, a fresh triple-cream cheese originating in Italy's Lombardy region, and probably first became known to us when tiramisu was the dessert du jour in the mid-1980s.

Like most wonderful things, there is no real substitute for mascarpone, but some recipes can be adapted to use soft cream cheese, sour cream or ricotta – or blends of all three.

2 tablespoons ground espresso coffee
1 cup (250ml) boiling water
½ cup (125ml) marsala
250g packet sponge finger biscuits
300ml thickened cream

¼ cup (40g) icing sugar
2 cups (500g) mascarpone cheese
2 tablespoons marsala, extra
2 teaspoons cocoa powder

1 Combine coffee and the water in coffee plunger; stand 2 minutes before plunging. Combine coffee mixture and marsala in medium heatproof bowl; cool 10 minutes.
2 Place half the biscuits, in single layer, over base of deep 2-litre (8-cup) dish; drizzle with half the coffee mixture.
3 Beat cream and sifted icing sugar in small bowl until soft peaks form; transfer to large bowl. Fold in combined mascarpone cheese and extra marsala.
4 Spread half the cream mixture over biscuits in dish. Submerge the remaining biscuits, one at a time, in coffee mixture, taking care the biscuits do not become so soggy that they fall apart; place over cream layer. Top biscuit layer with the remaining cream mixture. Cover; refrigerate 3 hours or overnight.
5 Serve tiramisu dusted with sifted cocoa.

nutritional count per serving 45g total fat (29.9g saturated fat); 2391kJ (572 cal); 25.8g carbohydrate; 6.5g protein; 0.5g fibre

sticky date pudding

PREP + COOK TIME 1 HOUR 10 MINS (+ STANDING) • SERVES 6

Both the pudding and sauce can be made a day ahead and stored, separately, covered, in the fridge. You can freeze the pudding for up to 3 months. Defrost and warm in a microwave oven while making the butterscotch sauce. Or, freeze wedges of the pudding, thaw in a microwave oven for about 30 seconds – an instant dessert to have with cream or ice-cream, with or without the sauce.

1¼ cups (200g) seeded dried dates
1¼ cups (310ml) boiling water
1 teaspoon bicarbonate of soda
50g butter, chopped
½ cup (100g) firmly packed brown sugar
2 eggs, beaten lightly
1 cup (150g) self-raising flour

butterscotch sauce
¾ cup (150g) firmly packed brown sugar
300ml cream
80g butter

1 Preheat oven to 180°C/160°C fan-forced. Grease deep 20cm-round cake pan; line base and side with baking paper.
2 Combine dates and the water in medium heatproof bowl. Stir in soda; stand 5 minutes.
3 Blend or process date mixture with butter and sugar until pureed. Add eggs and flour; blend or process until just combined. Pour mixture into pan.
4 Bake cake about 1 hour. Stand in pan 10 minutes; turn onto serving plate
5 Meanwhile, make butterscotch sauce.
6 Serve cake warm with butterscotch sauce.
butterscotch sauce Stir ingredients in medium saucepan over low heat until smooth.
nutritional count per serving 41.5g total fat (26.6g saturated fat); 3068kJ (734 cal); 82g carbohydrate; 6.5g protein; 4.2g fibre

Q&A

Why is it that every time I make a pavlova the results are different?

There are many factors that contribute to the success, or perceived failure, of the perfect pav. There are huge variations in the egg whites themselves and then there's the weather which affects the sugar in the pavlova. As soon as the weather becomes wet or humid, the sugar absorbs the extra moisture in the air and your pav becomes weepy. The best you can do is to follow a good recipe – make sure every grain of sugar is dissolved, bake the pavs carefully and thoroughly, and resign youself to the idea that every pav you make will be slightly different – and still edible, no matter what happens.

CAKES

Cakes

There is something incredibly heartening about the smell of a freshly baked cake. And eating it, perhaps still slightly warm, is one of life's unequivocal pleasures. In this chapter, we've assembled recipes for all the classic and impressive cakes you need to have in your repertoire.

THE BASICS

Take cold ingredients out of the fridge ahead of cooking so they have time to come to room temperature for cooking.

Follow recipes closely and always use the size and shape of cake pan as directed by the recipe: using a different size or shape requires a different oven temperature or baking time.

To grease a pan either spray it with a light, even coating of cooking-oil or brush melted butter lightly over the base and side(s). If a recipe calls for a greased and floured pan: brush the pan with melted butter and let it set for a minute before sprinkling a little flour evenly over the surface. Tap it to remove any excess flour.

Cakes that are high in sugar or contain golden syrup or treacle tend to stick to the pan; we recommend lining the pan with baking paper.

Spoon and cup measurements should be levelled off with a knife or spatula. Be fussy about levelling spoons when measuring ingredients like honey: more is not better in this case.

As a rule, we don't mix cakes in a food processor: use an electric mixer to mix the cake then a spatula or spoon to work in the other ingredients.

COOLING

Once cooked, stand the cake in its pan for 5 to 10 minutes. Turn the cake onto a wire rack to cool: the easiest way to do this is to hold the cake pan firmly and shake it, gently, to loosen the cake. Turn the cake upside down onto a wire rack, then turn the cake top-side up immediately using a second rack. Fruit cakes are the exception to this cooling process. Fruit cakes should be covered with foil and left to cool completely in the pan.

STORING

- Most cakes keep well for 2 to 3 days depending on the climate and type of cake. Generally, the higher the sugar content, the longer the cake will keep.
- The cake needs to be at room temperature before placing in an airtight container.
- Most cakes will freeze well: unfilled and uniced is best. Wrap or seal in plastic wrap or a freezer bag.
- Thaw a whole cake overnight in the refrigerator; slices of frozen cake need only 10 or 15 minutes at room temperature.

TYPES OF CAKES

BUTTER CAKES

Butter cakes are also called pound cakes – a term derived from the traditional balance of the main ingredients: a 'pound' each of butter, eggs, flour and sugar.
• When combining the dry ingredients and the liquid, be careful: there is a tendency to overmix and this will toughen the mixture. Add half the dry ingredients and half the liquid then beat on low speed until just combined. Add the remaining ingredients, beating on low speed until just combined, then increase the speed beating for about 30 seconds, until mixture is smooth.

HOW DO YOU TEST IF A BUTTER CAKE IS COOKED?
Take the cake out of the oven, push a skewer gently through the thickest part of the cake to the bottom of the pan. Pull the skewer out slowly: if the skewer is clean the cake is done: if the skewer has uncooked mixture on it, cook the cake further. For cupcakes: you can usually tell if they're cooked through simply by looking at them and touching them. If in doubt, use a skewer as you would a butter cake.

CHOCOLATE CAKES

The secret to a great chocolate cake lies in the quality of the chocolate you use. The better quality the chocolate, the better the results. The more bitter the chocolate, the higher the content of cocoa solids and more intense the chocolate flavour.
In most of our recipes, like the mud cake in this chapter, we recommend using good quality eating chocolate. Generally, try to avoid anything labelled compound chocolate (the cheaper chocolates) in which some of the cocoa butter is replaced with other vegetable fats such as palm, coconut or soya oil. Exceptions to this rule are when the recipe calls for chocolate melts or choc bits: these are sometimes specified for particular recipes because they keep their shape when baked.

HOW DO YOU TEST IF A CHOCOLATE CAKE IS COOKED?
Use the same method as for butter cakes above.

SPONGE CAKES

• Most recipes insist on triple-sifting the dry ingredients, to aerate the flour as much as possible.
• Use an electric mixer to beat the eggs. Start beating at a low speed and, as they thicken, increase to moderately high.
• When adding the sugar, add it a tablespoon at a time: keep the mixer beating until the grains dissolve after each addition and continue until all the sugar is used.
• The best way to fold in the dry ingredients of a sponge mixture is to use your hands: with fingers splayed like a rake, drag the flour up through the egg mixture, wiping the side of your hand around the edge of the bowl. You can also use a metal spoon, or a plastic or rubber spatula.
• A deep-sided cake pan gives the best results for a sponge – the high side(s) protect it from developing a crisp crust.

HOW DO YOU TEST IF A SPONGE IS COOKED?
Assess a sponge cake by its appearance and feel – piercing with a skewer will deflate it. Toward the end of baking time, open the oven gently: it should be well-risen, browned and not shrunken from the side of the pan. Feel the top of the cake – it should be slightly springy. Turn sponges out immediately as they continue to cook and dry out if left in the pan. Turn onto a wire rack, then quickly turn the right way up to prevent the wire racks from indenting the surface.

FRUIT CAKES

• Be guided by the recipe's cooking time, but check every half hour or so – it might need turning.
• Once you think your cake is cooked, feel the top with your fingers: there should be a feeling of a firm crust.

HOW DO YOU TEST IF YOUR FRUIT CAKE IS COOKED?
Rich fruit cakes are best tested using the blade of a sharp, pointed knife. The blade gives you a larger area to see and feel what's going on inside the cake. Push the knife into the centre of the cake and look at the blade: if it has uncooked mixture on it, continue baking; if the blade is shiny and feels clean, the cake is done.

SPECIAL FEATURE

Preparing cake pans

It's important to grease, flour and line your cake pans with care. It would be a sad thing to have gone to the trouble of making a wonderful cake only to have it break into pieces when you try to remove it from the pan.

GREASING WITH COOKING-OIL SPRAY
Hold the cake pan up with the base vertical, then spray lightly with cooking-oil spray, evenly coating the base and side(s). Ideally, do this by an outside door to avoid oil falling onto kitchen fittings.

GREASING WITH BUTTER
Melt butter and, with a pastry brush, brush it evenly over base and sides of pan. If butter collects in corners or where sides meet base, go back and dab with brush to even it out, or use your fingers.

FLOURING A PAN (1)
First grease the pan with cooking-oil spray or butter, as described previously, then sprinkle lightly but evenly with a little flour, tilting pan to flour side evenly too.

LINING A ROUND PAN (1)
Place round cake pan on baking paper (close to the edge to minimise waste) and trace around it with a pencil.

LINING A ROUND PAN (2)
Cut out the circle you have traced, cutting just inside the pencil line to allow for the thickness of the pan so it will fit the inside base exactly.

LINING A ROUND PAN (3)
Cut a strip of baking (or greaseproof) paper so that it's long enough to go round the pan with a little overlap, is wide enough to allow for a 2cm turn-up, and extends 5cm above the rim of the pan.

Q&A

if you're using baking paper to line a cake pan, do you have to grease the paper?

No. In fact you don't really need to grease the pan when you're using baking paper. The only reason you do it is to make the baking paper stick to the pan so you can smooth it out evenly.

FLOURING A PAN (2)
After flouring, hold pan upside down and tap firmly to shake out excess flour. This ensures that the cake browns evenly and there is no flour 'band' around the base of cake after baking.

LINING A RECTANGULAR OR SQUARE PAN
Mark width of pan on baking paper, and cut a strip of this width, long enough to line pan end-to-end with overhang. Mark length and cut another strip to line side-to-side with some overhang. Place strips in pan, overlapping.

LINING A LAMINGTON OR BAR PAN
Mark pan width on baking paper, and cut a strip of this width, long enough to line pan end-to-end and extend over. Place in pan with equal overhang at each end, smoothing to fit.

LINING A ROUND PAN (4)
Fold over long side of paper about 2cm from the edge, run a finger along to make a crease; open out and use scissors to make diagonal cuts, about 2cm apart, across the folded strip from edge to crease.

LINING A ROUND PAN (5)
Place paper around inside of pan, with the snipped edge flat on the base, securing it to the side or base, as needed, with melted butter or cooking-oil spray.

LINING A ROUND PAN (6)
Place the cut-out circle of paper into the pan and smooth it out, covering the snipped edges of the side lining, to fit neatly.

lemon syrup cake

PREP + COOK TIME 50 MINS • SERVES 10

Lemon syrup cake is probably the most well-known and popular of all. We love this recipe for its tangy taste and velvety texture.

125g butter, softened
3 teaspoons finely grated lemon rind
⅔ cup (150g) caster sugar
2 eggs
⅔ cup (160ml) buttermilk
2 tablespoons lemon juice
1½ cups (225g) self-raising flour

lemon syrup
⅓ cup (80ml) lemon juice
¼ cup (60ml) water
¾ cup (165g) caster sugar

1 Preheat oven to 180°C/160°C fan-forced. Grease 23cm baba pan or deep 22cm-round cake pan.
2 Beat butter, rind and sugar in small bowl with electric mixer until light and fluffy. Beat in eggs, one at a time. Transfer mixture to large bowl; fold in buttermilk, lemon juice and sifted flour, in two batches. Spread mixture into pan.
3 Bake cake about 30 minutes if using baba pan or about 40 minutes if using round pan. Stand cake 5 minutes; turn onto wire rack set over tray.
4 Meanwhile, make lemon syrup. Pour hot syrup over hot cake; serve warm.
lemon syrup Stir ingredients in small saucepan over heat, without boiling, until sugar dissolves. Simmer, uncovered, without stirring, 5 minutes.
nutritional count per serving 11.9g total fat (7.3g saturated fat); 1350kJ (323 cal); 48.8g carbohydrate; 4.4g protein; 0.9g fibre

A baba pan has a pretty fluted base, which becomes the top of the cake. Grease it well with softened butter.

Beat the butter, lemon rind and sugar in a small bowl with an electric mixer until it is light and fluffy.

Place the warm cake and wire rack on an oven tray (to catch the drips) then pour the hot syrup over it. Serve warm.

hummingbird cake

PREP + COOK TIME 1 HOUR 10 MINS • SERVES 12

This cake will keep for several days in an airtight container.

450g can crushed pineapple in syrup
1 cup (150g) plain flour
½ cup (75g) self-raising flour
½ teaspoon bicarbonate of soda
½ teaspoon ground cinnamon
½ teaspoon ground ginger
1 cup (200g) firmly packed brown sugar
½ cup (45g) desiccated coconut
1 cup mashed banana
2 eggs, beaten lightly
¾ cup (180ml) vegetable oil

cream cheese frosting
30g butter, softened
60g cream cheese, softened
1 teaspoon vanilla extract
1½ cups (240g) icing sugar

TIPS
• You need about 2 large overripe bananas (460g) for this recipe.

1 Preheat oven to 180°C/160°C fan-forced. Grease deep 23cm-square cake pan, line base with baking paper.
2 Drain pineapple over medium bowl, pressing with spoon to extract as much syrup as possible. Reserve ¼ cup (60ml) syrup.
3 Sift flours, soda, spices and sugar into large bowl. Using wooden spoon, stir in drained pineapple, reserved syrup, coconut, banana, egg and oil; pour into pan.
4 Bake cake about 40 minutes. Stand in pan 5 minutes; turn, top-side up, on wire rack to cool.
5 Meanwhile, make cream cheese frosting. Spread cold cake with frosting.
cream cheese frosting Beat butter, cream cheese and extract in small bowl with electric mixer until light and fluffy; gradually beat in icing sugar.
nutritional count per serving 21.1g total fat (6.6g saturated fat); 1881kJ (450 cal); 59.5g carbohydrate; 4.5g protein; 2.2g fibre

Tell me about hummingbird cake. Where did it come from?

Hummingbird cake is rich and sweet. Its first known sighting was in the 1970s in a magazine published in the southern United States. The cake is made from pineapple, bananas, spices and coconut and usually comes thickly iced with cream cheese frosting. It's the perfect cake to serve at parties or large gatherings because a little goes a long way.

moist chocolate cake

PREP + COOK TIME 1 HOUR 10 MINS (+ COOLING) • SERVES 20

3 cups (660g) caster sugar
250g butter, chopped
2 cups (500ml) water
⅓ cup (35g) cocoa powder
1 teaspoon bicarbonate of soda
3 cups (450g) self-raising flour
4 eggs

fudge frosting
90g butter
½ cup (110g) caster sugar
⅓ cup (80ml) water
1½ cups (240g) icing sugar
⅓ cup (35g) cocoa powder

1 Preheat oven to 180°C/160°C fan-forced. Grease deep 26.5cm x 33cm (3.5-litre/14-cup) baking dish; line base with baking paper.
2 Stir sugar, butter, the water and sifted cocoa and soda in medium saucepan over heat, without boiling, until sugar dissolves; bring to the boil. Reduce heat; simmer, uncovered, 5 minutes. Transfer mixture to large bowl; cool to room temperature.
3 Add flour and eggs to bowl; beat with electric mixer until mixture is smooth and pale in colour. Pour mixture into pan.
4 Bake cake about 50 minutes. Stand in pan 10 minutes; turn, top-side up, onto wire rack to cool.
5 Meanwhile, make fudge frosting. Spread cold cake with frosting.

fudge frosting Stir butter, caster sugar and the water in small saucepan over low heat, without boiling, until sugar dissolves. Sift icing sugar and cocoa into small bowl then gradually stir in hot butter mixture. Cover; refrigerate about 20 minutes or until frosting thickens. Beat with wooden spoon until spreadable.

nutritional count per serving 15.8g total fat (9.8g saturated fat); 1806kJ (432 cal); 67.3g carbohydrate; 4.3g protein; 1g fibre

Q&A

I know flourless chocolate cakes are extremely moist and I love them, but they're very expensive. Is there a recipe for a moist chocolate cake that won't cost me a fortune?

This moist chocolate cake is an excellent family cake. The mixture is boiled before it is baked, which gives the cake a lovely dense texture. And it's not all that expensive to make, using cocoa instead of chocolate.

orange cake

PREP + COOK TIME 50 MINS • SERVES 12

When making any cake by the quick-mix, one-bowl method, you should start by having the butter, eggs and milk at room temperature. You might also like to bake this cake in a loaf pan; line the pan base and bake the cake about 50 minutes.

150g butter, softened
1 tablespoon finely grated orange rind
⅔ cup (150g) caster sugar
3 eggs
1½ cups (225g) self-raising flour
¼ cup (60ml) milk
¾ cup (120g) icing sugar
1½ tablespoons orange juice

1 Preheat oven to 180°C/160°C fan-forced. Grease deep 20cm-round cake pan.
2 Beat butter, rind, caster sugar, eggs, flour and milk in medium bowl with electric mixer at low speed until just combined. Increase speed to medium, beat about 3 minutes or until mixture is smooth.
3 Spread mixture into pan; bake about 40 minutes. Stand cake 5 minutes; turn, top-side up, onto wire rack to cool.
4 Combine sifted icing sugar and juice in small bowl; spread over cake.
nutritional count per serving 12g total fat (7.3g saturated fat); 1129kJ (270 cal); 36.3g carbohydrate; 3.8g protein; 0.7g fibre

boiled fruit cake

PREP + COOK TIME 1 HOUR 45 MINS (+ COOLING) • SERVES 12

Cover the cake loosely with foil during baking if it starts to overbrown; and give the cake quarter turns several times during baking if it is browning unevenly. This cake can be made up to 3 months ahead. Store in an airtight container in a cool, dry place, or refrigerate if the weather is humid.

2¾ cups (500g) mixed dried fruit
½ cup (125ml) water
1 cup (220g) firmly packed brown sugar
125g butter, chopped
1 teaspoon mixed spice
½ teaspoon bicarbonate of soda
½ cup (125ml) sweet sherry
1 egg
1 cup (150g) plain flour
1 cup (150g) self-raising flour
⅓ cup (55g) blanched almonds
2 tablespoons sweet sherry, extra

1 Combine fruit, the water, sugar, butter, spice and soda in large saucepan. Stir over low heat, without boiling, until sugar dissolves and butter melts; bring to the boil. Reduce heat; simmer, covered, 5 minutes. Remove from heat; stir in sherry. Cool to room temperature.
2 Preheat oven to 160°C/140°C fan-forced. Grease deep 20cm-round cake pan; line base and side with two layers of baking paper, extending paper 5cm above side.
3 Stir egg and sifted flours into fruit mixture. Spread mixture into pan; decorate with almonds. Bake about 1½ hours. Brush top of hot cake with extra sherry. Cover cake with foil, cool in pan.
nutritional count per serving 12.2g total fat (6.1g saturated fat); 1718kJ (411 cal); 64.6g carbohydrate; 5g protein; 3.7g fibre

[1] orange cake
[2] boiled fruit cake
[3] genoise sponge [page 540]
[4] mississippi mud cake [page 540]

1

2

3

4

genoise sponge

PREP + COOK TIME 1 HOUR • SERVES 8

This classic sponge relies totally on the air incorporated into the egg mixture for its raising. It's correct that the recipe uses plain flour, so, beat the egg mixture well, and fold the flour in gently.

4 eggs
½ cup (110g) caster sugar
⅔ cup (100g) plain flour
60g butter, melted, cooled
300ml thickened cream
1 tablespoon icing sugar
¼ cup (80g) strawberry jam, warmed
500g strawberries, sliced thinly
1 tablespoon icing sugar, extra

1 Preheat oven to 180°C/160°C fan-forced. Grease deep 20cm-round cake pan; line base with baking paper.

2 Combine eggs and sugar in large heatproof bowl, place over saucepan of simmering water (do not allow water to touch base of bowl); beat with electric mixer about 10 minutes or until mixture is thick and creamy. Remove bowl from saucepan; beat mixture until it returns to room temperature.

3 Sift half the flour over egg mixture; carefully fold in flour. Sift remaining flour into bowl, fold into mixture. Working quickly, fold in melted butter.

4 Pour mixture into pan; bake about 20 minutes. Turn immediately, top-side up, onto baking-paper-covered wire rack to cool.

5 Beat cream and sifted icing sugar in small bowl with electric mixer until soft peaks form. Split sponge in half; place one half, cut-side up, on serving plate. Spread with jam and cream; top with strawberries, then remaining sponge. Decorate cake with extra sifted icing sugar, and strawberries, if you like.

nutritional count per serving 22.9g total fat (14g saturated fat); 1572kJ (376 cal); 35.1g carbohydrate; 6.6g protein; 2g fibre

mississippi mud cake

PREP + COOK TIME 1 HOUR 45 MINS (+ COOLING & STANDING) • SERVES 16

250g butter, chopped
150g dark eating chocolate, chopped coursely
2 cups (440g) caster sugar
1 cup (250ml) hot water
⅓ cup (80ml) coffee liqueur
1 tablespoon instant coffee granules
1½ cups (225g) plain flour
¼ cup (35g) self-raising flour
¼ cup (25g) cocoa powder
2 eggs, beaten lightly

dark chocolate ganache
½ cup (125ml) cream
200g dark eating chocolate, chopped coarsely

1 Preheat oven to 160°C/140°C fan-forced. Grease deep 20cm-round cake pan; line base and side with baking paper.
2 Combine butter, chocolate, sugar, the water, liqueur and coffee granules in medium saucepan. Using wooden spoon, stir over low heat until chocolate melts.
3 Transfer mixture to large bowl; cool 15 minutes. Whisk in combined sifted flours and cocoa, then egg. Pour mixture into prepared pan.
4 Bake cake about 1½ hours. Stand cake in pan 30 minutes before turning, top-side up, onto wire rack to cool.
5 Meanwhile, make dark chocolate ganache; spread over top of cake.
dark chocolate ganache Bring cream to the boil in small saucepan. Pour hot cream over chocolate in medium heatproof bowl; stir until smooth. Stand at room temperature until spreadable.
nutritional count per serving 23.7g total fat (14.9g saturated fat); 1910kJ (457 cal); 53.6g carbohydrate; 4.3g protein; 1g fibre

flourless chocolate and almond torte

PREP + COOK TIME
1 HOUR 15 MINS
(+ COOLING & STANDING)
SERVES 14

160g dark eating chocolate, chopped
160g unsalted butter, chopped
5 eggs, separated
¾ cup (165g) caster sugar
1 cup (120g) ground almonds
⅔ cup (50g) flaked almonds, roasted, chopped coarsely

⅓ cup (35g) coarsely grated dark eating chocolate
1 cup (150g) vienna almonds
dark chocolate ganache
125g dark eating chocolate, chopped
⅓ cup (80ml) thickened cream

Flourless (making this recipe gluten-free) cakes have a delightful texture and are now very popular in restaurants. They are simple to make, we're not sure why more home-cooks don't make them. Serve slim wedges of cake with whipped cream and some berries of your choice.

1 Preheat oven to 180°C/160°C fan-forced. Grease deep 22cm-round cake pan; line the base and side with two layers of baking paper.
2 Stir chopped chocolate and butter in small saucepan over low heat until smooth; cool to room temperature.
3 Beat egg yolks and sugar in small bowl with electric mixer until thick and creamy. Transfer mixture to large bowl; fold in chocolate mixture, ground almonds, flaked almonds and grated chocolate.
4 Beat egg whites in small bowl with electric mixer until soft peaks form; fold into chocolate mixture, in two batches. Pour mixture into pan.
5 Bake cake about 45 minutes. Stand cake in pan 15 minutes before turning, top-side up, onto wire rack to cool.
6 Meanwhile, make dark chocolate ganache.
7 Spread ganache over cake, decorate with vienna almonds; stand 30 minutes before serving.
dark chocolate ganache Stir ingredients in small saucepan over low heat until smooth.
nutritional count per serving 36.9g total fat (13.5g saturated fat); 2103kJ (503 cal); 32.6g carbohydrate; 9.7g protein; 2.9g fibre

date and walnut rolls

PREP + COOK TIME 1 HOUR 10 MINS • SERVES 20

If you can't buy new nut roll tins, look around in some second-hand shops or garage sales, you might be lucky. They will rust if they're not looked after properly, as they're made from tin. You can also make your own nut roll tins from tall 850ml (8cm x 17cm) fruit juice cans. You'll need to remove one end from each can by using a can opener that cuts just below the rims. Wash and dry cans thoroughly before greasing.

60g butter
1 cup (250ml) boiling water
1 cup (180g) finely chopped dried dates
½ teaspoon bicarbonate of soda
1 cup (220g) firmly packed brown sugar
2 cups (300g) self-raising flour
½ cup (60g) coarsely chopped walnuts
1 egg, beaten lightly

1 Preheat oven to 180°C/160°C fan forced. Grease two 8cm x 19cm nut roll tins; line bases with baking paper. Place tins upright on oven tray.
2 Stir butter and the water in medium saucepan over low heat until butter melts. Remove from heat; stir in dates and soda, then remaining ingredients. Spoon mixture into tins; replace lids.
3 Bake rolls about 50 minutes. Stand rolls in tins 5 minutes; remove ends (top and bottom), shake tins gently to release rolls onto wire rack to cool. Serve rolls sliced with butter.

nutritional count per serving 5g total fat (1.9g saturated fat); 702kJ (168 cal); 27.4g carbohydrate; 2.5g protein; 1.6g fibre

TIPS

• It is important that you do not fill nut roll tins with too much mixture. The nut rolls rise surprisingly high; both because the tin is narrow and because the cooking method approximates that of steaming. As a rough guide, the tins should be filled just a little over halfway.

• Some nut roll tins open along the side; be certain these are closed properly before baking.

• Some lids have tiny holes in them to allow steam to escape; make sure these are not used on the bottom of the tins.

Using a pastry brush, grease the nut roll tins generously with very soft butter. Place a round of baking paper inside the top and bottom lids.

Spoon the cake mixture into the tins, filling them to just above halfway.

When the rolls are cooked, remove both top and bottom lids and shake the tins gently to release the rolls. Cool them on a wire rack.

jam roll

PREP + COOK TIME 30 MINS • SERVES 10

Known as a jelly roll in the US, this filled and rolled sponge cake has long been a favourite there and in the UK. Quick and easy to make, yet very impressive-looking, slices of the roll are good served warm or at room temperature with a dollop of whipped cream.

3 eggs, separated
½ cup (110g) caster sugar
2 tablespoons hot milk
¾ cup (110g) self-raising flour
¼ cup (55g) caster sugar, extra
½ cup (160g) jam, warmed

1 Preheat oven to 200°C/180°C fan forced. Grease 25cm x 30cm swiss roll pan; line base with baking paper, extending paper 5cm over short sides.
2 Beat egg whites in small bowl with electric mixer until soft peaks form; add sugar, 1 tablespoon at a time, beating until dissolved between additions. With motor operating, add egg yolks, one at a time, beating until mixture is pale and thick; this will take about 10 minutes.
3 Pour hot milk down side of bowl; add triple-sifted flour. Working quickly, use plastic spatula to fold milk and flour through egg mixture. Pour mixture into pan, gently spreading evenly into corners.
4 Bake cake about 8 minutes.
5 Meanwhile, place a piece of baking paper cut the same size as pan on board or bench; sprinkle evenly with extra sugar.
6 Turn cake immediately onto sugared paper; peel away lining paper. Use serrated knife to trim crisp edges from all sides of cake.
7 Using paper as a guide, gently roll warm cake loosely from one of the short sides. Unroll; spread evenly with jam. Reroll cake from same short side. Cool.

nutritional count per serving 1.9g total fat (0.6g saturated fat); 819kJ (196 cal); 40.5g carbohydrate; 3.3g protein; 0.6g fibre

Place the cake on a piece of sugared baking paper and gently peel away the lining paper, using a spatula to press down on the paper. The weight of the spatula will prevent the sponge from breaking.

Using a serrated knife, trim away the crisp edges from all sides of the cake.

With no filling, and using the sugared baking paper as a guide, gently roll the warm cake loosely. You do this so that once you've spread it with jam, it will roll up easily.

carrot cake with lemon cream cheese frosting

**PREP + COOK TIME
1 HOUR 25 MINS
SERVES 12**

3 eggs
1⅓ cups (250g) firmly packed brown sugar
1 cup (250ml) vegetable oil
3 cups firmly packed, coarsely grated carrot
1 cup (120g) coarsely chopped walnuts
2½ cups (375g) self-raising flour
½ teaspoon bicarbonate of soda
2 teaspoons mixed spice

lemon cream cheese frosting
30g butter, softened
80g cream cheese, softened
1 teaspoon finely grated lemon rind
1½ cups (240g) icing sugar

TIP
• You need about 3 large carrots (540g) for this recipe.

1 Preheat oven to 180°C/160°C fan-forced. Grease deep 22cm-round cake pan; line base with baking paper.
2 Beat eggs, sugar and oil in small bowl with electric mixer until thick and creamy. Transfer mixture to large bowl; stir in carrot and nuts then sifted dry ingredients. Pour mixture into pan.
3 Bake cake about 1¼ hours. Stand in pan 5 minutes; turn, top-side up, onto wire rack to cool.
4 Meanwhile, make lemon cream cheese frosting. Spread cold cake with frosting.
lemon cream cheese frosting Beat butter, cream cheese and rind in small bowl with electric mixer until light and fluffy; gradually beat in icing sugar.
nutritional count per serving 32.1g total fat (6.1g saturated fat); 2416kJ (578 cal); 64.2g carbohydrate; 7g protein; 2.7g fibre

lamingtons

PREP + COOK TIME 1 HOUR • MAKES 16

6 eggs
⅔ cup (150g) caster sugar
⅓ cup (50g) cornflour
½ cup (75g) plain flour
⅓ cup (50g) self-raising flour
2 cups (160g) desiccated coconut

icing
4 cups (640g) icing sugar
½ cup (50g) cocoa powder
15g butter, melted
1 cup (250ml) milk

1 Preheat oven to 180°C/160°C fan-forced. Grease 20cm x 30cm lamington pan; line with baking paper, extending paper 5cm over long sides.
2 Beat eggs in large bowl with electric mixer about 10 minutes or until thick and creamy; gradually beat in sugar, dissolving between additions. Fold in triple-sifted flours. Spread mixture into pan.
3 Bake cake about 35 minutes. Turn cake immediately onto a baking-paper-covered wire rack to cool.
4 Meanwhile, make icing.
5 Cut cake into 16 pieces; dip each square in icing, drain off excess. Toss squares in coconut. Place lamingtons onto wire rack to set.
icing Sift icing sugar and cocoa into medium heatproof bowl; stir in butter and milk. Set bowl over medium saucepan of simmering water; stir until icing is of a coating consistency.

nutritional count per lamington 10.4g total fat (1.8g saturated fat); 1501kJ (359 cal); 59.6g carbohydrate; 5.1g protein; 1.9g fibre

strawberry jelly cakes

PREP + COOK TIME 50 MINS (+ REFRIGERATION) • MAKES 15

These jelly cakes are a popular variation of the traditional lamington. Experiment with other flavoured jellies such as passionfruit, lime, raspberry or cherry.

6 eggs
⅔ cup (150g) caster sugar
⅓ cup (50g) cornflour
½ cup (75g) plain flour
⅓ cup (50g) self-raising flour
80g packet strawberry jelly crystals
2 cups (160g) desiccated coconut
300ml thickened cream, whipped

1 Preheat oven to 180°C/160°C fan-forced. Grease 20cm x 30cm lamington pan; line base and long sides with baking paper, extending paper 5cm over sides.
2 Beat eggs in large bowl with electric mixer about 10 minutes or until thick and creamy; gradually add sugar, beating until dissolved between additions. Triple-sift flours; fold into egg mixture.
3 Spread mixture into pan; bake about 35 minutes. Turn cake immediately onto baking-paper-covered wire rack to cool.
4 Meanwhile, make jelly as per packet instructions; refrigerate until set to the consistency of unbeaten egg white.
5 Trim all sides of cake. Cut cake into 15 squares; dip squares into jelly, drain off excess. Place coconut into medium bowl; toss squares in coconut. Refrigerate 30 minutes. Halve cakes horizontally; sandwich cakes with whipped cream.

nutritional count per cake 16.6g total fat (11.7g saturated fat); 1087kJ (260 cal); 22.2g carbohydrate; 5g protein; 1.9g fibre

marble cake

PREP + COOK TIME 1 HOUR 40 MINS • SERVES 12

Pink, green and white also make a pretty marble cake. If this is your preference, omit the cocoa powder and extra milk from this recipe, and add a few drops of green food colouring into the mixture instead.

250g butter, softened
1 teaspoon vanilla extract
1¼ cups (275g) caster sugar
3 eggs
2¼ cups (335g) self-raising flour
¾ cup (180ml) milk
pink food colouring
2 tablespoons cocoa powder
2 tablespoons milk, extra

butter frosting
125g butter, softened
2 cups (320g) icing sugar
2 tablespoons milk

1 Preheat oven to 180°C/160°C fan-forced. Grease deep 22cm-round or 19cm-square cake pan; line base with baking paper.
2 Beat butter, extract and sugar in medium bowl with electric mixer until light and fluffy. Beat in eggs, one at a time. Stir in sifted flour and milk, in two batches.
3 Divide mixture among three bowls; tint one mixture pink. Blend sifted cocoa with extra milk in a cup; stir into second mixture; leave remaining mixture plain. Drop alternate spoonfuls of mixtures into pan. Pull a skewer backwards and forwards through cake mixture.
4 Bake cake about 1 hour. Stand cake in pan 5 minutes before turning, top-side up, onto wire rack to cool.
5 Make butter frosting. Spread frosting over top and side of cake.
butter frosting Beat butter in small bowl with electric mixer until light and fluffy; beat in sifted icing sugar and milk, in two batches.
nutritional count per serving 28.3g total fat (18g saturated fat); 2349kJ (562 cal); 70.8g carbohydrate; 5.6g protein; 1.1g fibre

Tint one third of the cake mixture pink using a few drops of pink food colouring. Stir in only a drop or two of colouring at a time – overcolouring produces an unattractive cake.

To flavour the chocolate third of the cake mix, combine cocoa powder with a little milk and stir into the mixture.

Drop alternate spoonsful of each cake mixture into the pan.

Use a skewer to 'marble' the cake by pulling it backwards and forwards through the mixture.

madeira cake

PREP + COOK TIME 1 HOUR 15 MINS • SERVES 12

180g butter, softened
2 teaspoons finely grated lemon rind
⅔ cup (150g) caster sugar
3 eggs
¾ cup (110g) plain flour
¾ cup (110g) self-raising flour
⅓ cup (55g) mixed peel
¼ cup (35g) slivered almonds

1 Preheat oven to 160°C/140°C fan-forced. Grease deep 20cm-round cake pan; line base with paper.
2 Beat butter, rind and sugar in small bowl with electric mixer until light and fluffy; beat in eggs, one at a time. Transfer mixture to large bowl, stir in sifted flours.
3 Spread mixture into pan; bake 20 minutes. Remove cake from oven; sprinkle with peel and nuts. Return to oven; bake about 40 minutes. Stand cake 5 minutes; turn, top-side up, onto wire rack to cool.
nutritional count per serving 15.5g total fat (8.6g saturated fat); 1137kJ (272 cal); 28.7g carbohydrate; 4.3g protein; 1.1g fibre

pound cake

PREP + COOK TIME 1 HOUR 20 MINS • SERVES 12

Many cooks believe the butter or pound cake to be the mother of all cakes and indeed it has been around so long and spawned so many variations that it deserves the title. The term pound cake comes from the balance of major ingredients – a pound of each.

250g butter, softened
1 cup (220g) caster sugar
1 teaspoon vanilla extract
4 eggs
½ cup (75g) self-raising flour
1 cup (150g) plain flour

1 Preheat oven to 180°C/160°C fan-forced. Grease deep 20cm-round cake pan; line base with baking paper.
2 Beat butter, sugar and extract in small bowl with electric mixer until light and fluffy. Beat in eggs, one at a time. Transfer mixture to large bowl; fold in sifted flours in two batches.
3 Spread mixture into pan; bake about 1 hour. Stand cake in pan 5 minutes before turning, top-side up, onto wire rack to cool. If you like, serve with whipped cream and strawberries, and dust with sifted icing sugar.
nutritional count per serving 19.1g total fat (11.8g saturated fat); 1325kJ (317 cal); 31.9g carbohydrate; 4.3g protein; 0.7g fibre

[1] madeira cake
[2] pound cake
[3] one-bowl sultana loaf [page 552]
[4] vanilla patty cakes with glacé icing [page 552]

1

2

3

4

one-bowl sultana loaf

PREP + COOK TIME 1 HOUR 45 MINS • SERVES 8

Loaf pans come in slightly different sizes and depths, also in different materials and finishes. The most common size is 14cm x 21cm inside-top measurement and about 5cm deep.

125g butter, melted
750g sultanas
½ cup (110g) firmly packed brown sugar
2 tablespoons marmalade
2 eggs, beaten lightly
¼ cup (60ml) sweet sherry
¾ cup (110g) plain flour
¼ cup (35g) self-raising flour
30g blanched almonds
2 tablespoons apricot jam

1 Preheat oven to 150°C/130°C fan-forced. Grease 15cm x 25cm loaf pan; line base with baking paper.
2 Beat butter, sultanas, sugar, marmalade, egg, sherry and flours in large bowl using a wooden spoon until combined. Spread mixture into pan; decorate top with blanched almonds.
3 Bake loaf about 1½ hours. Cover cake with foil; cool in pan. Brush cold cake with warmed sieved apricot jam

nutritional count per serving 16.8 g total fat (9g saturated fat); 2625kJ (628 cal); 106.7g carbohydrate; 7.1g protein; 5.3g fibre

vanilla patty cakes with glacé icing

PREP + COOK TIME 40 MINS (+ COOLING) • MAKES 24

You can make glacé icing without butter (or oil) but, a tiny amount of butter will add gloss to the icing and make it easy to cut neatly – without butter, glacé icing tends to shatter when you cut it.

125g butter, softened
1 teaspoon vanilla extract
⅔ cup (150g) caster sugar
3 eggs
1½ cups (225g) self-raising flour
¼ cup (60ml) milk

glacé icing
1½ cups (240g) icing sugar
1 teaspoon butter
2 tablespoons milk, approximately

1 Preheat oven to 180°C/160°C fan-forced. Line two deep 12-hole patty pans with paper cases.
2 Beat butter, extract, sugar, eggs, flour and milk on low speed in medium bowl with electric mixer until ingredients are combined. Increase speed to medium; beat about 3 minutes or until mixture is smooth and paler in colour.
3 Drop slightly rounded tablespoons of mixture into paper cases.
4 Bake cakes about 20 minutes. Turn cakes, top-side up, onto wire racks to cool.
5 Meanwhile, make glacé icing. Top cool cakes with icing.
glacé icing Sift icing sugar into small heatproof bowl; stir in butter and enough milk to give a firm paste. Place bowl over small saucepan of simmering water; stir until icing is spreadable.

nutritional count per patty cake 5.4g total fat (3.2g saturated fat); 627kJ (150 cal); 23.1g carbohydrate; 1.9g protein; 0.4g fibre

banana cake

PREP + COOK TIME 1 HOUR 15 MINS • SERVES 10

125g butter, softened
¾ cup (165g) caster sugar
2 eggs
1 cup mashed banana
1 teaspoon bicarbonate of soda
2 tablespoons hot milk
1 cup (150g) plain flour
⅔ cup (100g) self-raising flour

TIP
- You need about 2 large (460g) overripe bananas for this recipe.

1 Preheat oven to 180°C/160°C. Grease deep 20cm-round cake pan; line base and side with baking paper.
2 Beat butter and sugar in small bowl with electric mixer until light and fluffy. Beat in eggs, one at a time. Transfer to large bowl; stir in banana.
3 Combine soda and milk in small jug; stir into banana mixture then stir in sifted flours. Spread mixture into pan.
4 Bake cake about 50 minutes. Stand cake in pan 5 minutes before turning, top-side up, onto wire rack to cool. Serve dusted with sifted icing sugar, if you like.

nutritional count per serving 11.8g total fat (7.2g saturated fat); 1216kJ (291 cal); 40.8g carbohydrate; 4.5g protein; 1.5g fibre

cinnamon teacake

PREP + COOK TIME 45 MINS • SERVES 10

The secret to making a perfect cinnamon teacake is to beat the butter, sugar and egg mixture in a small bowl until it's as light and white as possible.

60g butter, softened
1 teaspoon vanilla extract
⅔ cup (150g) caster sugar
1 egg
1 cup (150g) self-raising flour
⅓ cup (80ml) milk
10g butter, melted, extra
1 teaspoon ground cinnamon
1 tablespoon caster sugar, extra

1 Preheat oven to 180°C/160°C fan-forced. Grease deep 20cm-round cake pan; line base with baking paper.
2 Beat butter, extract, sugar and egg in small bowl with electric mixer until light and fluffy, this will take about 10 minutes. Stir in sifted flour and milk. Spread mixture into pan.
3 Bake cake about 30 minutes. Turn cake onto wire rack then turn top-side up; brush top with extra butter, sprinkle with combined cinnamon and extra sugar. Serve warm with butter, if you like.

nutritional count per serving 6.8g total fat (4.2g saturated fat); 769kJ (184 cal); 27.8g carbohydrate; 2.5g protein; 0.6g fibre

TEATIME

Teatime

When friends drop around for a cuppa, it's nice to welcome them with a home-baked little something. A plate of still-warm scones or crunchy biscuits will always hit the spot. Watch them disappear while you chat, laugh and solve the world's problems. This chapter contains a selection of sweet sentimental favourites to accompany that freshly brewed pot of tea or coffee. It's always handy to have a supply in the freezer (or biscuit tin) for such an occasion.

SCONES & MUFFINS

WELCOME YOUR GUESTS WITH OPEN ARMS, WITH WARM MUFFINS AND SCONES. YOU CAN RUN UP A BATCH BETWEEN THE TIME YOU RECEIVE THE CALL TO SAY "WE THOUGHT WE MIGHT CALL IN" AND THE TIME THE DOORBELL RINGS.

FOR SCONES

Use a round-ended knife to 'cut' the milk through the flour and butter mixture. The finished dough should be soft and sticky, just holding its shape. If you need to add a little flour when you turn it onto the floured working surface, be sparing.

You can freeze uncooked scones and then bake them straight from the freezer.

It's easy to tell if scones are done. They should be well-risen and even in colour. Scones don't take long to cook through because they're small and are baked at a high temperature. The best test is to tap them with your finger: they have quite a distinctive hollow sound. Test the scones in the centre of the batch, as the ones on the outside will have cooked first. Slide the scones onto a wire rack and cover them loosely to cool.

FOR MUFFINS

Muffins are quick and low-fuss and most only require a single bowl for mixing. Use a large metal spoon or fork and mix with the edge, in a cutting motion, in as few strokes as possible. Stop when the dry ingredients are just moistened – the mixture should still be coarse and lumpy.

Muffins are cooked when risen, browned, firm to touch and beginning to shrink from the sides of the pan. Turn them onto a rack to cool.

STORAGE AND FREEZING SCONES AND MUFFINS ARE BEST EATEN THE DAY THEY ARE MADE, IDEALLY SOON AFTER THEY COME OUT OF THE OVEN. THEY CAN BE KEPT IN AN AIRTIGHT CONTAINER FOR 2 DAYS AND FROZEN FOR UP TO 2 MONTHS.

BISCUITS

- Don't overbeat the butter and sugar mixture: stop when they are well combined but still firm. Overbeating makes the mixture too soft, causing biscuits to spread.
- When cooking biscuits, it's important to use the correct trays. These should be flat, with little or no sides, to allow the heat to circulate and ensure even browning. Lightly coat trays with cooking-oil spray or brush with melted butter.
- If you bake two or more trays at once, swap the trays around mid-way through baking and rotate them as well, to help with even browning.
- Biscuits should develop a crust, but still feel slightly soft to the touch when you remove them from the oven. They will firm up as they cool.
- Don't stack biscuits on top of each other when cooling; most biscuits need air circulating around them to crisp.
- If the biscuits are too brown underneath, the tray may have been overgreased; incorrect oven position and temperature could also be the cause.

STORAGE AND FREEZING BISCUITS MUST BE COMPLETELY COLD BEFORE STORING IN AN AIRTIGHT CONTAINER, BETWEEN LAYERS OF BAKING PAPER. BISCUITS TO BE FILLED WITH JAM, CREAM OR ICING ARE BEST FILLED ON THE DAY OF SERVING. IF UNFILLED, UNICED BISCUITS BEGIN TO SOFTEN, RE-CRISP THEM BY PLACING THEM ON AN OVEN TRAY AND HEATING IN A MODERATE OVEN FOR AROUND 5 MINUTES. AS LONG AS THEY ARE UN-ICED AND UNFILLED, BISCUITS WILL FREEZE WELL.

SLICES

Slices are half-way between a cake and a tart – they can be made of one mixture, or can combine a base (biscuit or pastry) covered with a topping and/or a filling.

- Use aluminium trays: pans made from tin and stainless steel don't conduct heat as evenly.
- Preheating the oven is important for slices as they require less than 30 minutes of baking. Preheat for around 10 minutes before placing the food in the oven.

STORING AND FREEZING MOST SLICES KEEP FOR 2 TO 3 DAYS IN AN AIRTIGHT CONTAINER. REFRIGERATE THOSE CONTAINING DAIRY PRODUCTS. MOST SLICES CAN BE FROZEN FOR UP TO 2 MONTHS BUT THOSE WITH ICINGS AND CREAM FILLINGS MAY CRACK AND CHANGE IN APPEARANCE AS THEY THAW.

FRIANDS

Friands (French for small cakes) are perfect little morsels when you want a bite that is small and stylish but not too rich. One of their many charms is that they can be very quickly made. You can make them in muffin pans, but if you plan to make them often, there are sweet little oval or rectangular friand pans available. You can buy friand pans separately or in the form of 6-, 8-, 9- or 12-hole pans from good kitchen and cookware shops.

STORAGE AND FREEZING FRIANDS ARE BEST EATEN THE DAY THEY ARE MADE, BUT CAN BE STORED IN AN AIRTIGHT CONTAINER FOR 2 DAYS. THEY ALSO FREEZE WELL.

basic scones

PREP + COOK TIME 45 MINS • MAKES 35

The fear-of-failure-factor surrounding scones is very high. But once you've got the hang of them, you'll find them incredibly easy to make. Home-bakers seem to fall into two categories, those who can, and those who can't make scones. Read on for some tips to help you become an expert and a much-admired scone-maker.

4 cups (600g) self-raising flour
2 tablespoons icing sugar
60g butter
1½ cups (375ml) milk
¾ cup (180ml) water, approximately

1 Preheat oven to 220°C/ 200°C fan-forced. Grease 20cm x 30cm lamington pan.
2 Sift flour and sugar into large bowl; rub in butter with fingertips.
3 Make a well in centre of flour mixture; add milk and almost all the water. Use knife to "cut" the milk and water through the flour mixture, mixing to a soft, sticky dough. Knead dough on floured surface until smooth.
4 Press dough out to 2cm thickness. Dip 4.5cm round cutter in flour; cut as many rounds as you can from piece of dough. Place scones, side by side, just touching, in pan.
5 Gently knead scraps of dough together; repeat pressing and cutting of dough, place in same pan. Brush tops with a little extra milk.
6 Bake scones about 15 minutes or until just browned and sound hollow when tapped firmly on the top with fingers. Serve with jam and cream.

nutritional count per scone 2g total fat (1.2g saturated fat); 339kJ (81 cal); 13.2g carbohydrate; 2.1g protein; 0.7g fibre

VARIATIONS

sultana and lemon Add ½ cup sultanas and 2 teaspoons finely grated lemon rind to mixture after butter has been rubbed in.
blueberry and ginger Add 3 teaspoons ground ginger and ½ cup fresh or frozen blueberries to mixture after butter has been rubbed in.

Rub the butter into the sifted flour and icing sugar mixture, using your fingertips.

Add the milk and water to the bowl and, using a flat-bladed knife, slice through the flour mixture, mixing until the dough is soft and sticky.

Place the dough on a floured surface and knead until smooth. Press the dough out to a 2cm thickness with your fingertips.

Brush the tops of the scones with the extra milk. The scones should be arranged so they are sitting side by side in the pan and just touching.

almond friands

PREP + COOK TIME 45 MINS • MAKES 12

In France, these oval- or rectangular-shaped cakes are better known as financiers, because they were originally baked in tiny, gold-bar shaped pans. You can buy these traditionally-shaped pans individually from specialty kitchen stores or as baking dishes with multiple holes from most supermarkets. You might also choose to make tiny friands containing a single berry or piece of fruit using a mini-muffin pan, or larger friands in a regular muffin pan.

6 egg whites
185g butter, melted
1 cup (125g) ground almonds
1½ cups (240g) icing sugar
½ cup (75g) plain flour

1 Preheat oven to 200°C/180°C fan-forced. Grease 12 x ½-cup (125ml) pans; stand on oven tray.
2 Place egg whites in medium bowl; whisk lightly with fork until combined. Using wooden spoon, stir in remaining ingredients until just combined. Divide mixture among pans.
3 Bake friands about 25 minutes. Stand friands in pans 5 minutes; turn onto wire rack. Serve dusted with extra sifted icing sugar.
nutritional count per friand 18.5g total fat (8.7g saturated fat); 1195kJ (286 cal); 25g carbohydrate; 4.6g protein; 1.2g fibre

VARIATIONS

raspberry and white chocolate Stir 100g coarsely chopped white chocolate into the egg-white mixture. Top friands with 100g fresh or frozen raspberries.
lime coconut Stir 2 teaspoons finely grated lime rind, 1 tablespoon lime juice and ¼ cup (20g) desiccated coconut into the egg-white mixture; sprinkle unbaked friands with ⅓ cup (15g) flaked coconut.

rhubarb and custard muffins

PREP + COOK TIME 45 MINS (+ COOLING) • MAKES 12

2 cups (300g) self-raising flour
½ cup (75g) plain flour
¾ cup (165g) caster sugar
100g butter, melted
1 cup (250ml) milk
1 egg
3 cups (330g) finely chopped rhubarb
1 tablespoon demerara sugar

custard
2 tablespoons custard powder
¼ cup (55g) caster sugar
1 cup (250ml) milk
1 teaspoon vanilla extract

1 Make custard.
2 Preheat oven to 200°C/180°C fan-forced. Line 12-hole (⅓-cup/80ml) muffin pan with paper cases.
3 Sift flours and caster sugar into large bowl. Stir in butter, milk and egg. Do not over-mix. Stir in half of the rhubarb.
4 Spoon half of the mixture into cases; top with custard. Spoon in remaining mixture to cover custard. Sprinkle with remaining rhubarb and demerara sugar.
5 Bake muffins about 20 minutes. Stand muffins in pan 5 minutes; turn, top-side up, onto wire rack to cool.
custard Combine custard powder and sugar in small saucepan; gradually stir in milk. Stir custard over medium heat until mixture boils and thickens. Stir in extract. Cool.
nutritional count per muffin 9.3g total fat (5.8g saturated fat); 1233kJ (295 cal); 45.7g carbohydrate; 5.7g protein; 1.9g fibre

berry muffins

PREP + COOK TIME 30 MINS • MAKES 12

Buttermilk, despite its luscious-sounding name, is low-fat. It adds a unique quality to muffins, scones and cakes. Try it and taste the difference.

2½ cups (375g) self-raising flour
90g cold butter, chopped
1 cup (220g) caster sugar
1¼ cups (310ml) buttermilk
1 egg, beaten lightly
200g fresh or frozen mixed berries

1 Preheat oven to 180°C/160°C fan-forced. Grease 12-hole (⅓-cup/80ml) muffin pan.
2 Sift flour into large bowl; rub in butter. Stir in sugar, buttermilk and egg. Do not overmix; mixture should be lumpy. Add berries; stir through gently. Spoon mixture into pan holes.
3 Bake muffins about 20 minutes. Stand muffins 5 minutes; turn, top-side up, onto wire rack to cool.
nutritional count per muffin 7.5g total fat (4.6g saturated fat); 1095kJ (262 cal); 42.4g carbohydrate; 5.1g protein; 1.6g fibre

VARIATIONS

lemon poppy seed Omit berries. Add 2 teaspoons lemon rind and 2 tablespoons poppy seeds with the sugar.
date and orange Omit berries. Substitute self-raising flour with 1 cup wholemeal self-raising flour and 1½ cups white self-raising flour. Add 1½ cups seeded, chopped dried dates and 2 teaspoons finely grated orange rind with the sugar.
choc chip and walnut Omit berries. Add ¾ cup dark Choc Bits and 1 cup coarsely chopped walnuts with the sugar.

chocolate fudge brownies

PREP + COOK TIME 1 HOUR 25 MINS • MAKES 16

Despite the richness of these seriously chocolatey brownies, nobody can stop at one. It's great to think that something so good is so easy to make – all in one pan. If you like your brownies really fudgy, bake them for less time. Dust the brownies with a little sifted cocoa powder or icing sugar, or both.

150g butter, chopped
300g dark eating chocolate, chopped
1½ cups (330g) firmly packed brown sugar
3 eggs
1 teaspoon vanilla extract
¾ cup (110g) plain flour
¾ cup (140g) dark Choc Bits
½ cup (120g) sour cream
¾ cup (110g) roasted macadamias, chopped coarsely

1 Preheat oven to 180°C/160°C fan-forced. Grease 19cm x 29cm rectangular slice pan; line base with baking paper, extending paper 5cm over sides.
2 Stir butter and chocolate in medium saucepan over low heat until smooth. Cool 10 minutes.
3 Stir in sugar, eggs and extract then sifted flour, Choc Bits, sour cream and nuts. Spread mixture into pan.
4 Bake brownies 40 minutes. Cover pan with foil; bake a further 20 minutes. Cool in pan. Serve dusted with sifted cocoa powder, if you like.

nutritional count per serving 24.8g total fat (12.7g saturated fat); 1722kJ (412 cal); 42.8g carbohydrate; 4.2g protein; 1g fibre

chocolate caramel slice

PREP + COOK TIME 45 MINS (+ COOLING & REFRIGERATION) • MAKES 16

This recipe is an all-time favourite. To cut out a step, buy a can of condensed milk that has already been caramelised: it's called Top 'n' Fill, and you simply have to add the extra butter (melted) and the golden syrup to it then spread the mixture over the hot biscuit base.

½ cup (75g) self-raising flour
½ cup (75g) plain flour
1 cup (80g) desiccated coconut
1 cup (220g) firmly packed brown sugar
125g butter, melted
395g can sweetened condensed milk
30g butter, extra
2 tablespoons golden syrup
200g dark eating chocolate, chopped coarsely
2 teaspoons vegetable oil

1 Preheat oven to 180°C/160°C fan-forced. Grease 20cm x 30cm lamington pan; line with baking paper, extending paper 5cm over long sides.
2 Combine sifted flours, coconut, sugar and butter in medium bowl; press mixture evenly over base of pan. Bake about 15 minutes or until browned lightly.
3 Meanwhile, make caramel filling by combining condensed milk, extra butter and syrup in small saucepan. Stir over medium heat about 15 minutes or until caramel mixture is golden brown; pour over base. Bake 10 minutes; cool.
4 Make topping by combining chocolate and oil in small saucepan; stir over low heat until smooth. Pour warm topping over caramel. Refrigerate 3 hours or overnight.

nutritional count per piece 17.7g total fat (11.8g saturated fat); 1492kJ (357 cal); 44.6g carbohydrate; 4.1g protein; 1.2g fibre

[1] chocolate fudge brownies
[2] chocolate caramel slice
[3] date slice [page 564]
[4] portuguese custard tarts [page 564]

1

2

3

4

date slice

PREP + COOK TIME 1 HOUR 25 MINS (+ REFRIGERATION) • MAKES 24

This recipe works just as well with prunes instead of dates – or a combination of both dates and prunes would also be good.

1½ cups (225g) plain flour
1¼ cups (185g) self-raising flour
150g cold butter, chopped
1 tablespoon honey
1 egg
⅓ cup (80ml) milk, approximately
2 teaspoons milk, extra
1 tablespoon white sugar

date filling
3½ cups (500g) dried seeded dates, chopped coarsely
¾ cup (180ml) water
2 tablespoons finely grated lemon rind
2 tablespoons lemon juice

1 Grease 20cm x 30cm lamington pan; line base with baking paper, extending paper 5cm over long sides.
2 Sift flours into large bowl; rub in butter until mixture is crumbly. Stir in combined honey and egg and enough milk to make a firm dough. Knead on floured surface until smooth. Cover; refrigerate 30 minutes.
3 Meanwhile, make date filling.
4 Preheat oven to 200°C/180°C fan-forced.
5 Divide dough in half. Roll one half large enough to cover base of pan; press into pan, spread filling over dough. Roll remaining dough large enough to cover filling. Brush with extra milk; sprinkle with sugar. Bake about 20 minutes; cool in pan.
date filling Cook ingredients in medium saucepan, stirring, about 10 minutes or until thick and smooth. Cool to room temperature.
nutritional count per piece 5.7g total fat (3.6g saturated fat); 757kJ (181 cal); 28.2g carbohydrate; 2.6g protein; 2.7g fibre

portuguese custard tarts

PREP + COOK TIME 55 MINS • MAKES 12

Use a vegetable peeler to peel a strip of rind – about 5cm long and 1cm wide – from a washed and dried lemon. Avoid the white pith, and use a rough-skinned lemon for the best flavour.

½ cup (110g) caster sugar
2 tablespoons cornflour
4 egg yolks
300ml cream
⅓ cup (80ml) water
3cm strip lemon rind
1 teaspoon vanilla extract
1 sheet puff pastry

1 Preheat oven to 220°C/200°C fan-forced. Grease 12-hole (⅓-cup/80ml) muffin pan.

2 Combine sugar and cornflour in medium saucepan; whisk in egg yolks, cream and the water. Add rind; stir over medium heat until mixture comes to the boil. Remove from heat; discard rind. Stir extract into custard.

3 Cut pastry sheet in half; place halves on top of each other. Roll pastry tightly (like a swiss roll) from one short side; cut roll into twelve 1cm rounds.

4 Place pastry rounds, cut-sides up, on floured surface; roll each into a 10cm round. Push rounds into pan holes; spoon in custard.

5 Bake tarts about 20 minutes. Stand 5 minutes, before transferring to wire rack to cool.

nutritional count per tart 14.3g total fat (8.3g saturated fat); 849kJ (203 cal); 16.5g carbohydrate; 2.4g protein; 0.2g fibre

tangy lemon squares

PREP + COOK TIME 50 MINS • MAKES 16

Wonderful for an afternoon tea with a pot of earl grey. These squares are also delicious made with orange or mandarin rind and juice.

125g butter
¼ cup (40g) icing sugar
1¼ cups (185g) plain flour
3 eggs
1 cup (220g) caster sugar
2 teaspoons finely grated lemon rind
½ cup (125ml) lemon juice

1 Preheat oven to 180°C/160°C fan-forced. Grease shallow 23cm-square pan; line base and sides with baking paper, extending paper 2cm above edges of pan.

2 Beat butter and icing sugar in small bowl with electric mixer until smooth. Stir in 1 cup (150g) of the flour. Press mixture evenly over base of pan.

3 Bake base about 15 minutes or until browned lightly.

4 Meanwhile, whisk eggs, caster sugar, remaining flour, rind and juice in bowl until combined. Pour egg mixture over hot base.

5 Bake slice about 20 minutes or until firm. Cool in pan on a wire rack before cutting. Dust with extra sifted icing sugar, if you like.

nutritional count per square 7.5g total fat (4.5g saturated fat); 748kJ (179 cal); 24.9g carbohydrate; 2.6g protein; 0.5g fibre

vanilla slice

PREP + COOK TIME 55 MINS (+ COOLING & REFRIGERATION) • MAKES 16

It's best to store any leftover slice in large pieces, so if you think it won't all be eaten or you want to save some for later, keep a portion without cutting it into squares or bars. Keep the piece of slice as airtight as possible in a resealable plastic bag or an airtight container, and cut it when you're going to serve it.

2 sheets puff pastry
½ cup (110g) caster sugar
½ cup (75g) cornflour
¼ cup (30g) custard powder
2½ cups (625ml) milk
30g butter
1 egg yolk
1 teaspoon vanilla extract
¾ cup (180ml) thickened cream

passionfruit icing
1½ cups (240g) icing sugar
1 teaspoon soft butter
¼ cup (60ml) passionfruit pulp

1 Preheat oven to 240°C/220°C fan-forced. Grease deep 23cm-square cake pan; line with foil, extending foil 10cm over sides of pan.
2 Place each pastry sheet on separate greased oven trays. Bake about 15 minutes; cool. Flatten pastry with hand; place one pastry sheet in pan, trim to fit if necessary.
3 Meanwhile, combine sugar, cornflour and custard powder in medium saucepan; gradually add milk, stirring until smooth. Add butter; stir over heat until mixture boils and thickens. Simmer, stirring, about 3 minutes or until custard is thick and smooth. Remove from heat; stir in egg yolk and extract. Cover surface of custard with plastic wrap; cool to room temperature.
4 Make passionfruit icing.
5 Whip cream until firm peaks form. Fold cream into custard, in two batches. Spread custard mixture over pastry in pan. Top with remaining pastry, trim to fit if necessary; press down slightly. Spread pastry with passionfruit icing; refrigerate 3 hours or overnight.
passionfruit icing Place sifted icing sugar, butter and pulp in small heatproof bowl over small saucepan of simmering water; stir until icing is spreadable.
nutritional count per piece 12.6g total fat (7.6g saturated fat); 1158kJ (237 cal); 37.2g carbohydrate; 3.1g protein; 0.8g fibre

Once cooled, flatten each baked pastry sheet with your hands.

Add egg yolk and vanilla extract to the custard, stirring with a wooden spoon to combine.

Fold the whipped cream into the custard, in two batches.

Spread the custard mixture over the pastry in the cake pan. Smooth out the surface to make it even.

traditional shortbread

PREP + COOK TIME 55 MINS • MAKES 24

Shortbread is the national biscuit of Scotland and for some shortbread making has become a serious competition, featuring as a category at the annual Scottish highland games.

250g butter, softened
⅓ cup (75g) caster sugar
1 tablespoon water
2 cups (300g) plain flour
½ cup (100g) rice flour
2 tablespoons white sugar

1 Preheat oven to 160°C/140°C fan-forced. Grease oven trays.
2 Beat butter and caster sugar in medium bowl with electric mixer until light and fluffy; stir in the water and sifted flours, in two batches. Knead on floured surface until smooth.
3 Divide mixture in half; shape each, on separate trays, into 20cm rounds. Mark each round into 12 wedges; prick with fork. Pinch edges of rounds with fingers; sprinkle with white sugar.
4 Bake shortbread about 40 minutes; stand 5 minutes. Using sharp knife, cut into wedges along marked lines. Cool on trays.

nutritional count per piece 8.8g total fat (5.7g saturated fat); 644kJ (154 cal); 17g carbohydrate; 1.7g protein; 0.6g fibre

vanilla kisses

PREP + COOK TIME 25 MINS • MAKES 20

125g butter, softened
½ cup (110g) caster sugar
1 egg
⅓ cup (50g) plain flour
¼ cup (35g) self-raising flour
⅔ cup (100g) cornflour
¼ cup (30g) custard powder

vienna cream
60g butter, softened
½ teaspoon vanilla extract
¾ cup (120g) icing sugar
2 teaspoons milk

1 Preheat oven to 200°C/180°C fan-forced. Grease oven trays; line with baking paper.
2 Beat butter, sugar and egg in small bowl with electric mixer until light and fluffy. Stir in sifted dry ingredients, in two batches.
3 Spoon mixture into piping bag fitted with 1cm-fluted tube. Pipe 3cm rosettes about 3cm apart on trays.
4 Bake biscuits about 10 minutes; cool on trays.
5 Meanwhile, make vienna cream. Sandwich biscuits with vienna cream.
vienna cream Beat butter and extract in small bowl with electric mixer until as white as possible; gradually beat in sifted icing sugar and milk, in two batches.

nutritional count per kiss 8g total fat (5.1g saturated fat); 648kJ (155 cal); 20g carbohydrate; 0.9g protein; 0.2g fibre

[1] traditional shortbread
[2] vanilla kisses
[3] chocolate chip cookies [page 570]
[4] almond macaroons [page 570]

1

2

3

4

chocolate chip cookes

PREP + COOK TIME 40 MINS (+ REFRIGERATION) • MAKES 40

Don't overbeat the butter, sugar and egg mixture or the cookies will spread too much during baking. You can use dark or white chocolate in place of the milk chocolate if you like – or a mixture of any type of chocolate.

250g butter, softened
1 teaspoon vanilla extract
¾ cup (165g) caster sugar
¾ cup (165g) firmly packed brown sugar
1 egg
2¼ cups (335g) plain flour
1 teaspoon bicarbonate of soda
375g dark chocolate Melts, chopped coarsely

1 Preheat oven to 180°C/160°C fan-forced. Grease oven trays.
2 Beat butter, extract, sugars and egg in small bowl with electric mixer until light and fluffy. Transfer mixture to large bowl; stir in sifted flour and soda, in two batches. Stir in chocolate. Cover; refrigerate 1 hour.
3 Roll level tablespoons of mixture into balls; place about 3cm apart on trays.
4 Bake cookies about 12 minutes; cool on trays.

nutritional count per cookie 8.2g total fat (6g saturated fat); 665kJ (159 cal); 19.5g carbohydrate; 1.5g protein; 0.8g fibre

almond macaroons

PREP + COOK TIME 35 MINS • MAKES 22

Macaroons can be stored in an airtight container for up to 2 days.

For coconut macaroons, replace ground almonds with ¾ cup desiccated coconut and ¾ cup shredded coconut; replace almond essence with vanilla extract; omit blanched almonds.

2 egg whites
½ cup (110g) caster sugar
1¼ cups (150g) ground almonds
½ teaspoon almond essence
2 tablespoons plain flour
¼ cup (40g) blanched almonds

1 Preheat oven to 150°C/130°C fan-forced. Grease oven trays.
2 Beat egg whites in small bowl with electric mixer until soft peaks form; gradually add sugar, beating until dissolved between additions. Gently fold in ground almonds, essence and sifted flour, in two batches.
3 Drop level tablespoons of mixture about 5cm apart on trays; press one nut onto each macaroon.
4 Bake macaroons about 20 minutes or until firm and dry; cool on trays.

nutritional count per macaroon 4.8g total fat (0.3g saturated fat); 326kJ (78 cal); 6.1g carbohydrate; 2.2g protein; 0.8g fibre

monte carlo biscuits

PREP + COOK TIME 40 MINS • MAKES 28

180g butter, softened
1 teaspoon vanilla extract
½ cup (110g) firmly packed brown sugar
1 egg
1¼ cups (185g) self-raising flour
¾ cup (105g) plain flour
¼ teaspoon bicarbonate of soda
⅔ cup (50g) desiccated coconut
⅓ cup (110g) raspberry jam

vienna cream
60g butter
½ teaspoon vanilla extract
¾ cup (120g) icing sugar
2 teaspoons milk

1 Preheat oven to 200°C/180°C fan-forced. Grease oven trays; line with baking paper.
2 Beat butter, extract and sugar in small bowl with electric mixer until just combined; beat in egg. Stir in sifted flours, soda and coconut, in two batches.
3 Roll 2 level teaspoons of mixture into ovals; place on trays about 5cm apart. Flatten slightly; use back of fork to roughen surface.
4 Bake biscuits about 7 minutes.
5 Meanwhile, make vienna cream.
6 Transfer biscuits to wire rack to cool. Sandwich biscuits with vienna cream and jam.

vienna cream Beat butter, extract and sifted icing sugar in small bowl with electric mixer until fluffy; beat in milk.

nutritional count per monte carlo 8.5g total fat (5.7g saturated fat); 656kJ (157 cal); 18.3g carbohydrate; 1.5g protein; 0.7g fibre

Q&A

When I bake cookies at home I always make a few varieties and then store them in a clean, dry airtight container, yet some of them go soft and soggy within two days. What could I be doing wrong?

If biscuits are stored properly, they should retain their freshly baked taste and texture longer than two days. You may be combining soft and crisp-textured biscuits in the jar. If so, you need to store them in separate containers, otherwise the soft biscuits will make the crisp ones soft. Crisp biscuits can be stored in an airtight container – it's important to eliminate as much air as possible from inside the container too, either by keeping it full of biscuits, or using smaller containers. Biscuits with dairy-based centres should be filled just before serving.

pistachio and cranberry biscotti

PREP + COOK TIME 1 HOUR (+ REFRIGERATION & COOLING) • MAKES 60

60g unsalted butter, softened
1 teaspoon vanilla extract
1 cup (220g) caster sugar
2 eggs
1¾ cups (260g) plain flour
½ teaspoon bicarbonate of soda
1 cup (130g) dried cranberries
¾ cup (110g) coarsely chopped roasted pistachios
1 egg, extra
1 tablespoon water
2 tablespoons caster sugar, extra

Serve these biscuits with fruit tea, good strong coffee, or at the end of dinner with a tiny glass of limoncello (lemon-flavoured liqueur). For a change, use slivered almonds instead of pistachios.

1 Beat butter, extract and sugar in medium bowl until combined. Beat in eggs, one at a time. Stir in sifted flour and soda then cranberries and nuts. Cover dough; refrigerate 1 hour.
2 Preheat oven to 180°C/160°C fan-forced. Grease oven tray.
3 Knead dough on floured surface until smooth but still sticky. Halve dough; shape each half into 30cm log. Place logs on oven tray.
4 Combine extra egg with the water in small bowl. Brush egg mixture over logs; sprinkle with extra sugar. Bake 20 minutes or until firm; cool 3 hours or overnight.
5 Preheat oven to 160°C/140°C fan-forced.
6 Using serrated knife, cut logs diagonally into 1cm slices. Place slices on ungreased oven trays. Bake about 15 minutes or until dry and crisp, turning halfway through baking time; cool on wire racks.

nutritional count per biscotti 2.1g total fat (0.7g saturated fat); 259kJ (62 cal); 9.2g carbohydrate; 1.2g protein; 0.4g fibre

anzacs

PREP + COOK TIME 35 MINS • MAKES 25

1 cup (90g) rolled oats
1 cup (150g) plain flour
1 cup (220g) firmly packed brown sugar
½ cup (40g) desiccated coconut
125g butter
2 tablespoons golden syrup
1 tablespoon water
½ teaspoon bicarbonate of soda

1 Preheat oven to 160°C/140°C fan-forced. Grease oven trays; line with baking paper.
2 Combine oats, sifted flour, sugar and coconut in large bowl.
3 Stir butter, syrup and the water in small saucepan over low heat until smooth; stir in soda. Stir syrup mixture into dry ingredients.
4 Roll level tablespoons of mixture into balls; place about 5cm apart on trays, flatten slightly.
5 Bake biscuits about 20 minutes; cool on trays.

nutritional count per biscuit 5.5g total fat (2.8g saturated fat); 518kJ (124 cal); 17g carbohydrate; 1.2g protein; 0.7g fibre

[opposite] pistachio and cranberry biscotti

Christmas & other celebrations

Around the world, food is at the heart of all rituals and celebrations: when there is a special occasion in our lives, we celebrate it with special food.

Some foods might represent a specific important occasion, such as a wedding cake, while other foods may be simply part of a family tradition, like a celebration fruit cake. And other foods might signify 'party': delicious, tasty little morsels eaten off roaming platters at a great cocktail party.

Some food traditions are deeply ingrained, while others can change over time: the classic Australian Christmas lunch consisting of roast meats and a steaming pudding has relaxed over the years, in tune with our casual summers, to encompass food such as a barbecued seafood platter or white Christmas ice-cream puddings. In this chapter, we have assembled a glorious assortment of festive foods to accompany some of the special occasions in your lives: perhaps there is a recipe here that echoes, with some subtle changes, a favourite tradition in your family. Or perhaps you will create a tradition of your own.

PLANNING

Whatever the occasion – a small soiree with a few friends or a big party – the key to running a smooth event is in the planning. Without it, you can feel fraught instead of fabulous when you open your doors to your guests.

In the case of a big party, you should have a plan of action drawn up weeks in advance. A small party requires at least a week of planning.

It's a time for making lists. Make a list of the food and drink shopping that needs to be done. List all the equipment you'll need for the occasion (everything from extra cutlery pieces to extra chairs and napkins) and assess whether you need to buy, borrow or hire anything ahead of time.

MENU PLANNING

Make a list detailing all the foods you're aiming to cook, and when you plan to cook them. Think about whether the food will be competing for bench space and fridge and/or freezer space.

If you're organising a big party, think about which foods you can cook ahead of time and those suitable for freezing. Defrosting foods is much less stressful than cooking them all on the day.

On the day of your event, think about what can be done ahead of time – from preparing vegetables to making dressings. If you're hosting a traditional Christmas lunch, then you will need to start baking the meat from early in the morning and the steamed pudding will have been made weeks ahead.

KEEP IT MANAGEABLE THE FIRST RULE OF ENTERTAINING IS TO BE REALISTIC ABOUT HOW MUCH YOU CAN DO WITHOUT GETTING TOO FRAZZLED. YOU WANT TO BE ABLE TO SOCIALISE, NOT JUST SPEND YOUR TIME IN THE KITCHEN OR PLAYING WAITRESS FOR THE ENTIRE EVENT.

FINGER FOOD

HAVING A REPERTOIRE OF DELICIOUS MORSELS THAT CAN BE EATEN IN ONE OR TWO MOUTHFULS IS A VALUABLE ASSET WHEN ENTERTAINING. YOU CAN EITHER HAND AROUND PLATTERS OF FINGER FOODS, OR PLACE THEM STRATEGICALLY AROUND THE ROOM FOR GUESTS TO HELP THEMSELVES.

QUANTITIES

WHETHER IT'S A COCKTAIL PARTY OR LOW-KEY STAND-AROUND AFFAIR, ALLOW FOUR TO FIVE PIECES OF FINGER FOOD PER PERSON FOR THE FIRST HOUR, THEN FOUR PIECES FOR EACH HOUR AFTER THAT. FOR A FULL AFTERNOON OR EVENING, ALLOW 12 TO 14 PIECES PER PERSON FOR THE WHOLE PARTY.

HOME-MADE AND BOUGHT

When it comes to finger foods, don't worry about striving for a smorgasbord of offerings: just a few kinds will keep your guests happy. And don't think that you must make everything yourself: combine a few home-made appetisers with quality bought items (see Starters, page 74).

If you tend to host impromptu gatherings, then it's wise to keep some provisions on hand in the freezer: most savoury pastries and items such as pizzas or blini can be frozen and then half-thawed in the microwave.

EQUIPMENT

GLASSES Have an abundant supply of suitable, clean glasses on hand: classic wine glasses, champagne flutes, V-shaped, stemmed cocktail glasses and straight-sided tumblers will cover most needs. Chilling them beforehand (30 minutes in the refrigerator; 10 minutes in the freezer, space permitting) is a nice touch.

ICE You will need plenty of ice. Fill a large tub, such as a laundry tub, with ice and use it as a cooler for bottles and cans.

GARNISHES A fresh garnish adds colour and party glamour even to a mineral water: slices of lemon or lime placed on the rim of a glass; strawberries (cut in half with a slit to slide onto the rim of a glass); a pair of joined cherries dangling over the rim; or a sprig of mint, all look wonderful.

COCKTAIL PARTY DRINKS

While wine and beer are perfect party drinks, the offer of cocktail drinks elevates your event into a special occasion. You don't have to offer a full menu of cocktails, just a couple of crowd pleasers – like a champagne cocktail, bellini or a cosmopolitan, as we've included in this chapter. Make sure you practise making them beforehand and – ideally – ask a friend or family member if they could be your cocktail makers for the occasion. Alternatively, you could pre-make a punch, which still says 'special event' and can be made ahead of time. Because cocktails are quite powerful, it's important to offer enough food to help absorb the alcohol being consumed. Elegant finger food is the perfect match. It's customary to offer cocktails for only the first hour or so, then switch to wine, beer, mineral water and perhaps a freshly-squeezed juice.

QUANTITIES Ten guests will consume about 20 drinks at a cocktail party. If it's a full afternoon or evening affair, this increases to 40 drinks. Have a modest reserve of wine and beer and a larger one of non-alcoholic drinks.

CHAMPAGNE Champagne and other sparkling drinks should be chilled in a tub of ice or in the fridge (not the freezer) until needed. To pour champagne, add a little at a time to each glass so that they don't overflow.

WINE Glasses for both still and sparkling wines should be filled only half-full so that the bouquet (aroma) will collect in the top of the glass.

champagne cocktail

PREP TIME 5 MINS • SERVES 1

Use marginally less than ⅔ cup of champagne for each cocktail and you will be able to make five cocktails from one bottle of champagne.

5cm strip orange rind
1 sugar cube
5 drops Angostura bitters
⅔ cup (160ml) chilled champagne

1 Slice rind thinly.
2 Place sugar cube in champagne glass; top with bitters then champagne. Garnish with rind.
nutritional count per serving 0g total fat (0g saturated fat); 527kJ (126 cal); 6.9g carbohydrate; 0.3g protein; 0.1g fibre

bellini

PREP TIME 5 MINS • SERVES 8

2 medium peaches (300g), chopped coarsely
½ cup (125ml) peach schnapps
750ml chilled champagne
8 sugar cubes

1 Blend or process peach and schnapps until smooth. Combine peach mixture with champagne in large jug.
2 Place 1 sugar cube in each of eight champagne glasses; top with bellini mixture.
nutritional count per serving 0.1g total fat (0g saturated fat); 556kJ (133 cal); 12.6g carbohydrate; 0.5g protein; 0.4g fibre

sparkling burgundy and cranberry punch

**PREP TIME 15 MINS (+ STANDING & REFRIGERATION)
SERVES 8
(MAKES 2 LITRES)**

1¼ cups (310ml) cranberry juice
1 cup (220g) white sugar
1 black-leaf tea bag
125g raspberries
250g strawberries, hulled, quartered
125g blueberries
2 cups ice-cubes
750ml bottle sparkling burgundy

1 Combine juice and sugar in small saucepan; stir over heat until sugar dissolves. Bring to the boil, remove from heat. Add tea bag; stand 15 minutes; discard tea bag, cool tea.
2 Combine berries in a large jug. Stir in ice-cubes and cranberry mixture; refrigerate 2 hours. Stir in burgundy before serving.
nutritional count per serving 0.3g total fat (0g saturated fat); 882kJ (211 cal); 35.2g carbohydrate; 1.6g protein; 1.8g fibre

cosmopolitan

PREP TIME 5 MINS • SERVES 1

This refreshingly tart concoction is a favourite summer cocktail. You can double the quantities to make two at a time.

45ml vodka
30ml cointreau
20ml cranberry juice
10ml lime juice
1 cup ice cubes

1 Place ingredients in cocktail shaker; shake vigorously.
2 Strain into 230ml chilled martini glass.

nutritional count per serving 0.1g total fat (0g saturated fat); 991kJ (237 cal); 17.4g carbohydrate; 0.2g protein; 0g fibre

caipiroska

PREP TIME 5 MINS • SERVES 1

See page 581 for garnishing tips on making a curl with citrus peel.

1 lime, cut into eight wedges
2 teaspoons caster sugar
45ml vodka
½ cup crushed ice

1 Place lime wedges in cocktail shaker. Using muddler, crush lime with sugar. Add vodka and ice; shake vigorously.
2 Pour into 260ml old-fashioned glass. Garnish with a curl of lime rind.

nutritional count per serving 0.1g total fat (0g saturated fat); 585kJ (140 cal); 13.7g carbohydrate; 0.4g protein; 1.4g fibre

piña colada

PREP TIME 15 MINS • SERVES 1

This recipe makes 350ml of sugar syrup. Store any remaining syrup in an airtight container in the refrigerator for up to 1 month.

See page 580 for tips on garnishing with pineapple.

1 cup ice cubes
30ml white rum
30ml dark rum
80ml pineapple juice
40ml coconut cream
dash Angostura bitters

sugar syrup
1 cup (220g) caster sugar
1 cup (250ml) water

1 Make sugar syrup.
2 Blend ice, rums, juice, 20ml sugar syrup, coconut cream and bitters until smooth.
3 Pour into 400ml tulip-shaped glass. Garnish with pineapple piece and leaves.

sugar syrup Stir sugar and the water in small suacepan over low heat, until sugar dissolves; bring to the boil. Reduce heat; simmer, uncovered, 5 minutes. Cool.

nutritional count per serving 8.4g total fat (7.3g saturated fat); 1179kJ (282 cal); 19.8g carbohydrate; 1g protein; 0.7g fibre

SPECIAL FEATURE

Drink garnishes

These are the final flourishes that make drinks memorable. For a party, prepare garnishes ahead of time and refrigerate in covered containers.

CHERRIES
Choose pairs of ripe black, red or white cherries joined by their stalks. Hang over the rim of a tall glass of any fruity or creamy drink.

CITRUS SLICE
Cut a slit in a slice of lemon or lime (or both together) and place on the rim of a glass; for larger fruit, such as orange or blood orange, use half-slices, slit from the centre.

PINEAPPLE
Pull small leaves from a pineapple top, slit in half at the bottom end and place on the rim of a glass. A small wedge of pineapple can be placed alongside

DECORATED ICE CUBES
Fill an ice-cube tray half-full of water and freeze. Dip herb leaves, citrus-slice segments, edible flowers etc in iced water, place on top of the cubes and freeze until firm. Top up with iced water and freeze.

COCONUT CURLS
Bake a whole coconut in a moderate oven for about 10 minutes, then split by hitting it with a hammer. Remove the flesh and, using a very sharp knife, pare off thin peelings to make curls to hang on the rim of a glass.

FROSTING
Hold a glass upside down and wipe the outside of the rim with a cut lemon until evenly moistened, then dip the rim into a saucer filled with salt or caster sugar. Shake away excess.

Q&A

What is a frappé and how do I make one?

A frappé is a mixture of fresh fruit and crushed ice. You need a heavy-duty blender to crush the ice. Half-fill a blender with ice cubes and blend on high until crushed. Add whatever fruits you like, cut into chunks (unless they're berries). The most famous frappés are mango, pineapple, strawberry (or a mixture of berries) or you can make your own tropical mixture using whatever fruit you like. You must drink a frappé soon after it's made or it will separate. You can add iced water to a frappé if you feel it needs thinning.

STRAWBERRY
Choose firm, ripe strawberries with fresh green fixes; almost slit in half from the point, or make few slits and fan out. Place on the glass rim.

CELERY STICK
Cut celery into sticks about 4cm longer than the glasses to be used, leaving the leafy tops on if fresh and undamaged. Place in a bloody mary or vegetable juice as a stirrer.

MELON BALLS
Use a melon-baller to cut balls from melons of different colours. Thread alternately onto cocktail sticks and place in drinks in short glasses.

CUCUMBER
Using lebanese cucumbers, thinly slice the unpeeled cucumber. More than just a fresh garnish, these are also useful stirrers.

PEAR AND MINT
Cut a thin slice of pear and cut a slit from the bottom of the slice to the centre. Gently press a small fresh mint sprig into the pear and place in a drink.

CITRUS PEEL
Peel the rind from citrus fruit in a spiral. Place in a drink, hooking one end over the rim; or slice straight strips into narrow "strings", tie in knots and drop into drinks.

kingfish carpaccio

PREP TIME 30 MINS (+ FREEZING & REFRIGERATION) • SERVES 8

Specify sashimi-grade tuna, kingfish, bream, mackerel or jewfish when purchasing, and only buy from a reputable fish market. Wrap the fish tightly in plastic wrap and freeze until just firm. Immediately on removing from the freezer and unwrapping, use a heavy, sharp knife to slice the fish as thinly as possible.

400g piece sashimi kingfish
¼ cup (60ml) lemon juice
2 tablespoons olive oil
1 small red onion (80g), sliced thinly
1 cup loosely packed fresh flat-leaf parsley leaves
2 tablespoons drained baby capers, rinsed

1 Tightly wrap kingfish in plastic wrap; freeze 1 hour or until firm. Unwrap fish; slice as thinly as possible.
2 Arrange slices on platter; drizzle fish with juice. Cover; refrigerate 1 hour.
3 Combine oil, onion, parsley and capers in medium bowl. Drain juice from fish; serve with onion mixture.

nutritional count per serving 5.7g total fat (1g saturated fat); 410kJ (98 cal); 0.9g carbohydrate; 10.5g protein; 0.5g fibre

blini with chilli crab salad

PREP + COOK TIME 40 MINS (+ COOLING) • MAKES 24

You can buy cooked crab meat at the local fish markets or supermarket. Alternatively, buy fresh crabs and cook them (blue swimmer crabs are good). To tell if crabs are meaty, look at the claws; if they are pointy and sharp it means they have a new shell and don't have much meat. If the claws are rounded, they have an older shell and will have more meat.

⅔ cup (100g) wholemeal plain flour
¼ cup (35g) white self-raising flour
1 tablespoon plain flour
½ teaspoon cayenne pepper
2 eggs
¾ cup (180ml) buttermilk
2 green onions, sliced finely
40g butter, melted

chilli crab salad
150g cooked crab meat
1 tablespoon finely chopped fresh mint
1 tablespoon finely chopped fresh vietnamese mint
1 teaspoon finely grated lime rind
2 tablespoons lime juice
2 teaspoons fish sauce
½ lebanese cucumber (65g), seeded, chopped finely
1 fresh small red thai chilli, sliced thinly

1 Sift flours and pepper into medium bowl; whisk in eggs and buttermilk until smooth. Stir in onion and butter.
2 Heat oiled large frying pan; cook level tablespoons of blini mixture, in batches, until golden both sides; cool on wire racks.
3 Meanwhile, make chilli crab salad.
4 Serve blinis topped with salad.

chilli crab salad Combine ingredients in medium bowl; season to taste.

nutritional count per piece 2.1g total fat (1.1g saturated fat); 201kJ (48 cal); 4.6g carbohydrate; 2.5g protein; 0.6g fibre

[1] kingfish carpaccio
[2] blini with chilli crab salad
[3] tomato tarts [page 584]
[4] peppered beef and blue cheese canapés [page 584]

tomato tarts

PREP + COOK TIME 40 MINS • MAKES 16

Chervil is a delicate, lacy herb with a fresh, slightly anise flavour. It is one the four fines herbes (the others are parsley, tarragon and chives) that flavour a classic omelette aux fines herbes, and is good used as a garnish or sprinkled on salads, fish, cream soups or cooked vegetables. Chervil is available for much of the year but is at its best in spring.

4 medium vine-ripened tomatoes (600g), peeled, quartered, seeded
1 tablespoon brown sugar
1 tablespoon balsamic vinegar
½ sheet puff pastry
16 sprigs fresh chervil

1 Preheat oven 220°C/200°C fan-forced.
2 Combine tomato, sugar and vinegar in small baking dish; roast, uncovered, about 20 minutes or until tomato is soft.
3 Meanwhile, cut pastry sheet in half lengthways, cut each half into 4 squares; cut each square into triangles (you will have 16). Place pastry triangles on oiled oven tray; top with another oiled oven tray (the second tray stops the pastry from puffing up). Bake pastry, alongside tomato, about 10 minutes or until crisp.
4 Place a tomato piece on each pastry triangle. Serve topped with chervil.
nutritional count per tart 1.2g total fat (0.6g saturated fat); 117kJ (28 cal); 3.4g carbohydrate; 0.7g protein; 0.5g fibre

peppered beef and blue cheese canapés

PREP + COOK TIME 30 MINS • MAKES 48

Use a soft creamy blue cheese for the blue cheese mousse; the mousse can be made a day ahead and kept, covered, in the fridge. It's best to cook the beef as close to serving time as possible.

500g beef fillet, trimmed
¼ cup (60ml) olive oil
2 tablespoons finely cracked black pepper
180g packet lavash crispbreads
1 small bunch watercress
blue cheese mousse
100g blue cheese, softened
100g packaged cream cheese, softened
⅓ cup (60ml) cream

1 Halve beef lengthways; rub with oil and pepper. Cook beef on heated oiled grill plate (or grill or barbecue) until cooked to your liking, turning beef once. Cover beef; stand 10 minutes before slicing thinly.
2 Meanwhile, make blue cheese mousse.
3 Serve lavash topped with beef, a spoonful of mousse, and sprigs of watercress.
blue cheese mousse Stir ingredients together until smooth; season to taste.
nutritional count per piece 4.2g total fat (1.8g saturated fat); 272kJ (65 cal); 2.5g carbohydrate; 4g protein; 0.8g fibre

barbecued seafood platter

PREP + COOK TIME 1 HOUR (+ REFRIGERATION) • SERVES 8

- 16 uncooked medium king prawns (720g)
- 1 teaspoon finely grated lemon rind
- ½ teaspoon dried chilli flakes
- 1 clove garlic, crushed
- 1 tablespoon finely chopped fresh oregano
- 2 tablespoons olive oil
- 8 slices prosciutto (120g)
- 8 butterflied sardines (240g)
- 300g baby octopus, quartered
- 200g squid hoods, sliced into rings
- 2 tablespoons balsamic vinegar
- ¼ cup coarsely chopped fresh flat-leaf parsley
- 500g small black mussels
- ¼ cup (60ml) lemon juice
- 1 medium tomato (150g), seeded, chopped finely

1 Remove and discard prawn heads. Cut prawns lengthways, three-quarters of the way through (and down to 1cm before the tail), leaving shells intact; press down on prawns on board to flatten.
2 Combine prawns, rind, chilli, garlic, oregano and half the oil in medium bowl. Cover; refrigerate 1 hour.
3 Wrap a prosciutto slice firmly around each sardine.
4 Cook octopus and squid on heated oiled grill plate (or grill or barbecue). Combine octopus and squid in medium heatproof bowl with remaining oil, vinegar and 2 tablespoons of the parsley. Cover to keep warm.
5 Cook prawns and sardines on heated oiled grill plate (or grill or barbecue).
6 Meanwhile, cook mussels, covered, on heated oiled flat plate about 5 minutes or until mussels open (discard any that do not). Place mussels in medium heatproof bowl; drizzle with juice, sprinkle with tomato and remaining parsley. Serve seafood with lemon wedges, if you like.

nutritional count per serving 8.7g total fat (1.7g saturated fat); 836kJ (200 cal); 1.3g carbohydrate; 28.5g protein; 0.4g fibre

I'd like to buy more fresh fish and other types of seafood, but I'm not sure how to tell if they've been sitting there for days or arrived that morning. How do I know that the seafood I'm buying is fresh?

Fresh seafood (fish and shellfish) should always be bought from seafood markets or a reputable fishmonger. All seafood should look fresh and have a fresh "sea" smell – any seafood that smells "fishy" is no good to eat. Whole fish should have firm, not spongy, flesh with red gills; the skin should be shiny with close fitting scales and the eyes should be clear and bright. Fish fillets and cutlets should have moist flesh with a firm texture; there should be no signs of discolouration or dryness. Any bones should be firmly attached to the flesh. Crustaceans and molluscs should have brightly coloured shells or flesh, and the tentacles, heads, flesh or shells should be plump, firm and intact. Shells should be closed, or should close when tapped on a bench. There should also be no discolouration of the joints.

smoked salmon and dilled sour cream crêpe cakes

PREP + COOK TIME
1 HOUR (+ STANDING & REFRIGERATION)
MAKES 16

½ cup (75g) plain flour
2 eggs
2 teaspoons vegetable oil
1 cup (250ml) milk
2 tablespoons drained capers, rinsed, chopped coarsely
2 tablespoons finely chopped fresh dill
1 tablespoon grated lemon rind
2 teaspoons lemon juice
1 clove garlic, crushed
1 cup (240g) sour cream
500g sliced smoked salmon

For a vegetarian version, combine 250g spreadable fetta cheese, 2 tablespoons chopped fresh mint, 2 teaspoons finely grated lemon rind, 2 teaspoons lemon juice and 1 crushed garlic clove. Spread over crêpes; top with thin slices of roasted red capsicum, char-grilled eggplant, 50g chopped kalamata olives and 50g chopped semi-dried tomatoes.

1 Line base and side of deep 20cm-round cake pan with plastic wrap.
2 Place flour in medium bowl. Make well in centre; gradually whisk in combined eggs, oil and milk. Strain into large jug; stand 30 minutes.
3 Heat oiled 19cm frying pan; pour ¼ cup of the batter into pan, tilting pan to coat base. Cook over low heat, loosening around edge with spatula until browned lightly. Turn; brown other side. Remove from pan; repeat with remaining batter to make a total of five crêpes.
4 Combine capers, dill, rind, juice, garlic and sour cream in small bowl. Place a crêpe in cake pan; spread with ⅓ cup of sour cream mixture, cover with a quarter of the salmon. Continue layering with remaining crêpes, sour cream mixture and salmon, finishing with a crêpe. Cover; refrigerate overnight.
5 Gently turn crêpes cake onto chopping board; discard plastic wrap. Using sharp knife, carefully trim cake into a square; discard trimmings. Cut into 4cm squares; top squares with a little extra sour cream and dill, if you like.

nutritional count per piece 9.3g total fat (4.9g saturated fat); 585kJ (140 cal); 4.8g carbohydrate; 9.4g protein; 0.3g fibre

Pour ¼ cup of the batter into a frying pan (a crêpe or omelette pan is perfect). Tilt the pan so the mixture evenly coats the base.

Cook crêpes lightly on both sides and stack one on top of the other (they won't stick).

Place one crêpe in a plastic-wrap-lined cake pan and spread with sour cream mixture, top with smoked salmon slices, then another crêpe.

Remove the crêpe cake from the pan and cut into a square, then cut into 4cm squares for serving.

chicken and mayonnaise finger sandwiches

PREP TIME 10 MINS • MAKES 12

2 cups (320g) coarsely shredded barbecued chicken
2 tablespoons drained capers, chopped coarsely
2 tablespoons finely chopped fresh chives
⅓ cup (100g) whole-egg mayonnaise
8 slices brown bread
1 lebanese cucumber (130g), sliced thinly

1 Combine chicken, capers, chives and ¼ cup of the mayonnaise in medium bowl.
2 Spread chicken mixture over four bread slices; top with cucumber. Spread remaining mayonnaise over remaining bread; place on top of cucumber.
3 Remove and discard crusts; cut sandwiches into three strips.
nutritional count per finger 4.3g total fat (0.7g saturated fat); 422kJ (101 cal); 9.9g carbohydrate; 5.7g protein; 1.2g fibre

chermoulla prawn skewers

PREP + COOK TIME 30 MINS • MAKES 16

Soak bamboo skewers in water for an least an hour to prevent splintering or scorching during cooking.

16 uncooked medium king prawns (720g)
1 tablespoon olive oil
2 tablespoons finely chopped fresh flat-leaf parsley
2 tablespoons finely chopped fresh mint
2 tablespoons finely chopped fresh coriander
2 cloves garlic, crushed
2 teaspoons finely grated lemon rind
1 tablespoon lemon juice
1 teaspoon ground allspice
1 teaspoon caraway seeds

1 Shell and devein prawns, leaving tails intact.
2 Combine prawns with oil and remaining ingredients in medium bowl.
3 Preheat grill.
4 Thread prawns, tail-end first, onto 16 small bamboo skewers or strong toothpicks; grill prawns about 5 minutes or until changed in colour.
nutritional count per skewer 1.3g total fat (0.2g saturated fat); 130kJ (31 cal); 0.1g carbohydrate; 4.7g protein; 0.1g fibre

sticky pork on betel leaves

PREP + COOK TIME 55 MINS • MAKES 48

Use a splatter guard while deep-frying pork; these are handy to have and are available from supermarkets. The pork becomes sticky during the second cooking (stir-frying), so use a non-stick pan to make cleaning up easier. Use scissors to finely shred kaffir lime leaves.

- 1.2kg pork belly, skin and bones removed
- ⅓ cup (80ml) fish sauce
- 2 tablespoons grated palm sugar
- 1 star anise
- 1cm piece fresh ginger (5g), peeled, sliced thinly
- 2 cloves garlic, bruised
- 1 litre (4 cups) water
- vegetable oil, for deep-frying
- 1½ teaspoons white peppercorns
- ½ cup coarsely chopped fresh coriander root
- 8 green onions, chopped coarsely
- ½ cup (90g) grated palm sugar, extra
- ¼ cup (60ml) fish sauce, extra
- 48 betel leaves
- 4 fresh kaffir lime leaves, shredded finely

1 Cut pork into 1cm cubes. Place pork in medium saucepan with sauce, sugar, star anise, ginger, garlic and the water; bring to the boil. Reduce heat; simmer, covered, about 25 minutes or until pork is tender. Drain pork; discard liquid and spices. Dry pork well with absorbent paper

2 Heat oil in wok, deep-fryer or deep wide saucepan; deep-fry pork, in batches, until golden brown. Drain on absorbent paper.

3 Meanwhile, dry-fry peppercorns in small frying pan until fragrant. Using mortar and pestle, grind peppercorns until fine. Add coriander and onion, grind until smooth. Add extra sugar and extra sauce; grind until sugar is dissolved.

4 Stir-fry pork with coriander mixture in oiled wok over high heat until pork is crisp.

5 Place betel leaves on a serving platter, top with pork mixture and lime leaves.

nutritional count per leaf 6.9g total fat (2.1g saturated fat); 380kJ (91 cal); 2.6g carbohydrate; 4.9g protein; 0.2g fibre

Q&A

What are betel leaves and where can I find them? If they're not available what can I use as a substitute?

Betel leaves are mostly used as a little wrap or a tiny plate – the filling is placed on top and the diner picks up a leaf, folds it over the filling and pops it into his mouth. They are available at some greengrocers and most Asian food stores. If you can't find them, witlof leaves would work well or soft lettuce cups.

lace wedding cakes

PREP + COOK TIME 1 HOUR 45 MINS (+ COOLING) • MAKES 36

250g butter, softened
1¼ cups (250g) firmly packed brown sugar
4 eggs
2 tablespoons orange marmalade
1.5kg (7¾ cups) mixed dried fruit, chopped finely
1½ cups (225g) plain flour
½ cup (75g) self-raising flour
2 teaspoons mixed spice
½ cup (125ml) sweet sherry
¼ cup (30g) blanched whole almonds
2 tablespoons sweet sherry, extra

decorations
½ cup (80g) icing sugar
750g ready-made white icing
½ cup (160g) orange marmalade, warmed, strained
silver lustre

TIPS

• If your oven won't hold three sets of muffin pans, it's fine to leave the mixture standing at room temperature while the first batch bakes.

• Use an embossed rolling pin or plastic doily to mark the icing. These are available from haberdashery, craft and cake-decorating shops.

• We used three cake stands stacked on top of each other to display the cakes. They measured 17cm, 24cm and 34cm in diameter. Mix and match the colours of the plates, cakes and flowers to suit the occasion.

1 Preheat oven to 150°C/ 130°C fan-forced. Line three 12-hole (⅓-cup/80ml) muffin pans with silver foil and paper cases.

2 Beat butter, sugar and eggs in small bowl with electric mixer until just combined. Transfer mixture to large bowl, add marmalade and fruit; mix well.

3 Sift flours and spice over mixture, add sherry; mix well. Place 2 level tablespoons of mixture into each case; smooth surface.

4 Bake cakes about 50 minutes. Remove cakes from oven; brush tops with extra sherry. Cover pan tightly with foil; cool cakes in pan.

5 On surface dusted with sifted icing sugar, knead icing until smooth. Roll out to a thickness of 5mm. With an embossed rolling pin, gently press over icing to make a pattern. Using a 7.5cm round fluted cutter cut out 36 rounds.

6 Brush cakes with marmalade; top with icing rounds. Carefully brush silver lustre over pattern on icing.

nutritional count per cupcake 7g total fat (4g saturated fat); 1363kJ (326 cal); 58.7g carbohydrate; 3.4g protein; 3.6g fibre

Knead the icing with the heel of your hand on a surface dusted with icing sugar until the icing is smooth.

Roll out the icing until it is about 5mm thick. Then, using an embossed rolling pin, gently roll over the icing to make a pattern.

Cut out 36 rounds of icing using a 7.5cm round fluted cutter.

Carefully remove the scraps of icing between the rounds and lift the rounds on top of the marmalade-brushed cakes.

fruit mince pies

PREP + COOK TIME 1 HOUR 40 MINS (+ STANDING & REFRIGERATION) • MAKES 24

Mince pies will keep well in an airtight container for up to two weeks. Make double the quantity of fruit mince to bottle for gifts.

150g dried figs, chopped finely
½ cup (65g) dried cranberries
½ cup (75g) raisins, chopped coarsely
¼ cup (40g) mixed peel
¼ cup (55g) finely chopped glacé ginger
¼ cup (60g) finely chopped glacé peach
1 medium apple (150g), grated
½ cup (110g) firmly packed brown sugar
2 tablespoons fig jam
1 teaspoon finely grated orange rind
2 tablespoons orange juice
1 cinnamon stick, halved
1 teaspoon mixed spice
⅓ cup (80ml) brandy
1½ sheets shortcrust pastry, thawed
1 egg white

pastry
2 cups (300g) plain flour
⅓ cup (75g) caster sugar
150g cold butter, chopped coarsely
1 egg, beaten lightly

1 Combine fruit, sugar, jam, rind, juice, spices and brandy in medium bowl. Cover, stand for a week or up to a month; stir mixture every two or three days.
2 Make pastry.
3 Grease two 12-hole (2 tablespoon/40ml) deep flat-based patty pans. Divide pastry in half; roll one portion of dough between sheets of baking paper to 3mm thickness; cut 12 x 7cm rounds from pastry. Repeat with remaining pastry. Press rounds into pan holes; pricks bases all over with fork, refrigerate 30 minutes.
4 Preheat oven to 200°C/180°C fan-forced.
5 Cut whole shortcrust pastry sheet into 16 squares; cut each square into 6 strips. Cut the half pastry sheet into 8 squares, cut into 6 strips. Use 6 strips to make a lattice pattern. Cut a 6.5cm round from each latticed piece of pastry. Repeat with remaining strips.
6 Discard cinnamon from mince, spoon mince into pastry cases; top with lattice pastry rounds. Press edges to seal; brush pastry with egg white.
7 Bake pies about 20 minutes. Dust with a little sifted icing sugar before serving.
pastry Blend or process flour, sugar and butter until crumbly. Add egg; process until combined. Knead pastry on floured surface until smooth. Cover; refrigerate 30 minutes.
nutritional count per pie 8.5g total fat (5g saturated fat); 995kJ (238 cal); 34.7g carbohydrate; 2.9g protein; 2.1g fibre

rich chocolate christmas cakes

**PREP + COOK TIME
2 HOURS 15 MINS
(+ STANDING & COOLING)
MAKES 8**

1 cup (170g) seeded prunes
1 cup (140g) seeded dried dates
1 cup (150g) raisins
½ cup (75g) muscatels
1 cup (200g) dried figs
5 (100g) glacé orange slices
1½ cups (375ml) irish whiskey
1½ cups (330g) firmly packed dark brown sugar
185g butter, softened
3 eggs
½ cup (50g) ground hazelnuts
1½ cups (225g) plain flour
2 tablespoons cocoa powder
1 teaspoon mixed spice
½ teaspoon ground nutmeg
½ teaspoon bicarbonate of soda
150g dark eating chocolate, chopped finely
¼ cup (60ml) water
1 cup (150g) muscatels, extra
2 tablespoons cocoa powder, extra

Buy 200g muscatels for these cakes, use one-third in the cake mixture and the rest for decorating.

These cakes make fabulous Christmas gifts and you can make them weeks ahead – except for the decoration – and store them in airtight containers. Store the whiskey syrup in a screw-top jar, then stand the jar in hot water to thin it again when glazing muscatels.

1 Chop all fruit finely. Combine fruit and ¾ cup of the whiskey in large bowl. Cover with plastic wrap; stand overnight.
2 Preheat oven to 120°C/100°C fan-forced. Line eight deep 8cm-round cake tins with two thicknesses of baking paper, extending paper 5cm above sides of tins.
3 Stir remaining whiskey and ¾ cup of the sugar in small saucepan over heat until sugar dissolves; bring to the boil. Remove from heat; cool syrup 20 minutes.
4 Meanwhile, beat butter and remaining sugar in small bowl with electric mixer until combined; beat in eggs, one at a time. Add butter mixture to fruit mixture; mix well. Mix in ground hazelnuts, sifted dry ingredients, chocolate and ½ cup of the cooled syrup. Spread mixture into tins.
5 Bake cakes about 1¾ hours.
6 Bring remaining syrup and the water to the boil in small saucepan; boil for 3 minutes or until thickened slightly. Brush hot cakes with half of the hot syrup, cover cakes with foil; cool in tins.
7 Divide extra muscatels into eight small bunches; place bunches in remaining syrup. Stand in syrup until cool, drain.
8 Dust cakes with extra sifted cocoa, top with muscatel bunches.
nutritional count per cake 31.5g total fat (16.9g saturated fat); 4075kJ (975 cal); 132.5g carbohydrate; 10.9g protein; 10.4g fibre

boiled christmas pudding PREP + COOK TIME 6 HOURS 30 MINS (+ STANDING & COOLING) • SERVES 16

Sprinkle plain flour onto the boiled pudding cloth and spread it out to cover an area of about 40cm.

Gather pudding cloth evenly around pudding, avoiding deep pleats then pat the mixture into a round shape.

TIPS

• You need a 60cm square of unbleached calico for the pudding cloth. If calico has not been used before, soak in cold water overnight; next day, boil it for 20 minutes then rinse in cold water.

• To store pudding: remove cloth, then allow pudding to come to room temperature, wrap it in plastic wrap and seal tightly in a freezer bag or airtight container. Pudding can be stored in refrigerator up to two months or frozen up to 12 months.

• To reheat: thaw frozen pudding three days in refrigerator; remove from fridge 12 hours before reheating. To reheat in microwave oven: cover whole pudding with plastic wrap; microwave on medium (55%) about 15 minutes or until hot.

1½ cups (250g) raisins
1½ cups (240g) sultanas
1 cup (150g) dried currants
¾ cup (120g) mixed peel
1 teaspoon finely grated lemon rind
2 tablespoons lemon juice
2 tablespoons brandy
250g butter, softened
2 cups (440g) firmly packed brown sugar
5 eggs
1¼ cups (185g) plain flour
½ teaspoon ground nutmeg
½ teaspoon mixed spice
4 cups (280g) stale breadcrumbs

1 Combine fruit, rind, juice and brandy in large bowl. Cover tightly with plastic wrap; store in a cool, dark place overnight or up to a week, stirring every day.

2 Beat butter and sugar in large bowl with electric mixer only until combined. Beat in eggs, one at a time, beat only until combined between each addition. Add butter mixture to fruit mixture then sifted dry ingredients and breadcrumbs; mix well.

3 Fill large boiler three-quarters full of hot water, cover; bring to the boil. Have ready 2.5m of kitchen string and an extra ½ cup of plain flour. Wearing thick rubber gloves, dip pudding cloth in boiling water; boil 1 minute then remove and carefully squeeze excess water from cloth. Working quickly, spread hot cloth on bench, rub flour into centre of cloth to cover an area about 40cm in diameter, leaving flour a little thicker in centre of cloth where "skin" on the pudding needs to be thickest.

4 Place pudding mixture in centre of cloth. Gather cloth evenly around mixture, avoiding any deep pleats; then pat into round shape. Tie cloth tightly with string as close to mixture as possible. Pull ends of cloth tightly to ensure pudding is as round and firm as possible. Knot two pairs of corners together to make pudding easier to remove.

5 Lower pudding into boiling water; tie free ends of string to handles of boiler to suspend pudding. Cover with tight-fitting lid, boil for 6 hours, replenishing water as necessary to maintain level.

6 Untie pudding from handles; place wooden spoon through knotted calico loops to lift pudding from water. Do not put pudding on bench; suspend from spoon by placing over rungs of upturned stool or wedging handle in drawer. Pudding must be suspended freely. Twist ends of cloth around string to avoid them touching pudding. If pudding has been cooked correctly, cloth will dry in patches within a few minutes; hang 10 minutes.

7 Place pudding on board; cut string, carefully peel back cloth. Turn pudding onto a plate then carefully peel cloth away completely; cool. Stand at least 20 minutes or until skin darkens and pudding becomes firm.

nutritional count per serving 15.5g total fat (9.1g saturated fat); 2090kJ (500 cal); 79.7g carbohydrate; 7g protein; 3.3g fibre

wedding cake cookies

PREP + COOK TIME 55 MINS (+ REFRIGERATION & COOLING) • MAKES 12

These biscuits make the perfect wedding gift, or treat for your guests to take home after the big day. Drop a little food colouring into your royal icing if you want a variation to the all-white decorations we've used here – pastel pink or yellow would look sweet.

⅓ cup (55g) dried mixed fruit
2 tablespoons brandy
125g butter, softened
1 teaspoon finely grated orange rind
⅓ cup (75g) caster sugar
1 tablespoon golden syrup
1 cup (150g) self-raising flour
⅔ cup (100g) plain flour
½ teaspoon mixed spice

fondant icing
300g ready-made white icing, chopped coarsely
1 egg white
½ teaspoon lemon juice

royal icing
1½ cups (240g) pure icing sugar
1 egg white

1 Process fruit and brandy until smooth.
2 Beat butter, rind, sugar and syrup in small bowl with electric mixer until combined. Stir in sifted dry ingredients and fruit puree, in two batches.
3 Knead dough on floured surface until smooth; roll dough between sheets of baking paper until 5mm thick. Cover; refrigerate 30 minutes.
4 Preheat oven to 180°C/160°C fan-forced. Grease oven trays; line with baking paper.
5 Using 10.5cm wedding cake cutter, cut 12 shapes from dough. Place about 5cm apart on oven trays. Bake about 12 minutes. Cool on wire racks.
6 Make fondant icing. Use a metal spatula, dipped in hot water, to spread icing quickly over cookies; set at room temperature.
7 Make royal icing. Decorate cookies with royal icing.
fondant icing Stir white icing in small heatproof bowl over small saucepan of simmering water until smooth. Add egg white and juice; beat until smooth.
royal icing Sift icing sugar through fine sieve. Beat egg white until foamy in small bowl with electric mixer; beat in icing sugar, a tablespoon at a time. Cover surface tightly with plastic wrap.
nutritional count per serving 8.8g total fat (5.7g saturated fat); 1555kJ (372 cal); 67.1g carbohydrate; 3.2g protein; 1.5g fibre

Q&A

[1] wedding cake cookies
[2] white christmas ice-cream puddings [page 598]
[3] celebration fruit cake [page 598]
[4] steamed christmas pudding [page 599]

Have you got any suggestions for really simple Christmas desserts? My family finds pudding too heavy after the big meal, but we all want something festive to round off our celebrations.

The perfect dessert for a southern hemisphere Christmas is red fruits. Strawberries, raspberries, blueberries and cherries all mixed together and served in a big glass bowl with some good quality vanilla ice-cream not only looks festive, but it's light and fresh and a wonderful way to end a big lunch. The fruit doesn't need to be cooked and you don't need to add sugar. The only time-consuming part of the dish is stoning the cherries.

1

2

3

4

white christmas ice-cream puddings

**PREP + COOK TIME
1 HOUR (+ COOLING &
REFRIGERATION)
MAKES 8**

1 vanilla bean
1¾ cups (430ml) milk
600ml cream
180g white eating chocolate, chopped coarsely
8 egg yolks
¾ cup (165g) caster sugar
1 cup (130g) dried cranberries
2 tablespoons brandy
1 cup (140g) unsalted pistachios
2 teaspoons vegetable oil

It is considered that the black specks from the vanilla bean in a dish give it cachet as they show that the real thing has been used. Each bean can be washed, dried and re-used several times, and then be put into a jar of sugar to scent it for using in cakes and desserts.

1 Split vanilla bean lengthways; scrape seeds into medium saucepan. Add pod, milk, cream and 50g of the chocolate; bring to the boil.
2 Meanwhile, whisk egg yolks and sugar in medium bowl until thick and creamy; gradually whisk into hot milk mixture. Stir custard over low heat, without boiling, until thickened slightly. Cover surface of custard with plastic wrap; cool 20 minutes.
3 Strain custard into shallow container, such as aluminium slab cake pan, cover with foil; freeze until almost firm.
4 Place ice-cream in large bowl, chop coarsely; beat with electric mixer until smooth. Pour into deep container, cover; freeze until firm. Repeat process two more times.
5 Meanwhile, place cranberries and brandy in small bowl; stand 15 minutes.
6 Stir cranberry mixture and nuts into ice-cream. Spoon ice-cream into eight ¾-cup (180ml) moulds. Cover; freeze 3 hours or until firm.
7 Stir remaining chocolate and oil in small saucepan over low heat until smooth.
8 Dip each mould, one at a time, into a bowl of hot water for about 1 second. Turn ice-creams onto serving plates; top with warm chocolate mixture.
nutritional count per pudding 57.7g total fat (30.4g saturated fat); 3281kJ (785 cal); 53.1g carbohydrate; 11.5g protein; 2.3g fibre

celebration fruit cake

PREP + COOK TIME 4 HOURS 10 MINS (+ STANDING & COOLING) • SERVES 20

3 cups (500g) sultanas
1¾ cups (300g) raisins, halved
1¾ cups (300g) dried dates, chopped finely
1 cup (150g) dried currants
⅔ cup (110g) mixed peel
⅔ cup (150g) glacé cherries, halved
¼ cup (55g) coarsely chopped glacé pineapple
¼ cup (60g) coarsely chopped glacé apricots
½ cup (125ml) dark rum
250g butter, softened
1 cup (220g) firmly packed brown sugar
5 eggs
1½ cups (225g) plain flour
⅓ cup (50g) self-raising flour
1 teaspoon mixed spice
2 tablespoons dark rum, extra

1 Combine fruit and rum in large bowl. Cover tightly with plastic wrap. Store mixture in cool, dark place overnight or up to a week, stirring every day.
2 Preheat oven to 150°C/130°C fan-forced. Line deep 22cm-round cake pan with three thicknesses of baking paper, extending paper 5cm above side.
3 Beat butter and sugar in small bowl with electric mixer until just combined. Add eggs, one at a time, beating only until combined between additions.
4 Add butter mixture to fruit mixture; mix well. Mix in sifted dry ingredients; spread mixture evenly into pan.
5 Bake cake, uncovered, about 3½ hours. Brush cake with extra rum. Cover hot cake, in pan, tightly with foil; cool overnight.
nutritional count per serving 12g total fat (7.2g saturated fat); 1944kJ (465 cal); 77.2g carbohydrate; 4.9g protein; 4.5g fibre

steamed christmas pudding

PREP + COOK TIME
7 HOURS 45 MINS
(+ STANDING & COOLING)
SERVES 12

4 cups (750g) mixed dried fruit
½ cup (125ml) dark rum
250g butter, chopped
2½ cups (500g) firmly packed dark brown sugar
1 tablespoon parisian essence
4 eggs
1 cup (150g) plain flour
1 teaspoon mixed spice
4 cups (280g) stale breadcrumbs
1 large apple (200g), grated coarsely

Parisian essence is available from most supermarkets in the baking section.

This pudding can be made up to 3 months ahead and kept refrigerated, or made up to one year ahead and frozen. If the pudding was made in an aluminium steamer, remove the pudding from the steamer and wrap in plastic wrap before storing.

1 Combine fruit and rum in large bowl. Cover; stand overnight or up to a week, stirring every day.
2 Beat butter, sugar and essence in small bowl with electric mixer until just combined. Beat in eggs, one at a time. Add butter mixture to fruit mixture, then stir in sifted flour and spice, then breadcrumbs and apple; mix well.
3 Grease 2-litre (8-cup) pudding steamer; line base with baking paper. Spoon pudding mixture into steamer.
4 Place 30cm x 40cm sheet of foil on bench, grease foil; top with a sheet of baking paper. Fold 5cm pleat crossways through centre of both sheets. Place sheets, baking-paper-side down, over steamer; secure with string or lid. Make a handle with excess string. Crush surplus foil and baking paper firmly around the rim to help form a good seal; trim any excess.
5 Place pudding in large boiler with enough boiling water to come halfway up side of steamer. Cover with tight-fitting lid, boil 6–7 hours, replenishing water as necessary to maintain level. Stand pudding 15 minutes before turning onto a plate; cool.
6 Wrap pudding in plastic wrap, then place in an airtight container or freezer bag.
nutritional count per serving 20.4g total fat (12.2g saturated fat); 2867kJ (686 cal); 108.3g carbohydrate; 8.4g protein; 5.3g fibre

SPECIAL FEATURE

Cheeses

This is just a small sample of the many cheeses available to us today. Even supermarkets now carry a range of exceptional cheeses. Soft cheeses such as brie and camembert should be taken out of the fridge half an hour or so before you serve them, to allow their full flavours to develop.

BOCCONCINI
Italian for "little mouthfuls", bocconcini are bite-sized balls of fresh mozzarella. A delicate-flavoured, semi-soft cheese, traditionally made from buffalo milk but now mostly made from cow's milk. Sold fresh, it will only keep, refrigerated in brine, for 1-2 days.

BRIE
A soft-ripened cow's milk cheese with a delicate, creamy texture and a rich, sweet taste. After a brief period of ageing, brie should have a bloomy white rind and creamy, voluptuous centre which becomes runny on ripening. Best served at room temperature.

CAMEMBERT
A luscious, buttery cow's milk cheese with a thin edible, aromatic rind. It is probably the most famous and most popular soft French cheese in the world. For the best flavour, eat it at room temperature.

GOAT'S CHEESE (CHEVRE)
Made from goat's milk, this cheese has a very earthy, strong taste. It is available in soft, crumbly and firm textures, in various shapes and sizes, and is sometimes covered in a layer of edible ash (pictured), or herbs.

COTTAGE CHEESE
Its name comes from the description of where it is thought to have been made originally – in cottages from any milk leftover after making butter. This mild, fresh, unripened curd product, has a grainy consistency and a fat content of 15 to 55 per cent.

EDAM
Instantly recognisable from the coating of red paraffin wax on exported products, edam is a semi-hard Dutch cheese made from part-skimmed cow's milk. It is mild in flavour and supple in texture when young, but becomes dry and hard when mature.

Q&A

I recently tried haloumi cheese in a restaurant. What a delicious cheese it is. Can you tell me a simple recipe for using it please?

Place torn rocket leaves in a bowl. Cut some snow peas into thin strips and microwave briefly (1 minute), then plunge into cold water. Drain and add these to the rocket. Cut some baby eggplants into rounds and fry on both sides in olive oil – watch these carefully, they burn easily. Fry halved plum tomatoes in olive oil until soft. Lastly, fry slices of haloumi on both sides in olive oil. Drain all the fried ingredients on absorbent paper and pat with more paper to remove excess oil. Mix the salad together and sprinkle with a little balsamic vinegar. Serve warm.

FETA
crumbly textured goat- or sheep-milk cheese, with sharp, salty taste. Originally from Greece, other countries, including Denmark, now produce it with cow's milk. Ripened and stored in salted whey, it is particularly good tossed into salads.

FONTINA
A smooth, firm Italian cow's milk cheese with a creamy, nutty taste and brown or red rind. It is ideal for melting or grilling. The original fontina from Italy is fairly pungent and quite intense, while fontina produced in other countries tends to be much milder.

GORGONZOLA
Named after the Italian village, Gorgonzola, in Milan, where it was first made, this creamy blue-veined cheese has a mild, sweet taste. It is good as an accompaniment to fruit or used to flavour sauces (especially for pasta or gnocchi).

GRUYERE
hard-rind cow's milk cheese named after the town of Gruyères in Switzerland. It is sweet but slightly salty, with a flavour that varies widely with age – often described as creamy and nutty when young, becomes more assertive, earthy and complex with age. It is a popular cheese for soufflés.

HALOUMI
This Greek Cypriot cheese has a semi-firm, spongy texture and very salty sweet flavour, and is ripened and stored in salted whey. Best grilled or fried, it holds its shape well on being heated. Eat while still warm as it becomes tough and rubbery on cooling.

HAVARTI
Originating in Denmark, this traditional, creamy, semi-hard cow's milk cheese is washed-rind. It is quite mild in flavour and dotted with small holes and irregularities.

PRESERVES

Preserves

Don't dismiss preserving. Yes, it might have been something your Great Aunt did, but like a lot of those lovely, homespun notions we've returned to in recent years, there's a lot of wisdom in the practice. Preserving was a way of ensuring that the household had summer fruits all year round. These days, there isn't the urgency to stock up, but it's deeply rewarding nonetheless.

FOR ALL THE SAME REASONS THAT KNITTING HAS ENJOYED A COMEBACK, YOU SHOULD CONSIDER PRESERVING: IT'S A GENTLE ANTIDOTE TO OUR BUSY, BUSY TIMES AND A COUPLE OF HOURS IN THE KITCHEN ABSORBED IN THE CALM PLEASURE OF CREATING A JEWEL-LIKE JAM OR A TANGY CHUTNEY COULD BE JUST THE THERAPEUTIC OUTLET YOU'RE LOOKING FOR.

READY, SET?

JAM OR JELLY IS READY FOR TESTING when a candy thermometer reads 105°C. If you don't have a candy thermometer, dip a wooden spoon into the jam, hold it horizontal above the pan and tilt the bowl of the spoon towards you. When the mixture falls from the spoon in heavy drops, it is ready for testing.

TO TEST WHEN JAM IS READY remove the pan from the heat, allow the bubbles to subside and drop a teaspoon of mixture on a freezer-chilled plate. Return the plate to the freezer briefly to cool the jam to room temperature. When it has cooled, test the consistency: smooth jam should be of a spreadable consistency, jam with pieces of fruit should form a skin and wrinkle when pushed with a finger; jelly should be a firm mass.

If the mixture hasn't achieved the desired consistency, boil for a few more minutes and test again. Always take the jam or jelly off the heat and wait until it stops bubbling before testing.

JARS FOR BOTTLING

Use ultra-clean, just-sterilised glass jars without chips or cracks. Sterilise jars and metal funnels in one of the following ways:

DISHWASHER In the dishwasher, on the rinse cycle, without detergent, at the hottest temperature.

STOVE TOP Cover with cold water in a large saucepan, put the lid on, bring to the boil and boil for 20 minutes. Remove the jars, drain well and stand right-way up on a board (they'll dry by evaporation).

OVEN Stand the jars right-way up, not touching each other, on an oven tray in a cold oven. Heat the oven to very slow and leave for 30 minutes.

SAVOURY JOYS

A LITTLE RELISH OR CHUTNEY, OR SOME PICKLES, CAN ENLIVEN A SANDWICH AND SUDDENLY MAKE A SNACK OF LEFTOVER COLD MEATS ANYTHING BUT ORDINARY.

PICKLES are vegetables, and occasionally fruits, that are preserved in vinegar, brine or a mixture of the two, usually with flavourings like herbs or spices and sugar or mustard. The best-known pickles are pickled onions, pickled cucumbers (called dill pickles or gherkins), and mixed mustard pickles. Pickles are assertive, sharp and spicy in flavour.

RELISHES Usually based on a single vegetable such as corn or tomatoes, relishes are cooked on the stovetop and simmered for about an hour. Relishes are milder than pickles, being sweet/savoury and tangy rather than strong and sharp. These usually only keep for a few weeks, stored in the refrigerator.

CHUTNEYS Similar to relishes, they encompass a range of spicy, sweet and tangy fruit and/or vegetable mixtures that have been cooked to a thickened texture. Often combining ingredients as diverse as tomatoes, apples, mustard powder and sultanas, chutney mixtures are brought to the boil then simmered for about an hour. The most famous of these is mango chutney, which is superb with curries.

SAVOURY JAMS Onion and chilli jams are delicious, deep-flavoured accompaniments to meats and seafood or can be used to flavour a casserole or soup.

SWEET DELIGHTS

THERE IS SOMETHING SUBLIME ABOUT A DOLLOP OF CRIMSON JAM FILLED WITH REAL CHUNKS OF FRUIT: THE PERFECT PARTNER TO A SCONE OR PIECE OF TOAST.

JAMS are made with small pieces of fruit. The fruit is cooked until tender, then sugar is added and the mixture is cooked until it's of a spreadable but set consistency, achieved by the action of pectin, a substance in the cell walls of fruit. Fruits vary greatly in their pectin content – high-pectin ones include apples, citrus, plums, quinces and black or red currants. Low-pectin fruits such as cherries, figs, peaches, pears, pineapples, rhubarb, strawberries and raspberries can be mixed with high-pectin fruits to make jam set well.

CONSERVES are made with whole pieces of fruit, such as cherries or strawberries, or large pieces of fruits such as peaches or apricots.

MARMALADES are clear, bittersweet jams usually made from one or more citrus fruits. The bitterness comes from the pieces of citrus peel that are cooked into the jam with the fruit.

JELLIES are clear, lozenge-coloured mixtures made from cooked fruit that is strained overnight through a jelly bag. The clear juice is boiled with sugar until it reaches a consistency that will gel. Jelly bags are available from kitchen shops or you can make your own from a fine cloth.

STORING

HOME-MADE PRESERVES, OR HOME-STYLE ONES FROM SMALL-TIME PRODUCERS AT FARMER'S MARKETS, CAN BE STORED AT ROOM TEMPERATURE AWAY FROM SUNLIGHT UNTIL THEY'RE OPENED, AND THEN THEY NEED TO BE REFRIGERATED AND USED WITHIN A MONTH OR TWO.

spicy mustard pickles

PREP + COOK TIME 50 MINS (+ STANDING & COOLING) • MAKES 4 CUPS

This is an old-fashioned pickle that is splendid with cold roast lamb or cheddar cheese. For a delicious snack, mix it with grated cheese, pile it on toast and grill.

¼ medium cauliflower (400g), chopped coarsely
250g green beans, trimmed, chopped coarsely
3 medium brown onions (450g), sliced thickly
1 medium red capsicum (200g), sliced thickly
¼ cup (70g) coarse cooking salt
2 teaspoons dry mustard
2 tablespoons wholegrain mustard
3 teaspoons curry powder
¼ teaspoon ground turmeric
2 cups (500ml) white vinegar
1 cup (220g) firmly packed brown sugar
2 tablespoons plain flour

1 Combine vegetables and salt in large bowl. Cover; stand overnight.
2 Rinse vegetables; drain. Stir vegetables, mustards, curry powder, turmeric, 1¾ cups of the vinegar and sugar in large saucepan over heat, without boiling, until sugar dissolves; bring to the boil. Reduce heat; simmer, uncovered, about 10 minutes or until vegetables are just tender.
3 Stir in blended flour and remaining vinegar; stir over heat until mixture boils and thickens. Pour into hot sterilised jars; seal.

nutritional count per tablespoon 0.1g total fat (0g saturated); 113kJ (27 cal); 5.7g carbohydrate; 0.6g protein; 0.5g fibre

Place the salted vegetables in a pan with the spices, vinegar and brown sugar. Stir over low heat until sugar dissolves, then boil until vegetables are tender.

Add blended flour and vinegar to the cooked vegetables and stir over heat until the mixture boils and thickens.

Spoon the hot pickle mixture into hot, sterilised jars. Seal the jars while mixture is still hot.

tomato chutney

PREP + COOK TIME 1 HOUR 30 MINS (+ COOLING) • MAKES 1.5 LITRES (6 CUPS)

Tomato chutney makes a great addition to casseroles, rissoles, burgers and pot roasts.

- 10 medium ripe tomatoes (1.5kg), peeled, chopped coarsely
- 2 large apples (400g), peeled, chopped coarsely
- 2 medium brown onions (300g), chopped coarsely
- 1 cup (220g) firmly packed brown sugar
- 1½ cups (375ml) brown vinegar
- ¼ teaspoon chilli powder
- ½ teaspoon dry mustard
- ¾ cup (120g) sultanas
- 1 clove garlic, crushed
- 2 teaspoons curry powder
- 2 teaspoons ground allspice

1 Stir ingredients in large saucepan over heat, without boiling, until sugar dissolves; bring to the boil. Reduce heat; simmer, uncovered, stirring occasionally, about 1 hour or until mixture is thick.

2 Pour chutney into hot sterilised jars; seal immediately.

nutritional count per tablespoon 0g total fat (0g saturated fat); 100kJ (24 cal); 5.3g carbohydrate; 0.3g protein; 0.5g fibre

orange marmalade

PREP + COOK TIME 1 HOUR 40 MINS (+ STANDING & COOLING) MAKES 1.75 LITRES (7 CUPS)

- 5 large seville oranges (1.5kg)
- 1.25 litres (5 cups) water
- 2 teaspoons citric acid
- 2 tablespoons lemon juice
- 1.1kg (5 cups) white sugar, approximately

Seville oranges have a short season in winter, and they make a superb bittersweet marmalade. The seeds and pith are reserved because they contain high levels of pectin, which will help the marmalade to set.

1 Peel oranges thinly; cut rind into thin strips. Remove pith from all oranges; reserve half, discard remaining pith. Chop flesh coarsely, reserve seeds.

2 Combine flesh and rind in large bowl with the water. Tie reserved pith and seeds in muslin; add to bowl. Stand at room temperature overnight.

3 Place orange mixture and muslin bag in large saucepan; bring to the boil. Reduce heat; simmer, covered, 35 minutes or until rind is soft. Discard bag.

4 Measure fruit mixture; allow 1 cup (220g) sugar for each cup of mixture.

5 Return mixture and sugar to pan; stir over heat, without boiling, until sugar dissolves. Boil, uncovered, about 30 minutes or until marmalade gels when tested.

6 Pour marmalade into hot sterilised jars; seal immediately.

nutritional count per tablespoon 0g total fat (0g saturated fat); 326kJ (78 cal); 18.8g carbohydrate; 0.2g protein; 0.5g fibre

[opposite] tomato chutney

dark plum jam

PREP + COOK TIME 1 HOUR 45 MINS (+ COOLING) • MAKES 2 LITRES (8 CUPS)

When cooking jam, be sure to use a large wide-topped saucepan that allows for the necessary evaporation, otherwise you will end up with runny jam. Usually about half the liquid has to evaporate before the jam will gel.

28 medium blood plums (2kg)
1 litre (4 cups) water
⅓ cup (80ml) lemon juice
1.3kg (6 cups) white sugar

1 Cut plums into quarters; discard stones. Place plums and the water in large saucepan; bring to the boil. Reduce heat; simmer, covered, 1 hour.
2 Add juice and sugar, stir over heat, without boiling, until sugar dissolves. Boil, uncovered, without stirring, 20 minutes or until jam gels when tested.
3 Pour into hot sterilised jars; seal immediately.

nutritional count per tablespoon 0g total fat (0g saturated fat); 255kJ (61 cal); 14.7g carbohydrate; 0.1g protein; 0.4g fibre

apricot jam

PREP + COOK TIME 1 HOUR (+ COOLING) • MAKES 1.25 LITRES (5 CUPS)

Fruit for jam-making should be barely ripe, as overripe fruit results in a jam or jelly that does not set well. Remove any bruised or damaged pieces before you start.

25 medium apricots (1kg)
1½ cups (375ml) water
1.1kg (5 cups) sugar, approximately

1 Halve apricots; discard stones. Combine apricots and the water in large saucepan; bring to the boil. Reduce heat; simmer, covered, about 15 minutes or until apricots are soft.
2 Measure fruit mixture, allow 1 cup sugar to each cup of fruit mixture. Return fruit mixture and sugar to pan; stir over heat, without boiling, until sugar is dissolved. Bring to the boil; boil, uncovered without stirring, about 15 minutes or until jam gels when tested.
3 Pour jam into hot sterilised jars; seal immediately.

nutritional count per tablespoon 0g total fat (0g saturated fat); 334kJ (80 cal); 9.3g carbohydrate; 0.1g protein; 0.3g fibre

quince paste

PREP + COOK TIME 1 HOUR 25 MINS (+ STANDING) • MAKES 40 SLICES

It is really important that the puree and sugar mixture is cooked until it turns a deep rose colour. The cooking times may vary, depending on the pectin content of the individual fruit. If you have a food processor, puree cooked quinces in seconds, rather than using a sieve.

4 large quinces (2kg)
¼ cup (60ml) lemon juice
1¾ cups (430ml) water
1.1kg (5 cups) caster sugar, approximately
¼ cup (35g) shelled pistachios, chopped coarsely

1 Oil 15cm x 25cm loaf pan. Peel, quarter and core quinces; chop coarsely. Place in large saucepan with juice and the water, simmer, covered, about 40 minutes or until soft; cool.
2 Push quince mixture through sieve into medium bowl. Measure puree, for each cup allow 1 cup sugar. Stir puree and sugar in medium saucepan over heat 20 minutes or until thick and red; stir in nuts. Spread into pan; smooth top. Stand, uncovered, 24 hours.

nutritional count per slice 0.5g total fat (0.1g saturated fat); 539kJ (129 cal); 29g carbohydrate; 0.4g protein; 2.7g fibre

apple jelly

PREP + COOK TIME 1 HOUR 25 MINS (+ COOLING) • MAKES 3 CUPS

Sugar cubes have fewer impurities and are therefore more likely to result in a clearer jelly. Try adding ½ cup passionfruit pulp to this jelly just before bottling; it's delicious.

5 medium sour green apples (750g), chopped coarsely
1½ litres (6 cups) water
4 cups (880g) white sugar, approximately

1 Place apples (seeds, skin, cores and all) and the water in large saucepan; bring to the boil. Simmer, covered, 1 hour. Strain mixture through fine cloth; discard pulp.
2 Measure apple liquid; allow 1 cup (220g) of sugar for each cup of liquid.
3 Place apple liquid and sugar in large saucepan; stir over heat, without boiling, until sugar dissolves. Bring to the boil; boil, uncovered, 15 minutes or until jelly sets.
4 Pour jelly into hot sterilised jars; seal immediately.

nutritional count per tablespoon 0g total fat (0g saturated fat); 447kJ (107 cal); 26.2g carbohydrate; 0.1g protein; 0.3g fibre

strawberry conserve

PREP + COOK TIME 1 HOUR 10 MINS (+ COOLING) • MAKES 1.5 LITRES (6 CUPS)

TIPS

- You will need about 3 medium lemons (420g) to get the amount of juice needed for this recipe.

1.5kg strawberries, hulled
1.1kg (5 cups) white sugar
1 cup (250ml) lemon juice

1 Gently heat berries in large saucepan, covered, 5 minutes to extract juice from berries. Transfer berries with slotted spoon to large bowl; reserve.
2 Add sugar and lemon juice to strawberry juice in pan, stir over heat, without boiling, until sugar dissolves; bring to the boil. Boil, uncovered, without stirring, 20 minutes. Return reserved berries to pan; simmer, uncovered, without stirring, 25 minutes or until jam gels when tested.
3 Pour hot jam into hot sterilised jars; seal immediately.

nutritional count per tablespoon 0g total fat (0g saturated fat); 280kJ (67 cal); 15.9g carbohydrate; 0.4g protein; 0.5g fibre

Add lemon juice to the sugar and strawberry juice in the pan. (The lemon adds pectin to help the jam set.)

The way to test whether a jam is set is to put a spoonful of it onto a freezer-chilled saucer. Push the jam with your finger; if it wrinkles, the jam is set. If it doesn't wrinkle, cook for a little longer then test again.

Pour the hot jam into hot sterilised jars, taking the mixture right up to the top. Seal the jars while the jam is still hot.

TEACHING KIDS TO COOK

Teaching kids to cook

Children love to help in the kitchen, and it's wonderful to find the time to harness their enthusiasm. After all, food preparation and eating is a major part of our lives and it's natural for children to want to be a part of it.

The key is to choose a cooking project that's interesting and uncomplicated. You also need to accept that your assistant chef might create a little extra mess on the kitchen benchtop – and go with it.

Sharing the bench space with an enthusiastic helper takes patience and time, but it can be deeply rewarding for all parties: not only is there the simple joy of creating food together, but you get to see your little person grow up with a love of good food and a respect for the ways of the kitchen.

Bringing them into the kitchen also de-mystifies it for them, and they are more likely to follow the safety rules you lay down – they need to sit or stand safely at the benchtop; they mustn't don't go near the stove top, etc. There are many lessons to be learned in the kitchen, but more than anything teaching kids to cook needs to be fun, not stressful. The learning just happens. It's important for children to realise that cooking is more than getting food to the table: it's about creating healthy meals, sharing, passion and creativity.

HYGIENE

The first lesson for any budding young chef is in personal hygiene. They need to understand that they cannot begin to help you until they've washed their hands carefully with warm water and soap. It's wise to get girls into the habit of tying back long hair too.

Perhaps you could buy your child a special cooking apron of their own. Not only will it help to protect clothes, but donning the apron can be part of the ritual of helping in the kitchen: they can only put their apron on once they've washed their hands.

REMINDER Having washed hands is especially important when handling uncooked food, and everyone should wash their hands again after touching uncooked meat, seafood or poultry.

SAFETY

When there is a child in the kitchen, everyone needs to be super cautious and aware of potential dangers lurking within the arm-shot of darting, inquisitive hands.

Keep sharp knives and other pointy utensils out of reach. If there are pots on the stove top, make sure they are on the back hotplates, with handles facing towards the back wall.

If a kettle has recently boiled, make sure it is out of arm's reach.

Never, ever leave a young child alone in the kitchen – not even for a moment. Give children clear rules about what they can touch and what is strictly out of bounds.

A TACTILE EXPERIENCE

While safety is the priority, don't forget that cooking is an activity filled with sights, smells and sounds. Let your child feel the ingredients: encourage them to compare textures like sugar and flour; touch a cold raw chicken fillet; smell a cut onion, as well as herbs and spices. Let them taste the ingredients too, if they want to: teach about sweet and sour and bitter and 'sharp' tastes. And of course, get them into the good habit of washing their hands before proceeding.

START WITH THE SIMPLE THINGS

You don't want to be tackling a complicated recipe with your four year old in tow. Start with simple foods they love to eat like pizza or nachos. Let them stir the ingredients and spread the tomato paste. Encourage older children to read the recipe out loud. Talk through the steps of the instructions, what ingredients and utensils are needed: encourage your child to find the equipment and measure out the quantities.

FAMILIARISATION

As part of your child's orientation around the kitchen, it's important to explain the workings of the appliances in the room, and the utensils you're using – graters, whisks, beaters, measuring spoons, spatulas, pastry brushes, chopping boards etc – and where they live in the kitchen. The next time you're cooking together, you can ask for your child to help you to find the utensils (as long as they're safely located) which gives them a greater sense of involvement.

DEFROSTING MEAT

If you're working with meat, make sure you impart lessons on meat care as you go. Meat, seafood and poultry always needs to be thawed in the refrigerator, so if your menu calls for any of these, make sure you've thawed them ahead of time, making sure to place a tray under the meat to prevent drips. It's not ideal to defrost any of these items in the microwave because sometimes the outside edges of the meat can actually cook.

CLEANING UP

THIS IS THE PART WHERE YOUR ERSTWHILE ENTHUSIASTIC LITTLE HELPERS SUDDENLY LOSE INTEREST IN THE KITCHEN, BUT IT'S IMPORTANT FOR THEM TO KNOW THAT PACKING UP IS A PART OF THE PROCESS OF COOKING, TOO. EXPLAIN TO THEM THE IMPORTANCE OF CAREFULLY PUTTING AWAY ANY UNUSED FOOD. IF YOU'RE PUTTING AWAY UNUSED MEAT OR VEGETABLES, MAKE SURE THEY'RE PLACED IN A SEALED CONTAINER OR RESEALABLE PLASTIC BAG.

TIDY UP AS YOU GO

Keep the bench and the rest of the preparation area clean and tidy as you work. Wipe up any spills or grease spots when they happen.

Have one cloth for wiping the benchtop and a separate one for wiping spills on the floor. And use another cloth altogether for wiping hands. Rinse cloths constantly in hot soapy water.

Wash – or at least rinse – the equipment you're using after each use: don't let the food cement itself to the bottom of the bowls or pans.

TASTE-TESTING

This is the part where there is usually never any problem recruiting help. It's good to taste-test the food you're making and children love to learn about the flavours they're creating.

REMEMBER Don't taste from the stirring spoon and return it to the saucepan or mixing bowl. Use clean cutlery each time you taste.

ham and pineapple pizza

PREP + COOK TIME 1 HOUR (+ STANDING) • SERVES 8

2 teaspoons olive oil
⅓ cup (85g) bottled tomato pasta sauce
2 cups (200g) coarsely grated pizza cheese
100g sliced leg ham, chopped coarsely
⅔ cup (140g) coarsely chopped drained canned pineapple pieces

pizza dough
2 teaspoons (7g) dried yeast
1 teaspoon sugar
½ teaspoon salt
¾ cup (180ml) warm water
2½ cups (375g) plain flour
2 tablespoons olive oil

1. Make pizza dough.
2. Preheat oven to 250°C/230°C fan-forced.
3. Carefully lift each dough round onto oiled pizza pans or oven trays; using a pastry brush, brush oil over pizza bases. Spoon tomato pasta sauce on bases, using back of large spoon to spread sauce all over base.
4. Sprinkle half of the cheese over sauce, then top with ham and pineapple. Sprinkle remaining cheese over pizzas.
5. Bake pizzas, uncovered, 20 minutes. Serve cut into slices.

pizza dough Combine yeast, sugar, salt and the warm water in small bowl, cover; stand in warm place about 20 minutes or until mixture is frothy. Combine flour and oil in large bowl; stir in yeast mixture, mix to a soft dough. Knead dough on floured surface about 5 minutes or until smooth and elastic. Place dough in large oiled bowl, cover; stand in warm place about 1 hour or until dough doubles in size. Turn dough onto floured surface; knead until smooth. Divide dough in half; using rolling pin, flatten dough and roll each half out to a 32cm round.

nutritional count per serving 12.2g total fat (4.6g saturated fat); 1354kJ (324 cal); 36.8g carbohydrate; 15.2g protein; 2.5g fibre

Place the yeast, sugar, salt and warm water in a bowl and allow to stand for 20 minutes or until the mixture becomes frothy.

Set the dough mixture aside for about an hour or until it is well risen. The dough should double in size.

Divide the kneaded dough in half. Roll out each half to a 32cm round with a rolling pin. Drape the dough over the rolling pin and place onto the oiled pizza pans.

Sprinkle grated pizza cheese evenly over the tomato sauce, then top with chopped ham and pineapple pieces.

noodle and vegetable rice paper rolls

PREP + COOK TIME 40 MINS • MAKES 12

The rolls can be made at the table or made ahead of time and stored in the fridge for up to 3 hours. Cover them with a damp clean tea towel to keep them moist.

60g rice vermicelli noodles
1 small carrot (70g), grated coarsely
200g wombok, shredded finely
1 tablespoon fish sauce
1 tablespoon brown sugar
¼ cup (60ml) lemon juice
12 x 17cm square rice paper sheets
12 fresh mint leaves

1 Place noodles in medium heatproof bowl, cover with boiling water; stand about 10 minutes or until just tender, drain. Using kitchen scissors, cut noodles into random lengths.
2 Place noodles in same cleaned bowl with carrot, cabbage, sauce, sugar and juice; toss gently to combine.
3 To assemble rolls, place one sheet of rice paper in medium bowl of warm water until just softened; lift sheet carefully from water, placing it on a tea-towel-covered board with a corner point facing towards you. Place a little of the vegetable filling horizontally in centre of sheet, top with one mint leaf. Fold corner point facing you up over filling; roll sheet to enclose filling, folding in sides after first complete turn of roll. Repeat with remaining sheets, filling and mint.

nutritional count per roll 0.2g total fat (0g saturated fat); 130kJ (31 cal); 6g carbohydrate; 1.1g protein; 0.6g fibre
serving idea sweet chilli sauce for dipping.

With a corner pointing towards you, carefully lift a softened rice paper sheet onto a clean board covered with a tea towel.

Place a little of the filling in the middle of the sheet, then top with one mint leaf. Fold the corner point facing you over the filling and roll the sheet to enclose the filling.

As you roll the rice paper sheet over to enclose the filling, tuck in the sides after the first complete turn. Continue rolling the sheet to form a roll. Repeat for the remaining sheets and filling.

vegie nachos

PREP + COOK TIME 50 MINS • SERVES 4

Serve nachos straight from the oven so the corn chips remain crunchy and the cheese nice and oozy.

1 tablespoon olive oil
1 medium brown onion (150g), chopped finely
1 clove garlic, crushed
400g can chopped tomatoes
420g can mexibeans, drained, rinsed
230g packet corn chips
1 cup (120g) grated cheddar cheese
½ cup (120g) sour cream
1 tablespoon chopped fresh coriander

1 Preheat oven to 200°C/180°C fan-forced.
2 Heat oil in medium frying pan; cook onion and garlic, stirring, about 5 minutes or until onion softens. Stir in undrained tomatoes and beans.
3 Bring mixture to a boil; reduce heat, simmer, uncovered, 15 minutes, stirring constantly, until mixture thickens slightly.
4 Place corn chips onto large ovenproof plate; spoon bean mixture over chips, then sprinkle with cheese. Bake, uncovered, about 10 minutes or until cheese is melted. Serve topped with sour cream and coriander.

nutritional count per serving 43.4g total fat (21.3g saturated fat); 2867kJ (686 cal); 49.3g carbohydrate; 20.5g protein; 13.3g fibre

Add the onion and garlic to a heated, oiled frying pan and cook, stirring, until onion is soft.

Add tomatoes and beans to the pan with the onion mixture. Simmer, stirring constantly, for 15 minutes, until the mixture becomes thick.

Spoon the cooked bean mixture over the corn chips, arranged on an ovenproof plate.

meatballs napoletana

PREP + COOK TIME 1 HOUR • SERVES 4

The combination of pork and veal mince gives these meatballs a deliciously rich quality that you won't get with beef mince.

500g pork and veal mince
1 egg
½ cup (50g) packaged breadcrumbs
¼ cup (20g) finely grated parmesan cheese
¼ cup finely chopped fresh flat-leaf parsley
1 tablespoon olive oil
1 small brown onion (80g), chopped finely
1 clove garlic, crushed
700g bottled tomato pasta sauce
½ cup (60g) frozen peas
¼ cup coarsely chopped fresh basil
½ cup (60g) seeded green olives

1 Combine mince, egg, breadcrumbs, cheese and parsley in medium bowl. Roll level tablespoons of mince mixture into balls.
2 Heat half the oil in large frying pan; cook meatballs until browned and cooked through. Remove meatballs from pan.
3 Heat remaining oil in same pan; cook onion and garlic, stirring, until onion softens. Add sauce; bring to the boil. Add meatballs, reduce heat; simmer, uncovered, about 10 minutes or until sauce thickens slightly.
4 Add peas and basil to meatball mixture; simmer, uncovered, until peas are tender. Add olives to meatball mixture, season to taste; stir until heated through.
nutritional count per serving 18.2g total fat (5.7g saturated fat); 1831kJ (438 cal); 30.5g carbohydrate; 35.3g protein; 5.4g fibre
serving idea serve meatballs with spaghetti.

In a medium bowl, combine the pork and veal mince, egg, breadcrumbs, cheese and parsley, using clean hands.

Take a level tablespoon of mince mixture and roll it in your hands to form a ball. Repeat until you have used up all the mince.

Add the cooked meatballs to the pasta sauce and simmer, uncovered, for 10 minutes or until the sauce thickens slightly.

mango and raspberry jelly

PREP TIME 30 MINS (+ REFRIGERATION) • SERVES 8

If mangoes are in season, you can use one large fresh mango weighing about 600g for this recipe. Peel the mango over a small bowl to catch as much of the juice as possible, then cut off mango cheeks; slice cheeks thinly. Squeeze as much juice as possible from around the mango seed into the bowl with other juice; add enough cold water to make 1 cup of liquid to be added to the mango jelly crystals (see step 2).

425g can sliced mango
85g packet mango jelly crystals
2 cups (500ml) boiling water
150g raspberries
85g packet raspberry jelly crystals
1 cup (250ml) cold water
300ml thickened cream

1 Drain mango in sieve over small bowl; reserve liquid. Measure ¼ cup mango slices and reserve. Divide remaining mango slices among eight ¾-cup (180ml) glasses.
2 Combine mango jelly crystals with 1 cup of the boiling water in medium jug, stirring until jelly dissolves; stir jelly into reserved mango liquid. Divide evenly among glasses over mango, cover; refrigerate about 2 hours or until jelly sets.
3 Divide raspberries among glasses over jelly. Combine raspberry jelly crystals and remaining cup of the boiling water in medium jug, stirring until jelly dissolves; stir in the cold water. Divide evenly among glasses over raspberries. Cover; refrigerate about 2 hours or until jelly sets.
4 Beat cream in small bowl with electric mixer until soft peaks form. Using rubber spatula, spread equally among glasses; top with reserved mango.

nutritional count per serving 13.9g total fat (9.1g saturated fat); 1028kJ (246 cal); 26.8g carbohydrate; 2.9g protein; 1.5g fibre

Drain the mango in a sieve over a bowl and reserve the syrup.

Add the jelly mixture to the reserved mango syrup, stirring constantly to combine.

Carefullly pour the raspberry jelly mixture over the raspberries and mango jelly in each glass. Cover glasses and chill until jelly sets.

butterfly cakes

PREP + COOK TIME 50 MINS • MAKES 24

Use whatever jam you like, or some pureed fruit. Stewed fruit such as apple or stone fruits also make a lovely variation – it helps if they are not too thin in consistency though. Lemon butter is another popular filling.

125g butter, softened
1 teaspoon vanilla extract
⅔ cup (150g) caster sugar
3 eggs
1½ cups (225g) self-raising flour
¼ cup (60ml) milk
½ cup (160g) jam
300ml thickened cream, whipped

1 Preheat oven to 180°C/160°C fan-forced. Line two 12-hole (2 tablespoons/40ml) deep flat-based patty pans with paper cases.
2 Beat butter, extract, sugar, eggs, sifted flour and milk in small bowl on low speed with electric mixer until ingredients are just combined. Increase speed to medium; beat about 3 minutes or until mixture is smooth and pale in colour.
3 Drop slightly rounded tablespoons of mixture into paper cases.
4 Bake cakes about 20 minutes. Stand cakes in pans 5 minutes before turning, top-sides up, onto wire racks to cool.
5 Using sharp pointed vegetable knife, cut a circle from the top of each cake; cut circle in half to make two "wings". Fill cavities with jam and whipped cream; position wings on top of cakes.
nutritional count per cake 9.8g total fat (6.2g saturated fat); 702kJ (168 cal); 17.8g carbohydrate; 2.2g protein; 0.4g fibre
serving idea dust butterfly cakes with sifted icing sugar just before serving.

Beat together the butter, vanilla extract, sugar, eggs, sifted flour and milk with an electric mixer until the mixture is smooth and pale in colour.

Place tablespoons of cake mixture into the paper cases.

Cut a circle out of the top of each cake, using a pointed vegetable knife. Cut each circle in half to form two wings.

Fill the cavity of each cake with jam, then top with the whipped cream, before placing the two wings on top.

gingerbread men

PREP + COOK TIME 50 MINS • MAKES 20

You obviously need a gingerbread-man cutter to make this shape, but any decorative cutter – a star, diamond, heart or whatever shape you may already have in your kitchen – can be used for this recipe.

125g butter
⅓ cup (75g) firmly packed brown sugar
½ cup (175g) golden syrup
3 cups (450g) plain flour
2 teaspoons ground ginger
2 teaspoons ground cinnamon
½ teaspoon ground clove
2 teaspoons bicarbonate of soda
1 egg, beaten lightly
1 teaspoon vanilla extract

royal icing
1 egg white
1 cup (160g) pure icing sugar
food colourings

TIPS

• If the mixture in step 3 is dry and crumbly, add a little more beaten egg – enough to make it feel like play dough.

• To make a quick piping bag, cut off a corner of a small plastic bag.

1 Preheat oven to 180°C/160°C fan-forced. Grease oven trays.
2 Heat butter, sugar and golden syrup, in small microwave-safe bowl, uncovered, on HIGH (100%) in microwave oven about 1 minute or until butter has melted. Using oven mitts, remove bowl from microwave oven; cool butter mixture 5 minutes.
3 Sift combined flour, spices and soda into large bowl; add butter mixture, egg and extract, stir with wooden spoon until combined.
4 Divide dough in half; knead each portion of dough on floured surface. Using rolling pin, roll dough out to 5mm thickness. Using gingerbread-man cutter, cut out shapes; place on oven trays.
5 Bake gingerbread men about 10 minutes or until golden brown. Cool on trays.
6 Make royal icing. Decorate gingerbread men with royal icing.

royal icing Beat egg white in small bowl with electric mixer until just frothy; gradually add sifted icing sugar, beating between additions, until stiff peaks form. Tint icing as desired, using various food colourings.

nutritional count per gingerbread man 5.7g total fat (3.5g saturated fat); 1141kJ (273 cal); 51.4g carbohydrate; 3.2g protein; 0.9g fibre

decorating ideas you could also use coloured cachous or mini smarties to make buttons or other patterns.

Using a rolling pin, roll each portion of biscuit dough out to a thickness of 5mm.

Cut out shapes from the dough, using a gingerbread-man cutter.

Arrange the biscuits on an oven tray, leaving space between each one.

Pipe tinted royal icing onto gingerbread men. You can also use cachous or smarties to decorate.

TRICKS OF THE TRADE

Tricks of the trade

Even if you're a veteran cook there are always new tricks that you can learn to improve your cooking. Here are some tips and techniques from the experts that will get you cooking like a professional and eating like a king.

EGGS

ALWAYS CRACK EGGS INTO A SMALL BOWL OR CUP ONE AT A TIME, IN CASE THERE IS ONE THAT IS NOT FRESH.

TO TEST THE FRESHNESS OF EGGS, PLACE IN A BOWL OF WATER. ANY THAT FLOAT ARE NOT FRESH AS THEY HAVE A LARGER AIR SAC IN THEM (THE AIR SAC GETS BIGGER AS THE EGG AGES). THOSE THAT SINK ARE FRESHER.

WHEN POACHING EGGS, PLACE A TEASPOON OF VINEGAR IN THE WATER. THIS HELPS TO QUICKLY COAGULATE THE EGG WHITE, PREVENTING IT FROM SPREADING. ALSO CREATE A WHIRLPOOL IN THE WATER USING A SPOON. ADD THE EGG TO THE CENTRE OF THE WHIRLPOOL, THIS HELPS THE EGG TO KEEP A ROUND SHAPE.

TO MAKE PERFECT MASHED POTATOES

BOIL THE POTATOES UNTIL COMPLETELY TENDER, THEN DRAIN THEM WELL. TURN OFF THE HOTPLATE. RETURN THE POTATOES TO THE SAUCEPAN AND THE PAN TO THE SAME HOTPLATE FOR 1 MINUTE TO EVAPORATE ANY REMAINING LIQUID. THIS ALSO ALLOWS THE STARCH IN THE POTATOES TO DRY, MAKING THEM READY TO ACCEPT HOT MILK WHEN MASHED.

ALL ABOUT BAKING

Store vanilla beans in a jar of white or caster sugar. The sugar creates an airtight environment for the beans, keeping them fresh and you'll produce vanilla sugar that can be used in a variety of dishes.

When adding citrus rinds to cakes, always cream with the butter and sugar. This helps to release natural oils in the rind, giving more flavour.

Make sure the water is icy cold when making pastry. The key to flaky dough is suspending fat deposits of butter and shortening, rather than fully incorporating them into the dough. The colder the fat remains, the easier it is to turn out the ultimate pie.

To test if scones, damper or bread are cooked, tap the bottom, if it sounds hollow, it's cooked through.

To prevent meringues from "weeping" a liquid, sticky substance, ensure the sugar is dissolved properly in the meringue mixture. Beat whites to soft peaks then gradually add sugar, beating well between additions. To test if the sugar is dissolved, rub a little of the meringue between your fingers. If it's still grainy, continue beating.

When making cakes such as sponges, the fresher the eggs, the more volume you will get when whipping them, resulting in a light cake. Always have eggs at room temperature before whipping, you will get more volume.

When melting chocolate, stir with a metal spoon, if you use a wooden spoon, any moisture in the wood might cause the chocolate to seize.

When whipping egg whites, rub a cut lemon over the inside of the bowl before adding the egg whites. This neutralises any fat or grease that might be in the bowl. Fat prevents the whites from whipping.

If you don't have a pastry bag and need one for a recipe, take a resealable plastic bag and cut one of the corners off for an instant makeshift pastry bag.

Cooling a baked cheesecake in the oven with the door slightly ajar will prevent it from cracking on the surface. Cracks occur when the cheesecake is removed hot from the oven – the cold air causes the protein in the eggs to seize, and the cheesecake to shrink and crack.

THE PERFECT SAUCE

When you make a sauce and use a starchy thickener, like a roux (butter and flour mix), you have to take care of one crucial thing that will prevent lumping of the starch – you need to heat the starch evenly. What happens then is that the starch granules will swell up at the same time and eventually burst and release the starch particles into the sauce and thicken it. But if you don't heat up the starch evenly then granules will become sticky on the outside and start to aggregate with other starches. So what you need to do, practically, is simple: add the hot liquid sauce to the roux at a slow rate and make sure to stir at all time. Cook up the sauce between each addition. If you still get some lumps then you can always strain the sauce through a fine sieve

If your hollandaise or béarnaise sauce looks like it's about to split (curdle), whisk in a tablespoon of boiling water to emulsify it.

If a creamy sauce looks like it is splitting during cooking, add a little cold cream, this will make it smooth again.

STORAGE

STORE FRESH HERBS WRAPPED IN DAMP ABSORBENT PAPER IN AN AIRTIGHT CONTAINER IN THE FRIDGE, THIS KEEPS THEM FRESHER FOR LONGER.

TO RIPEN FRUITS, WRAP THEM IN NEWSPAPER OR A BROWN PAPER BAG AND PUT IN A WARM PLACE FOR 2-3 DAYS. THE ETHYLENE GAS THEY EMIT WILL MAKE THEM RIPE.

BUTTER AND OIL

Melt butter and oil together when pan-frying. The butter adds flavour and the oil prevents the butter from burning.

To test if oil is hot enough for deep-frying, add a cube of bread to see if oil sizzles or stand the end of a wooden spoon in oil. If the oil around the spoon sizzles it means any moisture in the wood is reacting with the oil, meaning the oil is hot enough.

Peanut oil is the best oil to fry with as it has a high smoking/heating point.

THE GOODNESS OF GARLIC

WHEN A RECIPE CALLS FOR CRUSHED GARLIC, CHOP THE GARLIC INTO SMALL PIECES. ADD A LITTLE PINCH OF SALT THEN CONTINUE TO CHOP, THEN MASH WITH THE BACK OF YOUR KNIFE. IT'S WORTH CRUSHING A LARGE QUANTITY AND PLACING IT IN ICE CUBE TRAYS WITH A LITTLE WATER, THEN COVER AND FREEZE. WHENEVER YOU NEED CRUSHED GARLIC, PLACE A CUBE STRAIGHT FROM THE FREEZER INTO THE PAN.

FRUIT

To prevent apples from browning when cutting a lot for pies, place peeled, cut apple in a bowl of cold water with 2 tablespoons of lemon juice. The acid prevents the enzymes that make the apple brown from reacting.

Freeze overripe bananas in a freezer bag. Defrost and use in banana cakes.

When squeezing a lemon or lime, first roll the fruit around on a work surface with your hands to start releasing some of the juices or you can place it in the microwave for about 30 seconds. Then cut the fruit in half and squeeze cut-side up so the seeds don't get into what you're doing. You can also stick a fork in the fruit to help squeeze without getting all the seeds everywhere.

VEGETABLES

To store a cut avocado, squeeze a little lemon on the cut surface then wrap in plastic wrap – this prevents the avocado from browning.

To stop your eyes from weeping when cutting onions, place peeled onions in water for about 20 minutes before chopping… or wear goggles!

When sautéing onions, add salt after the onions have started to turn brown or the salt will slow down the caramelisation process.

MEAT AND FISH

How to know if fish is fresh? There are several things to look for. One, the skin should be shiny. Two, the eyes should be clear and not opaque. Three, the gills should be pink-red. And four, the smell should be pleasant and not too fishy. Seawater fish should smell like the ocean coast, and freshwater fish should have a grassy smell.

An easy way to devein peeled prawns is to bend prawn exposing vein down the back. Insert a skewer or toothpick through the skin and behind the vein, then lift, this will pull the vein out. Rub a cut lemon on hands before washing with warm soapy water to remove the prawn smell.

Salt salmon skin before pan-frying then cook skin-side down first to get a crispy skin. The salt helps draw any moisture out of the skin to make it crisp.

When cooking steaks or fish, only turn once during pan-frying. Place the best side down first in the pan, this will be the presentation side. Cook until browned nicely then turn and cook until desired. Turning only once prevents any juices from the food being lost and making the food dry.

To test the doneness of a steak, insert a skewer for 30 seconds then place on your bottom lip. If the steak is medium, the skewer will be warm and juices that run out will be bloody, if it's well done, the skewer will be hot and juices will be clear. Or do the finger test, the firmer the steak, the more cooked it is.

GENERAL

SOAK WOODEN SKEWERS IN WATER BEFORE USING THEM TO PREVENT THEM FROM SCORCHING DURING COOKING.

PLACE PLASTIC WRAP OVER THE SURFACE OF CUSTARD WHEN STORING TO PREVENT A SKIN FROM FORMING.

WHEN MEASURING A REALLY STICKY SUBSTANCE SUCH AS HONEY OR MOLASSES, COAT THE UTENSIL OR MEASURING CUP WITH A LITTLE COOKING-OIL SPRAY – THE HONEY ETC WILL SLIDE RIGHT OUT LEAVING NOTHING BEHIND.

IF YOU NEED SOUR CREAM BUT DON'T HAVE ANY ON HAND, YOU CAN ALWAYS IMPROVISE. TAKE NORMAL CREAM AND ADD SOME LEMON JUICE TO IT. STIR THE MIXTURE AND USE IN THE RECIPE AS SOUR CREAM.

TO KEEP SALT FROM CLUMPING TOGETHER IN YOUR SALT SHAKER ADD SOME UNCOOKED RICE TO IT.

WHEN COOKING PANCAKES OR PIKELETS, THEY ARE READY TO TURN WHEN BUBBLES APPEAR ON THE SURFACE OF THE PANCAKE.

IF YOU HAVE BURNT THE BASE OF A FRYING PAN OR SAUCEPAN, ADD WATER AND BICARB AND BRING TO THE BOIL. BOIL FOR 5 MINUTES. THE BICARB HELPS TO SOFTEN THE BURNT BITS.

KNOW YOUR SPUDS

THERE IS AN AMAZING NUMBER OF VARIETIES NOW AVAILABLE SO CHOOSING WHICH TYPE TO USE CAN BE CONFUSING. GENERALLY POTATOES CAN BE DIVIDED INTO FLOURY AND WAXY VARIETIES. FLOURY VARIETIES SUCH AS RUSSET BURBANK, IDAHO, COLIBAN, KING EDWARD, SPUNTA AND KENNEBEC ARE LOW IN MOISTURE AND HIGH IN STARCH, MAKING THEM PERFECT FOR BAKING, FRYING AND MASHING. WAXY VARIETIES SUCH AS KIPFLER, PINK-EYE, PINK-FIR APPLE, NICOLA, PONTIAC AND BINTJE ARE LOWER IN STARCH AND HIGHER IN MOISTURE, AND WILL BOIL BEAUTIFULLY AND CUT INTO CLEAN SLICES FOR SALAD. DESIREE AND SEBAGO ARE ALL-ROUNDER VARIETIES THAT WILL BOIL, BAKE, FRY AND MASH WELL.

USING LEFTOVERS

SOUPS, FRITTATAS AND PASTA SAUCES ARE WONDERFUL WAYS TO USE UP LEFTOVER BITS AND PIECES. ANY LEFTOVER VEGIES LIKE A FLORET OF BROCCOLI, A FEW MUSHROOMS OR A PIECE OF CAPSICUM CAN EASILY BE CHOPPED UP AND SAUTEED WITH SOME ONION AND MADE INTO A VEGIE FRITTATA, ADDED TO A SOUP OR TURNED INTO A LOVELY HEALTHY PASTA SAUCE.

BREAD

BREAD IS ALWAYS BEST WHEN FRESH, BUT FEW OF US CAN GET THROUGH A WHOLE LOAF AT ONCE. IF YOU'RE ONLY STORING IT FOR A DAY OR TWO, KEEP IT IN A BREAD BOX OR PAPER BAG TO PREVENT IT FROM DRYING OUT. YOU MAY STILL NEED TO SLICE OFF AND THROW OUT THE EXPOSED SURFACE, BUT THE BREAD UNDER THAT SHOULD STILL BE OK. STORING BREAD IN THE FRIDGE MAKES IT GO STALE QUITE QUICKLY. BREAD FREEZES VERY WELL, SO IF YOU WANT TO STORE A FRESH LOAF FOR A LONGER PERIOD, CUT IT INTO SLICES, SEPARATE SLICES USING BAKING PAPER AND FREEZE THEM IN SEALED PLASTIC BAGS.

PASTRY PERFECT

TO LINE A PIE OR TART TIN WITH BUTTER-RICH PASTRY, COARSELY GRATE THE PASTRY STRAIGHT INTO THE TIN AND PRESS DOWN WITH YOUR FINGERTIPS. THIS HELPS TO MAKE SURE THAT THE PASTRY IS NOT OVERWORKED, WHICH CAN EASILY HAPPEN WHEN ROLLING IT. WHEN PASTRY IS OVERWORKED IT WILL TOUGHEN AND SHRINK DURING COOKING.

REFRESHING VEGETABLES

SOME VEGETABLES, IN PARTICULAR GREEN BEANS, SNOW PEAS AND SUGAR SNAP PEAS, TEND TO LOSE THEIR BRIGHT GREEN COLOUR AND CRUNCHY TEXTURE AFTER THEY'VE COOKED. TO PREVENT THIS, PLUNGE THEM INTO A BOWL OF ICED WATER STRAIGHT AFTER COOKING. THIS WILL STOP THEM FROM CONTINUING TO COOK AND KEEP THEM BRIGHT AND CRUNCHY.

PASTA PERFECT

IT IS A MYTH THAT ADDING OIL TO THE COOKING WATER WILL PREVENT THE PASTA FROM STICKING TOGETHER, AS IT SIMPLY SITS ON THE SURFACE. INSTEAD, MAKE SURE THAT YOU HAVE PLENTY OF RAPIDLY BOILING, WELL-SALTED WATER. ADD THE PASTA, GIVE IT A GOOD STIR AND REPLACE THE LID OF THE POT ONLY UNTIL THE WATER COMES BACK TO THE BOIL, THEN REMOVE THE LID. STIR THE PASTA FREQUENTLY AND DRAIN WHEN IT IS AL DENTE. TOSS HOT PASTA WITH HOT SAUCE QUICKLY WITHOUT RINSING IT.

YOU SHOULD ALWAYS RESERVE A CUP OR TWO OF THE PASTA COOKING WATER TO ADD TO THE PASTA AT A LATER STAGE, AS THE PASTA WILL ABSORB THE SAUCE YOU ARE SERVING IT WITH AND MAY DRY OUT. THE PASTA COOKING WATER, WHICH IS FLAVOURED BY THE SALT AND ENRICHED STARCH FROM THE PASTA, WILL REFRESH THE PASTA.

CHEESE PLEASE

CHEESE SHOULD ALWAYS BE EATEN AT ROOM TEMPERATURE, NOT STRAIGHT OUT OF THE FRIDGE, SO REMOVE IT FROM THE FRIDGE AN HOUR OR TWO BEFORE USING.

Conversion chart

MEASURES

One Australian metric measuring cup holds approximately 250ml; one Australian metric tablespoon holds 20ml; one Australian metric teaspoon holds 5ml.

The difference between one country's measuring cups and another's is within a two- or three-teaspoon variance, and will not affect your cooking results. North America, New Zealand and the United Kingdom use a 15ml tablespoon.

All cup and spoon measurements are level. The most accurate way of measuring dry ingredients is to weigh them. When measuring liquids, use a clear glass or plastic jug with the metric markings.

We use large eggs with an average weight of 60g.

DRY MEASURES

METRIC	IMPERIAL
15g	½oz
30g	1oz
60g	2oz
90g	3oz
125g	4oz (¼lb)
155g	5oz
185g	6oz
220g	7oz
250g	8oz (½lb)
280g	9oz
315g	10oz
345g	11oz
375g	12oz (¾lb)
410g	13oz
440g	14oz
470g	15oz
500g	16oz (1lb)
750g	24oz (1½lb)
1kg	32oz (2lb)

LIQUID MEASURES

METRIC	IMPERIAL
30ml	1 fluid oz
60ml	2 fluid oz
100ml	3 fluid oz
125ml	4 fluid oz
150ml	5 fluid oz
190ml	6 fluid oz
250ml	8 fluid oz
300ml	10 fluid oz (½ pint)
500ml	16 fluid oz
600ml	20 fluid oz (1 pint)
1000ml (1 litre)	1¾ pints

LENGTH MEASURES

METRIC	IMPERIAL
3mm	⅛in
6mm	¼in
1cm	½in
2cm	¾in
2.5cm	1in
5cm	2in
6cm	2½in
8cm	3in
10cm	4in
13cm	5in
15cm	6in
18cm	7in
20cm	8in
23cm	9in
25cm	10in
28cm	11in
30cm	12in (1ft)

OVEN TEMPERATURES

These oven temperatures are only a guide for conventional ovens. For fan-forced ovens, check the manufacturer's manual.

	°C (CELSIUS)	°F (FAHRENHEIT)	GAS MARK
Very slow	120	250	½
Slow	150	275-300	1-2
Moderately slow	160	325	3
Moderate	180	350-375	4-5
Moderately hot	200	400	6
Hot	220	425-450	7-8
Very hot	240	475	9

Glossary

ALLSPICE
Also called pimento or jamaican pepper; tastes like a combination of nutmeg, cumin, clove and cinnamon. Available whole or ground.

ALMONDS
Flat, pointy-tipped nuts having a pitted brown shell enclosing a creamy white kernel which is covered by a brown skin.
blanched brown skins removed.
flaked paper-thin slices.
ground also known as almond meal; nuts are powdered to a coarse flour-like texture.
slivered small pieces cut lengthways.
vienna toffee-coated almonds.

ARROWROOT
A starch made from the rhizome of a Central American plant, used mostly as a thickening agent.

ARTICHOKES
globe large flower-bud of a member of the thistle family; it has tough petal-like leaves, and is edible in part when cooked. See also page 216.
hearts tender centre of the globe artichoke; can be harvested from the plant after the prickly choke is removed. Cooked hearts can be bought from delicatessens or canned in brine.
jerusalem neither from Jerusalem nor an artichoke, this crunchy brown-skinned tuber tastes a bit like a water chestnut and belongs to the sunflower family. Eat raw in salads or cooked like potatoes. See also page 218.

ASAFOETIDA
The dried and ground resin of a giant fennel, notorious for its penetrating "rotten" smell which is toned down in cooking. Its pungent flavour suggests fermented garlic. Use this spice sparingly with lentils and in fish and vegetable curries. See also page 416.

BACON
Also known as bacon slices.

BAHARAT
An aromatic spice blend, includes some or all of the following: mixed spice, black pepper, allspice, dried chilli flakes, paprika, coriander seeds, cinnamon, clove, sumac, nutmeg, cumin seeds and cardamom seeds. It is used through the Middle East; here, it is often sold as lebanese seven-spice, and can be found in Middle-Eastern food stores, specialist food stores and some delicatessens. See also page 416.

BAKING POWDER
A raising agent consisting mainly of two parts cream of tartar to one part bicarbonate of soda. See also gluten-free baking powder.

BANANA LEAVES
Used to line steamers and wrap food; sold in bundles in Asian food shops, greengrocers and supermarkets. Cut leaves, on both sides of centre stem, into required sized pieces then immerse in hot water or hold over a flame until pliable enough to wrap or fold over food; secure with kitchen string, toothpicks or skewers.

BARLEY
A nutritious grain used in soups and stews. Hulled barley, the least processed, is high in fibre. Pearl barley has had the husk removed then been steamed and polished so that only the "pearl" of the original grain remains, much the same as white rice.

BAY LEAVES
Aromatic leaves from the bay tree available fresh or dried; adds a strong, slightly peppery flavour.

BEANS
adzuki small russet beans with a cream stripe. Thin-skinned and sweetish, they are used in Japan in a paste for desserts and cakes, and are also good in stews and for sprouting. See also page 496.
black also called turtle beans or black kidney beans; an earthy-flavoured dried bean completely different from the better-known chinese black beans (fermented soybeans). Used mostly in Mexican and South American cooking. See also page 496.
black-eyed also called black-eyed peas or cow peas. Mild-flavoured and thin-skinned, so they cook faster than most other beans. Often served in the American south with pork and cornbread. See also page 496.
borlotti also called roman beans or pink beans, can be eaten fresh or dried. Interchangeable with pinto beans due to their similarity in appearance – pale pink or beige with dark red streaks. See also page 216.
broad also called fava, windsor and horse beans; available dried, fresh, canned and frozen. Fresh should be peeled twice (discarding both the outer long green pod and the beige-green tough inner shell); the frozen beans have had their pods removed but the beige shell still needs removal. See also pages 216 & 497.
butter cans labelled butter beans are, in fact, cannellini beans. Confusingly butter is also another name for lima beans, sold both dried and canned; a large beige bean having a mealy texture and mild taste.
cannellini small white bean similar in appearance and flavour to other *phaseolus vulgaris* varieties (great northern, navy or haricot). Available dried or canned. See also page 497.
green also known as french or string beans (although the tough string they once had has generally been bred out

of them), this long thin fresh bean is consumed in its entirety once cooked. See also page 216

haricot the haricot bean family includes navy beans and cannellini. All are mild-flavoured white beans which can be interchangeable. See also page 496

kidney medium-sized red bean, slightly floury in texture yet sweet in flavour; sold dried or canned, it's found in bean mixes and is used in chilli con carne.

lima large, flat kidney-shaped, beige dried and canned beans. Also known as butter beans.

snake long (about 40cm), thin, round, fresh green beans, Asian in origin, with a taste similar to green or french beans. Used most frequently in stir-fries, they are also known as yard-long beans because of their (pre-metric) length. See also page 216

soy the most nutritious of all legumes; high in protein and low in carbohydrate and the source of products such as tofu, soy milk, soy sauce, tamari and miso. Also available dried and canned.

sprouts tender new growths of assorted beans and seeds germinated for consumption as sprouts.

white a generic term we use for canned or dried cannellini, haricot, navy or great northern beans belonging to the same family, *phaseolus vulgaris*.

BEEF

chuck inexpensive cut from the neck and shoulder area; good minced and slow-cooked.

corned beef also called corned silverside; little fat, cut from the upper leg and cured. Sold cryovac-packed in brine.

eye-fillet tenderloin, fillet; fine texture, most expensive and extremely tender.

gravy boneless stewing beef from shin; slow-cooked, imbues stocks, soups and casseroles with a gelatine richness. Cut crossways, with bone in, is osso buco.

minced also known as ground beef.

new-york cut boneless striploin steak.

oxtail a flavourful cut originally from the ox but today more likely to be from any beef cattle; requires long, slow cooking so it is perfect for curries and stews.

rump boneless tender cut from the upper part of the round (hindquarter). Cut into steaks, good for barbecuing; as one piece, great as a roast.

scotch fillet cut from the muscle running behind the shoulder along the spine. Also known as cube roll, cuts include standing rib roast and rib-eye.

silverside also called topside roast; the actual cut used for making corned beef.

skirt steak lean, flavourful coarse-grained cut from the inner thigh. Needs slow-cooking; good for stews or casseroles.

t-bone sirloin steak with bone in and fillet eye attached.

BEETROOT
Also known as red beets; firm, round root vegetable. See also page 216

BESAN
See flour.

BETEL LEAVES
Grown and consumed in India and throughout South-East Asia, betel leaves are used raw as a wrap, cooked as a vegetable, or chopped and used as both a herb and a medicine. They are available at some greengrocers and most Asian food stores, especially those specialising in Vietnamese produce. See also page 349

BICARBONATE OF SODA
Also known as baking soda.

BLACK BEAN SAUCE
An Asian cooking sauce made from salted and fermented soybeans, spices and wheat flour; used most often in stir-fries.

BREADCRUMBS
fresh bread, usually white, processed into crumbs.

japanese also called ponko; available in two kinds: larger pieces and fine crumbs; have a lighter texture than Western-style ones. Available from Asian food stores and some supermarkets.

packaged prepared fine-textured but crunchy white breadcrumbs; good for coating foods that are to be fried.

stale crumbs made by grating, blending or processing 1- or 2-day-old bread.

BRIOCHE
French in origin; a rich, yeast-leavened, cake-like bread made with butter and eggs. Available from cake or specialty bread shops.

BROCCOLINI
A cross between broccoli and chinese kale; long asparagus-like stems with a long loose floret, both completely edible. Resembles broccoli but is milder and sweeter in taste. See also page 217

BUCKWHEAT
A herb in the same plant family as rhubarb; not a cereal so it is gluten-free. Available as flour; ground (cracked) into coarse, medium or fine granules (kasha) and used similarly to polenta; or groats, the whole kernel sold roasted as a cereal product.

BUK CHOY
Also known as bok choy, pak choi, chinese white cabbage or chinese chard; has a fresh, mild mustard taste. Use stems and leaves, stir-fried or braised. Baby buk choy, also called pak kat farang or shanghai bok choy, is much smaller and more tender. Its mildly acrid, distinctively appealing taste has made it one of the most commonly used Asian greens. See also page 348

BURGHUL
Also called bulghur wheat; hulled steamed wheat kernels that, once dried, are crushed into various sized grains. Used in Middle Eastern dishes such as felafel, kibbeh and tabbouleh. Is not the same as cracked wheat. See also page 496

BUTTER
We use salted butter unless stated otherwise; 125g is equal to 1 stick (4 ounces). Butter is basically churned pasteurised cream with salted being the most popular one sold in supermarkets. Unsalted or "sweet" butter has no salt added and is perhaps the most popular butter among pastry-chefs.

BUTTER LETTUCE
Small, round, loosely formed heads with a sweet flavour; its soft, buttery-textured leaves range from pale green on the outer leaves to pale yellow-green inner leaves.

BUTTERMILK
See milk

CACHOUS
Also called dragées; minuscule metallic-looking-but-edible confectionery balls used in cake decorating; available in silver, gold or various colours.

CAPERBERRIES
Olive-sized fruit formed after the buds of the caper bush have flowered; they are usually sold pickled in a vinegar brine with stalks intact.

CAPERS
The grey-green buds of a warm climate (usually Mediterranean) shrub, sold either dried and salted or pickled in a vinegar brine; tiny young ones, called baby capers, are also available both in brine or dried in salt. Their pungent taste adds piquancy to a tapenade, sauces and condiments.

CAPSICUM
Also called pepper or bell pepper. Discard seeds and membranes before use.

CARAWAY SEEDS
The small, half-moon-shaped dried seed from a member of the parsley family; adds a sharp anise flavour when used in both sweet and savoury dishes. Used widely, in foods such as rye bread, harissa and the classic Hungarian fresh cheese, liptauer.

CARDAMOM
A spice native to India and used extensively in its cuisine; can be purchased in pod, seed or ground form. Has a distinctive aromatic, sweetly rich flavour and is one of the world's most expensive spices.

CASHEWS
Plump, kidney-shaped, golden-brown nuts having a distinctive sweet, buttery flavour and containing about 48 per cent fat. Because of this high fat content, they should be kept, sealed tightly, under refrigeration to avoid becoming rancid. We use roasted unsalted cashews in this book, unless otherwise stated; they're available from health-food stores and most supermarkets. Roasting cashews brings out their intense nutty flavour.

CAYENNE PEPPER
A thin-fleshed, long, extremely hot dried red chilli, usually purchased ground.

CELERIAC
Tuberous root with knobbly brown skin, white flesh and a celery-like flavour. Keep peeled celeriac in acidulated water to stop it discolouring. It can be grated and eaten raw in salads; used in soups and stews; boiled and mashed like potatoes; or sliced thinly and deep-fried as chips. See also page 217

CHAR SIU
Also called chinese barbecue sauce; a paste-like ingredient dark-red-brown in colour with a sharp sweet and spicy flavour. Made with fermented soybeans, honey and various spices; can be diluted and used as a marinade or brushed onto grilling meat.

CHEESE
blue mould-treated cheeses mottled with blue veining. Varieties include firm and crumbly stilton types and mild, creamy brie-like cheeses.
bocconcini from the diminutive of "boccone", meaning mouthful in Italian; walnut-sized, baby mozzarella, a delicate, semi-soft, white cheese traditionally made from buffalo milk. Sold fresh, it spoils rapidly so will only keep, refrigerated in brine, for 1 or 2 days at the most. See also page 600
brie soft-ripened cow-milk cheese with a delicate, creamy texture and a rich, sweet taste that varies from buttery to mushroomy. Best served at room temperature after a brief period of ageing, brie should have a bloomy white rind and creamy, voluptuous centre which becomes runny with ripening. See also page 600
camembert a luscious, buttery cheese with a thin edible, aromatic rind; it is probably the most famous and most popular soft French cheese in the world. It is best eaten at room temperature. See also page 600
cottage fresh, white, unripened curd cheese with a grainy consistency and a fat content of 15 to 55 per cent. See also page 600

cream commonly called philadelphia or philly; a soft cow-milk cheese, its fat content ranges from 14 to 33 per cent.
edam a semi-hard Dutch cheese made from part-skimmed cow's milk. Mild in flavour and supple in texture when young, it becomes stronger, dry and hard when mature. See also page 600
fetta Greek in origin; a crumbly textured goat- or sheep-milk cheese having a sharp, salty taste. Ripened and stored in salted whey; particularly good cubed and tossed into salads. See also page 601
fontina a smooth, firm Italian cow-milk cheese with a creamy, nutty taste and brown or red rind; an ideal melting or grilling cheese. See also page 601
fromage frais a light, fresh French cheese that has the consistency of thick yogurt with a refreshing, slightly tart taste. Low fat varieties are available.
goat's made from goat's milk, has an earthy, strong taste. Available in soft, crumbly and firm textures, in various shapes and sizes, and sometimes rolled in ash or herbs. See also page 600
gorgonzola a creamy Italian blue cheese with a mild, sweet taste; good as an accompaniment to fruit or used to flavour sauces (especially pasta). See also page 601
gruyère a hard-rind Swiss cheese with small holes and a nutty, slightly salty flavour. A popular cheese for soufflés. See also page 601
haloumi a Greek Cypriot cheese with a semi-firm, spongy texture and very salty sweet flavour. Ripened and stored in salted whey; best grilled or fried, and holds its shape well on being heated. Eat while still warm as it becomes tough and rubbery on cooling. See also page 601
havarti a traditional, creamy, semi-hard cow's milk cheese from Denmark. This washed-rind cheese is mild in flavour and peppered with small holes and irregularities. See also page 601

mascarpone an Italian fresh cultured-cream product made in much the same way as yogurt. Whiteish to creamy yellow in colour, with a buttery-rich, luscious texture. Soft, creamy and spreadable, it is used in Italian desserts and as an accompaniment to fresh fruit.
mozzarella soft, spun-curd cheese; originating in southern Italy where it was traditionally made from water-buffalo milk. Now generally made from cow milk, it is the most popular pizza cheese because of its low melting point and elasticity when heated.
parmesan also called parmigiano; is a hard, grainy cow-milk cheese originating in the Parma region of Italy. The curd for this cheese is salted in brine for a month, then aged for up to 2 years in humid conditions. Reggiano is the best parmesan, aged for a minimum 2 years and made only in the Italian region of Emilia-Romagna.
pecorino the Italian generic name for cheeses made from sheep milk. This family of hard, white to pale-yellow cheeses, traditionally made in the Italian winter and spring when sheep graze on natural pastures, have been matured for 8 to 12 months. They are classified according to the area in which they were produced – romano from Rome, sardo from Sardinia, toscano from Tuscany etc. If you can't find it, use parmesan.
pizza cheese a commercial blend of varying proportions of processed grated mozzarella, cheddar and parmesan.
provolone a mild stretched-curd cheese similar to mozzarella when young, becoming hard, spicy and grainy the longer it's aged. Golden yellow in colour, with a smooth waxy rind, provolone is a good all-purpose cheese used in cooking, for dessert with cheese, and shredded or flaked.
ricotta a soft, sweet, moist, white cow's milk cheese with a low fat content (8.5 per cent) and a slightly grainy texture. The name roughly translates as "cooked again" and refers to ricotta's manufacture from a whey that is itself a by-product of other cheese making.
roquefort considered the "king of cheeses", this is a blue cheese with a singularly pungent taste; made only from the milk of specially bred sheep and ripened in the damp limestone caves found under the village of Roquefort-sur-Soulzon in France. Has a sticky, bone-coloured rind and, when ripe, the sharp, almost metallic-tasting interior is creamy and almost shiny.
swiss generic name for a variety of slightly firm to hard Swiss cheeses, among them emmentaler and gruyère.

CHICKEN

barbecued we use cooked whole barbecued chickens weighing about 900g apiece in our recipes. Skin discarded and bones removed, this size chicken provides 4 cups (400g) shredded meat or about 3 cups (400g) coarsely chopped meat.
breast fillet breast halved, skinned and boned.
drumette small fleshy part of the wing between shoulder and elbow, trimmed to resemble a drumstick.
drumstick leg with skin and bone intact.
maryland leg and thigh still connected in a single piece; bones and skin intact.
small chicken also called spatchcock or poussin; no more than 6 weeks old, weighing a maximum of 500g. Spatchcock is also a cooking term to describe splitting a small chicken open, flattening then grilling.
tenderloin thin strip of meat lying just under the breast; good for stir-frying.
thigh skin and bone intact.
thigh cutlet thigh with skin and centre bone intact; sometimes found skinned with bone intact.
thigh fillet thigh with skin and centre bone removed.

CHICKPEAS
Also called garbanzos, hummus or channa; an irregularly round, sandy-coloured legume used extensively in Mediterranean, Indian and Hispanic cooking. Firm texture even after cooking, a floury mouth-feel and robust nutty flavour; available canned or dried (reconstitute for several hours in cold water before use). See also page 497

CHILLI
Use rubber gloves when seeding and chopping fresh chillies as they can burn your skin. We use unseeded chillies because the seeds contain the heat; use fewer chillies rather than seeding the lot.

ancho mild, dried chillies commonly used in Mexican cooking.

chipotle pronounced cheh-pote-lay. The name used for jalapeño chillies once they've been dried and smoked. Having a deep, intensely smoky flavour, rather than a searing heat, chipotles are dark brown, almost black in colour and wrinkled in appearance.

flakes also sold as crushed chilli; dehydrated deep-red extremely fine slices and whole seeds.

green any unripened chilli; also some particular varieties that are ripe when green, such as jalapeño, habanero, poblano or serrano.

jalapeño pronounced hah-lah-pain-yo. Fairly hot, medium-sized, plump, dark green chilli; available pickled, sold canned or bottled, and fresh, from greengrocers.

long red available both fresh and dried; a generic term used for any moderately hot, long, thin chilli (about 6cm to 8cm long).

powder the Asian variety is the hottest, made from dried ground thai chillies; can be used instead of fresh in the proportion of ½ teaspoon chilli powder to 1 medium chopped fresh red chilli.

sauce, sweet comparatively mild, fairly sticky and runny bottled sauce made from red chillies, sugar, garlic and white vinegar; used in Thai cooking.

thai also known as "scuds"; tiny, very hot and bright red in colour.

CHINESE BARBECUED DUCK
See duck

CHINESE BARBECUED PORK
See pork

CHINESE COOKING WINE
Also called hao hsing or chinese rice wine; made from fermented rice, wheat, sugar and salt with a 13.5 per cent alcohol content. Inexpensive and found in Asian food shops; if you can't find it, replace with mirin or sherry.

CHOCOLATE
Choc Bits also called chocolate chips or chocolate morsels; available in milk, white and dark chocolate. Made of cocoa liquor, cocoa butter, sugar and an emulsifier, these hold their shape in baking and are ideal for decorating.

couverture a term used to describe a fine quality, very rich chocolate high in both cocoa butter and cocoa liquor. Requires tempering when used to coat but not if used in baking, mousses or fillings.

dark cooking also called compounded chocolate; good for cooking as it doesn't require tempering and sets at room temperature. Made with vegetable fat instead of cocoa butter so it lacks the rich, buttery flavour of eating chocolate. Cocoa butter is the most expensive component in chocolate, so the substitution of a vegetable fat means that compounded chocolate is much cheaper to produce.

dark eating also known as semi-sweet or luxury chocolate; made of a high percentage of cocoa liquor and cocoa butter, and little added sugar. Unless stated otherwise, we use dark eating chocolate in this book as it's ideal for use in desserts and cakes.

Melts small discs of compounded milk, white or dark chocolate ideal for melting and moulding.

milk most popular eating chocolate, mild and very sweet; similar in make-up to dark with the difference being the addition of milk solids.

white contains no cocoa solids but derives its sweet flavour from cocoa butter. Very sensitive to heat.

CHOCOLATE HAZELNUT SPREAD
Also known as Nutella; made of cocoa powder, hazelnuts, sugar and milk.

CHOKO
Chayote or christophine are the other names for this South American tuber. Some describe its taste as bland, others say it is subtle. It can be used like a potato in recipes, but the skin has a tacky sap, so wear gloves when peeling it. Available early winter. See also page 217

CHORIZO
Sausage of Spanish origin, made of coarsely ground pork and highly seasoned with garlic and chilli.

CHOY SUM
Also known as pakaukeo or flowering cabbage, a member of the buk choy family; easy to identify with its long stems, light green leaves and yellow flowers. Stems and leaves are both edible, steamed or stir-fried. See also page 348

CIABATTA
In Italian, the word means slipper, the traditional shape of this popular crisp-crusted, open-textured white sourdough bread. Often used for bruschetta.

CINNAMON
Available both in the piece (sticks or quills) and ground; one of the world's most common spices, used universally as a sweet, fragrant flavouring in sweet and savoury foods.

CLOVES
Dried flower buds of a tropical tree; can be used whole or in ground form. They have a strong scent and taste so should be used sparingly.

COCOA POWDER
Also known as unsweetened cocoa; cocoa beans (cacao seeds) that have been fermented, roasted, shelled, ground into powder then cleared of most of the fat content.

COCONUT
cream obtained commercially from the first pressing of the coconut flesh alone, without the addition of water; the second pressing (less rich) is sold as coconut milk. Available in cans and cartons at most supermarkets.
desiccated concentrated, dried, unsweetened and finely shredded coconut flesh.
essence synthetically produced from flavouring, oil and alcohol.
flaked dried flaked coconut flesh.
milk not the liquid found inside the fruit, which is called coconut water, but the diluted liquid from the second pressing of the white flesh of a mature coconut (the first pressing produces coconut cream). Available in cans and cartons at most supermarkets.
shredded unsweetened thin strips of dried coconut flesh.

COINTREAU
See liqueurs

COOKING-OIL SPRAY
See oil

CORAL LETTUCE
A soft-leafed lettuce with either red or green tightly crinkled leaves. Its leaves have a delicate, sweet flavour, so they're perfect with a mixture of lettuces. You'll often find coral as part of a mesclun mix. Use within two days of purchase and dress lightly. See also page 106

CORNFLOUR
Also known as cornstarch. Available made from corn or wheat (wheaten cornflour, gluten-free, gives a lighter texture in cakes); used as a thickening agent in cooking.

CORNICHON
French for gherkin, a very small variety of cucumber. Pickled, they are a traditional accompaniment to pâté, and are also served with fondue or raclette.

COS LETTUCE
Also known as romaine lettuce; the traditional caesar salad lettuce. Long, with leaves ranging from dark green on the outside to almost white near the core; the leaves have a stiff centre rib giving a slight cupping effect to the leaf on either side. See also page 106

COUSCOUS
A fine, grain-like cereal product made from semolina, from the countries of North Africa. A semolina flour and water dough is sieved then dehydrated to produce minuscule even-sized pellets; it is rehydrated by steaming or adding a warm liquid and swells to three or four times its original size; eaten like rice with a tagine, as a side dish or salad ingredient. See also page 497

CRANBERRIES
Available dried and frozen; have a rich, astringent flavour and can be used in cooking sweet and savoury dishes. The dried version can usually be substituted for or with other dried fruit.

CREAM
pouring also known as pure cream. It has no additives and contains a minimum fat content of 35 per cent. If a recipe here calls for an unspecified cream, this is the one we use.
sour cream a thick, commercially-cultured sour cream with a minimum fat content of 35 per cent.
thickened a whipping cream that contains a thickener. It has a minimum fat content of 35 per cent.

CREAM OF TARTAR
The acid ingredient in baking powder; added to confectionery mixtures to help prevent sugar from crystallising. Keeps frostings creamy and improves volume when beating egg whites.

CREME FRAICHE
A mature, naturally fermented cream (minimum fat content 35 per cent) having a velvety texture and slightly tangy, nutty flavour. Crème fraîche, a French variation of sour cream, can boil without curdling and be used in sweet and savoury dishes.

CUCUMBER, LEBANESE
Short, slender and thin-skinned cucumber. Probably the most popular variety because of its tender, edible skin, tiny, yielding seeds, and sweet, fresh and flavoursome taste.

CUMIN
Also known as zeera or comino; resembling caraway in size, cumin is the dried seed of a plant related to the parsley family. Its spicy, almost curry-like flavour is essential to the traditional foods of Mexico, India, North Africa and the Middle East. Available dried as seeds or ground. Black cumin seeds are smaller than standard cumin, and dark brown rather than true black; they are mistakenly confused with kalonji.

CURLY ENDIVE
Also known as frisée, curly endive belongs to the chicory family and has its characteristic bitterness played against grassy freshness. Particularly good with beetroot and also used in mesclun. It will keep in the refrigerator, unwashed, for five days. See also page 106

CURRANTS, DRIED
Tiny, almost black raisins so-named after a grape variety that originated in Corinth, Greece.

CURRY PASTES
Make your own with the recipes found in this book or purchase the ready-made pastes from the supermarket. The heat intensity of ready-made pastes may differ from brand to brand, so adjust the amount used according to your taste.

green hottest of the traditional thai pastes; particularly good in chicken and vegetable curries, and a great addition to stir-fry and noodle dishes.

korma a classic north Indian sauce with a rich yet delicate coconut flavour and hints of garlic, ginger and coriander.

massaman rich, spicy flavour reminiscent of Middle Eastern cooking; favoured by southern Thai cooks for use in hot and sour stew-like curries and satay sauces.

panang based on the curries of Penang, an island off the north-west coast of Malaysia, close to the Thai border. A complex, sweet and milder variation of red curry paste; good with seafood and for adding to soups and salad dressings.

red probably the most popular thai curry paste; a hot blend of different flavours that complements the richness of pork, duck and seafood. Also works well stirred into marinades and sauces.

rogan josh a paste of medium heat, from the Kashmir region of India, made from fresh chillies or paprika, tomato and spices, especially cardamom. It sometimes has beetroot added to make it a dark red.

tikka in Indian cooking, the word "masala" loosely translates as paste and the word "tikka" means a bite-sized piece of meat, poultry or fish, or sometimes a cutlet. Tikka paste is any maker's choice of spices and oils, mixed into a mild paste, frequently coloured red. Used for marinating or for brushing over meat, seafood or poultry, before or during cooking instead of as an ingredient.

vindaloo a Goan combination of vinegar, tomatoes, pepper and other spices that exemplifies the Portuguese influence on this part of India's coast.

yellow one of the mildest thai pastes; similar in appearance to Indian curries as they both include yellow chilli and fresh turmeric. Good blended with coconut in vegetable, rice and noodle dishes.

CURRY POWDER
A blend of ground spices used for making Indian and some South-East Asian dishes. Consists of some of the following spices: dried chilli, cumin, cinnamon, coriander, fennel, mace, fenugreek, cardamom and turmeric. Available mild or hot.

CUSTARD POWDER
Instant mixture used to make pouring custard; similar to North American instant pudding mixes.

DAIKON
Also called white radish; an everyday fixture at the Japanese table, this long, white horseradish has a wonderful, sweet flavour. After peeling, eat it raw in salads or shredded as a garnish; also great when sliced or cubed and cooked in stir-fries and casseroles. The flesh is white but the skin can be either white or black; buy those that are firm and unwrinkled from Asian food shops. See also page 219

DASHI
The basic fish and seaweed stock that accounts for the distinctive flavour of many Japanese dishes, such as soups and various casserole dishes. Made from dried bonito (a type of tuna) flakes and kombu (kelp); instant dashi (dashi-no-moto) is available in powder, granules and liquid concentrate from Asian food shops.

DATES
Fruit of the date palm tree, eaten fresh or dried. About 4cm to 6cm in length, oval and plump, thin-skinned, with a honey-sweet flavour and sticky texture.

DRAGON FRUIT
The fruit of a pitaya cactus. The flesh, eaten raw, is tasty and mildly sweet, a little like the flavour of kiwifruit. Scoop the flesh and seeds out of the chilled fruit with a teaspoon. See also page 516

DRIED CHINESE SAUSAGE
Also called lap cheong; highly spiced, bright red, thin pork sausages. The meat is preserved by the high spice content and can be kept at room temperature.

DUCK
We use whole ducks in some recipes; available from specialty chicken shops, markets and some supermarkets.

breast fillets boneless whole breasts, with the skin on.

chinese barbecued traditionally cooked in special ovens in China; dipped into and brushed during roasting with a sticky sweet coating made from soy sauce, sherry, ginger, five-spice, star anise and hoisin sauce. Available from Asian food shops as well as dedicated Chinese barbecued meat shops.

maryland thigh and drumstick still connected, skin on.

DUKKAH
An Egyptian specialty spice mixture made up of roasted nuts, seeds and an array of aromatic spices.

DURIAN
Famous as the fruit which "smells like hell and tastes like heaven". To enjoy the taste without the smell, cut the sweet, aromatic flesh into pieces and soak in coconut milk for a day. See also page 517

EGGPLANT
Also called aubergine. Ranging in size from tiny to very large and in colour from pale green to deep purple. Can also be purchased char-grilled, packed in oil, in jars.
baby also called finger or japanese eggplant; very small and slender so can be used without disgorging.
pea tiny, about the size of peas; sometimes known by their thai name, "makeua puang". Sold in clusters of 10 to 15 eggplants, similar to vine-ripened cherry tomatoes; very bitter in flavour, a quality suited to balance rich, sweet coconut-sauced Thai curries. Available in Asian greengrocers and food shops, fresh or pickled.
thai found in a variety of different sizes and colours, from a long, thin, purplish-green one to a hard, round, golf-ball size having a white-streaked pale-green skin. This last looks like a small unripe tomato and is the most popular eggplant used in Thai and Vietnamese curries and stir-fries.

EGGS
We use large chicken eggs weighing an average of 60g unless stated otherwise in the recipes in this book. If a recipe calls for raw or barely cooked eggs, exercise caution if there is a salmonella problem in your area, particularly in food eaten by children and pregnant women.

FENNEL
Also called finocchio or anise; a crunchy green vegetable slightly resembling celery that's eaten raw in salads; fried as an accompaniment; or used as an ingredient in soups and sauces. Also the name given to the dried seeds of the plant which have a stronger licorice flavour. See also page 218

FENUGREEK
Hard, dried seed usually sold ground as an astringent spice powder. Good with seafood and in chutneys, fenugreek helps mask unpleasant odours. See also page 416

FISH SAUCE
Called naam pla if Thai-made, nuoc naam if Vietnamese; the two are almost identical. Made from pulverised salted fermented fish (most often anchovies); has a pungent smell and strong taste. Available in varying degrees of intensity, so use according to your taste.

FIVE-SPICE POWDER
Although the ingredients vary from country to country, five-spice is usually a fragrant mixture of ground cinnamon, cloves, star anise, sichuan pepper and fennel seeds. Used in Chinese and other Asian cooking; available from most supermarkets or Asian food shops.

FLOUR
besan also called chickpea flour or gram; made from ground chickpeas so is gluten-free and high in protein. Used in Indian cooking to make dumplings, noodles and chapati; for a batter coating for deep-frying; and as a sauce thickener.
buckwheat see buckwheat
cornflour see cornflour
plain also called all-purpose; unbleached wheat flour is the best for baking: the gluten content ensures a strong dough, which produces a light result.
rice very fine, almost powdery, gluten-free flour; made from ground white rice. Used in baking, as a thickener, and in some Asian noodles and desserts. Another variety, made from glutinous sweet rice, is used for chinese dumplings and rice paper.
self-raising all-purpose plain or wholemeal flour with baking powder and salt added; make it yourself in the proportion of 1 cup flour to 2 teaspoons baking powder.
wholemeal also known as wholewheat flour; milled with the wheat germ so is higher in fibre and more nutritional than plain flour.

FOOD COLOURING
A vegetable-based substance available in liquid, paste or gel form. Used to colour icings, cake mixtures or sugar.

FRENCH BREAD STICK
A long, narrow cylindrical loaf with a crisp brown crust and a light chewy interior. Also called french loaf.

FROMAGE FRAIS
See cheese

GAI LAN
Also called gai larn, chinese broccoli and chinese kale; green vegetable appreciated more for its stems than its coarse leaves. Can be served steamed and stir-fried, in soups and noodle dishes. One of the most popular Asian greens, best known as a dish at yum cha, where it's steamed then sprinkled with a mixture of oyster sauce and sesame oil. See also page 349

GALANGAL
Also known as ka or lengkaus if fresh and laos if dried and powdered; a root, similar to ginger in its use. It has a hot-sour ginger-citrusy flavour; used in fish curries and soups.

GARAM MASALA
Literally meaning blended spices in its northern Indian place of origin; based on varying proportions of cardamom, cinnamon, cloves, coriander, fennel and cumin, roasted and ground together. Black pepper and chilli can be added for a hotter version. See also page 417

GELATINE
A thickening agent. We use dried (powdered) gelatine; it's also available in sheet form known as leaf gelatine. Three teaspoons of dried gelatine (8g or one sachet) is about the same as four leaves. The two types are interchangable but leaf gelatine gives a much clearer mixture than dried gelatine.

GHEE
Clarified butter; with the milk solids removed, this fat has a high smoking point so can be heated to a high temperature without burning. Used as a cooking medium in Indian recipes.

GINGER
fresh also called green or root ginger; the thick gnarled root of a tropical plant. Can be kept, peeled, covered with dry sherry in a jar and refrigerated, or frozen in an airtight container.
glacé fresh ginger root preserved in sugar syrup; crystallised ginger (sweetened with cane sugar) can be used if rinsed with warm water and dried before using.
ground also called powdered ginger; used as a flavouring in baking but cannot be substituted for fresh ginger.
pickled pink or red coloured; available, packaged, from Asian food shops. Pickled paper-thin shavings of ginger in a mixture of vinegar, sugar and natural colouring; used in Japanese cooking.

GLACE CHERRIES
Also called candied cherries; boiled in heavy sugar syrup and then dried.

GLACE FRUIT
Fruit such as peaches, pineapple and orange cooked in heavy sugar syrup then dried.

GLUCOSE SYRUP
Also known as liquid glucose, made from wheat starch; used in jam and confectionery making. Available at health-food stores and supermarkets.

GLUTEN-FREE BAKING POWDER
Used as a leavening agent in bread, cake, pastry or pudding mixtures. Suitable for people with an allergic response to gluten or seeking an alternative to everyday baking powder. See also baking powder.

GOLDEN SYRUP
A by-product of refined sugarcane; pure maple syrup or honey can be substituted. Golden syrup and treacle (a thicker, darker syrup not unlike molasses), also known as flavour syrups, are similar sugar products made by partly breaking down sugar into its component parts and adding water. Treacle is more viscous, and has a stronger flavour and aroma than golden syrup (which has been refined further and contains fewer impurities, so is lighter in colour and more fluid). Both can be use in baking and for making certain confectionery items.

GOW GEE WRAPPERS
See wrappers

GRAND MARNIER
See liqueurs

GRAPEVINE LEAVES
From early spring, fresh grapevine leaves can be found in most specialist greengrocers. Alternatively, cryovac-packages containing about 60 leaves in brine can be found in Middle Eastern food shops and some delis; these must be rinsed well and dried before using. Used as wrappers of savoury fillings for Mediterranean foods.

GREEN PAPAYA
See Papaya. See also page 348

HARISSA
A North African paste made from dried red chillies, garlic, olive oil and caraway seeds; can be used as a rub for meat, an ingredient in sauces and dressings, or eaten as a condiment. It is available from Middle Eastern food shops and some supermarkets. See also page 417

HAZELNUTS
Also called filberts; plump, grape-sized, rich, sweet nut having a brown skin that is removed by rubbing heated nuts together vigorously in a teatowel.
ground also called hazelnut meal; is made by grounding the hazelnuts to a coarse flour texture for use in baking.
oil a mono-unsaturated oil, made in France, extracted from crushed hazelnuts.

HERBS
basil *holy* also called kra pao or hot basil; different from thai and sweet basil, having an almost hot, spicy flavour similar to clove. Used in many Thai dishes, especially curries; distinguished from thai basil by tiny "hairs" on its leaves and stems.
sweet the most common type of basil; used extensively in Italian dishes and one of the main ingredients in pesto. See also page 229
thai also called horapa; different from holy basil and sweet basil in both look and taste, having smaller leaves and purplish stems. It has a slight aniseed taste and is one of the identifying flavours of Thai food. See also page 229

chervil also called cicily; mildly fennel-flavoured member of the parsley family with curly dark-green leaves. Available fresh and dried but, like all herbs, is best used fresh; like coriander and parsley, its delicate flavour diminishes the longer it's cooked. See also page 228

chives related to the onion and leek; has a subtle onion flavour. Used more for flavour than as an ingredient; chopped finely, they're good in sauces, dressings, omelettes or as a garnish.

garlic chives also known as chinese chives; are strongly flavoured, have flat leaves and are eaten as a vegetable, usually in stir-fries. See also page 228

coriander also called cilantro, pak chee or chinese parsley; bright-green-leafed herb having both pungent aroma and taste. Used as an ingredient in a wide variety of cuisines. Often stirred into or sprinkled over a dish just before serving for maximum impact as, like other leafy herbs, its characteristics diminish with cooking. Both the stems and roots of coriander are used in Thai cooking: wash well before chopping. Coriander seeds are dried and sold either whole or ground, and neither form tastes remotely like the fresh leaf. See also page 228

dill also called dill weed; used fresh or dried, in seed form or ground. Its anise/celery sweetness flavours the food of the Scandinavian countries, and Germany and Greece. Its feathery, frond-like fresh leaves are grassier and more subtle than the dried version or the seeds (which slightly resemble caraway in flavour). Use dill leaves with smoked salmon and sour cream, poached fish or roast chicken; use the seeds with simply cooked vegetables, or home-baked dark breads. See also page 228

marjoram closely related to and similar in flavour to oregano, but milder and sweeter. Delicious in herb mixtures for omelettes, stuffings, herb scones and herb and cream cheese sandwiches. As with oregano, many chefs prefer dried marjoram to fresh. See also page 229

mint the most commonly used variety of mint is spearmint; it has pointed, bright-green leaves and a fresh flavour.

oregano a herb, also known as wild marjoram; has a woody stalk and clumps of tiny, dark-green leaves. Has a pungent, peppery flavour. See also page 228

parsley a versatile herb with a fresh, earthy flavour. There are about 30 varieties of curly parsley; the flat-leaf variety (also called continental or italian parsley) is stronger in flavour and darker in colour. See also page 229

rosemary pungent herb with long, thin pointy leaves; use large and small sprigs, and the leaves are usually chopped finely.

sage pungent herb with narrow, grey-green leaves; slightly bitter with a slightly musty mint aroma. Refrigerate fresh sage wrapped in a paper towel and sealed in a plastic bag for up to 4 days. Dried sage comes whole, crumbled or ground. It should be stored in a cool, dark place for no more than three months. See also page 229

tarragon french tarragon, with its subtle aniseed flavour, complements chicken, eggs and veal, and is perfect in a béarnaise sauce. It is also one of the herbs that make up the French fines herbs. Russian and mexican tarragons are slightly coarser in taste. See also page 229

thyme a basic herb of French cuisine is widely used in Mediterranean countries to flavour meats and sauces. A member of mint family, it has tiny grey-green leaves that give off a pungent minty, light-lemon aroma. Dried thyme comes in both leaf and powder form. Dried thyme should be stored in a cool, dark place for no more than three months. Fresh thyme should be stored in the refrigerator, wrapped in a damp paper towel and placed in a sealed bag for no more than a few days.

vietnamese mint not a mint at all, but a pungent and peppery narrow-leafed member of the buckwheat family. Not confined to Vietnam, it is also known as cambodian mint, pak pai (Thailand), laksa leaf (Indonesia), daun kesom (Singapore) and rau ram in Vietnam. It is a common ingredient in Thai foods, particularly soups, salads and stir-fries. See also page 228

HOISIN SAUCE

A thick, sweet and spicy Chinese barbecue sauce made from salted fermented soybeans, onions and garlic; used as a marinade or baste, or to accent stir-fries and barbecued or roasted foods. From Asian food shops and supermarkets.

HONEY

The variety sold in a squeezable container is not suitable for the recipes in this book.

HORSERADISH

A vegetable with edible green leaves but mainly grown for its long, pungent white root. Occasionally found fresh in specialty greengrocers and some Asian food shops, but commonly purchased in bottles at the supermarket in two forms: prepared horseradish and horseradish cream. These cannot be substituted one for the other in cooking but both can be used as table condiments. Horseradish cream is a commercially prepared creamy paste consisting of grated horseradish, vinegar, oil and sugar, while prepared horseradish is the preserved grated root.

IRISH CREAM
See liqueurs

JACKFRUIT
A huge fruit containing numerous seeds surrounded by golden, richly flavoured, sharp-sweet flesh. Used in fruit salads, ice-cream, milk drinks and soups. The seeds are edible boiled, then roasted in a pan with a little oil. See also page 516

JELLY CRYSTALS
A combination of sugar, gelatine, colours and flavours; when dissolved in water, the solution sets as firm jelly.

JUNIPER BERRIES
Dried berries of an evergreen tree; it is the main flavouring ingredient in gin.

KAFFIR LIME
Also known as magrood, leech lime or jeruk purut. The wrinkled, bumpy-skinned green fruit of a small citrus tree originally grown in South Africa and South-East Asia. As a rule, only the rind and leaves are used.

KAFFIR LIME LEAVES
Also known as bai magrood and looks like two glossy dark green leaves joined end to end, forming a rounded hourglass shape. Used fresh or dried in many South-East Asian dishes, they are used like bay leaves or curry leaves, especially in Thai cooking. Sold fresh, dried or frozen, the dried leaves are less potent so double the number if using them as a substitute for fresh; a strip of fresh lime peel may be substituted for each kaffir lime leaf. See also page 349

KAHLUA
See liqueurs

KALE
This strong-flavoured member of the cabbage family is very high in antioxidants. In the southern USA it's known as collard greens, while the Italians call it cavolo nero. Used like cabbage, kale is best during winter. The summer variety is paler and thinner. See also page 218

KALONJI
Also called nigella or black onion seeds. Tiny, angular seeds, black on the outside and creamy within, with a sharp nutty flavour that is enhanced by frying briefly in a dry hot pan before use. Typically sprinkled over turkish bread immediately after baking or as an important spice in Indian cooking, kalonji can be found in most Asian and Middle Eastern food shops. Often erroneously called black cumin seeds. See also page 417

KANG KONG
Also known as water spinach, this delicate green vegetable has long, hollow stems and thin leaves. Use the leaves and top half of the stems, cut into 5cm lengths. Stir-fry, dip in batter and deep-fry, or serve steamed with kecap manis or a savoury paste. See also page 349

KECAP ASIN
A thick, dark, salty Indonesian soy sauce.

KECAP MANIS
A dark, thick sweet soy sauce used in most South-East Asian cuisines. Depending on the manufacturer, the sauces's sweetness is derived from the addition of either molasses or palm sugar when brewed.

KIRSCH
See liqueurs

KIWIFRUIT
Also known as chinese gooseberry; it has a brown, somewhat hairy skin and bright-green flesh with a unique sweet-tart flavour. Used in fruit salads, desserts and eaten as is.

KOHLRABI
This round purple or green globe is a member of the cabbage family and develops a bulbous stem above ground. The bulb has a delicate cauliflower/turnip flavour and can be added to soups and casseroles, or used like potatoes. It comes into season in winter. See also page 218

KUMARA
The Polynesian name of an orange-fleshed sweet potato often confused with yam; good baked, boiled, mashed or fried similarly to other potatoes.

LAMB
backstrap also known as eye of loin; the larger fillet from a row of loin chops or cutlets. Tender, best cooked rapidly: barbecued or pan-fried.
chump Cut from just above the hind legs to the mid-loin section; can be used as a piece for roasting or cut into chops.
cutlet small, tender rib chop; sometimes sold french-trimmed, with all the fat and gristle at the narrow end of the bone removed.
diced cubed lean meat.
fillets fine texture, most expensive and extremely tender.
leg cut from the hindquarter; can be boned, butterflied, rolled and tied, or cut into dice.
minced ground lamb.
rolled shoulder boneless section of the forequarter, rolled and secured with string or netting.
shank forequarter leg; sometimes sold as drumsticks or frenched shanks

if the gristle and narrow end of the bone are discarded and the remaining meat trimmed.
shoulder large, tasty piece having much connective tissue so is best pot-roasted or braised. Makes the best mince.

LAMB'S LETTUCE
Also known as mâche or corn lettuce, this salad green has long, spoon-shaped dark leaves that resemble the shape of a lamb's tongue. They have a distinctive, tangy flavour and suit a light dressing. They can also be cooked. Available in the cooler months. See also page 106

LEEKS
A member of the onion family, the leek resembles a green onion but is much larger and more subtle in flavour. Tender baby or pencil leeks can be eaten whole with minimal cooking but adult leeks are usually trimmed of most of the green tops then chopped or sliced and cooked as an ingredient in stews, casseroles and soups.

LEMON GRASS
Also known as takrai, serai or serah. A tall, clumping, lemon-smelling and tasting, sharp-edged aromatic tropical grass; the white lower part of the stem is used, finely chopped, in many South-East Asian dishes. Can be found, fresh, dried, powdered and frozen, in supermarkets, greengrocers and Asian food shops. See also page 348

LENTILS (RED, BROWN, YELLOW)
Dried pulses often identified by and named after their colour. Eaten by cultures all over the world, most famously perhaps in the dhals of India, lentils have high food value.
french green lentils are a local cousin to the famous (and very expensive) French lentils du puy; green-blue, tiny lentils with a nutty, earthy flavour and a hardy nature that allows them to be rapidly cooked without disintegrating. See also page 496

LIMONCELLO
See liqueurs

LINSEED
The seed from the flax plant. Mostly used to produce linseed oil, the grain is also used in breads.

LIQUEURS
cointreau citrus-flavoured liqueur.
Grand Marnier orange liqueur based on cognac-brandy.
irish cream we used Baileys, a smooth and creamy natural blend of fresh Irish cream, the finest Irish spirits, Irish whiskey, cocoa and vanilla.
kahlua coffee-flavoured liqueur.
kirsch cherry-flavoured liqueur.
limoncello Italian lemon-flavoured liqueur; originally made from the juice and peel of lemons grown along the Amalfi coast.
rum we use a dark underproof rum (not overproof) for a more subtle flavour in cooking. White rum is almost colourless, sweet and used mostly in mixed drinks.
Tia Maria coffee-flavoured liqueur.

LOTUS ROOT
The crisp, delicately-flavoured root of a waterlily. Crossways slices are patterned with holes arranged like a flower. To prepare, simply peel and slice as the recipe directs, dropping the slices into acidulated water (water with lemon juice) to prevent them from browning. It is available canned or frozen and sometimes fresh.

LYCHEES
A small fruit from China with a hard shell and sweet, juicy flesh. The white flesh has a gelatinous texture and musky, perfumed taste. Discard the rough skin and seed before using in salads or as a dessert fruit. Also available canned in a sugar syrup. See also page 516

MACADAMIAS
Native to Australia; fairly large, slightly soft, buttery rich nut. Used to make oil and macadamia butter; equally good in salads or cakes and pastries; delicious eaten on their own. Should always be stored in the fridge to prevent their high oil content turning them rancid.

MANGO
Tropical fruit originally from India and South-East Asia. With skin colour ranging from green to yellow and deep red; fragrant, deep yellow flesh surrounds a large flat seed. Slicing off the cheeks, cross-hatching them with a knife then turning them inside out shows the sweet, juicy flesh at its best. Mangoes can also be used in curries and salsas, or pureed for ice-cream, smoothies or mousse. Mango cheeks in light syrup are available canned. Sour and crunchy, green mangoes are just the immature fruit that is used as a vegetable in salads, salsas and curries. See also page 517
green this is the unripe fruit of the mango tree. The flesh is deliciously tart. Used raw in many Asian salads or as a vegetable; it can also be bought pickled or dried. See also page 517

MANGOSTEEN
The shiny, purple-brown skin peels to reveal segments of white flesh whose refreshing, sweet-sour flavour is reminiscent of pineapple. Delicious eaten out of hand, like an orange, or chilled and mixed with other tropical fruits. See also page 517

MAPLE-FLAVOURED SYRUP
Is made from sugar cane and is also known as golden or pancake syrup. It is not a substitute for pure maple syrup.

MAPLE SYRUP
Distilled from the sap of sugar maple trees found only in Canada and about ten states in the USA. Most often eaten with pancakes or waffles, but also used as an ingredient in baking or in preparing desserts. Maple-flavoured syrup or pancake syrup is not an adequate substitute for the real thing.

MARINARA MIX
See seafood

MARSALA
A fortified Italian wine produced in the region surrounding the Sicilian city of Marsala; recognisable by its intense amber colour and complex aroma. Often used in cooking.

MAYONNAISE, WHOLE-EGG
Commercial mayonnaise of high quality made with whole eggs. Must be refrigerated once opened.

MERGUEZ SAUSAGES
A small, spicy sausage believed to have originated in Tunisia but eaten in North Africa, France and Spain; is traditionally made with lamb meat and is easily recognised because of its chilli-red colour. Can be fried, grilled or roasted; available from many butchers, delis and specialty sausage stores.

MESCLUN
Sold as a pre-mixed pile or bouquet of baby greens, which may include coral, mignonette, oak-leaf or butter lettuce, rocket, spinach, curly endive, mizuna and/or radicchio. If buying loose, grab more than you need and discard the tired-looking leaves. See also page 107

MIGNONETTE LETTUCE
This is a small, soft-leafed lettuce, but crisper and glossier than coral or oak-leaf. It has a good grassy flavour with just a delicate suggestion of bitterness. Its leaves vary from red to green. See also page 107

MILK
We use full-cream homogenised milk unless otherwise specified.
buttermilk in spite of its name, buttermilk is actually low in fat, varying between 0.6 per cent and 2 per cent per 100ml. Originally the term given to the slightly sour liquid left after butter was churned from cream, today it is intentionally made from no-fat or low-fat milk to which specific bacterial cultures have been added during the manufacturing process. It is readily available from the dairy department in supermarkets. Because it is low in fat, it's a good substitute for dairy products such as cream or sour cream in some baking and salad dressings.
evaporated unsweetened canned milk from which water has been extracted by evaporation. Evaporated skim or low-fat milk has 0.3 per cent fat content.
full-cream powder instant powdered milk made from whole cow milk with liquid removed and emulsifiers added.
sweetened condensed a canned milk product consisting of milk with more than half the water content removed and sugar added to the remaining milk.
top 'n' fill caramel a canned milk product made of condensed milk that has been boiled to a caramel.

MIRIN
A Japanese champagne-coloured cooking wine, made of glutinous rice and alcohol. It is used just for cooking and should not be confused with sake. A seasoned sweet mirin, manjo mirin, made of water, rice, corn syrup and alcohol, is used in dipping sauces.

MISO
Fermented soybean paste. There are many types of miso, each with its own aroma, flavour, colour and texture; it can be kept, airtight, for up to a year in the fridge. Generally, the darker the miso, the saltier the taste and denser the texture. Salt-reduced miso is available. Buy in tubs or plastic packs.

MIXED DRIED FRUIT
A combination of sultanas, raisins, currants, mixed peel and cherries.

MIXED SPICE
A classic spice mixture generally containing caraway, allspice, coriander, cumin, nutmeg and ginger, although cinnamon and other spices can be added. It is used with fruit and in cakes.

MIZUNA
A mustard green from Japan where it is traditionally used in soups and other cooked main dishes. It's often found in a mesclun, but its mild, aromatic jagged green leaves can also stand alone. Refrigerate in a plastic bag, unwashed, for up to five days. See also page 106

MOLASSES
A thick, dark brown syrup, the residue from the refining of sugar; available in light, dark and blackstrap varieties. Its slightly bitter taste is an essential ingredient in American cooking, found in foods such as gingerbread, shoofly pie and boston baked beans.

MORTAR AND PESTLE
A cooking tool whose design has remained the same over the centuries: the mortar is a bowl-shaped container and the pestle a rounded, bat-shaped tool. Together, they grind and pulverise spices, herbs and other foods. The pestle is pressed against the mortar

and rotated, grinding the ingredient between the two surfaces. Essential for curry pastes and crushing spices.

MOULI
Also known as food mill; an essential kitchen tool in terms of versatility, ease of use and multi-task function. It's a rotary grater large enough to fit over a saucepan or bowl which comes with variety of interchangeable plates for processing different textures; it strains, pulps, rices, mashes, purees and even dices. Unlike a blender or processor, it separates the peel, seeds, cores, etc., from the puree and allows the cook a degree of control over the final texture.

MUESLI
Also known as granola; a combination of grains (mainly oats), nuts and dried fruits. Can also be toasted in oil and honey, adding crispness and kilojoules.

MUSCATEL
Also known as muscat grapes; used to make the sweet dessert wine having the same name. This grape variety is superb eaten fresh; when dried, its distinctively musty flavour goes well with cheese, chocolate, pork and game.

MUSHROOMS
button small, cultivated white mushrooms with a mild flavour. When a recipe in this book calls for an unspecified type of mushroom, use button. See also page 441
chanterelle also called girolles or pfifferling; a trumpet-shaped wild mushroom, ranging in colour from yellow to orange. It has a delicate flavour and a chewy texture. Also available dried. See also page 441
chestnut are cultivated mushrooms with a firm texture and strong flavour. They are available only irregularly. See also page 441
dried porcini the richest-flavoured mushrooms, also known as cèpes. Expensive, but because they're so strongly flavoured, only a small amount is required. See also page 440
enoki cultivated mushrooms also called enokitake; are tiny long-stemmed, pale mushrooms that grow and are sold in clusters, and can be used that way or separated by slicing off the base. They have a mild fruity flavour and are slightly crisp in texture. See also page 440
flat large, flat mushrooms with a rich earthy flavour, ideal for filling and barbecuing. They are sometimes misnamed field mushrooms which are wild mushrooms. See also page 440
oyster also called abalone; grey-white mushrooms shaped like a fan. Prized for their smooth texture and subtle, oyster-like flavour. Also available pink. See also pages 348 & 440
pine also called the australian cep, are wild-picked in forests of introduced pine species in autumn and early winter. they are related to but not the same as the true european cep, but their fruity scent and deep, earthy flavour explain the common name. They are best served simply: fried quickly or added in the last few minutes of cooking to a soup. See also page 440
portobello are mature, fully opened swiss browns; they are larger and bigger in flavour. See also page 441
shiitake *fresh*, are also called chinese black, forest or golden oak mushrooms. Although cultivated, they have the earthiness and taste of wild mushrooms. Large and meaty, they can be used as a substitute for meat in some Asian vegetarian dishes. See also page 349
dried also called donko or dried chinese mushrooms; have a unique meaty flavour. Rehydrate before use.
shimeji cultivated mushrooms also called beech mushrooms, grow and are sold in clumps; are nutty in flavour and slightly crunchy. See also page 441
straw so named for the straw on which they are grown; are small and globe-shaped with internal stems. They are cultivated but are so fragile and deteriorate so quickly after harvesting that they are not a commercial proposition fresh so are usually canned. See also page 440
swiss brown also known as roman or cremini. Light to dark brown mushrooms with full-bodied flavour; suited for use in casseroles or being stuffed and baked. See also page 441

MUSLIN
Inexpensive, undyed, finely woven cotton fabric called for in cooking to strain stocks and sauces; if unavailable, use disposable coffee filter papers.

MUSTARD
american-style bright yellow in colour, a sweet mustard containing mustard seeds, sugar, salt, spices and garlic. Serve with hot dogs and hamburgers.
dijon also called french. Pale brown, creamy, distinctively flavoured, fairly mild French mustard.
english traditional hot, pungent, deep yellow mustard. Serve with roast beef and ham; wonderful with hard cheeses.
japanese hot mustard available in ready-to-use paste in tubes or powder form from Asian food shops.
wholegrain also known as seeded. A French-style coarse-grain mustard made from crushed mustard seeds and dijon-style french mustard. Works well with cold meats and sausages.

MUSTARD SEEDS
black also called brown mustard seeds, they are more pungent than the white variety; used frequently in curries.
white also called yellow mustard seeds; used ground for mustard powder and in most prepared mustards.

NAAN
The rather thick, leavened bread associated with the tandoori dishes of northern India, where it is baked pressed against the inside wall of a heated tandoor (clay oven). Now made by commercial bakers and sold in most supermarkets.

NOODLES
bean thread also called cellophane or glass noodles, these are made from a paste of water and mung bean flour. To soften bean thread noodles, it is best to soak them in hot water as they lose texture when boiled. They can also be fried directly from the pack until puffed. See also page 192
dried rice noodles also called rice stick noodles. Made from rice flour and water, available flat and wide or very thin (vermicelli). Must be soaked in boiling water to soften.
fresh egg also called ba mee or yellow noodles; made from wheat flour and eggs, sold fresh or dried. Range in size from very fine strands to wide, spaghetti-like pieces as thick as a shoelace. See also page 193
fresh rice also called ho fun, khao pun, sen yau, pho or kway tiau, depending on the country of manufacture; the most common form of noodle used in Thailand. Can be purchased in strands of various widths or large sheets weighing about 500g which are to be cut into the desired noodle size. Chewy and pure white, they do not need pre-cooking before use. See also page 193
fried also known as crispy noodles, these wheat flour and egg noodles have been deep-fried until crisp, then dried and packaged. Add directly to a stir-fry or place in boiling water for one minute before using. Often used for the popular chinese dish sang choy bow. See also page 192

hokkien also called stir-fry noodles; fresh wheat noodles resembling thick, yellow-brown spaghetti needing no pre-cooking before use. See also page 192
ramen popular Japanese wheat noodles, sold in dried, fresh, steamed and instant forms. A popular fast food in the many ramen houses of Japan, these noodles are also a diet staple for students. See also page 192
rice stick also called sen lek, ho fun or kway teow; especially popular South-East Asian dried rice noodles. They come in different widths (thin used in soups, wide in stir-fries), but all should be soaked in hot water to soften. The traditional noodle used in pad thai which, before soaking, measures about 5mm in width. See also page 193
rice vermicelli also called sen mee, mei fun or bee hoon. Used throughout Asia in spring rolls and cold salads; similar to bean threads, only longer and made with rice flour instead of mung bean starch. Before using, soak the dried noodles in hot water until softened, boil them briefly then rinse with hot water. Vermicelli can also be deep-fried until crunchy and used in salad or as a garnish or bed for sauces. See also page 193
shanghai fresh thick, round wheat noodles, similar to hokkien but paler in colour, and usually sold unoiled. Also available as dried thin white noodles, which need to be boiled for up to 15 minutes, or until soft; often used in stir-fries. See also page 192
singapore pre-cooked wheat noodles best described as a thinner version of hokkien; sold, packaged, in the refrigerated section of supermarkets.
soba thin, pale-brown noodle originally from Japan; made from buckwheat and varying proportions of wheat flour. Available dried and fresh, and in flavoured (for instance, green tea) varieties; eaten in soups, stir-fries and, chilled, on their own. See also page 192

somen extremely thin noodles made from hard wheat – if eggless, they are labelled somen and tamago if made with egg. These Japanese noodles are traditionally eaten in cold dishes but can be served in warm broth. Avoid overcooking, as they become gluggy. See also page 193
udon available fresh and dried. These broad, white, wheat Japanese noodles are similar to the ones used in home-made chicken noodle soup. See also page 193

NORI
A type of dried seaweed used in Japanese cooking as a flavouring, garnish or for sushi. Sold in thin sheets, plain or toasted (yaki-nori).

NUTMEG
A strong and pungent spice ground from the dried nut of an evergreen tree native to Indonesia. Usually found ground but the flavour is more intense from a whole nut, available from spice shops, so it's best to grate your own. Used most often in baking and milk-based desserts, but also works nicely in savoury dishes. Found in mixed spice mixtures.

OAK-LEAF LETTUCE
The curly leaves vary from reddish-brown to pale green and resemble the shape of oak leaves. This popular variety of lettuce has a soft texture with a sweet, mild flavour. It is an ideal lettuce to grow because the leaves can be harvested one at a time. See also page 107

OATMEAL
Also sold as oatmeal flour, is made from milled oat kernels; not the same product as rolled oats or oat bran. It is available at health food stores.

OIL

cooking spray we use a cholesterol-free cooking spray made from canola oil.
grapeseed comes from grape seeds; available from supermarkets.
hazelnut oil see hazelnuts
macadamia oil see macadamias
olive made from ripened olives. Extra virgin and virgin are the first and second press, respectively, of the olives and are therefore considered the best; the "extra light" or "light" name on other types refers to taste not fat levels.
peanut pressed from ground peanuts; the most commonly used oil in Asian cooking because of its high smoke point (capacity to handle high heat without burning).
sesame made from roasted, crushed, white sesame seeds; a flavouring rather than a cooking medium.
vegetable any of a number of oils sourced from plant rather than animal fats.

OKRA

Also known as bamia or lady fingers. A green, ridged, oblong pod with a furry skin. Native to Africa, this vegetable is used in Indian, Middle Eastern and South American cooking. Can be eaten on its own; as part of a casserole, curry or gumbo; used to thicken stews or gravies. See also page 218.

ONIONS

brown strongly-flavoured onions with a brown skin and creamy flesh; they are the most commonly used onion in cooking.
fried onion served as a condiment on Asian tables to be sprinkled over just-cooked food. Found in cellophane bags or jars at all Asian grocery shops; once opened, they will keep for months if stored tightly sealed. Make your own by frying thinly sliced peeled baby onions until golden and crisp. See also shallots
green also called scallion or (incorrectly) shallot; an immature onion picked before the bulb has formed, having a long, bright-green edible stalk.
red also known as spanish, red spanish or bermuda onion; a sweet-flavoured, large, purple-red onion.
spring crisp, narrow green-leafed tops and a round sweet white bulb larger than green onions.
white milder than brown onions, these white-skinned and white-fleshed onions are suitable in salads as well as cooking.

ORANGE FLOWER WATER

Concentrated flavouring made from orange blossoms.

OYSTER SAUCE

Asian in origin, this thick, richly flavoured brown sauce is made from oysters and their brine, cooked with salt and soy sauce, and thickened with starches. Use as a condiment.
vegetarian mushroom a "vegetarian" oyster sauce made from blended mushrooms and soy sauce.

PANCETTA

An Italian unsmoked bacon, pork belly cured in salt and spices then rolled into a sausage shape and dried for several weeks. Used, sliced or chopped, as an ingredient rather than eaten on its own; can also be used to add taste and moisture to tough or dry cuts of meat.

PAPAYA

The papaya family includes both the yellow-fleshed fruit called pawpaw and the pink-fleshed fruit called papaya. Their mild, sweet flavour is best with a squeeze of lime. See also page 517.
green are available at Asian food stores; look for one that is hard and slightly shiny, proving it its freshly picked. Papaya will soften rapidly if not used within a day or two. See also page 348

PAPRIKA

Ground dried sweet red capsicum (bell pepper); there are many grades and types available, including sweet, hot, mild and smoked.

PARSNIP

Their nutty sweetness is especially good when steamed and dressed with a garlic and cream sauce or in a curried parsnip soup, or simply baked. Can be substituted for potatoes. Available all year but the cold develops their sweet/savoury flavour in winter. See also page 218

PASSIONFRUIT, PANAMA

A member of the berry family, this fruit is filled with tart-sweet pulp with small black seeds. It is not as tart as the more common purple variety of passionfruit. See also page 517

PASTA

conchiglie "shellfish" or "shells", have concave, ridged shapes that hold sauces well. A dried type, great in hearty soups like minestrone, or added to a vegetable salad. Available in different sizes: conchigliette (small), conchiglioni (larger). See also page 146
farfalle bow-tie shaped short pasta; sometimes known as butterfly pasta. See also page 146
fettuccine fresh or dried ribbon pasta made from durum wheat, semolina and egg. Also available plain or flavoured. See also page 146
fresh lasagne sheets thinly rolled wide sheets of plain or flavoured pasta; they do not need par-boiling before being used in cooking. See also page 146

fusilli "Little spindles", also called corkscrews, are a dried spiral pasta. Fusilli can be topped with any sauce, makes a great addition to casseroles or can be turned into a wonderful salad. Also comes in a longer, coil-like shape, called *fusilli col buco*. See also page 147

gnocchi Italian 'dumplings' made of potatoes, semolina or flour; can be cooked in boiling water or baked with sauce. See also page 147

macaroni tube-shaped pasta available in various sizes; made from semolina and water, and does not contain eggs.

orecchiette "little ears" are named after their shape, resembling tiny human ears. It's a chewy pasta that's traditional in southern Italy's Puglia region, where it is made from semolina. See also page 147

pappardelle from the Italian verb *pappare*, meaning "to gobble up", pappardelle are broad, flat or frilly, ribbons of pasta. Go well with red meat sauces (rabbit is a Tuscan favourite), chunky tomato and mushroom sauces as in *pappardelle boscaiola*, or with cream. See also page 147

penne Italian for "pen", this dried pasta resembles a quill, and has angled ends and ridges to hold chunky sauces. Penne are also available in a smooth variety to complement finer sauces. See also page 146

ravioli "little turnips", squares of pasta stuffed with cheese, vegetables or meat. Usually made from fresh pasta either by hand or in moulds. Ravioli are a match for tomato-based sauces, including bolognese, or they can be served with butter, olive oil or cream. See also page 147

rigatoni Italian for "large, ridged", this dried ribbed, tubular pasta is perfect with any sauce, from cream or cheese (especially ricotta) to the chunkiest meat sauces. Rigatoni is also good for pasta bakes. See also page 147

risoni small rice-shape pasta; very similar to another small pasta, orzo.

spaghetti long, thin solid strands of pasta.

tagliatelle long, flat strips of wheat pasta, slightly narrower and thinner than fettuccine.

tortellini circles of fresh plain pasta that are stuffed with a meat or cheese filling, and then folded into little hats. See also page 146

PASTRY

fillo is unique in that no fat or margarine is added to the dough. The dough is very elastic in texture and not rolled like other pastries, but stretched to the desired thickness. This gives it its delicate, tissue-thin sheets. It is best brushed with butter or margarine before baking.

sheets packaged sheets of frozen ready-made puff and shortcrust pastries. Available in the freezer section from supermarkets.

PEANUTS

Also known as groundnut, not in fact a nut but the pod of a legume. We mainly use raw (unroasted) or unsalted roasted peanuts.

oil See oil

PEARL BARLEY

See barley

PEAS

green also known as garden peas, must be shelled and their pods never eaten. Peas in the pod will yield just under half their weight of shelled peas; 1kg will serve 4. Peas in the pod are available fresh; shelled peas, frozen. See also page 219

snow also called mangetout; a variety of garden pea, eaten pod and all (although you may need to string them). Used in stir-fries or eaten raw in salads. Snow pea sprouts are available from supermarkets or greengrocers and are usually eaten raw in salads or sandwiches. See also page 219

sugar snap also known as honey snap peas; fresh small pea which can be eaten, whole, pod and all, similarly to snow peas. See also page 219

PECANS

Native to the US and now grown locally; pecans are golden brown, buttery and rich. Good in savoury as well as sweet dishes; walnuts are a good substitute.

PEPITAS

Are the pale green kernels of dried pumpkin seeds; they can be bought plain or salted.

PINE NUTS

Also known as pignoli; not a nut but a small, cream-coloured kernel from pine cones. They are best roasted before use to bring out the flavour.

PIRI PIRI SAUCE

A Portuguese chilli sauce made from red chillies, ginger, garlic, oil and various herbs.

PISTACHIOS

Green, delicately flavoured nuts inside hard off-white shells. Available salted or unsalted in their shells; you can also get them shelled.

PITTA BREAD

Also known as lebanese bread. A wheat-flour pocket bread sold in large, flat pieces that separate into rounds. Also available in small pieces called pocket pitta.

PLUM SAUCE

A thick, sweet and sour dipping sauce made from plums, vinegar, sugar, chillies and spices.

POLENTA
Also called cornmeal; a flour-like cereal made of dried corn (maize). Also the dish made from it. See also page 497

POMEGRANATE
Dark-red, leathery-skinned fresh fruit about the size of an orange filled with hundreds of seeds, each wrapped in an edible lucent-crimson pulp having a unique tangy sweet-sour flavour.

POMEGRANATE MOLASSES
Not to be confused with pomegranate syrup or grenadine (used in cocktails); pomegranate molasses is thicker, browner and more concentrated in flavour – tart, sharp, slightly sweet and fruity. Brush over grilling or roasting meat, seafood or poultry, add to salad dressings. Buy from Middle Eastern food stores or specialty food shops.

POPPY SEEDS
Small, dried, bluish-grey seeds of the poppy plant, with a crunchy texture and a nutty flavour. Can be purchased whole or ground in most supermarkets.

PORK
american-style spareribs well-trimmed mid-loin ribs.
belly fatty cut sold in rashers or in a piece, with or without rind or bone.
chinese barbecued roasted pork fillet with a sweet, sticky coating. Available from Asian food shops or specialty stores.
cutlets cut from ribs.
fillet skinless, boneless eye-fillet cut from the loin.
ham hock the shank of the leg, which does not form part of the ham but is salted and smoked in the same way.
minced ground lean pork.
neck sometimes called pork scotch, boneless cut from the foreloin.
shoulder joint sold with bone in or out.
speck smoked pork.

POTATOES
bintje oval, creamy skin, yellow flesh; good all-purpose potato, great baked and fried, good in salads.
coliban round, smooth white skin and flesh; good for baking and mashing.
congo purple flesh, small, elongated, sweet, mealy; good boiled and in salads.
desiree oval, smooth and pink-skinned, waxy yellow flesh; good in salads, boiled and roasted.
idaho also known as russet burbank; russet in colour, fabulous baked.
king edward slightly plump and rosy; great mashed.
kipfler small, finger-shaped, nutty flavour; great baked and in salads.
lasoda round, red skin with deep eyes, white flesh; good for mashing or roasting.
new potatoes also known as chats; not a separate variety but an early harvest with very thin skin. Good unpeeled steamed, eaten hot or cold in salads.
pontiac large, red skin, deep eyes, white flesh; good grated, boiled and baked.
pink-eye small, off-white skin, deep purple eyes; good steamed and boiled, great baked.
pink fir apple elongated, rosy skin, waxy; good boiled, baked and in salads.
russet burbank also known as idaho, long and oval, rough white skin with shallow eyes, white flesh; good for baking and frying.
sebago white skin, oval; good fried, mashed and baked.
spunta large, long, yellow flesh, floury; great mashed and fried.

PRESERVED LEMON
Whole or quartered salted lemons preserved in olive oil and lemon juice and occasionally clove, cinnamon and coriander. A North African specialty, added to casseroles and tagines to impart a rich, salty-sour acidic flavour; also added to dressings or yogurt. Available from delis and specialty food shops. Use the rind only and rinse well under cold water before using.

PRESERVED TURNIP
Also called hua chai po or cu cai muoi, or dried radish because of its similarity to daikon. Sold packaged whole or sliced, is very salty and must be rinsed and dried before use.

PROSCIUTTO
A kind of unsmoked Italian ham; salted, air-cured and aged, it is usually eaten uncooked.

QUAIL
Related to the pheasant and partridge; a small, delicate-flavoured farmed game bird ranging from 250g to 300g.

QUINCE
Yellow-skinned fruit with hard texture and astringent, tart taste; eaten cooked or as a preserve. Long, slow cooking makes the flesh a deep rose pink.

RADICCHIO
A red-leafed Italian chicory with a refreshing bitter taste that's eaten raw and grilled. Comes in varieties named after their places of origin, such as round-headed Verona or long-headed Treviso. See also page 107

RAITA
Yogurt that is whipped and seasoned with salt, pepper and one or two piquant spices; often has mint stirred through it. Served as a condiment, it possesses cooling properties to help temper the heat of a curry.

RAMBUTAN
A relative of the lychee, with similar luscious, perfumed, grape-like flesh. To remove the leathery, tendril-covered shell, break open with a fingernail and peel like an egg. See also page 516

RAS EL HANOUT
The name means "top of the shop" and the mixture varies from one merchant to another, but is always subtly savoury with a touch of heat. See also page 416

READY-MADE WHITE ICING
Also known as soft icing, ready-to-roll and prepared fondant.

RHUBARB
A plant with long, green-red stalks; becomes sweet and edible when cooked.

RICE
arborio small, round grain rice well-suited to absorb a large amount of liquid; the high level of starch makes it especially suitable for risottos for its classic creaminess. See also page 173
basmati a white, fragrant long-grained rice; the grains fluff up when cooked. It should be washed several times before cooking. See also page 172
black also called purple rice, black rice is unmilled, leaving the dark husk in place, colouring the grain when cooked. It has a nutty taste and crunchy texture. There are hundreds of varieties across Asia, from Chinese black rice to Thai black sticky rice. See also page 173
brown retains the high-fibre, nutritious bran coating that's removed from white rice when hulled. It takes longer to cook than white rice and has a chewier texture. Once cooked, the long grains stay separate, while the short grains are soft and stickier. See also page 172
calrose the brand name of a medium-grain white rice developed as an all-purpose rice; it gives different results according to how it is cooked. Calrose brown rice is also available. See also page 173
doongara a white rice with a lower glycaemic index (GI) than most other rices, so it is more slowly absorbed into the blood stream, providing sustained energy release for endurance. Cooks to a firm, fluffy rice, even if it is overcooked.
glutinous also known as sticky rice, this variety is a stickier version of short-grain rice. Its plump, distinctively flavoured grains cling together when cooked, so they can be easily formed into small balls for dipping into savoury dishes and soaking up the sauce. See also page 173
jasmine or thai jasmine, is a long-grain white rice recognised around the world as having a perfumed aromatic quality; moist in texture, it clings together after cooking. Sometimes substituted for basmati rice. See also page 172
koshihikari small, round-grain white rice. Substitute white short-grain rice and cook by the absorption method. See also page 173
long-grain elongated grains that remain separate when cooked; this is the most popular steaming rice in Asia. See also page 172
nishiki a Japanese variety that's often sold as medium-grain rice, but is actually a slightly longer short-grain rice. Like koshihikari, nishiki cooks to the tender and lightly clinging texture that is right for sushi. This light, fresh-tasting grain is also grown in California. See also page 173
short-grain fat, almost round grain with a high starch content; tends to clump together when cooked.
white is hulled and polished rice, can be short-or long-grained.
wild not a member of the rice family but the seed of an aquatic grass native to the cold regions of North America. Wild rice has a strong nutty taste and can be expensive, so is best combined with brown and white rices in pulaos, stuffings and salads. See also page 172
wild rice blend a packaged blend of white long-grain rice and wild rice. With its dark brown, almost black grains, crunchy, resilient texture and smokey-like flavour, wild rice contrasts nicely with mild-tasting white rice. Perfect with lentils fish, in pulaos or added to soups. See also page 172

RISONI
See pasta

ROCKET
Also called arugula, rugula and rucola; peppery green leaf eaten raw in salads or used in cooking. Baby rocket leaves are smaller and less peppery. See also page 107

ROLLED OATS
Flattened oat grain rolled into flakes and traditionally used for porridge. Instant oats are also available, but use traditional oats for baking.

ROLLED RICE
Flattened rice grain rolled into flakes; looks similar to rolled oats.

ROLLED RYE
Flattened rye grain rolled into flakes and similar in appearance to rolled oats.

ROSEWATER
Extract made from crushed rose petals; used for its aromatic quality in many sweetmeats and desserts.

RUM
See liqueurs

SAFFRON
Stigma of a member of the crocus family, available ground or in strands; imparts a yellow-orange colour to food once infused. The quality can vary greatly; the best is the most expensive spice in the world. See also page 416

SAMBAL OELEK
Also called ulek or olek; an Indonesian salty paste made from ground chillies and vinegar.

SASHIMI
Fish sold as sashimi has to meet stringent guidelines regarding handling. Seek advice from local authorities before eating any raw seafood.

SAVOY CABBAGE
Large, heavy head with crinkled dark-green outer leaves; a fairly mild tasting cabbage.

SEAFOOD
abalone is a harvested single-shelled deep-water shellfish with a reputation for toughness, it is usually sliced and pounded before cooking. Tastes like lobster. See also page 446
balmain bugs also known as slipper or shovelnose lobster, or southern bay lobster; crustacean, a type of crayfish. Substitute with moreton bay bugs, king prawns or scampi. See also page 447
blue-eye also called deep sea trevalla or trevally and blue-eye cod; thick, moist white-fleshed fish.
blue swimmer crab also known as sand crab, blue manna crab, bluey, sand crab or sandy. Substitute with lobster, balmain or moreton bay bugs. See also page 447
bream (yellowfin) also known as silver or black bream, seabream or surf bream; soft, moist white flesh. Substitute with snapper or ocean perch.
clams also called vongole; we use a small ridge-shelled variety of this bivalve mollusc.
fish fillet use your favourite firm-fleshed white fish fillet.
marinara mix a mixture of uncooked, chopped seafood available from fishmarkets and fishmongers.
marron one of three types of Australian freshwater crayfish, marron is native to south western Australia and is the largest of these varieties. It is important to undercook, rather than overcook crayfish as they will continue cooking in residual heat. See also page 446
mussels should only be bought from a reliable fish market: they must be tightly closed when bought, indicating they are alive. Before cooking, scrub shells with a strong brush and remove the beards; do not eat any that do not open after cooking. Varieties include black and green-lip. See also page 447
ocean trout a farmed fish with pink, soft flesh. From the same family as the atlantic salmon; one can be substituted for the other.
octopus usually tenderised before you buy them; both octopus and squid require either long slow cooking (usually for the large molluscs) or quick cooking over high heat (usually for the small molluscs) – anything in between will make the octopus tough and rubbery. See also page 446
oysters available in many varieties, including pacific, bay/blacklip, and sydney or new zealand rock oyster. See also page 447
pipis small smooth-shelled triangular shaped bivalve mollusc. Available from fish markets and large seafood outlets, they can also be substituted with vongole and cockles. See also page 446
prawns also known as shrimp; varieties include, school, king, royal red, sydney harbour, tiger. Can be bought uncooked (green) or cooked, with or without shells. See also page 447
salmon red-pink firm flesh with few bones; moist delicate flavour.
scallops a type of bivalve; often eaten raw or barely seared, they should never be cooked more than 30 seconds as they will lose their juicy tenderness and be tough. See also page 446
squid also known as calamari; a type of mollusc. Buy squid hoods to make preparation and cooking faster. See also page 447
swordfish also known as broadbill. Substitute with yellowfin or bluefin tuna or mahi mahi.
tuna reddish, firm flesh; slightly dry. Varieties include bluefin, yellowfin, skipjack or albacore; substitute with swordfish.
white fish means non-oily fish; includes bream, flathead, whiting, snapper, dhufish, redfish and ling.
yabbies the most common type of Australian freshwater crayfish; found throughout south eastern Australia, in creeks and dams, but those available commercially are mostly farmed. Its fresh-tasting, moist meat is in the tail and claws. See also page 446

SEMOLINA
Coarsely ground flour milled from durum wheat; the flour used in making gnocchi, pasta and couscous.

SESAME SEEDS
Black and white are the most common of this small oval seed, however there are also red and brown varieties. The seeds are used as an ingredient and as a condiment. Roast the seeds in a heavy-based frying pan over low heat.

SEVEN-SPICE MIX (SHICHIMI TOGARASHI)
A Japanese blend of seven ground spices, seeds and seaweed. The mix varies but includes hot and aromatic flavours. Used as a seasoning with noodles and cooked meats and fish.

SHALLOTS
Also called french shallots, golden shallots or eschalots. Small and elongated, with a brown-skin, they grow in tight clusters similar to garlic.
fried can be purchased at Asian grocery stores; once opened, fried shallots will keep for months if stored in a tightly sealed glass jar. See also onions
purple also known as asian shallots; related to the onion but resembling garlic (they grow in bulbs of multiple cloves). Thin-layered and intensely flavoured, they are used in cooking throughout South-East Asia.

SHERRY
Fortified wine consumed as an aperitif or used in cooking. Sold as fino (light, dry), amontillado (medium sweet, dark) and oloroso (full-bodied, very dark).

SHRIMP PASTE
Also called kapi, trasi and blanchan; a strong-scented, very firm preserved paste made of salted dried shrimp. Used sparingly as a pungent flavouring in many South-East Asian soups, sauces and rice dishes. It should be chopped or sliced thinly then wrapped in foil and roasted before use.

SICHUAN PEPPERCORNS
Also called szechuan or chinese pepper, native to the Sichuan province of China. A mildly hot spice that comes from the prickly ash tree. Although it is not related to the peppercorn family, small, red-brown aromatic sichuan berries look like black peppercorns and have a distinctive peppery-lemon flavour and aroma. See also page 417

SILVER BEET
Also called swiss chard and incorrectly, spinach; has fleshy stalks and large leaves, both of which can be prepared as for spinach. See also page 217

SKEWERS
Metal or bamboo skewers can be used: rub oil onto metal skewers to stop meat sticking; soak bamboo skewers in water for at least 1 hour to prevent them splintering or scorching during cooking.

SOPRESSA
A salami from the north of Italy, can be found in both mild and chilli-flavoured varieties. If you can't find it easily, you can use any hot salami, but the taste won't be exactly the same.

SOUR CREAM
See cream

SOY SAUCE
Also called sieu; made from fermented soybeans. Several variations are available in supermarkets and Asian food stores; we use japanese soy sauce unless indicated otherwise.
dark deep brown, almost black in colour; rich, with a thicker consistency than other types. Pungent but not particularly salty; good for marinating.
japanese an all-purpose low-sodium soy sauce made with more wheat content than its Chinese counterparts; fermented in barrels and aged. Possibly the best table soy and the one to choose if you only want one variety.
light fairly thin in consistency and, while paler than the others, the saltiest tasting; used in dishes in which the natural colour of the ingredients is to be maintained. Not to be confused with salt-reduced or low-sodium soy sauces.

SPECK
See pork

SPINACH
Also called english spinach and incorrectly, silver beet. Baby spinach leaves are best eaten raw in salads; the larger leaves should be added last to soups, stews and stir-fries, and should be cooked until barely wilted.

SPLIT PEAS
Yellow or green varieties, both with a sweet, strong pea flavour. They are usually pre-soaked but may be cooked without soaking. See also page 497

SPONGE FINGER BISCUITS
Also called savoiardi, savoy biscuits or lady's fingers, they are Italian-style crisp fingers made from sponge cake mixture.

SPRING ROLL WRAPPERS
Also known as egg roll wrappers; they come in various sizes and can be purchased fresh or frozen. Made from a delicate wheat-based pastry, they can be used for making gow gee and samosas as well as spring rolls. See also wrappers

STAR ANISE
A dried star-shaped pod whose seeds have an astringent aniseed flavour; commonly used to flavour stocks and marinades. See also page 416

STAR FRUIT
Also known as carambola, five-corner fruit or chinese star fruit; pale green or yellow colour, it has a clean, crisp texture. Flavour may be either sweet or sour, depending on the variety and when it was picked. There is no need to peel or seed it and they're slow to discolour. See also page 516

SUGAR
We use coarse, granulated table sugar (crystal sugar), unless specified.
brown a soft, finely granulated sugar retaining molasses for its characteristic colour and flavour.
caster also known as superfine or finely granulated table sugar.
demerara small-grained golden-coloured crystal sugar.
icing also known as confectioners' sugar or powdered sugar; pulverised granulated sugar crushed together with a small amount of cornflour.
muscovado a fine-grained, moist sugar that comes in two types, light and dark. Light muscovado has a light toffee flavour and is good for sticky toffee sauce and caramel ice-cream. Dark muscovado is used in sweet and spicy sauces.
palm also called nam tan pip, jaggery, jawa or gula melaka; made from the sap of the sugar palm tree. Light brown to black in colour and usually sold in rock-hard cakes; use brown sugar if unavailable.
pure icing also known as confectioners' sugar or powdered sugar.
raw natural brown granulated sugar.

SUMAC
A purple-red, astringent spice ground from berries growing on shrubs that flourish wild around the Mediterranean; adds a tart, lemony flavour to dips and dressings and goes well with barbecued meat. Can be found in Middle Eastern food stores. See also page 417

SUNFLOWER SEEDS
Grey-green, slightly soft, oily kernels; a nutritious snack.

TAHINI
Sesame seed paste; found in Middle Eastern food stores and in the health food section of most supermarkets.

TAMARI
Similar to but thicker than japanese soy; very dark in colour with a distinctively mellow flavour. Good used as a dipping sauce or for basting.

TAMARIND
The tamarind tree produces clusters of hairy brown pods, each of which is filled with seeds and a viscous pulp, that are dried and pressed into the blocks of tamarind found in Asian food shops. Gives a sweet-sour, slightly astringent taste to marinades, pastes, sauces and dressings.

TAMARIND CONCENTRATE (OR PASTE)
The commercial result of the distillation of tamarind juice into a condensed, compacted paste.

TAT SOI
Also known as pak choy and chinese flat cabbage, tat soi is a variety of buk choy. Its dark green leaves are cut into sections rather than separated and used in soups, braises and stir-fries. Available from some supermarkets and greengrocers. See also page 348

TIA MARIA
See liqueurs

TOFU
Also called soybean curd or bean curd; an off-white, custard-like product made from the "milk" of crushed soybeans. Refrigerate fresh tofu in water (changed daily) for up to 4 days.
firm made by compressing bean curd to remove most of the water. Good in stir-fries as it can be tossed without disintegrating. Can also be flavoured, preserved in rice wine or brine.
fried packaged pieces of deep-fried soft bean curd; the surface is brown and crunchy and the inside almost totally dried out. Add to soups and stir-fries at the last minute so they don't soak up too much liquid.
sheets also called dried bean curd skins or yuba. Manufactured product made from the sweet, stiffened skin that forms on warm soybean liquid as it cools. Reconstitute before use.
silken not a type of tofu but reference to the manufacturing process of straining soybean liquid through silk; this denotes best quality.
soft delicate texture; does not hold its shape when overhandled. Can be used as a dairy substitute in ice-cream etc.

TOMATOES
bottled pasta sauce a prepared sauce; a blend of tomatoes, herbs and spices.
canned whole peeled tomatoes in natural juices; available crushed, chopped or diced. Use undrained.
cherry also called tiny tim or tom thumb tomatoes; small and round.
egg also called plum or roma, these are smallish, oval-shaped tomatoes much used in Italian cooking or salads.
paste triple-concentrated tomato puree used to flavour soups, stews and sauces.
puree canned pureed tomatoes (not tomato paste).
semi-dried partially dried tomato pieces in olive oil; softer and juicier than sun-dried, these are not a preserve thus do not keep as long as sun-dried.
sun-dried tomato pieces that have been dried with salt; this dehydrates the tomato and concentrates the flavour. We use sun-dried tomatoes packaged in oil, unless otherwise specified.
truss small vine-ripened tomatoes with vine still attached.

TURKISH BREAD
Also called pide. Sold in long (about 45cm) flat loaves and individual rounds; made from wheat flour and sprinkled with black onion seeds.

TURMERIC
Also called kamin; is a rhizome related to galangal and ginger. Must be grated or pounded to release its acrid aroma and pungent flavour. Known for the golden colour it imparts, fresh turmeric can be substituted with the more commonly found dried powder.

VANILLA
bean dried, long, thin pod from a tropical golden orchid; the minuscule black seeds inside the bean are used to impart a luscious vanilla flavour in baking and desserts. Place a whole bean in a jar of sugar to make the vanilla sugar often called for in recipes; a bean can be used three or four times.
extract obtained from vanilla beans infused in water; a non-alcoholic version of essence.

VEAL
osso buco also called veal shin, usually cut into 3cm to 5cm thick slices and used in the famous Italian slow-cooked casserole of the same name.
rack row of small chops or cutlets.
scaloppine a piece of lean steak hammered with a meat mallet until almost see-through; cook over high heat for as little time as possible.
schnitzel thinly sliced steak.

VERMOUTH
A wine flavoured with a number of different herbs, mostly used as an aperitif and for cocktails.

VINEGAR
balsamic originally from Modena, Italy, there are now many balsamic vinegars on the market ranging in pungency and quality depending on how, and for how long, they have been aged. Quality can be determined up to a point by price; use the most expensive sparingly.
brown malt made from fermented malt and beech shavings.
cider made from fermented apples.
rice a colourless vinegar made from fermented rice and flavoured with sugar and salt. Also called seasoned rice vinegar; sherry can be substituted.
white made from distilled grain alcohol.

WALNUTS
As well as being a good source of fibre and healthy oils, nuts contain a range of vitamins, minerals and other beneficial plant components called phytochemicals. Walnuts contain the beneficial omega-3 fatty acids.

WASABI
Also called wasabe; an Asian horseradish used to make the pungent, green-coloured sauce traditionally served with Japanese raw fish dishes; sold in powdered or paste form.

WATER CHESTNUTS
Resemble true chestnuts in appearance, hence the English name. Small brown tubers with a crisp, white, nutty-tasting flesh. Their crunchy texture is best fresh; however, canned water chestnuts are more easily obtained and can be kept for about a month in the fridge, once opened. Used, rinsed and drained, in salads and stir-fries.

WATERCRESS
One of the cress family, a large group of peppery greens used raw in salads, dips and sandwiches, or cooked in soups. Highly perishable, so it must be used as soon as possible after purchase. See also page 106

WITLOF
Also known as belgian endive; related to and confused with chicory. A versatile vegetable, it tastes as good cooked as it does eaten raw. Grown in darkness like white asparagus to prevent it becoming green; looks somewhat like a tightly furled, cream to very light-green cigar. The leaves can be removed and used to hold a canapé filling; the whole vegetable can be opened up, stuffed then baked or casseroled; and the leaves can be tossed in a salad with other vegetables. See also page 107

WOK CHAN
A long-handled, metal mini-shovel used in stir-frying to lift, toss and stir food in a wok. Invest in a wooden chan if you use a non-stick wok so that you don't scratch its surface.

WOMBOK
Also called chinese cabbage, peking or napa cabbage; elongated in shape with pale green, crinkly leaves, is the most common cabbage in South-East Asia. Can be shredded or chopped and eaten raw or braised, steamed or stir-fried. See also page 349

WORCESTERSHIRE SAUCE
Thin, dark-brown spicy sauce developed by the British when in India; used as a seasoning for meat, gravies and cocktails, and as a condiment.
japanese there are two types available, one similar to normal worcestershire and the other somewhat blander; both are made from varying proportions of vinegar, tomatoes, onions, carrots, garlic and spices.

WRAPPERS
Wonton wrappers and gow gee or spring roll pastry sheets, made of flour, egg and water, are found in the refrigerated or freezer section of Asian food shops and many supermarkets. These come in different thicknesses and shapes. Thin wrappers work best in soups, while the thicker ones are best for frying; and the choice of round or square, small or large is dependent on the recipe. See also spring roll wrappers

YEAST (DRIED AND FRESH)
Raising agent used in dough making. Granular (7g sachets) and fresh compressed (20g blocks) yeast can almost always be substituted one for the other when yeast is called for.

YOGURT
We use plain full-cream yogurt unless specifically noted otherwise. If a recipe in this book calls for low-fat yogurt, we use one with a fat content of less than 0.2 per cent.

ZA'ATAR
A Middle Eastern herb and spice mixture which varies but always includes thyme (for which it gets its Arabic name), with ground sumac and, usually, toasted sesame seeds. It is sprinkled on yogurt and flatbreads and can be used as a rub on lamb or chicken to grilled or roasted. See also page 417

ZUCCHINI
Also called courgette; small, pale- or dark-green or yellow vegetable of the squash family. Harvested when young, its edible flowers can be stuffed and deep-fried. See also page 219

Index

A

abalone 446, 660
accompaniments 25
    meatloaf, to 25
    soups, to 134–5
    stews, to 386–7
adzuki beans 496, 641
aïoli 280
    lemon 465
    mint 79
allspice 641
almonds 641
    almond friands 560
    almond macaroons 570
    flourless chocolate and almond torte 541
anchovies 315, 378
    chicken cacciatore 378
    pan-seared scallops with anchovy butter 474
    penne puttanesca 158
    spaghetti and meatballs 155
anchovy toasts 135
angel hair with rocket and chilli 166
anzacs 572
appetisers, mixed 74
apples 636
    apple crumble 521
    apple jelly 611
    apple pie 509
    apple sauce 326, 328–9, 332–3
    grilled pork chops with apples 452
    pork chops with apples and calvados 465
    pork cutlet with fennel and apple salsa 451
    quick apple sauce 330
    tarte tatin 518
apricot jam 610
arborio rice 171, 173, 659
arrabbiata sauce 279
arrowroot 641
artichoke
    artichoke hearts vinaigrette 220
    globe 216, 641

(*artichoke* continued)
    hearts 641
    jerusalem 218, 641
asafoetida 416, 641
asian crab and rice omelette 252
asian greens, steamed, with char siu sauce 238
asian vegetables 211, 348–9
    asian greens, steamed, with char siu sauce 238
    cooking 349
asparagus
    asparagus hollandaise 215
    prawn and asparagus risotto 176
avocado 95
    avocado salsa 84
    storage 636

B

baba ghanoush
bacon 469, 641
    bacon toasts 134
    cassoulet 376
    fried eggs and bacon 255
    gruyère, leek and bacon tart 404
    quiche lorraine 392
    sausages with pea and bacon mash 469
baharat 416, 641
baking 635
    butter cookies 44–6
    butter, using 40
    cakes *see* cakes
    citrus rind 635
    desserts 504
    essence or extract, using 40
    greasing pan 40
    powder 641
    sifting 40
    tips 635
    vegetables 211
    water bath, using 504
balmain bugs 447, 660
    garlic herbed butter, with 449
balsamic and garlic dressing 116
bamboo shoots 211

banana
　cake 553
　fritters 477
　golden 516
　leaves 641
　thai steamed fish in banana leaves 64
barbecue sauce, tangy 282
barbecues and grills 211, 434–5
　balmain bugs with garlic herbed butter 449
　barbecued baby octopus 450
　barbecued scotch fillet 452
　barbecued whole snapper 454–5
　cajun chickens 439
　care of barbecue 435
　cheeseburgers with caramelised onion 443
　chilli and honey barbecued steak 443
　garlic and rosemary smoked lamb 436
　grilled pork chops with apples 452
　grilled t-bone with three butters 442
　grilled vegetables with garlic herb dressing 455
　grilling 11, 434–5
　lemon and garlic lamb kebabs 454
　lemon-chilli butterflied chicken 444
　piri piri chicken thigh fillets 442
　pork cutlet with fennel and apple salsa 451
　salmon with dill and caper dressing 439
　texan-style spareribs 451
　using barbecues 434, 436
　veal cutlets with green olive salsa 450
barley 483, 641
basil 229, 649
　bruschetta with tomato, olives and capers 80
　thai 229, 649

(*basil* continued)
　thai basil chicken and snake bean stir-fry 350
basmati rice 171, 172, 659
bay leaves 641
bean thread noodles 191, 192, 200, 655
beans 482, 496–7, 641–2
　baked lima beans 490
　bean sprouts 642
　black bean, corn and chipotle stew 490–1
　black bean sauce 642
　black beans 496, 641
　black-eyed beans 641
　borlotti 216, 641
　broad 216, 497, 641
　broad beans and thyme 224
　cassoulet 376
　dried 365
　green 216, 641
　lentil and bean burger 492
　lima 642
　snake 216, 642
　white bean dip 80
　white bean puree 501
béarnaise sauce 264, 266, 269
béchamel sauce 265, 273
beef 24, 288–9, 642
　barbecued scotch fillet 452
　barbecuing steaks 434
　beef lasagne 160
　beef massaman curry 422
　beef pasties 405
　beef rendang 428
　beef stew with parsley dumplings 377
　beef stroganoff 368
　beef sukiyaki 346
　boeuf bourguignon 366
　carpaccio 91
　chilli and honey barbecued steak 443
　chilli con carne 370
　chow mein 199
　chunky beef and vegetable pie 396
　corned beef hash 372
　corned beef with parsley sauce 372

(*beef* continued)
　crispy shredded beef 341
　cuts for roasting 291, 294
　glazed meatloaf 26–7
　grilled t-bone with three butters 442
　hokkien mee 203
　marbling 28
　meat pies 402
　pastitsio 163
　peppered beef and blue cheese canapés 584
　prime steak cuts 28
　rare steak, judging 28
　roast, with espagnole sauce 270
　roast, with yorkshire puddings 290–3
　roasting 288–9
　satay sauce, in 342
　sausages with pea and bacon mash 469
　slicing 294
　spaghetti bolognese 151
　standing rib roast with roast vegetables 294–7
　steak and kidney pie 398
　steak diane 462
　steak sandwich 466
　steak with pepper sauce 30–1
　stock 124
　teriyaki beef 345
　testing for doneness of steak 637
　thai beef salad 102
　vietnamese beef pho 129
　wellington 51, 63
beetroot 95, 216, 642
　borscht 132
　caramelised onion and beetroot tart 223
　cooking 223
belgian endive 107
bellini 578
berry muffins 561
betel leaves 349, 589, 642
　sticky pork on betel leaves 589
beurre blanc 274
bicarbonate of soda 642

bircher muesli 498
biscuits/cookies 557
   anzacs 572
   baking tips 44–5
   basic butter cookies 46–7
   chocolate and hazelnut
     butter cookies 46–7
   chocolate chip cookies 570
   dried cranberry butter
     cookies 46–7
   lemon butter cookies 46–7
   monte carlo biscuits 571
   orange butter cookies 46–7
   pistachio and cranberry
     biscotti 572
   storage and freezing 557, 571
   vanilla butter cookies 46–7
   wedding cake cookies 596
black beans 496, 641
   black bean, corn and
     chipotle stew 490–1
   sauce 642
black-eyed beans 641
black olive tapenade 87
black rice 171, 173, 659
blini, poached eggs and smoked
   salmon on 247
blini with chilli crab salad 582
blowtorches 68
blue cheese 643
   blue cheese and caramelised
     onion dip 82
   blue cheese dressing 114
   blue cheese mousse 584
   peppered beef and blue
     cheese canapés 584
blueberry and ginger scones 558
bocconcini 600, 643
   caprese salad 111
boeuf bourguignon 366
boiling 211
borlotti beans 216, 641
borscht 132
braises and stews 362–3
   accompaniments 386–7
   beef stew with parsley
     dumplings 377
   beef stroganoff 368
   boeuf bourguignon 366

(*braises and stews* continued)
   braised pork with pears
     and cider 376–7
   braised sweet ginger duck 375
   cassoulet 376
   chicken cacciatore 378
   chicken, olive and preserved
     lemon tagine 385
   chilli con carne 370
   coq au vin 380
   corned beef with parsley
     sauce 372
   hungarian veal goulash 368
   irish stew 378
   lamb shank stew 371
   lamb with kumara and
     raisins 370–1
   octopus braised in
     red wine 381
   osso buco 380–1
   pork cabbage rolls 382
   seafood stew with
     chermoulla 384
bread 638
   filler 24
   grain and seed loaf 484
   pumpernickel 491
   storing 638
bread and butter pudding 524
breadcrumbs 642
brie cheese 600, 643
   baked eggs 258
brioche 642
broad beans 216, 497, 641
   thyme and 224
broccoli 217
broccolini 217, 642
   pork larb with broccolini 353
broth
   beef sukiyaki, for 346
   scotch 130
   udon noodle and prawn 207
brown rice 172, 659
   sushi 185
brownies, chocolate fudge 562
bruschetta with tomato, basil
   and capers 80
brussels sprouts with cream
   and almonds 227

buckwheat 483, 642
  noodles 191
buk choy 348, 642
bulb baster 11
burger, lentil and bean 492
burghul 483, 496, 643
  tabbouleh 100
burmese clam and mussel
  stir-fry 358
butter 40, 636, 643
  beans 641
  cakes see cakes
  frosting 548
  garlic herbed 449
  lemon herb 454–5
  mustard 442
  peppercorn 442
  satay 442
butter chicken 414
butter lettuce 643
butterfly cakes 629
buttermilk 643
butterscotch sauce 527
button mushrooms 441, 654

C

cabbage
  coleslaw 100
  mixed cabbage coleslaw 104
  pork cabbage rolls 382
cachous 643
caesar dressing 104, 117
caesar salad, classic 104
caipiroska 579
cakes 530–1
  bar ana 553
  basic butter 42–3
  boiled fruit 538
  butter 531, 550
  butterfly 629
  cake pans, preparing 532–3
  carrot cake with lemon cream
    cheese frosting 546
  celebration fruit 598–9
  chocolate 531
  chocolate butter 43

(cakes continued)
  cinnamon teacake 553
  cooling 530
  cupcakes 41
  date and walnut rolls 542
  featherlight sponge 38–9
  flourless chocolate and
    almond torte 541
  genoise sponge 540
  ginger fluff sponge 39
  hummingbird 536
  icing 41
  jam roll 545
  lace wedding 590
  lamingtons 546–7
  lemon syrup 534
  madeira 550
  marble 548
  mississippi mud cake 540–1
  moist chocolate 537
  one-bowl sultana loaf 552
  orange 538
  orange butter 43
  pound 550
  rich chocolate christmas 593
  slab sponge 39
  sponges 531
  storing 530
  strawberry jelly 547
  testing for readiness 531
  types of 531
  vanilla patty cakes with
    glacé icing 552
calasparra rice 171
calrose rice 171, 173, 659
calvados 465
calves' liver with persillade 466
camembert cheese 600, 643
canapés, peppered beef and
  blue cheese 584
cannellini beans 497, 641
cannelloni, spinach and ricotta 154–5
cantonese lamb 344
caperberries 643
capers 643
  bruschetta with tomato,
    olives and capers 80
  salmon with dill and
    caper dressing 439

(capers continued)
  smoked salmon, with 90
caprese salad 111
capsicum 95, 643
  roasted 215
caraway seeds 643
cardamom 414, 643
carnaroli rice 171
carpaccio
  beef 91
  kingfish 582
carrots 95
  carrot cake with lemon cream
    cheese frosting 546
  glazed, with hazelnuts 226
carving tools 17
cashews 643
casseroles see braises and stews
cassoulet 376
cauliflower 217
  gratin 239
cayenne pepper 643
celebrations 576–7
  see also Christmas
  barbecued seafood platter 585
  blini with chilli crab salad 582
  celebration fruit cake 598–9
  chermoulla prawn skewers 588
  chicken and mayonnaise
    finger sandwiches 588
  cocktail party drinks 577, 578–9
  see also drinks
  equipment 577
  finger food 577
  fruit mince pies 592
  kingfish carpaccio 582
  lace wedding cakes 590
  menu planning 576
  peppered beef and blue
    cheese canapés 584
  planning 576
  quantities 577
  smoked salmon and dilled sour
    cream crêpe cakes 586
  sticky pork on betel leaves
    589
  tomato tarts 584
  vegetarian crêpe cakes 586
  wedding cake cookies 596

celeriac 217, 643
    mash 233
    puree 233
celery 95
    garnish for drink 581
champagne 577
    cocktail 578
chanterelle mushrooms 441, 654
char-grilling 211, 435
char kway teow 204
    vegetarian 204
char siu sauce 342, 344, 643
charcuterie sauce, pork cutlets with 282
cheese 600–1, 639, 643–4
    baked eggs 258
    blue cheese and caramelised
        onion dip 82
    blue cheese dressing 114
    blue cheese mousse 584
    caprese salad 111
    cheese and spinach tortellini with
        gorgonzola sauce 166
    cheeseburgers with
        caramelised onion 443
    goat's cheese soufflé 260
    grilled parmesan polenta
        triangles 487
    gruyère, leek and bacon tart 404
    gruyère soufflé 59
    gruyère toasts 135
    lemon and ricotta-filled
        zucchini flowers 239
    macaroni cheese 154
    quiche lorraine 392
    sauce 160, 164
    spanakopita 404–5
    spinach and ricotta cannelloni
        154–5
    temperature for serving 639
    types 600–1
    witlof, pear and blue
        cheese salad 114
cheeseburgers with
    caramelised onion 443
cheesecake 505
    cooling 635
    new york 521
chermoulla 384
    prawn skewers 588

cherries 580
chervil 228, 584, 650
chestnut mushrooms 441
chiang mai pork and eggplant 344
chicken 17, 18–19, 288–9, 644
    barbecuing 434
    butter chicken 414
    butterflied 444
    buying 298
    cajun chickens 439
    chicken and leek pie 394–5
    chicken and mayonnaise
        finger sandwiches 588
    chicken and mushroom
        pasta bake 159
    chicken and olive
        empanadas 83
    chicken and vegetable
        soup 128–9
    chicken cacciatore 378
    chicken korma 429
    chicken liver pâté 51, 55
    chicken, mushroom and
        leek fricassee 34–5
    chicken, olive and preserved
        lemon tagine 385
    chicken pot roast with mustard
        cream sauce 306–9
    chicken salad 96
    chicken schnitzel 460
    chicken teriyaki 185
    chicken tikka 430
    coq au vin 380
    cream of chicken soup 128
    curried chicken pies 394
    cuts 32
    farmhouse chicken pie 395
    fillets, cooking 108
    green chicken curry 426
    keeping meat moist 298
    lemon and thyme baked
        chicken 298–301
    lemon-chilli butterflied
        chicken 444
    money bags 88
    piri piri chicken thigh fillets 442
    roast chicken with herb
        stuffing 18–19
    roasting 288

(*chicken* continued)
    singapore noodles 194
    skinless fillets 108
    stock 124
    sweet chilli plum chicken with noodles 353
    tandoori chicken 418
    terrine de campagne 56
    thai basil chicken and snake bean stir-fry 350
    thawing poultry 298
    vietnamese chicken salad 108
    vietnamese noodle and chicken salad 200
chicken liver pâté 55
chickpeas 497, 645
    chickpea and vegetable gratin 495
    felafel 486
    hummus 486
chicory 107
chilli 645
    angel hair with rocket and chilli 166
    chilli and herb swede crush 227
    chilli and honey barbecued steak 443
    chilli and tomato relish 492
    chilli citrus dressing 111
    chilli con carne 370
    chilli crab salad 582
    chilli fried shallots 358–9
    chilli lime dressing 354
    chilli parmesan crisps 134
    chilli prawn linguine 159
    garlic and chilli seafood stir-fry 358–9
    lemon-chilli butterflied chicken 444
    lime and sweet chilli dressing 64
    piri piri chicken thigh fillets 442
    singapore chilli crab 338
    sweet chilli dressing 200
    sweet chilli plum chicken with noodles 353
chinese cooking wine 645

chinese sausage
    char kway teow 204
    dried 647
    fried noodles with 203
    nasi goreng 186
chives 12, 650
    chive oil 223
    garlic 228, 650
chocolate 645
    cakes *see cakes*
    choc chip and walnut muffins 561
    chocolate and hazelnut butter cookies 47
    chocolate butter cake 43
    chocolate caramel slice 562
    chocolate fudge brownies 562
    chocolate fudge sauce 283
    chocolate self-saucing pudding 512
    mousse 513
    soufflé 67
    tart 513
chocolate hazelnut spread 645
choko 217, 645
chopping board 13
chopsticks 21
chorizo 645
    jambalaya 177
chow mein, beef 199
chowder, fish 141
choy sum 348, 645
Christmas 576–7
    see also celebrations
    boiled christmas pudding 594
    dessert suggestion 596
    fruit mince pies 592
    menu planning 576
    planning 576
    rich chocolate christmas cakes 593
    steamed christmas pudding 599
    white christmas ice-cream puddings 598
christmas pudding, boiled 594
chutney 605
    tomato 609
ciabatta 645

cinnamon 646
    cinnamon teacake 553
    cream 134
citrus and poppy seed dressing 118
citrus peel (garnish) 581
citrus slice (garnish) 580
clafoutis, plum 520
clams 660
    burmese clam and mussel stir-fry 358
    cleaning 167
    paella 182
    spaghetti alla vongole 167
classics 51
    see also showing off
    caesar salad 104
    fish and chips 470
    mayonnaise 118
    pulao 178
    trifle 520
cloves 646
cocktail party drinks *see drinks*
cocoa powder 646
coconut 646
    coconut curls (garnish) 580
    coconut macaroons 570
    coconut rice
    coconut rice with coriander 180
    yellow 181
coleslaw 100
    mixed cabbage 104
combination fried rice 186
conchigliette 146, 656
condiments 21
conserves 605
    strawberry 612
cookies *see biscuits/cookies*
cooking techniques 11
cooking utensils 10
cookware *see also pans*
    casserole dish 363
    cast-iron 307
coq au vin 380
coral lettuce 106, 646
coriander 228, 420, 650
corn fritters 237
corned beef hash 372
corned beef with parsley sauce 372

corned silverside 341
cornflour 646
    sponge cakes, in 36
cornichon 646
cos lettuce 106, 646
cosmopolitan 579
cottage cheese 600, 643
coulis, strawberry 283
couscous 385, 386, 483, 497, 646
crab 582
    asian crab and rice omelette 252
    blue swimmer 447, 660
    chilli crab salad 582
    crab and soba salad 206
    crab cakes with avocado salsa 84
    crab, fennel and herb quiches 398
    singapore chilli crab 338
cranberries 646
    dried cranberry butter cookies 47
cream 646
cream cheese 644
    cream cheese frosting 536
cream of chicken soup 128
cream of pumpkin soup 133
cream of tartar 646
creamy scrambled eggs 251
crème anglaise 283
crème brûlée 51, 68
crème caramel 506
crème fraîche 646
crêpes suzette 478
croûtons 123
    gruyère 136
crumble, apple 521
cucumber 95
    cucumber and onion salsa 135
    garnish 581
    lebanese 646
    raita 425
cumin 646
cupcakes 41
currants, dried 647
curried chicken pies 394
curried sausages 384–5
curries 410–11
    beef massaman curry 422
    beef rendang 428
    butter chicken 414
    chicken korma 429
    chicken tikka 430
    curry pastes 412–13
    dhal and paneer vegetable curry 428–9
    easy lamb curry 420
    fish curry with lime and coconut 420–1
    green 411
    green chicken curry 426
    green curry paste 412
    indian 411
    massaman curry paste 413, 647
    panang curry paste 413, 647
    panang fish curry 426
    pork and vegetable vindaloo 418
    pork jungle curry 421
    pumpkin and eggplant curry 430
    red 411
    red curry paste 412, 647
    rogan josh 425
    tandoori chicken 418
    thai 411
    yellow 411
curry pastes 412–13, 647
curry powder 647
custard 524, 560–1, 637
    baked 510
    powder 647

D

daikon 219, 647
dashi 647
dates 647
    date and orange muffins 561
    date and walnut rolls 542
    date slice 564
    sticky date pudding 527
decorations for lace wedding cakes 590

deep-fries *see also pan-fries*
  banana fritters 477
  batter 472, 473
  classic fish and chips 470
  salt and pepper squid 465
  vegetable tempura 472
  zucchini fritters 473
deep-frying 459
  equipment 459
  oils for 459
  safety 459
defrosting meat 617
deglazing 11, 29, 265
denver omelette 256
desserts 504–5
  apple crumble 521
  apple pie 509
  baked custard 510
  baking tips 504
  bread and butter pudding 524
  chocolate mousse 513
  chocolate self-saucing pudding 512
  chocolate tart 513
  classic trifle 520
  crème caramel 506
  frozen 505
  golden syrup steamed pudding 510
  lemon delicious puddings 524
  lemon meringue pie 514
  marshmallow pavlova 526
  meringue 504
  new york cheesecake 521
  plum clafoutis 520
  sticky date pudding 527
  summer pudding 523
  tarte tatin 518
  tiramisu 526
  vanilla bean ice-cream 512
  water bath 504
dhal and paneer vegetable curry 428–9
dhal, mixed 488
dhansak with caramelised onion rice 494–5
dill 228, 650
  cream 135
dinner party rules 50

dipping sauce 472
  hoisin 76
  peanut 88
dips
  baba ghanoush 82
  black olive tapenade 87
  blue cheese and caramelised onion dip 82
  white bean 80
doongara rice 659
dough for pizza 618
dragon fruit 516, 647
dressings 95
  see also vinaigrette
  balsamic and garlic 116
  blue cheese 114
  caesar 104, 117
  chilli citrus 111
  chilli lime 354
  citrus and poppy seed dressing 118
  french 115
  ginger miso 206
  green goddess 117
  honey mustard 117
  italian 115
  lemon 52
  lemon and macadamia 116
  lime and sweet chilli 64
  mustard honey 90
  ponzu 86
  ranch 115
  russian 117
  sesame soy 115
  shallot 86
  sun-dried tomato 103
  sweet chilli dressing 200
  thousand island 116
  vietnamese 108
dried fruit, mixed 653
drink garnishes 580–1
drinks
  bellini 578
  caipiroska 579
  champagne cocktail 578
  cocktail party 577
  cosmopolitan 579
  frappé 581
  garnishes 580–1

(*drinks* continued)
  matching 25, 299
  piña colada 579
  sparkling burgundy and cranberry punch 578
duck 289, 647
  braised sweet ginger duck 375
  buying 302
  caramelised crispy-skin 469
  fat 303
  peking duck 352
  rareness 303
  reheating 302
  slow-roasted duck marylands 302–5
  testing for doneness 303
duck eggs 242
dukkah 486, 648
dumplings, parsley 377
durian 517, 648

E

edam cheese 600, 644
egg noodles 191, 193
  fresh 655
egg pasta 145
eggplant 648
  baba ghanoush 82
  eggplant parmigiana 234
  pumpkin and eggplant curry 430
eggs 12, 15, 25, 39, 242–3, 634, 648
  asian crab and rice omelette 252
  baked 258
  beating egg whites 243
  benedict 248
  boiled 243, 247
  buying and storing 242
  denver omelette 256
  duck 242
  egg-white omelette 257
  egg-whites, whipping 635
  freezing yolks 257
  french toast 477
  freshness 634

(*eggs* continued)
   fried 243
   fried eggs and bacon 255
   goat's cheese soufflé 260
   hen 242
   herb omelette 14–15
   methods of cooking 243
   mini pea and pancetta frittatas 258
   poached 243, 244, 634
   poached eggs and smoked salmon on blini 247
   potato frittata with smoked salmon 261
   quail 242
   raw 346
   scrambled 243, 251
   separating 243
   sizes 242
   soufflés *see soufflés*
   spanish tortilla 260–1
   spinach scrambled eggs 255
   temperature for baking 635
   varieties 242
   zucchini and mushroom omelette 256–7
empanadas, chicken and olive 83
endive, curly 106, 747
enoki mushrooms 440, 654
espagnole sauce 265
   roast beef with 270

F

farfalle 146, 656
farmhouse chicken pie 395
fattoush 99
felafel 486
fennel 218, 648
   caramelised fennel tarts 222
   pork cutlet with fennel and apple salsa 451
fenugreek 416, 648
fetta cheese 601, 644
   greek salad 103
   spanakopita 404–5

fettuccine 146, 656
   alfredo 151
   boscaiola 158
   carbonara 152
fillo pastry 404
   spanakopita 404–5
finger food 577
finger sandwiches, chicken and mayonnaise 588
fish *see seafood*
fish sauce 648
five-spice powder 648
flat mushrooms 440, 654
flour 648
flourless chocolate and almond torte 541
fondant icing 596
fontina cheese 644
food colouring 648
forcemeat stuffing 312–13
frappé 581
freezing
   biscuits 557
   casseroles and braises 363, 365
   egg yolks 257
   friands 557
   muffins and scones 556
   slices 557
french bread stick 648
french dressing 115
french onion soup with gruyère croûtons 136
french, to 371
french toast 477
friands 557
   almond 560
   lime coconut 560
   raspberry and white chocolate 560
fricassee 32, 33
   chicken, mushroom and leek 33
frittata, potato, with smoked salmon 261
frittatas, mini pea and pancetta 258
fritters
   banana 477
   corn 237
   zucchini 473

fromage frais 644
frosting
   butter 548
   cream cheese 536
   fudge 537
   glass, on 580
   lemon cream cheese 546
frozen desserts 505
fruit cake, boiled 538
fruit cake, celebration 598–9
fruit mince pies 592
fruit, ripening 636
fruit tips 636
fruit, tropical 516–17
fudge frosting 537
fusilli 147, 657

G

gai lan 349, 648
   steamed, in oyster sauce 387
galangal 648
ganache
   dark chocolate 540–1
garam masala 187, 417, 494–5, 649
garlic 636
   garlic and chilli seafood stir-fry 358–9
   garlic and rosemary smoked lamb 436
   garlic herbed butter 449
   garlic prawns 468
   mongolian garlic lamb 352
garnishes 577
   drinks, for 580–1
gazpacho 140
gelatine 649
genoise sponge 540
ghee 488, 649
ginger
   braised sweet ginger duck 375
   ginger fluff sponge 39
   ginger miso dressing 206
gingerbread men 630
glacé cherries 649
glacé fruit 649

glacé icing 552
glasses 577
globe artichoke 216
glucose syrup 649
gluten-free baking powder 649
glutinous rice 171, 173, 659
gnocchi 147, 657
   vegetable, with cheese sauce 164
goat's cheese 600, 644
   soufflé 260
golden banana 516
golden syrup 649
   golden syrup steamed pudding 510
gorgonzola cheese 644
goulash, hungarian veal 368
grain and seed loaf 484
grains *see* pulses and grains
grapevine leaves 649
gratin
   cauliflower 239
   chickpea and vegetable 495
gravy 265, 292–3
greek roast lamb with skordalia and potatoes 322–5
greek salad 103
green beans 216, 641
green curry paste 412, 647
   green chicken curry 426
green goddess dressing 117
green mango 517, 652
   green mango and cucumber salsa 86
green olive salsa 450
green papaya 348
   salad 111
gremolata 134, 380–1
grill pans 435
grilling 11, 434–5 *see also* barbecues and grills
gruyère cheese 404, 601, 644
   gruyère croûtons 136
   gruyère, leek and bacon tart 404
   gruyère soufflé 59
   gruyère toasts 135

H

haloumi cheese 601, 644
   salad 601
ham
   denver omelette 256
   glazed baked 51, 60
   ham and pineapple pizza 618
   minestrone 126
haricot beans 496, 642
harissa 417, 649
hasselback potatoes 212
havarti cheese 601, 644
hazelnuts 649
herbs 228–9, 649 *see also by individual names*
   broad beans and thyme 224
   chilli and herb swede crush 227
   crab, fennel and herb quiche 398
   dried 229
   garlic and rosemary smoked lamb 436
   garlic herbed butter 449
   grilled vegetables with garlic herb dressing 455
   herb omelette 14–15
   herb stuffing 16, 18–19
   herbed rack of lamb with potato smash 316–17
   lamb and rosemary pies 4-6
   lemon and thyme baked chicken 300–1
   lemon herb butter 454–5
   oak-leaf and mixed herb salad 102
   parsley dumplings 377
   parsley sauce 372
   roast loin of pork, with 331
   salmon with dill and caper dressing 439
   smoked salmon and dilled sour cream crêpe cakes 586
   storage 636
   thai basil chicken and snake bean stir-fry 350
   tomato and herb salad 387
hogget 322
hoisin dipping sauce 76

hoisin sauce 650
hokkien mee 203
hokkien noodles 191, 192, 655
hollandaise sauce 215, 248, 264, 266
honey 650
honey mustard dressing 117
horseradish 650
horseradish cream 223
hummingbird cake 536
hummus 486
hungarian veal goulash 368
hygiene 616
    taste-testing 617

I

ice 577
    decorated ice cubes 580
    white christmas ice-cream puddings 598
ice-cream
    vanilla bean 512
icing 41, 547
    fondant 596
    glacé 552
    passionfruit 567
    ready-made white 659
    royal 596, 630
ingredients
    balanced 20
    quality 10
irish stew 378
italian dressing 115

J

jackfruit 516, 651
jalapeño chillies 177
jam 605
    apricot 610
    dark plum 610
    savoury 605
    testing for readiness 604
jam roll 545
jambalaya 177

jasmati rice 171
jasmine rice 171, 172, 659
    steamed 180
jellies 605
    apple 611
    mango and raspberry 626
    testing for readiness 604
jelly crystals 651
jerusalem artichoke 218
jungle curry, pork 421
juniper berries 56, 651

K

kaffir lime 651
kaffir lime leaves 349, 651
kale 218, 651
kalonji 417, 651
kang kong 349, 651
kebabs, lemon and garlic lamb 454
kecap asin 651
kecap manis 651
khitcherie 178
kidney beans 642
kidneys
    steak and kidney pie 398
kingfish carpaccio 582
kisses, vanilla 568
kiwifruit 651
knives
    sharp 12
kohlrabi 218, 651
koshihikari rice 171, 173, 659
kumara 651
    lamb with kumara and raisins 370–1

L

lace wedding cakes 590
laksa paste 139
laksa, seafood 139
lamb 288–9, 651–2
    buying 318
    cantonese 344

(lamb continued)
   cassoulet 376
   char siu lamb and noodle stir-fry 342
   crumbed lamb cutlets 468
   cuts 314, 318, 322
   dhansak with caramelised onion rice 494–5
   easy lamb curry 420
   fat 319
   garlic and rosemary smoked lamb 436
   greek roast lamb with skordalia and potatoes 322–5
   herbed rack of lamb with potato smash 314–17
   irish stew 378
   kumara and raisins, with 370–1
   lamb and rosemary pies 406
   lamb biryani 187
   lamb shank and vegetable soup 133
   lamb shank stew 371
   lemon and garlic lamb kebabs 454
   mongolian garlic lamb 352
   roast 288, 318–21
   rogan josh 425
   scotch broth 130
   shepherd's pie 400
lamb's lettuce 106, 652
lamingtons 546–7
larb 353
   pork larb with broccolini 353
lasagne 146, 656
   beef 160
   vegetarian 156
leeks 395, 652
   braised baby 226
   chicken and leek pie 394–5
   gruyère, leek and bacon tart 404
   vichyssoise 130
leftovers 25, 27, 299, 638
   chilli con carne 370
   freezing 365
   storing 311, 331
lemon grass 348, 652

lemons
   dressing 52
   juicing 636
   lemon aïoli 465
   lemon and garlic lamb kebabs 454
   lemon and macadamia dressing 116
   lemon and ricotta-filled zucchini flowers 239
   lemon butter cookies 47
   lemon-chilli butterflied chicken 444
   lemon cream cheese frosting 546
   lemon delicious puddings 524
   lemon herb butter 454–5
   lemon meringue pie 514
   lemon poppy seed muffins 561
   lemon syrup cake 534
   lemon tart 71
   pancakes with lemon and sugar 474
   preserved 658
   tangy lemon squares 565
lentils 482, 496, 652
   dhansak with caramelised onion rice 494–5
   lentil and bean burger 492
   mixed dhal 488
   puy 496
lettuce 94, 107
   oak-leaf and mixed herb salad 102
   varieties 106–7
lima beans 642
   baked 490
lime and sweet chilli dressing 64
lime coconut friands 560
linguine, chilli prawn 159
linseed 652
liqueurs 652
liver
   calves' liver with persillade 466
   chicken liver pâté 51, 55

loaf, grain and seed 484
long-grain rice 171, 172, 659
lotus root 211, 472, 652
lychee 516, 652

M

macadamias 652
macaroni 657
macaroni cheese 154
macaroons
   almond 570
   coconut 570
mache 106, 652
madeira cake 550
mango 517, 652
   green 517, 652
   mango and raspberry jelly 626
mangosteen 517, 652
maple-flavoured syrup 653
maple syrup 653
marble cake 548
marjoram 229, 650
marmalade 605
   orange 609
marron 446, 660
marsala 653
marshmallow pavlova 526
masala paste 494–5
mascarpone cheese 526, 644
massaman curry, beef 422
massaman curry paste 413, 647
mayonnaise 95
   classic 118
   whole-egg 653
measuring sticky ingredients 637
meat
   see also by individual names
   marbling 28
   rareness 28
   thermometer 318
   tips 637
meat pies 402
meatballs napoletana 625
meatloaf, glazed 26–7

medium-grain rice 171
mee goreng 202
mee krob 198–9
melba toasts 135
melon balls (garnish) 581
merguez sausages 653
meringue 504
    lemon meringue pie 514
    marshmallow pavlova 526
    weeping 635
mesclun 107, 653
mignonette lettuce 107, 653
milk 653
minestrone 126
mint 650
    aïoli 79
    sauce 269
    vietnamese 228
mirin 345, 653
miso 653
mississippi mud cake 540–1
mixed dried fruit 653
mixed spice 653
mizuna 106, 653
molasses 653
money bags 88
mongolian garlic lamb 352
monte carlo biscuits 571
mornay sauce 275
    fish mornay pie 401
mortar and pestle 653–4
mouli 654
mousse
    blue cheese 584
    chocolate 513
mozzarella cheese 644
mud cake, mississippi 540–1
muesli 654
    bircher 498
    roasted, with dried fruit and honey 498
muffins 556
    berry 561
    choc chip and walnut 561
    date and orange 561
    lemon poppy seed 561
    rhubarb and custard 560–2
    storage and freezing 556
mung bean noodles 191

muscatel 654
mushrooms 33, 95, 440–1, 654
    chicken and mushroom pasta bake 159
    mushroom risotto 174
    sautéed 238
    zucchini and mushroom omelette 256–7
muslin 654
mussels 358, 447, 660
    barbecued seafood platter 585
    burmese clam and mussel stir-fry 358
    paella 182
mustard 654
    american 452
    mustard butter 442
    mustard honey dressing 90
    spicy mustard pickles 606
mustard seeds 654
mutton 322

N

naan 655
nachos, vegie 622
napoletana sauce 279
nasi goreng 186
new york cheesecake 521
niçoise salade 114
nishiki rice 171, 173, 659
noodles 190–1, 655
    beef chow mein 199
    char kway teow 204
    char siu lamb and noodle stir-fry 342
    chilled soba 207
    crab and soba salad 206
    dried rice 655
    fried 191, 192, 655
    fried noodles with chinese sausage 203
    hokkien mee 203
    mee goreng 202
    mee krob 198–9
    noodle and vegetable rice paper rolls 621

(*noodles* continued)
   pad thai 197
   singapore noodles 194
   storing 190
   sweet chilli plum chicken with noodles 353
   sweet soy fried noodles 206
   types of 191
   udon noodle and prawn broth 207
   vegetarian pad thai 198
   vietnamese noodle and chicken salad 200
nori 655
nut roll tins 542
nutmeg 655

O

oak-leaf lettuce 107, 655
   oak-leaf and mixed herb salad 102
oatmeal 655
oats 483
   bircher muesli 498
   roasted muesli with dried fruit and honey 498
   rolled 659
octopus 660
   baby 446
   barbecued baby octopus 450
   barbecued seafood platter 585
   octopus braised in red wine 381
oils 636, 656
   deep-frying, for 459
okra 218, 656
olives
   black olive tapenade 87
   bruschetta with tomato, olives and capers 80
   chicken and olive empanadas 83
   chicken, olive and preserved lemon tagine 385
   green olive salsa 450

omelettes
   asian crab and rice 252
   denver 256
   egg-white 257
   herb 14–15
   spanish tortilla 260–1
   tips 12–13, 14
   zucchini and mushroom 256–7
one-bowl sultana loaf 552
onions 443, 656
   caramelised 443, 636
   caramelised onion and beetroot tart 223
   caramelised onion rice 494–5
   caramelised red onion 222
   cutting 136, 636
   french onion soup with gruyère croûtons 136
   roasted balsamic 237
orange flower water 656
oranges
   cutting 478
   orange butter cake 43
   orange butter cookies 47
   orange butterscotch sauce 284
   orange cake 538
   orange marmalade 609
   orange sauce 478
orecchiette 147, 657
oregano 228, 650
osso buco 380–1
oven temperature 318
oyster mushrooms 348, 654
oyster sauce 656
oysters 447, 660
   oysters with three toppings 86

P

pad thai 197
   vegetarian 198
paella 182
panama passionfruit 517
panang curry paste 413, 647
   panang fish curry 426
pancakes with lemon and sugar 474

pancetta 656
   mini pea and pancetta frittatas 258
pan-fries 458, 636, 637
   see also deep-fries
   calves' liver with persillade 466
   caramelised crispy-skin duck 469
   chicken schnitzel 460
   crêpes suzette 478
   crumbed lamb cutlets 468
   french toast 477
   garlic prawns 468
   pancakes with lemon and sugar 474
   pan-seared scallops with anchovy cream 474
   pork chops with apples and calvados 465
   sausages with pea and bacon mash 469
   steak diane 462
   steak sandwich 466
   veal parmigiana 464
   veal saltimbocca 462
pan-frying 11, 211, 458
   see also pan-fries
   suitable foods 458
pans 13, 29, 33
   see also cookware
   baking 37
   burnt 637
   cake pans *see* cakes
   friands 560
   frying pan 458
   greasing 40
   grill 435
papaya 517, 656
   green 517, 656
pappardelle 147, 657
paprika 656
paprika butter 134
parisian essence 599
parsley 12, 229, 650
   dumplings 377
   sauce 372
parsnips 218, 656
   mash 386
   roasted caramelised 224

parties *see celebrations*
passionfruit icing 567
passionfruit, panama 517, 656
pasta 144–7, 639, 656–7
    angel hair with rocket and chilli 166
    beef lasagne 160
    cheese and spinach tortellini with gorgonzola sauce 166
    chicken and mushroom pasta bake 159
    chilli prawn linguine 159
    cooking 144, 639
    dried 145
    egg 145
    fettuccine alfredo 151
    fettuccine boscaiola 158
    fettuccine carbonara 152
    flavoured 145
    fresh 145, 148
    macaroni cheese 154
    machines for making 148
    pasta salad 103
    pastitsio 163
    penne puttanesca 158
    prawn and scallop tortellini 52
    sauce, amount of 147
    shapes of 145
    spaghetti alla vongole 167
    spaghetti and meatballs 155
    spaghetti bolognese 151
    spaghetti with pesto 152
    spinach and ricotta cannelloni 154–5
    types of 146–7
    vegetable gnocchi with cheese sauce 164
    vegetarian lasagne 156
    wholemeal 145
pastes
    laksa 139
    quince 611
    spice 417
pasties, beef 405
pastitsio 163
pastry 392, 509, 513, 514, 518, 592, 639, 657
    fillo 404, 657
    puff 398

(*pastry* continued)
    resting 391
    storing 391
    temperature of ingredients 635
pastry bag 635
pâté, chicken liver 51, 55
pavlova 527
    marshmallow 526
pea and ham soup 132
peanut dipping sauce 88
peanuts 657
pear and mint (garnish) 581
peas
    green 219, 657
    mint butter, with 233
    pea and pancetta frittatas, mini 258
    sausages with pea and bacon mash 469
    snow 219, 657
    split *see split peas*
    sugar snap 219, 657
pecans 657
pecorino cheese 644
peking duck 352
penne 146, 657
    puttanesca 158
pepitas 657
pepper
    grinding 29
    peppered beef and blue cheese canapés 584
    salt and pepper squid 465
    salt and pepper tofu 354
    steak with pepper sauce 30–1
peppercorn butter 442
persillade 466
pesto, spaghetti with 152
pho, vietnamese beef 129
pickles 605
    spicy mustard 606
pies 390–1
    see also quiches; tarts
    beef pasties 405
    butter chicken filling 414
    chicken and leek pie 394–5
    chicken, mushroom and leek fricassee filling 35
    chunky beef and vegetable 396

(pies continued)
 crusts 391
 curried chicken 394
 dish for 390, 396
 farmhouse chicken pie 395
 fish mornay 401
 fruit mince 592
 lamb and rosemary 406
 lemon meringue 514
 meat 402
 one-crust 391
 pastry see pastry
 picnic, for 406
 reheating 402
 sagging in the middle, prevention 396
 shepherd's pie 400
 spanakopita 404–5
 steak and kidney 398
 two-crust 391
pilaf 387
piña colada 579
pine mushrooms 440, 654
pine nuts 657
pineapple (garnish) 580
pink oyster mushrooms 440
pipis 446, 660
piri piri chicken thigh fillets 442
piri piri sauce 657
pistachio and cranberry biscotti 572
pistachios 657
pistou 135
pitta bread 657
 fattoush 99
pizza
 cheese 644
 dough 618
 ham and pineapple 618
planning 50, 75, 576
plums
 dark plum jam 610
 plum clafoutis 520
 plum sauce 657
polenta 483, 497, 658
 grilled parmesan polenta triangles 487
 soft 386, 487

pomegranate 658
pomegranate molasses 658
ponzu dressing 86
poppy seeds 658
porcini mushrooms, dried 440, 654
pork 21, 289, 658
 braised pork with pears and cider 376–7
 buying 333, 452
 cassoulet 376
 chiang mai pork and eggplant 344
 crackling 327
 cuts 326
 grilled pork chops with apples 452
 meatballs napoletana 625
 mee goreng 202
 overcooking 327
 pad thai 197
 pork and vegetable stir-fry 22–3
 pork and vegetable vindaloo 418
 pork cabbage rolls 382
 pork chops with apples and calvados 465
 pork cutlet with charcuterie sauce 282
 pork cutlet with fennel and apple salsa 451
 pork jungle curry 421
 pork larb with broccolini 353
 rind, preparing 331
 roast leg of pork with apple sauce 326–9
 roast loin of pork 330–3
 sang choy bow 345
 singapore noodles 194
 sticky pork on betel leaves 589
 storing 326
 sweet and sour 357
 terrine de campagne 56
 texan-style spareribs 451
 vegetarian pad thai 198
 vietnamese pork rolls 331
portobello mushrooms 441, 654
portuguese custard tarts 564–5

potatoes 16, 405, 638, 658
 cajun wedges 232
 creamy mashed 387
 crushed 451
 greek roast lamb, with 323
 hasselback 212
 kipfler 450
 lemon pepper wedges 232
 perfect mashed 233, 634
 perfect potato chip 232
 potato frittata with smoked salmon 261
 potato salad 112
 roast 291, 386
 rösti stacks with prawns and mint aïoli 79
 rösti, the perfect 230
 sausages with pea and bacon mash 469
 scalloped 230
 smash 314
 spanish tortilla 260–1
 steakhouse chips 28
 topping 400
 varieties 638
 vegetable gnocchi with cheese sauce 164
 vichyssoise 130
 wedges 232
pot-roasting 362
pound cake 550
prawns 660
 barbecued seafood platter 585
 chermoulla prawn skewers 588
 chilli prawn linguine 159
 deveining 637
 garlic prawns 468
 king prawns 447
 nasi goreng 186
 pad thai 197
 prawn and asparagus risotto 176
 prawn and scallop tortellini 52
 prawn cocktail 84
 rösti stacks with prawns and mint aïoli 79

(*prawns* continued)
   spring rolls 91
   tom yum goong 140–1
   udon noodle and prawn broth 207
   vietnamese prawn rolls 76
preserved lemon 658
   chicken, olive and preserved lemon tagine 385
preserved turnip 658
preserves 604–5
   apricot jam 610
   dark plum jam 610
   jars for bottling 604
   orange marmalade 609
   quince paste 611
   savoury 605
   spicy mustard pickles 606
   storing 605
   strawberry conserve 612
   sweet 605
   testing for readiness 604
   tomato chutney 609
prosciutto 658
provolone cheese 644
puddings *see also desserts*
   boiled christmas 594
   bread and butter 524
   golden syrup steamed 510
   lemon delicious 524
   steamed christmas 599
   sticky date 527
   summer 523
   white christmas ice-cream 598
puff pastry 398
pulao, classic 178
pulses and grains 482–3
   baked lima beans 490
   bircher muesli 498
   black bean, corn and chipotle stew 490–1
   chickpea and vegetable gratin 495
   cooking pulses 482
   dhal and paneer vegetable curry 428–9
   dhansak with caramelised onion rice 494–5
   felafel 486

(*pulses and grains* continued)
   grain and seed loaf 484
   grilled parmesan polenta triangles 487
   hummus 486
   lentil and bean burger 492
   mixed dhal 488
   pumpernickel bread 491
   roasted muesli with dried fruit and honey 498
   semolina slice 501
   soaking pulses 482
   soft polenta 487
   split pea and vegetable tagine 488
   storing 483
   vegetarian diet 497
   white bean puree 501
pumpernickel bread 491
pumpkin
   baked pumpkin and spinach risotto 176–7
   cream of pumpkin soup 133
   pumpkin and eggplant curry 430
punch, sparkling burgundy and cranberry 578

Q

quail 658
quail eggs 242
quiches
   crab, fennel and herb 398
   quiche lorraine 392
quince 658
quince paste 611
quinoa 483

R

radicchio 107, 658
raita 658
   cucumber 425
rambutan 516, 658
ramen noodles 191, 192, 655

ranch dressing 115
ras el hanout 370, 416, 659
raspberry and white chocolate friands 560
ravioli 147, 657
recipes to know by heart
   basic butter cake 42–3
   basic butter cookies 46–7
   chicken, mushroom and leek fricassee 34–5
   featherlight sponge 38–9
   glazed meatloaf 26–7
   herb omelette 14–15
   pork and vegetable stir-fry 22–3
   roast chicken with herb stuffing 18–19
   steak with pepper sauce 30–1
red berry vinaigrette 116
red curry paste 412, 647
   pork jungle curry 421
red onion, caramelised 222
red wine vinaigrette 112
relish 605
   chilli and tomato 492
resting 11, 28, 289, 295, 321, 443
   pastry 391
rhubarb 659
rhubarb and custard muffins 560–2
rice 20, 170–3, 659
   asian crab and rice omelette 252
   baked pumpkin and spinach risotto 176–7
   boiled 170
   brown rice sushi 185
   caramelised onion rice 494–5
   classic pulao 178
   coconut rice with coriander 180
   combination fried rice 186
   cooking methods 170
   jambalaya 177
   khitcherie 178
   lamb biryani 187
   mushroom risotto 174
   nasi goreng 186
   paella 182

(*rice* continued)
   pilaf 387
   prawn and asparagus risotto 176
   rolled 659
   salmon kedgeree 181
   steamed jasmine rice 180
   storing 171
   types of 171, 173
   yellow coconut rice 181
rice noodles 191, 193
   dried 655
   fresh 655
rice paper sheets 191
   noodle and vegetable rice paper rolls 621
   softening 76
   vietnamese prawn rolls 76
rice stick noodles 191, 193, 655
   pad thai 197
   vegetarian pad thai 198
rice vermicelli 191, 193, 655
   mee krob 198–9
   spring rolls 91
ricotta cheese 644
   lemon and ricotta-filled zucchini flowers 239
   spinach and ricotta cannelloni 154–5
rigani 450
rigatoni 147, 159, 657
risoni 657
risotto
   baked pumpkin and spinach 176–7
   mushroom 174
   prawn and asparagus 176
roast meats/poultry 288–9
   barbecuing 434
   beef with yorkshire puddings 290–3
   browning the meat 307
   checking for doneness 289, 290, 295, 303, 313
   chicken pot roast with mustard cream sauce 306–9
   greek roast lamb with skordalia and potatoes 322–5

(*roast meats/poultry* continued)
   herbed rack of lamb with potato smash 314–17
   lemon and thyme baked chicken 298–301
   pot roasts 307
   roast lamb 318–21
   roast leg of pork with apple sauce 326–9
   roast loin of pork 330–3
   roast turkey with forcemeat stuffing 3100–13
   slow-roasted duck marylands 302–5
   standing rib roast with roast vegetables 294–7
   timing 291
   tips 11, 211, 288–9
   tying 327
rocket 107, 659
rogan josh 425
roll, jam 545
roll, vietnamese prawn 76
rolled oats 659
rolls, date and walnut 542
roquefort cheese 644
rosemary 650
   lamb and rosemary pies 406
rosewater 659
rösti 230
   rösti stacks with prawns and mint aïoli 79
royal icing 596, 630
russian dressing 117
rye 483
   rolled 659

S

sabayon 284
safety 33, 311, 365, 459, 616
saffron 416, 659
   scallops with saffron cream 87
sage 229, 650
salade composé 112
salade niçoise 114

salads 94–5
  caprese 111
  chicken 96
  chilli crab 582
  classic caesar 104
  coleslaw 100
  crab and soba 206
  fattoush 99
  greek 103
  green papaya 111
  leaves 94, 106–7
  mixed cabbage coleslaw 104
  oak-leaf and mixed herb 102
  pasta 103
  potato 112
  roast loin of pork, with 330
  salade composé 112
  salade niçoise 114
  strawberry coulis 283
  tabbouleh 100
  thai beef 102
  tomato and herb 387
  vietnamese chicken 108
  vietnamese noodle and chicken 200
  waldorf 96
  witlof, pear and blue cheese 114
salmon kedgeree 181
salmon with dill and caper dressing 439
salsa 264, 490–1 *see also sauces*
  avocado 84
  cucumber and onion 135
  green mango and cucumber 86
  green olive 450
  spicy tomato 439
  tuna 99
  verde 274
salt 315, 319, 637
salt and pepper squid 465
salt and pepper tofu 354
sambal oelek 659
sandwiches
  chicken and mayonnaise finger 588
  steak 466
sang choy bow 345
sashimi 660
satay butter 442

satay sauce 273
  beef in 342
sauces 264–5, 635 *see also dipping sauces; salsas*
  aïoli 280
  apple 326, 328–9, 332–3
  arrabbiata 279
  béarnaise 269
  béchamel 273
  beurre blanc 274
  butterscotch 527
  cheese 160, 164
  chicken and mushroom velouté 276
  chocolate fudge 283
  classic 265
  creamed spinach 260
  curdling 635
  deglazing 265
  egg and butter 264
  gravy 292–3
  hollandaise 215, 248, 266
  lumpiness 635
  Mars Bar 284
  mint 269
  mornay 275
  napoletana 279
  orange 478
  orange butterscotch 284
  parsley 372
  pork cutlets with charcuterie sauce 282
  roast beef with espagnole sauce 270
  sabayon 284
  salsa verde 274
  satay 273
  seafood 275
  skordalia 280
  sweet chilli 273
  tangy barbecue 282
  tartare 280, 470
  tips for making 635
  tomato 276, 464
  white 156
  white wine 274–5
sausages
  barbecuing 434
  pea and bacon mash, with 469
savoy cabbage 660

scallops 446, 474, 660
    pan-seared scallops with
        anchovy cream 474
    prawn and scallop tortellini 52
    scallops with saffron cream 87
schnitzel, chicken 460
scones 556
    basic 558
    blueberry and ginger 558
    storage and freezing 556
    sultana and lemon 558
scotch broth 130
seafood 446–7, 637, 660
    asian crab and rice
        omelette 252
    balmain bugs with garlic
        herbed butter 449
    barbecued baby octopus 450
    barbecued seafood platter 585
    barbecued whole
        snapper 454–5
    barbecuing 434
    burmese clam and
        mussel stir-fry 358
    buying 585, 637
    char kway teow 204
    chermoulla prawn
        skewers 588
    chilli prawn linguine 159
    classic fish and chips 470
    crab and soba salad 206
    crab cakes with avocado salsa 84
    crab, fennel and herb
        quiches 398
    fish chowder 141
    fish curry with lime and
        coconut 420–1
    fish mornay pies 401
    fish stock 125
    freshness 637
    garlic and chilli seafood
        stir-fry 358–9
    garlic prawns 468
    kingfish carpaccio 582
    laksa 139
    octopus braised in red wine 381
    oysters with three toppings 86
    paella 182
    panang fish curry 426

(seafood continued)
    pan-seared scallops with
        anchovy cream 474
    potato frittata with smoked
        salmon 261
    prawn and asparagus
        risotto 176
    prawn and scallop tortellini 52
    prawn cocktail 84
    rösti stacks with prawns
        and mint aïoli 79
    salmon kedgeree 181
    salmon with dill and caper
        dressing 439
    salt and pepper squid 465
    sauce 275
    scallops with saffron cream 87
    seafood stew with chermoulla 384
    singapore chilli crab 338
    smoked salmon and dilled sour
        cream crêpe cakes 586
    smoked salmon with capers 90
    spaghetti alla vongole 167
    spring rolls 91
    thai steamed fish in
        banana leaves 64
    tuna salad 99
    tuna tartare 90
    udon noodle and prawn broth 207
    vietnamese prawn rolls 76
semolina 660
    semolina slice 501
serving platter 16
sesame seeds 660
sesame soy dressing 115
seven-spice mix 660
shallots 660
    chilli fried shallots 358–9
    shallot dressing 86
shanghai noodles 192, 655
shepherd's pie 400
sherry 661
shiitake mushrooms 349, 654
shimeji mushrooms 441, 654
shortbread, traditional 568
short-grain rice 171, 659
showing off 50–1
    beef wellington 63
    chicken liver pâté 55

(showing off continued)
    chocolate soufflé 67
    crème brûlée 68
    glazed baked ham 60
    gruyère soufflé 59
    lemon tart 71
    prawn and scallop tortellini 52
    terrine de campagne 56
    thai steamed fish in
        banana leaves 64
shrimp paste 661
sichuan peppercorns 417, 661
sifting 76
silver beet 217, 661
singapore chilli crab 338
singapore noodles 194, 655
skewers 637, 661
    chermoulla prawn 588
skordalia 280, 323, 324–5, 473
slab sponge 39
slices 557
    chocolate caramel 562
    date 564
    semolina 501
    vanilla 567
slow cookers 363, 364–5
    cleaning 365
    cuts of meat 365
    dried beans and 365
    freezing leftovers 365
    hints on using 364
    safety 365
    settings 365
smoked salmon
    capers, with 90
    potato frittata with 261
    smoked salmon and dilled
        sour cream crêpe cakes 586
smoking chips 436
snake beans 216, 642
    thai basil chicken and
        snake bean stir-fry 350
snow peas 219, 657
soaking pulses 482
soba noodles 192, 655
    chilled 207
    crab and soba salad 206
    preparation 193

somen noodles 191, 193, 655
sopressa 661
soufflés 51
   chocolate 67
   egg whites 67
   goat's cheese 260
   gruyère 59
soups 122–3 *see also stocks*
   accompaniments 134–5
   borscht 132
   chicken and vegetable 128–9
   cream of chicken 128
   cream of pumpkin 133
   fish chowder 141
   french onion soup with gruyère croûtons 136
   gazpacho 140
   lamb shank and vegetable soup 133
   minestrone 126
   pea and ham soup 132
   scotch broth 130
   seafood laksa 139
   tom yum goong 140–1
   vichyssoise 130
   vietnamese beef pho 129
sour cream 637
soy beans 642
soy sauce 357, 661
spaghetti 657
   alla vongole 167
   bolognese 151
   meatballs and 155
   pesto, with 152
spanakopita 404–5
spanish tortilla 260–1
spice, mixed 653
spice paste 417
spices 416–17
   grinding 410
spicy mustard pickles 606
spicy tomato salsa 439
spinach 661
   baked pumpkin and spinach risotto 176–7
   cheese and spinach tortellini with gorgonzola sauce 166
   creamed 227
   creamed spinach sauce 260

(*spinach* continued)
   spinach and ricotta cannelloni 154–5
   spinach scrambled eggs 255
split peas 482, 497, 661
   dhansak with caramelised onion rice 494–5
   khitcherie 178
   mixed dhal 488
   split pea and vegetable tagine 488
sponge cakes 36–7, 531
   featherlight 38–9
   genoise 540
   ginger fluff 39
   slab 39
sponge finger biscuits 661
spring rolls 91
   wrappers 661
squares, tangy lemon 565
squid 447, 660
   barbecued seafood platter 585
   salt and pepper 465
star anise 375, 416, 661
star fruit 516, 661
starters 74–5
   baba ghanoush
   beef carpaccio 91
   black olive tapenade 87
   blue cheese and caramelised onion dip 82
   bruschetta with tomato, basil and capers 80
   chicken and olive empanadas 83
   crab cakes with avocado salsa 84
   money bags 88
   oysters with three toppings 86
   prawn cocktail 84
   rösti stacks with prawns and mint aïoli 79
   scallops with saffron cream 87
   smoked salmon with capers 90
   spring rolls 91
   tuna tartare 90
   vietnamese prawn rolls 76
   white bean dip 80
steak *see beef*
steakhouse chips 28
steaming 64, 211

sterilising jars for preserves 604
stews 11, 362–3 *see also* braises and stews
   accompaniments 386–7
   beef stew with parsley dumplings 377
   black bean, corn and chipotle stew 490–1
   irish stew 378
   lamb shank stew 371
   seafood stew with chermoulla 384
sticky date pudding 527
stir-fries 11, 211, 336–7
   accessories 337
   beef in satay sauce 342
   beef sukiyaki 346
   burmese clam and mussel 358
   cantonese lamb 344
   char siu lamb and noodle 342
   chiang mai pork and eggplant 344
   crispy shredded beef 341
   garlic and chilli seafood 358–9
   mongolian garlic lamb 352
   peking duck 352
   pork and vegetable stir-fry 22–3
   pork larb with broccolini 353
   salt and pepper tofu 354
   sang choy bow 345
   singapore chilli crab 338
   sweet and sour pork 357
   sweet chilli plum chicken with noodles 353
   technique 337
   teriyaki beef 345
   thai basil chicken and snake bean 350
   thai vegetable 359
   wok chan 22, 337, 663
   woks 336
stocks 122–3
   beef 124
   chicken 124
   fish 125
   vegetable 125
straw mushrooms 440, 654
strawberry (garnish) 581
strawberry conserve 612
strawberry coulis 283

strawberry jelly cakes 547
sugar 661
   cubes 611
sugar snap peas 219, 657
sugar syrup 501
sukiyaki
   beef 346
   egg, dipping in 346
sultana and lemon scones 558
sultana loaf, one-bowl 552
sumac 417, 662
summer pudding 523
sun-dried tomato dressing 103
sunflower seeds 662
sushi, brown rice 185
sushi vinegar 185
swede
   chilli and herb swede crush 227
sweet and sour pork 357
sweet chilli dressing 200
sweet chilli plum chicken with noodles 353
sweet chilli sauce 273
sweet soy fried noodles 206
swiss brown mushrooms 309, 441, 654
swiss cheese 644
syrup 510
   lemon 534
   sugar 501

T

tabbouleh 100
table etiquette 20
tagine 488
   chicken, olive and preserved lemon 385
   split pea and vegetable 488
tagliatelle 657
tahini 662
tamari 357, 662
tamarind 662
tamarind concentrate/paste 662
tandoori chicken 418
tapenade, black olive 87

tarragon 229, 650
tartare sauce 280, 470
tarte tatin 518
tart(s)
   caramelised fennel 222
   caramelised onion and beetroot 223
   gruyère, leek and bacon tart 404
   lemon 71
   portuguese custard 564–5
   roasted vegetable 400–1
   tomato 584
tat soi 348, 662
tea 21
teaching kids to cook 616–17
   butterfly cakes 629
   cleaning up 617
   defrosting meat 617
   gingerbread men 630
   ham and pineapple pizza 618
   hygiene 616
   mango and raspberry jelly 626
   meatballs napoletana 625
   noodle and vegetable rice paper rolls 621
   safety 616
   vegie nachos 622
teatime 556–7
   almond friands 560
   almond macaroons 570
   anzacs 572
   basic scones 558
   berry muffins 561
   blueberry and ginger scones 558
   choc chip and walnut muffins 561
   chocolate caramel slice 562
   chocolate chip cookies 570
   chocolate fudge brownies 562
   coconut macaroons 570
   date and orange muffins 561
   date slice 564
   lemon poppy seed muffins 561
   lime coconut friands 560
   monte carlo biscuits 571
   pistachio and cranberry biscotti 572
   portuguese custard tarts 564–5

(*teatime* continued)
   raspberry and white
     chocolate friands 560
   rhubarb and custard muffins 560–2
   sultana and lemon scones 558
   tangy lemon squares 565
   traditional shortbread 568
   vanilla kisses 568
   vanilla slice 567
tempura, vegetable 472
teriyaki
   beef 345
   chicken 185
terrine de campagne 56
texan-style spareribs 451
thai basil 229, 350
   thai basil chicken and
     snake bean stir fry 350
thai beef salad 102
thai steamed fish in
   banana leaves 64
thai vegetable stir-fry 359
thermometer, meat 318
thousand island dressing 116
thyme 650
tikka paste 430, 647
tiramisu 526
tofu 204, 662
   salt and pepper 354
   types of 354, 662
tom yum goong 140–1
tomato 94, 662
   bruschetta with tomato,
     basil and capers 80
   caprese salad 111
   chilli tomato relish 492
   chutney 609
   gazpacho 140
   sauce 276, 464
   spicy tomato salsa 439
   sun-dried tomato dressing 103
   tarts 584
   tomato and herb salad 387
torte, flourless chocolate
   and almond 541
tortellini 146, 657
   cheese and spinach tortellini
     with gorgonzola sauce 166
   prawn and scallop 52

tortilla crisps 134
tortilla, spanish 260–1
traditional shortbread 568
tricks of the trade 634–8
trifle, classic 520
tropical fruit 516–17
tuna salad 99
tuna tartare 90
turkey 289
   cooking guide 311
   food safety 311
   roast, with forcemeat
     stuffing 310–13
   size 310
   stuffing 311
   testing for doneness 313
turkish bread 662
turmeric 662
turnip, preserved 658

U

udon noodles 191, 193, 655
   udon noodle and prawn broth 207

V

vanilla, 662
   beans 598, 662
   butter cookies 47
   essence 40
   extract 40
   vanilla bean ice-cream 512
   vanilla bean storage 635
   vanilla kisses 568
   vanilla patty cakes with
     glacé icing 552
   vanilla slice 567
veal 464
   hungarian veal goulash 368
   meatballs napoletana 625
   osso buco 380–1
   veal cutlets with green
     olive salsa 450
   veal parmigiana 464
   veal saltimbocca 462

vegetables 17, 21, 23, 24,
    210–11, 216–19, 636
    see also by individual names
  artichoke hearts vinaigrette 220
  asian 211
  asparagus hollandaise 215
  braised baby leeks 226
  broad beans and thyme 224
  brussels sprouts with
    cream and almonds 227
  buying 210
  caramelised fennel tarts 222
  caramelised onion and
    beetroot tart 223
  caramelised red onion 222
  cauliflower gratin 239
  celeriac puree 233
  chickpea and vegetable
    gratin 495
  chilli and herb swede crush 227
  chunky beef and vegetable pie 396
  cooking 211
  corn fritters 237
  creamed spinach 227
  dhal and paneer vegetable
    curry 428–9
  eggplant parmigiana 234
  glazed carrots with
    hazelnuts 226
  grilled, with garlic herb
    dressing 455
  hasselback potatoes 212
  lemon and ricotta-filled
    zucchini flowers 239
  mashed potato, perfect 233
  noodle and vegetable rice
    paper rolls 621
  pan-frying 458
  peas with mint butter 233
  perfect potato chip, the 232
  pork and vegetable stir-fry 22–3
  pork and vegetable vindaloo 418
  potato wedges 232
  pumpkin and eggplant curry 430
  refreshing 639
  roast meat, with 291
  roasted capsicums 215
  roasted caramelised parsnips 224
  roasted vegetable tart 400–1

(vegetables continued)
  roasting 319
  rösti 230
  salads, for 95
  sautéed mushrooms 238
  scalloped potatoes 230
  seasonality 219
  split pea and vegetable tagine 488
  steamed asian greens with
    char siu sauce 238
  stir-frying 23
  stock 125
  storing and handling 210
  thai vegetable stir-fry 359
  vegetable gnocchi with
    cheese sauce 164
  vegetable tempura 472
  vegie nachos 622
vegetarian crêpe cakes 586
vegetarian lasagne 156
vegetarian pad thai 198
velouté 265
  chicken and mushroom 276
vermouth 663
vialone nano rice 171
vichyssoise 130
vienna cream 568, 571
vietnamese beef pho 129
vietnamese chicken salad 108
vietnamese dressing 108
vietnamese mint 228, 650
vietnamese noodle and
  chicken salad 200
vietnamese pork rolls 331
vietnamese prawn rolls 76
vinaigrette 95 see also dressings
  red berry 116
  red wine 112
vinegar 663

W

waldorf salad 96
walnuts 663
wasabi 663
water bath 504
water chestnuts 211, 353

watercress 106, 663
wedding cake cookies 596
wedding cakes, lace 590
wheat noodles 191
white beans 642
  dip 80
  puree 501
white christmas ice-cream
  puddings 598
white rice 659
white sauce 156
white wine sauce 274–5
wholemeal pasta 145
wild rice 172, 659
  blend 172, 659
wine 577
witlof 107, 663
  witlof, pear and blue
    cheese salad 114
wok 336
wok chan 22, 337, 663
wombok 349, 663
worcestershire sauce 663
wrappers 52, 663

Y

yabbies 446, 660
yeast 663
yellow coconut rice 181
yogurt, spiced 135
yorkshire puddings 292–3

Z

za'atar 417, 663
zucchini 95, 219, 473, 663
  flowers 219
  fritters 473
  zucchini and mushroom
    omelette 256–7

Published in 2010 by ACP Books, Sydney
ACP Books are published by ACP Magazines
a division of PBL Media Pty Limited

ACP BOOKS
General manager Christine Whiston
Editor-in-chief Susan Tomnay
Creative director & designer Hieu Chi Nguyen
Senior editor Stephanie Kistner
Design assistant Sarah Holmes
Contributing writers Liz Wilson, Raffaella Pugliese, Abby Pfahl
Food director Pamela Clark
Food editor Cathie Lonnie
Nutritional information Jordanna Levin
Sales & rights director Brian Cearnes
Marketing manager Bridget Cody
Senior business analyst Rebecca Varela
Operations manager David Scotto
Production manager Victoria Jefferys

Published by ACP Books, a division of ACP Magazines Ltd.
54 Park St, Sydney NSW 2000.
GPO Box 4088, Sydney NSW 2001.
Phone +61 2 9282 8618 Fax +61 2 9267 9438
acpbooks@acpmagazines.com.au
www.acpbooks.com.au

Chapter openers, special features and step-by-steps
Photographer Louise Lister
Stylist Kate Nixon
Photochefs Nicole Dicker, Lucy Nunes
Assistant photochef Tessa Immens

The publishers would like to thank the following
for props used in photography:
Le Creuset www.lecreuset.com.au; Wüsthof www.wusthof.com.au; Calphalon www.calphalon.com.au; KitchenAid www.petermcinnes. com; Profiline www.petermcinnes.com; Scanpan www.scanpan. dk; Furi ph 1800 209 999; Busatti wwwbusatti.com.au; The Essential Ingredient www.essentialingredient.com.au; Iced Affair ph 02 9519 3679; The Bay Tree www.thebaytree.com.au; tablekraft www.tomkin.com.au; Chef Inox www.tomkin.com.au

Printed by C&C Offset Printing, China.
Australia Distributed by Network Services, GPO Box 4088, Sydney, NSW 2001.
Phone +61 2 9282 8777 Fax +61 2 9264 3278
networkweb@networkservicescompany.com.au
United Kingdom Distributed by Australian Consolidated Press (UK),
10 Scirocco Close, Moulton Park Office Village, Northampton, NN3 6AP.
Phone +44 1604 642 200 Fax +44 1604 642 300 books@acpuk.com www.acpuk.com
Canada Distributed by Publishers Group Canada
Order Desk & Customer Service, 9050 Shaughnessy Street, Vancouver, BC V6P 6E5
Phone (800) 663 5714 Fax (800) 565 3770 service@raincoast.com
New Zealand Distributed by Southern Publishers Group, 21 Newton Road, Auckland, NZ.
Phone +64 9 360 0692 Fax +64 9 360 0695 hub@spg.co.nz
South Africa Distributed by PSD Promotions, 30 Diesel Road Isando, Gauteng Johannesburg.
PO Box 1175, Isando 1600, Gauteng Johannesburg.
Phone +27 11 392 6065/6/7 Fax +27 11 392 6079/80 orders@psdprom.co.za

Title: The AWW cooking school / food director Pamela Clark.
ISBN: 978-1-74245-002-5 (hbk.)
Notes: Includes index.
Subjects: Cookery.
Other authors/contributors: Clark, Pamela
Also titled: Australian women's weekly.
Dewey number: 641.5

© ACP Magazines Ltd 2010
ABN 18 053 273 546
This publication is copyright. No part of it may be reproduced or transmitted
in any form without the written permission of the publishers.

To order books, phone 136 116 (within Australia) or
online at www.acpbooks.com.au
Send recipe enquiries to: recipeenquiries@acpmagazines.com.au